WORKING

GEORGE RITZER
University of Maryland

DAVID WALCZAK
University of Maryland

WORKING
Conflict and Change

Third Edition

PRENTICE-HALL, Englewood Cliffs, New Jersey 07632

Library of Congress Cataloging-in-Publication Data

RITZER, GEORGE.
    Working, conflict and change.

    Includes indexes.
        1. Industrial sociology—United States.   2. Labor
and laboring classes—United States.   3. United
States—Occupations.   I. WALCZAK, DAVID, [date]
II. Title.
HD6957.U6R5   1986   306'.36'0973   85-28135
ISBN 0-13-967589-2

Editorial/production supervision: *Edith Riker*
Cover design: *20–20 Services, Inc.*
Manufacturing buyer: *Barbara Kittle*

Printed in the United States of America

10 9 8 7 6 5 4 3

ISBN   0-13-967589-2   01

Prentice-Hall International (UK) Limited, *London*
Prentice-Hall of Australia Pty. Limited, *Sydney*
Prentice-Hall Canada Inc., *Toronto*
Prentice-Hall Hispanoamericana, S.A., *Mexico*
Prentice-Hall of India Private Limited, *New Delhi*
Prentice-Hall of Japan, Inc., *Tokyo*
Prentice-Hall of Southeast Asia Pte. Ltd., *Singapore*
Editora Prentice-Hall do Brasil, Ltda., *Rio de Janeiro*
Whitehall Books Limited, *Wellington, New Zealand*

To the memory of LEONARD REISSMAN

To LUCILLE and KARL

CONTENTS

            AND PROPRIETORS   *258*

            Managers and Officials: Role Conflict, 258
            Proprietors: Economic Marginality, 285
            Conclusions, 290

ELEVEN   *CONFLICT IN A RANGE OF WHITE- AND BLUE-*
            COLLAR OCCUPATIONS   *292*

            White-Collar Clerical Workers, 292
            Salespeople, 303
            Skilled Crafts, 308
            Free Semiskilled and Unskilled Occupations, 315
            Conclusions, 326

TWELVE   *CONFLICT IN SEMISKILLED AND UNSKILLED*
            OCCUPATIONS IN ORGANIZATIONS   *328*

            Alienation, 328
            Coping with Social-Psychological Alienation, 339
            Coping with Structural Alienation, 354
            Conclusions, 372

THIRTEEN   *CONFLICT IN DEVIANT OCCUPATIONS*   *373*

            Coping with Conflict with Clients, Customers,
              and Victims, 375
            Coping with Other Conflicts, 384
            Ideology and Deviant Occupations, 391
            Conclusions, 401

FOURTEEN   *CONTEMPORARY WORK-RELATED PROBLEMS*   *402*

            Racism in the Workworld, 402
            Safety and Health Hazards, 415
            The Rationalization of Work, 422

APPENDIX   *OCCUPATIONAL STRUCTURE: REVISIONS IN U.S.*
            CLASSIFICATION SCHEME   *435*

            NAME INDEX   *439*

            SUBJECT INDEX   *448*

PREFACE

Given the passage of nine years since the publication of the second edition of this book, this third edition has obviously required some dramatic changes. In fact, the need for change was so great that a co-author, David Walczak, was brought in to help. The world of work had undergone some important changes in that period as had the sociological study of the workworld. This edition reflects both types of changes. Thus, in terms of changes in the world of work we find new (or expanded) concern with such topics as the dramatically altered position of women in the workworld, comparable worth, sexual harassment, the decline of America's "smokestack industries," robotization, the decline of the union movement, and the increasing rationalization of work. Reflective of changes within sociology is new (or expanded) coverage of such topics as the power approach to the professions, deprofessionalization, the proletarianization of the professions, the structural approach to alienation, labor market segmentation, and myths about retirement.

While there are dramatic changes in this edition, there is also continuity. The major concerns that animated earlier editions of this book remain at the core—careers, conflict, and conflict resolution.

Although written as a basic text for an undergraduate or graduate course in the sociology of work (or occupations), this book can also serve as a sourcebook for those interested in doing advanced work in the sociology of occupations. Effort has been made to deal with as many of the important classic and contemporary studies of work as possible. Adding to its utility as a sourcebook, this edition includes much more statistical information on work in America than previous editions.

We would like to thank Professor Gale Miller of Marquette University for his revisions of the chapter on deviant occupations as well as of the sections dealing with deviant occupations in Chapters 6 and 7.

George Ritzer
David Walczak
College Park, Maryland
August, 1985

ONE
INTRODUCTION

This book is about work in contemporary America. Of course, to understand work in the modern United States it is sometimes necessary to discuss occupations in other societies or at other times in history. In this book, our analysis is done from a sociological perspective; thus, this text is intended to be a compendium of current sociological knowledge about the workworld. This current knowledge has led us to focus on the *changing* nature of occupational life, the *careers* that individuals experience in their worklives, and the *conflicts* and efforts to *cope* with those conflicts that pervade the occupational world. In brief then, our four major themes are: change, careers, conflict, and conflict resolution. Naturally, many other issues will emerge in the course of discussing these focal themes—professionalization, health and safety hazards on the job, unemployment, and the status of women within the workworld, to name just a few.

In discussing these basic themes we will generally move between an analysis of social structures (such as bureaucracies, professions, labor unions, labor markets, technologies, and the structure of occupations) and individual workers. Of primary importance is the relationship between individual workers and the larger work-related structures in which they exist.[1]

---

[1]This largely microscopic (workers) and mesoscopic (work-related structures) orientation that is characteristic of the American study of work stands in contrast to the more macroscopic approach of British sociologists. This British orientation is reflected in, among other places,

The pivotal concept in this book is *occupation* which is defined in the following way:

> An occupation is the social role performed by adult members of society that directly and/or indirectly yields social and financial consequences and that constitutes a major focus in the life of an adult.[2]

We will be concerned with a wide array of broad types of occupations as well as innumerable specific occupations. For example, the professions as a type of occupation will concern us greatly, as will a number of specific professions such as physicians and lawyers.

Although we will generally operate on the assumption that the concepts of work and occupation are intimately related to one another, it is important to recognize, following Miller, that there are a number of important examples of "nonoccupational work."[3] *Nonoccupational work* involves work roles that are not organized as jobs from which income is derived. The most obvious example of nonoccupational work is the housewife. Amateurs of various kinds (such as amateur stamp collectors) would also fit into this category.[4]

While the occupations to be discussed throughout these pages currently exist, it is important to realize that occupations have a life history—they come into existence, reach maturity, and in some cases disappear. Where do occupations come from? One possibility is that new occupations split off from existing occupations. As a given occupation comes to encompass a disparate array of tasks, it may give birth to one or more new, more specialized occupations. The other major possibility is that an occupation develops over time out of a series of activities performed in the everyday world.[5] For example, people may perform a variety of voluntary activities without pay which, over time, come to be organized as an occupation. The effort to form an occupation is not a preordained success; some efforts may succeed but others will fail. Success occurs when distinctive activities are created "around which groups can be formed as their members seek autonomy and control over their

Salaman's interest in the "politics of work," or "the ways in which work experiences, rewards, activities, etc., are related to the organization and structure of power and interests within society" (p. 40). Although American studies of work also reflect a concern with the relationship of work to the larger society, that is much less of a concern than it is in British research. While the relationship to the larger society is of significance throughout this book, our main concern is with occupations and the workers who hold them. See, Graeme Salaman, "The Sociology of Work: Some Themes and Issues," in Geoff Esland and Graeme Salaman, eds., *The Politics of Work and Occupations* (Toronto: University of Toronto Press, 1980), pp. 1–41.

[2]Richard Hall, *Occupations and the Social Structure,* 2nd ed. (Englewood Cliffs, NJ: Prentice-Hall, 1975), p. 6.

[3]Gale Miller, "The Interpretation of Nonoccupational Work in Modern Society: A Preliminary Discussion and Typology," *Social Problems,* 27 (1980), 381–391.

[4]Robert Stebbins, *The Amateur: On the Margin Between Work and Leisure* (Beverly Hills, CA.: Sage, 1979); Robert Stebbins, "Amateur and Professional Astronomers: A Study of Their Interrelationships," *Urban Life,* 10 (1982), 433–454.

[5]Robert Dingwall. "In the Beginning Was the Work . . . Reflections on the Genesis of Occupations," *The Sociological Review,* 31 (1983), 605–624.

particular and distinctive work"[6] All existing occupations have achieved some measure of autonomy and control, but as we will see later in this book, it is the professions that have developed the greatest autonomy and control.

It is also the case that occupations can, over time, disintegrate; tasks that were once performed for money can come to be performed informally without pay. Thus, it is important to remember that the extant occupations we are discussing in this book arose out of informal, voluntary activities—and that they may some day return to the realm of everyday activities performed without pay.

We have not begun this book with the objective of rendering value judgments about the nature and quality of work in America. However, a careful reading of the sociological literature on work leads to a scathing indictment of work in America. The problems are evident in every chapter:

> The increasing rationalization, bureaucratization, specialization, and dehumanization of work, leaving many workers with little from which to gain any real meaning.
>
> Technological changes that deskill many occupations and threaten to eliminate many others.
>
> Persistently high rates of unemployment that leave millions of people out of work for weeks, months, even years.
>
> Safety and health hazards on the job that kill thousands of people each year and injure millions more.
>
> The efforts by professionals to protect, and even expand upon, their lucrative, prestigious, and powerful positions—even when the public they are supposed to serve suffers.
>
> The lack of any significant possibility for upward career mobility for most American workers.
>
> The mindless emphasis on educational credentials rather than skills and abilities to qualify for entry into many occupations.
>
> The plight of women in what we can call the "female semiprofessions" (nurses, social workers, schoolteachers, and librarians) who have been denied full professional status, in part at least, as a result of sexism in the larger society.
>
> The inability of the small proprietor to survive in the face of competition from franchises and large chain stores.
>
> The pathetic struggles for meager status symbols among white-collar clerical workers.
>
> The alienation of those in semiskilled and unskilled blue-collar occupations.
>
> The large number of deviant occupations.
>
> The overwhelming occupational problems that beset females, blacks, and members of other minority groups.

This list is merely suggestive of the enormous number of problems that are discussed in the ensuing pages. However, this list should not be taken to

---

[6]Eliot Freidson, "Occupational Autonomy and Labor Market Shelters," in Phyllis L. Stewart and Muriel G. Cantor, eds., *Varieties of Work* (Beverly Hills, CA: Sage, 1982), p. 54.

imply that there are no satisfying occupations, or that all workers are faced with insurmountable difficulties. Clearly, the American workworld operates quite satisfactorily for many millions of people.

The emphasis on problems in work in America should also not be taken as an indication that work in this country is more beset by difficulties than in other societies. It is clear that the worker in England, Sweden, the Soviet Union, and China faces a similar set of problems as well as many others that are specific to those societies. What this enumeration of problems does imply is that there is much that can—and must—be done to improve the quality of worklife in America.

PLAN OF THE BOOK

The book is organized into two parts: Part One which deals with social and individual change is composed of six chapters. Chapters 2 and 3 deal with an array of social changes taking place within the workworld. The first part of Chapter 2 is devoted to a brief history of work through the ages and to the present day. The second part of the chapter deals with the more recent history of work in America focusing on the increasing division of labor and various changes in the American labor force. Chapter 3 picks up where Chapter 2 leaves off and deals with a number of other changes including technological advances, bureaucratization, unionization, the revolution in education, and increasing leisure time. Chapter 4 deals in depth with one important social change—professionalization. The chapter also introduces a number of the theoretical and empirical issues that relate to a sociological understanding of the professions. Chapter 5 focuses in depth on another crucially important social issue—the changing position of women in the workworld. We will focus on both the gains made by women as well as the problems that continue to beset them. In Chapters 6 and 7 we shift from social to individual change, specifically to the careers and the career patterns in which individuals find themselves in their worklives.

Part Two also consists of six chapters in which the focus is on conflict and conflict resolution within the workworld. In each chapter we look at major types of occupations and distinctive forms of conflict and modes of conflict resolution found within them. In Chapter 8 we examine the professions (such as physicians, lawyers, scientists), differentiating between types of conflict and modes of resolution found among free professionals (those in private practice) and those characteristic of professionals employed in organizations. In Chapter 9 we turn to the professional marginality of such occupations as nurses, schoolteachers, chiropractors, and funeral directors and their efforts to deal with failure to achieve full professional recognition. Managers, officials, and proprietors are the subject of Chapter 10. While role conflict is characteristic of managers and officials, economic marginality is the most distinctive problem for (small) proprietors. Chapter 11 can be seen as a transitional chapter between the higher-status occupations dealt with in Chapters 8 to 10 and the lower-status occupations discussed in Chapters 12 to 13. Chapter 11 deals with conflict and conflict resolution among white-collar clerical workers, salespeople, skilled craftspeople, and free semi-skilled and unskilled occupations (for example, taxi drivers, waiters, police officers). Chapter 12 picks up the discussion of the occupational type dealt with at the end of Chapter 11, but focuses on the alienation characteristic of semiskilled and unskilled occupations employed in organizations. The final chapter (Chapter 13) in Part Two deals with a range of deviant occupations (such as prostitutes, strippers, bank robbers) and, as is the pattern in these chapters, the distinctive types of conflict and modes of conflict resolution in this type of occupation.

While a wide range of occupational problems are discussed throughout the book, the closing chapter, Chapter 14, singles out three problems for additional discussion—racism in the workworld, health and safety hazards on the job, and the increasing rationalization of work.

TWO
THE CHANGING NATURE OF WORK: I

The ultimate goal of this chapter, indeed of this book, is to communicate an understanding of the *contemporary* American workworld.[1] That workworld is not static, but is undergoing rapid social change.[2] Among these changes are the increasing division of labor, shifts in the labor force, technological advances (such as the rise of robot technology), increasing bureaucratization, the decline of the union movement, the revolution in education, and the growth in leisure time. To understand adequately the changing nature of the modern workworld, we must see what it was like historically. Therefore, let us begin with a brief discussion of the history of work through the ages.

WORK THROUGH THE AGES[3]

The Primitive World

In the primitive world there was no such thing as work or an occupation, at least as we understand these terms. Primitive peoples clearly labored, but work was virtually synonymous with life and certainly interpenetrated every

[1]We will find a number of occasions to discuss work in other societies, but our objective usually will be to shed light on work in America.

[2]Sar A. Levitan, "The Changing Workplace," *Society*, 21 (1984), 41–48.

[3]This section is based on Melvin Kranzberg and Joseph Gies, *By the Sweat of Thy Brow: Work in the Western World* (New York: G.P. Putnam's Sons, 1975).

facet of living.[4] A day generally consisted of waking, working primarily by gathering food, consuming the day's produce, and resting so that the process could begin anew the following day. To work was to live, for if one did not work, or was not successful in gathering enough food and providing sufficient warmth and shelter, then one died.

Work in the primitive world was virtually undifferentiated, that is, there was little division of labor. Almost everyone performed each and every required chore. The exceptions to this were the very old and the very young, and in many cases, the women. The aged were given sedentary tasks such as cooking, while the young were relegated to such relatively easy tasks as picking nuts and berries. Women spent a large portion of their life alternating between pregnancy and the nursing of their young; this meant they were generally excluded from such things as the hunt.[5] (Yet it should not be assumed that women were spared heavy work. As Kranzberg and Gies have written: "It has been said that woman is man's oldest beast of burden."[6])

Eventually work patterns became more and more differentiated. For example, potters came into being on at least a part-time basis to make objects. And when agriculture developed, skilled workers had to make the clothing that was no longer supplied solely by the furs and skins of animals killed in the hunt.

The development of agriculture, whereby crops and animals were systematically raised for consumption, was an important turning point. For the first time there was a modest surplus of food. This meant some people could devote all their time to specialties such as the manufacture of weapons and metal tools. Metalworkers were closely followed by makers of the luxury goods demanded by the community for the first time, as well as by priests and magicians to minister to the spiritual needs of the populace. These first divisions of labor set the stage for the rise of the great irrigation societies that came into being about 3000 B.C. in the Near, Middle, and Far East. According to Kranzberg and Gies, "In these civilizations the organization of work developed along lines that in their principal aspects remained unchanged for the next 5,000 years, that is, until the arrival of industrial machine power in the eighteenth century."[7]

These great irrigation societies required a disciplined and coordinated mass of laborers, who in turn needed a leadership group to exercise power

[4]This continues to be true of contemporary "nonmarket" ("primitive") societies. See, Herbert Applebaum, "Theoretical Introduction," in Herbert Applebaum, ed., *Work in Non-Market and Transitional Societies* (Albany, NY: State University of New York Press, 1984), p. 2

[5]In recent years a number of feminist anthropologists have come to question the view that biology mandated the place of women in the division of labor. See, for example, Michelle Zimbalist Rosaldo, "Woman, Culture and Society: A Theoretic Overview," in Michelle Z. Rosaldo and Louise Lamphere, eds., *Woman, Culture and Society* (Stanford, CA: Stanford University Press, 1974), pp. 17–42; Michelle Zimbalist Rosaldo, "The Use and Abuse of Anthropology: Reflections on Feminism and Cross-Cultural Understanding," *Signs: Journal of Women in Culture and Society,* 5 (1980), 389–417; Ruby Rohrlich-Leavitt, Barbara Sykes, and Elizabeth Weatherford, "Aboriginal Women: Male and Female Anthropological Perspectives," in Rayna R. Reiter, ed., *Toward an Anthropology of Women* (New York: Monthly Review Press, 1975), pp. 110–126.

[6]Kranzberg and Gies, *By the Sweat of Thy Brow,* p. 14.

[7]Ibid., p. 21.

over them. This was the beginning of the first organized and institutionalized form of state government. The new irrigation systems, with guidance from a leader "class," produced an even larger food surplus and this overproduction permitted the growth of still more specialized occupations, including merchants to trade in surplus products. Centers of trade that promoted the growth of villages and towns and cities developed. Stronger groups of politicians, soldiers, and clergymen helped to unify these entities into single kingdoms and empires.

The Classical World

These changes in work structure marked the end of the communal and egalitarian societies of the primitive era. Agriculture enabled families to become self-sufficient; this provided the basis for class differences, since some families produced greater surpluses than others. The affluent farmers joined with kings, nobles, warriors, and priests to make up the elites of society, and these elites expropriated more and more wealth for themselves. They used at least a part of these resources to solidify their position by building huge armies and government organizations to perform such tasks as tax collection. New specialized occupations evolved to provide for increasingly sophisticated needs and desires. The result, in such societies as Egypt and Mesopotamia, was a rather rigidified class system with the elites at the top; craftsmen, merchants, and peasant agriculturalists in the middle; and a mass of slaves at the bottom. One of the distinctive characteristics of the classical world was the denigration of manual labor. The existence of a mass of slaves allowed many to avoid manual labor and to spend their time philosophizing or following athletic pursuits. Slavery actually served to impede the application of scientific techniques to work, since the ready availability of expendable bodies made technological advance of little importance.

Even with the increasingly hierarchical structure of society, the vast majority of laborers in the classical world continued to toil on the farm. Family farms were the norm, with the result that farming was almost entirely done on a small scale. There was a minimal division of labor, and the classical farm resembled today's small family farm in many ways. Although, as today, there were many larger farms with a much more elaborate division of labor, workers on even these large farms were unable to produce a great deal more than they needed to consume to survive. Nevertheless some improvements did occur, including the invention of the wheeled plow and the water wheel. These innovations were not really applied intensively, however, until the Middle Ages.

The classical world of Greece and Rome was also characterized by other developments in work. Urban craftsmen proliferated as a result of larger markets and more sophisticated tastes. At first, these craftsmen traveled from market to market selling their wares, but as the number of consumers grew they began to stay in permanent locations. Cross-national commerce developed, and specific cities and areas began to specialize in the production of certain commodities. Athens, for example, was noted for its pottery, Pompeii for wool finishing. Specialization also occurred within crafts as different functions came to be divided up among, and even within, different shops. Thus, potting was divided among those who made cooking pots, jars, goblets, and so on. Out of these concentrations of craftsmen emerged the first guilds. Large shops also developed in which a number of craftsmen were employed under one master craftsman—there was even some specialization of function among these workers. Such systems were the rudiments of large-scale production. But this was unlike the specialization that was to occur later. A basic difference was that in the classical world workers were able to choose their tasks. In addition, they controlled their tasks, owned the means of production, and could see their contribution to the finished product. As we will see throughout this book, the later forms of the division of labor had much more profound—and odious—effects on workers.

Despite the impressive accomplishments of the classical world—the Egyptian pyramids, and Roman buildings, bridges, and aqueducts—work in this era was burdened by three basic handicaps: "the lack of powered machinery, the lack of sophisticated mechanical devices, and the lack of suitable harnesses to make the most of animal power."[8] The compensation for these handicaps was the ability to mass and organize an enormous number of workers. For example, the Great Pyramid at Giza, constructed about 2500 B.C., had a work force of about 30,000 throughout the project.

The Middle Ages

The next period, the so-called Dark (or Middle) Ages, from the fifth to the tenth centuries, managed to reverse or at least arrest many of the developments of the classical period. Scale of production was reduced as a result of declining demand. The larger production units were replaced by "small, self-sustaining feudal economic units [which] put a premium on the jack-of-all-trades in contrast to the specialized craftsman of more prosperous times."[9] While in many ways this was a period of regression, one countertrend that should be noted was the rapid decline of slavery.[10]

Another development associated with the Middle Ages was a growing respect for manual labor. And there were technological developments such as new types of plows, harnesses, and boats, as well as the change from the two-field agricultural system to a three-field system in which a third of a farm's land lay fallow each year, a third had traditional cereal crops in autumn, and a third had oats, barley, and legumes in the spring. This advance is said to have increased farm surplus by one-third to one-half, thereby allowing for the support of an even larger nonfarm population.

By the eleventh century there was a revival in the economic area. The fragmentation of the preceding 500 years began to give way to larger population aggregates. This led to a new era of stability, integration, and interdependence among the various facets of society.

In the eleventh and twelfth centuries the guilds revived and expanded. They provided a variety of welfare functions for the membership, protected

[8]Ibid., p. 49.
[9]Ibid., p. 57.
[10]Ibid.

the individual crafts, set "just" wages and "just" prices, and insured the quality of the product in a variety of ways:

> The officers of a guild took an oath on the relics of a saint to "guard the guild" carefully and loyally, and to spare neither friends nor relatives caught foisting substandard goods on the consuming public. Precise quantities and types of raw materials were specified . . . Inspection visits were made by guild officers, scales checked, substandard goods confiscated. A jeweler found using colored glass instead of stones paid a heavy fine.[11]

A major development within the guilds took place in the thirteenth century. Up to that time there had been two groups of workers—the master craftsmen and the apprentices who learned from them and performed most of the work. A new group developed in this period. The journeymen came to occupy an intermediate position between the masters above them and the apprentices below. The situation in the skilled crafts is not much changed today.

Although the Middle Ages was characterized by small-scale enterprises, some large-scale industries did manage to develop. One was the "putting-out" system of wool cloth manufacture in Flanders, in which the manufacturer bought a fleece and "put it out" to a weaver who in his home and with the help of his family produced cloth. The cloth was returned to the manufacturer, who finished the production process (for example, dyeing) or sold it to be finished in another establishment. This system led to an international division of labor; the fleece came from England, was woven into cloth in Flanders, dyed and finished by Italians, and sold to the Mediterranean Muslim states. Similarly specialized areas developed elsewhere (arms and armor in Milan, shoes and other leather goods in Cordoba, silk in Seville, rugs and tapestries at Limoges, glass in Venice). The cities of Western Europe boomed as a result of this economic activity.

The work involved in the construction of public projects was also transformed during the Middle Ages. Whereas the public works in the Classical Age had been the product of a massive number of slaves, in medieval times such projects as the construction of the great Gothic cathedrals were organized quite differently. In charge was a head architect-engineer who supervised the work of a large number of free, hired, and well-paid skilled craftsmen such as masons, carpenters, blacksmiths, plumbers, and glaziers.

The recovery underway during the twelfth and thirteenth centuries was abruptly ended by the advent of the bubonic plague as well as a variety of other adverse social and economic forces. But by the sixteenth century the recovery process resumed in a much more determined fashion. Among the work-related innovations at this time were double-entry bookkeeping, commercial credit, and marine insurance. Also underway were the further development of urban centers, improvements in plant and livestock breeding, creation of new farm equipment, and the replacement of the three-field method of farming with the even more efficient four-field method.

[11]Ibid., pp. 66–67.

An important byproduct of the new surplus productivity and the larger urban class that could be spared the task of food production was the creation of a "market for what had always been considered luxury goods—comfortable clothing, multi-room houses, pewter dishes and mugs, glassware, cabinets and other furniture, meat, spices, wine."[12] This, in turn, contributed to the overthrow of the old handicraft system and laid the groundwork for the first stages of the Industrial Revolution. The age of large-scale production organizations was beginning: craftsmen were to be subordinated to the owners of the means of production (materials, tools, and workplaces). Not only were the owners of increasing importance, but the state was also exercising greater control over the economic sphere. The worker was becoming progressively submerged in large and more powerful entities.

The Industrial Revolution

The founding of the New World during this period had a number of implications for work. The Americas were exploited both as a market for European goods and as a source of the needed raw materials. Slavery took on a new life after years of eclipse in Europe. In fact, the traffic in slaves reached new heights. The invention of the cotton gin—a simple, efficient, and easy-to-produce machine—led to a huge increase in cotton production in the southern United States. A flood of raw cotton fiber from America began to inundate the English midlands and this set the stage for the Industrial Revolution.

The Industrial Revolution was characterized by the development of the factory system of production. Large work sites were constructed and filled with machines that were powered by a central energy source. These machines were manned by a wide array of workers from the highly skilled to the almost totally unskilled, the latter frequently working at low pay for very long hours. In machine work, women and children with little or no training could be substituted for skilled craftsmen because the skill was already built into the machines. As a result, workers were transformed into machine tenders.

Another defining characteristic of this age was the elaborate division of labor whereby a single product went through the hands of a number of workers, each of whom performed a small step in the entire production process. This development was depicted by Adam Smith in his famous description of the new method of producing pins. Under the old system a single person producing a whole pin could produce only a few each day, but in the new division of labor a group of ten workers could produce almost 5000 pins each per day. Here is his description of the division of labor:

> One man draws out the wire, another straights it, a third cuts it, a fourth points it, a fifth grinds it at the top for receiving the head; to make the head requires two or three distinct operations; to put it on, is a peculiar business; to whiten the pins, is another; it is even a trade by itself to put them into the paper; and the important business of making a pin is, in this manner, divided into about eight-

[12]Ibid., p. 81.

een distinct operations, which, in some manufactories, are all performed by distinct hands, though in others the same man will sometimes perform two or three of them.[13]

Another result of the factory system was the shattering of the influence of the guilds, with their notions of a just price and a just wage. The relative freedom and individuality of the guild system was replaced by the discipline needed to run a large factory efficiently. Exploitation of employees by the capitalist owners of large factories became the norm. The well-known abuses of the factory system, some of which are with us to this day, led to a number of reactions, including government legislation about work, sabotage on the part of the workers, and the growth of the union movement.

The first factories were rather primitive affairs, but over the years they grew larger and more efficient; they came to involve mass production. Mass production had a variety of characteristics; products were standardized, parts were made interchangeable, precision tools were used so that parts could be made to fit universally, the production process was mechanized to yield high volume, the flow of materials to the machine and products from the machine was synchronized, and the entire process was made as continuous as possible. This, of course, led to the assembly-line type of production that we continue to know today in the auto industry, for example. These systems reached their fullest application in the United States in the mid-twentieth century and spread throughout the world.

Another development that occured at about the same time as the spread of large factories was the rise of the large-scale organization, especially the *bureaucracy*. It had many of the same effects on white-collar work that mass-production technology had on blue-collar workers.

Capitalism

The rise of industries and large-scale bureaucracies is coterminous with the development of capitalism. While industries and bureaucracies certainly have come to exist in noncapitalistic societies (such as the Soviet Union), their development is associated with the coming of age of capitalist society. The most important analyst *and* critic of capitalist society was Karl Marx.[14] The essence of the capitalist system, as far as Marx was concerned, was its system of two social classes in which one class exploited the other. One class, the *capitalist,* owned the means of production within capitalist society (that is, tools, raw materials, factories). The other class, the *proletariat,* was forced to sell its labor time to the capitalist in order to have access to the means of production. In other words, in capitalist society, the proletariat is unable to work unless it sells its labor time to the capitalist. The capitalist pays the workers for their labor time, but the secret of capitalist society is that the workers are paid *less* than they produce for the capitalist. In fact, in Marx's view, the proletariat is paid

[13]Adam Smith, *The Wealth of Nations* (New York: The Modern Library, 1937), pp. 4–5.
[14]Karl Marx, *Capital: A Critique of Political Economy,* Vol. 1 (New York: International Publishers, 1967).

only a subsistence wage which allows it to survive. Everything else that the proletariat produces is kept by the capitalists who reinvest most of it in the expansion of their business. In this way, the success of the capitalist grows ever greater, but the source of that success is the proletariat and the fact that the capitalists pay them less than they deserve to be paid. In other words, the success of the capitalist is based on the exploitation of the proletariat.

Writing in the middle 1800s, Marx was describing capitalism in its heyday. Over the years capitalism has changed tremendously and many neo-Marxian scholars have attempted to adapt Marx's ideas to the changing realities of capitalist society. For example, the capitalism of Marx's day may be thought of as *competitive capitalism*. Companies were comparatively small, with the result that no one capitalist, or small group of capitalists, could gain complete and uncontested control over a market. While Marx foresaw the growth of monopolies, it was Baran and Sweezy who described modern capitalist society as *monopoly capitalism*.[15] This means that one, or a few, capitalists control a given sector of the economy. Clearly, there is far less competition in monopoly capitalism than in competitive capitalism. Along with a change in competitiveness has come a change in the control structure of capitalist enterprises. In competitive capitalism the enterprise tended to be controlled by a single capitalist-entrepreneur. However, in monopoly capitalism the modern corporation is owned by a large number of stockholders, although it is often the case that a few stockholders own most of the stock in a given company. Although stockholders "own" the company, managers exercise the actual day-to-day control. Managers are crucial in competitive capitalism, whereas the entrepreneurs were central in competitive capitalism. One of the byproducts of this is that Marx's simple model of opposition between capitalist and proletariat no longer applies. Who are the capitalists? Are the millions of people who own a few shares of stock in General Motors capitalists? Are the managers of modern enterprises capitalists? Or are they members of the proletariat since they are employees of the organization? These are just a few of the questions raised by changes in the capitalist system in the last century.

Another significant change in capitalism has been the growth of white-collar and service workers and the decline of the blue-collar workers that Marx was thinking about when he wrote of the proletariat. Can Marx's theory of exploitation be extended to white-collar and service occupations? Braverman argued that the concept of the proletariat does not describe a specific group of people or occupations but is rather an expression of a process of buying and selling labor power.[16] Like blue-collar workers, white-collar workers and service workers are being forced to sell their labor time to capitalists. In Braverman's view, capitalist exploitation and control are being extended to white-collar and service occupations, although their impact is not yet as great as it has been on blue-collar occupations.

Braverman recognized economic exploitation, which was Marx's focus,

---

[15]Paul Baran and Paul M. Sweezy, *Monopoly Capital: An Essay on the American Economic and Social Order* (New York: Monthly Review Press, 1966).

[16]Harry Braverman, *Labor and Monopoly Capital: The Degradation of Work in the Twentieth Century* (New York: Monthly Review Press, 1974).

but concentrated on the issue of managerial *control* over workers. The issue of control is even more central to Edwards who sees it at the heart of "the transformation of the workplace in the twentieth century."[17] Following Marx, Edwards sees the workplace, both past and present, as an arena of class conflict, in his terms a "contested terrain." Within this arena, dramatic changes have taken place in the way in which those at the top control those at the bottom. In the era of nineteenth century competitive capitalism, "simple" control was utilized in which "bosses exercised power personally, intervening in the labor process often to exhort workers, bully and threaten them, reward good performance, hire and fire on the spot, favor loyal workers, and generally act as despots, benevolent or otherwise."[18] Although this system continues to survive in small businesses, it was undermined by the growth of large organizations. Simple personal control tended to be replaced by impersonal technical and bureaucratic control. On the one hand, modern workers came to be controlled by the technologies with which they worked. The classic example of this is the automobile assembly line in which the worker's actions are controlled by the incessant demands of the line. On the other hand, workers are controlled by the impersonal rules of bureaucracies rather than the personal control of supervisors. Capitalism is constantly changing and with it so are the means by which workers are controlled.

The Decline of American Capitalism

Having viewed the changing nature of capitalism, we might now wonder what is the fate of capitalism within American society? While it continues to dominate the capitalist world, American industry is not the powerful force it once was. The fact is that many American industries, especially steel and automobiles, have declined (what Bluestone and Harrison call, "the deindustrialization of America"[19]).

A number of factors are involved in the decline of at least some elements of American capitalism. The United States has been afflicted by aging industrial sectors, especially its "smokestack industries."[20] The inefficiencies of these outdated factories have, in turn, helped make it difficult for American industries to compete with foreign industries. On the other side, successes of foreign manufacturers on a variety of fronts have made them formidable competitors in the international marketplace.

Radios, TVs and video recorders.   Once dominated by American firms, the radio, TV, and video recorder industries are now controlled by Japanese companies as well as other Far Eastern manufacturers.

[17]Richard Edwards, *Contested Terrain: The Transformation of the Workplace in the Twentieth Century* (New York: Basic Books, 1979).

[18]Ibid., p. 19.

[19]Barry Bluestone and Bennett Harrison, *The Deindustrialization of America* (New York: Basic Books, 1982).

[20]Warren Brown, "Fading Muscle: Steel, Once Symbol of U. S. Might, Casts Shrinking Economic Shadow," *Washington Post* (April 24, 1983), pp. F1, F5.

The most striking case is the video tape recorder industry. Invented in 1956 by an American manufacturer (Ampex), about 90 percent of all video recorders sold in the world are now manufactured in Japan, with the only competition being Philips, a Dutch manufacturer. The video recorders marketed in the United States under names like Zenith and RCA are *all* produced by Japanese manufacturers. Japanese firms were willing and able to undertake the long-term risks involved in producing a low-priced video recorder; American firms were not. Instead, Zenith and other American firms concentrated on products that guaranteed them short-term profits. In the end, the short-run rationality of these firms led to the long-term irrationality (for Americans) that it is Japanese workers and companies that are reaping the rewards of dominating the market for a product invented in America.[21]

Automobiles.   Then there is the success of the Japanese automobile industry. Much of this success is traceable to the skills and abilities of Japanese managers and workers. For the most part, they did not create new technologies, but rather adapted American technologies and simply used them more effectively and efficiently.[22] The success of Japan can also be traced to the failures of their American counterparts. American automobile workers earned comparatively high wages and yet were characterized by high rates of absenteeism, sabotage, low productivity, and poor quality work.

For their part, managers of American automobile firms (as well as those in many other industries) seem to have grown arrogant, contented, and unresponsive to the impending challenge from Japan. By the time that challenge actually materialized, management reaction was both too little and too late.[23] The incompetence of top-level American management was underscored by John DeLorean (one-time top executive at General Motors, later head of the now bankrupt DeLorean Motors), in his critique of the top executives at GM:

> *First and most importantly, there are a great many incompetent executives . . . Most of our management mistakes today are not mistakes of commission, they are errors of omission. Missed opportunities—things left undone . . . we react rather than act . . . Our inability to compete with the foreign manufacturers is more due to management failure than anything else . . . The system and management are stifling initiative.*[24]

There is little doubt that part of the blame for the failure of some American industries must be borne by top American managers and their emphasis on short-term profitability rather than long-term growth.

---

[21]Paul Blumberg, *Inequality in an Age of Decline* (New York: Oxford University Press, 1980), pp. 122–25; Peter Behr, "Playing it Safe, and Losing Out," *Washington Post* (January 17, 1982), pp. A1, A17; "How Zenith Lost Its Competitive, Creative Edge," *Washington Post* (January 19, 1982), pp. C1, C10; "Serving Only the Present," *Washington Post* (January 20, 1982), pp. D1, D10.

[22]William Ouchi, *Theory Z* (New York: Avon, 1981).

[23]J. Patrick Wright, *On a Clear Day You Can See General Motors* (New York: Avon, 1979).

[24]Ibid., p. 261.

Disinvestment.   Another factor in the deindustrialization of America is what Bluestone and Harrison call the "systematic disinvestment in the nation's basic productive capacity."[25] To maintain productivity, as well as to allow it to grow, industries must invest in basic plant and equipment. It is through this kind of industrial investment that the United States became the world's greatest economic power. However, in recent years, much of that money has been diverted from such productive investment. For example, instead of investing in new plants and equipment in the United States, corporations are investing in similar facilities in other countries. While this may be good for these other nations, and even for the corporations doing the investing, it is not good for the American economy and it certainly does not help the employability of the American worker. Another example of disinvestment is the many billions of dollars spent in recent years in the mergers of huge corporations. From the point of view of the economy as the whole, as well as the workers in it, these billions would have been far better spent in investment in productive capacity. Mergers, in themselves, produce no new factories, technologies, or jobs. They do, however, help pad the bank accounts of speculators and stockholders.

The Postindustrial Society

Many of the changes discussed in the last few pages involve the movement of the United States through the industrial-capitalist age. But in the eyes of many observers we are now moving beyond that stage into a "postindustrial" society.

Daniel Bell, a major proponent of the idea of the postindustrial society, thinks that such a society is in the process of emerging in America.[26] The following data support Bell's thesis: In 1940, 51.4 percent of the American workforce was in goods-producing areas such as agriculture, mining, construction, and manufacturing. By 1972, the percentage in goods-production had dropped to 35.8 percent and the estimate for the 1980s is that less than 32 percent of the workforce will be in these areas. On the other hand, in 1940, 48.6 percent of the American workforce was in service areas such as transportation, wholesale and retail trade, finance, insurance, real estate, personnel administration, professional and business services, and local, state, and federal government. In 1972, that proportion had increased to 64.2 percent and in the 1980s it is forecast to be over 68 percent.[27] The Industrial Revolution that defined our workworld for many years is in the process of being supplanted by a "Service Revolution."[28] Occupying positions of increasing impor-

[25]Bluestone and Harrison, *The Deindustrialization of America,* p. 6.

[26]Daniel Bell, *The Coming of Post-Industrial Society: A Venture in Social Forecasting* (New York: Basic Books, 1973). For other viewpoints on the post-industrial society see, Alan Touraine, *The Post-Industrial Society. Tomorrow's Social History: Classes, Conflicts, and Culture in the Programmed Society* (New York: Random House, 1971); Robert L. Heilbroner, "Economic Problems of a 'Post-Industrial Society,' " *Dissent,* 20 (Spring, 1973), 163–176.

[27]Michael Urquhart, "The Employment Shift to Services: Where Did It Come From?" *Monthly Labor Review,* 107 (1984), 15–21.

[28]For cross-cultural data on this trend see, Joachim Singelmann, *From Agriculture to Services: The Transformation of Industrial Employment* (Beverly Hills, CA: Sage, 1978).

tance in this society are various types of professionals, scientists, and technicians. It is these groups that create and control the theoretical knowledge needed for decision making, innovation, and directing social change through the planning of technological growth. In fact, we are in the process of becoming a society in which knowledge itself will become the new form of technology. What we have created is a method of invention, and the keepers of these techniques are professional and technical workers.

So important is knowledge and information processing that some have challenged Bell's thesis on the emergence of a service society. For example, John Naisbitt[29] argues that we are changing from an industrial society to an information processing society rather than a service society. Occupations which in the past had been thought of as professional, clerical, or service occupations are really knowledge and information processing occupations. In terms of the latter, Naisbitt notes that "the overwhelming majority of service workers are actually engaged in the creation, processing, and distribution of information."[30] Naisbitt cites such examples of information processing occupations as systems analysts, computer programmers, teachers, librarians, clerks, secretaries, accountants, newspaper reporters, and lawyers. In contrast to Bell's thesis, Naisbitt argues that over 60 percent of us work in occupations where the "creation, processing, and distribution of information *is* the job."[31]

Given this brief excursion into the history of work in the world, let us turn to some more specific developments, particularly in the United States. First, we shall examine a topic that has concerned us throughout this section— the increasing division of labor—but this time we will look at it in terms of what it means for work in contemporary America.

INCREASING DIVISION OF LABOR

The starting point for any discussion of changes in the division of labor must be Emile Durkheim's seminal work, *The Division of Labor in Society.*[32] Durkheim saw primitive society defined by what he called *mechanical solidarity,* in which unity stemmed, in part, from the fact that everyone did essentially the same things. Such a society was also characterized by a powerful common morality that played a central role in making it cohesive. Primarily because of population growth and increased interaction among people (what Durkheim called *dynamic density*), mechanical solidarity was largely replaced over time by *organic solidarity,* characterized not by the similarities in the tasks performed by individuals, but by their differences. Societies of this type are held together by the fact that people who perform specialized jobs need the contributions of many other specialists to survive. Thus, people may specialize as butchers in the modern world, but to live they will need the services of grocers, bakers, law-

---

[29]John Naisbitt, *Megatrends: Ten New Directions Transforming Our Lives* (New York: Warner Books, Inc., 1982).

[30]Ibid., p. 14.

[31]Ibid., p. 15.

[32]Emile Durkheim, trans. George Simpson, *The Division of Labor in Society* (Glencoe, IL: Free Press, 1947).

yers, physicians, and many others. It is this mutual need for specialized work that is the primary force that holds modern society together.

While organic solidarity becomes dominant with increasing specialization and the division of labor, Durkheim seems to feel that society is not held together as tightly as it was in mechanical solidarity. Basically, the mutual needs created by a high degree of division of labor do not hold society together as well as did the strong common morality characteristic of mechanical solidarity. Durkheim had more specific criticisms of modern society noting three dysfunctional aspects of organic solidarity: (1) *anomie,* or a sense of normlessness or isolation, may increase with the division of labor; (2) there is a forced division of labor, where people are more likely to be compelled to perform tasks that are not congruent with their individual capacities; and (3) the division of labor may be so minute that a task does not seem meaningful to the worker. Although these problems seem to be most characteristic of lower-status occupations in our society (such as assembly-line workers), they are found in all types of occupations.

Contemporary American society may be viewed as an example of a society characterized by organic solidarity. This is true not only because of the high degree of the division of labor but also because of the kinds of problems Durkheim saw as concomitants of a high degree of specialization.

Highly Specialized Labor

There are roughly 20,000 occupations in the United States.[33] Among them are some remarkable examples of the high degree of occupational specialization:

> In the baking industry one can make a living as a cracker breaker, meringue spreader, a pie stripper, or pan dumper. In the slaughter and meat-packing industry one can specialize as: a large stock scalper, belly shaver, crotch buster, gut snatcher, gut sorter, snout puller, ear cutter, eyelid remover, stomach washer (sometimes called belly pumper), hindleg toenail puller, frontleg toenail puller and oxtail washer.[34]

It is quite clear that we have witnessed an enormous proliferation of occupations. More important, however, is the effect of this division of labor on workers. As work is subdivided and subdivided again, it becomes increasingly difficult for workers to find satisfaction in the intrinsic aspects of their jobs. One need only ponder how much satisfaction a worker can get from pulling hindleg toenails hour after hour 5 days each week. Work on the automobile assembly line is generally regarded as the ultimate form of the extreme division of labor. A typical worker may fasten a bolt on an automobile every 20 seconds with only a rare respite. Assembly-line work is one of the most

---

[33]For a list of the majority of these see, *Dictionary of Occupational Titles,* 4th ed. (Washington, D.C.: U.S. Department of Labor, 1977).

[34]Harold Wilensky, "The Early Impact of Industrialization on Society," in William A. Faunce, ed., *Readings in Industrial Sociology* (New York: Appleton-Century-Crofts, 1967), pp. 78–79.

alienating occupations (see Chapter 12) in contemporary America involving a high degree of meaninglessness, isolation, powerlessness, and self-estrangement.

Although specialization is clearest among semi- and unskilled workers (in particular, assembly-line workers), it has occurred throughout the occupational hierarchy. In medicine we have witnessed the decline of the general practitioner and the increasing number of doctors in such specialties as pediatrics, surgery, psychiatry, and gynecology. In the early days of personnel administration almost everyone was a personnel manager, but today we find specialists in labor relations, employment, benefits, and counseling. The examples are legion, but the basic point is that virtually every occupation has become more highly specialized.

While it remains true that we are a specializing society, there are at least two countertrends worth noting. First, there is considerable evidence that automation, to be discussed in Chapter 3, sometimes leads to the destruction of highly specialized jobs and the creation of less specialized occupations. In effect, many highly specialized jobs are exchanged for a few more generalized occupations and a sophisticated technological system. Second, the democratization of work (see Chapter 12) is oriented, among other things, toward the elimination of meaningless, highly specialized occupations. Despite these two trends, the dominant thrust in society continues to be in the direction of increasing specialization.

How do we account for this? The primary reason lies in the belief that the most specialized tasks are the most efficient. In part, this can be traced to the ideas of time and motion specialists like Frederick W. Taylor, who sought to subdivide work into its most basic components, and to the implementation of many of these ideas by Henry Ford. Ford described the principles on which his assembly line was based as:

> the reduction of the necessity of thought on the part of the worker and the reduction of his movements to a minimum. He does as nearly as possible only one thing with only one movement.[35]

Assembly lines built on these principles were highly efficient. But they also had negative consequences for those who worked on them. Henry Ford was aware not only of the efficiencies that this system produced, but also of the human problems that it created. However, while he saw repetition and monotony as a problem for him and other elite members of society, his disdain for workers led him to deny that workers would be similarly affected:

> Repetitive labour . . . is terrifying to me. I could not possibly do the same thing day in and day out, but to other minds, perhaps I might say the majority of minds, repetitive operations hold no terrors . . . The average worker, I am sorry to say, wants a job in which he does not have to put forth much physical exertion—above all, he wants a job in which he does not have to think.[36]

---

[35]Henry Ford (in collaboration with Samuel Crowther), *My Life and Work* (Garden City, NY: Doubleday, Page, and Co., 1922), p. 80.

[36]Ibid., p. 103.

A second reason for increasing specialization can be found in the boom in knowledge and technology that makes it difficult for any one person to master more than a small portion of the needed knowledge or a few of the numerous skills needed to complete a given task. Take the case of knowledge expansion in academia. Sociologists at the turn of the twentieth century could, given the limited amount of sociological knowledge at the time, be generalists knowledgeable about virtually every facet of their field. But today there are well over 10,000 practicing sociologists writing thousands upon thousands of books and articles on countless esoteric topics. It is literally impossible to be a generalist in contemporary sociology. One must specialize in the study of the family, the city, or work, and even then it is very difficult to keep up with the explosion of knowledge in one's sub-area. The same applies, of course, to all other academic fields as well as many other occupations.

A third and very different reason for specialization is found particularly in high-status occupations, especially professions like medicine and law. It is in the best interest of those in such prestigious occupations to push for more and more specialization since that tends to bring with it the ability to restrict entry to only a few chosen individuals, to charge higher prices, and gain higher status. Columnist Nicholas von Hoffman offers a resounding attack on the reasons behind professional specialization:

> In medicine specialization takes the form of coy little ads which read "Sharply P. Ripthroat, M.D., practice limited to diseases of the left eyeball, member, American College of Left Eyeball Surgeons." Years of advanced training permit Dr. Ripthroat to charge larger-than-usual prices for confining himself to blinding you in the left eye. In the old days before scientifc research had brought the healing arts to their present pitch of perfection, the same man was permitted to put out your right eye as well, but then he usually charged less and sometimes threw in six free lessons for your seeing-eye dog.[37]

While von Hoffman is obviously exaggerating for the sake of humor, the fact remains that specialization, particularly among high-status occupations, has its advantages for the professional and some disadvantages for the client.

CHANGES IN THE LABOR FORCE

There have been enormous shifts in the occupational structure of the United States since the turn of the century. Table 2.1 details the major changes in the labor force by occupational level.

Table 2.2 examines the same changes, but seeks to clarify what has taken place by collapsing the occupational categories used in Table 2.1. White-collar occupations include the first four occupational categories in Table 2.1, service occupations include occupational categories 5–6, manual occupations encompass 7–9, and farm occupations include categories 10–11.

---

[37]Nicholas von Hoffman, "Specialization: Raising the Standards—and the Prices," *Washington Post* (January 1, 1975), p. C1.

TABLE 2.1   Changes in Labor Force by Occupational Level

OCCUPATIONAL LEVEL	PERCENTAGE OF THE LABOR FORCE					
	1900	1930	1960	1970	1982	1995*
Professional, technical, and kindred workers	4.3%	6.8%	10.8%	14.0%	17.0%	17.1%
Managers, officials, proprietors, except farm	5.9	7.4	8.7	7.9	11.5	9.6
Clerical and kindred workers	3.0	8.9	14.1	16.9	18.5	18.9
Sales workers	4.5	6.3	7.2	6.8	6.6	6.9
Private household workers	5.4	4.1	2.7	1.4	1.0	0.7
Other service workers	3.6	5.7	8.9	10.4	12.8	15.6
Craftsmen, foremen, and kindred workers	10.6	12.8	13.8	12.9	12.3	11.6
Operators and kindred workers	12.8	15.8	17.5	16.3	12.9	12.1
Laborers, except farm and mine	12.5	11.0	5.1	4.2	4.5	5.6
Farmers and farm managers	19.9	12.4	3.9	1.7	1.5	1.1
Farm laborers and foremen	17.7	8.8	2.3	1.2	1.3	0.8
Not reported	—	—	5.0	6.3	—	—
Total percent	100.2	100.0	100.0	100.0	99.9	100.0
Employed civilian labor force Total number (in thousands)	29,073	45,480	65,778	78,678	99,526	127,110

*The figures for 1995 involve projections.

SOURCES: Percentages for 1900 and 1930 from Philip M. Hauser, "Labor Force," in Robert E.L. Faris, ed., Handbook of Modern Sociology (Chicago: Rand-McNally, 1964), p. 183. Percentages for 1960 and 1970 adapted from Constance Bogh DiCesare, "Change in the Occupational Structure of U.S. Jobs," Monthly Labor Review (1975), p. 24. Percentages for 1982 and total employed civilian labor force for 1930 through 1982 from Employment and Earnings (30) 1, (Washington D.C.: U.S. Department of Labor, 1983), pp. 140, 157. Data for 1995 from George T. Silvestri, John M. Lukasiewicz, and Marcus E. Einstein, "Occupational Employment Projections Through 1995," Monthly Labor Review 106, 11 (1983), 37–49. Totals are rounded.

In the following pages we will highlight some of the major changes that are reflected in Tables 2.1 and 2.2.

The Decline of the Farm

One of the most striking changes in the American labor force is the remarkable decline in the number of people who work on the farm, or in farm-related activities. The statistics on farm laborers in Tables 2.1 and 2.2 indicate the well-known fact that over the last century America has shifted from an agrarian society to an industrial, service, and knowledge producing society.[38]

[38]It should be noted that the statistics on farm laborers—indeed, all labor force statistics—can be somewhat deceptive. It could be argued that a large number of people are in farm-related occupations, even though they are included in other occupational categories. For example, the old-time farmer repaired his own equipment, but as equipment became more complex, specialists were needed. Thus, the tractor repairman is engaged in farm work, but he is not included in the farm category. There are many workers who, while not categorized as farm workers, are engaged in farm-related work.

TABLE 2.2   Changes in Labor Force by Occupational Group

OCCUPATIONAL LEVEL	PERCENTAGE OF THE LABOR FORCE					
	1900	1930	1960	1970	1982	1995*
White-collar	17.6%	29.4%	40.8%	45.6%	53.7%	52.5%
Service	9.1	9.8	11.6	11.8	13.8	16.3
Manual	35.8	39.6	36.4	33.4	29.7	29.3
Farm	37.5	21.1	6.2	2.9	2.7	1.9
Not reported	—	—	5.0	6.3	—	—
Total	100.0	100.0	100.0	100.0	99.9	100.0

*The figures for 1995 involve projections.

SOURCES: Data for 1900 and 1930 adapted from Philip M. Hauser, "Labor Force," in Robert E.L. Faris, ed., *Handbook of Modern Sociology* (Chicago: Rand-McNally, 1964), p. 183. Data for 1960 and 1970 adapted from Constance Bogh DiCesare, "Change in the Occupational Structure of U.S. Jobs," *Monthly Labor Review* (1975), p. 24. 1974 Statistics from *Handbook of Labor Statistics—1975—Reference Edition* (Washington D.C.: U.S. Department of Labor, 1975), p. 41. Data for 1982 from *Employment and Earnings* (30) 1, Washington, D.C.: U.S. Department of Labor, 1983), p. 157. Data for 1995 from George T. Silvestri, John M. Lukasiewicz, and Marcus E. Einstein, "Occupational Employment Projections Through 1995," *Monthly Labor Review* 106, 11 (1983), 37–49. Totals are rounded.

Accounting for the decline of farm workers would in itself require an entire book, but we can at least mention a few of the factors involved. First, of course, is the fact that because of technological advances far fewer people are required to produce much more food. Included in these advances are improved machinery such as mechanical harvesters and packing machines; better seed, fertilizer, insecticide, and animal feed; and improved veterinary medicine. Another factor is the economies of scale produced by having a few large farms rather than innumerable small family farms. These factors have forced many people in the last century to leave the farm. While people were being "pushed" off the farms, the increasing number of comparatively lucrative jobs in the industrial and service sectors served to "pull" others from the farms as well as providing work for those who were forced off the farm. Another factor, intimately related to the others, is the urbanization that was both a cause and a result of the decline of the farm. The new jobs were found in and around the cities and the flow of people from the farms generally ended in urban areas.

While these declines have slowed dramatically over the last two decades,[39] we have not yet reached the end of this process.

Today the independent farmer is virtually on the verge of extinction and in a short time the United States Department of Labor predicts that a few large farms will control food production.[40] Bankruptcies and foreclosures

[39] Patricia A. Daly, "Agricultural Employment: Has the Decline Ended?" *Monthly Labor Review,* 104 (November, 1981), 11–17.

[40] David Kline, "The Embattled Independent Farmer," *New York Times Magazine* (November 29, 1981), p. 138.

reached levels in the early 1980s unseen since the Great Depression. The sound of the auctioneer is increasingly heard throughout America's farm land.[41] Today, the largest 7 percent of all farms control more than half of agricultural sales. By the year 2000 the United States Department of Agriculture predicts that half the current U.S. farmers will be driven from the land. One percent of the farmers who remain will control about half the farm land and food supply.

Currently, it is the medium-sized farmers (those working between 200 and 1000 acres) who are being hardest hit. There are many reasons for this, but basically it is a matter of simple economics, that is, declining profits. Increasing costs due to high interest rates, high energy costs, and high fertilizer costs, and low prices resulting, among other things, from bumper crop yields, have all contributed to this profit squeeze and the resultant decline of the number of medium-sized independent farmers.

To survive, such farmers are often forced to earn the majority of their income from nonfarm employment in local businesses and factories. In this way, they generate enough income to subsidize the farm. In contrast, the bigger corporate megafarms have assets, resources, tax advantages, and sufficient volume of production to remain profitable.

The Rise of the Professions

Although the number of people in the professions and related occupations nearly quadrupled between 1900 and 1982, growth in this category has stabilized and the percentage of the labor force in the professions in 1995 will be about the same as it is in 1982. In 1982 there were about 16.9 million people in the professional category and by 1995 it is expected that about 22 million people will be employed in these occupations.

A variety of factors were involved in the growth of this category in the twentieth century. Such a range of factors is involved because this category encompasses a wide array of occupations from established professions such as law and medicine to semiprofessions such as teaching and nursing to technical occupations such as the health therapy field or computer specialization. One factor is the increasing sophistication of our knowledge, techniques, and machinery, which has led to a burgeoning demand for technically trained people to handle these areas. A second factor is the increasing wealth and sophistication of the American population, which leads people to demand more and more services from such diverse occupations as psychoanalysts, tax accountants, divorce lawyers, and architects. A third factor is the internal pressure from these occupations to either coerce us, or create a desire within us, to use their services. Thus, for example, psychiatrists may have created the idea that psychological problems are illnesses similar to cancer and tuberculosis in order to get us to use their services.[42] On another level, lawyers have helped

---

[41]Ward Sinclair, "Hard Times Keep Spirits Down—on the Farm," *Washington Post* (December 26, 1981), p. A1.

[42]Thomas Szasz, *The Myth of Mental Illness* (New York: Delta, 1961); *The Myth of Psychotherapy* (New York: Doubleday, 1978).

make the real estate transaction so complex that we are almost compelled to use their services in buying or selling a house. Finally, and at another level, the growth in the professional category is fueled by the growing number of occupations that are striving for and achieving (at least in their own eyes) professional status. Professional recognition is a desirable goal for many occupations because it carries with it gains in power, economic position, and prestige. Thus people in many occupations (such as, personnel managers, morticians, librarians) are now actively seeking the elusive professional label. Those in other occupations (such as, schoolteachers, nurses, social workers) feel that they have made it, although the amount of time they devote to an analysis of their professional status raises questions about whether they believe their own claims. The point here is that pressure from a variety of occupations for professional recognition has swelled the number of people found in this category.

Although the number of people found in the professions and related occupations will continue to increase in the future, there is a growing countertrend that constitutes an attack on the basic concept of a profession. This process of deprofessionalization will be discussed in some detail in Chapter 4.

The Clerical Revolution

Although a leveling off in the growth of this occupational category (for example, general office clerks, typists, office machine operators, receptionists, cashiers, and bookkeepers) is expected by 1995, it will continue to be *the* largest occupational category. In 1970 there were over 13 million clerical workers. In 1982 there were 18.4 million workers in clerical occupations, and it is expected that there will be about 24 million workers in 1995.

A major reason for the massive growth in this occupational category is the proliferation of large-scale bureaucracies. Although we will discuss bureaucratization in the next chapter, we must note at this point that a large-scale organization requires innumerable clerical workers to handle the paperwork that is its lifeblood. In addition to increasing the numbers of people employed in this category, bureaucratization has also radically altered the nature of white-collar work. Whereas white-collar clerical work formerly brought with it higher status than blue-collar work, the growing "factory-like" structure of many bureaucracies, as well as the fact that many factory and office workers are doing similar work with computers, has reduced the status of white-collar work by making it indistinguishable, in many cases, from blue-collar factory work. We will devote much more attention to this important issue in Chapter 11.

Another factor in the growth of at least some occupations in this category is technological change. As of 1970 there were almost 3 million typists and secretaries in the United States, and these occupations obviously exist because of the development and use of the typewriter. The effect of the computer is clearer because it is a far more recent technological advance. For example, in 1960 there were less than 2000 operators of computers and computer-related equipment in the United States, but by 1982 that number had grown to over 434,000 workers. The computer also cuts the other way, serving to reduce those employed in certain routine clerical jobs such as filing and billing. But the increase in those needed to prepare material for the computer more than compensates for this decline. Overall, technological change has led, and will continue to lead, to increases in this occupational category.

The Decline in Blue-Collar Workers

In 1900 the number of blue-collar (manual, or what we call "semi- and unskilled workers" in this book) workers was a close second to the number of those employed on the farm. By 1930, reflecting the burgeoning industrialization and the accelerating decline of the farm, the blue-collar worker was, by a wide margin, the largest occupational category. Technological advances in the factory and the growth of bureaucracies were already being felt in 1930 and this was reflected in the increased number of white-collar workers, but this category was still a distant second to blue-collar workers. But by 1956 the number of people in white-collar occupations was greater than the number in blue-collar occupations and that gap increased greatly between 1960 and 1982. The percentage of workers in the manual category has been declining and the forecast is for a further modest decline through the mid-1990s.

There are a number of reasons for this decline—the most notable being various technological advances in factories and other settings that have allowed for an increase in production with a decline in the number of blue-collar employees. The decline in America's traditional "smokestack industries" like steel and automobiles has cost this country hundreds of thousands of blue-collar jobs. Then there is the general shift in our society from goods production to the offering of services with the corresponding movement from blue-collar to white-collar employees.

Other Occupational Changes

The proportion of sales workers in the labor force increased by almost 50 percent between 1900 and 1982. However, the rate of growth has leveled off. Between 1960 and 1982 there was actually a slight decline in the proportion of sales workers and this percentage is expected to remain almost constant over the next decade. One reason for this leveling off of growth among sales workers can be traced to changed merchandising techniques such as self-service and vending machines that have reduced the need for sales workers in various types of stores. Within the sales occupation, the majority of workers remain in retail establishments, although that group is growing less rapidly than those in service organizations such as insurance and real estate. With more money, people can afford to buy more life insurance or purchase a new, or even a vacation, home. This, of course, reflects once again the transformation in our society from goods production to service offering.

The number of private household workers[43] continues its steep decline. Employing private household workers is simply not as fashionable—or affordable—as it once was. In Lewis Coser's view this occupational category

---

[43] Allyson Sherman Grossman, "Women in Domestic Work: Yesterday and Today," *Monthly Labor Review*, 103 (1980), 17–21.

has become "obsolete."[44] Families seem to desire more privacy than they did in the past, the growing cost of living space has made household help prohibitively expensive; and the extended family has contracted, leaving fewer people in the home to be cared for.[45] Then, many of the services once provided by private household workers are now offered by such outside agencies as laundry services, diaper services, babysitting agencies, and the like. Also involved in this change are a variety of technological changes (such as self-cleaning ovens and frost-free refrigerators) that have allowed middle- and upper-class families to dispense with household workers without increasing their workload appreciably. To this we add the fact that fewer and fewer people are willing to accept these low-paying, manual jobs even when they are available. Finally, changing attitudes of women toward this type of work (especially increasing resistance to it) has had a marked impact, especially since over 96 percent of the private household workers in 1982 were women.

Excluding private household workers, other types of service workers[46] have grown substantially and that trend will continue. This, of course, is part of the increasing desire for, and ability to afford, services in American society. A variety of specific changes helps account for this broad development. In the health field,[47] for example, a growing number of service workers are being employed to provide services that can no longer be provided by the limited number of professionals and semiprofessionals. This is reflected in the increase in nurses' aides, physicians' aides, and paraprofessionals in the health field. This trend is expected to continue through this decade. Further, as more families have both wives and husbands working, the demand for food service occupations and child care workers is also expected to continue to grow. On the other hand, some service occupations have declined in spite of the increase in the category as a whole. For example, the number of elevator operators has almost disappeared as a result of the installation of self-service elevators. All in all, however, the need for service workers in our increasingly service-oriented society has led to a substantial and continuing growth in this category.

We can see from this discussion that the American labor force is highly volatile, with a complex series of large- and small-scale changes resulting in major overall shifts. (See the Appendix on page 435, for a discussion of changes in the classifications of occupations in America.) It is clear that the American labor force has undergone major changes in the twentieth century and that the rest of the century should continue to bring some significant changes.

[44]Lewis Coser, "Servants: The Obsolescence of an Occupational Role," *Social Forces,* 52 (1973), 31–40.

[45]David Chaplin, "Domestic Service and the Negro," in Arthur B. Shostak and William Gomberg, eds., *Blue-Collar World: Studies of the American Worker* (Englewood Cliffs, NJ: Prentice-Hall, Inc., 1964), pp. 535–44.

[46]Michael Urquhart, "The Employment Shift to Services: Where Did it Come From?"

[47]Edward S. Sekscenski, "The Health Services Industry: A Decade of Expansion," *Monthly Labor Review,* 104 (1981), 9–16.

CONCLUSIONS

This chapter began with a discussion of the history of work through the ages, from the earliest times through America in the 1980s. In addition to this broad historical background, two more specific changes were discussed in this chapter: the growing specialization of work that has come to characterize a wide array of occupations, and the changing nature of the American labor force. In most cases, we started with 1900 data and traced labor force changes not only to the present day, but beyond in terms of projections for 1995. In the next chapter we continue this line of discussion with a number of other changes in work in the United States.

THREE
THE CHANGING NATURE
OF WORK: II

In Chapter 2 we reviewed some of the broadest changes affecting work in America—the history of work through the ages, the increasing division of labor, and the changing nature of the labor force. In this chapter we turn to a series of more specific changes beginning with technological advances.

TECHNOLOGICAL ADVANCES

As is clear from our discussion of the American labor force, technological change has had a pervasive and profound impact upon the workworld. Before discussing some of these recent technological developments, we need to define precisely what we mean by technology. We can conceive of *technology* as the complex interplay among various elements (including materials, tools, machines, skills, knowledge, and procedures) in the production process. The way these various elements are combined determines the type of technology that is employed. This is a very broad definition of technology that allows us to see that it is not just something that applies to the production of automobiles, but also to the provision of medical services, the production of television programs, and even the election of a president. Our concern in this section is with "all innovations which result from the application of scientific and engineering knowledge and techniques to the process of production and distribution and other economic operations."[1]

A key technological development, and one about which we will have more to say throughout this book, is *automation*. The important factor that distinguishes automation from other technological changes is the mechanization of the control of the production process. The key development is *cybernation*, or the ability of the system itself to adjust to imperfections, abnormalities, and problems.

During the 1960s and most of the 1970s, computerized automation was theoretically possible but limited applications and high costs made large-scale automation impractical. As of 1978, less than 7 percent of American workers were in beginning or advanced automated industries.[2] However, with recent advances and refinements in microprocessor technology, a much more widespread utilization of automated (and robot) technology is underway. These developments have led many social scientists to suggest that we are on the verge of another technological revolution.

We will have much more to say about automation (and robots) shortly, but before we do we will look at a range of types of occupations and a number of technological changes that have had a profound effect on them.

Professions

Because, in many cases, they deal primarily with knowledge, the professions have been radically altered by technological change. We often overlook this fact because we tend to equate technological change with changes in tools and machinery. Yet when we include knowledge and equipment as part of technology, we can see how the professions have undergone substantial change. Not only are the professions affected by technological changes, but they themselves have played a central role in producing those changes.

As legal knowledge grows and the number of potentially precedent-setting cases multiply, lawyers have been forced to become more specialized, carving out ever-smaller spheres of practice so that they can be sure that they can knowledgeably handle their area. The legal profession has also been altered to some degree by the development of Lexis, a computerized system for storing and retrieving information on cases.[3] Now, instead of poring over mountains of law books, lawyers can utilize Lexis to retrieve relevant cases.

Physicians have been affected by a tremendous increase in knowledge and have reacted with a like tendency toward specialization. But physicians have also been affected by dramatic changes in medical equipment. A recent study of the effect of technology on the medical profession concludes:

[1]Seymour Wolfbein, "The Pace of Technological Change and the Factors Affecting It," in Simon Marcson, ed., *Automation, Alienation, and Anomie* (New York: Harper & Row, 1970), p. 54.

[2]William Faunce, *Problems of an Industrial Society*, 2nd ed. (New York: McGraw-Hill, 1981), p. 47.

[3]Eve Spangler and Peter M. Lehman, "Lawyering as Work," in Charles Derber, ed., *Professionals as Workers: Mental Labor in Advanced Capitalism* (Boston: G.K. Hall, 1982), p. 71.

> . . . modern medicine has now evolved to a point where diagnostic judgments based on "subjective" evidence—the patient's sensations and the physician's own observations of the patient—are being supplanted by judgments based on "objective" evidence, provided by laboratory procedures and by mechanical and electronic devices.[4]

The increasing sophistication of diagnostic tests and diagnostic machinery has rendered the physician who practiced solely from his or her "little black bag" a thing of the past. Physicians have grown ever more dependent on machinery created and run by others. A whole new set of technical occupations has been created to run these machines and provide meaningful information to the physician. The relationship between these new technicians and specialists and the physician has added a whole new dimension to the practice of medicine, as well as a new set of conflicts between the establishment medical professions and technical occupations that aspire to that status, as well as a share of the power currently wielded by physicians. As a result of these changes and many others, the practice of medicine has been transformed, at least in part, into ordering a patient to undergo a series of sophisticated tests and then depending on others to administer them and help interpret them. The occupation is very different from what it was only a few years ago.

Almost by definition, the professional occupation most affected by technological change is that of scientists. On the one hand, virtually all technological changes are derived from basic scientific research. On the other hand, the sciences are, in turn, propelled into making new discoveries by technological advances. For example, it was basic scientific research that led to the technological development of the atomic reactor, and the proliferation of atomic reactors has created new scientific questions as well as many more nuclear scientists. As both a cause and a result of technological change, the scientific occupations have undergone enormous growth in recent years. It was estimated in the 1950s that 90 percent of all the scientists who *ever* lived were alive then,[5] and that percentage has certainly increased with the dramatic growth in the number of scientists since that time. The number of doctorates in science grew from 60 in 1885[6] to over 17,000 *per year* from 1976 through 1982.[7] As of 1977 there were over 250,000 doctoral scientists in the United States[8] and it is likely that by the time this book is read that number will be in excess of one-half million.

[4]Stanley Joel Reiser, *Medicine and the Reign of Technology* (Cambridge, MA: Cambridge University Press, 1978), p. ix.

[5]Derek J. De Solla Price, "The Exponential Curve of Science," *Discovery,* 17 (1956), 240–43.

[6]Harriet Zuckerman and Robert K. Merton, "Age, Aging and Age Structure in Science," in Robert K. Merton, *The Sociology of Science* (Chicago: University of Chicago Press, 1973), pp. 497–559.

[7]U.S. Bureau of the Census, *Statistical Abstract of the United States: 1984,* 104th ed. (Washington, D.C., 1983), p. 600.

[8]*Characteristics of Doctoral Scientists and Engineers in the United States: 1977* (Washington, D.C.: National Science Foundation, 1979).

While it is true that engineers have made crucial contributions to technological change,[9] our concern here is with the fact that the growth of engineering is a product of technological advance.[10] Engineering was virtually unknown in the early 1800s. Technological advances that allowed for the development of such public works as canals and railroads led to some growth, so that by 1850 there were about 2000 civil engineers in the United States.

In the 40-year period between 1880 and 1920, the engineering profession grew by 2000 percent—from 7000 to 136,000,[11] largely because of technological and other developments. These developments also changed the nature of the occupation. The civil engineer who was predominant in the mid-1800s was replaced by new types of engineers needed by industry, such as those in mining, metallurgical, mechanical, electrical, and chemical fields. As the twentieth century has progressed new technological changes have led to still other engineering specialties, and the number of engineers in the country grew to about 1.1 million in 1972 and to almost 1.6 million in 1982.[12] Similar growth has occurred among engineers in other industrial and industrializing nations.[13]

In addition to the increase in scientific and engineering personnel, there has been a considerable growth in technical occupations. This is almost a direct measure of the degree of technological change. Individuals in these occupations serve primarily as adjuncts to scientists or as operators of the complex technological mechanisms that stem from scientific research. Examples of occupations in this category include the computer programmer as well as technicians in a variety of fields including medicine, dentistry, and engineering. The technician generally combines some professional expertise with manual skills. Thus, engineering technicians, to give one example, know something about engineering theory, but their primary responsibility is "the testing and development, the application, and the operation of engineering or scientific equipment or processes."[14] The rapidity of growth in this category is reflected by the fact that a technical occupation such as computer programmer was not even listed in the 1949 *Dictionary of Occupational Titles*.[15] The number of computer operators grew by almost 350 percent between 1970 and 1980[16] and the coming years are likely to bring with them continued substantial growth.

---

[9]David F. Noble, *America by Design: Science, Technology, and the Rise of Corporate Capitalism* (New York: Alfred A. Knopf, 1982).

[10]Edwin Layton, "Science, Business, and the American Engineer," in Robert Perrucci and Joel E. Gerstl, eds., *The Engineers and the Social System* (New York: John Wiley, 1969), pp. 51–72.

[11]Ibid., p. 53.

[12]*Statistical Abstract of the United States: 1984*, p. 419.

[13]See, for example, Peter Whalley, *The Social Production of Technical Work: The Case of British Engineers* (London: Macmillan, 1985).

[14]William M. Evan, "On the Margin—The Engineering Technician," in Peter Berger, ed., *The Human Shape of Work* (New York: Macmillan, 1964), p. 88.

[15]Ibid., p. 84.

[16]Andrew Hacker, *US: A Statistical Portrait of the American People* (New York: Viking Press, 1983), p. 126.

Managers

New types of managerial occupations have been spawned by technological changes. A good example is the manager of computer services, now an important position in industry, government, and medical service facilities. Similarly, a number of traditional managerial positions have been altered by technological change. As a result, many managers have been forced to school themselves in the theory and functioning of computers.

Executive computer work stations hooked to company, industry, national, and international data bases are now widely used. Managers use computers for plotting sales trends, pricing and budget analysis, and inventory control. Analyses which previously were produced by several staff members over an extended period of time can now be summarized and neatly printed on easily readable and colorful graphs and charts generated by the manager him/herself.

Teleconferencing is another innovation that is changing the way managers work. Costly travel time is being eliminated and expenses reduced as managers visually confer simultaneously with other managers at various domestic and international locations from the comfort of their personal offices.

In the future, it is likely that much managerial work will not be conducted in the office at all. Portable computers and stationary personal computers make it possible to have an office wherever the manager is—at home, in an airplane, on a train, and so forth. While we are not suggesting that the office will be completely eliminated, there is little doubt that the traditional centralized office is being altered by these recent developments.

Clerical Workers

The machines and tools of clerical workers have radically changed over the last 100 years and with these developments have come important alterations in the nature of their work. We can divide technological change in the office into five basic stages:[17]

1. *Craft*—Before the mechanization of the office, all a clerk needed was a pen, a ledger, and the ability to count and write.
2. *Early Mechanization*—In the late nineteenth century typewriters, adding machines, and dictating machines appeared; they performed single functions and did not radically alter traditional clerical tasks.
3. *Multi-Function Business Machines*—After World War I, more skills were needed to operate office machines.
4. *Punched-Card Data Processing*—After World War II this development produced revolutionary changes in many office jobs.
5. *Electronic Data Processing*—In 1951 the first commercial computers appeared, with the built-in capacity for speed, accuracy, storage, and the ability to perform long, complex, uninterrupted operations. In the late 1970s and 1980s, the coming of age of the minicomputer and the personal computer revolutionized the office by permitting word processing and sophisticated data analysis.

---

[17]Jon Shepard, *Automation and Alienation: A Study of Office and Factory Workers* (Cambridge, MA: The M.I.T. Press, 1971).

As was the case with managers, many clerical workers now work with electronic work stations hooked to a central computer with access to several data bases and support systems. Rather than performing one function, that is, recording sales, billing, crediting accounts, or keeping track of correspondence for many customers, one account "manager" now handles several functions for fewer customers. Other common office equipment now includes desktop computers, word processors, electronic switchboards, and electronic mail systems.

Machine Operators

It is perhaps in the machine operator category that technological advances have been felt most. In the early days of industrialization much production was still done in the home, but with the advent of steam power and new, large machines, the early factories developed. Operatives were moved out of their homes and their ability to control their own work behavior was greatly reduced. The early machines required tending by the operatives, but these machines did not have the total control over the workers that were characteristic of some later machinery. Nevertheless, the shift from home to factory was a difficult adjustment for most people, and with each technological change and advance new adjustments were required. Unemployment and technological obsolescence were feared by all early industrial workers and were realities for many.

The next great technological change that had a profound effect on the operative was the development of the assembly line, which proved to be both highly efficient for the organization and highly alienating for the worker. While home workers had a great deal of control over their work behavior, and machine tenders had some control, assembly-line workers were almost totally controlled by the machine. Examining the impact of the assembly line on workers, many observers saw increasingly dark days ahead. It was felt that further technological advances would only mean increasing alienation for them. Thus the advent of automation was viewed fearfully by many blue- (and white-) collar workers.

When automation comes on a partial basis to assembly-line industries, the worst fears of blue-collar workers seem to be realized. In discussing the partial automation of automobile factories, Faunce contends that the advent of automation climaxes the long trend toward decreasing control of work pace by the industrial worker.[18]

However, the situation in totally automated factories, such as oil or chemical plants, appears to be considerably different. Interestingly, there seems to be a substantial increase in control and decline in alienation in these industries. Operative positions in totally automated factories offer greater responsibility and freedom. However, whether automation gives the operative more or less control is somewhat irrelevant to the concern in this section. The fact is, automation is a continuing process of technological change and, as

---

[18]William A. Faunce, *Problems of an Industrial Society*, 1st ed. (New York: McGraw-Hill, 1968).

such, it is a cause of considerable real and imaginary insecurity to the operative.

Farm Workers

Technological advances have also been an important factor in the changes that have occurred in farm occupations. Historically, improved farm machinery reduced the need for hand labor, causing both considerable unemployment and migration to the industrialized cities. For those who remained on the farm, much of the work was transformed from hand labor to machine tending. In short, the sickle, scythe, and horsedrawn plow were replaced by the gang plow, modern combine, and mechanical harvester which dig, plant, harvest, and clean crops.

Changes in farm machinery continue to affect farming as an occupation. Friedland, Barton, and Thomas show how a machine capable of harvesting tomatoes revolutionized the handling of that crop.[19] In 1962, 1 percent of the tomato crop was machine harvested, but by 1970 it had risen to 99.9 percent. They predict a similar revolution in lettuce harvesting once remaining technological problems are worked out.

Added to the increasingly sophisticated farm machinery is the growth in knowledge about farming and farm-related activities. Thus, the development of effective (and hopefully harmless to humans) insecticides has also radically altered the nature of farming. Other innovations include better soil techniques, improved varieties of crops, and more advanced systems of irrigation.

The mechanization of farming and the corresponding improvement in farming techniques has led to a tremendous rise in productivity. In 1875, the United States produced 314 million bushels of wheat, but by 1982 productivity had grown to 2.8 billion bushels.[20] Over the past several years, the agricultural output per man-year has increased at a rate close to 6 percent per year. This stands in contrast to 2.5 percent for all other U.S. industries.[21] Compared to 100 years ago, only a miniscule percentage of the workforce is needed to produce more than enough food for a population that has increased fourfold.

TECHNOLOGICAL ADVANCES: RECENT DEVELOPMENTS

As previously mentioned, recent technological advances in microprocessor technology have led some to suggest that we are on the verge of a revolution which could far surpass the Industrial Revolution of the nineteenth century in its consequences for the way we work. Microprocessor technology, that is, the miniaturization of computer technology, is made possible by the silicon chip. In essence, the silicon chip is a "miniaturized system of integrated circuits

[19]William H. Friedland, Amy E. Barton and Robert J. Thomas, *Manufacturing Green Gold: Capital, Labor, and Technology in the Lettuce Industry* (Cambridge, MA: Cambridge University Press, 1981).

[20]*Statistical Abstract of the United States: 1984*, p. 675.

[21]Wayne D. Rasmussen, "The Mechanization of Agriculture," *Scientific American*, 247 (1982), 48–61.

which can direct electrical current and, thereby, generate vast computational power."[22] Hence, numerous calculations and large storage capacity is made possible by a chip 1 square centimeter in size. This reduction in size makes possible a reduction in the costs associated with production and use, rendering microprocessor technology economically competitive.

Computers[23] and Robots[24]

There is a near endless number of applications of microprocessor technology in both the factory and office. In the office, typewriters are being replaced by electronic wordprocessors. The wordprocessor helps workers complete assignments faster and easier with fewer errors.[25] Computers are also used for information storage and retrieval, as well as writing, editing, and delivering correspondence.

While the advantages are many, a series of concerns have recently emerged about the use of computers in the office. Health issues (such as low level radiation from video display terminals) are a concern in the office, but most of the debate about the impact of widespread implementation of computers centers around the issue of unemployment and worker displacement. The issue is will modern technology create enough jobs to employ those it displaces or will it create a permanent, unemployed and unemployable class of people? We will return to this issue after we discuss the role of robots and computers in the modern factory.

In the factory, robots are now a reality in Japan[26]—the world leader— and the United States.[27] By the end of this decade, over 200,000 robots are expected to be in operation in various U.S. industries. The range of jobs that a robot can perform expands daily.[28]

Industrial robots[29] are basically mechanical limbs linked to reprogrammable and hence multifunctional computers. Robots are now used in the manufacture of coal, refrigerators, tanks, aircraft, guns, and ammunition. Robots are used to spray paint cars and bridges, test thermometers, and assemble TV sets and typewriter ribbon cartridges. In agriculture, robots are used in spraying and crop dusting. Robots with vision systems are now being

---

[22]Sar A. Levitan and Clifford M. Johnson, "The Future of Work: Does it Belong to Us or to the Robots?" *Monthly Labor Review* (November, 1982), 10.

[23]The entire May, 1979 issue of *Sociology of Work and Occupations* was devoted to computers and work.

[24]The entire November, 1983 issue of *The Annals of the American Academy of Political and Social Science* was devoted to the issue of robots and work.

[25]Jeffery L. Sheler and Jeannye Thornton, "The Paperless Office—How Workers Adapt," *U.S. News and World Report* (Feburary 22, 1982), p. 77.

[26]Leonard Lynn, "Japanese Robotics: Challenge and Limited Exemplar," *The Annals of the American Academy of Political and Social Science*, 470 (1983), 16–27.

[27]Gail M. Martin, "Industrial Robots Join the Work Force," *Occupational Outlook Quarterly*, 26 (1982), 2–11.

[28]Ibid.

[29]Martha M. Hamilton, "High-Tech Revolution Makes, Breaks Jobs," *Washington Post* (July 27, 1982), p. C1; Otto Friedrich, "The Robot Revolution," *Time* (December 8, 1980), p. 73.

developed and applied.[30] In the future we can expect robots that will explore and extract materials in subsurface mines and beneath the seas, as well as engage in satellite repair.[31]

The current generation of robots cannot react to unforeseen circumstances or altered conditions, nor can they improve their performance based on past experience. In short, the robots that are available today are found in industrial environments where variability and decision making is minimal.[32] That is likely to change in the future as robots gain additional capacities.

The service industry is also affected by computers and robotics. While computers make possible tellerless banks and unmanned gasoline stations, robots that will cut your hair or deal you a blackjack card game are being developed. Police departments and the military can now use the services of bomb-disposing robots. Currently on the drawing board are robotic servants designed to assist handicapped persons in wheelchairs, quadriplegics, and bedridden patients.[33]

Benefits of Computers and Robots

Modern computer and robot technology is attractive for many reasons, The robot's advantages over human beings include the precision and speed at which it accomplishes its task. Further, not only can the robot work 24-hour shifts, but it "takes no coffee breaks, does not call in sick on Mondays, does not become bored, does not take vacations, or qualify for pensions—and does not leave Coca-Cola cans rattling around inside the products it has helped assemble."[34] In addition, robots have no fear of dangerous tasks or poor working conditions. They work fearlessly with plutonium, radiation, or in extreme temperatures.

Not only are robots superior workers, they are also cheaper and more productive than their human counterparts. In the automobile industry, where approximately $20 per hour is needed to cover a worker's pay and benefits, robots can be operated for about $6 per hour.[35] Overall, the average robot costs about $40,000 and can be operated for approximately $4.80 an hour.[36] In general, it is estimated that the typical robot pays for itself in about a year and a half.

Along with cheaper operating costs comes the added benefit of greater productivity. A robot operated by Digital Electronic Automation assembles a compressor valve unit composed of twelve separate parts. Without error, the robot operates for 24 hours a day and produces 320 units an hour. This is the approximate equivalent output of ten human beings. At Chrysler, fifty robot

[30]Paul Kinnucan, "Machines That See," *High Technology*, (April, 1983), pp. 30–36.

[31]Robert U. Ayres and Stephen M. Miller, "Robotic Realities: Near-Term Prospects and Problems," *The Annals of the American Academy of Political and Social Science*, 470 (1983), 33.

[32]Ibid., 28–45.

[33]Philip Faflick, "Here Come the Robots," *Time* (March 7, 1983), pp. 46–47.

[34]Otto Friedrich, "The Robot Revolution," p. 73.

[35]Sar A. Levitan and Clifford M. Johnson, "The Future of Work: Does it Belong to Us or to the Robots?"

[36]Otto Friedrich, "The Robot Revolution," p. 73.

welders have replaced 200 human welders with an increase in productivity of almost 20 percent.[37] It is predicted that automation will raise productivity from sixteen cars to twenty cars per hourly job. At this rate, by 1990 it will take 115,000 fewer workers to produce the same number of cars manufactured in 1978.[38] At a General Electric Company plant in Erie, Pennsylvania, robots and other automated computerized systems are expected to produce an engine frame in 16 hours—down from 16 days.[39] Similar benefits are derived from the application of modern technology in the office.

Computers, Robots, and Job Loss

One of the key issues in computerization and robot technology is the degree to which they jeopardize peoples' jobs. Meaningful generalizations about job elimination and worker displacement are difficult because of the large number of variables that need to be considered. Some of these variables include elasticity of demand for products due to lower costs, market conditions outside the firm or industry introducing the new technology, new legislation, and government regulation or deregulation.[40]

While projections are difficult, they are nonetheless being made. Sar A. Levitan and Clifford M. Johnson suggest that nearly "one-third of *all* manufacturing employment" could be eliminated by 1990.[41] It is estimated that in less than 30 years it will be technologically possible to replace "almost all operative jobs in manufacturing, about 9 percent of today's workforce, as well as a number of skilled manufacturing jobs and routine nonmanufacturing jobs."[42]

Everyone concerned with this issue agrees that the technological capabilities exist (or will soon exist) to eliminate millions of jobs. Writes Naisbitt: "In Australia, microprocessors are called 'job killers,' and in England, a program entitled 'The Chips Are Down' portrayed widespread job loss and economic upheaval because of micro-electronics."[43] Although, as we have seen, middle level managerial positions will be affected, those most likely to be displaced are manual workers in the manufacturing industries and those in lower level white-collar clerical positions, that is, file clerks, bookkeepers,

[37]Ibid.

[38]"Detroit's Jobs That Will Never Come Back," *Business Week* (May 23, 1983), pp. 91–92.

[39]Monroe W. Karmin, "Industry: Lean, Mean and Ready for Recovery," *U.S. News & World Report* (May 9, 1983), pp. 141–142.

[40]For an elaboration of these points see the following: Harvey Brooks, "Technology, Competition, and Employment," *The Annals of the American Academy of Political and Social Science,* 470 (1983), 115–122; Doris B. McLaughlin, "Electronics and the Future of Work: The Impact on Pink and White Collar Workers," *The Annals of the American Academy of Political and Social Science,* 470 (1983), 152–162.

[41]Sar A. Levitan and Clifford M. Johnson, "The Future of Work: Does it Belong to Us or to the Robots?" 11, (Emphasis added); see also, M. Eugene Merchant, "Flexible Manufacturing Systems: Robotics and Computerized Automation," *The Annals of the American Academy of Political and Social Science,* 470 (1983), 123–135.

[42]Ayres and Miller, "Robotic Realities," 51.

[43]John Naisbitt, *Megatrends,* p. 29.

typists, etc. Under this scenario, according to Harley Shaiken: "Ultimately, retraining will not be possible, because there will be no jobs for workers to be retrained for."[44]

Less pessimistically, others believe that such wholesale elimination of jobs will occur but that various occupations will remain. However, what jobs do remain will require skills that the unemployed and displaced have not been trained for, leaving the jobless and unskilled "forced to compete with illegal immigrants and refugees for the few unskilled jobs available."[45] Increasingly, an even more polarized, two-tiered workforce could emerge, with a few high-paying, high-skilled jobs at one end of the occupational order and a large number of low-paying, low-skilled jobs at the other extreme.

Still another scenario suggests that widespread implementation of auto-mated technologies and expanding employment are not incompatible as long as the rate of technological expansion is no "faster than the natural rate of worker attrition, which now runs as high as 15% in the metalworking plants that are ripe for robotization."[46] Slow, steady, piecemeal technological change is seen as a workable solution.

According to this scenario, new jobs will be created in such high-tech in-dustries as computer and robot manufacturing, telecommunications, and aerospace. Jobs in information processing (gathering, storing, manipulating, communicating) are expected to be plentiful. Occupations such as tape librar-ians, word processor operators, robotics specialists, office machine mainte-nance workers, systems analysts, and service technicians will grow. By the early part of the next century it is predicted that business and commerce will need over 3.5 million software writers. Further, programming, monitoring, and repairing industrial robots will employ over 2 million workers.[47] Over the next decade, the following occupations are expected to grow: computer serv-ice technicians (97 percent); computer system analysts (85 percent); computer operators (76 percent); computer programmers (77 percent); miscellaneous electronic data processing equipment operators (63 percent).[48]

Even this more optimistic scenario, however, acknowledges the difficulties current jobless and future displaced workers will face if they are not properly trained for the new tasks which will emerge. As one analyst sug-gests: "Millions of new jobs will be created . . . but they'll be so different that today's laid-off workers will be hard pressed to fill them."[49] Said one corporate president, "It's unfortunate, but the kind of people we will need are not un-employed steelworkers."[50]

Which of these scenarios is most likely to be an accurate prediction of the

[44]Otto Friedrich, "The Robot Revolution," p. 78.

[45]Martha M. Hamilton, "High-Tech Revolution Makes, Breaks Jobs," p. A16.

[46]Otto Friedrich, "The Robot Revolution," p. 78.

[47]Monroe W. Karmin, "Industry: Lean, Mean and Ready for Recovery."

[48]George T. Silvestri, John M. Lukasiewicz, and Marcus E. Einstein, "Occupational Em-ployment Projections Through 1995," *Monthly Labor Review*, 106 (1983), 37–49.

[49]Jeremy Main, "Work Won't Be the Same Again," *Fortune* (June 28, 1982), p. 58.

[50]William D. Marbach et al., "High Hopes for High Tech," *Newsweek* (February 14, 1983), p. 55.

future is difficult to predict.[51] However, several authors do agree that automation will not come as rapidly as many fear; steady, piecemeal technological adaptation is seen as the most likely future scenario. Levitan and Johnson see various market forces working to slow the pace of technological implementation. The size of capital investment, the rate of plant utilization, and current massive investments in existing facilities are seen as "economic governors" which could slow the rate of technological adoption.[52] Brooks argues that the rate of adoption will be checked by several factors including an underestimation of training needs, breakdowns and repairs that inevitably accompany the introduction of new technology, and the failure to realize expected productivity gains.[53] Martin suggests that while robots are getting less costly every year, the cost may still be prohibitive for the small and medium size firms.[54] Finally, Uttal points out that much office work is not routine and the rate of adoption of sophisticated office equipment will be slowed until the precise steps by which managers and professionals do their jobs can be specified and programmed.[55]

Regardless of the ultimate outcome, what seems certain is that workers will need to be trained or retrained in the skills that will be needed in the future. According to Groff, no issue in the next decade "is more important than the relationship between occupational education and the economy."[56] If the pessimists are correct and millions of jobs are eventually eliminated, the retrained workers will not be needed for many years. If the optimists are correct and plenty of new jobs are created, the displaced workers must be retrained much more rapidly.[57]

While the United States has for some time spent money to upgrade the skills of various groups, the nature and scope of current training/retraining efforts is changing. As one analyst notes, "We have focused our attention in the past on young and disadvantaged workers, but now it is absolutely necessary to focus our attention on the whole workforce."[58] With this change in mind, it seems that a multifaceted approach involving schools, unions, industry, and various governmental bodies is essential to insure the acquisition of skills necessary to survive in a fast-paced, high-tech society.

Currently, we are beginning to see the retraining issue being addressed by these various institutions. Vocational schools, community colleges, and universities are developing programs to train students and displaced workers in robotics operation and maintenance. In 1980, 14.1 percent of the collective

---

[51]Quoted in Martha M. Hamilton, "High-Tech Revolution Makes, Breaks Jobs," p. A16.

[52]Sar A. Levitan and Clifford M. Johnson, "The Future of Work: Does it Belong to Us or to the Robots?"

[53]Harvey Brooks, "Technology, Competition, and Employment."

[54]Gail M. Martin, "Industrial Robots Join the Work Force."

[55]Bro Uttal, "What's Detaining the Office of the Future," *Fortune* (May 3, 1982), pp. 176–196.

[56]Warren H. Groff, "Impacts of the High Technologies on Vocational and Technical Education," *The Annals of the American Academy of Political and Social Science*, 470 (1983), 82.

[57]Pat Choate and Noel Epstein, "Workers of the Future, Retool: Nothing to Lose But Your Jobs," *Washington Post* (May 9, 1982), p. D1.

[58]Jeremy Main, "Work Won't Be the Same Again," p. 60.

bargaining agreements between industry and major unions included some provision for retraining workers affected by the introduction of new technology.[59] A report prepared by American businessmen and academic leaders in 1983 called for a national displaced workers' program providing training and educational benefits.

While these efforts are just a beginning, these private and public organizatons are at least starting to cope with what may be one of the most important domestic issues facing the United States in the coming decades.

BUREAUCRATIZATION

Still another sweeping change that has had an enormous impact on occupational life has been the increasing employment of American workers in bureaucracies. The long-term shift of workers into organizations has changed some occupations and created others. Historically, members of such professions as law or medicine practiced on their own, but in recent years we have seen many of the "free" professions moving into organizational life. The physician, for example, is now likely to be involved in a group practice or a small clinic and is almost certainly affiliated with a hospital. The small independent proprietor is also rapidly being forced out of business by larger retail organizations such as Safeway and Sears. In contrast, managers and officials were created by the spread of organizations, and it is only within organizations that they are needed to supervise the work of subordinates. The same is true of white-collar workers; they came into existence to handle the enormous amount of paperwork generated by large-scale organizations. Blue-collar workers existed before the growth of organizations, but they generally worked alone or in small groups as skilled craftsmen. Technological advances created the need for large organizations, and these organizations lured workers into their employ. Even organized crime, in some cases, has found it more efficient to set up fairly large-scale organizations.

Just as any discussion of the division of labor must deal with the ideas of Emile Durkheim, a discussion of the process of bureaucratization must focus on the work of Max Weber.[60]

The Ideal-Typical Bureaucracy

It is in the context of his theoretical and historical discussion of the rationalization of the Western world that Weber developed his concept of the ideal-typical bureaucracy. Large-scale organizatons were seen as a major way of rationally (that is, efficiently) organizing work. Before discussing the characteristics of the ideal-typical bureaucracy, we need to say a few words about the concept of an ideal type. Weber made great use of the ideal type throughout his work and his ideal-typical bureaucracy is but one example. However,

---

[59]Gail Martin, "Industrial Robots Join the Work Force."
[60]See his *Economy and Society* (Totowa, NJ: Bedminster Press, 1968).

contrary to the implication that can be drawn from the term, an ideal type, as used by Weber, is *not* in any sense an ideal or best possible form.

Rather, Weber's ideal type is a methodological device. It is a logical, exaggerated, and integrated model that can be used for empirical research. In this sense, the ideal-typical bureaucracy was intended by Weber as a tool to be employed in the study of actual organizatons. With it in hand, we can discover which characteristics of the ideal type an actual organization possesses and to what degree it possesses each of them. Weber's ideal–typical bureaucracy is not a description of what we could, or should, expect to find in reality. Rather, it is a set of "sensitizing concepts" with which we can examine reality. In actual operation bureaucracies are quite different from Weber's ideal type.

The ideal-typical bureaucracy consists of a hierarchy of offices with each lower office under the control and supervision of the one above it. Each office is delegated the task of performing a set of official functions and what goes on in each office is defined by a set of official rules. What takes place in one office is clearly delimited from the functions of other offices. Individuals in each office are granted just enough authority to carry out the functions attached to it; they are not granted generalized authority. Thus, for example, they may not interfere with the home life of subordinates. Or, they may reprimand, or perhaps even fire, insubordinate underlings, but they cannot imprison, torture, or execute them for their insubordination.

According to Weber's model, for bureaucrats to apply the rules attached to their positions rationally, they must receive specialized training. In general, only those who have acquired the required knowledge through specialized training are entitled to a position within a bureaucracy. Bureaucrats do not own the "means of production," the offices, desks, machines, and so on. These are owned by the organization and are provided to the bureaucrats as needed. This includes the position of the bureaucrat, which is not the possession of the individual who fills it, but of the organization. The written word is the hallmark of a bureaucracy as administrative acts, decisions, and rules are all put into writing.

Only the supreme authority within the ideal-typical bureaucracy is able to obtain his or her position without going through bureaucratic selection procedures (such as testing) or without the need for certain educational credentials (for example, an M.B.A.). The chief may appropriate his or her position, may be elected to it, or may be designated supreme authority by a predecessor. Despite the fact that the position may be obtained via nonbureaucratic means, the authority of the head, like that of all those in a bureaucracy, is limited to a well-defined sphere of competence.

In Weber's model, all bureaucrats are free; that is, they are able to freely choose their position and to choose to leave it. All bureaucrats are paid a salary and how much they are paid is usually directly related to how high they stand in the bureaucratic hierarchy. Bureaucrats usually have a right to a pension. The office is the sole, or at least the primary, occupation of the bureaucrat. It is usually part of a career. This means that the bureaucrat has the possibility of moving to ever-higher positions within the organization. Upward mobility is based on merit, seniority, or a combination of the two. Whether one is promoted is determine by superiors within the organization.

Interestingly, although Weber felt that the bureaucracy was the most efficient form of organization, he was very ambivalent about it. He deplored the effect of bureaucracy on the individual. He saw it as an alienating and dehumanizing force. Yet he saw no alternative.

Given Weber's ideal-typical bureaucracy and his view that these huge rational structures were going to become increasingly important in the modern world, let us now discuss the historical development of bureaucratic structures in the United States. The growth of bureaucracies can be documented, at least in part, by looking at their increasing size. When organizations grow to a size in which hundreds or even thousands of people are involved, one can be sure that many of the ideal-typical characteristics of bureaucracy have accompanied their increasing size within various sectors of American society.[61]

Growth of Industrial Bureaucracies

The twentieth century has been characterized by the ever-increasing predominance of large-scale industrial bureaucracies. Means pointed out that between 1860 and 1929 there was marked change in the structure of various business organizatons:

> Mass production and big corporate enterprises took over much of manufacturing; the railroads were consolidated into a few great systems; public utility empires and the big telephone system developed; and, even in merchandising, the big corporation played a part.[62]

By 1929 the

> 200 largest corporations legally controlled 48 percent of the assets of all nonfinancial corporations, that is, of all corporations other than banks, insurance companies, and similar financial companies. If we focus on land, buildings and equipment—the instruments of physical production—the 200 largest corporations had legal control of 58 percent of the net capital assets reported by all nonfinancial corporations. Thus, by 1929, the predominantly small-enterprise economy which prevailed in 1860 had been largely replaced by one in which the huge corporation was the most characteristic feature.[63]

Since 1929 there has been a variety of cross-currents affecting the further bureaucratization of the business world. Operating against it were government antitrust legislation and increasing public interest in such less easily bureaucratized sectors as health and recreation. On the other hand, continued massive shifts of people from the farm to the city and economies of scale have continued to support greater bureaucratization.

Means attempted to trace what happened between 1929 and 1962. He looked at the total assets (less stock) of all manufacturing corporations owned

[61]Anthony Downs, *Inside Bureaucracy* (Boston: Little Brown, 1967).

[62]Gardner Means, "Economic Concentration," in Maurice Zeitlin, ed., *American Society, Inc.* (Chicago: Markham, 1970), p. 5.

[63]Ibid.

by the 100 largest manufacturing corporations. In 1929 those firms owned 40 percent of these assets, but by 1962 the percentage had grown to 49 percent. Similarly, the net capital assets of all manufacturing corporations owned by the 100 largest had grown from 44 to 58 percent.

Mueller attempted to gather more recent and more reliable data on some of the trends underscored by Means.[64] He looked at changes in the assets of manufacturing firms between 1950 and 1962 and found that while assets of manufacturing corporations had grown by 111 percent over the period, the assets of the 200 largest manufacturing corporations had grown by 141.3 percent.

Since the early 1960s, the percent of assets controlled by the largest 100 and largest 200 manufacturing concerns has remained high but stable. In 1965, the 100 largest manufacturing firms held 46.5 percent of all manufacturing assets, while in 1980 they controlled 46.7 percent. Similarly, in 1965 the 200 largest manufacturing concerns controlled 56.7 percent of all manufacturing assets, and in 1980 they controlled 59.7 percent.[65] Similar trends can be established for the nonmanufacturing sectors of the economy, electric and gas utilities, life insurance,[66] and retailing.[67]

A further development in the direction of the evolution of large, industrial bureaucracies is the growth of American-based multinational corporations. George Modelski has studied the world's fifty largest international industrial companies.[68] Taken together, the fifty companies alone account for up to 15 percent of the Western world's industrial output and control as much as 33 percent of all international investment. Of these worldwide industrial giants, oil, chemical, automotive and electrical companies predominate. Most of the very largest of these companies (e.g. Exxon, General Motors, IBM) are based in the United States.

Modelski analyzed these fifty industrial companies in terms of international production and sales. He found that 96 percent of these corporations in 1975 were either multinational or global in scope. This contrasts with 68 percent so classified in 1955. In other words, multinational corporations are growing in significance.

Finally, we should mention the trend in recent years toward the merger of large corporations. Rather than entering into new undertakings, many corporations have found it increasingly attractive to merge with existing, successful firms. One of the results of the merger movement (as well as the growth of multinationals) is the tendency to create ever-larger bureaucratic systems.

---

[64]Willard Mueller, "Recent Changes in Industrial Concentration and the Current Merger Movement," in Zeitlin, *American Society, Inc.*, pp. 19–41.

[65]U.S. Bureau of the Census, *Statistical Abstract of the United States: 1981*, 102nd ed. (Washington, D.C., 1981), p. 541.

[66]Timothy Hannan, "Who Controls What in the U.S. Economy?" *Harvard Business Review*, 59 (September/October, 1981), 18.

[67]*Statistical Abstract of the United States: 1981*, p. 814.

[68]George Modelski, "International Content and Performance Among the World's Largest Corporations," in George Modelski, ed., *Transnational Corporations and the World Order* (San Francisco: W.H. Freeman and Company, 1979), pp. 45–65.

The Growth of Government Bureaucracy

The bureaucratization of the industrial sector of the United States has been paralleled in other spheres of the workworld. Government at all levels has undergone similar growth. At the federal level, there were only 49,000 employees in 1870. In 1900 that number had grown to 256,000, and by 1941 it was 1,370,000. By the close of World War II that number had skyrocketed to 3,569,000. In 1968, during the Vietnam War, total government employment had grown to over 5.6 million workers composed of 3.5 million military and 2.1 civilian employees. By 1980, owing to a peacetime economy and attempts to reduce the federal behemoth, government employment totaled 4.4 million with military and civilian employment about equally divided. In the 1980s federal government military and civilian employment is expected to remain constant with about 4.4 million workers expected to be employed by 1990.[69]

At the state and local levels employment has nearly tripled over the last 25 years. In 1955, 4.7 million workers were employed at the state and local levels. This figure had jumped to over 13 million in 1980. Similar to the federal government, this figure is expected to remain essentially stable during the next decade with 13.5 million in projected employment by 1990.[70]

There are other aspects of the massive expansion of the federal government. Take for example statistics on federal receipts and outlays given in Table 3.1.

Another useful statistic is the level of the national debt, as seen in Table 3.2. The economic growth of the federal bureaucracy has been paralleled by similar expansion at the state and local levels.

TABLE 3.1   Federal Budget Receipts and Outlays, Select Years (in millions of dollars)

FISCAL YEAR	BUDGET RECEIPTS	BUDGET OUTLAYS
1925	3,641	2,924
1935	3,706	6,497
1945	45,216	92,690
1955	65,469	68,509
1965	116,833	118,430
1975	280,997	326,151
1980	520,050	579,613
1983 (estimate)	809,209	817,254

SOURCE: *Budget of the United States Government*, (Washington, D.C., Office of Management and Budget, 1982), p.613.

[69]Norman C. Saunders, "The U.S. Economy Through 1990—An Update," *Monthly Labor Review*, 104 (August, 1981), 18–27.

[70]Ibid.

TABLE 3.2 Total National Debt

YEAR	DEBT
1940	$ 43.0 billion
1950	$ 256.1 billion
1960	$ 284.1 billion
1970	$ 370.1 billion
1975	$ 533.2 billion
1980	$ 907.7 billion
1982	$1,142.0 billion
1983 (est)	$1,383.7 billion

SOURCES: *Statistical Abstract of the United States: 1984*, pp. 315, 322.

There are many reasons for the spread of governmental bureaucracies. On one level, the very efficiency of this mode of organization has made it the natural form of governmental development. On another, the growing size and complexity of American society has made it necessary for the government to develop a bureaucratic mechanism to handle its burgeoning business. A more specific factor in the growth of government bureaucracy has been war. Warfare has always made necessary an expansion of governmental activities, and the end of a war has never been characterized by a return to pre-war levels of bureaucratization. Still another specific factor was the changed philosophy of the American government as a result of the Depression and the resulting New Deal. Government involvement in what can be broadly labeled welfare programs expanded greatly between the 1930s and 1970s, with a resulting boom in bureaucratization.

The Growth of Bureaucracies in Other Sectors

The labor movement has shifted from a series of isolated groups to several huge regional, national, and international organizations. Regional, state, national, and international unions have replaced the local as the center of the labor movement. According to Freeman and Medoff: "In 1948–50, 25 percent of all union members in the private sector were in the five largest unions; in 1962, 30 percent of private-sector members were in the five largest unions; and in 1974, 34 percent were."[71]

In the news and entertainment fields, similar bureaucratization has taken place. Newspapers used to be primarily independent, local dailies. However, the number of independents has dropped dramatically—from about 2,600 in 1909 to 1,711 in 1982.[72] The newspaper world is dominated by large corporations, naturally organized on a bureaucratic basis. The same is true of television: three major networks dominate the field. (The movie industry is an exception: for years it moved in the direction of greater and greater

[71]Richard B. Freeman and James L. Medoff, *What Do Unions Do?* (New York: Basic Books, 1984), pp. 35–36.

[72]*Statistical Abstract of the United States: 1984*, p. 565.

bureaucratization, but more recently the huge movie studios have been broken up and replaced by numerous small, independent companies.)

Thus, we see that the first 85 years of the twentieth century can be viewed as an unparalleled era of bureaucratization in American society, a social change which has had a dramatic effect on the modern workworld.

UNIONIZATION

An important change in occupational life has been the growth (and more recent decline) of labor unions. In 1900 only 3 percent of the labor force in the United States belonged to labor unions, but spurred on by, among other things, the competition between the AFL and the CIO, the percentage grew to 23 percent by the end of World War II. Through 1970 that figure had remained stable at slightly less than a quarter of the labor force. Between 1970 and 1980 there was a decline in the percentage of workers belonging to unions. In 1980, union membership had dropped to 20.9 percent of the workforce. However, there were 1 million more union members in 1980 than 1970.[73] This percentage decline but numerical increase is accounted for by the absolute growth of the labor force during the decade. Thus unions have been working hard just to maintain their position in terms of the percentage of the workforce that is unionized. However, the most recent evidence is that they are losing the battle. As of 1984 union membership had declined to 18.8 percent of the labor force. Even more striking is the fact that the total number of people belonging to labor unions has actually *dropped* to 17.3 million.[74] Looking more specifically at the membership of the AFL-CIO, it was 12.6 million when the union was founded in 1955, it reached a peak of 14.1 million members in 1975 and it has declined since, so that in 1983 the AFL-CIO had 13.8 million members.[75] A number of specific unions have also suffered significant declines in recent years. Between 1970 and 1982, the United Automobile Workers (UAW) declined by 20 percent from 1.5 million to 1.2 million members. The United Rubber Workers which once had 200,000 members, had only 90,000 members in 1982. The Oil and Chemical and Atomic Workers claimed to have 180,000 members in 1970, but by 1980 membership had declined to 120,000.[76] These declines are a major factor in the finding in one survey that more than 50 percent of union officials feel there is a crisis in the union movement.[77]

[73]George Ruben, "Organized Labor in 1981: A Shifting of Priorities," *Monthly Labor Review,* 105 (January, 1982), 21–28.

[74]Paul O. Flaim, "New Data on Union Members, and Their Earnings," *Employment and Earnings,* 32 (1985), 13.

[75]George Ruben, "Economy Improves: Bargaining Problems Persist in 1983," *Monthly Labor Review,* 107 (1984), 33–43. Excluded in this is the temporary high of 14.5 million members reached in 1981 as a result of the reaffiliation of the UAW with the AFL-CIO.

[76]Stanley Aronowitz, *Working Class Hero: A New Strategy for Labor* (New York: The Pilgrim Press, 1983), p. 128.

[77]Brian Heshizer and Harry Graham, "Are Unions Facing a Crisis? Labor Officials are Divided," *Monthly Labor Review,* 107 (1984), 25.

There are many reasons for the decline in union success in recent years. By the early 1950s unions had already organized a large proportion of the group most prone to unionization, blue-collar factory workers, and thus had to look elsewhere for members. Other occupations proved far more resistant to their membership drives. The scandals that rocked the union movement certainly did not help: names such as Dave Beck, James Hoffa, and Tony Boyle[78] became symbols of union corruption. The merger of the AFL and the CIO in the early 1950s removed much of the competitiveness and dynamism from the union movement. In addition, many nonunionized companies made the conditions of employment (wages, hours, and working conditions) equal to or better than those in unionized firms. Faced with these obstacles, the union movement has tried, largely unsuccessfully, to recruit members outside its traditional domain. In such industrialized states as Michigan, New York, Pennsylvania, and West Virginia, between 34 and 39 percent of nonagricultural workers were in unions in 1980; but in many less industrialized southern and southwestern states, the percentage is far lower.[79] Nor does union strength in these states seem to be growing. Between 1970 and 1980, the percentage of unionized workers dropped from 11.6 to 7.8 in South Carolina and from 21.4 to 15.8 in Arizona.[80] As of 1977, only 18 percent of southern blue-collar workers were unionized, while 38 percent of blue-collar workers in both the Northeast and the central United States were union members.[81]

Unions have also lacked success in organizing white-collar workers. In 1955, 13.6 percent of all union members were white-collar workers. In 1978 this figure increased to 18.7 percent.[82] However, as a percentage of all white-collar workers, union membership has decreased over the last 25 years. In 1956, 12.9 percent of all white-collar workers were in unions, but by 1978 that figure had dropped to less than 9 percent. A much higher proportion of white-collar workers is unionized in countries such as Sweden, Norway, Belgium, England, and Australia.

A variety of factors account for the failure to organize white-collar workers. Many white-collar workers are women and women are less likely to join labor unions. Thus, while 27 percent of males belong to unions, only 11 percent of females are union members.[83] Why have females been so much less likely to join unions? The most common view is that women simply are more likely to not desire to be union members. However, Freeman and Medoff attribute the underrepresentation of females largely to structural factors. For one thing, women are more likely to be in sectors of the economy (industries, occupations, firms) where unionization is less common. For another, women

[78]For a discussion of some of Boyle's crimes as head of the mine workers, see Paul F. Clark, *The Miners' Fight for Democracy* (Ithaca, NY: New York State School of Industrial and Labor Relations, Cornell University, 1981).

[79]Although one recent study found more support than expected for unions among Southern textile workers, see James A. McDonald and Donald A. Clelland, "Textile Workers and Union Sentiment," *Social Forces*, 63 (1984), 502–521.

[80]*Statistical Abstract of the United States: 1984,* p. 440.

[81]Freeman and Medoff, *What Do Unions Do?*, p. 27.

[82]*Statistical Abstract of the United States: 1981,* p. 412.

[83]Freeman and Medoff, *What Do Unions Do?*, p. 27; based on 1977 data.

are likely to have less tenure in their occupation and employing organization with the result that unions are "less likely to expend time and effort to organize their workplaces."[84] Third, the fringe benefits that can be won by unions are less valuable to women because they are more likely to be receiving them under plans that cover their spouses. Freeman and Medoff conclude:

> In total, over 80 percent of the male-female differential in unionization appears due to differences in the characteristics of the jobs held by men and by women and in the economic interests of each group, rather than to any innately lower desire for union membership by females.[85]

There are other factors involved in the failure to organize large numbers of white-collar workers. White-collar workers tend to associate unions with blue-collar workers and hence consider it beneath their dignity to join. Many white-collar workers cling to the dream that they will eventually rise to management positions and regard union membership as a hindrance to the attainment of that goal.[86] Among professionals in particular, there are many associations that perform functions similar to those performed by unions. Examples of such associations include the American Medical Association, the National Education Association, and the American Sociological Association. As a result of barriers such as these, many union leaders have largely given up hope of organizing large numbers of white-collar workers employed in the private sector. Says Aronowitz:

> . . . except for public employee unions and a minority of the older industrial unions, union leaders often consider professionals, managers, and clerical workers in the private sector as unorganizable. The hard fact is that the American labor movement has been too preoccupied with the survival of its traditional jurisdictions to pay much attention to the growing sectors of the economy.[87]

Latta has provided insight into the general problems of unions in this area in his discussion of the failure to unionize engineers.[88] He begins with the first serious effort to organize engineers in 1915. This first effort and much of what occurred in ensuing years was marked by failure. An exception was some inroads made by independent unions controlled by employers during and just after World War II. In 1952, a number of these independent unions combined to form the Engineers and Scientists of America, but this organization did not last very long. Little progress was made until 1968, when some increase in elections involving engineers began to be seen. Between 1968 and 1980, however, unions won only four major elections and in two of these they lost decertification elections within a few years. Thus, Latta concludes that "as

[84]Ibid., p. 28.

[85]Ibid.

[86]For a study that shows at least some similarities between blue-collar and white-collar unionists in Great Britain see, Frederick G. Cook, et al., "Are White-Collar Trade Unionists Different?" *Sociology of Work and Occupations*, 5 (1978), 235–245.

[87]Aronowitz, *Working Class Hero*, p. 126.

[88]Geoffrey W. Latta, "Union Organization Among Engineers: A Current Assessment," *Industrial and Labor Relations Review*, 35 (1981), 29–42.

the 1980s commence, the little momentum the unions had achieved is slowing markedly."[89]

Latta identifies four major reasons for the failure to unionize engineers, of which the first two are of utmost importance. The first factor is the opposition of employers. Once organizing campaigns are underway, employers often seek to placate engineers with a variety of concessions such as dental plans or increased travel allowances. Employers have also taken a negative approach by using a variety of threats and underscoring the negative results of unionization. Among the latter are claims that a union would result in a barrier between management and engineers, the loss of the ability to complain as individuals, high dues, the loss of professional status, and strike activity that most engineers find abhorrent. Finally, in the rare cases where unions overcame this opposition and succeeded in organizing engineers, management proceeded to adopt a very tough stance toward them.

The second barrier to unionization is the attitudes and values of the engineers themselves. The main factor here is the professionalism of engineers and their fear that unionization would threaten that status.

Third, there is the relatively weak bargaining power of engineers. A strike by engineers cannot paralyze the vast majority of organizations in which they are employed. Further, engineers are often unwilling to apply sanctions to their employing organization or even to be in conflict with it.

Finally, the unions themselves created problems. For example, engineers are very sensitive to the blue-collar orientation of most labor unions as well as the problem of corruption within the labor movement.

In addition to these four specific factors, Latta links the failure to unionize engineers to the more general problems facing the American labor movement; especially the decline in the percentage unionized and increasing hostility by employers to *all* unions.[90]

Another problem facing the union movement is its failure to attract young people. While 25 percent of blue-collar workers under 25 years of age belong to unions, that rises to 37 percent for those between 25 and 44, to 42 percent for those between 45 and 54, and then drops to 34 percent for those over 55 years old. [91] As with the underrepresentation of women, the reason for this is not primarily a lack of desire (at least in the year of the study, 1977) to join unions, but the result of a series of structural factors. For example, young people are often in temporary jobs where they work for short periods of time before moving on to something more permanent. Temporary workers are clearly less interested in unions and more difficult to organize than permanent employees. Second, nonunionized sectors of the economy have been growing faster than unionized sectors and it is the growing sectors that are more likely to hire young people. Freeman and Medoff conclude: "Unionization is low among young workers because of the jobs they hold, not because they are averse to unionism."[92]

[89]Ibid., 33.
[90]Ibid., 40.
[91]Freeman and Medoff, *What Do Unions Do?*, p. 27.
[92]Ibid., p. 32

If unions have ceased to grow and are even in decline (at least for the time being), why are they included in this section on social change? For one thing, historically they have had an important effect on occupational life. More important, they continue to have an impact, albeit more indirectly. Management continues to be alert to the needs of its workers in order to try to prevent unionization. Managers of nonunionized firms study the terms of collective bargaining agreements in unionized locations and seek to meet or exceed them. [93] Thus, unionized firms often serve as models for nonunionized ones. Further, unions often serve to put pressure on professional and employee associations and to push them into a more union-like posture. A good example is the more militant position that the National Education Association has taken as a result of pressure from the American Federation of Teachers, an AFL-CIO affiliate. Finally, although the percentage of unionized workers has not increased, new groups of workers are being drawn into unions. Within the last few years, for example, gains have been made among various government workers. In 1956, 5.1 percent of all union members were employed in the government, but by 1978 that proportion had jumped to 16.7 percent.[94]

REVOLUTION IN EDUCATION

Another important trend in contemporary America is the increasing educational level of the populace. Of focal concern to us here is the fact that a high level of education has come to be associated with entry into, and success in, high-status and high-paying occupations.

In 1870 there were only 80,000 people enrolled in secondary schools in the United States; by 1960 there were nearly 10 million. Secondary school enrollment peaked in the 1970s at well over 15 million students. By 1982 this figure had dropped somewhat to 14.3 million.[95] Continuing modest declines are expected during the current decade. Also striking has been the dramatic changes in university and college enrollments. In 1870, there were only 52,000 young adults in colleges and universities in the United States, but by 1970 this figure had jumped to over 7 million. In 1982, enrollments in institutions of higher learning peaked when 12.4 million students were enrolled.[96] Similar to secondary schools, enrollment in colleges and universities is expected to decline modestly through 1990. However, in 1980 more high school graduates were enrolled in college than ever before. In 1960, 23.7 percent of high school graduates were enrolled, but by 1982 this figure increased to 33 percent.[97]

Additional statistics reveal the importance of education in contemporary

[93]Joseph W. Garbarino, "Unionism Without Unions: The New Industrial Relations," *Industrial Relations*, 23 (1984), 41.

[94]*Statistical Abstract of the United States: 1981*, p. 412

[95]*Statistical Abstract of the United States: 1984*, p. 137.

[96]Ibid.

[97]Ibid., p. 161.

American society. In 1960 there were 1,968 private and public universities, colleges, professional schools, and junior and teacher colleges in the United States. By 1981, this figure had increased to 3,253.[98] In 1960, 24.7 billion dollars was spent by all public and private, elementary and secondary schools, and institutions of higher learning. This figure represented 5 percent of the gross national product (GNP). In 1980, 6.9 percent of the GNP, approximately 166 billion dollars, was spent by these institutions.[99]

The importance of education is also revealed in the increasing educational attainment of the American workforce.[100] The revolution in education has affected virtually every occupational level. It means that a vastly increasing number of people have the training needed to qualify for professional positions. Many graduates will continue to flow into high-level managerial and official positions. For example, one of the areas of biggest growth has been, and promises to continue to be, in business schools. The old type of manager who rose from the bottom to the pinnacle of the organization will be even more uncommon in the future. Today, a significant number of managers and officials are highly trained individuals with both college [101] and professional degrees.

One example of this trend is what has happened in the personnel occupations.[102] A brief look at the history of these occupations will demonstrate why they have come to require even higher levels of educational attainment by aspiring personnel adminstrators. With the growth of industry came a huge expansion of the functions handled by the personnel department. At first, these were what has been called "trashcan" functions–that is, tasks that no one else in the organization wanted. Examples included running the company cafeteria, parking lots, and similar kinds of relatively "unimportant" services. But changes within industry brought an increasing number of "important" functions into the personnel department. The development of industrial psychology, with its psychological and manual tests, was a big spur, and the testing of applicants and regular employees soon found its way into the personnel department. Unionism led to the need for an agency to handle collective bargaining and union relations for management, and these too became an accepted part of the personnel function. Government legislation in the 1930s and 1940s forced companies, and consequently personnel departments, to become increasingly concerned with the question of benefits such as health insurance and pensions. Finally, the growing field of human relations, with its emphasis on group problems at work, forced companies to abandon their focal concern with monetary factors. Personnel was given the job of

[98]Ibid.

[99]Statistical Abstract of the United States: 1981, p. 134.

[100]Anne McDougall Young, "Trends in Educational Attainment Among Workers in the 1970's," Monthly Labor Review, 103 (1980), 44–47.

[101]Anne McDougall Young, "Recent Trends in Higher Education and Labor Force Activity," Monthly Labor Review, 106 (1983), 39–41; Anne McDougall Young and Howard Hayghe, "More U.S. Workers are College Graduates," Monthly Labor Review, 107 (1984), 46–51.

[102]George Ritzer and Harrison M. Trice, An Occupation in Conflict: A Study of the Personnel Manager (Ithaca, NY: New York State School of Industrial and Labor Relations, Cornell University, 1969).

studying and handling problems of communication, motivation, leadership, job satisfaction, and intergroup relations.

It is clear that the knowledge and abilities required of a modern personnel administrator far exceed those needed by early personnel officers. Labor relations representatives need to be lawyers or at least well-versed in law to handle union contract negotiations and grievance settlements. The complexity of benefit programs requires highly trained personnel. The human problems of the workworld, as well as testing and training, require a thorough knowledge of the behavioral sciences. Modern personnel adminstrators must often be highly and specifically trained for their positions. Thus there has been a huge growth in personnel administration as a field of study at most colleges and universities. Most business schools offer a variety of graduate and undergraduate courses in personnel administration, and there are even a number of American schools that are focally concerned with the study of personnel administration. It is now extremely difficult for anyone to find work in personnel adminstration without a bachelor's degree. And few will be able to rise to high-level positions within this field without an advanced degree.

Thus personnel administration represents what has taken place in almost all managerial positions: a great rise in the educational level needed to enter, and succeed in, the occupation.

Another occupational group that has been most profoundly affected by the revolution in education is that of the semiskilled worker. In the early days of industralization it was possible for a talented blue-collar worker to attract the attention of top management and gradually move on to higher level managerial positions. However, the revolution in education has all but eliminated this possibility. Managerial positions now usually require at least an undergraduate degree and in many cases advanced degrees. Even the position of foreman is increasingly filled with new college graduates who are given this job to gain experience before moving on to higher-level positions. Management can now afford to fill its ranks with college graduates because so many people graduate from college. This leaves the blue-collar worker (usually with no more than a high-school diploma) with little hope of achieving a managerial position.

Although the professionals, managers, and blue-collar workers have been most affected by the increasing educational attainments of the population, all occupational levels have been affected to some degree. Nonmanagerial white-collar workers must have more training to fill the same level jobs they filled before, without any real preoccupational training. Their chances, like those of the blue-collar workers, of moving into managerial positions, have also been reduced because of the greater education required to fill managerial positions. Salespeople now sometimes need advanced training or college degrees to handle their jobs. The computer salesperson of today bears little resemblance to the door-to-door salesperson of yesterday. Many storekeepers even find that the complexity of modern business requires at least some college-level training. Finally, even those in illegal deviant occupations have come to recognize the need for education if they are to make it to the top. Note, for example, the case of the Mafia:

Cosa Nostra members occupying the higher echelons of organized crime are orienting their sons to the value of education. . . . They are sending their sons to college to learn business skills, on the assumption that these sons will soon be eligible for "family" membership.[103]

In short, in virtually every occupation education has become a prerequisite to success.

An Overeducated Society?

An offshoot of this revolution in education has been the birth of a new problem in occupational life. We are in danger of becoming an overeducated society.[104] Positions that formerly required only a high school education now require bachelor's or even master's degrees. The problem is that many positions have not been altered to fit the new occupants; jobs that require a high school degree often remain unchanged although they are now filled by college graduates. Thus college graduates frequently find themselves in positions which they consider unworthy of their ability and training—positions that do not make full use of their education.

In part, the fault lies with the colleges and universities; they lead students to believe that they will immediately be placed in responsible positions. This is particularly true of business schools. Thus there is much disillusionment and turnover in the first few years on the job. The major fault, however, lies with organizations that have not revised the jobs to suit the training and abilities of the new type of occupant. Nevertheless, they continue to seek employees with higher and higher levels of education.

Ivar Berg offers useful insights into this increased demand for higher education.[105] In conducting research of his own and reviewing the work of other researchers, Berg concludes that there is no hard evidence that higher levels of education are related to any of the positive ends sought by management when it hires those with advanced education. Among these management goals are lower turnover, lower absenteeism, increased productivity, higher job satisfaction, and so forth. Instead, there is considerable evidence of higher turnover rates and more job dissatisfaction among those with higher levels of education.[106] Rumberger argues that overeducation may also adversely affect job performance, the physical and mental health of workers, and lead to higher rates of absenteeism, strikes, drug problems, and sabotage in the workplace. Berg concludes that business executives in charge of recruiting

---

[103]Donald R. Cressey, *Theft of the Nation* (New York: Harper & Row, 1969), p. 241.

[104]Richard B. Freeman, *The Overeducated American* (New York: Academic Press, 1976); Russell W. Rumberger, *Overeducation in the U.S. Labor Market* (New York: Praeger, 1981); Val Burris, "The Social and Political Consequences of Overeducation," *American Sociological Review,* 48 (1983), 454–467; Beverly Burris, *No Room at the Top: Underemployment and Alienation in the Corporation* (New York: Praeger, 1983).

[105]Ivar Berg, *Education and Jobs: The Great Training Robbery* (Boston: Beacon Press, 1971).

[106]See also Rumberger, *Overeducation in the U.S. Labor Market;* Val Burris, "The Social and Political Consequences of Overeducation."

have a blind faith in the value of education and are mistaking what they would like for what they actually need.

> The tendency on the part of employees to raise educational requirements without careful assessments of their needs, in both the short and the long run, can benefit neither managers nor the system they extol.[107]

What has been created by all this attention to education is the growing need for *credentials* throughout the occupational world.[108] It often does not seem to be the content or quality of education that is important to employers, but rather the piece of paper that duly accredits one as a B.A., B.S., M.B.A., or L.L.B. A college degree has come to be a sort of union card that people must have to obtain good jobs. This emphasis has led to a new class system in the United States based on educational credentials. This obviously operates to the advantage of those social groups that value education and to the detriment of those that do not. The accident of being born into one group or the other is obviously crucial.

A focus on credentials makes life easier for the personnel officer in charge of hiring. Credentials are far easier to evaluate than "competence," "ability," etc. But the fact is that credentials often tell us very little about the individual. Worse, this system eliminates from consideration many able people who lack the proper credentials. The remarkable thing is that all of this has been accomplished with no hard evidence that more education makes one a better employee. In fact, as we've seen, there is considerable evidence that the reverse may often be the case. Although we must not conclude from this that education is useless or harmful, the evidence points to the fact that we have created what is, at best, an overemphasis on education and, at worst, an orientation toward credentials that adversely affects both work and workers.

INCREASING LEISURE TIME

What exactly do we mean by the term "leisure?"[109] This is not an easy question for as Kando puts it, leisure "is an ambiguous term."[110] However, he takes as the key to the idea of leisure "a state of freedom from everyday necessity." While leisure is "intrinsically rewarding," work requires "extrinsic justifica-

---

[107]Berg, *Education and Jobs*, p. 190.

[108]Randall Collins, *The Credential Society: An Historical Sociology of Education and Stratification,* (New York: Academic Press, 1979); Michael A. Faia, "Selection by Certification: A Neglected Variable in Stratification Research," *American Journal of Sociology,* 86 (1981), 1093–1111.

[109]For a review of various approaches to leisure see, John R. Kelly, *Leisure Identities and Interactions* (London: George Allen and Unwin, 1983), Chap.1. The difficulties involved in answering this question have led Carter to abandon the work-leisure dichotomy in favor of the concepts of work and nonwork. See Reginald Carter, "The Myth of Increasing Non-Work vs. Work Activities," *Social Problems,* 18 (1970), 52–67.

[110]Thomas M. Kando, *Leisure and Popular Culture in Transition,* 2nd ed. (St. Louis: C.V. Mosby Co., 1980), p. 14.

tion."[111] Stanley Parker offers us a more complex approach to this issue by dividing up our "life space"[112] on the basis of the amount and type of constraint on what people do:

1. Work, working time, subsistence time. Hours on job.
2. Work-related time. Time related to one's work that one must put in. Examples include travel time and forced "voluntary" overtime.
3. Existence time. Nonwork time that is taken up meeting basic physiological needs like sleeping and eating.
4. Nonwork obligation. Activities the individual considers mandatory; they are related to leisure, but are not in themselves leisure activities (e.g., repairing the home, maintaining lawn or garden). These activities may only be classified as leisure when a person is not forced to do them.
5. Leisure. Free time, time that the individual can fill in any way he or she pleases. (Going to the office can be leisure as long as there is no compulsion involved. On the other hand, working in the garden may not be leisure if the individual is forced to do it.)

The issue of constraint on choice is only part of a further clarification of leisure offered by Gunter and Gunter.[113] They begin with several basic assumptions about leisure. First, leisure is not automatically equated with time free from work or other obligations, with engagement in culturally defined leisure activities, or a specific state of mind. Their point is that these conditions may make leisure more likely, but they do not guarantee that leisure will occur. Second, some amount of leisure, involving choice and freedom, may occur in virtually all types of activities. Thus, there is usually some work in leisure and some leisure in work. In other words, they reject a rigid separation of work and leisure. Third, not only are there varying degrees of leisure, but there are different types of leisure as well. Fourth, leisure is seen as multidimensional involving the interaction of various individual and situational factors. Finally, their primary focus is on leisure at the individual rather than the societal level.

Gunter and Gunter posit two key dimensions of leisure. The first is a psychological dimension of the degree of individual involvement in activities. The second is a structural dimension involving the degree of constraint on individual choice on how to spend time. From the intersection of these two continua, Gunter and Gunter identify four basic styles of leisure.

The first is *pure leisure* involving high individual involvement and maximum freedom of choice. This is an ideal both from a personal and social point of view and is achieved only sporadically in such activities as travel or immersion in music. Pure leisure is what we most often think of when we think of leisure. However, it is not the only type of leisure. Next, is *anomic leisure* involving low individual involvement and high freedom of choice. In this situ-

[111]Ibid.

[112]Stanley Parker, *The Future of Work and Leisure* (New York: Praeger, 1971).

[113]B.G. Gunter and Nancy C. Gunter, "Leisure Styles: A Conceptual Framework for Modern Leisure," *Sociological Quarterly* 21, (Summer, 1980), 361–374.

ation, an individual has a great deal of free time, but doesn't know what to do with it. Gunter and Gunter give several examples of life circumstances that produce this kind of leisure including the "old, the infirm, the unemployed and unemployable, some retirees, and many women in the 'empty nest' phase of the family life cycle."[114] Third, is *institutional leisure,* in which the individual does not have much choice, but nevertheless is deeply engaged in the activities. The best known example of this type of leisure is the "workaholic" who is constrained by the work setting, but who is nevertheless deeply engaged in it. The workaholic is likely to choose to take work along even on vacation. Finally, their is *alienated leisure* in which the individual's choices are constrained and he or she is not deeply involved in the activities. An example is a spouse who is forced by the other spouse's work to be involved in various kinds of social affairs. In addition to making clear that there are various types of leisure, Gunter and Gunter also show that leisure time is often a cause of problems rather than a solution to life's problems. We will return to this issue shortly.

When we compare the worker of today to the worker of 100 years ago, it is clear that there has been a significant increase in the amount of nonwork time. As Nels Anderson puts it, this was an "unintended creature of technological efficiency," and a "child not planned for."[115] However, when we take a longer time perspective we see that people of earlier eras had considerably more nonwork time than we do today. Wilensky argues: "The twentieth-century decline in work has been grossly exaggerated by selective comparison with the shocking schedules of early English textile mills."[116] Echoing this position, Parker argues that "the urban worker today has only regained the position of his thirteenth-century counterpart."[117] Similarly, Kando argues that "comparing ourselves with most of the world's past societies, we seem to be working as hard as ever."[118]

It is only when we take the narrower view of the last 100 to 150 years that we see a steady decline in hours on the job. According to Faunce, the average workweek has gone from about 65 hours to about 40.[119] More specifically, Kando reports data on a decline of the workweek from 69.7 hours in 1850 to 37.2 hours in 1978.[120] The future promises further cuts in the workweek and, as a result, a substantial increase in nonwork time.

There are various factors involved in the boom in nonwork time in the last century and a half. One is the increase in vacation periods; it is not uncommon in some organizations for a worker to have a month's vacation every year. Retirement is another source of increasing nonwork time, for the age at

[114]Ibid., 370.

[115]Nels Andersen, *Dimension of Work: The Sociology of a Work Culture* (New York: David McKay, 1964), p. 90

[116]Harold Wilensky, "The Uneven Distribution of Leisure: The Impact of Economic Growth on Free Time," *Social Problems,* 9 (1961), 32–56.

[117]Stanley Parker, "The Sociology of Leisure: Progress and Problems," *British Journal of Sociology,* 26 (1975), 92.

[118]Kando, *Leisure and Popular Culture in Transition,* p. 114.

[119]Faunce, *Problems of Industrial Society,* 1st ed., p. 73.

[120]Kando, *Leisure and Popular Culture in Transition,* p. 109.

which one may retire has declined and at the same time life expectancy has increased. Thus the person who retires at 60 or 62 may have many nonwork years to cope with.

While we have had an increase in nonwork time in recent years, this does not necessarily mean that we have had an increase in satisfying leisure-time activities. Of the four types of leisure discussed by Gunter and Gunter, only pure leisure is clearly positive and satisfying. The increase in nonwork time does not mean that we have more pure leisure. Rather, it may well be that our increase in nonwork time has led to an increase in such clearly unsatisfying forms of leisure as alienated and anomic leisure. For example, a large proportion of the population "moonlights." That is, extra nonwork time is used to hold down a second job. Second, many people are forced to work overtime rather than take time off to enjoy their nonwork hours. Third, many people are "victims" of anomic leisure. That is, they would prefer to work, but are forced by a variety of circumstances into leisure. Included here are many retirees and the unemployed.

It should be noted that work itself may have become less playful, less like leisure. In other words, we may have less institutional leisure than we had in the past. Thus, while we may have more nonwork hours, our predecessors may have been better at combining work and leisure. In contrast to the rather grim atmosphere in most contemporary work settings, here is a description of work among the primitive Basuto tribe:

> These are gay, sociable affairs comprising about 10–50 participants of both sexes. . . . These matsema are useful though not very efficient. They assemble in the morning . . . and work, with frequent breaks for light refreshment, until . . . the afternoon, to the accompaniment of ceaseless chatter and singing.[121]

Thus, although nonwork time has certainly increased in the last 100 to 150 years, it is far from a simple, unilinear, and uniformly positive development.

Leisure may have created problems, but is has also been a boon to occupational life, creating many new organizations and occupations. The automobile and related industries owe much of their existence to the growth of leisure, and many occupations exist primarily because of it — such as, baseball players, actors, movie projectionists, and tourist agents. A large part of the American economy is based on supplying those who need things for their leisure-time activities.

Finally, it is worth noting that leisure time has different implications for different occupational levels. For example, many professionals find leisure in their work (institutional leisure). Hence one is likely to find professionals working after the formal workday ends. On the other end of the occupational spectrum, many of those in semi- and unskilled occupations cannot find satisfying activities in their work and thus literally flee from work in search of pure leisure-time activities at the 5 o'clock whistle. Thus, in seeking to understand leisure, we must take into consideration the nature of the occupation of the person involved in such activities.

---

[121]Parker, *The Future of Work and Leisure,* p. 40.

CONCLUSIONS

In this chapter, we continued the discussion of the major changes that have affected work in America. We focused on several changes—technological advances, bureaucratization, unionization, the revolution in education, and increasing leisure time. The subject of social change will continue to concern us in the next two chapters. In Chapter 4 we turn to the increasing professionalization of the workforce. We already have presented the data on this change in Chapter 2. Our concern in the next chapter is a presentation of the theoretical tools needed to understand this process. Concluding the discussion of social change is Chapter 5 in which the concern is the changing position of women in the workplace.

FOUR
PROFESSIONALIZATION

We have touched upon the growth of the professions in Chapter 2. In this chapter we go beyond the bare statistics of growth to an analysis of the dynamics by which occupations become professions, retain their professional standing, and even seek to expand on their professional base. The study of professionalization has been the preeminent concern of sociologists interested in the workworld.[1] Although this may reflect an elitist bias, the fact remains that some of the best work in the field has been done on this topic.

Much of the early work in occupational sociology dealt with the role of

---

[1]For the period 1946–1952, Smigel reports that 58 percent of all studies in the field of occupational sociology dealt with the professions; later (1953–1959) Smigel et al. report a decline in interest, with 48 percent of occupational studies concerned with the professions. Despite this decrease in interest, studies of the professions continued to dominate, with their nearest rival being studies of proprietors, managers, and officials (22 percent of all studies from 1953–1959). More recently, Hall did a similar study in which he reported "the decline and almost disappearance of papers on the professions and professionalization." However, we believe that Hall greatly overstates the decline of the studies of the professions. As we will see in this chapter, studies on the professions are still very much alive, especially in books and the British journals, neither of which were included in Hall's study. See Erwin Smigel, "Trends in Occupational Sociology in the United States: A Survey of Postwar Research," *American Sociological Review*, 19 (1954), 398–404; Erwin Smigel et al., "Occupational Sociology: A Re-examination," *Sociology and Social Research*, 47 (1963), 472–77; Richard Hall, "Theoretical Trends in the Sociology of Occupations," *The Sociological Quarterly*, 24 (1983), 5–23.

the professions in the larger society. Then, for a time, sociologists tended to focus their attention on the characteristics that seemed to make the professions distinctive as well as their internal structures and processes. However, in the last two decades a new orientation has come to question many assumptions about the structures and processes of the professions; this has sparked a rebirth of interest in the reciprocal relations between the professions and the larger society. Before discussing these more contemporary developments, let us look briefly at the work of one of the early masters of sociology, Max Weber, who was acutely aware of the relationship between the professions and society.[2] Max Weber is best known for his ideas on the relationship between the Protestant Ethic, in particular Calvinism, and the rise of bureaucratization, capitalism, and rationalization (for example, the emphasis on efficiency) in the Western world. Less well-known, but of central interest to us, is the fact that Weber linked professionalization to these social forces. Weber believed that Calvinism was an important factor in the development of what he called a "spirit of capitalism" in the West. Capitalism, in turn, was a part of the broader process of rationalization that also included the development of highly efficient bureaucracies to do much of the work of this new society. In Weber's view, Calvinism helped promote the development of a disciplined and methodical organization of conduct, and it was the professional who represented this type of behavior. But at the same time, professionalization, in its turn, played a role in the development and expansion of rationalization, bureaucratization, and capitalism. All of these forces, then, were involved in a mutually reinforcing process that gave the Western world its distinctive orientation.

Weber, then, postulated a general process of professionalization that was related to a variety of other social changes, most generally the rationalization of the West and the corresponding failure to develop rational systems in the rest of the world. He was attuned to, and acutely interested in, the relationship between the professions and the social structure of various societies. While this orientation was not totally lost,[3] the thrust of the modern sociological study of the professions has, at least until recently, been away from such macroscopic questions. The focus shifted internally to the nature of the professions themselves and what differentiates them from all other occupations. Let us turn now to an analysis of the more contemporary status of the study of the professions.

---

[2]This section is based on George Ritzer, "Professionalization, Bureaucratization, and Rationalization: The Views of Max Weber," *Social Forces,* 53 (1975), 627–34.

[3]Major exceptions to this trend away from broad societal issues include the following: Alexander Carr-Saunders and P.A. Wilson, *The Professions* (Oxford: Clarendon Press, 1941); Talcott Parsons, "The Professions and Social Structure," *Social Forces,* 17 (1939), 457–67; N.S. Timasheff, "Business and Professions in Liberal, Fascist, and Communist Society," *American Journal of Sociology,* 45 (1940), 863–69; W.J. Reader, *Professional Men* (New York: Basic Books, 1966); and a variety of recent works to be discussed in this chapter and associated with the now dominant power approach to the study of the professions.

CONTEMPORARY STUDY OF THE PROFESSIONS[4]

In this section we will examine the three basic approaches to studying the professions.[5] The first approach focuses on *process,* on the historical steps an occupation must go through en route to professional status and on the internal processes that characterize professions. The second, the *structural-functional* orientation, focuses on the distinctive characteristics of a profession and on the structure of established professions.[6] These approaches dominated the field until the 1970's, when the *power* perspective burst upon the scene. Here, the focus is on the power needed by an occupation to acquire professional recognition as well as on the power such an occupation wields once it has achieved that position. Because the power perspective has now gained preeminence in sociology and it seems capable of subsuming the other two approaches, the emphasis here will be on criticisms of the first two by the supporters of the power approach, as well as on a discussion of the ways in which the three can be integrated into a stronger and more inclusive method of studying the professions.

The proponents of the three approaches disagree in two chief areas: (1) over what exactly differentiates an occupation from a profession, and (2) on the basic nature of the professions. Before getting to these differences, we can begin with a point of basic agreement. The vast majority of occupational sociologists subscribe to the notion that there are *degrees of professionalization* rather than a simple dichotomy between professions and nonprofessions. That is, all occupations can be placed on a continuum ranging from the nonprofessions on one end to the established professions on the other. The idea of a continuum grows out of the focus on social change that is characteristic of both the process and power perspectives. Those who favor the process approach tend to be concerned with how an occupation rises and falls in status, especially what historical stages it needs to navigate en route to the professional end of the continuum. The power theorists are more concerned with why an occupation moves up or down: they focus on the power needed to move up, and the loss of it that causes an occupation to slip down. We will use

[4]The following discussion is based, in some part, on George Ritzer, "The Emerging Power Perspective in the Sociological Study of the Professions," paper presented at the meetings of the American Sociological Association, San Francisco, California, August 1975; as well as a similar discussion of the professions in the second edition (1977) of this book.

[5]It is possible to identify a fourth, more microsociological approach focusing on the status claims made by professionals in the everyday workworld. Although such microsociological approaches hold promise, and are in line with the rise of micro-sociological theory in general, they are not yet widely accepted in the sociology of the professions. On this micro-approach to the professions see, Robert Dingwall, "Accomplishing Professions," *Sociological Review,* 24 (1976), 331–349. On the growth of micro-theories in general see George Ritzer, "The Rise of Micro-Sociological Theory," *Sociological Theory,* 3 (1985), 88–98.

[6]We are combining the closely related trait and structural-functional approaches under the heading of structural-functionalism. For an approach that differentiates between them see, Mike Saks, "Removing the Blinkers? A Critique of Recent Contributions to the Sociology of the Professions," *The Sociological Review* (February, 1983), 1–21.

the term *professionalization* for movement toward the professional end of the continuum and *deprofessionalization* for movement toward the nonprofessional end.

The place of an occupation on the professional continuum is determined by how many professional characteristics it has or is believed to have, and to what degree it possesses or is believed to possess each of them. This leads us to our definition of a *profession: an occupation that has had the power to have undergone a developmental process enabling it to acquire, or convince significant others (for example, clients, the law) that it has aquired a constellation of characteristics we have come to accept as denoting a profession.* We can see from this definition how professions may gain their stature by actually acquiring certain characteristics (which we discuss shortly) or by merely convincing significant others that they have acquired them whether or not they, in fact, actually have. This definition combines elements of all three theoretical approaches: it (1) deals with a process; (2) focuses on power; and (3) gives importance to the possession, or belief in the possession, of a constellation of characteristics (a product of the structural-functional school).

We can use the concept of a profession to theoretically evaluate the status of all occupations; however, it really makes little sense to use this analytical tool on occupations that have never aspired to, or been thought to seek, professional status. Thus few janitors have sought to have their occupation accorded the status of a professional, and hence it would not be very useful to analyze the occupation of janitor from this point of view.[7] One occupation that is often *inappropriately* analyzed from the viewpoint of professionalization is the police officer.[8] In our view, police officers are better thought of as free semiskilled workers and will be discussed under that heading in this book (see Chapter 11). Thus Menke, White, and Carey are correct when they conclude that "police claims to professional status are hollow."[9]

In contrast, we can use the concept of a profession to analyze many occupations that, with a reasonable chance of success, either have sought that status or been thought of as professions or professional aspirants. Thus we can see that medicine is a good example of an occupation that stands at the professional end of the continuum, since it has had the power to undergo the process of professionalization and thereby acquire, or convince others that it has acquired, the major professional characteristics. Social work is one of many occupations that has made a great effort to move to the professional end of the continuum, but it has made it only part way because of its inability to acquire, or convince others that it has acquired, the needed characteristics. Managers, especially personnel managers, have been even less successful in

---

[7] We will soon see, however, that the concept of professional*ism* can be usefully applied to such occupations.

[8] Michael K. Brown, *Working the Street: Police Discretion and the Dilemmas of Reform* (New York: Russell Sage Foundation, 1981).

[9] Ben A. Menke, Mervin F. White, and William L. Carey, "Police Professionalization: Pursuit of Excellence or Political Power?" in Jack R. Green, ed., *Managing Police Works: Issues and Analysis* (Beverly Hills, CA: Sage Publications, 1982), pp. 75–106.

their efforts than social workers.[10] The clergy is a good example of an occupation that once was at or near the professional end but has undergone a process of deprofessionalization in recent years.[11] There are even occupations (such as public lecturing) that tried to win professional recognition in the past, failed, and have now disappeared as independent occupations.[12] It is to these types of occupations that the professional model is best and most usefully applied.

Although there have been efforts to develop a total occupational continuum,[13] the most useful effort from our point of view is Albert Reiss' classification system, which focuses on the professional end of the continuum:[14]

1. *Old established professions*—Occupations in this category include physicians, lawyers, and college professors.

2. *New professions*—Occupations here include the natural and social scientists.[15]

3. *Semiprofessions*—Although they are professionalized to some degree and have made a great effort to make it to the professional end of the continuum, this group of occupations has lacked the power to win widespread recognition as professions.[16] Included in the semiprofessions are public school teachers, nurses, social workers, and librarians.

4. *Would-be professions*—These are occupations that have sought or are actively aspiring to professional status, but which, for a variety of reasons, have had even less power than the semiprofessions and have had less success in convincing the relevant audiences that they have acquired the needed characteristics. Examples include personnel managers and funeral directors.

5. *Marginal professions*—Included here are a variety of occupations that work "hand in hand" with the professions, perform many of the same functions, but lack the capacity to acquire professional status in their own right, partly because they

[10]George Ritzer and Harrison Trice, *An Occupation in Conflict: A Study of the Personnel Manager* (Ithaca, NY: New York School of Industrial and Labor Relations, Cornell University, 1969); Tony Watson, *The Personnel Managers: A Study in the Sociology of Work and Employment* (London: Routledge and Kegan Paul, 1977).

[11]Hernan Vera, *Professionalization and Professionalism of Catholic Priests* (Gainesville, Florida: University Presses of Florida, 1982); Sherryl Kleinman, *Equals Before God: Seminarians as Humanistic Professionals* (Chicago: University of Chicago Press, 1984).

[12]Donald M. Scott, "The Profession that Vanished: Public Lecturing in Mid-Nineteenth-Century America," in Gerald L. Geison, ed., *Professions and Professional Ideologies in America* (Chapel Hill, NC: The University of North Carolina Press, 1983), pp. 12–28.

[13]See, for example, Everett Hughes, "Personality Types and the Division of Labor," in Hughes, *Men and Their Work* (Glencoe, IL: Free Press, 1958), pp. 23–41; Robert Hodge, Paul Siegel, and Peter Rossi, "Occupational Prestige in the United States: 1925–1963," in Reinhard Bendix and Seymor M. Lipset, eds., *Class, Status and Power: Social Stratification in Comparative Perspective*, 2nd ed. (New York: Free Press, 1966), pp. 322–33.

[14]Albert Reiss, Jr., "Occupational Mobility of Professional Workers," *American Sociological Review*, 20 (1955), 693–700.

[15]It might be useful to add another category at this point, "declining professions," to include occupations like the clergy that are undergoing deprofessionalization.

[16]Amital Etzioni, ed., *The Semi-Professions and Their Organization* (New York: Free Press, 1969), pp. xiii–xiv.

very often labor in the shadow of the established professions. Occupations in this category include laboratory and scientific technicians as well as various paraprofessionals.

The bulk of this chapter deals in varying degrees with the broad types of occupations delineated by Reiss, although our primary focus will be on the established professions. Although not all of them are recognized as professions, analysis of them in light of the theory of professionalization reveals much about their basic character. Later in this book we will take a more detailed look at the distinct categories of professions; in Chapter 8 we will deal with individuals in old established and new professions, while Chapter 9 will analyze individuals in semiprofessions, would-be professions, and marginal professions.

Professionalism

Just as occupations vary in terms of their degree of professional*ization,* individuals in any occupation vary in their degree of professional*ism.* Occupational sociologists have addressed in a variety of ways the question of what factors determine the position of an occupation on the professional continuum. Comparatively ignored has been the important question of professionalism at the individual level.[17] In this book we will use *professionalism* when we are discussing individuals and *professionalization* when we are examining occupations.[18]

In every occupation there are individuals who are (or who are at least regarded as such) more professional than others. Thus while medicine is a profession, individual doctors vary in their degree of professionalism. The majority of physicians exhibit a high degree of professionalism since they are, for the most part, competent, efficient, and effective. At least some, however, are inept or are quacks or violate the profession's code of ethics, and they have a relatively low degree of professionalism. The same point holds for occupations in the middle or toward the low end of the professionalization continuum. That is, there is a range of professionalism in every occupation. However, the more nonprofessional the occupation, the less likely we are to find large numbers of individuals with a high degree of professionalism. In other words, the lower the level of professionalization, the lower the average level of professionalism.

A similar differentiation has been made by Richard Hall, who contends that the professional model consists of both structural (that is, "professionalization") and attitudinal ("professionalism") variables.[19] We believe that combining both these levels into one professional model confuses the issue. The

---

[17]This discussion is based on George Ritzer, "Professionalism and the Individual," in Eliot Freidson, ed., *The Professions and Their Prospects* (Beverly Hills, CA: Sage Publications, 1973), pp. 59–73.

[18]This differentiation has also been made by Eliot Freidson, *The Profession of Medicine* (New York: Dodd, Mead, 1970).

[19]Richard Hall, "Professionalization and Bureaucratization," *American Sociological Review,* 33 (1968), 92–104.

two levels are conceptually and analytically distinct, as Hall himself discovered.[20]

There is not one professional model; rather, there are two. And although they are highly correlated, we must keep them distinct.[21]

Professionalization

Where an *occupation* lies on the professional continuum depends on how much power it possesses and whether it is sufficient to allow it to undergo a process of professionalization whereby it has been able to acquire, or convince significant others that is has acquired, the constellation of professional characteristics.

It is at this point that it will be helpful to return to a discussion of the three basic approaches to the sociological study of the professions.

THE PROCESS APPROACH

Those who favor this approach, you will remember, tend to focus on the steps an occupation must go through to achieve professional status. Caplow, for example, sees four steps in the process of professionalization:

1. A professional association must be established.
2. There must be a change of name that dissociates the occupation from its previous nonprofessional status and provides it with a title that is its exclusive domain.
3. There is the development and adoption of a code of ethics.
4. There is political agitation to gain popular and legal support and the setting up of a mechanism controlled by the profession to train new members.[22]

Wilensky outlines a five-step process approach to professionalization that is very close to that of Caplow:

1. Creation of a full-time occupation.
2. Establishment of a training school.
3. Establishment of a national association.
4. Efforts to win legal support.
5. Establishment of a code of ethics.[23]

[20]Ibid., 103.

[21]Among the more recent studies to deal with the issue of professionalism are Vera, *Professionalization and Professionalism of Catholic Priests;* and Thomas Keil and Charles Ekstrom, "Police Chief Professionalism: Community, Departmental, and Career Correlates," *Sociology of Work and Occupations,* 5 (1978), 470–486.

[22]Theodore Caplow, *The Sociology of Work* (Minneapolis: University of Minnesota Press, 1954), pp. 139–40.

[23]Harold Wilensky, "The Professionalization of Everyone?" *American Journal of Sociology,* 70 (1964), 137–58.

If we combine the two lists, we can define the process approach as having the following characteristics:

1. Full-time occupation.
2. Change of name, which becomes the occupation's exclusive domain.
3. National association.
4. Training school.
5. Code of ethics.
6. Political agitation to win popular and legal support.

The above steps can be in any order, and some steps may take place concurrently.

The process approach attunes us, of course, to the historical development of occupations. But one basic problem is that it leads to a rather routinized procedure. We are advised to simply examine the history of an occupation for the existence of these stages, and if they have occurred, we can label an occupation a profession. A most damning criticism of this approach is its tendency to generalize from the past to the present and future. Yet it is clear that occupations that underwent professionalization some years ago were involved in a very different occupational world than those that seek it today. Portwood and Fielding make the point that, in the case of some British professions (for example, barristers), their present status is the result of a combination of historical and contemporaneous conditions.[24] (Macdonald[25] makes a similar point about accountants in Scotland.) Given the partial reliance of such professions on historical conditions that no longer exist, Portwood and Fielding conclude that "it is logically impossible for any current or future profession to attain a similar pre-eminence."[26] Perhaps the most important fault of the process orientation is that it underestimates the significance of the political process, that is, the power wielded by professions in their drive toward professionalization and the power of opposing forces that must often be overcome. *Political variables* are relegated to secondary status in this approach, while in more recent thinking they have assumed center stage.

Akin to the process approach, although not directly aligned with it, are studies of the history of specific occupations and their efforts to achieve professional recognition. These studies do not adopt a set series of stages and then determine whether an occupation has passed through them. Rather, they look at the actual history of an occupation to see what really went on in the process of professionalization.

One important example of such an historical approach, of which we will have more to say later, is Paul Starr's *The Social Transformation of American Med-*

---

[24]Derek Portwood and Alan Fielding, "Privilege and the Professions," *The Sociological Review* 29 (1981), 749–773.

[25]Keith M. Macdonald, "Professional Formation: The Case of Scottish Accountants," *British Journal of Sociology*, xxxv (1984), 174–189.

[26]Portwood and Fielding, "Privilege and the Professions," 768. Those occupations that play a vital role in *contemporary* society can, in their view, achieve professional status.

icine.[27] Starr sees the history of professions in general, and medicine in particular, as examples of collective mobility. In the mid-nineteenth century, medicine was not a secure profession;[28] indeed, it was in a very weak position on a variety of counts. The prestige of a physician was much lower than it is today and the occupation was rarely a path to economic wealth. There was no set educational criteria and no fixed career path. Medicine was not able to command deference and merely maintained a "front of propriety and respectability."[29] The American Medical Association had been founded in 1846, but in Starr's opinion it had little impact through the remainder of the nineteenth century. The occupation itself was wracked by a series of bitter internal feuds caused by the existence of a variety of medical sects.

Having detailed the weak position of medicine in the mid-nineteenth century, Starr turns to the issue of the rise of the medical profession through the nineteenth and into the twentieth century. The 1870s and 1880s witnessed the growth of medical licensing. General reforms in the educational system led to improvements in medical schools. The improved medical schools, in turn, "greatly increased the homogeneity and cohesiveness of the profession. The extended period of training helped to instill common values and beliefs among doctors, and the uniformity of the medical curriculum discouraged sectarian divisions."[30] Whereas nostrum makers had been a major source of competition to physicians, the medical profession now began to gain control over the pharmaceutical business. The AMA came to stand between physicians and drug manufacturers and, in fact, the substantial income from drug advertisements helped the AMA expand its power. Then there were successes (for example, in public hygiene and immunology) and technological advances (the stethoscope) that contributed to medicine's growing power. External changes also aided medicine. For example, the growing prestige of science in general was a boon to medicine. Hospitals were transformed from places of dread to centers of science, and they became centers of medical education and practice as well. The efforts of corporations to control physicians and turn them into employees were warded off. In these and other ways by the 1920s "the medical profession had successfully resolved the most difficult problems confronting it."[31] In other words, medicine had taken the many steps needed to turn itself into the most powerful profession in the United States. We will return shortly to Starr's work because, to its credit, it is relevant not only to the process approach to the professions, but to the other two approaches as well.

[27]Paul Starr, *The Social Transformation of American Medicine* (New York: Basic Books, 1982). Others are Keith M. Macdonald, "Professional Formation: The Case of Scottish Accountants;" Daniel Duman, "The Creation and Diffusion of a Professional Ideology in Nineteenth Century England," *The Sociological Review*, 27 (1979), 113–138.

[28]Gelfand contends that the professionalization of medicine in France predated that development in the United States by about a half century; see Toby Gelfand, *Professionalizing Modern Medicine: Paris Surgeons and Medical Science and Institutions in the 18th Century* (Westport, CT: Greenwood Press, 1980).

[29]Starr, *The Social Transformation of American Medicine*, p. 85.

[30]Ibid., p. 123

[31]Ibid., p. 232.

Professional Segments

Stemming from the process approach in general, and the work of **Rue Bucher** in particular, is the idea of professional *segments,* a concept which offers a great deal of insight into the internal and external forces leading to change within the professions. In one of her early studies, Bucher focused on the profession of pathology.[32] Like many other professions, pathology has been subjected to much social change and this has resulted in the growth of segments within the profession. Pathology has become less of a science and more of a clinical specialty that serves physicians, and because of these changes it has split into two segments. The *practitioner segment* views pathology as a medical specialty that must focus on clinical diagnostic activities and efforts to build closer ties with the medical profession. In contrast, the *scientific segment* is primarily concerned with scientific investigation and the communication of results to fellow professionals. Further, it is devoted to the idea of "maintaining the scientific position of the specialty." These two segments were found to be so distinct that members of one segment were generally not interested in, or informed about, the activities of the other.

The practitioners constitute the newer segment and are seeking to carve out a niche for themselves despite the resistance of the entrenched old-liners. Pathology to the practitioner is not just the study of disease, and they have declared new missions for the science including acting as servant, consultant, and educator to the physician. In addition, they have developed a new self-image that dissociates them from the old image of pathologist as a laboratory worker. They have sought to solidify their position by developing their own professional associations, which press for the establishment of practitioner-pathologist positions in hospitals. They have also sought to recruit new pathologists who accept their ideology and who will ultimately fill the positions they are developing.

In contrast, the primary interest of the long-established scientific pathologists is research, an interest which is threatened by the service ideal of the practitioners. This conflict is not only over mission, but has extended to a battle between the two segments to attract recruits. In the face of the threat from practitioners the scientific pathologists have taken a number of steps "to rejuvenate pathology as a science." They are trying to move away from the old techniques and emphasize the exciting new methods being utilized by the modern scientific pathologists. However, they also continue to defend the old techniques because those methods constitute their exclusive domain. The scientists are redefining their research mission to include traditional techniques as well as new scientific developments.

More recently, Pawluch has examined the changing nature of pediatrics

---

[32]Rue Bucher, "Pathology: A Study of Social Movements Within a Profession," *Social Problems,* 10 (1962), 40–51. See also Rue Bucher and Anselm Strauss, "Professions in Process," *American Journal of Sociology,* 66 (1961), 325–34, in which professions are seen as "loose amalgamations of segments pursuing different objectives in different manners and delicately held together." This idea was formulated in reaction to the overwhelming static view of the professions developed by the structual-functionalists and enunciated in William Goode, "Community Within a Community: The Professions," *American Sociological Review,* 22 (1957), 194–200.

from the point of view of professional segments.[33] Primary-care pediatricians who were mainly concerned with treating children's diseases once dominated the profession. By about 1950, however, the need for such pediatricians declined as there were fewer and milder childhood diseases, the result of an array of medical advances. In the face of declining need, some pediatricians sought to move away from biological problems and toward treating the "behavioral, emotional, and social problems of children."[34] Conflict has arisen between these "new pediatricians" and academic and research pediatricians, many of whom are unwilling to move into these new and less "scientific" areas. How this ongoing conflict between segments in pediatrics will be resolved is not yet clear.

Conflict between segments often results in large-scale social changes within professions. The examples from pathology and pediatrics may be extended to every professional occupation. Conflict within a profession may revolve around its mission, work activities, methodology and techniques, clients, colleagues, interests and associations, recruits, and public recognition. Segments form around these issues, and new ones do battle with the established ones, which are seeking to maintain tradition. However, just as it is erroneous to view professions as monoliths, it is equally erroneous to view segments as monolithic. Segments are internally differentiated and constantly in flux. A profession may witness the rise of a segment, its later decline and replacement by a new segment, or the resurgence of an older segment.

Viewing professions in this way has enormous implications for the overall study of these occupations. The places in which they work are the arenas for the battle between members of the rival segments. This conflict is affected by, and affects, the organization in which the profession operates. Careers within professions are not a well-defined series of steps but vary between segments. Further, career ladders may disappear or come to the fore when one segment declines or a new segment arises. Socialization is not a simple process of indoctrination into the profession: instead, it involves a conflict between segments for recruits, and it involves among recruits a choice of the segment by which each chooses to be socialized or a compromise among the demands of the various segments.[35] In training schools, recruits are treated to the spectacle of competing segments vying for their commitment. Segments disagree on the image they wish to convey to the public and may seek to project distinct ones. Finally, segments may relate differently to other professions and may each possess their own leaders. In sum, looking at professions as segmental affects virtually all areas in the study of professions. The examples of pathology and pediatrics demonstrate some of the internal and external forces leading to change in the professions.

Let us now move on to the structural-functional interpretation, keeping

---

[33]Dorothy Pawluch, "Transitions in Pediatrics: A Segmental Analysis," *Social Problems*, 30 (1983), 449–465.

[34]Ibid., 450.

[35]Kath M. Melia, "Student Nurses' Construction of Occupational Socialization," *Sociology of Health and Illness*, 6 (1984), 132–151.

in mind that the process approach provides us a useful tool in its emphasis on process, historical development, and dynamism.

THE STRUCTURAL-FUNCTIONAL (OR TRAIT) APPROACH

The structural-functionalists are best known for their development of a constellation of characteristics used to differentiate the professions from other occupations. We have selected the six most frequently cited characteristics for discussion here. The degree to which an occupation has these six characteristics is held to determine whether it is a profession or not. Established and new professions have—or are believed to have—all of these characteristics and to a high degree. Would-be professions may be lacking one or two, and those that it possesses are thought to be less pronounced than in the established or new professions. Nonprofessions have—or are believed to have—few, if any of these characteristics, and those that they do possess are likely to be of a low degree. In enumerating these characteristics, the structural-functionalists have generally argued that these are "real" qualities that professions possess and nonprofessions do not. But the recent work of the power advocates has made it clear that a profession may not really possess these traits; it may simply have the power to *convince* the public, the law, and other sectors that it possesses them. We have been influenced by the power advocates, and thus the six professional characteristics should be seen as either characteristics a profession has or traits it has simply been able to convince others that it possesses.

Let us turn to a discussion of these characteristics. We will also present the critical analyses of each offered by the power advocates; these will focus on the role power plays in the creation of these traits, or of the illusion that they exist. In fact, it is in the power advocates' critique of the structural-functionalists' six characteristics that we begin to get a better sense of the power approach to the professions.

General, systematic knowledge. Intellectually, the professions possess, or are thought to possess, general systematic knowledge. In contrast, the knowledge of other occupations is said to be less general and systematic. The knowledge base of the professions supposedly can only be transmitted formally from one professional to another in a lengthy training program existing within a professional school, or informally between a senior member of the professional establishment and the neophyte. Those in professions argue that nonprofessional occupations do not require such an elaborate system of training because their knowledge base is less general, less systematic and, as correlates, less complex and less important to the functioning of society. The structural-functionalists tend to accord this variable a central role in the constellation of characteristics:

> The crucial distinction between professions and non-professions is this: the skills that characterize a profession flow from and are supported by a fund of knowledge that has been organized into an internally consistent system called a body of

theory. A profession's underlying body of theory is a system of abstract propositions that describe in general terms the classes of phenomena comprising the
profession's focus of interest.[36]

The power advocates argue that while it is true that the professions do
have a knowledge base, so do many nonprofessional occupations. There
seems to be no basis for arguing that there is a qualitative difference between
the knowledge base of the professions and many nonprofessions, although
few would argue with the idea that there is a quantitative difference. Professionals often argue that their knowledge is their own, while other occupations
such as social work and business management are said to have knowledge derived from a number of different fields and over which they have little control. To the degree that this is true, it is a result of the power of the professions to create information, or integrate information, into a body of
knowledge that they control and that they keep from various other segments
of society. But of course, this is not totally true. The professions must rely on
information provided by a variety of other occupations. Modern medical
knowledge is composed of insights from various nonmedical sources—
biology, chemistry, psychology, even sociology.

Those in the professions also argue that their knowledge is theoretical
while that of other occupations is much more practical. Again, the evidence
fails to support this contention. For example Freidson, in his study of the
medical profession, found that physicians tend to rely on their own tested
remedies for various maladies rather than using the latest medical discoveries;
physicians are found to be profoundly practical people. Finally, it is often argued that the knowledge base of the professional is systematic, while there are
grave inconsistencies in the knowledge base of nonprofessionals. Roth, however, has argued that just as with the knowledge in other occupations, the
knowledge of the professional possesses great gaps, numerous inconsistencies, and even grave paradigmatic differences that lead to controversies over
the most fundamental issues.[37] Although there are no real qualitative differences between professional and nonprofessional knowledge, the professions
often engage in a systematic effort to create the illusion that there is something distinctive about their knowledge. Sometimes a profession might even
go further and artificially produce a distinctive body of knowledge and then
deny others access to it in order to improve its power position.

Based on the criticisms of the power advocates, we can conclude that although there are no inherent qualitative differences between professions and
nonprofessions in terms of knowledge, there are quantitative differences.
Where qualitative differences exist, they have been artificially created by professionals denying access to their knowledge by others. Yet we must also recognize that even where there are no artificially produced qualitative differences, the professions have been able to convince the public, the law, and so
forth that such differences do exist. Believing in this myth, many people act

---

[36]Ernest Greenwood, "Attributes of Profession," *Social Work,* 2 (1957), 46.

[37]Julius Roth, "Professionalism: The Sociologist's Decoy," *Sociology of Work and Occupations,*
1 (1974), 6–23.

toward the professions as if there was something inherently distinctive about their knowledge base.

Norm of autonomy.   The professions have developed the idea that they should be free of external control—that is, the norm of autonomy, that outside interference would supposedly reduce the quality of professional service. Believing this, the community often surrenders to the profession the right to control its own activities. In Hughes' terms the community yields a "license" to the profession to perform its activities as it sees fit. Of course, a profession is rarely satisfied with the limited rights it receives and seeks to expand them by enlarging its "mandate."[38] Even without expanding its mandate, the profession is usually able to carve out areas in which professionals can only be evaluated by their peers. Thus the profession is allowed to select its own recruits, train them as it sees fit in its own schools, determine what constitutes unprofessional behavior, and punish it accordingly. To accomplish these last functions the profession develops codes of ethics, sets of principles by which the actions of professionals are supposed to be guided. The codes are developed and policed by the professions themselves.

The professional emphasis on the norm of autonomy, or self-control, is criticized by supporters of the power approach on a variety of grounds. While the professions have often been able to gain a measure of autonomy, this has certainly not always been the case. Johnson, for example, has demonstrated how both clients and the state (e.g., though licensing requirements) have often exercised considerable control over the professions.[39] Thus, the history of every profession is studded with incidents of external control. Furthermore, ongoing changes in at least some professions threaten to erode their autonomy even further. For example, Starr describes the "coming of the corporation," or for-profit institutions, to medical practice. The medical profession's involvement in such

> corporate work will necessarily entail a profound loss of autonomy. Doctors will no longer have control over such basic issues as when they retire. There will be more regulation of the pace and routines of work. And the corporation is likely to require some standard of performance, whether measured in revenues generated or patients treated per hour.[40]

Thus professional autonomy has always been limited, and there are ongoing changes in at least some professions that threaten to erode it even further.

A second criticism stems from the evidence that the professions have not used their autonomy as they promised, to improve their service to clients: "The history of professions and professionalism does not really seem to support the contention that professional autonomy contributes to high standards of professional service."[41] Related to this are the criticisms leveled at the pro-

[38]Hughes, "License and Mandate," in Hughes, *Men and Their Work,* p. 79.

[39]Terence Johnson, *The Professions and Power* (London: Macmillan, 1972).

[40]Starr, *The Social Transformation of American Medicine,* p. 446.

[41]Arlene Daniels, "How Free Should Professions Be?" in Eliot Freidson, ed., *The Professions and Their Prospects* (Beverly Hills, CA: Sage Publications, 1973), p. 55.

fessions' codes of ethics. Many argue that the ethical codes are not set up to protect the welfare of the clients, but rather the interests of professionals.[42] These codes conceal the professions and their activities from public scrutiny by allowing for in-group punishment of those who violate professional norms. This serves to insulate the professions from external control by keeping their abuses from public visibility. Worse yet, many believe that the professions do not do a good job of policing themselves.[43] In Abbott's view, there are far more violations of professional codes than there are prosecutions of such offenses. Those relative few that are prosecuted are likely to be highly visible offenses, those that would be hard to conceal. Roth is one of the most outspoken critics of the professions' codes of ethics:

> The evidence we do have about realtors, lawyers, psychologists, insurance agents, physicians, and other occupational groups with codes of ethics shows overwhelmingly that, although these codes sometimes curb competition among colleagues, they have almost no protective value for the clientele or the public. Indeed, the existence of such codes is used as a device to turn aside public criticism and interference.[44]

In recent years, the medical profession has come under increasing attack for failing to adequately "police itself and protect the public's health."[45] This attack primarily took the form in the 1970s of a dramatic increase in patient malpractice suits against physicians for incompetence and negligence. This, in turn, led to a dramatic increase in malpractice insurance premiums. The federal, state, and local governments, as well as the AMA, were impelled to take steps to better police the medical profession.

Finally, it should be noted that critics argue that codes of ethics do not really differentiate professions, since a wide variety of occupations have such ethical codes.[46]

Despite these criticisms, we can say that the professions have been able to convince many to respect their right to autonomy. Thus, the professions have often been able to function quite autonomously and to police themselves (however badly) through their codes of ethics. These realities do not contradict the arguments that the professions have never been as autonomous as they would like us to believe, do not really require this autonomy, and often use it to the detriment of clients and the public.

[42]Andrew Abbott, "Professional Ethics," *American Journal of Sociology*, 88 (1983), 862.

[43]See, for example, Eliot Freidson and Buford Rhea, "Processes of Control in a Company of Equals," *Social Problems*, 11 (1963), 119–31; Eliot Freidson, *Doctoring Together: A Study of Professional Social Control* (New York: Elsevier, 1975); Vern Bullough and Sheila Groeger, "Irving W. Potter and Internal Podalic Version: The Problems of Disciplining a Skilled but Heretical Doctor," *Social Problems*, 30 (1982), 109–116.

[44]Roth, "Professionalism: The Sociologist's Decoy," 10.

[45]Carol Klaperman Morrow, "'Sick Doctors': The Social Construction of Professional Deviance," *Social Problems*, 30 (1982), 95.

[46]Abbott, "Professional Ethics."

Norm of altruism.   Those in the professions contend that they have imbued in their members a norm of altruism, or community interest rather than
self-interest. This is supposedly related to the professional's greater interest in
symbolic rather than economic rewards.

It is interesting to note that it was the major figure in the structural-
functional approach, Talcott Parsons, who first called this differentiation into
question many years ago. Parsons contended that professionals and
businesspeople were both interested in the same goal—success. Thus the difference between them (if there is any) lies not in goals but simply in means to
the same goal: the professional can be *successful* by being, or seeming to be,
altruistic, while egoism leads the businessperson to success. Parsons concluded:

> The typical motivation of professional men is not in the usual sense "altruistic,"
> nor is that of businessmen typically "egoistic." Indeed there is little basis for
> maintaining that there is any broad difference of motivation in the two cases, or
> at least any of sufficient importance to account for the broad differences of so-
> cially expected behavior.[47]

Parsons seemed to conclude from this that the businessperson was as "good"
as the professional, while modern power advocates have used the same evidence to argue that professionals are as "bad" as businesspeople.

Interesting new light is cast on this issue by the rise of professionals (especially physicians) in business, or entrepreneurial professionals. Says
Goldstein:

> At a time when traditional entrepreneurial approaches are being fostered in
> medicine, it seems reasonable to assert that physicians who are entrepreneurs or
> favorably disposed to becoming entrepreneurs will take on increasing impor-
> tance. It is our impression that, at least in some areas of the country, physician
> entrepreneurs have emerged as important elements in the provision of certain
> medical services. Pathology labs, radiology groups, health promotion centers,
> obesity and substance abuse clinics, chains of local emergency rooms, proprie-
> tary hospitals, long-term care facilities, and nursing homes are some examples.[48]

Hence, the line between professionals and businesspeople, never clear-cut, is
growing even fuzzier.

The power advocates argue that the service ethic is a myth created and
perpetuated by professionals to enhance their status[49] and to "silence the critics of monopoly, privilege, and power to which professionals are attempting
to cling."[50] It is a myth created by the professions to give them autonomy and
authority by convincing the public and various significant others that they can

---

[47]Parsons, "Professions and Social Structure," 465.

[48]Michael S. Goldstein, "Abortion as a Medical Career Choice: Entrepreneurs, Community
Physicians, and Others," *Journal of Health and Social Behavior,* 25 (1984), 211–229.

[49]Freidson, *The Profession of Medicine,* p. 82.

[50]Paul Halmos, Introduction to Paul Halmos, ed., *Professionalization and Social Change: The
Sociological Review Monograph* (Staffordshire, England: The University of Keele, 1973), p. 6.

be trusted to handle crucial matters because they are not self-interested. Many have found this hard to accept, given the high salaries and enormous power accruing to many professionals. For example, in 1982 the average *net* income for physicians in the United States was about $90,000. This is take-home pay since it is income *after* taxes, expenses, malpractice insurance, and so on. The median net annual income for dentists in 1983 was approximately $66,000, while for lawyers the average was $52,000 per year.[51]

Doubt about the altruism of the professions has increased in recent years as a result of "exposés of the backstage activities of the professions regarding fees and fee-splitting, unnecessary referral and intervention, ritualistic procedures, or billing for work that was never undertaken."[52] Attacking the idea of a service ethic, Roth argues that although the professional is supposed to give service to all, "there is a mass of evidence already publicly available on the bias of professional workers and their service organizations against deviant youth, the aged, women, the poor, ethnic minorities, and people they just didn't like the looks of."[53] Based on these criticisms, we can conclude that the professions do not operate according to altruistic principles, although they have often been able to convince many clients that they do. Altruism is a myth in the professions, but, like many others, it is a highly effective myth.

Intimately related to the claim of altruism is the professionals' argument that they are "called" to their vocation. As McKinlay sees it, this implies "either that professionals are specially selected by some higher authority, or that they respond to some higher idealism."[54] To McKinlay, this notion is, at least in part, a vestige of the time that professionals were either clergymen or intimately connected with the church. He dismisses the professional claim of a "calling" as either deceptive or false:

> We are still told that people are "called" to the ministry or priesthood, but suspect that no God called them. Similarly, in the field of law, we hear that people are "called to the bar," although again we know that nobody called them and that the initiative was entirely theirs. . . . Since a disproportionate number of those in dominant professions are from families already in or associated with them it would appear whoever's doing the calling is doing it on a highly biased and self-protective fashion.[55]

The idea of a professional calling is a myth to increase the profession's power over significant others.

Norm of authority over clients. The professionals argue that they should have virtually uncontested authority over clients. They argue that they have

[51]John Wright, *The American Almanac of Jobs and Salaries* (New York: Avon, 1984).

[52]John B. McKinlay, "On the Professional Regulation of Change," in Halmos, *Professionalization and Social Change,* pp. 67–68. See also, John J. Lally and Bernard Barber, "The Compassionate Physician: Frequency and Social Determinants of Physician-Investigator Concern for Human Subjects," *Social Forces,* 53 (1974), 289–96.

[53]Roth, "Professionalism: The Sociologist's Decoy," 10–11.

[54]McKinlay, "On the Professional Regulation of Change," p. 67.

[55]Ibid.

always had it and must continue to have it to provide high-quality service to clients. Somehow a questioning clientele would reduce the quality of their service, presumably by distracting them from the highly important and complex tasks at hand. Professionals, and some sociologists, usually differentiate between clients and customers. The professions have clients while all other occupations have customers. Clients are supposed to be incapable of judging their own needs or the ability of a given professional to satisfy those needs. In contrast, customers, such as people shopping for a car, are supposed to be able to evaluate their own needs and judge the ability of a given dealer to satisfy those needs. In the latter situation, the power is supposed to rest with the customer ("the customer is always right"), while in the former case it is the professional who is supposed to have uncontested authority over the client. One problem with this, of course, is that it simply does not mesh with reality, either past or present. Rothstein, among others, has shown how professions historically have never had complete authority and, in fact, how clients wielded considerable control over them.[56] In contemporary terms, Freidson has shown that the physician has far from unlimited control over the patient. Freidson points out that doctors do not have the ability to define a patient, at least initially, as ill;[57] doctors must wait for patients to first define themselves as ill and then seek out a physician. Physicians, especially general practitioners, also have their authority limited because they must be responsive to the lay culture. It is by pleasing this culture that general practitioners get and keep patients. In contrast to general practitioners, doctors who deal only with patients referred by other doctors have much more authority and have therefore much greater freedom from lay control. But instead they must be more responsive to fellow doctors, and this places a limitation on their authority, too. In sum, the more professional the occupation, the greater the authority, but this authority is rarely absolute.

Furthermore, it can be argued that the changing nature of medical work is further reducing the authority of physicians over patients. Physicians are less and less likely to be confronted with acute illnesses that can be cured with a single treatment. Instead they are more likely to deal with chronic illnesses, such as cancer, heart disease, or mental illness, in which they are almost always unable to demonstrate their competence in a single stroke. To deal with such illnesses, physicians need the active support of the patient, since treatment is likely to take place over long periods of time. Furthermore, they must also rely on a variety of other occupations (such as therapists, technicians, counselors) to help with such patients. Such a sharing of patients serves to further dilute the authority of the physician.[58]

Roth has generalized this point by arguing that clients always have con-

[56]William Rothstein, "Professionalization and the Employer Demands: The Case of Homeopathy and Psychoanalysis in the United States," in Halmos, ed., *Professionalization and Social Change*, p. 172.

[57]Eliot Freidson, "Client Control and Medical Practice," *American Journal of Sociology*, 65 (1960), 374–82.

[58]Irving Kenneth Zola and Stephen J. Miller, "The Erosion of Medicine from Within," in Eliot Freidson, ed., *The Professions and their Prospects*, pp. 105–16.

siderable power over professionals.[59] At the extreme, the client may fire the professional or simply sever the relationship. Clients can, and often do, ignore the professional's advice and recommendations. Beyond this, some have argued that we have experienced a "revolt of the client," which means that for a variety of reasons (some of which will be discussed later in this chapter) clients are becoming even more questioning of the authority of professionals.[60]

Thus a number of people have come to the conclusion that the uncontested authority of the professional never existed and does not now exist; moreover, whatever authority does exist is likely to decline in the future. Absolute authority over clients is a myth developed by professionals to enhance their ability to control clients by imbuing in them the idea that they are supposed to be passive consumers of professional services. Nevertheless, the myth has had some success; many clients do subscribe to the idea that they cannot, or should not, question the decisions of professionals, at least to the extent that they are likely to question the decisions of the butcher or hairdresser. The professions do seem to have at least some greater degree of authority over their clients.

Another critical issue here is whether the professions need this unquestioned authority. Professionals would argue that they can provide better and more rapid service if they are not bothered by a questioning clientele. Further, they would undoubtedly contend that their work entails such skill and knowledge that a layperson could not possibly ask a useful question. These are largely rationalizations. The fact is that a more responsive client could provide the professional with far better information with which to make a decision. Further, a questioning clientele is likely to prod the professional into a higher, not lower, level of performance.[61]

A distinctive occupational culture. Those in the professions claim that they develop an occupational culture different from that developed in a nonprofessional occupation. Formal organizations that help to create a distinctive culture are professional associations, training schools and organizations in which professionals work; supplementing these formal structures is a series of informal groupings within the profession. The culture that develops is composed of a number of distinctive values, norms, and symbols.[62] Some typical professional values include the importance of their professional service to the community, authority over clients, self-control, and theoretical objectivity. In addition, there are numerous norms within a profession that serve as specific guides for behavior. Some examples from the legal profession include norms governing how to get into law school, how to attract a sponsor, and how to find clients. Such norms are so pervasive that Greenwood contends that "there is a behavior norm covering every standard interpersonal situation

---

[59]Roth, "Professionalism: The Sociologist's Decoy," 6–23.

[60]Marie Haug and Marvin Sussman, "Professional Autonomy and the Revolt of the Client," *Social Problems,* 17 (1969), 153–61.

[61]Douglas Rosenthal, *Lawyer and Client: Who's in Charge?* (New York: Russell Sage, 1974).

[62]Greenwood, "Attributes of a Profession," 51.

likely to recur in professional life."[63] Finally, there are the symbols of the profession, which reflect the culture and are in addition part of it: included are "its insignias, emblems, and distinctive dress; its history, folklore, and argot; its heroes and its villains; and its stereotypes of the professional, the client, and the layman."[64] Training in a profession is focally concerned with transmitting this culture to the neophyte through formal training schools or informal devices such as sponsorship.

The idea of a professional culture has been expanded by Goode. He views a profession as a community[65] because the members are bound by a common identity; it is terminal—in the sense that once in a profession few leave; it has common values, role definitions, and language; it has power over members; it has clear boundaries; and it has powers of reproduction via transmission of culture to succeeding generations.

Although we can readily acknowledge that the professions do develop highly elaborate cultures,[66] that does not mean that they are qualitatively different from the cultures developed in nonprofessional occupations. After all, most occupational cultures are composed of values, norms, symbols, language, power over members, and the like. Professional cultures are simply more elaborate—that is, they are quantitatively rather than qualitatively different from nonprofessional cultures. One thing that does stand out about the professional culture is its greater power to maintain itself and keep itself free of external control. Thus the professional culture simply has more of everything, most notably more power.

Recognition by the community and law that the occupation is a profession.   Although the structural-functionalists tend to see the communal and legal recognition of a profession's status as only one of the factors that serves to differentiate occupations, this legitimization assumes a far more central role in the analysis presented here. All of the myths promulgated by the professions are aimed at acquiring this recognition, since once the recognition is obtained all other facets of the professional model fall into place. The public and law come to recognize formally and/or informally that the professions possess the following traits, irrespective of whether they actually possess them:

1.   A body of general systematic knowledge that is their exclusive possession.
2.   A norm of autonomy that the public and law are bound to respect.
3.   A norm of altruism that entitles the profession to special treatment and respect.

---

[63]Ibid, 52.

[64]Ibid.

[65]William J. Goode, "Community Within a Community: The Professions."

[66]Not all professions have a community. For a discussion of one that does not, see Robert Perrucci and Joel Gerstl, *Profession Without Community: Engineers in American Society* (New York: Random House, 1969).

4. A norm of authority over clients that the public feels is its duty to obey.
5. A distinctive occupational culture.

Throughout this section we have discussed how all of these traits are myths developed and promoted by the professions. Yet they become realities when treated by the public and law as if they are real. To understand how this transformation of myth into reality takes place, we need to turn to a discussion of the dynamics of professionalization. In the preceding pages we have presented a summary of the basic characteristics of a profession offered by the structural-functionalists. And while enumerating them, we have also included criticisms of each offered by supporters of the power approach. Although much of the structural-functional approach has been rejected, the characteristics it developed are useful.[67] We shall see how they fit into a broadened theory of professionalization in the next section.

THE POWER APPROACH

We have caught only glimpses of the power perspectives in the criticisms leveled by its supporters at the structural-functionalist's constellation of characteristics. It is now time to articulate explicitly the power approach. We will then consider to what degree it can be reconciled with the other two orientations—the process and structural-functionalist theories—in a new, broader approach to the professions.

We define *power*, in this context, to mean the ability of an occupation (really its leaders) to obtain and retain a set of rights and privileges (and obligations) from societal groups that otherwise might not grant them. This implies the resistance, or the potential for resistance, among various societal groups (the public, the state) that must be overcome by the profession.[68]

As was mentioned earlier, the power approach has now become the dominant orientation in the study of the professions. The emphasis on power has been articulated by a number of authors. For example, Klegon concludes: "the ability to obtain and maintain professional status is closely related to both concrete occupational strategies, as well as wider social forces and arrangements of *power*."[69] In his recent review of the field, Hall concludes: "The key to

---

[67]For a defense of the structural-functional approach see Ernest Greenwood, "Attributes of a Profession Revisited," in Neil Gilbert and Harry Specht, eds., *The Emergence of Social Welfare and Social Work*, 2nd ed. (Itasca, IL: F.E. Peacock, Inc., 1980), pp. 255–276.

[68]In his study of the military, Abrahamsson offers a similar view: "I define *military political power* as the overcoming of resistance in the making of decisions concerning objectives . . . that have (perceived or actual) consequences for the military establishment." See Bengt Abrahamsson, *Military Professionalization and Professional Power* (Beverly Hills, CA: Sage, 1972), p. 140.

[69]Douglas Klegon, "The Sociology of Professions: An Emerging Perspective," *Sociology of Work and Occupations*, 5 (1978), 281–282 (italics added).

the nature of the professions is thus the possession of power."[70] While others have underscored the importance of professional power,[71] some have begun to question whether we have gone too far in emphasizing power.

In fact, one of the pioneers of the power approach to the professions, Eliot Freidson, has recently come to question the adequacy of a single-minded focus on power: "no single truly explanatory trait or characteristic—including such a recent candidate as 'power' . . . can join together all occupations called professions beyond the actual fact of coming to be called professions."[72] In fact, Freidson now urges that we give up the task of isolating the essence of professions and satisfy ourselves with "an intrinsically ambiguous, multifaceted folk concept" of the professions.[73]

While more of the limitations of the power approach are likely to be exposed in coming years, it remains the strongest approach to the study of the professions. In its most extreme form, the power approach operates from the assumption that there are no qualitative differences between the professions and nonprofessions other than the greater power of the professions. McKinlay adopts this position when he notes that except for their power position the professions are "indistinguishable from most other occupations."[74] He is even more explicit when he contends that "there is no logical basis for distinguishing between so-called professions and other occupations."[75]

A less extreme variant of this position is that while power is the defining characteristic of the professions, one or more distinctive characteristics are derived from that power. In a sense, it could be argued that all of the characteristics discussed in the preceding section stem from the power of the professions. That power allows them to either create these traits or to convince significant others that they possess them when they really do not. In fact, it is often difficult to draw a hard line between the professions convincing others that they have these characteristics and actually possessing them. A successful effort to convince the public that they have authority over them ends with the professions actually having that power.

Few would argue with the fact that the professions possess power and use it to develop a set of characteristics that win for themselves an exalted place in society, but how did they accomplish this historically? Larson deals with this in terms of an historical analysis of the "collective mobility" of the

[70]Richard Hall, "Theoretical Trends in the Sociology of Occupations," 12.

[71]Portwood and Fielding, "Privilege and the Professions;" Robert A. Rothman, "Occupational Roles: Power and Negotiation in the Division of Labor," *The Sociological Quarterly*, 20 (1979), 495–515.

[72]Eliot Freidson, "The Theory of the Professions: State of the Art," in Robert Dingwall and Philip Lewis, eds., *The Sociology of the Professions*, p. 32.

[73]See also, Topsy Murray, Robert Dingwall, and John Eekelaar, "Professionals in Bureaucracies: Solicitors in Private Practice and Local Government," in Dingwall and Lewis, eds., *The Sociology of the Professions*, p. 97. Saks makes the point that many supporters of the power approach (and others as well) have been content to make bald and unsubstantiated criticisms rather than basing their critiques on serious research; Mike Saks, "Removing the Blinkers?"

[74]McKinlay, "On the Professional Regulation of Change," p. 63.

[75]Ibid., pp. 65–66.

professions and their effort "to constitute *and control* a market for their expertise."[76]

The modern professions really came into existence with the rise of capitalism. Since capitalism was a market system, and the professions were tied to that system, the professions were defined by their effort to create and control the market for their services. However, unlike others in capitalism, professionals did not have a commodity to sell. Instead of controlling the market for their goods, they had to control the production of new professionals, that is, control their training. Since their markets were new and therefore unstable, professionals first had to make the case for their service and show its superiority to competing services. They did this through the standardization of their services. This standardization made the professional's "commodity" both distinct from those of others and recognizable to potential publics. The professions also needed to gain control over their markets to guarantee recruits that their training would pay off. As they were gaining control of the markets for their services, the professions were also able to engage in collective mobility in order to gain higher status and greater social standing. It was the history of medicine, of course, that best expressed this model of market monopoly and collective mobility.

One important issue is the source of professional power. Where does it come from in the first place? The power advocates have made a beginning toward answering this difficult question.

Indeterminacy and Uncertainty

In their study of French medical practice, Jamous and Peloille concluded that the professions (in this case the medical profession)

> perpetuated their definition only by emphasizing the *margin of indetermination* [italics ours] inherent in the production process and, by the same token, the rules, the norms and the institutions which are their supports. . . . These criteria, which specialized sociology considers to be characteristics of a profession, are in fact an expression of the professional ideology of the dominant members.[77]

Jamous and Peloille make it clear that sociologists have emphasized the derived characteristics of the professions—the elements of their ideology—while they have ignored a source of the power of the professions—the margin of indetermination.

What is this margin of indetermination? Unfortunately, Jamous and Peloille are not as clear as they might have been, but they seem to mean the degree to which an occupation's task(s) cannot be routinized—that is, made available to masses of people. Tasks that can be broken down into a series of

---

[76]Magali Sarfatti Larson, *The Rise of Professionalism: A Sociological Analysis* (Berkeley, CA: University of California Press, 1977), p. xvi.

[77]H. Jamous and B. Peloille, "Changes in the French University-Hospital System," in J.A. Jackson, ed., *Professions and Professionalization* (London: Cambridge University Press, 1970), pp. 111–52.

simple actions that virtually everyone can quickly learn do not lend themselves to professionalization. On the other hand, tasks that defy such routinization are the basis of professionalization. It can be argued that at least a portion of the power of physicians is derived from their margin of indetermination. It must be recognized, however, that physicians have never been content to rely on the level of indetermination inherent in the nature of their tasks but have actively used the power derived from it to protect it from routinization, as well as to expand it.[78]

In their analysis of the concept of indeterminacy, Atkinson et al. argue that Jamous and Peloille use this concept in an absolute sense *and* a political/ ideological sense.[79] On the one hand, Jamous and Peloille argue that indeterminacy is an objective (absolute) quality that professions have to a high degree. Atkinson et al. reject this usage on a variety of grounds, not the least of which is that it moves us away from the power approach and back to the trait orientation of the structural-functionalists. To be true to a power approach, Atkinson et al. opt for the political/ideological usage of indeterminacy. Indeterminacy is a *claim* made by professionals through which, if it is accepted, "areas of their day-to-day work governed by indeterminate means will be defined as beyond the scrutiny of fellow professionals and laymen alike. . . . The claims of indeterminacy serve to ensure the privacy of the individual practitioner, as well as enhancing the mystique of the profession at large."[80]

Although there is merit in the position of Atkinson et al., it leaves us without a sense of the basis of successful or unsuccessful claims of indeterminacy. Why does one occupation succeed in having its claims accepted while another fails? If we do not accept the idea that among the successful professions there is indeterminacy in some objective sense, then we are forced to argue that they succeed because they are powerful. In other words, the power of the professions is traced to their power. Such a circular argument will not do and as a result we are forced to accept the idea of indeterminacy in some absolute sense. That is not to deny that it is also a political/ideological mechanism by which professions seek to enhance their power.

A related source of professional power may be labeled the *level of uncertainty*. Johnson points to the importance of this factor in the genesis of professional power: "Occupational activities vary in degree to which they give rise to a structure of uncertainty and in their potentialities for autonomy."[81] Thus, returning to the example of physicians, we can see that they deal with an area of acute uncertainty to their clients, and this is an important source of their power. Again, of course, professionals ordinarily seek to protect as well as to expand this area of uncertainty and thereby increase their power.

We are suggesting that the professionals' margin of indetermination and

---

[78]Paul Boreham, "Indetermination: Professional Knowledge, Organization and Control," *The Sociological Review,* 31 (1983), 697.

[79]Paul Atkinson, Margaret Reid, and Peter Sheldrake, "Medical Mystique," *Sociology of Work and Occupations,* 4 (1977), 243–280.

[80]Ibid., 257–258.

[81]Johnson, *The Professions and Power,* p. 43. While Johnson equates uncertainty with indeterminacy, we see them as different sources of professional power.

control over areas of uncertainty are two major sources of their power.[82] There are undoubtedly a number of other sources, but these seem to be the most important.

It is important to note, following Johnson, that uncertainty and indeterminacy may not apply to all groups and for all time. What is indeterminate and uncertain in one era may not be indeterminate and uncertain in another. Thus, for example, the secularization of society has made religion less uncertain to people and the result has been a diminution in the power, and professionalization, of the clergy. Similarly, uncertainty and indetermination may vary from group to group. Thus, some groups may continue to accord professional status to the clergy while others have withdrawn such recognition.

In general, we can see from this explanation how physicians, the clergy, and even military officers gained professional status. They all clearly controlled, at least historically, problems of acute uncertainty and/or indetermination to most, if not all, groups in society. But what of the lawyer or the accountant? Did they achieve professional status because of the power they derived from control over areas of uncertainty or indetermination? The answer is clearly no. Rather, they acquired professional status by artificially creating areas of uncertainty or indetermination over which they then exercised control. Thus, indeterminacy and uncertainty can be either intrinsic to a task or can be artificially produced. Lawyers, for example, have certainly mystified the process of a divorce, and in the process they have artificially created an area of uncertainty and indetermination over which they exercise control. Accountants have done the same thing with income tax.

If an occupation can artificially produce areas of uncertainty or indetermination, we are once again confronted with the problem of the source of the power to perform such a feat. It seems clear that occupations that already possess some independent source of power are more likely to produce such areas. One example might be occupations that develop from some already powerful institution or occupation. Already possessing a power base, such occupations can use it to create areas of uncertainty and indetermination. Another example is the occupation that recruits people (or the children of people) who rank high in the social hierarchy. Still another would be those occupations that, already controlling one area of uncertainty or indetermination, expand into other areas. Thus, independent power sources are of crucial importance to aspiring professions.

However an occupation acquires areas of indeterminacy and/or uncertainty, naturally or artificially, it can and often does seek to deliberately ex-

---

[82]These factors have been found to be important in other intergroup situations. In his study of French bureaucracy, Michael Crozier [*The Bureaucratic Phenomenon*, (Chicago: University of Chicago Press, 1964)] found that skilled craftsmen derived power in the organization from their control over uncertainty. In their essay on intergroup power within organizations, D.J. Hickson et al. ["A Strategic Contingencies Theory of Intraorganizational Power," *Administrative Science Quarterly*, 16 (1971), 216–29] contend that uncertainty (and the ability to cope with it) as well as substitutability and routinization (which resemble the idea of margin of indetermination) are crucial sources of power. They also give a key role to the centrality of the group within the organization, but this factor seems less relevant to an analysis of the professions in society.

pand those areas. Johnson makes this argument: "Uncertainty is not, therefore, entirely cognitive in origin, but may be deliberately increased to serve manipulative or managerial ends."[83] Physicians, the clergy, military officers, lawyers, and accountants have all engaged in such expansion. This brings us to a central variable to those who follow the power approach—ideology.

Ideology

Almost all of the criticisms leveled by the power advocates at the basic characteristics of the professions can be subsumed under the heading of ideology. Daniels makes this point: "What professions say about themselves in justification of their privileged status above ordinary occupations might better be studied as political ideology than as an indication of intrinsic difference between professions and other types of occupations."[84]

Although there is a tendency to think of professional ideologies as consciously constructed efforts at self-aggrandizement, this need not be the case. Says Geison:

> . . . Professionals have usually constructed their ideologies unself-consciously and sincerely . . . whatever deception may be embodied in professional ideology and rhetoric is partly a matter of self-deception as well. Even in the case of the medical profession . . . there is evidence to suggest that many American physicians have genuinely believed in the extreme laissez-faire ideology that organized medicine has so long exploited in its efforts to avoid government interference.[85]

The professions have used (and traditional sociologists have accepted) these idealized characteristics as ideological tools in their efforts to enhance their power. For those occupations with historic control over areas of indeterminacy or uncertainty, ideology has been used to expand areas of their control and hence their power. For occupations without such control, ideologies have been employed to win control over these areas and then to expand control once it has been acquired.

Ideology also plays a defensive role for those occupations that have won professional status. Ideology is used to protect the established position of the professions from external and internal threats to its powerful position. As Jamous and Peloille note, the medical profession had to defend itself against a double threat:

> (1) The threat born of socio-economic struggles and changes which sought to redefine the social aim of medical activity by calling in question the conditions of production of medical care and the quality of such care. (2) The other threat produced by scientific and technical changes—issuing partly, therefore, from the "professional group" itself—which set itself the task of redefining the nature

[83]Johnson, *The Professions and Power*, p. 43.

[84]Arlene Daniels, "How Free Should Professions Be?" p. 56.

[85]Gerald L. Geison, "Introduction," in Geison, ed., *Professions and Professional Ideology in America* (Chapel Hill: The University of North Carolina Press, 1983), p. 7.

of medical knowledge and disputing the quality of what was produced and transmitted."[86]

More generally, we can say that the professions inevitably face threats from both within and without and that one of the major ways they seek to cope with these threats is through the development, and use, of sophisticated ideological systems. This leads to a dialectical view of the professions. As they become increasingly powerful and entrenched, external social changes and internal technical changes inevitably lead to threats to that position. Similarly, new technical developments take place internally that the "old guard" finds difficult to assimilate. Younger professionals, adept in the new areas, come to oppose, and be opposed by, the established professionals. Although ideologies and other defenses will work for a time, the established professions must be transformed by these forces. This presumably leads to a new entrenched group that will again be transformed when external and internal changes overwhelm it.

The Process of Professionalization

What we have now arrived at in our discussion is a multicausal, multidirectional approach to analyzing professionalization that focuses on the variables of power, of uncertainty and indeterminacy, and of ideology. It is impossible to construct a simple linear model because, as we have seen, all of these factors are interrelated in a highly complex manner. It is possible, however, to offer in summary a few partial statements about this process as long as we recognize that they are being extracted from a dialectical process and can only be understood in the context of that process.

1. An occupation that controls areas of indeterminacy and/or uncertainty is likely to have great power.
2. An occupation with such power is likely to use it to win the prestigious title of profession.
3. An occupation is likely to use ideology as a weapon in its effort to gain professional status.
4. The power of an occupation is likely to be enhanced once it acquires professional status.
5. A profession is likely to employ ideology in order to help it maintain or even improve its position.
6. Despite its power and the strength of its ideological system, a profession can lose its position as a result of external and internal social changes.

Where does all of this leave the constellation of characteristics most often focused on by the traditionalists, in particular the structural-functionalists? They are derived from the basic process outlined above and are used as ideological weapons by professionals. A profession may or may not actually possess them, but this is secondary to their utility as tools in an effort to gain and maintain professional status. Unfortunately, traditional analysts of the professions have tended to focus on these derived characteristics rather than the far more important process outlined above.

[86]Jamous and Peloille, "Changes in the French University-Hospital System," pp. 120–21.

RECONCILING THE THREE APPROACHES TO THE PROFESSIONS

It is relatively easy to reconcile the power and process interpretations. As we have seen, many of the advocates of the latter dealt with the power variable, and in fact much of their work stands as the intellectual precursor of the power approach.[87] Many of those once aligned with the process approach have even made the relatively easy transition to a power orientation (for example, Freidson). It is not necessary to choose between these two approaches; both should focus on the process by which occupations strive for professional status. But the focus should be on the roles played by such factors as power and ideology in this development and on the ongoing events (for example, segmentalization) within the professions (a traditional concern of the process advocates). Thus, despite criticisms by the power advocates (many of which are valid), there is no necessary contradictions between the process and power approaches. Indeed, they are eminently compatible.

The same is not true of the relationship between the power and structural-functional approaches. In our judgment, the power orientation at many points contradicts the structural-functional position. We believe—and it is now a consensus among sociological students of the professions—that the power approach has greater explanatory capacity than the structural-functional approach and that the functionalist orientation must therefore be subsumed under a power-process model. Although some elements of the structural-functional approach must simply be discarded, others can be integrated into the broader model being developed here. Of greatest utility is the constellation of characteristics developed by the functionalists. But these can no longer be viewed as necessarily "real" things that professions possess and occupations do not. Rather, they must be seen either (1) as traits that are derived from the power of the professions and are of secondary importance or (2) as a set of deceptive "traits" that the professions do not actually possess but have been able to convince significant others that they have. Thus the constellation of characteristics can be real, mythical, or some combination of the two. The structural-functional approach remains useful, but as an adjunct to a power-process model.

Let us turn to a more substantive concern of those who hold the power perspective—the role of the professions in society. On this issue, the power supporters are returning to a historical but long lost concern of the field.

THE PROFESSIONS AND SOCIETY

In the view of most power advocates, the power of the professions has been exaggerated and it is likely to decline even further in the future. This view debunks many myths and shows the professions to be far less menacing than many believe.

In his historical study of selected professions, Rothstein shows the enor-

[87]Saks ("Removing the Blinkers?") singles out Everett Hughes and Howard Becker as particularly important in this respect.

mous power clients have exercised over the professional. In contradiction to the myth that the professions exercised unquestioned authority over clients, Rothstein argues:

> Clients who patronized medical practitioners . . . wanted the best possible treatment, and if they could not obtain it from a physician who used one form of treatment, they would seek out physicians who used other forms of treatment. Wealthy clients in particular were able to impose demands on their physicians because they provided their physicians with their greatest remuneration . . . when advances occurred in medical practice such that new forms of safe and effective . . . treatments became available, patients insisted that physicians administer those treatments.[88]

Rothstein demonstrates how the professions are buffeted by a wide variety of forces that are beyond their control: "The history of homeopathy and psychoanalysis in the United States appears to support the conclusion that the individual physician in independent practice operates in a network of powerful economic and technical forces over which he has little individual control."[89] Professionals seem much less powerful when we recognize that they are subjected to pressure from clients and a variety of social forces beyond their influence.

Others have pointed to a variety of structural factors that greatly reduce the power of the professions. Jamous and Peloille's analysis of the development of the French medical system shows that, even though physicians had developed great power and influence in the early 1800s, that power was threatened and ultimately undermined in later years by government legislation.[90] Daniels shows how the structure of the military transformed the military psychiatrist from a helper of the sick to a social control agent operating in behalf of the military establishment.[91] Larkin underscores the existence of other occupations with their own desire for power as constraints on the power of the professions, in particular the medical profession.[92] Professions must often compromise with other occupations in order to maintain their position within the occupational hierarchy. At another level of generality, Johnson demonstrates how the nature of the British colonial system in the third world inhibited the development of a professional system as we know it.[93]

In Freidson's view, the success of the professions is primarily in the hands of society's dominant elites.[94] A profession's privileged position is given

---

[88]Rothstein, "Professionalization and Employer Demands," in Halmos, ed., *Professionalization and Social Change,* p. 172.

[89]Ibid.

[90]Jamous and Peloille, "Changes in the French University-Hospital System."

[91]Arlene Daniels, "The Captive Professional: Bureaucratic Limitations on the Practice of Military Psychiatry," *Journal of Health and Social Behavior,* 10 (1969), 255–65.

[92]Gerald Larkin, *Occupational Monopoly and Modern Medicine* (London: Tavistock Publications, 1983).

[93]Terence Johnson, "Imperialism and the Professions: Notes on the Development of Professional Occupations in Britain's Colonies and the New States," in Halmos, *Professionalization and Social Change,* pp. 281–309.

[94]Freidson, *The Profession of Medicine.*

by, not taken from, societal elites. He acknowledges that the would-be professions must endeavor to convince the elites of their worth, but the elites always have the power to deny their claims. The elites can allow a profession's status to lapse, or they can even actively remove it. The profession must continue to convince the elites of its worthiness (or at least its harmlessness) if it is to continue to be accorded professional status. Beyond this, Freidson sees the success of the professions determined by the sponsorship of the societal elites, which use their influence to "drive competing occupations out of the same area of work . . . [which] discourages others by virtue of the comparative advantages conferred on the chosen occupation, and [which] requires still others to be subordinated to the profession."[95] Thus the professions are viewed as almost helpless protectorates of this societal elite. They are allowed to exercise power within their domain, but only at the behest of the elites.[96]

Another theme in this approach is the ebb and flow of professional power, a perspective that is well illustrated in William Ray Arney's study, *Power and the Profession of Obstetrics.*[97] Arney outlines a long history in which developments served to enhance the power of obstetrics. The primarily male obstetricians wrested control of the birth process from primarily female midwives. They succeeded in defining one birth position, "the lithotomy position," as *the* standard, permitting "the obstetrician to 'stand before' the woman and watch for the potential pathology of delivery, and . . . [permitting] timely intervention should anything go wrong."[98] They succeeded in making a minor surgical procedure (episiotomy) on the vaginal opening almost routine even though such an operation was "done more in response to obstetrician's concerns about repairing perineal tears than in the interests of women."[99] Another procedure that was developed by obstetricians, largely for their own interests, was induced labor. All of these efforts were unified prior to the middle of the twentieth century by an effort to search out and contain potential pathologies associated with birth.

However, around 1950 the profession began to shift its philosophy from dealing with potential pathologies to the monitoring of, and surveillance over, *all* births. The domain of the obstetrician shifted from pathologies to "every aspect of birth and every aspect of the environment surrounding birth."[100] On the one hand, this enhanced the power of obstetrics because "every birth became subject to its gaze."[101] On the other, it set in motion a series of changes

---

[95]Ibid., p. 72.

[96]In an interesting study Jeffrey Berlant [*Profession and Monopoly: A Study of Medicine in the United States and Great Britain* (Berkeley, CA: University of California Press, 1975)] comes to a conclusion similar to Freidson's on the importance of societal elites in the success of the professions: "To the degree that there is a favorable constellation of interests between the profession and elite groups, the collective interests of the profession can be furthered through progressive monopolization" (p. 306). Berlant, by the way, is squarely in the power approach, using Weber's ideas on monopolization to analyze the medical profession.

[97]William Ray Arney, *Power and the Profession of Obstetrics* (Chicago: University of Chicago Press, 1982).

[98]Ibid., p. 64.

[99]Ibid., p. 70.

[100]Ibid., p. 94.

[101]Ibid., p. 100.

that served to reduce the power of the obstetrician. In effect, it served to reduce the margin of indetermination in obstetrics by making it clear to those outside the field what had, and could be, done.

> With monitoring so thoroughly deployed, with the proper course of pregnancy recorded in journals and texts accessible to anyone who learns the language, and with each small part of every pregnancy documented and accessible in the medical record, obstetricians became . . . visible to the inquiring eye. . . . The sovereignty of the obstetrician is gone.[102]

Laypeople, in the form of consumers and government groups, now can learn what obstetricians are doing, monitor their activities, and impose controls on them. In other words, some of the power has now shifted away from obstetricians as a result of changes they themselves set in motion.

The last few paragraphs lead us, first, to the conclusion that the professions have never been as powerful as has been assumed. And second, structural changes now taking place within the larger society are further reducing whatever power the professions possessed. In this context, we need to examine the processes of deprofessionalization and the proletarianization of the professions.

Deprofessionalization

A good measure of the success of the power approach in the sociology of the professions is the shift in attention from the process of professionalization to the process of deprofessionalization.[103,104] Deprofessionalization is attractive to the power advocates because it constitutes a critique of, rather than an apology for, the professions. Proponents of the structural-functional and process interpretations were often apologists for the professions.

One of the first to enunciate the deprofessionalization thesis was Marie Haug.[105] "Deprofessionalization is defined as the professional occupations' loss of their unique qualities, particularly their monopoly over knowledge, public belief in their service ethos, and expectations of work autonomy and authority over client."[106] What are the causes of this likely loss of power?

The "revolt of the client."   Clients, for a variety of reasons, have grown in-

---

[102]Ibid., p. 153.

[103]Nina Toren, "Deprofessionalization and its Sources: A Preliminary Analysis," *Sociology of Work and Occupations,* 2 (1975), 323–337.

[104]That *both* professionalization and deprofessionalization exist is made clear by Portwood and Fielding in their study of five English professions: "Thus, for the earliest professions there is no inalienable right to privilege for all time, and conversely this does not mean that latecomers will be denied privilege simply by virtue of their relative youth." Portwood and Fielding, "Privilege and the Professions," 760.

[105]Marie Haug, "Deprofessionalization: An Alternative Hypothesis for the Future," in Halmos, ed., *Professionalization and Social Change,* pp. 195–211. See also, Marie Haug and Marvin Sussman, "Professional Autonomy and the Revolt of the Client," *Social Problems,* 17 (1969), 153–61; Marie Haug, "The Deprofessionalization of Everyone?" *Sociological Focus,* 8 (1975), 197–213.

[106]Haug, "Deprofessionalization," 197.

creasingly likely to question the authority of the professional. Although clients have always questioned professionals, this attitude has apparently grown in recent years, and there is evidence that it is likely to spread in the future.

Diminution in level of indetermination.[107]   As a result of the specialization, routinization,[108] computerization, and rationalization of at least some of their functions,[109] some professions have suffered a diminished level of indetermination.

Artistic abilities.   The converse of the last point, but still pointing in the same direction, is the growing realization that many professional tasks require artistic abilities (e.g., diagnostic ability, social skills) rather than scientific skill. This means that such skills can, in many cases, be acquired by anyone who gains the needed experience. This has led to burgeoning movements of paraprofessionals who claim the right to perform these functions. Examples of these functions include the physician's "bedside manner," the lawyer's debating ability, and the like.

Narrowing of the competence gap.   The client has become increasingly knowledgeable about matters (for example, medical, legal) that were once virtually the exclusive domain of the professions. Rothman has recently called this the "narrowing of the competence gap" between professionals and the public.[110] Among other things, this can be traced to the increasing educational level of the population as well as the expansion of information emanating from the mass media.

Professional abuses.   Increasing revelations of professional abuse and malpractice have led to critical assaults on the professions (accusations of elitism, being money-hungry, disinterest in clients, and so on). Such revelations, along with the increasing sophistication of clients, has led to more questioning of the authority of the professional.[111] For example, medical patients want more information, more precise performance standards, and "redress of grievance whenever a transaction is deemed unfair."[112]

Increasing control by outsiders.   Johnson argues: "The conditions which gave rise to the institution of professionalism are no longer dominant in industrialized societies.[113] To Johnson, this means that professionalization as a

---

[107]Horobin argues that modern advances, while making some things more determinate, have also created new areas of indeterminacy which serve to maintain the power of the medical profession. Gordon Horobin, "Professional Mystery: The Maintenance of Charisma in General Medical Practice," in Dingwall and Lewis, eds., *The Sociology of the Professions*, pp. 84–105.

[108]Robert A. Rothman, "Deprofessionalization: The Case of Law in America," *Work and Occupations*, 11 (1984), 183–206.

[109]See also, Toren, "Deprofessionalization and Its Sources."

[110]Robert A. Rothman, "Deprofessionalization: The Case of Law in America," 189.

[111]Michael Betz and Lenahan O'Connell, "Changing Doctor-Patient Relationships and the Rise in Concern for Accountability," *Social Problems*, 31 (1983), 84–95.

[112]Ibid., 91.

[113]Terence Johnson, "Imperialism and the Professions."

form of control is being replaced by the other forms of control/patronage and other mediative systems. So the trend is in the direction of greater control by consumers and/or third parties.

In his study of the medical profession, Starr details two emerging external sources of control that contribute to deprofessionalization, or in his terms "the weakening of professional sovereignty."[114] One is a combination of government and employers who are desperately searching for ways to deal with the spiralling costs of medical care. They may eventually hit upon techniques that impose severe constraints on the medical profession. The other is the rise of corporate enterprise (for example, for-profit hospitals) within the medical field. In these enterprises, physicians are likely to have the principles of efficient business practice imposed upon them.

Many observers believe that the increasing likelihood that professionals will be found in bureaucracies contributes to deprofessionalization.[115] However, while bureaucracies do limit professionals in a variety of ways, it is by no means simply the case that bureaucracies and professions stand in total opposition to one another.[116]

Encroachment by allied professions.   Rothman argues in the case of the legal profession that "allied professions have met with considerable success in breaching traditional monopolies."[117] He gives examples of realtors and title insurers taking over functions previously controlled by the legal profession.

Thus, a wide number of factors have been identified that are contributing to the ongoing process of deprofessionalization. Those who foresee deprofessionalization are generally predicting a modest decline in the power, prestige, and income of the professions in coming years. There are those, however, who see a much more dramatic decline, in fact the "proletarianization" of the professions. But among the proponents of deprofessionalization, many reject the notion of proletarianization. Starr, for example, writes:

> Doctors are not likely, as some sociologists have suggested, to become "proletarianized" by corporate medicine. "Proletarianization" suggests a total loss of control over the conditions of work as well as a severe reduction in compensation. Such a radical change is not in prospect.[118]

Despite this, there are a number of sociologists who support the view that the professions are being proletarianized.

[114]Paul Starr, *The Social Transformation of Medicine*, p. 421.

[115]See for example, Rothman, "Deprofessionalization: The Case of Law in America"; Betz and O'Connell, "Changing Doctor-Patient Relationships and the Rise in Concern for Accountability."

[116]See Ritzer, "Professionalization, Bureaucratization and Rationalization: The Views of Max Weber."

[117]Rothman, "Deprofessionalization: The Case of Law in America," 195.

[118]Starr, *The Social Transformation of Medicine*, p. 446.

Proletarianization

Oppenheimer was one of the first to articulate this perspective: "My thesis is that a white-collar proletarian type of worker is now replacing the autonomous professional type worker in the upper strata professional-technical employment."[119] The proletarianization of the professions involves several dimensions, many of which have also been described by those who see the professions undergoing a process of deprofessionalization. First, the professions are undergoing an accelerating division of labor, resulting in a professional who performs an ever-narrower range of tasks. This, of course, is a process that has already occurred to a great extent in most other occupations. Second, the authorities overseeing the professional in public or private bureaucracies increasingly determine such things as work pace, nature of the workplace, nature of the product, uses to which the product may be put, and market conditions. In other words, the professions are increasingly subject to external, nonprofessional controls. Third, wages are no longer determined by face-to-face bargaining between professional and client, but rather by large-scale market conditions and economic processes—dynamics over which the professional has little control. Professionals, in the face of these trends, are seen as growing increasingly discontented[120] with their work and, in self-defense, are forced to move toward collective bargaining or a more militant professional association.

Proletarianization connotes a Marxist orientation,[121] rather than the more mainstream sociological perspective of *deprofessionalization*. This leads to a number of additional concerns. For one thing, the traditional Marxian distinction is between those (the capitalists) who own the "means of production" (tools, raw materials, machines) and those who do not (the proletariat) and must sell their labor time in order to obtain access to them. In this context, Derber argues that "technological developments leading to the introduction of complicated and expensive machinery in many forms of professional work make it impossible for individual professionals to raise the necessary capital to own and control their own means of production.[122] Thus, more and more professionals are forced into the "proletariat" because they can no longer afford to own the means of production and must sell their labor time to others to get access to them.

In a similar way, public and private capital has begun to pour into the medical field, as well as into other professional domains. Private corporations and the state have come to dominate these areas, and professionals are increasingly forced to accept positions as employees within these larger capitalistic structures. Professionals are therefore seen as employees indistinguish-

[119]Martin Oppenheimer, "The Proletarianization of the Professional," in Halmos, ed., *Professionalization and Social Change*, p. 213.

[120]Charles Derber, "Professionals as New Workers," in Charles Derber, ed., *Professionals as Workers: Mental Labor in Advanced Capitalism* (Boston: G.K. Hall and Co., 1982), p. 4.

[121]Mike Saks, "Removing the Blinkers? A Critique of Recent Contributions to the Sociology of Professions."

[122]Derber, "Professionals as New Workers," p. 6.

able in many ways from other members of the proletariat. Of course, even supporters of this viewpoint are forced to recognize that professionals "are relatively privileged workers, often well paid, usually exempt from 'punching in,' and typically equipped with at least modest levels of knowledge and skill."[123] Thus, not all members of the proletariat are equal, although what does tie them together is the fact that they are subject to external managerial control. "The proletarianization of the professional does not imply that professionals are becoming an *industrial* proletariat but that, like industrial workers, their labor is effectively subjected to the aims and controls of capitalist production."[124]

Derber makes a useful distinction between *technical* and *ideological* proletarianization.[125] Technical proletarianization is defined as "the loss of control over the process of the work itself (the means), incurred whenever management subjects its workers to a technical plan of production and/or rhythm or pace of work which they have no voice in creating."[126] In contrast, ideological proletarianization refers "to a loss of control over the goals and social purposes to which one's work is put . . . powerlessness to choose or define the final product of one's work, its disposition in the market, its uses in the larger society, and the values or social policy of the organization which purchases one's labor."[127] While industrial workers have been exposed to both types of proletarianization, professionals have thus far been primarily subjected to ideological proletarianization.

This differentiation helps us understand why the notion of "deskilling" does not (at least to this point in history) apply to the professions. One of the key characteristics of capitalistic enterprises is an effort to progressively reduce the skill level of work by dividing the work up into specialized tasks, developing technologies into which the skills are built, and recruiting less well-trained people to fill these specialized positions and operate the new technologies. Although this has happened to blue-collar work, and to a lesser degree to lower-level white-collar work, it has yet to have a major impact on professional work. In other words, we cannot yet talk of the deskilling of professional work.[128]

In sum, although there are differences between the theses of deprofessionalization and proletarianization, it seems clear that a careful analysis shows that the power of the professions, never the imposing societal force many have believed, now is undergoing changes that will further undermine

---

[123]Ibid., 8.

[124]Charles Derber, "The Proletarianization of the Professional: A Review Essay," in Derber, *Professionals as Workers*, p. 31.

[125]Charles Derber, "Managing Professionals: Ideological Proletarianization and Mental Labor," in Derber, ed., *Professionals as Workers.* pp. 167–190.

[126]Ibid., p. 169.

[127]Ibid.

[128]Peter Whalley, "Deskilling Engineers? The Labor Process, Labor Markets, and Labor Segmentation," *Social Problems,* forthcoming; Peter Meiksins, "Science in the Labor Process: Engineers as Workers," in Derber, ed., *Professionals as Workers,* pp. 121–140.

it.[129] The central issue appears to be how far and how fast the professions will fall. Those who subscribe to the deprofessionalization perspective foresee only a modest decline, whereas those who adopt the proletarianization orientation see much darker days ahead for the professions.

CONCLUSIONS

In this chapter we have examined the general process of professionalization. The sociological study of professionalization is divided into three schools—the structural-functional, the process, and the power approach. Although we have emphasized the power approach, we have also attempted to derive useful ideas from the other two orientations. In order to professionalize, an occupation must have control over areas of uncertainty and/or indeterminacy. Some occupations (for example, medicine and law) have historic control over these areas while others (for example, accounting) gain control because of their alternate sources of power—such as the ability to recruit members from elite groups, prior association with elite institutions, and control over other areas of uncertainty and indeterminacy. Once an occupation controls focal areas of uncertainty and/or indeterminacy, it uses the power derived from them to win the professional label. Ideology is a prime tool employed by occupations in the effort to professionalize. The power of an occupation is likely to be enhanced when professional status is acquired. Once that status is gained, an occupation is likely to use ideology to maintain its position and even improve on it. Despite the additional power an occupation derives from professional status, it can lose its position as a result of internal and external social changes. A good example of one area in which there has been loss of professional status (deprofessionalization) is the clergy.

In addition to examining the theoretical process of professionalization, we have also discussed the position of the professions in the larger society. Although most laypersons attribute much power to the professions, we have seen how sociologists have come to question the past, present, and future power of the professions. In this context, we examined the ideas that the professions are undergoing processes of deprofessionalization and/or proletarianization. Whichever of these perspectives one accepts, it seems clear that the future will bring with it a decline in the power of the professions.

---

[129]It is only fair to note that a number of observers still view the professions as powerful and, in fact, fear that power as well as the possibility that it might increase in the future. See, for example, Irving K. Zola, "Medicine as an Institution of Social Control," *The Sociological Review*, 20 (1972), 487–504. See also Henry Steadman, "The Psychiatrist as a Conservative Agent of Social Control," *Social Problems*, 20 (1972), 262–71. Zola sees medicine as a growing instrument of social control. He argues that more and more facets of life are coming to be defined in terms of health and illness with the growth of a belief in such approaches as comprehensive medicine, psychosomatic diseases, etc. As a result, physicians are gaining the right to intervene in such areas as a person's sleeping habits, eating preferences, and sexual proclivities. Physicians are propelling themselves and being propelled by societal attitudes about health, into a position in which they can exercise increasing control over areas heretofore not defined as medical areas. Others take a more general position, arguing that the professions are conservative forces, a part of the societal power elite, that often act to retard meaningful social change.

FIVE
THE CHANGING PLACE
OF WOMEN
IN THE WORKWORLD

Our main concern in this chapter will be the many changes in the position of women in the workworld. In spite of these changes, it remains clear that sexism is a pervasive phenomenon in that institution. This is manifested in the occupational realm as sexist attitudes, discriminatory behavior against women, and above all institutional sexism. *Institutional sexism* means that the day-to-day operation of the workworld operates against females. Thus, even if we eliminated all remnants of individual sexist attitudes and behavior, women would still be at a severe disadvantage at work. For example, despite recent changes, women still have the major responsibility for childrearing. As a result, the absence of adequate childcare facilities makes it difficult for many women to work on a full-time basis. In this and many other ways, the operation of our institutions adversely affects the ability of women to enter the workworld and to succeed once they are there.[1]

---

[1]Although much of what is said in this chapter applies to both black and white women, we will not directly deal with the somewhat unique position of the black female worker in this chapter. However, it should be pointed out that in all but a few cases (e.g., some of the professions) black females face greater problems in the workworld than white females.

LABOR FORCE PARTICIPATION

As we will see, the workworld has remained stubbornly sex-segregated. However, the number of women in the workforce has increased substantially in this century.[2] This can be documented in two ways. First, we can look at the percentage of women in the total (male and female) labor force. We can also look at the percentage of all women of working age who are in the labor force.

Looking at Table 5.1, by 1982 we can see that 42.8 percent of the total labor force[3] was composed of women, while over 50 percent of all women of working age were participating in the labor force. This compares with around 17 percent of women in both categories about a century ago.

The growth of female participation in the labor force has been characterized by the entry of successive waves of new groups of women into the workworld.[4] Prior to World War II the female labor force consisted of mostly young, single women. Grossman estimated that between 1890 and 1940 approximately 50 percent of working women were single.[5] In the two decades after World War II, older married women began entering or reentering the labor market in large numbers.[6] Since 1960 we have seen increases in participation rates for all women, but the greatest increases have been among young

TABLE 5.1   Labor Force Participation Rates for Women: 1890, 1950, 1982

	1890	1950	1982
Total labor force	23.3*	63.9	111.9
Total women in labor force	4.0*	18.4	47.9
Women as percent of labor force	17.2%	28.8%	42.8%
Total women of working age†	23.1*	54.3	90.9
Percent in labor force	17.3%	33.9%	52.7%

*In millions.
†Age 10 and over in 1890, age 16 and over in 1950 and 1982.

SOURCE: Data for 1890 and 1950 from Linda J. Waite, "U.S. Women at Work," *Population Bulletin,* 36, 2 (1981), 4. Data for 1982 from *Employment and Earnings* 30, 1 (Washington, D.C.: U.S. Department of Labor, 1983), p. 8.

[2]A similar trend has occurred in Great Britain; see, George Joseph, *Women at Work: The British Experience* (Oxford: Philip Allan, 1983).

[3]The labor force includes civilian employed, resident armed forces, and the unemployed.

[4]Francine D. Blau, "Women in the Labor Force: An Overview," in Jo Freeman, ed., *Women: A Feminist Perspective* (Palo Alto, CA: Mayfield Publishing Co., 1975), p. 221.

[5]Allyson Sherman Grossman, "Women in the Labor Force: The Early Years," *Monthly Labor Review,* 98 (1975), 3–9.

[6]Mary Frank Fox and Sharlene Hesse-Biber, *Women at Work* (Palo Alto, CA.: Mayfield Publishing Company, 1984).

married women, especially those with children. Table 5.2 shows the number of married women in the labor force and the percent within each category who participated in the labor force between 1960 and 1982. Overall, the participation rate among married women increased from 30.5 percent to 51.2 percent. In particular, notice the large percentage increase in the participation rate for married women with children 6 to 17 years old and with children under 6 years of age.

While the participation rate for married women with children has increased substantially, the rate might be even greater were it not for the constraints of child care. As Presser and Baldwin have shown,[7] a substantial minority (approximately 20 percent) of women with preschool-age children said they would look for work *if* suitable childcare was available at a reasonable cost. In general, black women with children, young women (18 to 24 years old), unmarried mothers, as well as women who did not graduate from high school or whose family income was under $5000, were most likely to feel the barriers to participating in the labor force from the lack of available, reasonably priced child care facilities.

How do we account for the changes and increases in female labor force participation? Clearly, there is no one reason or cause. The change has been gradual and the causes of this growth are difficult to pinpoint. Thus Smith has referred to this change as *The Subtle Revolution*.[8]

Yet there are several causative factors that can be suggested for this rise in women's employment. Of major importance is the increased *demand* for female workers. In recent years employers have needed more and more female workers, and this demand has been caused, in part, by the increase in white-collar clerical and service categories—occupations that have typically been thought of as female domains. In addition, there has been an increase in new "female" occupations (legal aides, computer operators) that have further

TABLE 5.2   Participation Rates for Married Women with Husband Present by Age of Child, 1960 to 1982

| | PARTICIPATION RATE PERCENT | | | | |
	1960	1970	1975	1980	1982
Married women, husband present, total:	30.5	40.8	44.4	50.1	51.2
No children under 18	34.7	42.2	43.9	46.0	46.2
Children 6–17 only	39.0	49.2	52.3	61.7	63.2
Children under 6	18.6	30.3	36.6	45.1	48.7

SOURCE: Janet L. Norwood, "The Female-Male Earnings Gap: A Review of Employment and Earnings Issue," Report 673 (U.S. Department of Labor: Bureau of Labor Statistics, 1982), p. 6.

[7]Harriet B. Presser and Wendy Baldwin, "Child Care as a Constraint on Employment: Prevalence, Correlates, and Bearing on the Work and Fertility Nexus," *American Journal of Sociology*, 85 (1980), 1202–1213.

[8]Ralph E. Smith, ed., *The Subtle Revolution* (Washington, D.C.: The Urban Institute, 1979).

served to bring women into the labor market. Evidence of the importance of the demand factor in the growth of female employment is found in the fact that female employment generally grows during periods of economic boom or warfare and declines when these periods end.

Also significant in accounting for the increasing number of women workers is changing societal norms and values regarding women working outside the home. (We should remember that women have always worked, but not always in the paid labor force.) It has clearly become far more acceptable for all types of women (young and old, single and married, with or without children) to work outside the home on a full-time basis. Moreover, women are more likely to want to work and employers are more likely to accept them in that setting.

Further, the structure of the American family has changed. First, women are choosing to enter marriage later than in the past. Once married, the trend toward smaller families also helps explain the increase in labor force participation among women. Additionally, even though there is still much resistance on the part of men, the increasing acceptance of the idea of a "househusband" has also had a positive effect on female employment.[9]

Economic necessity is another factor in the increase in labor force participation among women. With inflation running at a high rate through the 1970s and into the early 1980s, an increasing number of families/married couples found that they could only survive with two breadwinners. Many of the women who entered the labor force during the 1970s were married to men whose earnings hovered just above the subsistence level.[10]

Also significant is the rise in female-headed families. Between 1955 and 1970, the number of such families hovered around 10 percent. Since 1970 we have witnessed a steady increase in female-headed families. By 1982, one out of every six families was maintained by a woman.[11] Hence, more women are forced to work full-time in order to support these families.

Increasing educational attainments among women and legislation are two other factors in this "subtle revolution." In 1960, a little more than one out of three people enrolled in college were women. By 1980, this figure had increased to 50.6 percent.[12] Hence, at the beginning of this decade more women were enrolled in college than men. While more men than women received degrees in 1980 (52.5 percent to 47.5 percent respectively[13]) it is clear that women now have the educational credentials to qualify for more and better jobs. Finally, and far from least important, legislation has made it illegal to discriminate in employment on the basis of sex. Although this legislation is far

[9]Gary Kiger, "Working Women and their Children," *The Social Science Journal*, 21 (1984), 49-57.

[10]Nancy S. Barrett, "Women in the Job Market: Occupations, Earnings, and Career Opportunities," in Ralph E. Smith, ed. *The Subtle Revolution*, p. 69.

[11]Janet L. Norwood, "The Female-Male Earnings Gap: A Review of Employment and Earnings Issues," Report 673 (U.S. Department of Labor: Bureau of Labor Statistics, September, 1982), p. 6.

[12]U.S. Bureau of the Census, *Statistical Abstract of the United States: 1981*, 101st ed. (Washington, D.C., 1982), p. 159.

[13]Ibid., p. 165.

from totally effective, it has served to reduce the formal barriers to female employment in at least some occupations.[14]

OCCUPATIONAL SEX SEGREGATION

Institutional sexism continues to be reflected in the workworld in the phenomenon of the segregation of occupations by sex.[15] That is, some occupations are virtually the exclusive domain of males while others are virtually the exclusive province of females. The semiprofessions and white-collar clerical occupations are overwhelmingly female, while the professions, scientific occupations, management, and the skilled crafts are predominately male. It is safe to say that the highest paying, most powerful, and most prestigious occupations are taken by males while females are relegated to residual fields and to those that fit male stereotypes about the kinds of work women should do.

While females continue to be locked into a relatively small number of occupations, Table 5.3 shows that females have made gains in some high-paying, high-prestige occupations. However, these gains are deceptive. They conceal the fact that women generally occupy the lowest positions *within* these categories. Within the professions, the majority of females are in the semiprofessions. Table 5.4 reveals that since 1962 women have made gains into the traditionally male-dominated professions, but they also continue to dominate the traditional female semiprofessions. For example, in 1982 women comprised about 35 percent of all teachers in colleges and universities. This compares to 19 percent in 1962, an 86 percent increase for women in this profession. However, over 82 percent of the lower-paying, less prestigious, lower-skilled elementary school teachers are women, and this represents only a modest decline in the last twenty years. The health profession offers another example. Although only 14.8 percent of physicians were women in 1982, women represent over 95 percent of all nurses. Again, modest gains have been made, but women still dominate the lower positions within the professional category.

Another way to look at the relatively small number of occupations in which women are concentrated, is to look at the sex segregation of occupations by percentage of women who work in female-dominated occupations. In Table 5.5 the data generally illustrate that during this century the sex segregation of occupations has increased. Looking only at women who worked in occupations that were 80 percent or more female, in 1900 about 42 percent of all working women were so employed, whereas by 1982 nearly 50 percent were in this situation. Further, whereas 60 percent of all employed women worked in occupations that were 50 percent or more female in 1900, 75 percent of working women were employed in similarly sex-segregated occupations by 1982. The only sign of sex desegregation has been the decline in the

[14]Fox and Hesse-Biber, *Women at Work*; Elizabeth Waldman and Beverly J. McEaddy, "Where Women Work—An Analysis by Industry and Occupation," *Monthly Labor Review*, 97 (1974), 3–13.

[15]Valerie K. Oppenheimer, *The Female Labor Force in the United States* (Berkeley, CA: University of California Press, 1970).

TABLE 5.3   Comparison of Occupational Distribution of Female Workers (1900–1982) with Males (1982)

OCCUPATION	PERCENT WOMEN					PERCENT MEN
	1900	1950	1960	1975	1982	1982
Professional, technical, kindred	8.2	12.2	13.3	14.5	17.7	16.4
Managers, officials, proprietors, except farm	1.4	4.3	3.8	4.8	7.4	14.6
Clerical and kindred	4.0	27.4	30.9	34.7	34.4	6.3
Sales	4.3	8.6	8.3	6.8	6.9	6.4
Private household	28.7	8.9	8.4	3.5	2.3	0.6
Other service workers	6.8	12.6	14.4	18.0	17.3	9.3
Craftsmen, foremen, kindred	1.4	1.5	1.3	1.5	2.0	20.1
Operatives and kindred	23.8	20.0	17.2	13.6	9.6	15.4
Laborers, except farm and mine	2.6	0.9	0.6	1.1	1.2	7.1
Farmers and farm managers	5.9	0.7	0.6	0.3	.4	2.2
Farm laborers and foremen	13.1	2.9	1.3	1.1	.7	1.7

SOURCE: Data for 1900, 1950, 1960 from Philip Hauser, "Labor Force," in Robert E.L. Faris, ed., *Handbook of Modern Sociology* (Chicago: Rand-McNally, 1964), p. 183. Data for 1975 from *Handbook of Labor Statistics—1975: Reference Edition* (Washington, D.C.: U.S. Department of Labor, 1975), p. 41. Data for 1982 from *Employment and Earnings,* 30, 1 (Washington, D.C.: U.S. Department of Labor, 1983) pp. 158–159.

percentage of women in the most segregated occupations, those with 90 percent or more females.

The most sex-segregated occupations according to the percentage of women employed are presented in Table 5.6. This table lists about twenty occupations that were 90 percent or more female in 1982. Clerical and service work clearly dominate. Nearly 75 percent of the occupations listed are in these two broad occupational categories.

Male-dominated occupations represent the other end of the sex segregation continuum. Table 5.7 lists twenty-four occupations that were less than 2 percent female in 1982.

THE EARNINGS GAP

In addition to occupational sex segregation, institutional sexism is also reflected in the income differences between men and women. From Table 5.8 we can see that the income gap between the sexes increased between 1955 and 1981. In 1955, income for women employed on a full-time, year-round basis averaged 64.5 percent of what similarly employed men earned that year. By

TABLE 5.4 Women in Select Professions and Semiprofessions: 1962, 1974, 1982

OCCUPATION	PERCENTAGE OF TOTAL EMPLOYED		
	1962	1974	1982
Profession			
Physicians and Surgeons	6%	10%	14.8%
Lawyers and Judges	3	7	15.4
Accountants	19	24	38.6
College and University Teachers	19	31	35.4
Chemists	9	14	20.3
Semiprofession			
Librarians	86%	82%	83.4%
Nurses	98	98	95.6
Social Workers	60	61	66.4
Elementary School Teachers	86	84	82.4

SOURCE: Data for 1962 and 1974 compiled from Stuart H. Garfinkle, "Occupations of Women and Black Workers, 1962–1974," *Monthly Labor Review*, 98 (1975), 28. Data for 1982 from *Employment and Earnings*, 30, 1 (Washington, D.C.: U.S. Department of Labor, 1983), p. 158.

1965 the figure dropped to 58 percent. Over the ensuing 15-year period this earnings ratio has remained fairly constant, averaging around 60 percent. However, this is about 5 percentage points *less* than it was 25 years earlier. In other words, females are worse off in terms of comparative earnings than they were in 1955.

Typically, the earnings gap is smaller for younger workers and widens with age.[16] For example, during the second quarter of 1983 average median weekly earnings for women age 16 to 24 were 86.5 percent of male earnings. For women 25 years and over the earnings ratio stood at 65.7 percent.[17]

TABLE 5.5 Segregation of Working Women into Female-Dominated Occupations, 1900–1982

Percentage of Occupation Female	CUMULATIVE PERCENT OF EMPLOYED WOMEN IN THESE OCCUPATIONS			
	1900	1940	1960	1982
90 or more	38%	34%	28%	31.58%
80 or more	42	40	42	48.73
70 or more	54	49	50	61.42
60 or more	56	61	56	65.30
50 or more	60	65	73	74.59

SOURCE: Data from 1900, 1940, and 1960 from Linda J. Waite, "U.S. Women at Work," *Population Bulletin*, 36, 2 (1981), 26. Data for 1982 compiled from *Employment and Earnings*, 30, 1 (Washington, D.C.: U.S. Department of Labor, 1983), pp. 158–159.

[16]Linda J. Waite, "U.S. Women at Work," *Population Bulletin*, 36 (1981), 30.

[17]*Employment and Earnings*, 30 (Washington, D.C.: Department of Labor, 1983), p. 71.

TABLE 5.6   Occupations with 90 Percent or More Female, 1982

OCCUPATION	TYPE	PERCENT FEMALE
Secretary; includes medical and legal	Clerical	99.2
Prekindergarten and kindergarten teachers	Professional	98.5
Dental assistant	Service	98.0
Receptionist	Clerical	97.5
Practical nurse	Service	97.0
Private household worker, includes childcare, cleaners, servants & housekeepers	Service	96.9
Typists	Service	96.6
Dressmakers, except factory	Operative	96.4
Child care, personal service	Service	96.2
Lodging quarter cleaner	Service	96.2
Sewers and stitchers	Operative	95.4
Keypunch operators	Clerical	94.5
Demonstrators	Sales	94.0
Welfare service aides	Service	93.3
Teachers' aides, except school monitors	Clerical	92.5
Bank tellers	Clerical	92.0
Telephone operators	Clerical	91.9
Nurses, dietitians, and therapists	Professional	91.8
Bookkeepers	Clerical	91.8

SOURCE: *Employment and Earnings*, 30, 1 (Washington, D.C.: U.S. Department of Labor, 1983), pp. 158–159.

Median weekly earnings during the second quarter of 1983 for full-time wage and salary white, black, and hispanic women averaged 66, 63, and 59 percent of men respectively. Within the races, white women earned 65 percent of white male salaries, black women 82 percent of black men, and hispanic women 80 percent of hispanic men.[18]

Another way to look at the earnings gap is to consider lifetime earnings estimates for men and women. In 1979, it was estimated that 25-year-old male, college graduates would earn $1,165,000 through age 64.[19] A 25-year-old female college graduate would earn $772,000. Hence, women in this category are expected to earn only 66 percent of men's earnings over the course of their lifetime. More striking is the fact that 25-year-old, male *high school* graduates are expected to earn more through age 64 ($861,000) than female *college* graduates. It is expected that females with college degrees will earn only about 90 percent of male high school graduates over the course of their lifetimes.

Finally, as reported in Table 5.9, we can look at median weekly earnings

[18]Ibid.

[19]Neale Baxter, "The Millionaires: Lifetime Earnings Estimates for Men and Women, 1979," *Occupational Outlook Quarterly* (Fall, 1983), 14–16.

TABLE 5.7 Occupations with Less than 2 Percent Female, 1982

OCCUPATION	TYPE	PERCENT FEMALE
Cement and concrete finishers	Craft	.0
Structural-metal workers	Craft	.0
Millwrights	Craft	.0
Air-conditioning, heating, and refrigeration mechanics	Craft	.0
Farm implement mechanics	Craft	.0
Drillers, earth	Operative	.0
Railroad switch operators	Transport Equipt.	.0
Firefighters	Service	.5
Brickmasons and stonemasons	Craft	.7
Plumbers and pipefitters	Craft	.8
Roofers and slaters	Craft	.8
Crane, derrick, and hoist operators	Craft	.8
Automobile mechanics	Craft	.9
Electric power-line and cable installers and repairers	Craft	.9
Dry wall installers and lathers	Operative	1.1
Timber cutting and logging workers	Nonfarm Laborer	1.1
Carpet installers	Craft	1.2
Excavating, grading, and road machinery operators	Craft	1.3
Mine operatives, not elsewhere classified	Operative	1.4
Heavy equipment mechanics, including diesel	Craft	1.5
Automobile body repairers	Craft	1.5
Surveyors	Professional	1.5
Electricians	Craft	1.6
Carpenters	Craft	1.7

SOURCE: *Employment and Earnings,* 30, 1 (Washington, D.C.: U.S. Department of Labor, 1983), pp. 158–159.

of full-time, male and female wage and salary workers by occupation. According to information in the table, the earnings gap is smallest between male and female mechanics and repairers and largest in the sales category. Female executives, administrators, and managers also experience a large pay differential, and we will have more to say about this later when we discuss in detail the plight of the female manager.

Nancy F. Rytina[20] has found that the most highly paid occupations for men and women tend to be similar, but that the median weekly earnings of men in these occupations far exceeds that of women. Using 1981 median weekly earnings for men and women employed full-time in wage and salary jobs, Rytina ranked the twenty highest paid occupations for each sex. Overall, men's weekly earnings ranged from $507 to $619, while the range for women was $318 to $422.

[20]Nancy F. Rytina, "Earnings of Men and Women: A Look at Specific Occupations," *Monthly Labor Review,* 105 (April, 1982), 25–31.

TABLE 5.8   Median Income of Full-Time, Year-Round Workers by
Sex, 1955–1981

| YEAR | 1981 DOLLARS | | WOMEN'S INCOME AS PERCENT OF MEN'S |
	MEN	WOMEN	
1955*	$14,405	$ 9,289	64.5%
1960	16,688	10,122	60.7
1965	19,019	11,000	57.8
1970	21,511	12,742	59.2
1975	21,856	13,044	59.7
1981†	20,692	12,457	60.2

*1955 through 1975 for persons 14 years old and over.
†1981 for persons 15 years old and over.
SOURCE: *Economic Report of the President* (Washington, D.C.: United
States Government Printing Office, 1983), p. 194.

Rytina found that the earnings differential between men and women was lowest in public sector occupations, namely public administrators, secondary school teachers, vocational and educational counselors, and postal clerks. As Rytina notes, while these jobs might not pay as well as jobs in the private sector, at least the earnings are more equitable.

COMPARABLE WORTH

A current issue related to both the sex segregation of occupations and the earnings gap is comparable worth. Equal pay for equal work is mandated by the Equal Pay Act of 1963. Two similarly qualified people doing the same job are required by law to be equally rewarded. Exceptions based on seniority, piece work, and merit are allowed under the Equal Pay Act. As we have seen, women are, more often than not, segregated into occupations that are predominantly female (for example, nurse, secretary, and so on). Because women often do work that is different from the type of work men do, many legal issues related to pay equity are not governed by the Equal Pay Act.[21] The advocates of comparable worth argue that even though men and women do work that is different, both may do work that is of essentially comparable value to their employer and should therefore be equally rewarded. If women are in jobs that are comparable to those held by men but are not similarly rewarded, then, the proponents argue, this is just another form of sex discrimination and legal recourse is sought under Title 7 of the Civil Rights Act of 1964 which outlaws discrimination in employment practices, including discrimination based on sex.

The legal issues involved in the battle over comparable worth are com-

[21]For more detail on the legal dimensions of this issue see the following: Clarence Thomas, "Pay Equity and Comparable Worth," *Labor Law Journal*, 34 (1983), 3–12; John B. Golper, "The Current Legal Status of 'Comparable Worth' in the Federal Sector," *Labor Law Journal*, 34 (1983), 563–580; *Pay Equity and Comparable Worth* (Washington, D.C.: The Bureau of National Affairs, 1984), pp. 13–34.

TABLE 5.9   Women's Median Weekly Earnings as a Percentage of Men's, Full-time, Wage and Salary Workers by Occupation—2nd Quarter, 1983

OCCUPATION	WOMEN'S EARNINGS AS PERCENT OF MEN'S
Managerial and professional specialty	67%
Executive, administrative, and managerial	62
Professional specialty	71
Technical, sales, and administrative support	63
Technicians and related support	69
Sales occupations	53
Administrative support, including clerical	69
Service occupations	69
Private household	*
Protective service	67
Service, other than above	81
Precision production, craft, and repair	63
Mechanics and repairers	92
Construction trades	*
Other precision production, craft, repair	56
Operators, fabricators, and laborers	67
Machine operators, assemblers, and inspectors	63
Transportation and material-moving occupations	80
Handlers, equipment cleaners, helpers, and laborers	87
Farming, forestry, and fishing	78

*Data not shown where base is less than 100,000. For private household there were less than 100,000 men, while in the construction trades there were an insufficient number of women.

SOURCE: *Employment and Earnings*, 30, 1 (Washington, D.C.: U.S. Department of Labor, 1983), p. 73.

plicated and unsettled. Recent court decisions can be found that support or oppose, in part or in whole, comparable worth. However, while the legality of the issue is far from resolved, the proponents of pay equity for women will continue to pursue comparable worth as a means of eliminating the pay gap between the sexes.

There are many difficulties in establishing the comparability of jobs. However, regardless of the technique(s) used and the methodological difficulties involved,[22] the comparable worth of different jobs is typically established by evaluating job content in terms of one or more of the following broad job characteristics: effort, skill, knowledge, working conditions, challenge, accountability, and responsibility. More specific characteristics of the job, for example years of formal training or total number of people supervised, can also be used to compare job content. Once comparability is established, it can be shown that female-dominated jobs are consistently underpaid compared to male-dominated jobs.[23]

The comparable worth issue is an emotional one. On the positive side,

[22]Ronnie Steinberg and Lois Haignere, "Separate But Equivalent: Equal Pay for Work of Comparable Worth," in *Gender at Work: Perspective on Occupational Segregation and Comparable Worth* (Washington, D. C.: Women's Research and Educational Institute, 1984), pp. 13–24.

[23]Ibid., pp. 17–18; *Pay Equity and Comparable Worth*, pp. 5–12.

arguments for comparable worth include a higher standard of living and greater financial independence for women, reduced hostility between the sexes, and a victory for women's rights. On the negative side, critics argue that comparable worth will lead to the destruction of the free market system, higher employer costs, male resistance, subjectivity and bias in the selection and application of criteria used to evaluate comparability of jobs, and a legal nightmare.[24]

Currently, politicians, the courts, employers, union leaders, the media and various women's and civil rights groups are taking sides on the comparable worth issue. However, one thing is certain. As long as women continue to be segregated into various occupations and as long as these jobs pay substantially less then comparable jobs held by men, concern for redress on the basis of comparable worth will persist as a means of reducing the pay gap between the sexes.

FEMALE PROFESSIONALS

Although Table 5.3 indicates a substantial increase in female professionals, we have already noted that this is deceptive since it includes the female semiprofessions. A more accurate picture of females in the established professions can be derived from Table 5.4. The clear implication of this table is that females have been underrepresented in the established professions, although their position has improved somewhat in the last two decades. Let us look at the changing position of females within a few of the established professions.

Academic Women

As in most other professions, women have been making gains in college and university academic employment. In fact, between the years 1962 and 1974 the proportion of women in this area showed a big increase, from 19 to 31 percent.[25] Since then women have continued to enter academia and, as of 1982, 35.4 percent of college and university teachers were women.[26] Furthermore, since 1970 both the absolute number of women receiving Ph.D.'s (a virtual *sine qua non* for academic positions) and their percentage of the total (see Table 5.10) have continued to grow. As a result, in 1981 nearly one in three Ph.D. recipients were women, compared with one in eight just eleven years earlier.

Despite these gains, discrepancies between males and females in academia remain. Women continue to be more highly represented in lower-status colleges and universities. They also continue to be overrepresented at the bottom of the academic hierarchy (nontenured instructors and assistant

[24]For a discussion see, Benson Rosen, Sara Rynes, and Thomas A. Mahoney, "Compensation, Jobs, and Gender: Should a Female Nurse Make as Much as a Male Truck Driver?" *Harvard Business Review,* 61 (1983), 170–190; see also, Steinberg and Haignere, "Separate but Equivalent," pp. 18–20 and *Pay Equity and Comparable Worth,* pp. 26–28.

[25]Stuart H. Garfinkle, "Occupations of Women and Black Workers, 1962–1974," *Monthly Labor Review,* 98 (1975), 28.

[26]*Employment and Earnings,* 1983, p. 158.

TABLE 5.10 Total Number of Ph.D. Recipients and Percent Female, 1970, 1975, 1980, 1981

YEAR	TOTAL Ph.D. RECIPIENTS	PERCENT FEMALE
1970	29,900	13.4
1975	34,100	21.4
1980	32,800	29.6
1981	31,319	31.5

SOURCE: Data for 1970, 1975, and 1980 taken from the *Statistical Abstract of the United States: 1981*, p. 165. Data for 1981 is from the *Chronicle of Higher Education*, 35, 6 (October 6, 1982), p. 8.

professors) and underrepresented among tenured associate and full professors.

In 1981, for all academically employed science and engineering faculty, 64.6 percent of the men were tenured while only 37.6 percent of the women were in such positions.[27] On the other hand, 28.9 percent of the women across all fields held nontenure track positions compared to 13.2 percent of the men. Nontenure track positions are those that hold out no hope to the individuals holding them of ever receiving tenure.

As is the case with most employed women, females in the academic setting continue to be paid less than their male colleagues. In 1981, the average salary for female doctoral scientists and engineers employed in educational institutions was $25,700 per year. This was 80 percent of the average salary ($32,100) of similarly employed men. Compared with most other occupations, the earnings difference between men and women in academia is less pronounced. However, while conditions are changing in American colleges and universities, women still have some way to go to match male salaries.

Women in the academic world continue to be afflicted by a number of problems that their male peers escape. For example, they are likely to spend approximately eighteen hours a week on household chores.[28] This clearly takes time away from research and writing, the tasks that are most rewarded in the academic world. Women still tend to be overrepresented in low-status institutions and at low ranks. As such, they are likely to be faced with heavy teaching loads, and this too tends to adversely affect their ability to do research and to write. Despite these and other pressures, women are productive, with some research showing that their productivity approximates that of males. What is striking is that even when they are equally productive, they tend not to be rewarded as well as men.[29] Many other factors operate against women academics. For example, many universities have antinepotism rules—if a woman academic's husband is already employed in the university, she will be unable to obtain a job in that university. This is an especially press-

[27]All the data in this section is taken from *Science, Engineering, and Humanities Doctorates in the United States* (Washington, D.C.: National Academy Press, 1982).

[28]Helen S. Astin, *The Woman Doctorate in America: Origins, Career and Family* (New York: Russell Sage Foundation, 1969).

[29]Marianne A. Ferber and Jane W. Loeb, "Performance, Rewards, and Perceptions of Sex Discrimination among Male and Female Faculty," *American Journal of Sociology*, 78 (1973), 995–1002.

ing problem in small university towns where there may be no other university to turn to. Some academic couples are now coping with this problem by sharing appointments, working in alternate years, or commuting hundreds, and in some cases thousands, of miles.

Finally, we cannot ignore the fact that male college professors are often a barrier to their female peers. Like males in many other occupations, many prefer not to have female colleagues.[30] Although the formal barriers erected against female admittance in the past have largely been removed in recent years, male opposition to female academics continues in the form of informal barriers. Many male academics now believe that there is a process of "reverse discrimination" taking place in academiá, with women being favored with higher starting salaries, better starting positions, and a greater likelihood of gaining professional rewards such as fellowships and positions in professional associations. Reverse discrimination, real or imagined, has served to buttress some age-old male antagonisms to female professors.

Female Physicians[31]

Despite the rise in the proportion of women in medicine from 6 percent in 1960 to 15 percent in 1982 (see Table 5.4), women are still grossly underrepresented in medicine. More impressive is the increase in the number of females receiving medical degrees—from 5.5 percent in 1960 to 24.7 percent in 1981.[32] Even with this dramatic gain, however, women continue to be underrepresented among new physicians.

Even though more women are now receiving medical degrees, they are still confronted by what Bourne and Wikler describe as a discriminatory environment in medical school.[33] While the formal barriers have been demolished, women in medical school are constantly confronted with an array of subtle messages that convey the "maleness" of the medical profession. Bourne and Wikler discuss the covert forms that male discrimination takes in medical school, many of which focus on women's supposedly questionable commitment to medicine. For example, male faculty members express reservations about the "payoff" in training women to be physicians. A male faculty member states: "I just have a feeling that we get considerably less working years out of women; it's variable and it's intermittent."[34] Underlying this is the male attitude that what women really value is marriage and that they will eventually choose family before career. As a result, only certain specialties are deemed appropriate for female students, and they are channeled into them. These specialties are those that are thought to minimize women's conflict between work and family, including pediatrics, psychiatry, pathology, and public

---

[30]Jessie Bernard, *Academic Women* (University Park: Pennsylvania State University Press, 1964).

[31]See, for example, Judith Lorber, *Women Physicians: Careers, Status and Power* (New York: Tavistock Publications, 1984).

[32]*Statistical Abstract of the United States: 1984*, p. 170.

[33]Patricia G. Bourne and Norma J. Wikler, "Commitment and Cultural Mandate: Women in Medicine," *Social Problems*, 25 (1978), 430–440.

[34]Ibid., 433.

health. A quotation from a female medical student reflects the kind of discrimination that women continue to face in medical school:

> I've learned that you're supposed to say that you want to have children because that's normal. And you're supposed to have plans set and assume that you'll work in a group practice. And you're supposed to say that you'll wait until you're out (to have children) and you'll go into a field like pathology where you'll have good hours.[35]

As a practicing physician, the female is confronted with a series of distinctive problems.[36] For one thing, a good portion of the public continues to be reluctant to accept a female physician. Second, the female physician is not fully accepted by her male colleagues. This lack of professional acceptance may take many forms. Male doctors may refuse to refer their patients to female physicians, or they might seek to prevent females from holding offices in local or national associations. Sherman and Rosenblatt found that female physicians are underrepresented among medical administrators and overrepresented among teachers.[37] It appears that, as in other occupations, males have succeeded in keeping females out of the most powerful positions (administrative) within the occupation. Third, merely being a female in American society causes the woman doctor problems in balancing sex roles and occupational expectations. Although the female physician may, in fact, be well equipped to handle this conflict, it remains a source of difficulty.[38] Expectations associated with being a wife and mother often come into conflict with professional expectations.

Female Lawyers

Many of the same sorts of things can be said about women in law. Clearly, gains have been made. In 1972 women represented only 3.8 percent of all lawyers (and judges) in the United States, but a decade later that figure had jumped to 15.4 percent.[39] As with medicine, the gain in the proportion of females receiving degrees in law is even more impressive. In 1960 women received only 2 percent of all law degrees, but by 1981 that proportion had leaped to 32 percent.[40] But once again we must caution that despite impressive gains women continue to be underrepresented in the legal profession, even among new entrants.

Cynthia Epstein, in her recent study *Women in Law*, has uncovered prob-

[35]Ibid., 438.

[36]John Kosa and Robert E. Coker, Jr., "The Female Physician in Public Health: Conflict of the Sex and Professional Roles," *Sociology and Social Research*, 49 (1965), 294–305; see also, John Kosa, "Women and Medicine in a Changing World," in Athena Theodore, ed., *The Professional Woman* (Cambridge, MA: Schenkman, 1971).

[37]Susan R. Sherman and Aaron Rosenblatt, "Women Physicians as Teachers, Administrators and Researchers in Medical and Surgical Specialties: Kanter Versus 'Avis' as Competing Hypotheses," *Sex Roles*, 11 (1984), 203–209; see also, Lorber, *Women Physicians*.

[38]Carol Lopate, *Women in Medicine* (Baltimore: Johns Hopkins Press, 1968).

[39]*Statistical Abstract of the United States: 1984*, p. 419.

[40]Ibid., p. 170.

lems for the female lawyer.[41] For example, she found that female lawyers are disproportionately likely to do the kinds of legal work that are consistent with traditional sex roles—"family and government law, public interest and defender work."[42] And these are the areas in law that are likely to be less rewarded economically and to be lower in professional prestige. Thus, as in the other professions, women have made significant progress but still have a considerable distance to go.

THE FEMALE MANAGER AND OFFICIAL

In turning now to the female manager[43] and official,[44] we are obviously dealing with occupations that are considered even more of a male province than the professions. As Cussler put it some years ago, "If there is a thing women are not supposed to be it is the boss."[45]

Between 1970 and 1981 the proportion of female managers and officials increased from 16.6 percent to 27.4 percent.[46] Nevertheless, in 1982 only 7.4 percent of female workers were employed as managers and officials, while 14.6 percent of male workers were employed in this category.

In the early 1970s, in a study conducted by Lyle and Ross, it was found that 76 percent of the firms surveyed had no women in top management positions. Women were more likely to be found in lower-level managerial positions, although there were still not very many of them.[47] More recently, Fox and Hesse-Biber report that women held only 1 percent of the positions of vice-president and 6 percent of middle management positions in the United States.[48]

Granted, during the last decade women have made some modest gains into upper-level managerial positions. For example, in the 1,300 largest U.S. companies in 1981, there were 477 female corporate officers and over 300 women directors.[49] Modest gains are reflected in one specific, traditionally male-dominated industry—banking. In 1971 Citibank reported appointing its first female vice-president. By 1982, 150 women were employed at the level of vice-president. This figure, however, represents only 9 percent of the vice-presidents at Citibank.[50]

[41]Cynthia Epstein, *Women in Law* (New York: Basic Books, 1981).

[42]Ibid., p. 381.

[43]Max S. Wortman, Jr., "An Overview of the Research on Women in Management: A Typology and a Prospectus," in H. John Bernardin, ed., *Women in the Workforce* (New York: Praeger Publishers, 1982), pp. 1–28.

[44]Managerial positions exist in profit-making organizations, while official positions exist in nonprofit organizations.

[45]Margaret Cussler, *The Woman Executive* (New York: Harcourt, Brace, 1958), p. 3.

[46]Janet Norwood, "The Female-Male Earnings Gap," 8.

[47]Jerolyn R. Lyle and Jane L. Ross, *Women in Industry* (Lexington, MA: Lexington Books, 1973).

[48]Mary Frank Fox and Sharlene Hesse-Biber, *Women at Work*, p. 135.

[49]Lynn Langway, et al., "Women and the Executive Suite," *Newsweek* (September 14, 1981), p. 65.

[50]Peter W. Bernstein, "Women: The New Stars in Banking," *Fortune* (July 12, 1982), p. 84.

While these gains are encouraging, women are still highly unlikely to reach the very top of the corporate hierarchy. As one woman notes, "The top half of the pyramid is still virtually all male."[51]

And as observed in the professions, female managers tend to be concentrated in areas of the economy that are more consistent with female sex roles. Thus Brown points out that female managers tend to cluster in fields like health administration and restaurant, bar, and cafeteria management.[52]

Women are in a similar situation in official positions. In 1956, there were 29 women in elected or appointed official positions in 176 national and international unions. In 1976, only 47 women were in such official positions.[53] In terms of national elected political office, as of 1983 there were only 2 female senators and 22 representatives. Hence, women accounted for less than 5 percent of the 535 members of Congress. The situation is only a little better at the state level where 13 percent of statewide offices are held by women.[54]

Another index of the scarcity of women in high-ranking managerial positions is to be found in employment statistics for the federal government. Table 5.11 enumerates the general service grades for government jobs (the higher the better in terms of skill level, responsibility, status, and income) and the proportion of women in each grade. Although some improvement has been made over the last decade, as the reader might expect, women continue to represent a smaller percentage of each category as we ascend the grade system.

In addition to being fewer in number and generally restricted to low-ranking positions, female managers have other problems. They are very likely to be paid less than male managers for essentially the same work. In the sec-

TABLE 5.11   Women as Percentage of Full-time White-Collar Employees in Federal Government, 1970 and 1981

GENERAL SCHEDULE (GS) GRADE	WOMEN AS PERCENT OF TOTAL EMPLOYED	
	1970	1981
Grade 1–6	72.2%	74.1%
Grade 7–10	33.4	47.6
Grade 11–12	9.5	20.8
Grade 13–15	3.0	9.2
Grade 16–18	1.4	6.4

SOURCE: U.S. Bureau of the Census, *Statistical Abstract of the United States: 1984*, 104th ed. (Washington, D.C., 1983) p. 335.

[51]Lynn Langway, et al., "Women and the Executive Suite," 65.

[52]Linda Keller Brown, "Women and Business Management," *Signs*, 5 (1979), 268.

[53]Linda H. LeGrande, "Women in Labor Organizations: Their Ranks Are Increasing," *Monthly Labor Review*, 101 (August 1978), 13.

[54]John W. Hashek with Patricia Avery, "Women Politicians Take Off the White Gloves," *U.S. News & World Report* (August 15, 1983), p. 41.

ond quarter of 1983 median weekly earnings for women in executive, administrative, and managerial positions were only 62 percent of men in similar positions (see Table 5.9).

The situation does not improve for female M.B.A.s, whose mean salary at entry level was found to be $9300 less than that of men with the same degree and at the same career position.[55] The fate of the experienced female M.B.A. is no better. A study of 33 women graduates in 1973 from the Harvard Business School found that 15 percent were earning more than $100,000 per year. But for the class as a whole (males and females), 35 percent were in this income category.[56] Male discrimination, the relatively small size of the companies for which they worked, and interrupted careers were cited as the major reasons for the lower earnings of female M.B.A.s.

The place of women in management is changing less rapidly than in many other occupations, in particular the professions. Let us examine some of the reasons why women have made fewer inroads into this occupation.

First, is the socialization process that, at least historically, clearly indicates that women should not aspire to management positions. Although this is changing, the fact remains that most women still believe that management is not a viable career for them. This socialization, coupled with discrimination that has been practiced by business schools, has served to keep the number of female managers down. Although the formal barriers have been removed, and despite the fact that there has been considerable progress, we are still a long way from equality in the business schools. For example, in 1971 only 4 percent of the graduates of the Harvard Business School were women.[57] In 1983, nearly 26 percent of the graduates were women.[58] These figures parallel those on the national level.[59] Hence, while progress is being made, women are still underrepresented in M.B.A. programs throughout the nation.

As in many other occupations and professions, entry and success in management are facilitated by having a sponsor. Cussler gives several examples of how sponsorship aided the careers of female managers and officials:

> The head of an institution had been remembered by her professor at Columbia, and when the opportunity came, she was recommended for the position. A hospital administrator said that a good friend, a hospital physician, got her to leave the South and come to New England for a better job. The head of a catalog department urged his protege to go get a library school degree; he foresaw that specialized training would help toward her advancement on the library staff.[60]

The problem however, is that relatively few female managers have such a

[55]Lynn Langway, et al., "Women and the Executive Suite," 65.

[56]Roy Rowan, "How Harvard's Women MBAs are Managing," *Fortune*, July 11, 1983, pp. 58–59.

[57]Phyllis A. Wallace, "Sex Discrimination: Some Societal Constraints on Upward Mobility for Women Executives," in Eli Ginzberg and Alice M. Yohalem, eds., *Corporate Lib: Women's Challenge to Management* (Baltimore: Johns Hopkins Press, 1973), pp. 69–84.

[58]Roy Rowan, "How Harvard's Women MBAs Are Managing," p. 72.

[59]Lynn Langway, et al., "Women and the Executive Suite," 66.

[60]Margaret Cussler, *The Woman Executive*, p. 17.

sponsor. This is mainly traceable to the fact that most successful managers are men, and they are generally reluctant to sponsor women.

This brings us to the most central problem for the aspiring female manager or official—the opposition of the male manager. Goode catches the essence of this opposition:

> I do not believe that male managers can be easily persuaded that they should make room for even able women. We should not underestimate either their cunning or their staying power, and least of all, their motivation. They are convinced of their own special superiority, and will yield only grudgingly and slowly. Where they do yield, they will try to put women in the jobs that pay less, have less influence and offer less opportunity for advancement, in short, jobs fit for women.[61]

Male managers are unlikely to yield their power willingly or gracefully. As one woman notes:

> Men will accept women in certain staff jobs, where their talent and dedication can help. [However], let the women try to invade the male turf and whap-o, the curtain comes down.[62]

In part, this is related to the general propensity for people with power to hold onto it. But there is more here; male managers have a negative stereotype of female managers. Goode contends that the dominant view of female managers is that "they are tough, cold, bitchy, and castrating women."[63] This view is based on irrational fears. As Joan Cooney, a successful executive notes:

> Men don't like women as peers. They fear them in positions of power, and that's as old as the myths about women, you know: it's a very old unconscious, primordial thing.[64]

This image would change if many more women were allowed into managerial positions, but that seems unlikely to happen soon. As another female executive observes:

> [I]n big corporations it's not as easy to promote a woman as a man. And I don't think that's going to change for a long time.[65]

Subordinates pose another barrier to the female manager. Comparatively few males are willing to accept a female superior. As Cooney states:

> What a man can't imagine is working *for* a woman. That's what won't yield in American business, and I've been told that men, good men, have threatened to

[61]William Goode, "Family Life of the Successful Woman," in Ginzberg and Yohalem, *Corporate Lib*, p. 97.

[62]Lynn Langway, et al., "Women and the Executive Suite," 65–66.

[63]William Goode, "Family Life of the Successful Woman," p. 104.

[64]Eliza G.C. Collins and Allison I. Esposito, eds., "A Woman in the Boardroom: An Interview with Joan Ganz Cooney," *Harvard Business Review*, 56 (January/February, 1978), 85.

[65]Roy Rowan, "How Harvard's Women MBAs Are Managing," 72.

quit if a woman were appointed over them. I have always said, "You'll have to bite that bullet sooner or later." But they won't, not yet, anyway.[66]

Interestingly, the same attitude sometimes holds true for female subordinates. For example, during the early 1970s a Harris poll showed that women preferred a male boss to a female by a ratio of 8 to 1. Further, and more recently, Powell and Butterfield studied male and female business students and found that a good manager was defined in masculine terms by *both* sexes.[67]

However, recent evidence has called these findings into question.[68] These recent studies suggest that preference for male or female bosses is dependent upon factors other than simply the sex of the subordinate. To take just one example, Ferber, Huber, and Spitze have shown that preference for men as bosses is conditional upon one's educational attainment.[69] In a study of academically and nonacademically employed men and women, Ferber et al. showed that the more highly educated women and men were least likely to prefer men as bosses. And men who were married to employed professional or academic women showed preference for women bosses. Such a preference was also found to be related to the number and quality of interactions one has had with a female boss. The more and the better the interactions, the more likely one is to prefer a female boss.

Successful executives need a number of informal contacts who can aid their careers, but female executives tend to be excluded from the largely male informal groups. This inability to make contacts limits her effectiveness, and it may drive her into more social contacts with other females who are not as likely to be in positions where they will be able to do her much good in her work.

On the job the female manager must exhibit competency, but she must also be extremely careful that she is not threatening to male peers and superiors. But the line between "competency" that is nonthreatening and threatening is thin, and this complicates her worklife. Her male counterparts may frequently treat her as a female stereotype, yet the stereotypes may be highly inconsistent. Some males believe females have "a tendency to think in broad terms," while others view women as "too fussy about details." The female manager may want to move still higher in the organization, but wary of appearing too aggressive, she must often wait to be summoned to a higher position by male superiors. Perhaps her biggest liability is the noncompetitiveness that is an expected part of the female role in American society. She is at a decided disadvantage when she deals with male executives who are supposed to act in a highly competitive manner.

Being in an executive position affects every aspect of the female's life.

[66]Collins and Esposito, "A Woman in the Boardroom," 82.

[67]Gary N. Powell and D. Anthony Butterfield, "The 'Good Manager': Masculine or Androgynous?" *Academy of Management Journal,* 22 (1979), 395–403.

[68]James R. Terborg et al., "Organizational and Personal Correlates of Attitudes Toward Women as Managers," *Academy of Management Journal,* 20 (1977), 89–100; Christopher Stitt et al., "Sex of Leader, Leader Behavior, and Subordinate Satisfaction," *Sex Roles,* 9 (1983), 31–42.

[69]Marianne Ferber, Joan Huber, and Glenn Spitze, "Preference for Men as Bosses and Professionals," *Social Forces,* 58 (1979), 466–476.

High-ranking females are less likely to be married. In the 1958 Cussler study only one-third of the executive females were married, while in society as a whole two-thirds of all females were married. In a follow-up study of women who graduated from Harvard's MBA program in 1973, it was found that 27 percent never married and 18 percent have separated or divorced. As one of the most highly paid women executives in the United States notes:

> Had I married, there would have been the assumption that I would leave to wash socks and have babies. I knew I couldn't have it all.[70]

Given the nature of her position, the female manager often finds it more difficult to date. As an executive, she is threatening to many males. She makes a good salary, and this often precludes the possibility of her dating, let alone marrying, one of the large number of men who earns less than she does. The longer the woman is an executive, the more difficult it is for her to marry because she becomes increasingly unwilling to give up her executive life.

Even if the female executive is married, her position and the money she commands can still be threatening to other men or her husband. In terms of the former, Cooney notes:

> When I was married, whenever I went to a party, a male friend would come up to me and say, "I couldn't take it, I couldn't be married to you," meaning someone more famous than himself, more successful than himself.[71]

An executive wife who outearns her husband acknowledges the sense of threat when she notes, "We try to pretend it is a 50–50 partnership."[72]

For female executives who are married, a major problem is to combine the frequently incompatible expectations of home and office. Said one female executive in this situation:

> It took me a long time to accept the fact that personal ambition conflicts with what's best for my husband, my baby, and me in the long run.[73]

To help overcome these conflicting expectations, more equal responsibility in performing the daily domestic chores is essential. Often, executive women with children will hire others to do the domestic chores they do not have time to do themselves. As one married, female executive says, "We've hired ourselves a full-time housewife."[74] At a cost of $27,000 a year, one successful female Harvard M.B.A. employs a staff of three women—for housework, shopping, caring for the children, and so forth.[75]

[70]Lynn Langway, et al., "Women and the Executive Suite," 65.

[71]Eliza G.C. Collins and Allison I. Esposito, eds., "A Woman in the Boardroom: An Interview with Joan Ganz Cooney," 81.

[72]Peter W. Bernstein, "Women: The New Stars of Banking," p. 95.

[73]Roy Rowan, "How Harvard's Women MBAs are Managing," p. 64.

[74]Peter W. Bernstein, "Women: The New Stars of Banking," p. 95.

[75]Roy Rowan, "How Harvard's Women MBAs are Managing," p. 64.

FEMALES IN BLUE-COLLAR OCCUPATIONS

We jump now from women in high-status professional and managerial occupations to those in lower-status, blue-collar occupations. In the process we skip over some important occupational categories (the semiprofessions, white-collar clerical workers) that will be dealt with later in this book, with a focus on the role of women in them.

In the elite subcategory within blue-collar occupations, the skilled crafts, women have always been underrepresented. Women have not been attracted by the manual skills and the male subculture that tends to characterize the trades. For their part, male skilled craftsmen have resisted the entrance of women into their occupation. Thus, between 1900 and 1970 the proportion of women in the skilled crafts generally ranged between 2 and 3 percent. Significant inroads were made in the 1970s, and by 1982 women represented 7 percent of the craft workers.[76]

The exclusion of women from the skilled crafts is illustrated in a study of butchers.[77] Although women have made inroads in supermarkets as meat wrappers, male meatcutters "were prepared to fight against hiring women on the grounds that women [all women] could not do meat cutting tasks and especially not, they anticipated, the heavy lifting of whole lambs and sides of beef."[78] The more basic reason for their vehement opposition is that females would threaten the tough, male image of the craft and would disrupt the male subculture associated with it:

> "Butchers' talk," a common male skill occupationally specialized, would also be downgraded or driven underground if women were constantly present. Meat cutters enjoy swearing, talking and joking about women. They feel inhibited about talking this way in a woman's presence . . . [79]

Reimer reports a similar situation among construction workers: "The building construction industry is one of the last bastions of male supremacy in the work world."[80] He reports that women hold approximately 1 percent of all building construction jobs and are even less well represented in many building construction apprenticeship programs. As with the case of butchers, the "occupational culture of the building trades is by nature male oriented and male dominated."[81] Male construction workers resist the entrance of females into that culture. Among reasons for this resistance is a belief that females cannot do their fair share of the work and that they cannot be trusted not to endanger fellow (male) workers.

Although many of the old, formal barriers that prevented women from

[76]*Statistical Abstract of the United States: 1984,* p. 420.

[77]Hannah Meara, "Honor in Dirty Work: The Case of American Meat Cutters and Turkish Butchers," *Sociology of Work and Occupations,* 1 (1974), 259–283.

[78]Ibid., 274.

[79]Ibid.

[80]Jeffrey Reimer, *Hard Hats: The Work World of Construction Workers* (Beverly Hills, CA: Sage Publications, 1979), p. 81.

[81]Ibid., p. 86.

entering predominantly male, skilled occupations have been eliminated, recent evidence suggests that new, more informal barriers may be emerging. This is the finding of a study of women in nontraditional blue-collar jobs.[82]

In 1978, after several years of negotiations with the federal government, a manufacturing company signed a voluntary, national affirmative action agreement designed to increase the number of women in nontraditional blue-collar jobs. Many women were hired and enrollment of females in the company's apprenticeship program grew.

While many barriers were removed by the formal agreement, new forms of employer discrimination have emerged. First, among the men and women hired after 1978, more women (black and white) were hired in unskilled jobs, while more men (black and white) were hired in skilled jobs. This is basically the same situation that existed prior to the 1978 agreement. Furthermore, the prospects for upward mobility for those women hired in unskilled jobs were limited since large numbers of the higher-ranking positions were recently filled by new (largely male) employees. The women hired after 1978 tended to be in jobs with short career ladders; they were dead-end positions. The women placed in the apprenticeship programs will experience upward mobility, but interestingly many of them aspired to management positions. While this is encouraging it will do little to increase the number of women in skilled, blue-collar jobs.

In spite of the barriers, old and new, some women do succeed in entering the skilled crafts. Walshok has analyzed these women who she calls "pioneers on the male frontier."[83] In her view, success in such nontraditional occupations depends on three interrelated factors. First, women must show their competence on the job. Many prejudices can be overcome, informal barriers eliminated, and male acceptance gained "simply" by proving oneself on the job. This was the case, for example, of a female forklift operator:

> They did all kinds of tricks to me. . . . One time . . . they came and got me to stack tires. . . . They thought it was funny that I had to stack over four hundred tires. . . . They weren't just little VW tires, they were the big four-wheel tires. . . . But I did it . . . you know after I proved myself, after they seen me stack all them tires and they saw all the other things I went through, they respect me now. There are even guys under me now and they respect me.[84]

Secondly, Walshok found that work savvy helps women become successful. Not only must women learn specific skills, they must also learn the informal norms that determine the behavior of members of the occupation. In other words, to be successful in nontraditional occupations women must learn the occupational culture and, as a result, how to behave as members of that culture. Finally, women in such occupations need a strong sense of commitment. Dedication to a particular job helped many of the women in Walshok's study

[82]Sharon L. Harlan and Brigid O'Farrell, "After the Pioneers: Prospects for Women in Non-Traditional Blue-Collar Jobs," *Work and Occupations,* 9 (1982), 363–386.

[83]Mary Lindenstein Walshok, *Blue-Collar Women: Pioneers on the Male Frontier* (Garden City, NY: Anchor Books, 1981).

[84]Ibid., p. 223.

overcome prejudices and informal barriers; they entered, and succeeded in, nontraditional occupations.

Finally, we need to discuss the position of women within another type of blue-collar occupation, the police officer. Here, too, we have a situation of miniscule female representation coupled with a significant increase in recent years. In 1972 females accounted for only 2.6 percent of the police (and detective) category, but by 1982 that had increased to 6.7 percent.[85] As Walshok did with mainly skilled workers, Susan Martin depicts the women who have entered the police force as pioneers.[86] Focusing on patrol women she makes the point that, while women are not new to the police force, they are relatively new to patrol work. (Although the first female police officer was sworn in in 1910, the extensive use of females on patrol duty began only in the 1970s.)

Martin identifies a number of factors that led police departments to alter their procedures in the 1970s and begin hiring a significant number of female officers. First, legal changes made it mandatory that police departments stop discriminating against women on the basis of sex. Second, there was the rising crime rate and the demand that the police take radical new steps to curb it. Third, there was a gap between the white male police and the communities they served, a demand that they bring in black males, females, and so forth to help bridge those gaps. Fourth, there was a shift away from the idea that police work required strength and aggressiveness to the perspective that what was needed was interpersonal skills in dealing with the larger community. Fifth, as a result of the preceding change, police departments in the 1970s began trying to recruit in new areas such as colleges, but here they were often thwarted in their efforts because of the bad image that the police had ("pigs") in that decade; the resulting manpower shortage led them to look more toward women as potential police officers. Sixth, increases in crimes committed by juveniles and females, as well as increasing attention to the crime of rape, led to the need for more female officers. Finally, a set of changes in the larger society—such as the women's movement and the changing role of women within the labor force (as well as the legal changes mentioned above)—facilitated the movement of women into the police force.

In spite of all of these changes, and the significant increase in female officers in the the last decade, Martin makes it clear that barriers remain. For example, some tests (for example, for physical agility) operate against female candidates. Another barrier is that police departments give preference to military veterans, and only 2 percent of those veterans are female. Because of these and other barriers, Martin concludes:

> Despite the legal and social changes that have led to an increasing number of policewomen who are performing a wider variety of policing duties including patrol during the last five years, opposition to policewomen remains strong. Underlying the continued resistance to compliance with the law is the view of most policemen of all ranks that women are inherently unfit for police work.[87]

[85]*Statistical Abstract of the United States: 1984,* p. 420.

[86]Susan Ehrlich Martin, *Breaking and Entering: Policewomen on Patrol* (Berkeley, CA: University of California Press, 1982), p. xi.

[87]Ibid., p. 49.

For those women who overcome the barriers and become police officers, a variety of problems exist generally involving male co-workers and citizens. Martin differentiates between two broad types of coping mechanisms. The first is *police*women who "react by overachievement, invisibility, staunch loyalty to the department, and adherence to the rules in order to prove themselves exceptions among women. Successful as officers, they pay a price in terms of pressure to perform, social isolation, and self-distortion."[88] The second is police*women* who "adopt the stereotypic roles into which they are cast, tend to fail as police officers, and thus 'prove' women's incapacity for policing."[89] Most women, however, seek a position between these two extremes, or they seek to avoid the conflict altogether by opting for nonpatrol police assignments.

Perhaps the crucial point in terms of the police, as well as other nontraditional occupations, is that whatever resolution women adopt they are in double jeopardy. They must deal with the same set of conflicts as males in those occupations as well as a whole other set of conflicts traceable to their position as women in a predominantly male occupation. Thus, all officers must deal with the threats posed by those they police, and females face an additional set of difficulties traceable largely to opposition from male peers and members of the public.

INCREASING CONCERN WITH SEXUAL HARASSMENT IN THE WORKWORLD

We close this chapter with a discussion of a phenomenon that has attracted increasing concern in recent years, but which undoubtedly always existed in the workworld—sexual harassment of women. Note the following statement made by a woman seeking a job in the nineteenth century:

> The eldest clerk, with the foxy head, wheeled around, and took his turn to stare. He had hairy hands and large goggle eyes. . . . He perused me up and down with his small pig's eyes, as if he were buying a horse, scrutinizing my face, my figure, my hands, my feet.[90]

Sexual harassment in the workplace is difficult to define, but the Equal Employment Opportunity Commission has defined it as any "unwelcome sexual advances, requests for sexual favors, and other verbal or physical conduct of a sexual nature" when:

1. "submission to such conduct is made either explicitly or implicitly a term or condition of an individual's employment,"
2. "submission to or rejection of such conduct by an individual is used as the basis for employment decisions affecting such individual," or

[88]Ibid., p. 205.
[89]Ibid., p. 206.
[90]Catherine MacKinnon, *Sexual Harassment of Working Women: A Case of Sex Discrimination* (New Haven, CT: Yale University Press, 1979), p. 176.

3. "such conduct has the purpose or effect of unreasonably interfering with an individual's work performance or creating an intimidating, hostile, or offensive working environment."[91]

This definition provides a beginning, but what *specifically* is an unwelcome sexual advance? Or what specific verbal or physical conduct constitutes sexual harassment? Not only are these specific behaviors not spelled out, but, as Linenberger points out, even the courts have tended to resist translating these general guidelines into specific positions on verbal statements or physical behaviors.[92] Hence, does whistling at a woman as she enters the work area constitute sexual harassment?[93] Are sexually derogatory comments or lewd jokes sexual harassment? Some people will see these things as offensive while others will not.[94] We cannot resolve these problems here, but readers should bear them in mind as we discuss sexual harassment and its implications.

These problems aside, the three aforementioned guidelines are helpful in the definition of sexual harassment. They have been accepted by the courts as sufficient grounds for pursuing legal action under Title VII of the 1964 Civil Rights Act.[95] In other words, when it can be ascertained that one of the three conditions has been met, sexual harassment becomes another form of sex discrimination on the job.

It is not clear how frequently sexual harassment occurs, or how severe a problem it is within the workplace. However, a recent study casts light on these issues. Gruber and Bjorn interviewed women employed mostly as unskilled workers in an automobile final-assembly plant.[96] Of the 138 women interviewed, 36 percent reported experiencing a total of 160 incidents of sexual harassment while on the job. Unmarried women, blacks, and young women (26–35) were more likely to experience sexual harassment. The frequency of sexual harassment was found to be negatively related to job status and positively related to the female composition of the work area, that is, the greater the concentration of females in the work area, the greater the sexual harassment.

Gruber and Bjorn categorized types of harassment in terms of low, moderate, or high degrees of severity. Forty-eight percent of the women experienced moderate forms of sexual harassment—sexual propositions (28.1%), verbal innuendo (9.4%), social derogation (5.6%), and body language (5.0%).

[91]Equal Employment Opportunity Commission, "Discrimination Because of Sex Under Title VII of the Civil Rights Act of 1964, as Amended: Adoption of Interim Interpretive Guidelines," *Federal Register,* 29 (March 11, 1980).

[92]Patricia Linenberger, "What Behavior Constitutes Sexual Harassment?" *Labor Law Journal,* 34 (1983), 238–247.

[93]Although there is sexual harassment of males, we will not deal with that issue in this chapter since it is far less common than the harassment of females.

[94]Eliza G.C. Collins and Timothy B. Blodgett, "Sexual Harassment: Some See It . . . Some Won't," *Harvard Business Review,* 59 (March/April 1981), 76–94.

[95]Linenberger, "What Behavior Constitutes Sexual Harassment?"; Catherine A. MacKinnon, *Sexual Harassment of Working Women: A Case of Sex Discrimination.*

[96]James E. Gruber and Lars Bjorn, "Blue-Collar Blues: The Sexual Harassment of Women Autoworkers," *Work and Occupations,* 9 (August, 1982), 271–298.

An additional 20.7 percent experienced severe forms of sexual harassment: 14.4 percent experienced physical attacks and 6.3 percent sexual bribery. Hence, nearly 70 percent of the women experienced moderate or severe forms of sexual harassment on the job. As with frequency, black women were more likely than white women to experience more severe forms of harassment. In addition, and also as with frequency, severity was found to be positively related to the female composition of the work area.[97]

How did these women respond to their experiences? Gruber and Bjorn grouped the responses to sexual harassment into three categories. A *passive* response would be to ignore or to walk away from the situation. A *deflecting* response would involve joking or stalling. An *assertive* response would include a serious verbal reprimand or threatening to take—or actually taking—the complaint to someone in a position of authority. Gruber and Bjorn found responses to sexual harassment to be about equally divided among the three types. However, those women who suffered the most severe forms of sexual harassment were the most likely to respond in an assertive manner.

As previously mentioned, women can also go to court and seek redress under Title VII of the 1964 Civil Rights Act. In addition, women can seek legal redress through tort actions.[98] For example, when physical force is used, legal action based on assault and battery can be pursued. Infliction of emotional distress, intentional interference with a contractual relationship, invasion of privacy, libel, and slander are additional legal bases for pursuing tort action.

All of the responses discussed thus far are individual in nature, but there are also steps that an organization can take. In fact, since under certain conditions employers can be held liable for the actions of their employees,[99] organizations are required to take certain steps. In terms of prevention, the organization's policy should make it clear that sexual harassment will not be tolerated. Management and employees could be provided with training sessions on what is and is not appropriate behavior in the workplace. An intraorganizational grievance procedure for sexual harassment cases would be useful.[100] Those guilty of sexual harassment could be penalized by the employer and counseling could be recommended.

CONCLUSIONS

While much has changed in the place of women in the workworld, and while there have been dramatic improvements in a variety of areas, there is still a

[97]Similar results on the frequency and severity of sexual harassment are found in a study of students at the University of California at Berkeley; see, Donna J. Benson and Gregg E. Thomson, "Sexual Harassment on a University Campus: The Confluence of Authority Relations, Sexual Interest and Gender Stratification," *Social Problems*, 29 (1982), 236–251.

[98]Linenberger, "What Behavior Constitutes Sexual Harassment?"; MacKinnon, *Sexual Harassment of Working Women*.

[99]Donna E. Ledgerwood and Sue Johnson-Dietz, "Sexual Harassment: Implications for Employer Liability," *Monthly Labor Review*, 104 (April, 1981), 45–47.

[100]Judith Berman Brandenberg, "Sexual Harassment in the University: Guidelines for Establishing a Grievance Procedure," *Signs*, 8 (1982), 320–336.

considerable distance to go before we have gender equality in the occupational domain.

One of the dramatic changes in this century has been the substantial increase in the number of women in the labor force. In recent years the greatest increases in the female workforce have been among young married women, especially those with children. Factors involved in this influx of women include the increased demand for female workers, greater cultural acceptance of women who work, changes within the family (fewer children, greater willingness on the part of males to share responsibilities), the economic need of many women, the rise of female-headed families, increasing education of women, and legislation against discrimination on the basis of sex.

In spite of the influx of women, the occupational world remains highly sex-segregated. That is, a number of occupations are overwhelmingly female while many others exclude women almost entirely. Also remaining despite the increase in women workers is a significant gap between the earnings of males and females. In general, women are likely to earn about 60 percent of comparable males' salaries.

In addition to examining such general issues, we looked at the changing position of women within a number of specific occupations—academics, physicians, lawyers, managers and officials, and an array of blue-collar occupations (butchers, construction workers, police officers). In most cases we find both significant changes and continuing problems for women. We conclude that women are in double jeopardy in most occupations. Not only do they face the same difficulties as male workers, but they face as well still other pressures traceable to being women in the workworld.

We concluded the chapter with a discussion of sexual harassment. While not a new problem, there is a growing awareness of the extent of, and degree of harm caused by, sexual harassment on the the job.

SIX

INDIVIDUAL CHANGE: PRE-CAREER STAGES

To this point we have focused on change at the occupational level, but in this chapter and the next we shift to individuals, and how they undergo change in their work-related careers. Studying the careers of individuals yields insights not only into individuals, but also into occupations and even the broader society.[1]

On the *individual* level, one's career is "the moving perspective in which the person sees his life as a whole and interprets the meaning of his various attributes, actions, and the things which happen to him."[2]

On the *occupational* level, the career patterns open to individuals tell us a great deal about the structure of the occupation. Some occupations have elongated hierarchical structures that allow individuals the chance of considerable vertical mobility. Others offer considerable horizontal mobility but little vertical mobility. And some offer little mobility of any kind. Careers offering considerable mobility are most often found in higher-status, higher-paying occupations; it is this that leads Krause to argue that a "career is a minority elite institution in Western society."[3] Tellingly, Hearn labels the careers associated

---

[1]Jeff Hearn, "Toward a Concept of Non-Career," *The Sociological Review*, 25 (1977), 273–288.

[2]Everett Hughes, *Men and Their Work* (Glencoe, IL: Free Press, 1958), p. 63; see also, John Van Maanen, "Introduction: The Promise of Career Studies," in John Van Maanen, ed., *Organizational Careers: Some New Perspectives* (London: John Wiley & Sons, 1977), p. 1.

[3]Elliott A. Krause, *The Sociology of Occupations* (Boston: Little, Brown, and Co., 1971), p. 41.

with higher-status occupations "pure careers," while those linked to lower-status occupations involve "careerlessness."[4]

At the *societal* level, it is clear that a society is extremely rigid when careers consist of a series of clearly defined statuses and offices.[5] In contrast, in more open societies careers tend to be more highly variable. By studying careers we can "throw light on the nature of our institutions and reveal the nature and 'working constitution' of a society."[6]

Following Stebbins, we can differentiate between three basic aspects of career.[7] The *career pattern* is the series of stages associated with a given occupation. In a sense this is an "ideal" pattern of occupational movement, and few individuals ever follow it totally. Because of this gap between the ideal and the actual, we need the concept of *individual objective career,* the series of stages through which individuals actually traverse during their worklives. Finally, there is the concept of a *subjective career,* or the recognition and interpretation by individuals of their individual objective careers in light of the career patterns associated with their occupations.[8,9] Individuals evaluate how well they are doing in their careers in light of their personal aspirations, their peers' career progress and the ideal career pattern in their occupation.

Although most of this chapter and the next deals with career patterns, we must keep in mind that individuals' objective careers are likely to vary greatly from the ideal being described. More importantly, individuals are constantly interpreting, constructing, and reconstructing their own careers in their own minds. Individual careers are a product of people's analysis of their progress, actions that result from that analysis and the reactions of significant others to those actions.[10] To put it another way, one's career position is never fixed but rather is subject to negotiation and, in that sense, is open at least to a degree.[11]

Time Tables

An important component of people's subjective careers is *time.*[12] Individual workers are constantly attuned to cues that indicate whether or not they

[4]Hearn, "Toward a Concept of Non-Career."

[5]Hughes, *Men and Their Work.*

[6]Ibid., p. 67.

[7]Robert Stebbins, "Career: The Subjective Approach," *Sociological Quarterly,* 11 (1970), 32–49; see also, Robert Stebbins, "The Subjective Career as a Basis for Reducing Role Conflict," *Pacific Sociological Review,* 14 (1971), 383–402.

[8]A study of professional hockey players and symphony orchestra musicians has emphasized the subjective career; see, Robert Faulkner, "Coming of Age in Organizations: A Comparative Study of Career Contingencies and Adult Socialization," *Sociology of Work and Occupations,* 1 (1974), 131–73.

[9]Van Maanen offers a differentiation between "internal" and "external" careers that is similar to the ideas of subjective career and individual objective career; see, Van Maanen, "Summary: Towards a Theory of the Career," in Van Maanen, ed., *Organizational Careers,* pp. 166–167.

[10]Ralph Blankenship, "Organizational Careers: An Interactionist Perspective," *Sociological Quarterly,* 14 (1973), 88–98.

[11]Van Maanen, "Introduction," p. 20.

[12]Julius Roth, *Timetables: Structuring the Passage of Time in Hospital Treatment and Other Careers* (Indianapolis: Bobbs-Merrill, 1963); see also, Barney G. Glaser and Anselm L. Strauss, *Status Passage* (Chicago: Aldine/Atherton, 1971), especially Chap. 2.

are progressing "on time." Thus, for example, in academia one expects to be promoted from assistant professor to associate professor to full professor in approximately 10 to 15 years. Those who reach the rank of full professor earlier are likely to have positive feelings about themselves because they are ahead of the timetable.

People not only compare their progress to some abstract norm, they also compare their pace to members of their reference group. If many peers are moving faster, that is a source of considerable concern. In contrast, if individuals are moving faster than their peers, they might consider themselves "comers." Finally, individuals may also measure themselves by self-imposed standards. Positive and negative feelings are created by the rate of movement people attain according to their personal guidelines. Whether individuals compare themselves to some abstract norm, to peers, or to some self-imposed standard, it is clear that time plays a key role in people's subjective careers.

Occupations are not all alike in terms of the timetables associated with career patterns. Some occupations offer rather clear, rigid, and standardized timetables; others are far less certain. For example, the timetable associated with the career of the politician is highly uncertain, given the vagaries of being elected to public office. Those who labor in occupations with uncertain or unclear timetables are often made quite uncomfortable by the absence of clear guidelines to help them ascertain whether or not they are progressing "on schedule." They often seek to reduce their unease by trying to impose at least a semblance of order on the uncertain career. Roth suggests a variety of ways in which at least some order is imposed. For example, individuals can split up potentially long blocks of time between career moves. With these shorter, and therefore often more palatable, time periods, people can set up various signposts that allow them to determine for themselves whether they are progressing satisfactorily. Failure to progress as fast as one's reference group might necessitate a shift to another, slower reference group in order to keep self-esteem high. Individuals can also shift time perspectives, or revise expectations, when they have not reached a given career point at the expected time. Thus the assistant professor who remains unpromoted after seven years might shift to a goal of promotion in ten years.

> People will not accept uncertainty. They will make an effort to structure it no matter how poor the materials they have to work with and no matter how much the experts try to discourage them. . . . One way to structure uncertainty is to structure the time period through which uncertain events occur."[13]

Cyril Sofer, in his study of British business managers, found:

> . . . a sensitive awareness of the connection between age and grade as an indication of one's prospects for attaining senior managerial rank. Men in both samples were constantly mulling over this and asking themselves whether they were on schedule, in front of schedule or behind schedule, showing quite clearly that they had a set of norms in mind as to where one should be by a given age.[14]

[13]Roth, *Timetables*, p. 93.

[14]Cyril Sofer, *Men in Mid-Career: A Study of British Managers and Technical Specialists* (London: Cambridge University Press, 1970), p. 239.

Reaching a position late was cause for great anxiety because the manager was behind schedule, but once the position was attained, no matter how late, relief was felt at finally having made it. Never making the position was a major crisis necessitating a reorientation of the attitudes of managers toward themselves and their work. This consciousness of time and timing exists among virtually all workers and, indeed, exists in many other spheres of life as well.

Faulkner has underscored the importance of time and timing of occupational careers in a comparative study of professional symphony musicians in middle-level orchestras and of minor-league professional hockey players.[15,16] In both of these fields it is important to demonstrate one's ability early in one's career in order to be able to move up the career ladder. For instance, in the words of a hockey player:

> Hockey is a race with time. You feel you have to move up a level a year in the minors and make it into the National by 24 or 25, maybe 26 at the latest. This axe is always hanging over your head. . . . you can't waste any years.[17]

And a musician says:

> Some places will not look at you if you're over a certain age, like 35 or 36; so you have to move fast, audition, and. . . . you have to improve your position with each move.[18]

Because very few make it to the top, people must tone down their high expectations when it becomes clear that movement up is unlikely. Here is the way one rather honest musician reflects this changed orientation:

> Look, let's not kid ourselves, I'm nearly 40 years old. . . . I'm not going to be first in the New York Philharmonic anyway, not at my age.[19]

After scaling down ambitions, people must adapt to lower-status positions. This is done in a variety of ways. Individuals may take a new look at their present position and begin to accentuate the benefits to be derived from remaining in it. Upward mobility may be downgraded by emphasis on the high personal costs involved in moving to the big time. Or, people can adjust aspirations downward by seeking recognition within the present level. Or the focus may be shifted from work to other areas of life—in particular, family. Finally, a very calculating orientation may be adopted toward work—what can be gotten out of it (money, for example) and for how long?

Disorderly Careers

Much of this chapter tends to focus on orderly career patterns. But we must recognize that most people experience disorderly individual objective

[15]Robert R. Faulkner, "Career Concerns and Mobility Motivations of Orchestra Musicians," *Sociological Quarterly,* 14 (1973), 334–49.

[16]Faulkner, "Coming of Age in Organizations."

[17]Ibid., 150.

[18]Ibid., 150–51.

[19]Ibid., 154–155.

careers, and this disorder has important implications for their subjective careers.

Wilensky relates the disorder of individual careers to the disorder in the larger society:

> Rapid technological change dilutes old skills, renders others obsolete and creates demand for new ones; a related decentralization of industry displaces millions, creating the paradox of depressed areas in prosperous economies; metropolitan deconcentration shifts the clientele of service establishments, sometimes smashing or re-structuring careers; and recurrent crises such as wars, depressions, recessions, coupled with the acceleration of fad and fashion in consumption add to the general unpredictability.[20]

Hardest hit by these chaotic conditions tend to be individuals in semi- and unskilled occupations, and Wilensky finds that their careers are marked by considerable disorder. Thus, people at the lower end of the occupational continuum are likely to have disorderly careers, or even no careers at all. In contrast, those at the top (for example, professionals) have careers, and quite orderly ones.[21]

We turn next to the stages that precede the actual beginning of a career—occupational choice, occupational socialization, job search, and recruitment.

OCCUPATIONAL CHOICE

Initial occupational choices are usually shaped by a variety of childhood experiences.[22] Choosing an occupation is a progressive process in which unrealistic childhood wishes are gradually replaced by more and more realistic adolescent and adult choices. As this process progresses individuals are constantly forced to compromise personal desires with the realities of the situation.[23]

In a study of dental students, Helfrich has shed light on the process of career choice by identifying four different paths into professional school.[24] The first, "the striders," make a career choice early in their educational experience and follow a path directly through college and into professional school. The second, "the strivers," also make an early decision, but take a detour into the workworld between high school and college. The third, "the stragglers," remain in the educational system but make a late decision to enter dental

---

[20]Harold Wilensky, "Work, Careers and Social Integration," *International Social Science Journal*, 12 (1960), 554.

[21]For a discussion of at least some career disorder among physicians see, Jill S. Quadagno, "Career Continuity and Retirement Plans of Men and Women Physicians: The Meaning of Disorderly Careers," *Sociology of Work and Occupations*, 5 (1978), 55–74.

[22]Eli Ginzberg et al., *Occupational Choice: An Approach to a General Theory* (New York: Columbia University Press, 1951); "Toward a Theory of Occupational Choice: A Restatement," *Vocational Guidance Quarterly* (March, 1972), 169—76.

[23]Julienne Ford and Stephen Box, "Sociological Theory and Occupational Choice," in W.M. Williams, ed., *Occupational Choice* (London: George Allen and Unwin, Ltd., 1974), p. 112.

[24]Margaret Helfrich, "Paths Into Professional School: A Research Note," *Sociology of Work and Occupations*, 2 (1975), 169–181.

school. Finally, there are the "strugglers," who both make a late decision and leave school for the workworld between college and dental school. We can generalize that there is more than one path into the thousands of occupations available to people.

The realities confronted later on the job can serve to either reinforce or change people's attitudes toward their initial occupational choices. Mortimer and Lorence[25] have studied how the values that initially led to the selection of a particular occupation were altered after ten years of occupational experience. Their sample consisted of males concentrated at the professional and managerial levels. Ten years earlier, as students, the respondents had been asked for their assessment of the importance of seventeen work features. The responses were broken down into three categories, each representing a particular value orientation (income-generating, opportunities to work with people, self-expression in one's work). It was hypothesized that respondents who valued the income-generating potential of an occupation would choose an occupation for such "extrinsic" reward values. Respondents who valued occupations providing opportunities to work with people or those who valued self-expression in their work would select occupations that would satisfy these people-oriented or "intrinsic" values, respectively. It was further hypothesized that ten years of occupational experience would either reinforce or change the values that led to the initial occupational choice, depending of course, on whether the values were or were not realized.

In general, the findings of their study support the hypotheses. Respondents with extrinsic reward values selected occupations that could provide high incomes. Similarly, respondents with people-oriented or intrinsic work values selected occupations that could help them realize these values. Further, if the respondents seeking extrinsic values realized high income during their ten years of work experience, this experience not only reinforced but further increased the salience of these values. While working with people did not significantly change or reinforce the people-oriented values, the reinforcement effect was significant for those who expressed the importance of intrinsic reward values. For this group, realizing self-expression (autonomy, innovation, challenge) in their work greatly reinforced the values that led to their initial occupational choice. All this leads Mortimer and Lorence to conclude that even though one's initial occupational choice is shaped by a variety of early experiences, the values that led to the original choice can be reinforced or changed by one's occupational experience.

FORMAL OCCUPATIONAL SOCIALIZATION

Occupational socialization occurs in a number of ways. We start by focusing on the more elaborate, formally constituted forms—for example, those in medical or business school. Although we call it "formal," much of what really goes on in these training centers is informal—that is, it develops in an

---

[25]Jeylan T. Mortimer and Jon Lorence, "Work Experience and Occupational Value Socialization: A Longitudinal Study," *American Journal of Sociology,* 86 (1979), 1361–1385.

unplanned and spontaneous fashion. These informal processes play at least as great a role in the socialization of those in high-status occupations as do structured courses and lectures. Later we will discuss the socialization of those in less skilled, less prestigious occupations where, with little formally structured training, most socialization occurs informally on the job. To illustrate these process of informal socialization we will focus on the socialization for deviant occupations.

While our concern in this section is with the socialization for one's first occupation, it should be noted that occupational socialization, like socialization in general, occurs throughout one's lifetime as one changes jobs, organizations, or simply requires a refresher course after some years on the job.

Professionals

Most professional schools have courses designed both to communicate knowledge and to offer practical experience for recruits to learn the skills they need. Medical schools, for example, offer both formal and practical training. In most graduate schools the focus is on formal course work designed to enable the student to pass preliminary examinations—but opportunities to gain some practical experience are also offered. A graduate school may require students to assist in a course or in a research project to gain experience in research design, methodology, and analysis; dissertation research is also designed to give the student practical experience. However, some professional schools do not accomplish both of these goals. In Lortie's view, law schools are almost totally involved in communicating knowledge,[26] with little time allowed for the student to learn the practical side of law—how to handle clients and opposing lawyers, and how to handle the value conflicts inherent in the legal profession.

No matter how well they perform their formal tasks, professional schools leave many of the important aspects of professional training to an informal system. In medical school, for example, while the focus is formally on communicating knowledge and teaching skills, professional norms and values are acquired informally through contact with instructors and peers, patients, and members of the health team.

Changing Students' Idealism to Realism

Students, on entering professional schools, generally have an unrealistic picture of the nature of the profession. The informal system in such schools serves to communicate the norms and values of the profession and, in the process, generally changes initial idealism into a more realistic view. According to Lortie, supporting a position put forth by Hughes, there is in law school a "gradual replacement of the exotic and dramatized image by one which takes account of routine and pedestrian elements."[27]

Newly graduated law students are often dissatisfied with their prepara-

[26]Dan C. Lortie, "Layman to Lawman: Law School, Careers and Professional Socialization," *Harvard Educational Review,* 29 (Fall, 1959), 352–69.

[27]Ibid.

tion because they do not know what to expect in their first jobs. Although other professional schools perform this task better than do law schools,[28] there is inevitably *reality shock* in the transition from school to practice. That is, the reality of actual practice is strikingly different from the image of that practice conveyed in professional schools.

Medical students.   Becker and Geer examined the change in idealism that takes place in medical schools.[29] Freshman enter medical school imbued with the wonders of medicine and the desire to save humankind, but the first year proves to be a rude shock. They are disillusioned because their courses seem irrelevant and, furthermore, they are not even taught by doctors. They soon learn to "play the game" by concentrating on passing examinations, pleasing the faculty, and utilizing shortcuts to learn the mass of facts. They view the first year as unimportant and become cynical about their activities. They retain the hope, however, that subsequent years will prove better and that the knowledge learned will be more applicable to their lingering idealistic desires to help humankind. The second year proves to be little different, although there is some contact with "real" medical problems such as autopsies. In the third and fourth years they do have contact with patients, and their performance is assessed by doctors, but instead of helping these patients their primary concern is to understand them as a specific form of a general medical problem. "The student becomes preoccupied with the technical aspects of the case . . . because the faculty requires him to do so."[30] In addition, medical students are plagued by their low status in the hospital system and are not in reality central participants in the actual care of patients. As a result, they tend to look at patients in terms of the problems they create for them. In the end, however, the medical school provides students with an out. Although they have become more cynical, their cynicism is directed at the school; they are able to retain their idealistic belief that once they graduate they will be able to help society. As their student years come to an end their cynicism about medical school recedes and idealism about the profession regains center stage. However, this is quite different from the idealism they had when they entered medical school: they have acquired a more realistic picture of the profession, which will enable them to handle the blows to idealism (reality shock) they will face in private practice or hospital work.

A recent study by Haas and Shaffir of students in an innovative medical school also examines the loss of idealism.[31] Although Becker and Geer found the loss of idealism—cynicism—to be situational and transitional, Haas and Shaffir found it to be more general and permanent. As these medical students became increasingly professionalized, they grew less idealistic. One example of this is that their early closeness with patients was replaced by increasing

[28]Ibid., 353.

[29]Howard Becker and Blanche Geer, "The Fate of Idealism in Medical School," *American Sociological Review*, 23 (1958), 50–56.

[30]Ibid., 53.

[31]Jack Haas and William Shaffir, "The 'Fate of Idealism' Revisited," *Urban Life*, 13 (April, 1984), 63–81.

psychological distance from them. Such changes were not tied to the limited domain of the medical school, but the more general character of the profession as a whole:

> Our data suggest that students perceived the loss of idealism as inherent in the very demands of professionalization; medicine is organized on the assumption that practitioners will maintain a psychological distance from patients, and the profession's gatekeepers consciously or unconsciously insist that neophytes assume this posture. . . . If they are to complete the passage to professionalism, idealistic attitudes must go. Initial accommodations develop into acceptance of the identification with the way the profession solves its problems.[32]

Dental students. Growing cynicism was also observed by Morris and Sherlock in a study of socialization in dental school.[33] About one-third of the first-year students were highly cynical, but, despite a decline in cynicism in the middle years of dental school, fully one-half of the graduating class expressed cynicism toward dentistry. Much of the growing disillusionment is attributed to the clinical experience in dental school, which does not live up to the high expectations students have of it.

Sociology students. Graduate students in sociology frequently enter school with the same kind of vague idealism that is found among medical students:

> [The student] may see sociology in a rather vague way as being an avenue for the betterment of mankind, a discipline sensitive to the sore spots in civilization and dedicated to alleviating them. This appeals to his idealism, since he is likely to be a person who would want his life in some way to serve the cause of human welfare and progress.[34]

During their years in graduate school students quickly learn the realities of life in sociology. They are not given answers to society's ills; instead, the subject matter tends to be ambiguous, with the professors more concerned with getting the graduate students to "show initiative, imagination, and a self-starting capacity"[35] than they are with teaching them facts. Like medical students, sociology students learn that there is much more to sociology than they can possibly master. More frightening is the realization that "truth in sociology is provisional and problematic,"[36] and they begin to realize that, because of limitations in themselves and the field, they may never find the answers they originally sought. If they survive the process, graduating sociologists are in many ways changed people. They are concerned with more realistic goals, such as passing their dissertation defense, getting a good job, and above all,

---

[32]Ibid., 65.

[33]Richard R. Morris and Basil Sherlock, "Decline of Ethics and the Rise of Cynicism in Dental School," *Journal of Health and Social Behavior,* 12 (1971), 290–99; see also, Basil Sherlock and Richard Morris, *Becoming a Dentist* (Springfield, IL: Charles C. Thomas, 1972).

[34]Alan P. Bates, *The Sociological Enterprise* (Boston: Houghton Mifflin, 1967), p. 116.

[35]Ibid., p. 117.

[36]Ibid.

accepting the basic goal of professional sociologists: "the search for reliable scientific knowledge about human social behavior."[37]

Altering Student Commitment

In trying to understand what happens during professional socialization, an important factor is the nature of the entering student's commitment to the profession. Although most students who enter the training schools of the established professions already have a deep commitment to the profession in question, with students entering the training schools of some less well-established professions this is not always the case: in many cases they have entered the training schools for a number of nonprofessional reasons. Hence, some professional schools must be concerned with engendering a sense of professional commitment.

Much light is cast on this question by the comparative study of graduate students in physiology, philosophy, and engineering conducted by Becker and Carper.[38] In all three cases we will see that the way a graduate school socializes its students depends on the nature of their initial commitment to the field.

Physiology students.   A majority of the physiology students in the Becker and Carper study had originally planned a medical career and decided on graduate work in physiology only after they were rejected by medical schools. In general, they entered graduate work in physiology as a stopgap, planning to enter medical school after the end of the first year of graduate school. Even those students who planned to study physiology entered without a strong commitment to the field. But the first year of coursework makes it clear to the students that the field lacks many answers and is a fertile area for original work. This discovery, as well as developing skill in physiological techniques, makes for some degree of commitment by the end of the first year. Some may then reapply to medical school but, as medicine becomes more of an unattainable goal, physiology grows as a meaningful alternative. In the second year students begin laboratory work, and they find themselves in intimate contact with committed students and faculty, increasing their own commitment. By the end of the second year they are fairly well committed to physiology and "can even envision turning down a place in medical school if one materializes."[39] Their developing dedication is the result of two factors: a growing identity with the field and a reluctance to give up the "investments" (for example, the year of training) they have already made in physiology.

Engineering students.   Engineering students are in a much different situation: they have developed a commitment to engineering long before they entered graduate school. Thus in the first year little attention is paid to developing commitment, since it already exists. Instead, the first year of graduate

[37]Ibid., 120.

[38]Howard S. Becker and James W. Carper, "The Development of Identification with an Occupation," *American Journal of Sociology*, 61 (1956), 289–98.

[39]Ibid., 292.

school is seen as a way of enhancing the salary offers the student will ultimately receive; attention is primarily on coursework and gaining additional expertise.

Philosophy students.   Philosophy students enter graduate school with a view, acquired as undergraduates, of themselves as wide-ranging intellectuals. Many have chosen graduate training in philosophy not because of an intrinsic interest in the field, but because it offered them the widest range of intellectual interests. The graduate department offers them a variety of courses that serve to maintain this original inclination. Contacts with the faculty are limited by both parties, and this allows students to maintain broad-scale interests without facing the question of their ultimate occupational goal. Instead, the commitment to philosophy gradually grows as they learn that it is only philosophy that offers them the opportunity to remain wide-ranging intellectuals. Furthermore, by now they too have made a number of investments in philosophy that makes it costly for them to switch fields.

Merchant marine students.   Very different from preceding examples, maritime training illustrates the negative effect socialization can have on the commitment of students to an occupation. In their study of students in maritime academies, Bassis and Rosengren found that upperclassmen were actually *less* committed to a career in the merchant marine than new inductees into the academies.[40] Although these schools intended to foster greater commitment to the occupation, they were in fact fostering a declining attachment to the merchant marine. How is this possible? One answer is that students entering such schools have a romantic and naive conception of the occupation. Once they are exposed to some of the realities of shipboard life (for example, "the physical dangers, the stress, and the boredom of the occupation"[41]), students tend to grow less committed to the occupation.

Other Changes in Students

Identity.   Many other changes take place informally throughout the student's training years. For example, a change in identity takes place. Huntington was concerned with the process by which first-year medical students come to identify themselves by their fourth year as doctors.[42] In a survey of three medical schools she found that only 31 percent of the first-year students but 83 percent of the fourth-year students thought of themselves as doctors.

Huntington's view is that a clearer professional identity develops over time among medical students. Although this is a fair generalization about pro-

[40]Michael S. Bassis and William R. Rosengren, "Socialization for Occupational Disengagement: Vocational Educational in the Merchant Marine," *Sociology of Work and Occupations,* 2 (1975), 133–149.

[41]Ibid., 140.

[42]Mary Jean Huntington, "The Development of a Professional Self-Image," in Robert K. Merton, George Reader, and Patricia Kendall, eds., *The Student Physician: Introductory Studies in the Sociology of Medical Education* (Cambridge: Harvard University Press, 1957), pp. 179–88.

fessional training, Kleinman studied a seminary in which ministry students developed an ambivalent professional identity.[43] In the socialization process, these ministry students were exposed to both the traditional and the more humanistic orientations toward being a minister. In the traditional orientation ministers are seen as "special," different from and superior to parishoners; whereas in the humanistic orientation ministers and the public are seen as essentially alike—there is equality between them. As a result of exposure to these conflicting orientations, this group of professional students emerged from the socialization experience with identity problems rather than a clear sense of their professional identity. The ministry students

> . . . generally adopt a humanistic stance in "public"—in the classroom, in ministry projects, in their leisure pursuits in the seminary, at meals, and so on. Traditional elements of the role show up mostly in private. . . . They individually and collectively become familiar with, but do not fully adopt, either role.[44]

Kleinman places much of the blame for this ambivalence on the faculty and its failure to "provide a clear and coherent image of the profession as a distinctive and special occupation."[45]

Handling uncertainty. One of the latent functions of medical education is to train students to handle uncertainty inherent in the occupation. Renee Fox has outlined a number of ways in which medical school formally and informally prepares students to deal with such uncertainty.[46] Courses are not presented with clear expectations of what should and should not be learned. Students are expected to decide for themselves the boundaries of the subject matter. Students do not receive grades, and thus they must rate themselves subjectively. Each course covers an enormous amount of material, and the students learn that they cannot master all there is to know. Further, each course demonstrates the great gaps in medical knowledge. In contact with teachers, the students learn that they know far less than the instructors. When they get to actual practice, they make errors (for example, improper autopsies); they also learn of the unpredictability of death, the inability to prevent it, and the incorrect diagnoses that may have hastened it. Thus as the students learn more they also learn of the gaps in knowledge and of the uncertainty in the field. In learning more they also learn to differentiate between personal inadequacy and inadequacies in the discipline, and in their relationships with peers they soon learn that they are not alone in their sensitivity to these dual sources of uncertainty. Thus in addition to learning of uncertainty, medical students have also been taught informally to cope with it.

[43]Sherryl Kleinman, "Making Professionals into 'Persons': Discrepancies in Traditional and Humanistic Expectations of Professional Identity," *Sociology of Work and Occupations,* 8 (1981), 61–87; Sherryl Kleinman, *Equals Before God: Seminarians as Humanistic Professionals* (Chicago: University of Chicago Press, 1984).

[44]Kleinman, *Equals Before God,* p. 37.

[45]Ibid., p. 101.

[46]Renee Fox, "Training for Uncertainty," in Merton, Reader, and Kendall, eds., *The Student Physician,* pp. 207–44.

Postgraduate Socialization

Formal professional socialization often continues beyond graduate or professional school. Medical students enter the period of internship[47] and then residency, during which training is continued, although with larger and larger portions of actual hospital experience. Many scientists and academicians enter postdoctoral programs to continue their training in a highly specialized area. An interesting example of postgraduate socialization is the psychiatric resident.[48]

The psychiatric resident. Donald Light extends Fox's work on training for uncertainty in his study of residents who work in a psychiatric hospital.[49] Light found kinds of uncertainty among psychiatric residents that parallel those found by Fox among medical students. First, they experience uncertainty because they are unable to master all there is to know: "psychiatric residents are overwhelmed by what they have to learn."[50] Second, psychiatric residents learn the weaknesses in the knowledge base of the field. They are exposed to many theories, but to few systematic observations to support those theories. As psychiatric residents proceed in the program, they begin to wonder whether they know enough to treat a case, or whether the field as a whole has enough knowledge to deal with the problem.

Light extends his inquiry to uncertainties that arise later as the resident begins to take on cases. For one thing, it is often difficult to discern the nature of a patient's psychiatric problem. Residents are also unclear about the most effective treatment. How precisely will alternative treatments affect the patient? Light also identifies uncertainties in relationships with colleagues. The resident who has been trained to be in a superordinate position may have difficulty operating as simply one member of a psychiatric team. Or uncertainties in the relationships between residents and their subordinates, especially nurses, may cause problems. While residents give nurses orders, nurses teach residents many things about the day-to-day operations of hospitals. Nurses often have considerable practical experience that lead them to resent bad recommendations and decisions by residents. This resentment is often translated into disrespectful behavior toward psychiatric residents.

Light's most important conclusion about this is that, as the resident's clinical responsibilities grow, *"training for uncertainty becomes training for control."*[51] Light details a variety of techniques by which residents learn to control uncertainty. One strategy is an effort to define and master *necessary* knowledge. While it is impossible to learn everything, residents learn what they

[47]For a detailed study of internship see Emily Mumford, *From Students to Physicians* (Cambridge: Harvard University Press, 1970).

[48]Donald Light, *Becoming Psychiatrists: The Professional Transformation of Self* (New York: W. W. Norton, 1980); Bud Khlief, "Professionalization of Psychiatric Residents," in Phyllis Stewart and Muriel Cantor, eds., *Varieties of Work Experience: The Social Control of Occupational Groups and Roles* (New York: Schenkman, 1974), pp. 301–312.

[49]See also Rue Bucher, Joan Stelling, and Paul Dommeruth, "Differential Prior Socialization: A Comparison of Four Professional Training Programs," *Social Forces*, 48 (1969), 213–223.

[50]Light, *Becoming Psychiatrists*, p. 279.

[51]Ibid., p. 282.

need to know to handle a given case; they then move on to the next case and the next body of needed knowledge. A related strategy is for residents to divide up the work among themselves, share knowledge, and become experts in particular areas. By limiting what they know, residents also reduce uncertainties about diagnosis and procedures. Residents also adopt a particular school of psychiatry and this limited perspective also provides them with a sense of greater certainty.

Another important method of controlling uncertainty, especially uncertainty over diagnosis and treatment, is by deferring to those who have clinical experience. In fact, clinical experience is considered more important than technical knowledge:

> In psychiatric residency, it is the person in the room who has the most experience with the kind of case at hand whose opinion prevails, and the person is usually a senior clinician. Thus deferring to clinical experience clarifies collegial relations.[52]

Not only does the existence of people with experience help in controlling uncertainty, but the residents themselves are guaranteed increasing authority simply as a result of the fact that they will be accumulating more and more experience.

Control over uncertainty is also obtained by shifting "from considering technique as a means to considering it as an end."[53] One is deemed competent if one uses a technique well, *not* whether it in fact helps the patient.

Control over the uncertainties involved in relations with others is obtained when residents gain autonomy. Part of that autonomy stems from membership in a profession (psychiatry) that has a legal and administrative monopoly over an area. Control is enhanced by actions taken by individual residents such as regarding clients as ignorant on psychiatric matters and acting to keep them that way.

Thus, there are a variety of ways in which psychiatric residents can gain control over uncertainty. In fact, Light concludes that there is a real danger of overcontrol:

> Thus in gaining control over their work by acquiring a treatment philosophy and exercising individual judgment without question, residents run the danger of gaining too much control over the uncertainties of their work. Their emphasis on technique can make them oblivious to the needs of patients as patients define them; yet the patients trust that professionals will solve their complex problems provides the foundation of professional power.[54]

Semiprofessionals

Although semiprofessional training programs are not nearly as elaborate as those of the established professions, there are many similarities. For

[52]Ibid., p. 286.
[53]Ibid., p. 287.
[54]Ibid., pp. 294–295.

example, Simpson feels that the socialization of nurses[55] in particular, and professionals in general, takes place in three stages, "each involving some learning of the cultural content of the role and some self-identification with it."[56] In the first stage students must learn to become proficient in the required tasks. Second, out of the number of reference groups available, they select the one that will serve as their major reference group. Finally, they come to internalize the basic values of the profession and adopt the proper modes of behavior.

Nursing students.   Nursing students, like medical students, enter school with notions of helping the sick, but this goal is quickly thwarted. In the first stage, emphasis is on classroom work and learning such skills as the "21 consecutive steps" needed to properly make a bed. They soon learn that their status as nurses is based not on "nurturant relationships with patients," but on how well they perform their daily chores. In time, this emphasis leads to a basic change in the view of the nursing role: "the primary concern of the student shifted from helping a patient to playing a role of a nurse."[57] In the second stage, gradually co-workers who prize technical skill become the student nurse's major reference group. By the middle of the sophomore year, the students begin working in the hospital and the views of doctors and established nurses become important. As these significant others come to recognize and approve of the student nurses, the latter begin viewing themselves as "real" nurses. In the third stage they become truly "professional" as they come to believe that it is only the view of fellow "professional" nurses that is important. It is this last stage of socialization that proves difficult for nursing schools to accomplish. If nurses are unable to achieve this third stage it is because they interact with doctors; higher-ranking professionals whose views are often valued more than those of fellow nurses.

Psathas has studied the fate of idealism in nursing school in much the same way Becker and Geer analyzed that phenomenon in medical school.[58] He compared the perceptions of groups of freshmen and senior nursing students and found that freshmen nurses were much more idealistic and optimistic than their senior counterparts. In their attitudes toward patients, seniors tended to be technique-oriented while the freshmen were more patient-centered. Although they were confident of the outcome, freshmen nurses were much more uneasy about handling new or unstructured situations. Seniors had a clearer idea of the status system in the hospital and, interestingly, were less likely to see themselves "as a valuable contributor to the physician in providing better patient care."[59] In general, entering student nurses had idealized images of the significant others in the hospital, while sen-

[55]Ida Harper Simpson, "Patterns of Socialization into Professions: The Case of Student Nurses," *Sociological Inquiry,* 37 (1967), 47–54.

[56]Ibid., 47.

[57]Ibid., 50.

[58]George Psathas, "The Fate of Idealism in Nursing School," *Journal of Health and Social Behavior,* 9 (1968), 52–65.

[59]Ibid., 62.

iors had a much more realistic view of what significant others do and what they could expect them to do. Thus the socialization of nurses is in this sense—and many others—similar to the socialization of professionals.

Some Apparent Failures of Semiprofessional Socialization

Although the socialization of semiprofessionals is sometimes successful, in many instances it fails to achieve its goals. A study by Davis, Olesen, and Whittaker[60] indicates that the socialization of nurses fails to achieve at least some important objectives. For one thing, nursing school frequently fails to produce the kind of people needed to assume leadership positions within the occupation. As evidence of this, Davis et al. found that 89 percent of the nurses on entering nursing school ranked home and family their first priority; by graduation 90 percent *still* ranked home and family first. With this type of attitude, there is little chance that many graduates will aspire to leadership positions within nursing.

A study conducted in Great Britain casts additional light on the lack of commitment of nurses.[61] Based on interviews with student nurses, Melia found that their socialization is profoundly affected by the existence of two segments within nursing in general and within the nursing school in particular. One is the education segment which emphasizes becoming a professional nurse. The other is the service segment, the leaders of which are far more interested in the accomplishment of day-to-day nursing chores. The student nurses are forced to compromise between these two segments, moving between the work setting where the service segment is dominant and the college setting where the education segment reigns supreme. Students adopt a transient attitude toward their professional training, moving freely back and forth between these segments. However, this "supports a transient approach to nursing work itself, and so implicitly supports a lack of commitment to nursing as an occupation."[62]

Davis and his colleagues also believe that collegiate nursing often fails to instill in students the desire to work in hospital settings. Because a large proportion of the positions in nursing exist in this setting, this is perpetuating the trend toward filling these positions with the lesser-trained graduates of junior college or hospital-run programs. Although many college-trained nurses are initially drawn to the occupation by the image of hospital work, by the end of their training they tend to develop a humanistic, antibureaucratic orientation that leads them away from the hospital and into such fields as public health and psychiatric nursing. Supporting this development is the growing propen-

[60]Fred Davis, Virginia Olesen, and Elvi Waik Whittaker, "Problems and Issues in Collegiate Nursing Education," in Fred Davis, ed., *The Nursing Profession* (New York: Wiley, 1966), pp. 138–175.

[61]Kath M. Melia, "Student Nurses' Construction of Occupational Socialisation," *Sociology of Health and Illness*, 6 (1984), 132–151.

[62]Ibid., 149.

sity of many hospital administrators to view college-trained nurses as either overtrained, too rebellious, or knowledgeable in esoteric areas that are of little use in the hospital setting.

Formal Socialization in Total Institutions

Total institutions are places "of residence and work where a large number of like situated individuals, cut off from the wider society for an appreciable period of time, together lead an enclosed, formally administered round of life."[63] Total institutions—for example, military and police academies—are characterized by the fact that all aspects of life take place in the same location under one authority; all "students" work together doing the same things, and all are treated alike; all activities are tightly scheduled by a single plan; there is a large gap between superiors and subordinates, with little mobility between their positions; work is on a 24-hour-a-day basis; and there is a gulf between the total institution and the rest of society.

The military academy. There are three basic components of the socialization of officers in the military academy. The first involves the formal learning, usually through classroom exposure, of the basic doctrines of military theory. Second, military socialization is oriented, both formally and informally, to the inculcation of a set of ethical norms and rules for dealing with clients, the public, and military peers. For example, the following is an ethical rule for the Swedish army officer:

> The soldier's speech shall be honest. Swear words and coarse words must not be used.[64]

Finally, there is the goal, primarily achieved through informal means, of creating a feeling of corporateness and solidarity among military officers.

The military academy is physically isolated from civilian institutions (an exception is ROTC), and the recruit, in particular during the early phases of his or her stay in the academy, is isolated from civilian society and friends. This isolation is created for a variety of reasons. First, it speeds up the assimilation of military values since there is little or no interference from outside agencies. Second, it allows for the "mortification" of the self-concepts that recruits bring with them to the academy. Once that self-concept is destroyed, or at least reduced in significance, it is then possible for the academy to create a new military self. Third, the isolation reduces the possibility that the military will be embarrassed by young officers engaging in social upheavals and political controversy.

The logic behind making the military academy a total institution was best expressed by a West Point professor in 1906:

[63]Erving Goffman, *Asylums* (Garden City, NY: Anchor Books, 1961), p. xiii.

[64]Bengt Abrahamsson, *Military Professionalization and Political Power* (Beverly Hills, CA: Sage Publications, 1972), p. 67.

At the period of adolescence, when character is plastic and impulse wayward, before the stereotype has set, control and constraint are the essential forces for impressing permanent form upon young manhood. If the material can be removed from contaminating impurities, fused in the furnace of hard work, and kept in its mold until it has set, the best has been done that education can do for character provided the mold is a noble one.[65]

The first year is the most severe at West Point,[66] as well as at other military institutions.[67] Ten percent of the West Point recruits resign in the first two months and 18 percent leave in the first year. The first two months are devoted to physical and military training; there is no pretense at this point of education. The raw recruits are labeled "beasts." On the day of arrival they are given regulation haircuts, issued regulation service clothing, deprived of all civilian apparel and most possessions.

To create solidarity, assignments are structured so that recruits must cooperate with each other. Isolation from external life is designed to mute differences in social status and permit the development of a cohesive group. This overall unity is enhanced by hostility to outsiders.

The military academy, unlike most other total institutions, is structured in such a way that the control over the members is progressively reduced over the course of their tenure so that, in the end, they emerge with a strong, albeit altered, self.[68] At West Point they take away your rights and give them back as privileges.[69]

The police academy.   Although it lacks some of the military academy's defining characteristics (for example, a 24-hour day), the police academy is certainly a total institution by most definitions.[70] Formally, rookies are trained in equipment handling and are offered courses in law, government, police procedures and techniques, and human relations. Informally, they are trained to recognize and defer to those above them in the police hierarchy. Likewise, they acquire the "art" of police work: "an instinct for the proper time to be masterly or to genuflect, to be warm and sympathetic or cold and imperious toward his future clientele."[71] Like medical students and student nurses, police academy students begin with idealism that is soon transformed into cynicism. In class they are led to believe that they are, or soon will be, people of great power and responsibility. Yet,

[65]Cited in John P. Lovell, "The Professional Socialization of the West Point Cadet," in Morris Janowitz, ed., *The New Military* (New York: John Wiley & Sons, Science Editions, 1964), p. 119.

[66]Richard C. U'Ren, "West Point: Cadets, Codes and Careers," *Society*, 12 (May/June, 1975), 23–29, 36; see also, Joseph Ellis and Robert Moore, *School for Soldiers: West Point and the Profession of Arms* (New York: Oxford University Press, 1974).

[67]Sanford Dornbusch, "The Military Academy as an Assimilating Institution," *Social Forces*, 33 (1955), 316–321.

[68]We would like to thank professor John Blair for this insight.

[69]U'Ren, "West Point," 24.

[70]Arthur Niederhoffer, *Behind the Shield: The Police in Urban Society* (Garden City, NY: Anchor Books, 1969).

[71]Ibid., pp. 45–46.

. . . outside of class the department indicates in many ways that it does not trust the young probationer. It sets curfews for him; it declares stores where liquor is sold "off limits." The recruit measures this treatment against the frequent appeals to him to conduct himself like a professional. Doubts assail him.[72]

More cynicism is created when, in contact with established members of the force, recruits are told that they will have to forget everything they learned in training when they get a regular position. Unlike medical students, police recruits may not outgrow their cynicism.

In a detailed study of a single police academy in which he was a participant observer, Harris found that police socialization focused on creating norms of defensiveness, professionalization, and depersonalization in the new recruit.[73]

Recruits are taught, through a variety of formal and informal means, the ethos of defensiveness, to be constantly alert to the ever-present possibility of danger. On another level, they are taught to be very suspicious of a variety of out-groups (politicians, students, blacks, the press, females, lawyers, judges—and even personal friends). Recruits are trained to "play act" with the out-groups in order to disarm them and thereby prevent them from committing harmful acts. They are also trained to be secretive so that out-groups do not gain information that they can use against the police.

Harris' police academy also seeks to instill a sense of "professionalism" in recruits, though not in the sense used in Chapter 4. It is simply a generally positive image of responsibility the police hope to communicate to the public in order to achieve greater autonomy in their work. To accomplish this, the leaders of the academy place a great emphasis on the value of education. The recruits are told that they are "super professionals" who require the combined skills of the various established professions—lawyers, judges, physicians, and so forth. At the same time, the recruits are told disparaging things about these established professions in order to raise their self-image relative to them.

The emphasis on professionalism not only involves changing the recruits' self-image, it also involves communicating this new image to the public. Thus, for example, the academy stresses the importance of appearance and moral image. The recruits are urged to show the public that they are respectable, conventional, virtuous, and honorable. Above all, they are urged to be courteous in their contacts with the public.

Finally, the academy both intentionally and unintentionally teaches the recruits the norm of depersonalization, "characterized by categorizing persons and interacting with them on the basis of these categories rather than on each actor's individual merits."[74] Recruits are depersonalized by the public and are likely to be treated as stereotypes rather than as individuals. They are generally regarded as little more than performers of society's dirty work, such as "the tasks of touching diseased bodies, and crawling under trains to tie up a bloody stump on the end of a leg."[75] The department also depersonalizes re-

[72]Ibid., p. 46.
[73]Richard Harris, *The Policy Academy: An Inside View* (New York: John Wiley & Sons, 1973).
[74]Ibid., p. 67.
[75]Ibid., p. 114.

cruits by treating them as a category at the bottom of the police hierarchy. At another level, the recruits are taught that they cannot afford to deal with people on an individual basis. They must categorize them; they are on safer grounds if they follow general rules in dealing with the public. Treating people as objects helps reduce potentially dangerous personal involvement with them. Furthermore, reliance on general rules and categories serves to lessen the need of the police to use their own judgment in potentially troublesome and dangerous encounters with the public.

Interestingly, Harris seems to view the police academy as a failure.[76] On the one hand, its efforts to help recruits deal with their work problems often seem to only exacerbate the problems. For example, when recruits employ the norm of defensiveness, it only serves to increase public hostility to the police. On the other hand, it is also a failure in the sense that the formal lessons in the academy prove to have little effect on recruits once they leave the academy. What the academy does accomplish is to create a sense of solidarity among the recruits that has both positive and negative effects on their later work. While this enables them to later lean on one another during times of stress, the "in-group" character of their relationship often leads to greater hostility toward them among the out-groups with which they come in constant contact.

Formal Socialization: The Active Role of Trainees

Much of the work on professional socialization implies that it is a one-way process—from those in educational structures doing the socializing to those being socialized. This view has been challenged in a study by Bucher and Stelling on the socialization of students in professional schools of psychiatry, internal medicine, and graduate students in biochemistry.[77] They make it clear that socialization is *not* a unidirectional process: "Trainees, it is quite clear, are not simply responding to events around them; they are actively evaluating those events and constructing their own responses to them."[78]

Bucher and Stelling detail a variety of ways in which trainees play an active role in constructing their professional identities. For example, trainees are highly selective in which attributes they emulate and which they reject. They also assess the information they are receiving, adopting parts and ignoring the rest. Trainees also decide how they will handle various professional functions and how they will fill professional roles. Furthermore, trainees grow more selective as they progress through the training program and develop a greater sense of professional mastery. They increasingly discount external criticisms and use their own judgment. They grow less dependent on external sources of validation and more likely to become self-evaluating. It is this active orientation that allows for the emergence of an autonomous professional with a strong professional identity. While this process is certainly affected by an array of structural factors, Bucher and Stelling emphasize the role played by neophytes in constructing their own professional identities.

---

[76]A similar point is made by Bassis and Rosengren about military-type merchant marine academies. See Bassis and Rosengren, "Socialization for Occupational Disengagement."

[77]Rue Bucher and Joan Stelling, *Becoming Professional* (Beverly Hills, CA: Sage Publications, 1977).

[78]Ibid., p. 278.

INFORMAL OCCUPATIONAL SOCIALIZATION: DEVIANT
OCCUPATIONS[79]

Up to this point we have dealt primarily with formally structured socialization programs in the professions, semiprofessions, and "total institutions." But the socialization that occurs in most other occupations is primarily, or even exclusively, of an informal character. As we have seen, even in those occupations discussed above, a great deal of informal socialization takes place both during the formal training period and after it is over and the actual career is begun. For most occupations, informal socialization is the norm. For example, while skilled craftsmen receive some formal training in the classroom, most of their socialization occurs informally on the job during a lengthy apprenticeship program. With reference to the latter, Riemer, in his study of 195 construction electrician apprentices, shows how on-the-job socialization processes involve the adoption of specific brand-name tools, a particular costume (such as a hard hat), as well as jargon peculiar to the electrical trade.[80] Metz has shown how ambulance workers, emergency medical technicians, get relatively little formal socialization (the standard course involves 81 hours of class work, 10 hours of clinical experience, and study time), and that in many ways the most important socialization takes place informally on the job.[81]

For most other occupations, socialization is exclusively an informal process. Included here are such varied occupations as assembly-line workers, laborers, taxi drivers, and prostitutes. In their study of western Kentucky coal miners, Vaught and Smith show how informal socialization processes are used to develop in the novice a sense of mechanical solidarity that requires the worker to subordinate his or her will to that of the group thereby ensuring the safety of the group.[82] Although we could discuss a large number of different types of occupations in this section, we have chosen to focus on informal socialization in that most interesting category, deviant occupations.

Although the specific skills that are needed for success within deviant occupations are typically different from the skills required for other occupations, it is a mistake to assume that all deviant occupations require few or no high-level skills. As with conventional occupations, deviant occupations can be ranked along a continuum in terms of the number, type, and sophistication of the skills and knowledge that are required for success. The status hierarchies that make up many deviant occupations are often based on the differential possession of skills among occupational members.

As with conventional occupations, deviant occupations vary in the types of skills that are emphasized. Some, such as safecracking, involve a relatively isolated work setting in which the person does not have to deal directly with

[79]This section on deviant occupations was written primarily by Gale Miller. For more on this see, Gale Miller, *Odd Jobs: The World of Deviant Work* (Englewood Cliffs, NJ: Prentice-Hall, Inc., 1978).

[80]Jeffrey W. Riemer, "Becoming a Journeyman Electrician: Some Implicit Indicators in the Apprenticeship Process," *Sociology of Work and Occupations*, 4 (1977), 87–98.

[81]Donald Metz, *Running Hot: Structure and Stress in Ambulance Work* (Cambridge, MA: Abt Books, 1981).

[82]Charles Vaught and David L. Smith, "Incorporation and Mechanical Solidarity in the Underground Coal Mine," *Sociology of Work and Occupations*, 7 (1980), 159–187.

outsiders. In this case, the emphasis is placed on the development of a high level of skill and knowledge about the technical aspects of the work process. In other cases, deviant occupations involve the manipulation of situations and persons, and in these occupations the emphasis is on the development of social, or interpersonal, skills. It should be noted that most deviant occupations require the effective use of both social and technical skills, but the nature of the occupational activities often make one type of skill more important than the other.

A related aspect of deviant occupations is the process through which the appropriate skills are acquired. Although few involve a formal training process, most are characterized by standardized patterns of socialization. Within the worlds of deviant occupations there are three general and interrelated training processes. First, there is a type of on-the-job training in which novices learn their jobs by doing them. Very often this training procedure is characteristic of the least skilled deviant occupations, but it may be found in more highly skilled deviant occupations as well. A second training process is characterized by an adaptation of the apprentice-master relationship in which novices are instructed by experienced members of the occupation within the occupational setting. In this case, novices enter the occupation through the efforts and teachings of sponsors. Finally, there is a form of training in which novices learn their occupational skills while outside the work setting. Perhaps the best-known example of this type of training is the criminal instruction that takes place within prisons. In other cases, however, deviant occupational skills may be learned through involvement in different but related occupations or through nonoccupational activities. As the training process continues, several or all of these training procedures may be combined, but the initial training is typically concentrated around only one of the three training procedures.

Taxi-dancers.   Highly popular in the 1920s and 1930s, taxi-dancing is again gaining attention in some U.S. cities.[83] Taxi-dancers are female dancers who provide companionship for their male clientele.

In their research, Hong and Duff were interested in studying the *neutralization techniques,* that is, the rationalizations, taxi-dancers use to cope with some of the unpleasant aspects of their jobs. Most of these techniques are learned during the informal socialization processes that occur on the job.

During the first week on the job, the taxi-dancer can easily find her job stressful and depressing. Most suffer anxiety or stress as a result of customers expecting more romantic or sexual involvement than the dancer is employed to provide. In addition, age, race, and cultural differences with the clientele compound the hostess's anxieties and doubts.

According to Hong and Duff, it is after these initial negative interactions that management takes the first steps toward socializing the taxi-dancer in neutralization techniques. At this stage, the intrinsic rewards of the job are highlighted: "She is informed that her job is like 'a social worker or a counselor' trying to help these 'lonely men who are far away from home' or 'who

[83]Lawrence K. Hong and Robert W. Duff, "Becoming a Taxi-Dancer: The Significance of Neutralization in a Semi-Deviant Occupation," *Sociology of Work and Occupations,* 4 (1977), 327–342.

are unhappy with their wives.'"[84] When the dancers are not busy, they sit around in informal gatherings. It is during these gatherings that the new dancers are informally socialized in additional neutralization techniques. These techniques are used to soothe guilt feelings, resolve moral dilemmas, and reduce the stress and anxiety created in interactions with clients. For example, an experienced hostess used the following technique to help reduce the guilt feelings of a novice who thought she was leading her clients on:

> They deserve it. I don't care. All they want is to get you to bed with them. This guy dances with me all the time, and asks me to go to breakfast with him after work. I know what he wants, but he is not going to get anything from me.[85]

Many such neutralization techniques are learned on the job and they are an important part of learning to cope with work that is not necessarily accepted by the dominant culture.

Male strippers. While there is some anticipatory socialization prior to entering the job, most male strippers learn what they need to know informally on the job.[86] Most work skills are learned through conversations and observations. Among these skills are "the appropriate way to remove one's clothes, how to wear a G-string properly, and various tips about grooming and other factors in presenting oneself to the audience."[87] They learn how to maximize their attractiveness and provocativeness since tips, which are ordinarily placed in the dancers' G-strings, are an important source of their income.

The male strippers also are informally socialized into the occupational code of ethics relating to relationships with the employing organization, customers, and fellow dancers. For example, strippers learn the importance of coming to work on time, not allowing "audience members to touch their genitals,"[88] and not to copy the acts or dress of fellow dancers.

Male (homosexual) prostitution. The male homosexual who works in the male house of prostitution[89] has two distinguishing occupational features: an extremely short career (usually 3 years or less) and the lack of any formal training program for novices.[90] The basis for these distinctive features is the extreme emphasis placed by clients on youth and physical attractiveness. Because this emphasis is basic to occupational success, most male prostitutes tend to be young and attractive. Within this group, however, those persons who are newest to the occupation tend to be most successful because the clients are continually looking for new and different sexual partners. Pittman notes, for

[84]Ibid., 332.

[85]Ibid., 335.

[86]Paula L. Dressel and David M. Peterson, " Becoming a Male Stripper: Recruitment, Socialization and Ideological Development," *Work and Occupations*, 9 (1982), 387–406.

[87]Ibid., 398.

[88]Ibid., 399.

[89]Charles Winick and Paul M. Kinsie, *The Lively Commerce: Prostitution in the United States* (New York: Signet, 1971).

[90]David J. Pittman, "The Male House of Prostitution," *Transaction*, 8 (1971), 21–27.

example, that the new male prostitute may receive as many as seven calls during a 24-hour period, but this initial success is short-lived, usually ceasing after a few weeks.

The significant skills that are necessary for success in male prostitution are few and simple; initial socialization is limited to a few grooming techniques and rules about the nature of the prostitute-client relationship as well as relationships among the prostitutes. It is presumed that the male prostitute already possesses the necessary technical skills and knowledge.

Female prostitutes.   While limited on-the-job training is characteristic of male prostitutes, female prostitutes are likely to be trained in some form of apprentice system.

There are two general career lines for prostitutes: (1) that of the streetwalker, who solicits in houses of prostitution, bars, hotel lobbies, on the street and the like, and (2) that of the call girl (or party girl), who cultivates a more select and regular clientele. Although the skills involved in either type are not highly sophisticated, each involves an apprenticeship training program.

The training of the streetwalker usually involves a pimp and, less frequently, another prostitute or a madam.[91] The pimp first teaches the novice prostitute some of the technical skills that are useful in the occupation; however, most of the technical and social skills that are required are learned on the job. It is usually the pimp, for example, who teaches the novice how to check customers for venereal disease, to get them to wear condoms, and so on.[92] Gray notes, for example, that only about one-third of the streetwalkers in her sample were taught such important skills "as watching for cops, guarding against pregnancy, picking up customers, or locating trick houses."[93] Even the most basic types of sexual acts continually requested by customers are not taught to the novice prostitute by her pimp. She must already have acquired such knowledge or must learn these skills from her customers.

Not all pimps choose to train their own prostitutes; some use the services of others. An example of such an arrangement is the house of prostitution described by Barbara Heyl.[94] The house is operated by Ann who has been involved in prostitution for over twenty years. Ann's house is somewhat unique because it is exclusively staffed by new prostitutes in training and, although some of the women are independent, many of them have been sent by their

[91]A pimp is technically defined as a man who solicits for female prostitutes. This definition is somewhat deceiving because many contemporary pimps do not solicit; pimp is more often used as a synonym for "player"—meaning a man who is able to move easily in many different social circles and is able to manipulate the settings and the persons in them to his advantage. Thus, the modern pimp is more accurately a player who is involved with a prostitute. See Christian Milner and Richard Milner, *Black Players: The Secret Life of Black Pimps* (New York: Bantam Books, Inc., 1973).

[92]Diana Gray, "Turning-Out: A Study of Teenage Prostitution," *Urban Life and Culture*, 1 (1973), 401–425. Trick houses are places where the prostitute can take her customer to consummate their arrangement. Very often the trick house is a hotel in a central district of a large city, although it can be any other "safe place."

[93]Ibid., 413.

[94]Barbara Sherman Heyl, "The Madam as Entrepreneur," *Sociological Symposium*, 11 (1974), 62–81; "The Madam as Teacher," *Social Problems*, 24 (1977), 545–555; *The Madam as Entrepreneur* (New Brunswick, NJ: Transaction Books, 1979).

pimps. The training period usually takes two to three months, and it ends whenever the woman and her pimp decide that she is ready to work on her own. The decision is often difficult because Ann is dependent on the earnings of her trainees and often attempts to keep her women working within the house as long as possible.

While in the employ of Ann, the women receive considerable instruction in the techniques of prostitution. Not only are they taught the most important sex acts that they will be required to perform, but Ann observes their performances during the early phases of the training period. The women are also taught how to protect themselves from physical abuse by customers and how to "hustle" their customers—that is, how to talk the customer into a more expensive sex act than he initially desired. Finally, the women are taught basic rules. The most important rules are loyalty to one's pimp, fairness with other prostitutes in the house, and honesty with Ann. Unlike the training process directed by pimps, then, Ann's house is an organized training center where on-the-job experience is supplemented with formal instruction. The effectiveness of Ann's operation is reflected in the number of pimps who send their prostitutes back for periodic "refresher courses."

A somewhat different training process characterizes the career of the call girl or party girl.[95] Typically, the call girl is trained through a more elaborate apprenticeship process. As with most streetwalkers, most of the technical skills that are required by the occupation are not directly taught; rather, the mentor concentrates on the teaching of the social skills involved in the call girl-customer relationship and the communication of subcultural values. Although there is a greater emphasis on social skills in training the call girl as opposed to the streetwalker, these skills can be learned relatively quickly and easily. The primary social skills taught center around the proper ways to interact with the customer (both face-to-face and over the telephone) and how to manipulate the situation so that the customer does not cheat or physically harm the call girl.

Most of the call girl's training is centered in the communication of the values of the subculture. The novice is taught that she should pursue her interests over the interests of "squares," that she should be loyal to her pimp, that she should be fair to other call girls, that she should not become emotionally involved with customers, and that all men are corrupt and should be exploited with no sense of guilt. Although these values are stressed in the training process, it does not appear that they are taken seriously by most of the novices. Bryan notes, for example, that the ultimate break-up of the novice and her mentor is often based on mutual suspicions about the other party not being fair in their relationship. Further evidence for the limited significance of the values taught in the training process is found in a later study of Bryan's in which he discovered that call girls do sometimes become emotionally involved with their regular customers, and this is a clear violation of the value code.[96]

[95]James H. Bryan, "Apprenticeships in Prostitution," *Social Problems,* 12 (1965), 287–297.

[96]James H. Bryan, "Occupational Ideologies and Individual Attitudes of Call Girls," *Social Problems,* 13 (1966), 441–450.

It may appear, then, that the training process of call girls provides few benefits for either the novice or the sponsor. There are, however, two benefits, although neither is explicitly a part of the training process. If the sponsor has a large clientele that she cannot service by herself, it is to her advantage to bring in a novice to help. The novice is an especially appealing partner because she must pay a percentage of her earnings to her trainer in exchange for her training. Thus, the sponsor solves her problem without a loss of income. For the novice, the primary advantage is the chance to build a clientele that she can take with her when she leaves the sponsor. Because the call girl does not solicit on the street or in other public places, it is necessary that she locate and build a clientele in a more indirect manner. The training period provides her with such an opportunity and after she has built a sufficient clientele, usually in 2 or 3 months, she leaves the sponsor.

The third type of training in deviant occupations occurs when the initial socialization takes place outside the work setting and is then applied and refined when the individual enters the work setting. One example of this type of occupational training is found in the prison and reformatory.

Professional criminals.   Entry into the occupations of professional crime and bank robbery typically involves two stages of progressive criminal activity and commitment. The first stage is involvement in juvenile delinquency. This stage is important because it provides the individual with many of the basic skills and values of the criminal world. The skills involved in delinquency are usually unsophisticated and the delinquent often treats his criminal activities as adventures that are unrelated to his future occupational goals. Many teenagers never go beyond this stage, but those who do may become occupationally committed to safecracking or bank robbery and these people experience a second stage of occupational involvement—the reformatory stage.

During incarceration in a reformatory, the previously "uncommitted" juvenile delinquents are presented with a type of training in criminal activity that is not formalized, nor does it involve a mentor. They can learn techniques and values that may later form the basis for an occupational commitment. Letkemann suggests that the reformatory, and later the prison, operate to create a situation of "career crystallization" in which individuals begin to assess their occupational futures in terms of their previous experiences, their present criminal skills, and their chances in the noncriminal world.[97]

Upon release from the reformatory, the occupationally oriented criminals may attempt to put these newly learned criminal skills to use. If they are successful, they are likely to become involved with other persons who are also committed to crime as an occupation. Through these associations they learn more about the skills required for success and the values of the world they have joined. If they are unsuccessful in their initial criminal attempts, they are likely to be sent to prison, where they receive further informal instruction about their occupation. Thus, occupational entry and commitment evolve through a process of increasing involvement in the world of crime. As Letkemann notes:

[97]Peter Letkemann, *Crime as Work* (Englewood Cliffs, NJ: Prentice-Hall, 1973).

Respondents suggested that on-the-job training or apprenticeship is unusual. More common is a gradual progression, beginning with awkward juvenile efforts, refined by prison experience, and followed by trial and error combined with informal, intermittent advice from the more experienced.[98]

The skills that must be learned in order to participate in criminal activity are varied in both their content and their degree of sophistication. In the case of safecrackers, their skills are primarily of a technical nature and involve a high degree of knowledge about the physical principles on which safes are constructed. Bank robbers, on the other hand, tend to be more skilled at manipulating social settings to their advantage. As Letkemann notes, most bank robbers have only a rudimentary knowledge of the physical layouts of banks and of the principles of alarm systems; rather, they rely on surprise and speed in completing their task. Thus, bank robbers must be able to manipulate both bank personnel and other victims in an attempt to complete the robbery in a minimum amount of time.

In this section, we have examined a wide range of socialization processes. We have discussed the informal processes found in formal training programs in various professional and semiprofessional occupations. We then analyzed the formal aspects involved in the training of military and police cadets. Finally, we discussed the entirely informal training processes found in deviant occupations. Once people have undergone some type of training, they are often ready to begin the process of searching for a job. It is to this that we now turn.

JOB SEARCH

For some, searching for a job may be encompassed by the training program. Thus, when a prostitute or an assembly-line worker completes the training program, she or he is already in the job and no search is necessary. In such cases job search really occurs before the training program. In most other cases job search is undertaken after the training program is completed.

What is involved in the process of searching for a job? The answer, of course, depends on the nature of the occupation being sought. Looking for jobs as a lawyer, a personnel manager, a laborer, or a pimp clearly involve very different steps. For most occupations, however, a variety of formal steps may be taken. Individuals can go to an employment agency, or to the personnel offices of the various organizations that have the kind of work sought. They can reply to a public notice or an advertisement in the newspaper. Those who seek an occupation—usually a skilled craft—in which the union does the hiring would probably go to the union hiring hall. These, and many other formal devices, are open to the person in search of work.

However, one of the consistent findings in the study of work is that people in a wide array of occupations are more likely to use informal, rather than formal, means in searching for a job. For some occupations, such as the deviant occupations discussed earlier, there simply are no formal means available.

[98]Ibid., p. 134.

Among the informal means of job search most often used are the reliance on contacts through family, friends, or acquaintances.

A number of studies indicate that blue-collar workers,[99] skilled craftspeople,[100] and professionals[101] all rely on informal personal contacts in finding their jobs. Corcoran, Datcher, and Duncan[102] studied the role informal personal contacts played in finding jobs among 3,759 black and white men and women representing all major occupational categories. Nearly 50 percent of all workers in this study heard about their current job through personal contacts, friends, or relatives. Further, about the same percentage knew of someone employed by their current employer before they were hired. Professional workers and workers with college and advanced degrees were the least likely to use personal contacts, friends, or relatives in finding their current job.

One might think that reliance on informal rather than formal means of job search would lead to inefficiency in the process. But again, various studies have pointed in the opposite direction. Graves found informal contact networks to be very effective in the pipeline industry, where people are usually needed quickly for short-term jobs. In such a setting it would clearly be impossible to rely on more formal and more cumbersome methods of job search. Similarly, in a wide-ranging study of job-search behavior, Reid concludes that those using informal job-search methods "were no worse off in terms of frictional unemployment, wages or job preference" than those using formal methods.[103] Granovetter found that professionals, technicians, and managers obtain better jobs through personal contacts than through more formal methods.[104] Among other things, they were more likely to be highly satisfied with their work and to earn high salaries when they found their positions through personal contacts.

Although informal job-search methods seem to work well in various settings, we must not overlook the fact that they tend to be discriminatory. Those who have the contacts are more likely to find jobs than those who don't, and those who lack contacts are the ones who, in our society, are most often discriminated against because of sex, race, age, or religion. However, contrary to expectations, Corcoran, Datcher, and Duncan found that white men were *not* more likely than black men to have heard about their current job from a friend, relative, or the like. On the other hand, women, both black and white, *were* less likely than either group of men to have used such informal contacts.[105]

[99]Graham Reid, "Job Search and the Effectiveness of Job-Finding Methods," *Industrial and Labor Relations Review,* 25 (1972), 479–495.

[100]Bennie Graves, "Particularism, Exchange and Organizational Efficiency: A Case Study of a Construction Industry," *Social Forces,* 49 (1970), 72–81.

[101]Theodore Caplow and Reece McGee, *The Academic Marketplace* (New York: Basic Books, 1958); Mark S. Granovetter, *Getting a Job: A Study of Contacts and Careers* (Cambridge, MA: Harvard University Press, 1974); Stephen O. Murray, Joseph H. Rankin, and Dennis W. Magill, "Strong Ties and Job Information," *Sociology of Work and Occupations,* 8 (1981), 119–136.

[102]Mary Corcoran, Linda Datcher, and Greg J. Duncan, "Most Workers Find Jobs Through Word of Mouth," *Monthly Labor Review* (1980), 33–35.

[103]Reid, "Job Search," 493.

[104]Granovetter, *Getting a Job.*

[105]Corcoran, Datcher and Duncan, "Most Workers Find Jobs Through Word of Mouth."

When we are discussing job search we are looking at the interface between potential employer and employee, but from the point of view of the employee. Now we turn to the employer's side and the recruiting devices used to locate potential employees.

RECRUITMENT

As defined by Glaser, recruitment "is a process of screening, wooing, and eliminating before the career actually starts."[106] The elaborateness of the recruiting procedure depends upon the status of the occupation. Organizations seeking those in high-status occupations (lawyers, college professors) employ far more complex procedures than those used to recruit individuals in lower-status occupations (assembly-line workers, janitors). In part, this is due to the high demand and low supply of professionals. In addition, an organization can live with poor choices at its lower levels because mistakes there are unlikely to upset the entire organization. An error in the hiring of high-status people, however, is likely to have enormous repercussions throughout the organization. Finally, it costs the organization so much to train a professional that is is likely to be very careful who it recruits, and it is much more difficult to fire a professional than it is to fire a low-status employee. This is due to the investment in training costs and the difficulty in finding a qualified replacement.

In an attempt to fill a research gap in this area, Breaugh[107] studied biology and chemistry research scientists to establish which sources of recruitment were most strongly related to job performance, absenteeism, and work attitudes. Four sources of recruitment were analyzed: college placement offices, advertisements in professional journals and at conventions, newspaper advertisements, and self-initiative. Overall, those recruited from journal/convention advertisements and self-initiated contacts proved to be better employees than those recruited from the other two sources. These employees also proved to be more dependable. Recruits from journal/convention advertisements were most satisfied with their jobs and relations with their supervisors, while college placement recruits were least satisfied with their jobs. Employees recruited through newspaper advertisements were about twice as likely to be absent from work than any other type of recruit. Breaugh concludes that the recruits from journal/convention advertisements and self-initiated contacts are better and more satisfied employees because of the more accurate and complete information that was available to them compared with the amount and type of information available through newspaper and college placement sources.

In the next few pages we will discuss the recruiting of professionals and managers, since it is in these high-status occupations that the most elaborate forms of recruitment are employed.

---

[106]Barney G. Glaser, ed., *Organizational Careers: A Sourcebook for Theory* (Chicago: Aldine, 1968), p. 56.

[107]James A. Breaugh, "Relationships Between Recruiting Sources and Employee Performance, Absenteeism, and Work Attitudes," *Academy of Management Journal*, 24 (1981), 142–147.

College professors.   To understand the process of academic recruitment, some basic facts of academic life need to be clarified. Following Caplow and McGee, we can divide universities into three broad types—major universities (for example, Harvard, Michigan), minor universities (including most state universities and some private universities), and academic Siberia (all the rest of the universities, colleges, junior and community colleges).[108] Although this tripartite differentiation is simple enough, it is complicated by the fact that departments within universities vary in terms of their prestige. Thus, one can find major departments in minor universities and minor departments in major universities. Although there are a few exceptions, schools in the Siberia category are likely to be homogenous; that is, all of their departments are likely to be of rather low prestige.

We can broadly divide academic recruitment into two types. The first is the process involved in recruiting new, assistant professors from the ranks of those just finishing their graduate training. The second is the recruiting of already established academicians from other universities, usually for positions at the rank of associate or full professor.

Although there are differences in the two types of recruiting, a characteristic that applies to virtually all types in major and minor universities, and even some in the Siberia category, is the elaborateness of the recruiting process.

> The average salary of an assistant professor is approximately that of a bakery truck driver, and his occupancy of a job is likely to be less permanent. Yet it may require a large part of the time of twenty highly skilled men for a full year to hire him.[109]

In part, the great effort expended in recruiting academicians can be explained by the significant role they play in society and the great responsibility they have in educating young people. Beyond this, elaborate recruiting has become an expected part of the academic subculture and academicians are often very fond of the opportunity to make free trips to distant universities, have cocktail parties given in their honor, and have considerable attention showered on them over the course of a normal two-day recruiting trip.

Whether the candidate is a new Ph.D., or an established professor at another university, the recruiting process takes the same general form once the candidates have been narrowed to those who will be invited to campus for a visit. These visits are fairly expensive, especially when the university decides to examine several candidates. Before the visit letters of recommendation are solicited from professors who are familiar with the recruit. Such references are considered one piece of evidence and are rarely in themselves sufficient to cause acceptance or rejection. Once on the scene, the applicant generally meets individually with most members of the department. In these interviews the main topic of conversation is past and present research as well as future research plans. Although these interviews are primarily for the members of the recruiting department, they also serve to pass on information about the

[108]Caplow and McGee, *The Academic Marketplace.*
[109]Ibid., p. 97.

members of the department that can help recruits make a decision if they are offered a job. A seminar may be required in which recruits are asked to make a presentation to the faculty and graduate students; this presentation yields some insight into teaching ability. A party is also part of the typical recruiting visit, with the faculty and applicant given a chance to evaluate each other socially. Finally, the recruit frequently meets with the dean, who often has veto power over the recruiting department's choice. (Sometimes a visit with the dean is a formality devoted primarily to discussing the fringe benefits offered by the university.) At the completion of this process the recruiting department theoretically has all the information it needs to make a decision. Once all applicants have been seen, a departmental meeting is held in which the final choice is made. In general, those faculty members at or above the rank of the opening will vote. The applicant receiving the most votes will be offered the position. After the offer has been made, applicants are given a limited period of time to make a decision. If one refuses, the offer may be made to the second choice, or a new group of applicants may be brought in for interviews.

Until the 1970s academic recruiting was, especially for higher-level positions (associate and full professor) in major universities, a closed and informal process. Jobs were rarely, if ever, publicly announced. Instead, discreet feelers were sent out by ranking members of the department doing the recruiting to their peers in similar ranking departments that were considered suitable training grounds.

However, the informal practices of the major and minor universities have, at least on the surface, been radically altered by the recent pressure from minority groups like females, blacks, and Chicanos. Consequently, today there is more use of the formal recruiting processes long used by lesser universities. Now one is likely to see job openings at elite institutions like Harvard publicly announced, advertised and job applicants screened through more formal interview practices.

In many ways this change is more apparent than real. In the end the positions are often still filled by those with informal contacts in the recruiting department. Informal recruiting procedures now exist side by side with the new formal practices. Nevertheless, the form, if not the substance, of academic recruitment has been radically altered in recent years, particularly in the major universities.[110]

Despite the time and energy expended, academic recruiting is not totally rational. On the surface such factors as publications, teaching ability, and letters of recommendation would seem to be of utmost importance. However, letters of recommendation are rarely crucial, and they often focus on such irrelevant factors as appearance, friendliness, degree of conformity, and qualities of the spouse.[111] Little attention is paid to teaching ability. Publications are considered to be of central importance, especially at major universities. Para-

[110]This discussion is loosely based on Caplow and McGee's *The Academic Marketplace*, but much has changed since they did their research. Confirmation of at least some of their positions can be found in Diana Crane, "The Academic Marketplace Revisited: A Study of Faculty Mobility Using the Cartter Ratings," *American Journal of Sociology*, 75 (1970), 953–964.

[111]Lionel Lewis, "The University and the Professional Model," in Eliot Freidson, ed., *Professions and Their Prospects* (Beverly Hills, CA: Sage Publications, 1973), pp. 267–288.

doxically, however, publications of a recruit are rarely read by the members of the recruiting department, because people "are hired for their repute, and not for what the repute is based upon."[112] The quality of the publications is often not crucial; rather, of central importance is where the publications appeared. In effect, the department often hires the person it feels will most enhance its reputation in the eyes of the discipline.

Wall street lawyers.   In many ways the recruiting of Wall Street lawyers resembles academic recruitment,[113] especially in the elaborateness of the process. Wall Street firms strive, before beginning active recruitment, to create a favorable image among law students. They use alumni in their employ and brochures to set the stage for their visits to campuses. The active stage of the process begins when representatives of the firm visit law schools. In the Wall Street firms, the high-status partners frequently perform this function. University placement officials arrange for interviews with interested students.

The firm pays the travel expenses of law students invited for an interview and sometimes entertainment expenses. During their visit, law students are interviewed by many of the important figures in the firm. Those who ultimately receive offers often have influence or contacts within the firm. Part of the explanation for the elaborate recruiting procedure lies in the high income of starting lawyers in major firms. Other factors include the supply of and demand for top-flight young lawyers, sensitivity of the position they will occupy, the expense involved in training, and the difficulty in firing lawyers who don't work out.

Business executives.   For many of the same reasons that organizations use complex procedures in recruiting professionals, they also employ involved procedures in hiring managers and officials.[114] Industry recruitment is so active on university campuses that it has had a profound effect on the structure of the university, the curriculum, and the student. Universities have adjusted a large part of their curriculum to mesh with industry by instituting many courses that provide students with skills and knowledge they will need when they enter the workworld. By the same token, industry has striven to adjust itself to the university by making the first few years of organizational life little more than an extension of academia.

Although industry has pervaded much of academia, its most profound influence has been in the business schools. The number of students majoring in business has risen markedly. By 1955 business majors "had become the largest single undergraduate group,"[115] and as of 1982, more students were still enrolled in business and commerce than any other major field of study. Almost 24 percent (about 2.6 million) of the nearly 11 million students enrolled in college were in business and commerce. In fact, about twice as many

[112]Caplow and McGee, *Academic Marketplace,* p. 110.

[113]Erwin Smigel, *The Wall Street Lawyer* (Bloomington: Indiana University Press, 1969).

[114]There are some important exceptions to the above generalization. In voluntary organizations in particular, an official position frequently goes to the most interested individual, with little or no recruiting involved. For example, the position of local union president often goes to the person who is most active in the organization. Frequently, an individual interested in the presidency is unopposed because there is no one else in the union who wants the position.

[115]William H. Whyte, Jr., *Organization Man* (NY: Anchor Books, 1957), p. 93.

students were enrolled in business programs than in each of its nearest competitors, health and engineering.[116] Added to this has been the proliferation of graduate schools of business administration, many of which offer M.B.A.s and Ph.D.'s. In recruiting future managers, industry focuses its attention on the graduates of these programs.

In most universities the recruiting season lasts for virtually the entire year. There is a constant procession of potential employers through the placement center. Preceding them is a barrage of advertisements on the center's walls and in the college newspaper. When the recruiters appear on campus, the real action begins. Prior to their visits, recruiters have often checked with faculty and placement officers for suitable candidates for their organization. Frequently they are alumni of the university they visit, with contacts among the administration, the faculty, and the students. The actual recruiting interview usually takes about a half an hour, with both parties feeling each other out. If the interviewer is impressed, the recruit is invited for a visit to the company, mainly for a series of interviews with company officials. Many companies also insist on a battery of tests to be sure the recruit is the type of individual who will fit into the company and the specific department. After the recruit has left, a meeting is held in which the results of the interviews and tests are evaluated. Should the recruit be considered acceptable, a job offer is made.

The recruiting process does not end with the hiring of an individual. In many cases the first few years on the job are seen as an extension of the recruiting process. Many companies have formal training programs for recruits who are potential managers, and these programs perform a variety of functions. They allow the company to assess the potential of their new acquisition under circumstances that pose no threat to the organization if that person should fail. Many recruits are in reality not hired until they have successfully negotiated the trials of the training program. These training programs are similar in many ways to university life and they therefore serve to ease the transition from university to industry. Some organizations have a separate "campus" on which the recruits receive their training before they are allowed in the "real" world of industrial life. Another function of the training period is to allow recruits to get some exposure to various areas of industrial life. They are frequently given a series of different assignments, and they rotate among these positions during their training period. Only after they have "graduated" from such training programs (and some organizations even give diplomas) can we say that they have completed the recruiting process.

CONCLUSIONS

In this chapter we have examined some of the major aspects of the stages prior to an occupational career. We began with the assumption that an individual had made at least a provisional occupational choice. We then looked at some of the ways in which an individual is socialized into an occupation. These

---

[116]U.S. Bureau of the Census, *Statistical Abstract of the United States: 1984*, 104th ed. (Washington, D.C., 1983), p. 162.

methods can range from the highly elaborate formal programs (such as medical school) to on-the-job instruction of little more than a few minutes (for example, a streetwalker). We examined the nature of formal programs, the informal processes that develop within them, as well as the almost totally informal socialization of those in deviant occupations.

Once socialized, an individual must often search for a job, although some jobs are obtained at the time one is socialized into them. Our overriding conclusion on the issue of job search is that it is more often successful through informal, personal contacts than through formal means, such as placement services or newspaper advertisements. Finally, we looked at some of the recruiting practices used by employers in search of employees. The end of this process of socialization, search, and recruitment is, for most, the beginning of an occupational career. In the next chapter we pick up this discussion with an analysis of the patterns that careers typically take once one has entered the workworld.

SEVEN
INDIVIDUAL CHANGE:
LABOR MARKETS,
CAREER PATTERNS,
AND RETIREMENT

In this chapter we pick up the discussion of the individual career with an analysis of the various types of career patterns associated with some of the major types of occupations. Some of the key sociological concepts needed to understand these career patterns will be investigated—sponsorship, career contingencies, demotion, reality shock, and others. Although these concepts will typically be discussed in the context of a particular type of occupation, they are clearly applicable to the analysis of career patterns in all types of occupations. In addition, we will introduce the major similarities and differences in the career patterns associated with a wide range of occupational types. There will be discussions of occupations of different statuses, each of which is typified by specific career patterns. Some of these offer the individual the possibility of a great deal of mobility: others, particularly middle-level and semi- and unskilled occupations, offer much less mobility to the individual.

For some, the first job will be the beginning of a long career in that occupation. Others will move from job to job until they find the one they like, or until they are forced by personal or family responsibilities to remain in one that is less than they hoped for. Some never find a career and spend their lives hopping from job to job, or in and out of the labor market. Our concern in this chapter is the career patterns that confront individuals once they have settled on an occupation, either by choice or coercion, or some combination of the two.

Before discussing the career patterns of some specific occupations, it is important that we introduce the reader to the structure of the labor market within which careers occur—specifically, the idea of *labor market segmentation.*

LABOR MARKET SEGMENTATION

Peter Blau and Otis Duncan[1] were instrumental in initially assessing what variables influenced an individual's occupational (status) attainment. They analyzed the effects of four individual variables on occupational attainment. Father's educational and occupational attainment as well as the respondent's educational attainment and entry-level occupation were found to influence the individual's ultimate occupational attainment. Shortly after this pathbreaking analysis, William Sewell et al.[2] added several important psychological and social-psychological variables to Blau and Duncan's original model. Sewell agreed with Blau and Duncan that one's family status (education/occupation) could certainly affect an individual's educational attainment, which in turn could affect one's initial and ultimate occupational status and income. However, an individual's educational and/or occupational aspirations might also intervene and hence should also be considered. Sewell also included the influence of significant others in his analysis. In Sewell's more refined model, not only are family background and individual attainment variables important, but so also are individual psychological motivations, desires, aspirations, and the like.

These *status attainment* models assume a homogeneous labor market wherein all jobs are open to anyone possessing the requisite skills, ability, knowledge, and so on. Motivation is important, and it is implied that anyone having the desire to secure the requisite skills can achieve the highest occupational status. Wages are influenced by competitive supply-and-demand market characteristics. Individual achievements will lead to a similar return in wages. Those who receive poverty wages do so because of their inadequate personal resources. Job instability and/or immobility is the result of a low commitment to work or low motivation to achieve. Hence, occupational rewards are distributed through individual achievement. Hard work and individual striving are important: but while inequality of outcome is the result, it is equality of opportunity that is emphasized.

Although most analysts have long recognized the importance of individual characteristics in the achievement of a particular income or occupational status, only recently has widespread attention become focused on more structural, macro-level variables. Many terms have been used to describe this particular structural emphasis and those concerned with it. We will follow Baron and Bielby[3] and refer to this new style of thought as the *new structuralism* and those advocating it as the *new structuralists.*

In general, the new structuralists agree that individual-level attributes

[1]Peter Blau and Otis Dudley Duncan, *The American Occupational Structure* (New York: John Wiley & Sons, 1967).

[2]William Sewell, Archibald Haller and Alejandro Portes, "The Educational and Early Occupational Attainment Process," *American Sociological Review,* 34 (1969), 82-92.

[3]James N. Baron and William T. Bielby, "Bringing the Firms Back In: Stratification, Segmentation, and the Organization of Work," *American Sociological Review,* 45 (1980), 737–765.

are *not* the only variables important in considering occupational attainment. To understand occupational and wage attainment, career advancement, mobility, promotion potential, and so forth, we must locate the worker in a particular structure that is located in a particular sector of an ever-changing economy. Supraindividual characteristics are considered to have important mediating effects on both individual attributes and psychological variables. Career advancement is conditioned by the structural organization of society, which includes national economic, industrial sector, and organizational variables.

What emerges from this conceptualization is the idea that there is more than one homogeneous labor market within which individuals are employed. Further, there are differential consequences for the workers depending on which sector of the labor market they are in.

One major theoretical perspective advocated by some of the new structuralists is the *dual labor market* approach. The dual labor market theorists suggest that the labor market is divided either by structural-level entry barriers;[4] by race, sex, and age;[5] or by occupations[6] themselves.

Focusing on occupations, Piore divides the labor market into two sectors—primary and secondary. The *primary labor market* is subdivided into upper and lower tiers with the professional and technical as well as the managerial and administrative groups belonging to the upper tier, and sales, clerical, and skilled crafts comprising the lower tier. The *secondary labor market* is made up of semiskilled and unskilled nonfarm laborers and service workers.

The upper tier of the primary labor market consists of occupations that are supposed to have a generalized and diffuse body of knowledge and to be more creative and less routinized than most other jobs. Occupations in the upper tier are typically highly rewarded. Because of a highly developed internal labor market (a point we will return to shortly), the workers in the primary market often experience more job security and better opportunities for career advancement. The occupations in the secondary labor market do not pay as much as positions in the primary sector and are more routinized. Further, because of low employer investment in updating worker skills and knowledge, the occupations in the secondary labor market offer little opportunity for career development. Finally, because of the differences in skills and knowledge required by the occupations in the various markets, little mobility occurs between the secondary and primary labor markets. Hence, two labor markets exist and it is important to know where individuals and their occupations are located if we are to understand career development (and many other things as well).

A more recent, and we think more fruitful, way of conceptualizing the structural duality of labor markets is to consider the organizational and/or in-

---

[4]Clark Kerr, "The Balkanization of the Labor Markets," in E.W. Bakke et al., eds., *Labor Mobility and Economic Opportunity* (New York: John Wiley & Sons, 1954), pp. 92–110.

[5]Peter B. Doeringer and Michael J. Piore, *Internal Labor Markets and Manpower Analysis* (Lexington, MA: D.C. Heath, 1971).

[6]Michael J. Piore, "The Dual Labor Market: Theory and Implications," in David M. Gordon, ed., *Problems in Political Economy: An Urban Perspective* (Lexington, MA: D.C. Heath, 1971), pp. 90–94.

dustrial sector of the economy within which a worker is employed. Various economists[7] and sociologists[8] argue that there are two industrial sectors. *Core* (or monopoly, oligopoly) and *periphery* (or competitive) are the terms used most frequently to describe the two major industrial sectors of the economy. (Recently, Hodson has offered empirical evidence to justify differentiating among three industrial sectors—monopoly, regional, and local.[9])

A similar differentiation is made at the company level of analysis.[10] Companies, like industries, can be in either the core or peripheral sector of the economy. (If a tripartite model is preferred, a company can be in the monopolistic, regional, or local sector of the economy.)

In sociology there is disagreement over the number of industrial sectors as well as over the number and types of variables that should be used to differentiate among sectors. As a result, many different schemes have been offered.[11] There are some variables, however, that are frequently used to differentiate companies and industries into two (or three sectors) of the economy. In general, industries or companies in the core have high sales volume, hold many assets, and employ a large number of people. They are further characterized by high rates of profit, have diverse product lines, and a large market share. They are also capital intensive and highly unionized. Companies and industries in the periphery have lower sales, hold fewer assets, and employ fewer workers than those in the core. Firms in the periphery have a low rate of profit, are typically single-product in nature, and have a low market concentration. They are also labor intensive and are not highly unionized. (If a tripartite model is used, regional companies and industries typically fall somewhere between the core and the periphery in terms of the variables discussed above.)

Some core industries include: metal mining, food products, farm machinery, tobacco, and textile mills. Included in the periphery are agriculture, construction, and taxicab service.[12] In the regional sector we find various wholesale and retail businesses.

[7]See, for example, Paul A. Baron and Paul M. Sweezy, *Monopoly Capitalism* (New York: Monthly Review Press, 1966); Robert Averitt, *The Dual Economy: The Dynamics of American Industry Structure* (New York: W.W. Norton and Company, 1968); David M. Gordon, *Theories of Poverty and Underemployment* (Lexington, MA: D.C. Heath, 1972); Barry Bluestone, William M. Murphy, and Mary Stevenson, *Low Wages and the Working Poor* (Ann Arbor, MI: Institute of Labor and Industrial Relations, 1973).

[8]See, for example, Robert Bibb and William H. Form, "The Effects of Industrial, Occupational and Sex Stratification on Wages in Blue-Collar Markets," *Social Forces,* 55 (1977), 974–996; E.M. Beck, Patrick M. Horan, and Charles M. Tolbert II, "Stratification in a Dual Economy: A Sectoral Model of Earnings Determination," *American Sociological Review,* 43 (1978), 704–720; E.M. Beck, Patrick M. Horan and Charles M. Tolbert II, "Industrial Segmentation and Labor Market Discrimination," *Social Problems,* 28 (1980), 112–130.

[9]Randy Hodson, "Companies, Industries, and the Measurement of Economic Segmentation," *American Sociological Review,* 49 (1984), 335–348.

[10]Ibid; see also, James N. Baron and William T. Bielby, "Bringing the Firms Back In: Stratification, Segmentation, and the Organization of Work."

[11]Lynne G. Zucker and Carolyn Rosenstein, "Taxonomies of Institutional Structure: Dual Economy Reconsidered," *American Sociological Review,* 46 (1981), 869–884.

[12]Randy Hodson, "Companies, Industries, and the Measurement of Economic Segmentation."

Mostly the result of favorable market position, financial success, and a high level of unionization, it is hypothesized that workers employed in core industries will be paid higher wages and enjoy a higher quality of worklife, that is, better working conditions and higher fringe benefits. More job stability and greater opportunities for career advancement, promotion, and career development are also thought to accrue to those employed in the core industrial sector. While there are several beneficial consequences for those employed in the core sector, it is important to remember that these consequences stem largely from the structural organization of society and not mainly from the attributes and psychological characteristics of the individual.

Seymour Spilerman[13] offers us some useful theoretical insights into how structural variables can affect an individual's career development. Spilerman is interested in both organizational- and industrial-level variables. For example, in terms of an organization's promotion rules, upgrading from within or hiring from outside the firm can obviously impact on a person's career development. If an organization has a well-developed internal labor market, opportunities for career advancement will be greater for the employees within the organization. An organization in the core may have invested much time and money in training some workers in complex, organizationally specific tasks. The skills acquired make the employees more productive and more important to the firm, and high pay and strong promotion possibilities are offered as incentives to remain. Obviously this can also be the case with the larger, more profitable firms in the periphery or regional sectors, but it is considered more pronounced in the core firms. As Spilerman points out, an organization's promotion rules depend on several factors—the skills gaps separating various occupations, historical circumstances, and union contracts that specify promotion procedures. However, all of these conditions add further to the importance of considering the structural impact on career development.

Other structural variables are also important. Career advancement might be greater for semi-skilled workers in industries (for example, the chemical-processing industry) with a high ratio of skilled to semiskilled workers than in industries (textile manufacturing) where semiskilled labor predominates. The rate of growth within a particular organization as well as a particular industry might also be important. If a person is employed in an expanding firm or a growing industry, new skilled, technical, and upper-level administrative positions would be created and could be filled by promotion from within. Conversely, if a firm is on the verge of bankruptcy or an industry is declining in importance, fewer positions are likely to be available and chances for career development will be lessened.

Promotion rules as well as organizational and industry-wide occupational composition and growth rates are important structural variables that need to be considered if we are to more fully understand an individual's career development.

Most empirical research conducted by the new structuralists comes from

---

[13]Seymour Spilerman, "Careers, Labor Market Structure, and Socio-economic Achievement," *American Journal of Sociology,* 83 (1977), 551–593.

the dual-industrial-sector perspective. Further, most of these studies are concerned with predicting income differences between core and periphery workers.[14] Simply put, workers in the core make more money than workers in the periphery, and the difference between the two is *not* solely the result of individual variables. To cite just one recent example, Hodson found that core employees earned $4,200 more than those in the periphery.[15] Other findings that emerge from this body of research relate to sex and race. Women[16] and minorities[17] are consistently found to be overrepresented in the periphery. Again, to take just one example, Hodson found that 22.4 percent of the workers in the core were women whereas over 55 percent of the workers in the periphery were women.[18]

Tolbert analyzed career mobility patterns within and between core and periphery industrial sectors for men in their early and late careers.[19] In their early to middle careers (first occupation in late 1930s to occupation held in 1966), occupational mobility was high. Overall, 74 percent of the respondents experienced some form (upward, horizontal) of job change. However, most of these changes were within the same industrial sector; only 35.6 percent of the workers changed industrial sectors. In other words, nearly two-thirds of the respondents who started their careers in a particular industrial sector were in the same sector at mid-career. Hence, while there is much occupational mobility, industrial sector *im*mobility is also typical of a person's early career. The changes that do occur between sectors are more likely to occur from the periphery to the core than vice versa. Of those who changed industrial sector, 10.6 percent moved from the core to the periphery while more than 25 percent moved from the periphery to the core.

Finally, bigger gains in upward career mobility were made within the core than the periphery. Mean occupational prestige scores for men in the core were higher at career outset and in 1966. Men who were in the core sector by 1966 experienced a greater average range of upward occupational prestige mobility than those in the periphery. Men whose occupational mobility was exclusively within the periphery experienced the smallest occupational prestige gains.

After mid-career, occupational and sectoral mobility decrease dramatically. Overall, between 1966 and 1975, only 33 percent of the men changed

[14]Robert Bibb and William Form, "The Effects of Industrial, Occupational, and Sex Stratification on Wages in Blue-Collar Markets;" E.M. Beck, Patrick M. Horan and Charles M. Tolbert II, "Stratification in a Dual Economy: A Sectoral Model of Earnings Determination;" Arne L. Kalleberg, Michael Wallace, and Robert P. Althuser, "Economic Segmentation, Worker Power, and Income Inequality," *American Journal of Sociology*, 87 (1981), 651–683.

[15]Randy Hodson, "Companies, Industries, and the Measurement of Economic Segmentation."

[16]Bibb and Form, "The Effects of Industrial, Occupational, and Sex Stratification on Wages in Blue-Collar Markets;" E.M. Beck, Patrick Horan, and Charles Tolbert II, "Stratification in a Dual Economy: A Sectoral Model of Earnings Determination."

[17]E.M. Beck, Patrick M. Horan, and Charles M. Tolbert II, "Industrial Segmentation and Labor Market Discrimination."

[18]Randy Hodson, "Companies, Industries, and the Measurement of Economic Segmentation."

[19]Charles M. Tolbert II, "Industrial Segmentation and Men's Career Mobility," *American Sociological Review*, 47 (1982), 457–476.

jobs. Further, only 14.9 percent of these changes were between industrial sectors. Hence, while both occupational and sectoral mobility is less during the late career than the early career, the mobility that does occur is mostly within the same industrial sector. However, while the mobility between sectors that occurs during the early career is most likely to flow from the periphery to the core, this is not the case during the late career. Between 1966 and 1975 about an equal percent of the men went from the core to the periphery (8 percent) as went from the periphery to the core (6.9 percent). As during the early career, occupational prestige scores were higher for workers in the core than in the periphery. However, these higher prestige scores were shown to be a function of gains made during the early career.

Similar results emerge from analysis of the same data by Richard Wanner and Lionel Lewis.[20] Unlike Tolbert, Wanner and Lewis analyzed sectoral mobility by race. During the early part of one's career, sectoral immobility is the rule. Over 63 percent of the whites and 56 percent of the nonwhites who started their careers in the core or periphery were in the same sector by mid-career. Of those whites and nonwhites who changed industrial sectors during their early career, the majority went from the periphery to the core. Sectoral immobility is also characteristic of a person's later career. Only 16.5 percent of the white men and 18.7 percent of the nonwhite men changed sectors during the later part of their careers. However, unlike the early years, sectoral mobility is now more likely to be from the core to the periphery.

With reference to occupational prestige gains over the course of their careers, white men in both the core and the periphery start out with higher occupational status than nonwhites. During the early part of their careers, the gap between whites and nonwhites increases dramatically and then essentially remains unchanged during the later part of their careers.

We can get an idea of the effect of industrial segmentation on women and minority career patterns from an analysis conducted by Rachel Rosenfeld.[21] Drawing on the assumptions of both the dual labor market and the dual economy perspectives, Rosenfeld studied the career dynamics of white and nonwhite (mostly black) men and women.

It will be recalled that white men are more likely to be in the core industrial sector. This puts them in an advantageous position for higher starting wages and greater wage increases and offers them greater opportunities for advancement. On the other hand, women and minorities are likely to be overrepresented in the periphery, placing them in a sector offering lower financial rewards and less opportunity for advancement. Hence, higher starting wages and greater income and status gains could be expected to accrue to white men. This is exactly what Rosenfeld found. On average, white men began their careers with the highest starting hourly wage and also gained more in wages than any other group studied. Nonwhite men, white women, and nonwhite women ranked second to fourth respectively in terms of starting

[20]Richard A. Wanner and Lionel S. Lewis, "Economic Segmentation and the Course of the Occupational Career," *Work and Occupations,* 10 (1983), 307–324.

[21]Rachel A. Rosenfeld, "Race and Sex Differences In Career Dynamics," *American Sociological Review,* 45 (1980), 583–609.

hourly wage and income gained over the periods observed. Further, while white women began their careers at an occupational status somewhat higher than any of the three groups, it was, as expected, white men who experienced the greatest amount of upward status mobility. The speed at which the various groups reached their highest wage levels also reflects the differing structures of opportunity open in each sector. It took longer for white men to reach their highest wage level than any other group. This confirms the idea that there are more rungs on career ladders in the core sector and consequently it will take longer for those in this sector to reach their maximum wage level. Women and minorities, who have fewer rungs to climb, reach their highest income levels more quickly. In Rosenfeld's study, white women were the first group to reach their peak wage level, followed by black women and black men.

Although there is empirical support for some of the major hypotheses generated by the concept of labor market segmentation, it is important to note that the structuralists have no shortage of critics. Recently Hodson and Kaufman[22] have summarized the major criticisms, and Zucker and Rosenstein[23] have shown the empirical inconsistencies that leave many of the hypotheses unconfirmed or contrary to expectations. Both Sorensen and Tomaskovic-Devey argue that the labor market segmentation approach is hampered by methodological problems.[24]

While much theoretical and empirical work still needs to be done, the criticisms in no way diminish the importance of taking a more structural perspective toward understanding career mobility and status attainment. Since researchers in the status attainment tradition have tended to ignore structural concerns and since the new structuralists have often ignored individual characteristics, it is our position that neither perspective is correct all the time. What is needed in sociology in general,[25] and in segmentation studies in particular,[26] is a wholistic perspective that focuses on the broad spectrum of social phenomena ranging from societal-wide to individual characteristics and including sectoral, organizational, and occupational criteria. An integrated approach points to the complexity of the social world and guards against overly simplistic, unidimensional social-scientific explanations.

Let us now turn our attention from the structural context of careers to the career patterns characteristic of some specific occupations.

---

[22]Randy Hodson and Robert L. Kaufman, "Economic Dualism: A Critical Review," *American Sociological Review*, 47 (1982), 727–739.

[23]Lynne G. Zucker and Carolyn Rosenstein, "Taxonomies of Institutional Structure: Dual Economy Reconsidered."

[24]Aage B. Sorensen, "Sociological Research on the Labor Market: Conceptual and Methodological Issues," *Work and Occupations*, 10 (1983), 261–287; Donald Tomaskovic-Devey, "A Methodological Comment on 'Economic Segmentation, Worker Power, and Income Inequality,'" *American Journal of Sociology*, 89 (1983), 444–446.

[25]George Ritzer, *Toward an Integrated Sociological Paradigm: The Search for an Exemplar and an Image of the Subject Matter* (Boston: Allyn and Bacon, Inc., 1981).

[26]James N. Baron and William T. Bielby, "Bringing the Firms Back In: Stratification, Segmentation, and the Organization of Work."

CAREER PATTERNS

Professionals

Within the professions we find an array of types of career patterns. Some offer the individual a great deal of career mobility, while others offer fairly constricted career patterns.

Lawyers. Some interesting insights into careers in the legal profession can be drawn from Heinz and Laumann's study of 777 Chicago lawyers.[27] One of the most interesting career issues explored in the study is the relationship between type of law school attended and the type of practice in which lawyers are found. Heinz and Laumann deal with four types of law schools, of which the elite schools are on the top and local schools on the bottom. They also deal with six types of law practice, of which the large law firm is the most prestigious and solo practice offers the lowest status. The strongest findings are that graduates of elite law schools are greatly overrepresented in large law firms, while graduates of local schools are greatly underrepresented in such firms. On the other side, graduates of local law schools are substantially overrepresented among solo practitioners, while graduates of elite schools are underrepresented in solo practice. As the authors put it, "there is a rather strict and precise correspondence between the prestige hierarchies of the suppliers of trained personnel (i.e., the law schools) and of the buyers (the employers or employment context)."[28]

Another important career issue explored by Heinz and Laumann is the relationship between entry job into law and present position within the legal profession. Within all of the types of legal practice explored by them, there is a high level of retention of legal personnel. More than 50 percent of all those studied stayed in the type of practice in which they started. The greatest career stability was in the prestigious large law firms where 77.9 percent of those who started in such firms remained in them. The least career stability was in government work where only 32.5 percent of those who started in such a setting remained there. For many government lawyers, time spent in the government is seen as a prelude to moving on to legal work in one of the more prestigious settings. Interestingly, 56.4 percent of those who started their careers as solo practitioners remained there. Although it is likely that a large proportion of those in large law firms are anxious to remain in those settings, a large number of solo practitioners probably would have liked to move on to other settings. However, solo practice is often a career trap from which it is hard to extricate oneself. Thus, career stability can stem from a desire to stay in, as well as the inability to get out of, a setting.

Turning to career patterns of lawyers, as we have seen in the preceding chapter, Wall Street lawyers have a great deal of career mobility. Upon entering the firm, new Wall Street lawyers are made beginning associates. In this position they are socialized into the life of the firm, since they work closely

[27]John P. Heinz and Edward O. Laumann, *Chicago Lawyers: The Social Structure of the Bar* (New York: Russell Sage Foundation; and Chicago: American Bar Foundation, 1982).

[28]Ibid., p. 193.

with established lawyers. Law school has probably best prepared them to do research, but as beginning associates they learn how to "write memoranda and briefs, give advice, learn the 'ins and outs,' of the courts. . . . also confer with partners, learn to dictate, gain familiarity with the filing system, and compete with older women stenographers for small power symbols."[29] Such a position is very important to new lawyers since, as was pointed out earlier, law schools tend to do a poor job of communicating many of the realities of legal life. This first job serves to change idealism into realism in much the same way as this function is performed in medical, professional, and graduate schools. After four to eight years, lawyers may expect a promotion to middle-range associate. At this level they become more specialized and take on greater responsibility: for example, they may personally negotiate a contract for the sale of a house. In their eighth year in the firm Wall Street lawyers may expect to be promoted to the position of senior associate. Here they have more wide-ranging responsibilities, although they have less status and responsibility than the partners. The next step is permanent associate; this is a critical stage because it is at this point that they may be asked either to be a partner or to leave the organization. There are three steps once a lawyer has become a partner: junior, middle, and senior partner. Junior- and middle-partner positions are viewed as testing points for those who aspire to the summit, senior partnership. "When he arrives at that position he becomes the final interpreter of the law for the firm, its overall manager, and advisor to colleagues, clients and government, as well as in civic organization."[30] The careers of Wall Street lawyers thus follow well-defined patterns. Early in their careers they are generalists, then specialists, and ultimately they become again generalists, although at a much higher level in the organizational hierarchy.

College professors.   Within the university the professor's career generally involves four well-defined steps. In most cases the first step is the position of instructor. In minor-league universities instructors are usually those who have not yet received their Ph.D. In major-league universities the instructor position is generally filled by new Ph.D.'s. Instructors in lesser universities are virtually assured of promotion once they get their degrees. In contrast, instructors in top universities will only be promoted when they have demonstrated professional competence by their publication record.

An assistant professorship is the next step. In minor-league universities some publications will ensure progress to the next step, but in the best schools this position is often terminal. Those assistant professors in major league universities who are promoted must have demonstrated exceptional publication ability. The third step, associate professor, is therefore more difficult to achieve in a high-status university. The final step, a full professorship, is the most difficult to achieve in both types of universities, although the requirements are much greater at the major ones. In most universities one or more books and a number of articles are required in order to be considered for full

---

[29]Erwin Smigel, *The Wall Street Lawyer: Professional Organization Man?* (Bloomington, IN: Indiana University Press, 1969), p. 143.

[30]Ibid., p. 160.

professorship. (Smaller teaching colleges place less emphasis on research and promote more on the basis of teaching ability.)

Academicians are usually confronted with a much more constricted career pattern than lawyers. There are only a few steps, and once people become full professors there are very few alternatives open to them. Full professors at minor universities may seek similar positions at major universities or endowed chairs at their present schools, or perhaps leave academia for industry or government. However, only a small number of full professors take any of these options.

A central variable in analyzing the career patterns of academicians is the status of the university. One general rule is that new Ph.D.'s will find it difficult to obtain jobs at universities with greater prestige than those from which they received their degrees. Thus, Ph.D.'s from Ohio State are unlikely to get their first job at Ivy League universities; they are more likely to receive offers from state universities or private colleges at or below the level of Ohio State. This first step down in the prestige hierarchy is perfectly acceptable in academia. More important for graduates of major universities is their second position, which should be a step back toward the major league or directly into that level. Ph.D.'s from Harvard may take their first job at the University of Missouri, but their second job should represent a step up (for example, to Berkeley or right into the Ivy League) or should at least be a parallel move.

Ph.D.'s from minor universities have different career patterns. Their first jobs, following the aforementioned rule, is likely to be at universities of lower status. They thus begin in colleges or universities with lesser prestige, and it is virtually impossible for them to ever make the major leagues. They typically have not received the proper socialization and lack the contacts or prestigious label needed to ever be considered by major universities. Ordinarily, they can only hope to return to the level of the universities from which they received their degree. There are some exceptions to this rule: the prolific publisher from a minor university might ultimately be considered for a position at a major university. However, there are few (if any) Ph.D.'s from the University of Southern Mississippi at universities like Harvard.

It should be noted that in recent years academia has undergone a profound recession. The result is that many professors are happy to have academic positions at any type of college or university. In fact, there are large numbers of Ph.D.'s who are unemployed, employed on temporary or part-time bases, or who have even dropped out of academia completely. In other words, the typical career patterns described above have been profoundly disrupted in recent years by the hard times in academia.

Physicians.   Other professions offer virtually no mobility career pattern. Once individuals have become full-fledged doctors (that is, completed their residency), they have in most cases reached the pinnacle of their careers. Although this is formally correct, there is a great deal of informal mobility in the medical profession, and physicians may still have a number of informal career steps open to them.[31]

[31]Oswald Hall, "The Stages of a Medical Career," *American Journal of Sociology*, 53 (1948), 327–336.

Once established, physicians still stand on the outskirts of the informal organization of the medical profession. At the center of the medical profession is the inner fraternity, a group of high-status specialists who control a variety of rewards, for example, access to important posts in medicine. Newly established doctors often turn to the informal career pattern in an effort to gain acceptance in the inner fraternity. The best way to gain such acceptance is to be sponsored by someone who belongs. Those who successfully move into the inner fraternity of the medical profession have experienced considerable informal career mobility even though they have little formal career mobility.

Career Contingencies

Occupations are characterized by career patterns that are continually disrupted by *career contingencies,* events that occur at critical points in a career and may have a dramatic effect on the future course of that career. It is interesting to note that such contingencies do occur in the professions—the occupational group that should have career patterns that are most resistant to disruption. The success of new doctors may depend on whether they can attract the sponsorship of established physicians. A college professor may decide to change jobs after a chance meeting with a friend at another university. Professionals in the military probably exemplify best the duality in the professions of order and contingency in the career pattern. After graduation from a military academy, the formal steps in the career of an officer are clear. However, movement up the hierarchy is dependent on a series of factors, many of which may be considered career contingencies. One such contingency is the time when cadets graduate from the academy: if it is just before wartime, their chances of rapid promotion are greatly enhanced; there is a greater need for officers and there is more opportunity to display one's abilities. Another contingency is visibility of action. New officers who act bravely will not be promoted unless their actions are seen or heard about by those in a position to promote. On a formal level there are continuous appraisals of officers to determine whether they are worthy of promotion, but beyond these formal rankings the opportunity for informal contacts with highly placed officers is an important contingency determining when, and if, an individual will be promoted.[32]

Although our focus here is on contingencies affecting the careers of professionals, it should be clear that career contingencies play an even greater role at lower levels in the occupational hierarchy.

Occupational Obsolescence

Another important sociological concept is the growing likelihood that individuals will experience *occupational obsolescence.* That is, they are likely to become obsolete in terms of their knowledge or technical ability given the rapid growth in these areas. Such developments help make many professionals obsolete just a few years after they complete their training. It is simply impossi-

---

[32]Morris Janowitz, *The Professional Soldier: A Social and Political Portrait* (New York: Free Press, 1960).

ble to keep up with the massive number of new developments. As a result, the best-trained professionals are often those who have just completed their degrees and are beginning their careers. Obsolescence also results from the deterioration of previously held knowledge through disuse or decline in intellectual vigor. Professionals who find themselves obsolete have both their current career status and their future prospects jeopardized. The reality of this problem is underscored by the existence of various "updating" programs run by professional associations and universities.[33]

Although obsolescence is almost inevitable, it is not evenly distributed among all types of professionals. Those who choose to spend at least part of their careers in administrative positions are more likely to become obsolete than those who continue to remain in the mainstream of their profession and practice on a full-time basis. Professionals who are employed in organizations that do not support professional activities are more likely to focus on narrow organizational questions and, as a result, lose touch with new developments in the profession.

Although particularly troublesome in the professions, obsolescence is a problem that affects virtually all occupations in one way or another. The personnel manager, for example, must try to keep up with recent developments in the law, labor relations, the social sciences, and many other fields. The librarian must keep abreast of new books published, new acquisitions, new computer techniques. The taxi driver must keep up with new rules, changes in city routes, and new construction projects that cause traffic jams. Even the stripper must be attuned to new forms of music, new dances, and changes in public tastes in exotic performance.

In his analysis of middle managers, Kay concluded that they can become obsolete in five basic areas.[34] They may find it difficult, or impossible, (1) to keep up with new knowledge; (2) to keep in touch with the newer ideas of younger employees; and (3) to keep up with changing societal norms and values that have an impact on their work. In addition, (4) the changing political realities of life in their employing organization may pass unnoticed; and (5) their economic goals may fall behind the changing economic objectives of the employing organization.

Sponsorship

Already encountered in passing in this book, *sponsorship* is a key process by which those who have "made it" in a given occupation, profession, or organization aid those who are trying to make their way up in the hierarchy. In effect, those who have already made it stake their reputations on the likelihood that certain individuals will perform well if they are promoted to the next career stage.

[33]Robert A. Rothman and Robert Perrucci, "Organizational Careers and Professional Expertise," *Administrative Science Quarterly*, 15 (1970), 282–293; see also, Robert Rothman and Robert Perrucci, "Vulnerability to Knowledge Obsolescence among Professionals," *Sociological Quarterly*, 12 (1971), 147–158.

[34]Emanuel Kay, "Middle Management," in James O'Toole, ed., *Work and the Quality of Life: Resource Papers for Work in America* (Cambridge, MA: The M.I.T. Press, 1974), pp. 106–129.

Kram analyzes the development of sponsorship (or mentoring[35]) among business managers.[36] During this development, several career and psychosocial functions are provided by the sponsor. Among the career functions are giving the aspirant exposure and visibility within the organization, providing coaching when needed, affording protection in difficult situations, and providing the neophyte with challenging assignments. Among the psychosocial functions provided by the sponsor are serving as a role model to be emulated, providing support and acceptance, offering counseling, and providing friendship.

The aspirant is not the only one to benefit from sponsorship. While there are clearly some risks to the sponsors,[37] there are also reciprocal rewards. Those whom they sponsor are in their debt and can be used in a variety of ways when the sponsor needs help. They may be called on to help, for example, during a political battle in which the sponsor is one of the participants. The sponsors also gain psychic gratification in seeing those they have aided make their way up the career ladder:

> I can tell you that the biggest satisfaction that I get is seeing someone that you have some faith in really go beyond where you expect and really seeing them get recognized. . . . You know you had faith in these people, you've helped them along, but you haven't told them what to do. . . . you see those people get promoted and you're really pleased. And you say, "You know, I've had something to do with that."[38]

Progress in medicine, law, and the military (among other professions and occupations) is aided by the possession of a sponsor. In academia, a powerful sponsor is a tremendous advantage to the upwardly mobile young academician.[39] In his study of Hollywood studio musicians, Faulkner[40] found sponsorship to be of central importance. In the business world, sponsorship is so crucial to success that it has prompted such claims as this:

> I don't know that anyone has ever succeeded in any business without having some unselfish sponsorship or mentorship . . . For some the help comes with more warmth than for others, and with some it's done with more forethought,

[35]We will use the concept of mentor as synonymous with sponsor. It should be noted, however, that Auster argues that mentors are differentiated from sponsors by the protege's stronger identification, greater intimacy, and deeper emotional involvement with mentors than sponsors. See Donald Auster, "Mentors and Proteges: Power-Dependent Dyads," *Sociological Inquiry*, 54 (1984), 142–153.

[36]Kathy E. Kram, "Phases of the Mentor Relationship," *Academy of Management Journal*, 26 (1983), 608–625; see also, Nancy W. Collins, *Professional Women and Their Mentors* (Englewood Cliffs, NJ: Prentice-Hall, Inc., 1983).

[37]Auster, "Mentors and Proteges: Power-Dependent Dyads."

[38]Kathy Kram, "Phases of the Mentor Relationship," 616.

[39]Diana Crane, "Scientists at Major and Minor Universities: A Study of Productivity and Recognition," *American Sociological Review*, 30 (1965), 669–713.

[40]Robert R. Faulkner, *Hollywood Studio Musicians: Their Work and Careers in the Recording Industry* (Chicago: Aldine/Atherton, 1971).

but most people who succeed in a business will remember fondly individuals who helped them in their early days.[41]

More systematically collected data lends support to such claims. Gerald R. Roche[42] studied the mentor-protege relationship among 1,250 business executives. Roche found that approximately 60 percent of the executives did report some form of sponsorship during their climb up the corporate ladder. In fact, Roche found that each male executive averaged not one but two mentors during their career, while women executives averaged three. Hence, not only is sponsorship important, but in today's complex, mobile society more than one mentor seems essential.

Roche found that business executives who had a sponsor were better educated, earned more money at a younger age, and were more satisfied with their jobs than those executives who did not have a mentor.

Although mentor-protege relationships are prevalent in the corporate world, it is interesting to note that many of the executives interviewed by Roche did not consider their relationship with their sponsor(s) to be an important component of their career success. Business executives with sponsors report the ability to work long hours, complete assignments, make decisions, and lead and motivate others as more important ingredients in their career success. Individual motivation, high energy levels, and simple luck were also reported as important in one's success.

Although the sponsorship process exists throughout the occupational spectrum,[43] it is most frequently found, and most important, in higher-status occupations.

In this discussion of sponsorship we have touched upon managers and officials. We now turn to a more specific discussion of career patterns in this occupational category.

Managers and Officials

We will focus in this section primarily on the career mobility of managers in profit-making organizations. Many of the ideas and concepts discussed in this section also relate to officials in nonprofit organizations, but it is well to remember that there are some important career pattern differences between managers and officials. For example, union and political officials are often elected, and the possibility of losing an election is an important career difference between these officials and the managers discussed in this section. Careers of nonelected officials, such as those in universities and hospitals, resemble those of managers much more closely.

[41]Eliza G.C. Collins and Patricia Scott, "Everyone Who Makes It Has a Mentor," *Harvard Business Review*, 56 (July/August, 1978), 100.

[42]Gerald R. Roche, "Much Ado About Mentors," *Harvard Business Review*, 57 (January/February, 1979), 14–28.

[43]See, for example, Muriel Faltz Lembright and Jeffrey W. Riemer, "Women Truckers' Problems and the Impact of Sponsorship," *Work and Occupations*, 9 (1982), 457–474.

Who are the mobile managers today and what does it take to get to the top? Swinyard and Bond[44] studied more than 11,000 executives who were promoted to the vice presidential or presidential level of major U.S. business organizations between 1967 and 1976. During this period, educational attainment became increasingly important. By 1976, only 11 percent of the top executives did not have a college education; it was 18 percent in 1967. At the same time, there was a 39 percent increase in the number of executives holding master's degrees. In 1967, 22 percent of the executives held an advanced degree with a concentration in business administration and management while 22 percent were in engineering. In 1976, these two concentrations still ranked first and second, but those reporting their highest degree in business administration jumped to 33 percent while engineering decreased to 18 percent. In both years, law was the third main area of concentration.

Intraorganizational mobility was the typical career path to the top for the executives studied. For all executives, the median length of time spent with their companies was 12 years. While most executives spend a relatively long period of time with one company, they do not necessarily stay in one position very long: the median number of years spent in their previous position was 3.4 years.[45]

Intraorganizational mobility does not preclude geographic relocation. While most managers stay with one organization, 35 percent of all career moves involve geographic relocation by mid-career.[46] Sell presents evidence that the number of such geographic relocations is increasing.[47] Many managers relocate more than once, and for many relocation fatigue is typical. One manager notes:

> I've transferred several times since I started working here. . . . I'd just like to stay a little longer this time. . . . You know, I'm not even sure what my address and phone number are sometimes.[48]

Currently, many corporations are being confronted by managers and executives who are resistant to relocation. It is estimated that up to 80 percent of employees refuse their first relocation.[49] Morrison notes that changing values, dual career families, high costs, and concern about uprooting families are some of the major reasons for this resistance.[50]

In an attempt to break resistance to relocation, companies have started

[44]Alfred W. Swinyard and Floyd A. Bond, "Who Gets Promoted?" *Harvard Business Review,* 58 (September/October, 1980), 6–15.

[45]For a similar set of results see, John F. Veiga, "Do Managers on the Move Get Anywhere?" *Harvard Business Review,* 59 (March/April, 1981), 20–38.

[46]Ibid.

[47]Ralph Sell, "Transferred Jobs: A Neglected Aspect of Migration and Occupational Change," *Work and Occupations,* 10 (1983), 179–206.

[48]Ibid.

[49]Ann M. Morrison, "The Going Gets Lusher for Employees on the Move," *Fortune* (June 16, 1980), p. 159–173.

[50]For some mixed results on this issue see, John F. Veiga, "Mobility Influences During Managerial Career Stages," *Academy of Management Journal,* 26 (1983), 64–85.

to offer lucrative inducements to their employees. Some companies offer to pay their employees an interest rate differential, that is, a cash amount paid over a period of time based on the employee's new- and old-home mortgage rates. Other companies offer supplemental equity assistance—low-interest or no-interest guaranteed loans. Other corporations offer their employees cost-of-living adjustments when the relocation involves a move to a more expensive living area.

Promotion

It is commonly believed that those managers who move rapidly through the hierarchy to the pinnacle of their employing organization are the ones who are the most able, most aggressive, most innovative, and most daring. Many analysts of the business world tend to support this point of view. A major exponent of this position is Peter Drucker, who contends that being a manager requires "competence and performance of a high order."[51] Elsewhere he says:

> The constant temptation of every organization is safe mediocrity. The first requirement of organizational health is a high demand on performance. . . . The one man to distrust . . . is the man who never makes a mistake, never commits a blunder, never fails in what he tries to do. He is either a phony, or he stays with the safe, the tried, and the trivial. . . . The better a man is, the more mistakes he will make for the more new things he will try.[52]

Although Drucker is expressing the dominant view, many sociologists have a very different conception of what it takes to move up in the organization.

Before discussing the question of ability, it is important to underscore the fact that there are a great many lower-level managers, but far fewer within the top echelon. There is not enough room at the top for all of those who desire lofty status, and many management careers are therefore terminated at relatively low levels. Many competent individuals in low-level managerial positions remain there because the organization feels they do not have the abilities to move up. Others decide that the struggle for promotion is not worth the effort. Such individuals may remain low-level bureaucrats or leave the organization altogether.

There are those who do move steadily up in their organization. However, it is quite clear that it is not ability alone that determines whether an individual will reach the top. Dynamic, aggressive decision makers who fight their way to the top often seem to be a thing of the past. Those who succeed often seem to be those who are best able to understand the system and manipulate it for their own benefit. Brilliant decision making is not required; as a matter of fact, it frequently appears that the top positions go to those who avoid "sticking their necks out" by making decisions. Another important quality is the ability to understand what superiors want and give them exactly that,

---

[51]Peter Drucker, *Management: Tasks, Responsibilities and Practices* (New York: Harper & Row, 1974), p. 398.
[52]Ibid., pp. 456–457.

no more and no less. All of these points are neatly summarized by Mills in his discussion of success in the business world:

> So speak in the rich, round voice and do not confuse your superiors with details. Know where to draw the line. Execute the ceremony of forming a judgment. Delay recognizing the choice you have already made, so as to make the truism sound like the deeply pondered notion. Speak like the quiet competent man of affairs and never personally say No. Hire the No-man as well as the Yes-man. Be the tolerant Maybe-man and they will cluster around you, filled with hopefulness. Practice softening the facts into the optimistic, practical, forward-looking, cordial brisk view. Speak to the well-blunted point. Have weight: be stable: caricature what you are supposed to be but never become aware of it much less amused by it. And never let your brains show.[53]

Mills is being ironic, but the same thesis has been repeated many times in both the sociological and popular literature on management.

What it really takes to get ahead in an organization is often at variance with what is formally stated. In his study, Dalton points out a number of informal conditions required if one was to move up in the organizations he examined.[54] For one thing, it was informally recognized that one had to be a Mason in order to move ahead. Collins' study of a New England factory revealed the same processes:[55] virtually all of the top management positions at this New England factory went to Yankees. In contrast, almost all of the foremen positions were manned by the Irish. In Dalton's study the vast majority of managers were either Anglo-Saxon or German.[56] In addition, most managers were members of the yacht club and all had to be, at least officially, Republicans. These informal factors may vary from organization to organization, but it is clear that they are important for upward mobility. It is often not what you know but *who* you know that counts. Related to this is the informal importance of sponsorship in managerial life, a factor we have already noted.

Another informal factor that can prove beneficial for upward mobility is image management.[57] Image management can include a Dale Carnegie course on how to influence people; or it can mean hiring an image consultant, someone who advises managers on how they and their spouses should dress, what civic organizations to join, which luncheons to go to, and how to choose assistants who will help further their careers. Interpersonal communications specialists will advise executives on how to sit, stand, talk, what words to use, and the general art of body language. Cosmetic surgery, from face lifts to eyelid operations, are also being performed on executives who want to make a youthful impression on their superiors.

[53]C. Wright Mills, *The Power Elite* (New York: Oxford University Press, 1959), pp. 142–143.

[54]Melville Dalton, *Men Who Manage* (New York: John Wiley & Sons, 1959).

[55]Orvis Collins, "Ethnic Behavior in Industry: Sponsorship and Rejection in a New England Factory," *American Journal of Sociology*, 51 (1946), 293–298.

[56]Such factors are also important in a variety of other occupational categories, including the professions. For a study of the importance of ethnic groups in medicine, see David N. Solomon, "Ethnic and Class Differences among Hospitals as Contingencies in Medical Careers," *American Journal of Sociology*, 66 (1961), 463–471.

[57]Herbert Meyer, "Remodeling the Corporate Climb," *Fortune* (July 16, 1979), pp. 82–92.

Even if individuals have all the informal attributes, they are not guaranteed a series of inalterable steps to the top. There is much zigzagging in the career of the typical manager or official.

A useful concept in understanding the functions of promotion for at least some managers is the idea of *career anchorage*.[58] The basic idea here is that some managers value higher-level positions and actively strive for them, others focus on their past accomplishments, while still others are ambivalent and anchor their careers neither progressively nor retrospectively. Those managers who are oriented toward future promotion are likely to devote a significant proportion of their time to their work. The organization motivates this overachievement by offering promotions. Thus, the reward of a promotion provides valuable functions to the organization, in particular by eliciting prodigious efforts from ambitious managers.[59] Interestingly, only a small minority of managers anchor their careers on higher-level positions toward which they are aspiring. In a recent study on this issue, only 14 percent of managers were upwardly anchored, while 42 percent were ambivalent and 44 percent were downwardly anchored. Goldman concludes, "there are comparatively few who set their sights on the top positions in the organization. The American myth of success, that all who try can reach the top, just does not appear to inspire the vast majority of managers studied."[60]

Although promotion within organizations provides a number of positive functions, it also has negative consequences. Let us look first at the upwardly mobile manager. We can assume that the constant need to "get ahead" is a source of occupational stress. In fact, upwardly mobile managers, who typically have extraordinary workloads and great pressure and responsibility, have a far greater incidence of heart disease, ulcers, arthritis, stroke, and various forms of mental illness. Then too, job-related stress may manifest itself in a series of behaviors such as alcoholism, drug abuse,[61] and even suicide.[62] Even those who are successful in their efforts to move up in the organization are subjected to stress.

The promotion process can also have disastrous effects on the larger organization. One of the most provocative and interesting concepts in understanding these negative consequences is the so-called "Peter Principle."[63] The

[58]Curt Tausky and Robert Dubin, "Career Anchorage: Managerial Mobility Motivations," *American Sociological Review*, 30 (October, 1965), 725–735.

[59]Daniel R. Goldman, "Managerial Mobility Motivation and Central Life Interests," *American Sociological Review*, 38 (1973), 119–126; Daniel R. Goldman, "Career Anchorage: Managerial Mobility Motivations—A Replication," *Sociology of Work and Occupations*, 5 (1978), 193–208.

[60]Goldman, "Career Anchorage," 207.

[61]For a general discussion of the relationship of alcohol and drugs and work, see Harrison M. Trice and Paul M. Roman, *Spirits and Demons at Work: Alcohol and Other Drugs on the Job* (Ithaca, NY: Cornell University Press, 1972).

[62]Harry Levinson, "On Executive Suicide," *Harvard Business Review*, 53 (1975), 118–122.

[63]Lawrence J. Peter and Raymond Hull, *The Peter Principle: Why Things Always Go Wrong* (New York: Bantam Books, Inc., 1969). This book was so successful that in 1972 Peter published a sequel entitled *The Peter Prescription* (New York: Bantam Books, 1972). This book was so bad that it demonstrated Peter's principle. Based on the success of his first book, Peter had risen to his level of incompetence in the second book!

basic tenet of the Peter Principle is: "In a hierarchy, every employee tends to rise to his level of incompetence."[64] This process results because competent people are likely to be promoted. Each time they do well in a new position they are promoted again. This process is repeated until individuals reach positions that they can no longer handle—their level of incompetence. And that is where managers are likely to stay. They can no longer be promoted and the organization is unlikely to demote anyone. Thus, an organization is peopled by managers who are either incompetent or on the road to incompetence.

There are several possible solutions to this problem. First, the organization should drop the assumption that everyone should be moved ahead at a rapid pace. The organization should allow people who are happy in a given position, and performing well at it, to stay put. Second, the criteria for promotions should not be how well managers handle their present positions, but rather how well they are likely to handle *future* positions. Finally, individual managers can try to stay at positions that they find interesting, rewarding, and challenging. But if they turn down promotions, the organization is likely to think there is something wrong with them and penalize them with lower raises, or maybe even demotions. Peter offers a solution to managers who want to stay where they are and not be penalized for it: "creative incompetence." One cannot be incompetent on tasks directly related to one's work, since that would entail great risks. Thus, to avoid promotion one must demonstrate incompetence in areas peripheral to one's tasks. For example:

"Accidentally" spill coffee on the boss on one or two occasions.
Wear bizarre types of clothing, at least a few days a week.
Back your car into the boss' car in the company parking lot.
Throw away your deodorant and mouthwash.

An interesting question arises: If the Peter Principle is at least partially accurate, how does any real work get done in the organization? Taking Peter's often ironic work seriously, Lane Tracy offers us some insight into why more things don't go wrong in the organization.[65]

Peter claims that it is the people who are not yet at their levels of incompetence who do the real work in an organization. Tracy argues, however, that an organization's real work is done by those who are excluded from the organization's vertical hierarchy—those who are generally excluded from the promotion process. Tracy labels all such people "members of the subordinate class," and it is these workers—because they are shielded from the negative effects of promotion by discrimination against them—who really make the organization.

One of the first such occupations to come to mind is the secretary. This is a position usually filled by women, the major subordinate class in our society. Excluded from the vertical hierarchy and promotion opportunities, many secretaries are doomed to a life of greater competence than the manager. An-

[64]Ibid., p. 7.
[65]Lane Tracy, "Postscripts to the Peter Principle," *Harvard Business Review*, 50 (1972), 65–71.

other primarily female occupation, nursing, performs the same function in the hospital. Blue-collar workers are often heavily overrepresented by minority group members. Finding it difficult to move up, they too may spend their lives working competently and staying in one place in their career. In sum, we could say that our organizations are able to operate as efficiently as they do almost in spite of some managers. The success of these organizations, from this perspective, is based primarily on the exploitation of the lowest status people in the organization.[66]

Commitment to the Organization

Although it is certainly true that many young to middle-aged managers move from one organization to another in their careers,[67] most spend the majority of their careers in a single organization. One of the most interesting questions in the sociology of occupations is why so many managers (and other types of workers) do this.

In the course of their training programs, potential managers develop a commitment to their employing organizations. In Gouldner's terms, they begin their careers with a *local* rather than a *cosmopolitan* orientation.[68] That is, they are more committed to the immediate employing organization than to some external entity (e.g. a professional association). As their years in the organization pass, this initial loyalty is often transformed into a strong commitment. One of the major factors in this transformation is the "investments" managers make in their employing organization. The more they have invested, the more committed they will be. What are some of the investments individuals make in their organization? They may develop a series of skills that are useful in their organization, but that do not apply to others. They learn the informal workings of their organization and the shortcuts that make their jobs easier. Another investment lies in the fringe benefits most organizations offer. People may develop a great deal of equity in a retirement program, which would be lost if they left the organization. Or they may acquire, through stock-option plans, a considerable investment in the company and would lose this too if they left.[69] Other investments are managers' (and their families') friends within the community and the organization whom they may be reluctant to lose. Finally, the mere passing of time is an investment. The more years managers spend in one company, the more difficult it will be for them to move. All of these investments increase with the passing of years. And the older the managers are, the more difficult it will be for them to find alternative positions.

[66]We need hardly mention that few managers, officials, or experts on management (like Peter Drucker) would agree with this position.

[67]John F. Veiga, "The Mobile Manager at Mid-Career," *Harvard Business Review*, 51 (1973), 115–119.

[68]Alvin Gouldner, "Cosmopolitans and Locals: Toward an Analysis of Latent Social Roles—I," *Administrative Science Quarterly*, 2 (1957), 281–306.

[69]Peter Drucker calls these investments the "golden fetters" that serve to impede the free flow of managers between organizations. See Peter F. Drucker, *The Age of Discontinuity* (New York: Harper & Row, 1968).

Becker has called the investments described above "side-bets."[70] He contends that the more side-bets, the greater the commitment. While the concept is extremely useful, an empirical test by Ritzer and Trice has indicated that Becker's side-bet theory is overstated.[71] In the Ritzer and Trice study a number of investments were correlated with a score on commitment to the organization, and very few of the correlations were statistically significant. It was concluded that commitment to organization cannot be explained solely by structural side-bets: the additional component is the initial psychological commitment. As was pointed out earlier, in the process of going through the transition from college to organizational life, new managers often make a psychological commitment to their organization. Once they have accepted a position, they go through a process of emphasizing the strong points of the organization they have chosen and downgrading organizations that rejected them, or that they rejected. This commitment is enhanced by the first few years on the job in the management training program, for one of the functions of this program is to sell recruits on the company and allow recruits to convince themselves of the organization's worth. A process of self-selection also occurs here—those who are not sold, or who cannot sell themselves, leave the organization by the end of their training program. Those who remain are in all likelihood already highly committed to the company. It is at this point that the side-bets or investments play a role in enhancing this initial commitment. However, because the commitment is already strong, investments, while certainly important, are not the only factors involved in developing commitment.[72]

The relative significance of structural versus psychological factors has received continuing attention from sociologists. A replication of the Ritzer and Trice study on a sample of nurses and teachers indicated stronger sup-

[70]Howard S. Becker, "Notes on the Concept of Commitment," *American Journal of Sociology,* 66 (1960), 32–42.

[71]George Ritzer and Harrison M. Trice, "An Empirical Study of Howard Becker's Side-Bet Theory," *Social Forces,* 47 (1969), 475–478.

[72]For more on the commitment see, Robert A. Stebbins, "On Misunderstanding the Concept of Commitment: A Theoretical Clarification," *Social Forces,* 48 (1970), 526–529; Ritzer and Trice, "On the Problem of Clarifying Commitment Theory," *Social Forces,* 48 (1970), 530–533; Mary Sheldon, "Investments and Involvements as Mechanisms Producing Commitment to the Organization," *Administrative Science Quarterly,* 15 (1970), 473–481; Michael P. Johnson, "Commitment: A Conceptual Structure and Empirical Application," *Sociological Quarterly,* 14 (1973), 395–406; H.L. Hearn and Patricia Stoll, "Continuance Commitment in Low-Status Occupations: The Cocktail Waitress," *Sociological Quarterly,* 16 (1975), 105–114; Robert M. Steers, "Antecedents and Outcomes of Organizational Commitment," *Administrative Science Quarterly,* 22 (1977), 46–56; R.A. Flude, "The Development of an Occupational Self-Concept and Commitment to an Occupation in a Group of Skilled Manual Workers," *The Sociological Review,* 25 (1977), 41–49; Neena L. Chappell, "Paid Labor: Confirming a Conceptual Distinction Between Commitment and Identification," *Sociology of Work and Occupations,* 7 (1980), 81–116; Arthur P. Brief and Ramon J. Aldag. "Antecedents of Organizational Commitment Among Hospital Nurses," *Sociology of Work and Occupations,* 7 (1980), 210–221; Harold L. Angle and James L. Perry, "Organizational Commitment: Individual and Organizational Influences," *Work and Occupations,* 10 (1983), 123–146; Thomas S. Bateman and Stephen Strasser, "A Longitudinal Analysis of the Antecedents of Organizational Commitment," *Academy of Management Journal,* 27 (1984), 95–112; Derek Layder, "Sources and Levels of Commitment in Actors' Careers," *Work and Occupations,* 11 (1984), 147–162.

port for structural rather than attitudinal factors in explaining commitment.[73] However, in a study of federal and state park and forest rangers, Shoemaker, Snizek, and Bryant found that social-psychological factors were better predictors of organizational (and occupational) commitment than were structural factors.[74] More recently, Snizek and Little examined the same park and forest rangers five years later. [75] They found little change over time in the effect of structural and attitudinal factors on organizational commitment, but structural factors had become more important than social-psychological factors in explaining occupational commitment. Snizek and Little also found a decline over the five years in both occupational and organizational commitment as well as a decline in the explanatory power of both structural and psychological factors. The clear implication is that there may be other factors that are important in understanding commitment.

Lateral Movement

Given the commitment of managers to their employing organization, and the fact that there are relatively few opportunities for upward mobility (at least in comparison to the large numbers of lower-echelon people desirous of promotion), we should not be surprised to find considerable opportunity for horizontal (lateral) mobility within organizations. Lateral mobility takes a variety of forms.

Often people are moved laterally from department to department so they can gain experience needed to be considered for top positions. In personnel administration, for example, it is generally believed that people must have experience in many areas in the field before they can fill the position of personnel manager.

Sometimes, a person is moved laterally into a position that serves as a *testing point*; here it is determined "whether he moves on along a line to intermediate or higher management, horizontally to other staff or line jobs, or terminates his career at the level involved."[76] Success generally means continued upward movement, but timing now becomes a problem. To promote, the organization must have higher-level positions open. Frequently, however, it finds the next higher positions filled by job incumbents who cannot be moved up, down, or laterally. Since organizations are unlikely to fire such individuals, the people below who are ready to move are blocked. As a result, they may become unhappy over their prospects and seek to transfer, or to leave the company.

[73]Joseph A. Alutto, Lawrence G. Hrebiniak, and Ramon C. Alonzo, "On Operationalizing the Concept of Commitment," *Social Forces*, 51 (1973), 448–454.

[74]Donald J. Shoemaker, William E. Snizek, and Clifton D. Bryant, "Towards a Further Clarification of Becker's Side-Bet Hypothesis as Applied to Organizational and Occupational Commitment," *Social Forces*, 56 (1977), 598–603.

[75]William E. Snizek and Robert E. Little, "Accounting for Occupational and Organizational Commitment: A Longitudinal Reexamination of Structural and Attitudinal Approaches," *Sociological Perspectives*, 27 (1984), 181–196.

[76]Norman H. Martin and Anselm L. Strauss, "Patterns of Mobility within Industrial Organizations," *Journal of Business*, 29 (1956), 101–110.

Lateral moves may also constitute subtle demotions, as we will see shortly. Or one may move horizontally simply because there is nowhere else to go: if upward mobility is blocked, the organization may move individuals around laterally to give the illusion, at least, that they are progressing.

Demotion

In addition to moving vertically or horizontally, it is also possible for managers to move down in organizations. Goldner is concerned with the ways in which organizations make failure (demotion) "socially acceptable."[77] Outstanding performance is often not needed to move up, and adequate performance is generally sufficient to maintain one's position. Even when performance is inadequate, however, the organization is unlikely to fire individuals.[78] By rarely firing and gently demoting, the company removes most of the fear elements from its environment. However, anxiety is not totally eliminated from managers' lives. An occasional firing or outright demotion serves to keep them on their toes. Thus, demotion at a later point in the career is accepted as likely by most of Goldner's respondents.

The most fascinating portion of Goldner's study centers on the ways in which organizations and individuals adapt to demotion. The following outlines some methods organizations use to ease the impact of demotion:

1. Demotions are often obscured. Organizations hide them in a mass of ambiguity and constant movement between positions, which makes it difficult to be certain a move has been a demotion. These ambiguities tend to soften the blow.
2. Equally ambiguous is the demotion to a less desirable geographic location, even though the position remains the same.
3. Some companies give along with the demotion a reward, such as a free trip or no reduction in pay.
4. Since many demotions may be followed by promotions, it is difficult to differentiate managers demoted for further training so that they can fill higher jobs from managers demoted for inadequate performance.

Individuals who have been demoted also have a variety of means of adaptation.

1. Redefining themselves, both before and after demotion. For example, they may emphasize the high "price" one must pay to move up in the organization.
2. Shifting attention to other activities such as leisure time and community involvement.
3. Managing embarrassment in facing others in the organization after demotion.

---

[77]Fred H. Goldner, "Demotion in Industrial Management," *American Sociological Review*, 30 (1965), 714–725.

[78]On a more general level Goode has argued that the protection of the inept is ubiquitous. He notes that groups do not expose or expel members because of lack of achievement or talent. In fact, one of the major reasons for the effectiveness of industrial societies is their ability to use the inept and restrict the amount of destruction they can cause. William J. Goode, "The Protection of the Inept," *American Sociological Review*, 32 (1967), 5–19.

Dalton points out that the "assistant-to" office is an effective place into which to demote people. Such offices rarely have any real function, but at least it appears as if the individual has been promoted rather than demoted. These may also be used as holding positions for individuals who will be promoted when a position opens up.

Douglas More develops a more elaborate typology of demotion than does Goldner.[79] In addition to the types described by Goldner, More adds:

1. Lowered status with lower compensation.
2. Retention of the same job with a cut in salary.
3. Being bypassed for a promotion.
4. Being moved to a less desirable function.
5. Keeping the same job but having some subordinates moved.
6. Being bypassed in a general increase in salary.
7. Having steps added in the hierarchy above one's position.
8. Lateral movement from the high-status "line" (production) to the lower-status "staff" (for example, personnel department).
9. Staying essentially where one is, but being moved out of the line of promotion.
10. Elimination of one's position and reassignment.

Some of More's types of demotion are so subtle that fellow workers may be unaware that a person has been demoted. Others (for example, lowered status with lower compensation) are so blatant that they are likely to have important repercussions.

More also discusses individual reaction to demotion. The individual who has been demoted may show "increasing negativism, bitterness, resistance to direction within the firm, and may go as far as to express a defeatist attitude with respect to his total life goals."[80] Demotion may also have positive functions, causing a person "to work hard to recapture former status, resulting in increased effort and output. The man may become more realistically self-critical and may drive himself toward more thoroughness and perfectionism."[81] Others may be happy that they are no longer in positions they found too difficult to handle.

Demotion may have a number of impacts on middle-level managers in general. Because of a demotion, or a series of them, productivity, creativity, loyalty, and protective cliques may decrease, while turnover, illness, and absenteeism, abuse of privileges, and moonlighting may increase. While demotion may have some positive functions for the middle-management group in general, its negative effects are likely to be dominant. For this reason, most demotions are handled in the subtle way outlined by More and Goldner.

The comparatively gentle way in which demotion is handled contradicts the image of a ruthless American industry. In fact, there is little difference between industry and the civil service in the virtual impossibility of taking extreme actions against less than competent employees. In his study of British

---

[79]Douglas More, "Demotion," *Social Problems,* 9 (1962), 213–221.
[80]Ibid., 219.
[81]Ibid.

industry, Sofer found much the same phenomenon.[82] He uncovered a number of reasons for the reluctance to identify failures and deal with them severely. First, there is a genuine concern for others and a desire to protect their self-esteem. Second, those taking the action are, in effect, admitting their past failures in promoting such a person; it is therefore in their interests not to make demotion an abrupt and public event. Finally, extreme actions are avoided because of the threat to morale they pose for the entire organization.

On the basis of his analysis, Sofer concludes: "Whatever the complex of reasons it is clear that the difference between the reported Japanese practice of retaining industrial employees indefinitely once they have been appointed and Western practice is only one of degree."[83] The Japanese method of dealing with employees to which Sofer refers is outlined by Abegglen in this way:

> At whatever level of organization in the Japanese factory, the worker commits himself on entrance to the company for the remainder of his working career. The company will not discharge him even temporarily except in the most extreme circumstances. He will not quit the company for industrial employment elsewhere. He is a member of the company in a way resembling that in which persons are members of families, fraternal organizations, and other intimate and personal groups in the United States.[84]

Although this is our image of Japanese business practice, Ouchi cautions us that lifetime employment is true of only about one-third of the Japanese labor force.[85] Nonetheless, it is still the case that American and British organizations are not nearly as paternalistic as Japanese organizations. There are surprising resemblances, however, including their unwillingness to employ extreme methods of punishment.

If organizational leaders are unlikely to demote anyone, they like even less to fire anyone,[86] or for that matter take *any* form of extreme action. Despite this, we should recognize that demotions do occur. In a historical study of the St. Louis Police Department, Maniha shows that as the department became more and more bureaucratized, the tendency to demote increased slightly, while all other forms of negative personnel action such as dismissal and forced resignation declined.[87] Maniha believes that demotion is the control mechanism most compatible with bureaucratic structures. For one thing, in order to demote one needs a hierarchical bureaucratic structure with its

---

[82]Cyril Sofer, *Men in Midcareer: A Study of British Managers and Technical Specialists* (London: Cambridge University Press, 1970).

[83]Ibid., p. 24.

[84]James C. Abegglen, *The Japanese Factory: Aspects of Its Social Organization* (Glencoe, Il: Free Press, 1958), p. 11; see also, Robert E. Cole, "Permanent Employment in Japan: Facts and Fantasies," *Industrial and Labor Relations Review*, 26 (1972), 615–630.

[85]William G. Ouchi, *Theory Z: How American Business Can Meet the Japanese Challenge* (New York: Avon, 1982), p. 15.

[86]Diane Rothbard Margolis, *The Managers: Corporate Life in America: Work, Family and Community* (New York: William Morrow and Co., 1979), p. 73.

[87]John K. Maniha, "Organizational Demotion and the Process of Bureaucratization," *Social Problems*, 20 (1972), 161–173. See also, John K. Maniha, "The Standardization of Elite Careers in Bureaucratizing Organizations," *Social Forces*, 53 (1974), 283–288.

myriad of finely graded positions. Such a structure makes demotion, and the obscuring of it, more possible. Another aspect of bureaucracies, pension programs, means those who are demoted are unlikely to quit since they might well lose their pension rights. Thus demotion fits into the structure of the bureaucratized world, as long as it is done quietly and with discretion.

Professionals, managers, and officials are the occupational roles with the widest array of steps in career patterns; the rest of the occupational categories offer far fewer mobility opportunities. Let us turn to a discussion of some of these categories and see why they have constricted career patterns.

Constricted Mobility in Middle- and Lower-level Occupations

Clerical workers. There are few upward steps open to the white-collar clerical worker. Most clerical workers are not college graduates. After a few early job moves, most must reconcile themselves to the fact that there are very few better positions open to them. In this sense they are little different from blue-collar workers. Top management is unlikely to consider clerical workers for management positions, even if they perform their work in an outstanding manner. Increasingly, the managerial positions to which such people might aspire are filled by college graduates, as well as those with advanced degrees. With no possibility of movement up, they take some pride that their white-collar status has more prestige than blue-collar workers,[88] in spite of the fact that many blue-collar workers earn more money.

If one examines the nature of various white-collar clerical occupations, other reasons for the immobility experienced in them become clear. One barrier, in a society where sexism continues to exist, is the fact that they are almost always female ("pink-collar" workers). Furthermore, the skills of clerical workers have few applications at the managerial level. If secretaries excel at word processing, typing, and shorthand, they can expect job security but little in the way of promotions. Bookkeepers may be very skilled at making computer runs or ledger entries, but this does not prepare them to be managers of a highly complex accounting department. Yet it should be remembered that a lack of skill does not necessarily prevent a person at the managerial level from being promoted to high ranks. The most basic reason for the immobility of white-collar workers is that there is a chasm in most organizations between higher-level managers and clerical workers. This chasm is a result of the greater educational credentials of higher-level managers as well as the fact that clerical workers are generally drawn from a subordinate class (women) and are, as a result, not considered for—and even actively kept from—promotional opportunities.

Although white-collar clerical workers find it difficult to move up, they may find some solace in the fact that they are also unlikely to move down. Status differences within white-collar work have been leveled. Thus the white-collar clerical workers in any office are at essentially the same level. Poor performance, within bounds, is unlikely to have any impact on careers. Demotion

---

[88]The fact that this is changing and that white–collar workers find it increasingly difficult to derive this kind of satisfaction will concern us in Chapter 11.

to the ranks of blue-collar work is extremely unlikely in most organizations. White-collar workers know that merely adequate performance is likely to be enough to ensure them of their position for life. If they are in the civil service, they are even more secure because the civil service rules make it very difficult to fire white-collar workers.

Semiprofessionals.[89]   There is also little upward mobility in the semi-professions of teaching, social work, nursing, and librarianship. The only alternative open to most are administrative positions, and there are few of these to accommodate the many teachers, social workers, nurses, and librarians. Further, not many semiprofessionals see such movement as a meaningful goal, for it is in effect a move out of the occupation. Movement down, in any formal sense, is also a very remote possibility for semiprofessionals. Their most viable mobility route is through horizontal moves. This is shown in Becker's study of the schoolteacher, although the same ideas apply to the other semiprofessions.

As Becker points out, horizontal mobility is often an ignored dimension in the study of career patterns. There are clearly important differences among occupations that are on the same level. Becker writes:

> All positions at one level of work hierarchy, while theoretically identical, may not be equally easy or rewarding places in which to work. Given this fact, people tend to move in patterned ways among the possible positions, seeking that situation which affords the most desirable setting in which to meet and grapple with the basic problems of their work.[90]

The schoolteacher's major problem at work is students, and this career pattern typically consists of moving from school to school until the "right" kind of student is found.[91] Becker found that the teachers he studied in Chicago placed students in three categories: (1) lower-class and black students who were viewed as "difficult to teach, uncontrollable and violent in the sphere of discipline, and morally unacceptable on all scores;" (2) middle-class students, who were viewed as "hardworking but also slow to learn, extremely easy to control, and most acceptable on the moral level;" (3) upper-class students, who "were felt to be quick learners and easy to teach, but somewhat 'spoiled' and difficult to control and lacking in the important moral traits of politeness and respect for elders."[92] And in addition to the right kind of students, there were (4) the "right" kinds of principals, colleagues, and parents.

A desirable teaching position is one in which are found the desired types in each of the four categories. Lower-class slum schools are least desirable on all counts. Therefore, there are many requests to transfer out of these schools and few requests to transfer into them. Slum schools are typically staffed by new teachers, who generally transfer out as soon as they can. How quickly

---

[89]This section was written primarily by Richard Bell.

[90]Howard S. Becker, "The Career of the Chicago Public Schoolteacher," *American Journal of Sociology*, 57 (1952), 470.

[91]In recent years this option has not been open to most teachers because of the dearth of teaching positions.

[92]Becker, "The Career of the Chicago Public Schoolteacher."

transfers occur is based on a number of career contingencies. For one thing, teachers must have enough information to judge what is in fact a good school. Second, if they are black, or are labeled as troublemakers, it will be difficult to move to a "better" school. Finally, patience is required to wait for the "right" opening, rather than accepting the first available change of location.

A second type of career pattern exists for those teachers who adjust to the lesser school in which they began. They learn to live in that school, to be satisfied with lesser accomplishments, and to understand the behavior of the students they once found repugnant. A number of factors serve to keep them in the lower-class schools: acquisition of status among colleagues, a reputation as a disciplinarian that helps to keep the students from misbehaving, and stable relationships with the parents. These adjustments help to commit teachers to their schools and make them afraid to move because of what they would lose.

Through either of these adjustments the teacher achieves a relatively stable worklife, but this stability is continually threatened by external changes. If the social-class composition of the students should change, a desirable location then becomes undesirable. The age distribution in a community might change, leaving fewer children and a smaller need for public school teachers. Finally, a new, unsympathetic principal might upset the teacher's stable worklife.

The concept of reality shock applies particularly well to the careers of semiprofessionals.[93] There is often a rather large gap between what semiprofessionals are taught in school to expect from their occupations and what they actually encounter when they enter the workworld.

Potential teachers often enter schools of education with a high degree of idealism,[94] and these idealistic notions are at least formally perpetuated by the educational system. When they teach their own classes, they expect to help humanity, train the young, and help them become future successes. But these hopes and aspirations are very often dashed in the first weeks on the job. Idealism is quickly shattered by the reality shock of the position.

The first stage in the transition from idealism to reality is the formal orientation meeting that occurs over the course of several days prior to the opening of school. In one sense, this is a rite of passage marking the transition from student to teacher status.[95] But more important, for our purposes, it constitutes the new teacher's first reality shock. At these sessions, idealistic discussions of educational principles are of a low priority. Rather, the emphasis is on demonstrating to teachers that their primary role will be that of custodian and guardian to a captive and disruptive student body. They are initiated into a bureaucracy that tries to regulate and routinize children and teachers alike in order to run smoothly. The teachers are expected to conform

---

[93]For an application of the concept of reality shock to a profession, see Dan C. Lortie, "Layman to Lawman: Law School, Careers, and Professional Socialization," *Harvard Educational Review*, 29 (1959), 252–369.

[94]Benjamin D. Wright and Shirley A. Turner, "Career Dreams of Teachers," in Athena Theodore, ed., *The Professional Woman* (Cambridge, MA: Schenkman, 1971), pp. 334–345.

[95]Elizabeth M. Eddy, *Becoming a Teacher: The Passage to Professional Status* (New York: Columbia University Teachers College Press, 1971).

strictly to the rules laid down by the administration so that they may act as effective transmitters of these rules to pupils.

A second aspect of socialization into the reality of teaching is the initiation into the formal normative system and status hierarchy within the school. The informal group of teachers introduces neophytes into the culture and folklore of the school. It is made clear that new teachers must internalize this normative system. The neophytes are also socialized into the informal status hierarchy among teachers. While not recognized by the administration, this group, in particular those who stand at the top of it, exercise a profound influence on the day-to-day operation of the school. New teachers, especially young ones, soon learn that they stand at the bottom of the hierarchy, subject to control by a variety of subgroups that stand above. From these groups are gleaned such things as the proper dress, correct topics of conversation, and proper behavior. These informal rules, largely oriented toward nonacademic matters, constitute a second reality shock for the new teachers. It is in the famous (or infamous) teacher's lounge that these norms are inculcated and policed.[96]

A third source of reality shock are the students. Teachers usually expect to encounter students who are dutiful, dependent on them, responsive to their rewards and punishments, and anxious, or at least willing, to learn. What the teachers often encounter, however, is a very different kind of student:

> In general, I am appalled. . . . I have to remind myself that I have a very different background from theirs, but I keep putting myself in their place. I keep remembering when I was in school, how I wanted to learn, how I was respectful—not that I was a perfect angel. . . . This utter lack of respect and the slamming of doors, using filthy words, telling me to drop dead is really the thing that shocked me these past few months.[97]

Thus, in a variety of ways, the reality of teaching comes as quite a shock to the new teacher.

Social workers have career patterns typified by a largely theoretical education that fails to prepare them for real-life problems that will be faced on the job. The faculties in schools of social work are often interested in highly esoteric and theoretical issues.[98] And social work schools may be more interested in their own prestige than in the adequacy of their training programs. Hence the schools tend to hire faculty on the basis of their academic pedigree, or publication record, rather than on the basis of their ability to understand real-life problems. Such professors may be hostile to practitioners, regarding them as "conceptually and theoretically illiterate."[99]

Despite the academic character of training, social workers are still likely

---

[96]Frank Musgrove and Philip H. Taylor, *Society and the Teacher's Role* (London: Routledge and Kegan Paul, 1969).

[97]Eddy, *Becoming a Teacher,* p. 11.

[98]Scott Briar, "Practice and Academia," *Social Work,* 18 (1973), 2.

[99]John L. Ehrlich and Jessie F. McClure, "The Grassroots and the Ivory Tower," *Social Work,* 19 (1974), 653.

to enter the agency with a commitment to helping clients with real problems, but this commitment is in for a great shock. Social workers are subordinated to superiors who "are physically and operationally removed from the worker's daily activities because they are located in the agency's central office."[100] Furthermore, the administrators are often pressed by the realities of agency life into resolving any conflicts of interest in the direction of the agency rather than the client. Faced with distant administrators who are forced politically to be oriented more toward the organization than the clients, new social workers must learn to "work the system" in order to be able to service clients. But they are confronted daily by formal rules and administrative decisions that make helping clients more and more difficult. As the ability to assist the client recedes, the social worker's initial idealism and enthusiasm is frequently replaced by cynicism and defeatism.

The ability of social workers to help clients is undermined in a variety of ways. For one thing, social workers have entered the field with the notion that help must be provided to the "whole" client.[101] But the realities of bureaucratic life make it easier to divide up the labors and therefore divide up the client into a set of psychological problems, economic problems, family problems, and so forth. Another factor in reducing the ability of social workers to help clients is the constant supervision by superiors in the organization. Deviations from the norm in order to help a client, or for any other reason, are likely to be sanctioned by the ever-present supervisor.

The realities of life in the semiprofessions are a great shock to newcomers. It is for this reason, at least in part, that there is such high turnover here. This is likely to be especially true of the most creative and innovative semiprofessionals.

> Evidence might be found that the creative type of teacher tends to be an itinerant drifter moving from district to district . . . finally giving up. Even where tenure provides a semblance of security, a teacher who displays originality and creativity can be made so uncomfortable that he finally leaves the profession.[102]

This same pressure is likely to confront those in other semiprofessions, as well as those in a wide array of other occupations.

Semiskilled and unskilled workers.   People who work in semiskilled and unskilled occupations have little chance of career mobility, in particular upward mobility. This fact, supported by a number of studies,[103] contradicts the

[100]Henry Wasserman, "The Professional Social Worker in a Bureaucracy," *Social Work,* 16 (1971), 89–95.

[101]Nina Toren, *Social Work: The Case of a Semi-Profession* (Beverly Hills, CA: Sage Publications, 1972).

[102]Arthur F. Corey, "Overview of Factors Affecting the Holding Power of the Teaching Professions," in T.M. Stinnett, ed., *The Teacher Dropout* (Bloomington, IN: Phi Delta Kappa, Inc., 1970), p. 5.

[103]The major study of this genre is Peter M. Blau and Otis Dudley Duncan's *The American Occupational Structure.*

widely held notion that there is no limit to the horizons of a person with ability and ambition.

Chinoy's study of the automobile worker emphasized the highly limited possibility of upward mobility in that industry.[104] Focusing on semiskilled workers, he found that once in the occupation individuals found few places to which they could move. Quitting the automobile industry and moving into independent business is not a viable alternative for the automobile workers: for one thing, the small, essential industries that formerly were independent of the major automobile companies have been swallowed up by the large firms; and few automobile workers possess the skills and capital needed for success as independent small entrepreneurs. Movement *up* the organization's hierarchy has also become highly unlikely. The automobile industry is composed of huge plants within enormous organizations, and this makes it difficult for low-status employees to get the recognition that would enable them to rise. Technical and managerial occupations are increasingly beyond the levels of education that most blue-collar workers attain. As college graduates become more and more common, management is able to fill even lower managerial and technical positions with them.

Even such positions as skilled tradesman and foreman are unrealistic goals for upwardly mobile automobile workers. Increasing mechanization has expanded the number of semiskilled positions and reduced the number of skilled occupations. Hence there are a large number of semiskilled workers vying for a decreasing number of skilled positions. And even the position of foreman is now often being filled with college graduates. (However, it should be clear that many blue-collar workers would not desire the position in any case, for the pay differential between foreman and blue-collar worker is relatively small, and many do not find it worth the greater responsibility they must carry as foreman. Further, many blue-collar workers do not want to be in the uncomfortable position of supervising former peers, whose resentment they are likely to incur if they accept the position. They are also faced with the problem of gaining enough "social distance" between themselves and their former co-workers.)

With all sources of upward mobility virtually closed to blue-collar automobile workers, one might expect them to seek "better" jobs within the blue-collar category. Chinoy reports, however, that this too offers little hope for the auto workers, who find that the pay and status differences between semiskilled occupations are so slight that it is hardly worth the effort. Furthermore, union seniority rules have all but ruled out even this possibility of mobility.

Chinoy's study of the automobile industry does not take into account the realities of the automobile industry in the 1980's. For one thing, as the industry has shrunk as a result of foreign competition, there are fewer positions within the industry. For another, technological change is beginning to rapidly reduce the number of blue-collar workers needed on the assembly-line. As a result of these changes, modern automobile workers are much more inter-

---

[104]Ely Chinoy, *Automobile Workers and the American Dream* (Boston: Beacon Press, 1955).

ested in holding on to their present jobs than they are in their limited possibilities of moving up in the organization.

Lastly, Mars and Nicod studied the careers of waiters in hotels in Great Britain.[105] For those waiters who work in low-status hotels, there are few if any career options, with only slight status differences among the various positions open to them. On the other hand, those who work in high-status hotels do have some career steps open to them:

1. *Commis* Waiter—This is a trainee position in which the newcomer does most of the menial jobs in the hotel restaurant.
2. *Demi-chef*—This is not a chef, but simply the next step up the waiter career ladder.
3. *Chef de rang*—This is a relatively senior waiter position in which the individual is often in charge of two or more junior waiters.
4. Station head waiter—This is a senior waiter in charge of a station, including three or more junior waiters.
5. First head waiter.
6. Restaurant manager.

In addition to this formal hierarchy, there is also an elaborate informal system. A key element is the increasing ability to supplement one's income through pilferage and theft ("fiddling"). A variety of items are open to fiddling, including illicitly obtained food, soap, toilet paper, tablecloths, and even money. This example of deviance within a conventional occupation brings us to careers within deviant occupations.

Deviant Occupations[106]

As with semiskilled and unskilled occupations, deviant occupations offer little formal organization mobility. They are however, often organized as informal status hierarchies reflecting the values and work circumstances of the occupational communities. The status hierarchies are a major avenue of mobility for persons in deviant occupations.

Professional gamblers. Based on his study of the poker cardrooms of Gardens, California, Hayano describes four major types of professional gamblers.[107] Although there are variations in skill among professional gamblers, they are primarily distinguished from one another based on their sources of income and the stakes of the games in which they play. Some support themselves exclusively on their gambling winnings, and others have other sources of income. As a group, professional gamblers are distinguished from other

[105]Gerald Mars and Michael Nicod, *The World of Waiters* (London: George Allen and Unwin, 1984).

[106]This section was written by Gale Miller. For a general discussion of the study of careers in deviant occupations see, David F. Luckenbill and Joel Best, "Careers in Deviance and Respectability: The Analogy's Limitations," *Social Problems*, 29 (1981), 197-206.

[107]David M. Hayano, *Poker Faces* (Berkeley: University of California Press, 1982).

gamblers who are often described as "losers" because of their lack of skill and need to hold nongambling jobs to support themselves and cover their losses. Professional gamblers may have nongambling sources of income, but they are capable of supporting themselves through gambling.

The four types identified by Hayano are the worker professional, outside-supported professional, subsistence professional, and career professional. Professional gamblers do not spend their entire careers in only one category, however; rather, their involvement in gambling may vary over time based on the circumstances of their lives. Worker professionals are persons who earn a substantial part of their incomes from full-time and part-time jobs. For these people, "security in predictable paychecks and the social appearance of legitimacy are more valued alternatives than attempting to live and work full-time in the poker cardroom."[108] Outside-supported professionals are gamblers who do not hold jobs but have regular incomes from pensions, trust funds, social security, or similar sources. These gamblers usually play in small-stakes games, and their winnings are used to supplement their primary incomes.

Subsistence professionals are full-time gamblers who are totally dependent on their winnings for their income. They desire a moderate level of winnings each day and quit for the day when the desired level is attained. They usually play in small- and medium-stakes games where they are reasonably certain that they can win enough money to meet their daily needs. Career professionals are also dependent on their gambling winnings for their livelihoods. Unlike subsistence professionals, however, career professionals are interested in big winnings, and they seek games that test their skills. These persons are committed to gambling as a way of life and, in addition to money, they are interested in developing their skills and being recognized as outstanding players. Successful career professionals are the elite of gambling.

Female prostitution[109]   At the bottom of the hierarchy of female prostitution are the streetwalkers, who are receptive to any man able to pay the price, which is comparatively low. These are women who operate almost exclusively in lower-class areas. Near the bottom are the women who work in houses of prostitution. There are several types of prostitutes who fall somewhere in the middle of the hierarchy, although their status is not exactly clear. One is the party girl, who goes out on no more than one date a night and never explicitly discusses the question of a fee. However, the fact that there is a fee involved has been made clear by the person arranging the contact. Party girls are much more selective than streetwalkers or house girls and frequently will refuse a customer if he is unappealing. Another category is the kept woman, who "usually gives her favors to only one man at a time in return for financial secu-

---

[108]Ibid., p. 22.

[109]Harold Greenwald, "The Social and Professional Life of the Call-Girl," in Simon Dinitz et al., eds., *Deviance* (New York: Oxford University Press, 1969), p. 408. Also see, Jennifer James, "Prostitutes and Prostitution," in Edward Sagarin and Fred Montanino, eds., *Deviants* (Morristown, NJ: General Learning Press, 1977), 369–428; Barbara Sherman Heyl, "Prostitution: An Extreme Case of Sex Stratification," in Freda Adler and Rita James Simon, eds., *The Criminology of Deviant Women* (Boston: Houghton and Mifflin Company, 1979), 196-212.

rity during the time that the arrangement is in effect."[110] At the top is the call girl "who operates on an appointment basis, maintaining her own residence, which may or may not serve as a place for entertaining clients."[111] In many cases, it is unrealistic to differentiate between party girls, kept women, and call girls because the same women may alternately occupy each of these positions at one time or another. By the same token, the streetwalkers, house girls, and others at this level are also, in most cases, indistinguishable. Thus, we are left with two basic levels and there is little possibility of career mobility between them. That is, streetwalkers seldom become call girls and call girls seldom become streetwalkers.

One of the puzzling aspects of the status hierarchy that characterizes prostitution is the inverse relationship between skills and status. That is, the streetwalker holds lower status than the call girl, although the range of skills involved in public solicitation are greater. A key factor in accounting for this aspect of prostitution appears to be related to the selectivity of the prostitute. As mentioned above, the call girl is much more selective in her clientele than is the streetwalker; the streetwalker is more likely to solicit strangers. A second aspect of the status division involves the setting of the relationship. The call girl does not publicly solicit, nor does she use public facilities as meeting places with her customers. Rather, she is more likely to meet her customer at either her residence or the customer's residence. The streetwalker, on the other hand, must use the facilities that are available. Female prostitution, then, is an occupation that does not possess a status hierarchy based on the differential possession of skills; rather, it is based on the nature of the work setting and the nature of the customers.

The loss of physical attractiveness is an important problem for the female prostitute. Winick and Kinsie, for example, claim that the average prostitute in the United States is between the ages of 25 and 40.[112] Although there are some women who work as prostitutes well into their 60s, most leave the occupation relatively early in life. The importance of physical attractiveness in the occupation is further demonstrated through the activities of those women who remain in it for an extended period of time. Most older prostitutes must adapt to the problems of age by seeking a new clientele or by specializing in sexual acts that other prostitutes avoid. Thus, the older prostitute is more likely to ply her trade in skid-row areas of cities or to become involved in sadistic and masochistic sexual activities. This represents severe downward mobility.

Madams. A career goal for some prostitutes is to become a madam.[113] While most women who become madams had experience as prostitutes,

---

[110]Harold Greenwald, "The Social and Professional Life of the Call-Girl."

[111]Ibid.

[112]Charles Winick and Paul M. Kinsie, *The Lively Commerce: Prostitution in the United States* (New York: Signet, 1971).

[113]Paul J. Goldstein, "Occupational Mobility in the World of Prostitution: Becoming a Madam," *Deviant Behavior* (1983), 267–279.

Goldstein found that such experience is not mandatory. Another surprising finding is that madams are not necessarily aging prostitutes who can no longer attract a clientele. On the contrary, many prostitutes who become madams do so at the peak of their careers when they find themselves with more clients than they can service themselves. Rather than lose clients (and all the income), the prostitute begins referring clients to other prostitutes. As one prostitute turned madam said:

> My business was very good. It got so good that I had to call in another girl, and then another girl, and then another girl. I had eight women, eventually, working for me. And eventually I didn't do anything. I sat around and reaped the profit.[114]

Goldstein suggests that there are three basic requirements for becoming a madam—certain personality characteristics and the ability to secure and maintain an adequate supply of customers and prostitutes. In terms of personality, a madam would need to be ambitious, to have the ability to organize and to lead, as well as the capacity to manage finances. Securing an adequate number of customers depends on developing a series of avenues of communication directly with customers or indirectly with those (such as taxi drivers, bartenders) who can refer customers. Finally, the madam must be able to secure and to negotiate with a sufficient number of prostitutes.

As a manager, the madam is seen as a position offering higher status, greater responsibility, and greater rewards than a prostitute. However, there are problems associated with the position. For one thing, there are the pressures that come with managerial responsibility. These pressures are undoubtedly greater than those confronting conventional managers as a result of the deviant character of the work. For another, prostitutes may end up earning more money than madams. For these reasons, it is questionable whether becoming a madam necessarily marks a step upward in the career of the prostitute. However, it does offer an alternative career for some prostitutes (and a few others as well).

Strippers.   As with the relatively unskilled occupation of female prostitution, the status hierarchy and career mobility of female stripping is only partially related to the differential possession of skills. At the top of the status system is the feature performer, or the star of the show. The feature performer is more likely than other strippers to have been formally trained in the occupation and, presumably, she is a more skilled performer. A more important aspect of her position, however, is her geographic mobility and her identification with the occupation as a whole. The feature performer is more likely to travel from nightclub to nightclub in pursuing her career, and her commitment to the occupation is, thereby, expanded beyond any single

[114]Ibid., 272–273.

nightclub in which she performs. A second stratum of strippers is made up of those women who work in one night club on a full-time basis. These strippers are often called "house girls" and their primary source of identification is with the nightclub and its personnel. Between the house girls and the feature performer is the co-feature. The co-feature's status and identification is not entirely clear, but she appears to combine many of the characteristics of both the feature performer and the house girls.

Stripping is another occupation in which emphasis is placed on physical attractiveness and the career patterns of the stripper reflect this. Salutin claims that most strippers fear growing old and "they will work desperately to create the illusion that their bodies are firm and still sexy."[115] Once it becomes clear that the stripper is no longer sexually attractive, she may remain in the occupation but her position changes. The older stripper is often relegated to the comedy segment of the show, where she acts as "the butt of the MC's dirty jokes."[116] Many older strippers are married and they leave the occupation by becoming full-time housewives, whereas others remain involved in the occupation by making and selling costumes.[117]

Criminals.   Because of the direct relationship between occupational success and the possession of the proper skills, it should not be surprising that the status hierarchies of criminal occupations are highly related to the differential possession of the required skills by occupational members. Letkemann indicates that there are four strata of criminals based on the possession of criminal skills.[118] The first is represented by the "rounder;" this person is the truly committed criminal. In many ways, the rounder is very conventional in his occupational pursuits; that is, "according to some criteria, such as dedication to a job, stability, and reliability, the true criminal or rounder is actually more like a 'square-john' than those who are not true criminals."[119] A second group of criminals is the category of "bums." These people make up the bulk of the criminal and prison populations. Their distinctive feature is the absence of any long-term or serious commitment to crime as an occupation. The category of "young punks" makes up a third stratum and it is distinguished by the youthful and unskilled nature of its population. Finally, the lowest stratum is made up of alcoholics, drug addicts, rapists, and others who are deemed undesirable by the rounders. The primary reason for the low prestige of the alcoholics and drug addicts stems from their addiction—they are seen as committed to something other than crime and, therefore, are considered unreliable. The rapist, on the other hand, receives his low status based on the immorality of his crime.

[115]Marilyn Salutin, "Stripper Morality," *Transaction,* 8 (1971), 21.

[116]Ibid

[117]Jacqueline Boles and A.P. Garbin, "Stripping for a Living: An Occupational Study of the Night Club Stripper," in Clifton Bryant, ed., *Deviant Behavior: Occupational and Organizational Bases* (Chicago: Rand-McNally, 1974), pp. 312–335.

[118]Peter Letkemann, *Crime as Work* (Englewood Cliffs, NJ: Prentice Hall, 1973).

[119]Ibid., p. 20.

RETIREMENT: THE CLOSE OF THE CAREER

While for some death marks the end of the occupational career,[120] for many others, retirement means the career is over.[121] The retirement age in our society is typically age 65, although some people may work beyond their sixty-fifth year. Currently, there are over 26 million retirees in the United States. Over the last 30 years the labor force participation rate for older workers has steadily declined. This trend has continued during recent years despite economic hard times and the 1978 Amendments to the Age Discrimination and Employment Act, which specifies age 70 as the mandatory retirement age.[122] In 1960, of men age 65 and over, 33.1 percent participated in the labor force. By 1982, this figure had dropped sharply to 17.8 percent. For women, the figures are 10.8 and 7.9 percent, respectively. This trend is similar for men between the ages of 55 and 64. Of the men in this age category, 86.8 percent participated in the labor force in 1960, while only 70.2 percent worked in 1982. However, labor force participation rates for women in this age group showed a slight increase from 37.2 percent in 1960 to 41.8 percent in 1982.[123]

In general, wage and salary workers are likely to retire earlier than the self-employed.[124] A self-employed owner of a printing firm in Washington, D.C. explains:

> If you stop working, you can only do so much yardwork. . . .I've seen too many people get messed up when they retire. This company has been a part of my life. I have no desire to run away from it.[125]

The occupational groups with the largest number of older workers are managerial and administrative, sales, service, and farm. On the other hand, in professional and technical occupations, as well as in operative, craft, and labor, those over 60 are underrepresented.[126]

Rones highlights some of the reasons for the over/under-representation of older workers in certain occupational categories. Among the professional

---

[120]While our focus in this section is on retirement from conventional occupations, it is useful to note that it is possible to discuss retirement from deviant occupations. See, for example, Patricia A. Adler and Peter Adler, "Shifts and Oscillations in Deviant Careers: The Case of Upper-Level Drug Dealers and Smugglers," *Social Problems*, 31 (1983), 195–207; Neal Shover, "The Later Stages of Ordinary Property Offender Careers," *Social Problems*, 31 (1983), 208–217; Thomas Meisenhelder, "Becoming Normal: Certification as a Stage in Exiting from Crime," *Deviant Behavior*, 3 (1982), 137–153.

[121]It should be noted that a sizable number of people continue to work on a part-time basis after their retirement. See, Alan L. Gustman and Thomas L. Steinmeier, "Modeling the Retirement Process for Policy Evaluation and Research," *Monthly Labor Review*, 107 (1984), 26–33.

[122]Philip L. Rones, "The Retirement Decision: A Question of Opportunity," *Monthly Labor Review*, 103 (November, 1980), 14–17; Jeffery L. Sheler, "No Letup in Trend to Retiring Early," *U.S. News & World Report* (February 15, 1982), pp. 55–56.

[123]U.S. Bureau of The Census, *Statistical Abstract of The United States: 1984*, 104th ed. (Washington, D.C., 1984), p. 407.

[124]Mildred Doering, Susan R. Rhodes, and Michael Schuster, *The Aging Worker: Research and Recommendations* (Beverly Hills, CA: Sage Publications, 1983), p. 158.

[125]Sheler, "No Letup in Trend to Retiring Early," p. 56.

[126]Philip L. Rones, "Older Men—The Choice Between Work and Retirement," *Monthly Labor Review*, 101 (November, 1978), 3–10.

and technical occupations, physicians, dentists, and lawyers continue to work well after retirement age, but this overrepresentation is more than offset by the early retirement of technical workers whose skills have become obsolete or who are not able to keep pace with younger, more highly educated technicians. Further, many professionals are self-employed, meaning flexibility to set hours, days worked, vacation time, and so forth, which makes it easier to remain active in the labor force.

One of the reasons why blue-collar workers are likely to retire early is that they are highly concentrated in industries that are represented by collective bargaining and hence are covered by well-maintained pension plans. (This is not the case with sales and service workers who are much less likely to be covered by unionized pension plans, and they also earn less over the course of their careers and can therefore expect lower levels of Social Security. Both factors help keep the retirement rates relatively low in these occupational categories.) Health of course is another reason why blue-collar workers are likely to retire early. As we will see in the final chapter in this book, operatives, craftworkers, and laborers are more likely to experience an injury on, or an illness related to, the job than any other category of worker. Even for older blue-collar workers who are in good health, the work may be just too hard.

Managerial and administrative occupations, on the other hand, are less physically trying, and this helps to maintain the over-representation of older workers in this occupational category. Further, experience is very important in these occupations, and older managers and administrators may possess skills, knowledge, and/or authority that puts them in a position which, for personal or organizational reasons, they cannot easily retire from. None of this is to suggest that some managers do not retire early, especially when the challenge is gone or the promotion hierarchy is blocked. A retired, 59-year-old manager states:

> I felt I had reached my maximum potential with the firm, and some of the challenge wasn't there anymore. . . . I felt I would leave the pressures and frustrations to a younger man.[127]

Similar to the professional, many farmers are self-employed and this brings with it the flexibility to remain active in the labor force. Other factors keeping the labor force paticipation rates high for farmers include a rising age structure—due to fewer and fewer new farmers—and low incomes that either permit farmers to work while still receiving Social Security or that force them to continue earning their livelihood.

An adequate understanding of retirement is contingent on a proper analysis of the functions that work can perform for the individual. Friedmann and Havighurst point out that work performs five functions for the individual: "income, regulating of life activities, identification, association, and meaningful life-experience."[128] Let us look at retirement in light of each of these five functions.

---

[127]Sheler, "No Letup in Trend to Retiring Early," p. 56.

[128]E.A. Friedmann and R.J. Havighurst, "Work and Retirement," in Sigmund Nosow and William H. Form, eds., *Man, Work and Society* (New York: Basic Books, 1962), p. 41.

Income

Most people who retire suffer a diminution in income.[129] In 1960, slightly over 8 million retired workers were receiving monthly benefit checks averaging $74 from Social Security. By 1980, nearly 20 million retired workers were receiving benefit checks averaging $341 monthly.[130] While our Social Security program is large and growing rapidly, few people can live in our economy solely on their income from it. Many people are, of course, also covered by various types of pension plans. In 1960, 18.7 million workers, or 37.2 percent of all private sector employees, were covered by some form of private retirement plan. In 1975, these figures had climbed to 30.3 million or 46 percent.[131] The assets of these private pension plans rose from $57 billion in 1960 to $573 billion in 1982.[132]

Writing in the early 1970s Cook, paraphrasing Winston Churchill, said of these programs, "never has so much done so little for so few."[133] Although conditions improved with the passage of the Employee Retirement Income Security Act (ERISA) of 1974, many of the pension problems described by Cook have not disappeared.[134] For one thing, many companies find it in their best interest to fire employees who are nearing the retirement age so that they do not have to pay them their pension money. (Although malevolent business executives have certainly played a role in this national disgrace, it is important to note that several firms are currently involved in offering larger pension benefits, cash bonuses, and other benefits to induce older workers to retire.[135] While these current efforts are motivated by a concern over rising costs and unemployment, they have the effect of making retirement more appealing to many workers.) More impersonal factors also contribute to the fact that few people get the pension money they deserve. For example, if a company goes out of business, or merges with another company, workers are likely to lose their pension benefits. Still another factor is the lack of portability of most pension plans. This means that when workers move from one company to another it is unlikely that their pensions will move with them. In our era of high occupational mobility, a great many people lose their pension benefits because they change jobs frequently. For most retirees, the loss of regular income combined with the inadequacy of our Social Security system and the failings of our private pension plans makes it likely that many will experience economic difficulties when they retire. In their study, Streib and Schneider found that, on the average, a retiree's income declined by 56 percent after retire-

---

[129]Ann Foner and Karen Schwab, "Work and Retirement in a Changing Society," in Matilda White Riley, Beth B. Hess, and Kathleen Bond, eds., *Aging in Society: Selected Reviews of Recent Research* (Hillsdale, NJ: Lawrence Erlbaum Associates, 1983), pp. 71–93.

[130]*Statistical Abstract of the United States: 1984,* p. 329.

[131]Ibid., p. 333.

[132]Ibid., p. 384.

[133]Fred J. Cook, "The Case of the Disappearing Pension," *New York Times Magazine* (March 19, 1972), p. 30.

[134]Lawrence Meyer, "Pensions: Many Pay, but Few Collect," *Washington Post* (September 6, 1982), pp. A1, A10.

[135]Jeffery Sheler, "As More Firms Nudge Out Employees," *U.S. News & World Report* (February 28, 1983), pp. 65–66.

ment.[136] However, contrary to popular opinion, many of the retirees seemed to be able to cope with their economic situation.

The passage of ERISA by Congress in 1974 eliminated some of the worst pension abuses. Minimum standards were established for the regulation and supervision of pension plans. Greater protection was afforded workers so that they were more likely to get the pension benefits they earned. Workers were also allowed to transfer pension benefits from one company to another. Employers were required to permit employees over the age of 25 to participate in a pension program if they worked for their employer for more than one year. ERISA also allowed people to set up their own Individual Retirement Accounts (IRAs). However, IRAs have tended to benefit the middle classes rather than lower-income people who need them the most.

Regulating Life Activity

Before retirement, people's daily activities are largely structured by the work routine. When retirement comes, they must adjust to a lack of such external structuring. Commenting on the loss of the stabilizing force of the corporate routine, a retired executive, Leland Bradford, said:

> When retirement comes, most of these routines stop. At first it seems heavenly: no clock ruling you, no secretary reminding you of your luncheon appointment, no hurried breakfast, no train to catch. So I found it; but not for long. Besides, inasmuch as my day no longer had its ready-made structure, I was left with the aggravating necessity of making many small decisions.[137]

It is untrue, however, that the only thing that structures people's lives is their work. Clearly other activities (television viewing, hobbies, club meetings) structures one's time. And many of these structuring factors continue to exist after an individual retires.[138] Although most retirees do not radically transform their lives, some alterations are likely. In Bradford's case, for example, there were informal morning rendezvous at the post office with other retirees. Golf dates, card games, cocktail parties, and dinners became established routines. Adding to the activities of retirees is the fact that between 15 and 25 percent of them find employment, usually part-time work.[139]

Identification

For those people who have been able to identify strongly with their work, retirement can constitute a serious problem. But we should remember that many people do not identify significantly with their occupation or em-

---

[136]Gordon F. Streib and Clement J. Schneider, *Retirement in American Society: Impact and Process* (Ithaca, NY: Cornell University Press, 1971); similar, and later, data are reported in Ann Foner and Karen Schwab, *Aging and Retirement* (Monterey, CA: Brooks/Cole Publishing Co., 1981), p. 33.

[137]Leland P. Bradford, "Can You Survive Your Retirement?" *Harvard Business Review,* 57 (November/December, 1979), 105.

[138]Foner and Schwab, *Aging and Retirement.*

[139]Ibid.

ploying organization, and for these people retirement does not constitute a significant break with their prior worklife.[140] Professionals[141] and managerial personnel are more likely to have identified with their occupation and employing organization and find retirement difficult. For others, like assembly-line workers, typists, or switchboard operators, retirement may be a welcome event.[142]

Association with Workmates

A fourth source of satisfaction with work is meaningful association with fellow workers. Upon retirement, most of these personal contacts are severed. Bradford recalls

> I felt the alienation of no longer being a part of groups I had belonged to for 40 or more hours a week for more years than I cared to remember. Even in my childhood, when I had been temporarily ostracized by playmates, I had not felt so keenly excluded, bereft, outside, disposable.
>
> I thought again of my friend who had returned hungrily to the office to seek the companionship of his past subordinates. What was different for him, and now for me, was the apparent lack of an arena offering equal challenges and companionship. I found it harder than I ever expected to say a permanent good-bye to a lifetime work career. It took time and suffering to find an adequate solution.[143]

Those peers and colleagues who retire at the same time may move to a new location, or they may die within a short period of time. The retired person must find a way to adapt to this. It is true that most people are able to make new contacts outside the work setting, and this makes retirement less isolated than many believe. However, there is certainly some loneliness and isolation, as is reflected by the proliferation of such groups as Golden Age clubs.

Meaningful Life Experience

Finally, many occupations also often offer an opportunity to gain a meaningful life experience. As defined by Friedmann and Havighurst, this may include "purposeful activity," "self-expression," "new experience," and "service to others."[144] As we have made clear, all occupations do not offer such opportunities; for example, blue-collar assembly-line work has few intrinsic characteristics that might be considered meaningful by those in them. Nevertheless, to many professionals, managers, skilled craftsmen, and so forth, life is work, and it is precisely in these categories that we find individuals most troubled by retirement. Again Bradford illustrates this point.

---

[140]Jill S. Quadagno, ed., *Aging, the Individual and Society: Readings in Social Gerontology* (New York: St. Martin's Press, 1980), p. 299.

[141]Jill S. Quadagno, "Career Continuity and Retirement Plans of Men and Women Physicians: The Meaning of Disorderly Careers," *Sociology of Work and Occupations*, 5 (1978), 55–73.

[142]Foner and Schwab, "Work and Retirement."

[143]Bradford, "Can You Survive Your Retirement?" 104.

[144]Friedmann and Havighurst, "Work and Retirement," pp. 41–55.

I found that golf did not fill a day. The consultation and volunteer work I did was not satisfying. Other interests paled before the challenges I had faced. Life felt empty. I was not aged, just a little older. I had plenty of energy and I felt just as competent as I had been.[145]

How is the doctor to compensate for losing the satisfaction of curing or helping patients? How is the college professor to compensate for losing contact with students? How is the manager to compensate for losing the thrill of competing, and at times winning? How is the skilled craftsman to compensate for the loss of the pleasure of completing a difficult task? In most cases such compensation is impossible, and this can make retirement very difficult.

It is interesting to note that for some high-status workers retirement may, in fact, constitute the beginning of a new career. Some professionals, of course, simply continue to practice into their seventies or eighties or until they die. Others may leave one profession for another. Doctors or lawyers may serve as consultants after they formally retire from their own practice. Top-ranking military officers have even more postretirement opportunities than most other professionals, partly because they may retire at a relatively early age. In addition, upon retirement they may have training, skills, and prestige, as well as contacts in government and the military, that make them highly useful to industry, particularly one involved in defense contracts. Reissman found that retired generals are likely to be employed at relatively high levels, such as president, manager, vice president, assistant to the vice president, chairman of the board, member of the board, and divisional manager.[146]

Myths About Retirement

An elaborate study of retirement conducted by Streib and Schneider challenged many myths about retirement.[147] For example, a surprisingly large 37 percent of men in their study were found to be willing to retire—in fact, a larger proportion of men than women. They also found that the act of retiring does not, in itself, lead to a deterioration in health. There was no clear decline in psychological health and apparently no significant increase in feelings of uselessness as a result of retirement. All in all, the Streib and Schneider data indicate that most retired people are satisfied with their lives, and a number of studies over the years have tended to confirm this fact.

Based on much of this research, Foner and Schwab address four myths about retirement in more general terms.[148] Overall they confirm the conclusion that "there is little support for the image of retirement as an affliction imposed on older workers."[149] A number of facts are marshaled in support of this general position.

[145]Bradford, "Can You Survive Your Retirement?" 103.

[146]Leonard Reissman, "Life, Careers, Power and the Profession: The Retired Army General," *American Sociological Review*, 21 (1956), 215–222.

[147]Streib and Schneider, *Retirement in American Society.*

[148]Foner and Schwab, "Work and Retirement"; see also, Herbert S. Parnes and Gilbert Nestel, "The Retirement Experience," in Herbert S. Parnes, ed., *Work and Retirement: A Longitudinal Study of Men* (Cambridge, MA: M.I.T. Press, 1981), pp. 155–197.

[149]Foner and Schwab, "Work and Retirement," p. 72.

First, most workers do *not* retire as a result of mandatory retirement rules. This is due, in part, to the fact that most older workers are not even covered by such rules. Furthermore, even many of those covered by these rules retire *before* it is required. Finally, many of those who retire at the mandatory age do so willingly; they are not resistant to retirement.

Second, retirees are generally *not* eager to reenter the labor force. Some are not able to return to work, while many others are simply not interested in working again.

Third, most retired people are satisfied with their retirement. In research carried out over a number of years, people have generally expressed satisfaction with retirement, feeling among other things, "that it had fulfilled their expectations, it was enjoyable, they were glad they retired when they did, these were the best years of their lives, or that they felt good about their lives since retiring."[150] Retirees compare favorably to older workers in terms of satisfaction with their lives. Of course, there are retirees who do not express satisfaction with their lives, but such feelings are usually associated with poor health[151] and low incomes.

Finally, there is no clear answer on the issue of the effect of retirement on health. While the health of retirees is not as good as their peers within the workforce, it does not appear that retirement itself is the cause of this situation. Retirees may have been in poor health *before* they retired; in fact, it may have been poor health that led them to retire. Foner and Schwab conclude:

> A case can be made that the link between poor health and retirement is more in the direction of health status as an influence on the decision to retire rather than a physical decline when individuals are removed from the labor force.[152]

How do we explain the fact that retirees seem far more satisfied with retirement than is generally assumed?

For one thing, a variety of social changes have served to make retirement a more satisfying experience. Attitudes toward retirement have changed in recent years. In the 1950s retirement might have been considered appropriate only for those with physical impairments but now many people regard retirement "as a right earned after a lifetime of employment . . . a well-earned rest or reward."[153] Furthermore, more and more people are actually looking forward to retirement.

Not only have attitudes toward retirement grown more positive, but an increasing number of people have the economic resources to maintain an adequate standard of living after retirement. This is traceable to such developments as the expansion of Social Security coverage (about 90 percent of all employees are now covered), the increase in benefits paid by Social Security, the indexing of Social Security to inflation, and enlargement of pension cov-

---

[150]Ibid., p. 74.

[151]Neal Schmitt, J. Kenneth White, Bryan W. Coyle, and John Rauschenberger, "Retirement and Life Satisfaction," *Academy of Management Journal*, 22 (1979), 282–291.

[152]Foner and Schwab, "Work and Retirement," p. 75.

[153]Ibid., p. 77.

erage. Also of crucial importance is the Medicare program, which removed the threat of catastrophic medical costs for individuals. Various other programs (for example, reduced taxes, discounts of various types) have eased the economic burdens on retirees.

Another factor is the increasing number of social supports for retirees. For one thing, there are simply more retirees, and this serves to make the status more acceptable and to give retirees more peers with whom to interact. Then there are a variety of organizations of retired persons—for example, the National Retired Teachers Association and the American Association of Retired Persons, with a combined membership in 1979 of over 11 million persons.

In addition to the social changes outlined above, a variety of changes in individuals that occur over the life cycle serve to ease the strains of retirement. For one thing, people lower their expectations as they approach retirement and as they progress through their retirement years. Likewise, people come to redefine their reward system. They come to value leisure time more and money less. They emphasize the power over their own lives rather than the power they may have exercised in the past over others. Finally, the changes associated with retirement are minimized as people seek to maintain their familiar activity patterns in spheres other than the work setting.

There are other steps that can be taken to ease the transition to retirement even further. For example, more can be done in the area of *anticipatory socialization,* "the process of learning attitudes and behaviors associated with a role before the individual is actually in the role."[154] Relatively few people carefully plan ahead for their retirement. More planning would obviously make the transition easier and more comfortable. There are counseling programs for future retirees in companies and unions, too, although clearly not enough.

More practically, Bradford[155] discusses several ways the organization can help the worker cope with retirement. First, employees should be encouraged to widen their personal interests and develop skills that could be used in leisure or in pursuit of a second career after retirement. These interests and skills counter the boredom and loneliness of retirement and provide meaning in one's life. Bradford also suggests that employing organizations conduct training programs during the early and middle years of employment. If geared toward maintaining or improving one's self-awareness and self-confidence, these programs could help bolster the individual's self-image, an important ingredient of satisfaction with life during retirement. Finally, Bradford emphasizes that the focal point of any organizational action should be a preretirement program one or two years ahead of one's scheduled retirement. These programs, designed to include the employee's spouse, should deal realistically with the potential problems associated with retirement.

Although we have focused on retirement and the problems associated with it, we should bear in mind that they are but part of a more general set of

---

[154]Foner and Schwab, *Aging and Retirement,* p. 60.
[155]Bradford, "Can You Survive Your Retirement?"

problems related to the increasing number of older people in American society. As Olson concludes: "The list of unresolved social ills faced by older people is endless."[156]

CONCLUSIONS

This chapter opened with a discussion of the labor markets within which occupational careers occur. Next we examined the careers associated with a wide array of occupations. We found that some professionals, managers, and officials experience a considerable amount of upward mobility during their careers. However, the vast majority of people face a worklife that offers little or no upward career mobility. This reality stands in stark contrast to the myth, widely held in American society, that upward mobility is available to anyone with ambition. However, although few workers can expect much upward career mobility, they can take some solace in the fact that they are unlikely to be demoted at any time in their careers. Demotion has a number of unpleasant side effects, and organizations are unlikely to use it as a social-control device, if it can be avoided. This contradicts another American myth—the idea that those who do not perform well will be treated ruthlessly. Although true upward and downward mobility are relatively rare, many occupations do offer a variety of informal career moves, or formal horizontal steps.

In addition to introducing the student to the career patterns associated with various occupations, this chapter has also been concerned with demonstrating the utility of a number of sociological concepts in understanding the nature of occupational careers. Among the concepts discussed are sponsorship, career contingencies, occupational obsolescence, investments in the job, reality shock, and demotion. Although these concepts are discussed in this chapter within the context of a particular type of occupation, they are applicable to virtually every occupation.

The chapter closed with a discussion of retirement. The focus was on problems associated with retirement as well as on the myths that abound about retirement's negative impact on workers.

---

[156]Laura Katz Olson, *The Political Economy of Aging: The State, Private Power, and Social Welfare* (New York: Columbia University Press, 1982).

EIGHT
CONFLICT IN THE
PROFESSIONS

In Chapter 4 we dealt in general terms with the process of professionalization. In this chapter we turn our attention to individual professionals and their position in the workworld, their conflicts and the resolutions employed to those conflicts. We differentiate between three broad types of professionals: (1) professionals who are employed, or spend a large portion of their worklives, in formal organizations; (2) "free professionals" who are not employed in large organizations or, if they are, are not seriously constrained by those organizations; and (3) scientists. Although most modern scientists are found in organizations (and a few issues relating to them will be discussed in the section on professionals in organizations), they have been singled out for mainly separate discussion because of their increasing importance in our "post-industrial society," as well as for their unique occupational conflicts and methods of resolution.

PROFESSIONALS IN ORGANIZATIONS

One of the most interesting and hotly debated issues in the sociology of occupations is the relationship between professionalization and bureaucratization. The most widely held position until recently declared that these two processes—and the resulting structures: professions and bureaucracies—are at least to some degree antithetical. This antithesis surfaces most clearly in the argument that professionals, when employed in bureaucracies, are confronted with conflict because of the basic differences between these two normative systems.[1] However, both the classic work of Max Weber and a number of more recent studies have tended to cast doubt on this assumption.

Weber on Professionalization and Bureaucratization

To Weber, bureaucratization and professionalization are complementary processes involved in the rationalization of the Western world.[2] Furthermore, the process of professionalization is seen by Weber as occurring largely within bureaucracies. In fact, the two processes are inseparably intertwined. Weber is generally concerned with the "bureaucratic-professional," that is, with the professional who exists within a bureaucracy and seeks to balance the two systems. To Weber, the priest[3] and the soldier are examples of bureaucratic-professionals.

What distinguishes Weber's thinking from that of American sociologists who saw an inevitable antithesis between professionalization and bureaucratization? One element is that Weber's thinking was embedded in his broader orientation toward the rationalization of the West.[4] When one is examining rationality, it is relatively easy to see that professionalization and bureaucratization are related causes, and consequences, of growing rationality. In contrast, American occupational sociologists tended to look at these processes in isolation and therefore failed to see their linkages.

A second factor in the difference between Weber and many American occupational sociologists is the disproportionate amount of attention the latter group gave to one specific occupation—the physician in private practice. It is our contention that this focus on a single, in many ways aberrant, occupation served to distort American thinking on the relationship between professionalization and bureaucratization. Unlike most occupations, the physician existed apart from formal organizations, at least between the late 1800s and the mid-1900s.[5] In those years physicians developed an ethic of autonomy and therefore found themselves in conflict with bureaucracies when they were em-

[1]See, for example, W.R. Scott, "Professionals in Organizations: Areas of Conflict," in Howard Vollmer and Donald Mills, eds., *Professionalization* (Englewood Cliffs, NJ: Prentice Hall, Inc., 1966), pp. 265-275.

[2]This section is derived from George Ritzer, "Professionalization, Bureaucratization, and Rationalization: The Views of Max Weber," *Social Forces,* 53 (1975), 627-634.

[3]Contemporary support for this is found in Vera's study of Catholic priests in which he found commitment to occupation positively correlated with commitment to the organization. See Hernan Vera, *Professionalization and Professionalism of Catholic Priests* (Gainesville, FL: University of Florida Press, 1982), p. 66.

[4]On this issue see, Arnold Eisen, "The Meanings and Confusions of Weberian 'Rationality'," *British Journal of Sociology,* 29 (1978), 57-70; Stephen Kalberg, "Max Weber's Types of Rationality," *American Journal of Sociology,* 85 (1980), 1145–1179; Donald Levine, "Rationality and Freedom: Weber and Beyond," *Sociological Inquiry,* 51 (1981), 5–25; Rogers Brubaker, *The Limits of Rationality: An Essay on the Social and Moral Thought of Max Weber* (London: George Allen and Unwin, 1984).

[5]Paul Starr, *The Social Transformation of American Medicine* (New York: Basic Books, 1982).

ployed in them. It is largely from this single case that occupational sociologists generalized about the antithesis between bureaucratization and professionalization. However, most professions never existed outside of bureaucracies and hence never faced the conflict experienced by physicians. As mentioned earlier, in recent years even physicians have found themselves employed in organizations, and the occupational sociologist is discovering that the medical profession can survive (although perhaps in an altered form) within bureaucracies.

Examples of the linking of professionalization and bureaucratization are frequently found in Weber's work. On a general level he argued that "bureaucratization of all domination very strongly furthers the development of 'rational-matter-of-factness' and the personality type of the professional expert."[6] In addition to such general statements, Weber also linked professionalization and bureaucratization in specific settings:

> [Military] Only the bureaucratic army structure allows for the development of the professional standing armies.[7]

> [Religion] The rise of a professional priesthood . . . must occur in some kind of compulsory organization.[8]

> [Religion] This worldly asceticism as a whole favors the breeding and exaltation of the professionalism needed by capitalism and bureaucracy.[9]

It is clear from these quotations, and the thrust of his work, that Weber saw professionalization and bureaucratization as complementary processes involved in the rationalization of the West.

Professional-Bureaucratic Conflict

Although the issue of professionals in organizations was of some importance in Weber's era (the late 1800s and early 1900s), it has become even more important in recent years. Today, more and more professionals spend a greater proportion of their time in organizations, very often as employees of those organizations. Although Weber's views on the linkage between professionalization and bureaucratization are sound, it is nevertheless true that at least some professionals in at least some types of organizations experience conflicts. In general, bureaucracies are based on control from the top, while professions are premised on the idea of peer control. When bureaucratic superiors are not professionals, or are professionals who identify with the organization, there is at least the potential for conflict for the professionals in such an organization.

To get a better grasp of the nature and degree of this conflict we need to

---

[6]Max Weber, *Economy and Society* (Totowa, NJ: Bedminster Press, 1968), p. 998.
[7]Ibid., p. 981.
[8]Ibid., p. 1164.
[9]Ibid., p. 1200.

differentiate between three types of organizations in which professionals are found:[10]

Professional organizations are those in which at least 50 percent of the employees are professionals and the goals of the organization generally coincide with the goals of the professionals. There are two subtypes of professional organizations:

1. *Autonomous professional organizations* are those in which the professionals are in control of the organization, including managerial positions. Examples include large law firms and medical clinics.

2. *Heteronomous professional organizations* are professional organizations in which nonprofessionals—or professionals oriented to the needs of the organization rather than the profession—are in control. Examples include public schools and social work agencies.[11]

Service organizations are those in which professionals are provided with facilities but are neither employed by the organization nor under its control. A good example is the physician who, while affiliated with a hospital, is not employed by it.

Nonprofessional organizations are those in which professionals are in a small, subordinate subunit within the organization. The scientist (to be discussed extensively in the last section of this chapter), physician,[12] or lawyer[13] in industry exemplify this type.

Before we turn to a few examples of the conflict faced by professionals in some organizations, we need to return to the general issue of the relationship of professionals to bureaucracy—that is, to research suggesting that a greater degree of bureaucratization does not *necessarily* mean greater conflict for the professional.

Hall, for example, examined the degree of bureaucratization of three major work settings of professionals: autonomous professional organizations; heteronomous professional organizations; and the professional department that is part of a larger, nonprofessional organization.[14] The general assumption is that the professional department in the nonprofessional organization is the most bureaucratized and, as a result, the professional in this setting will experience the greatest conflict. However, Hall found that while autonomous professional organizations are the least bureaucratic, the differences between heteronomous professional organizations and professional departments are not great. In fact, professional departments are actually less bureaucratic than heteronomous professional organizations on some dimensions of bureaucra-

---

[10]Amitai Etzioni, ed., *The Semi-Professions and Their Organization* (New York: Free Press, 1969), pp. xii–xiii.

[11]Richard Hall, "Some Organizational Considerations in the Professional-Organizational Relationship," *Administrative Science Quarterly*, 12 (1967), 461–478.

[12]Vivienne Walters, "Company Doctors' Perceptions of and Responses to Conflicting Pressures from Labor and Management," *Social Problems*, 30 (1982), 1–12.

[13]For a discussion of the corporate lawyer and the role conflicts and ambiguities attendant to that role see, John D. Donnell, *The Corporate Counsel: A Role Study* (Bloomington, IN: Bureau of Business Research of the Graduate School of Business, Indiana University, 1970).

[14]Hall, "Some Organizational Considerations." •

tization. On the basis of these findings Hall cautions us that we must not merely assume that because professionals are employed in professional departments or heteronomous professional organizations they will inevitably face conflict.

Gloria Engel selected one dimension of professionalization—professional autonomy—and related it to the degree of bureaucratization.[15] Seeking "to demonstrate empirically that it is not bureaucracy per se but the degree of bureaucracy that can limit professional autonomy,"[16] Engel was specifically concerned with the autonomy of physicians in their relationships with patients (clinical practice) and in clinical research. In reviewing the contradictory literature, she concluded that the highly bureaucratic organization does indeed act to limit the professional autonomy of physicians. Somewhat surprisingly, Engel also concluded that solo practice limits professional autonomy.

> The solo practitioner may thus be limited in, or suffer a loss of, autonomy, not as the result of any administrative restrictions, as might be experienced by those employed within the bureaucracy, but from not having ready access to the various physical facilities typically available in the complex organization.[17]

Thus she hypothesizes that it is the moderately bureaucratic organization that affords physicians more autonomy than either the nonbureaucratic or highly bureaucratic work setting.

To this end she compared doctors in three settings: solo or small group practice; "a privately owned, closed panel medical organization;" and a government medical organization. She found differences between autonomy in clinical practice and in clinical research. Physicians in moderately bureaucratic settings are more likely to have a high degree of autonomy in their clinical practice than those in the other two settings. But surprisingly, those in highly bureaucratic settings are most likely to have a high degree of professional autonomy in clinical research. In explaining this second finding Engel noted, "In the highly bureaucratic setting, administrative procedures are less formal, and fewer rules and regulations are imposed upon physicians who are interested in pursuing research activities."[18] This latter finding further muddies the relationship between professionalization and bureaucratization. It points to the fact that perhaps we cannot even discuss organizations as a whole in terms of their degree of bureaucratization. An organization may be highly bureaucratic on one factor (for example, clinical practice), moderately bureaucratic on a second (clinical research), and have a low degree of bureaucratization in terms of still a third factor.

A number of other studies have suggested that professionalization and bureaucratization are not necessarily irreconcilable. Some see them, in fact, as interdependent rather than antagonistic. Litwak points to the existence of a

[15]Gloria Engel, "The Effect of Bureaucracy on the Professional Authority of Physicians," *Journal of Health and Social Behavior*, 10 (1969), 30–41.

[16]Ibid., 31.

[17]Ibid., 34.

[18]Ibid., 37.

"professional bureaucracy," an organization that synthesizes the professional and bureaucratic models.[19] Similarly, Smigel terms what he finds in the Wall Street law firm a professional bureaucracy.[20] This phenomenon was also uncovered in Montagna's study of the Big Eight public accounting firms.[21] In these firms, accountants spend relatively little of their time on nonprofessional administrative duties: they are freer of this burden because most are involved in a *small* amount of administrative detail, thereby spreading it evenly among them. Broader decision making is centralized, removing this burden from most of the accountants. In addition, external rules formulated by professional associations were far more important than internal rules of the organization. Because of rotation through administrative positions, there are no full-time administrators who have vested interests in retaining and expanding the bureaucratic structure. The codification of formerly "mystical" procedures is seen as a threat to the accountant since: "The power of the expert disappears as soon as the area of uncertainty (professional judgment) can be translated into rules and programs."[22] Yet accountants have responded to even this threat by expanding into new areas of uncertainty. In these and other ways they have created for themselves a new type of organization, one which combines the professional and bureaucratic models.

Lengermann has further refined our knowledge on this issue in a study of certified public accountants.[23] He addressed himself to the paradox that although accountants thought that they had more autonomy in solo practice, the best of them sought careers in large accounting firms. In fact, Lengermann did find greater autonomy among accountants in solo practice than among those in large firms. However, when he controlled for level of position in the organization, that relationship ceased to exist. It is being in lower-level positions that accounts for lower autonomy, not the mere fact of being in an organization. Since, by virture of their size, larger organizations have more lower-level positions, they offer less autonomy, at least to those on the bottom rungs of the organization.

Further contradicting the idea of a basic incompatability between professionalization and bureaucratization are those cases, many of which were the focus of Weber's analysis, in which the profession and the organization are virtually indistinguishable. One example is the clergy, in which the profession and the church hierarchy are very difficult to differentiate.[24] Supe-

[19]Eugene Litwak, "Models of Bureaucracy which Permit Conflict," *American Journal of Sociology*, 69 (1961), 182.

[20]Erwin Smigel, *The Wall Street Lawyer: Professional Organization Man?* (Bloomington, IN: Indiana University Press, 1969).

[21]Paul Montagna, "Professionalization and Bureaucratization in Large Professional Organizations," *American Journal of Sociology*, 74 (1968), 138–145.

[22]Ibid., 143.

[23]Joseph J. Lengermann, "Professional Autonomy in Organizations: The Case of CPA's," in Phyllis Stewart and Muriel Cantor, eds., *Varieties of Work Experience: The Social Control of Occupational Groups and Roles* (New York: Schenkman, 1974), pp. 173–187. For a somewhat different point of view on this issue see, James E. Sorenson and Thomas L. Sorenson, "The Conflict of Professionals in Bureaucratic Organizations," *Administrative Science Quarterly*, 19 (1974), 98–106; A. Hastings and C.R. Hinings, "Role Relations and Value Adaptation: A Study of the Professional Accountant in Industry," *Sociology*, 4 (1970), 353–366.

[24]Vera, *Professionalization and Professionalism of Catholic Priests*.

riors within the organization are at the same time professional peers. The other prime example is the military officer in the armed forces. Here again we have an at least partial fusion of organization and profession. Military officers are not likely to find themselves in an employer-employee relationship within the military. In fact, they are not likely to view the military as an employer, but rather as a means for efficiently coordinating their professional activities with those of their peers. Although most military officers experience little professional-bureaucratic conflict, exceptions are those officers who stand at the top of the military hierarchy. They are answerable to civilian officials representing the state. While the military often tries to reduce or eliminate civilian control, there usually remains at least some strain between the two. Without the strain, the military might emerge completely autonomous, and such an outcome would have enormous implications for society.[25]

Bucher and Stelling attack the assumption that organizations in which professionals are employed are bureaucratic.[26] By starting with this assumption, most researchers are led to the idea of an inevitable conflict between professional and bureaucratic norms. Yet when professionals control an organization (such as in some types of hospitals), Bucher and Stelling contend that they create an organization that is neither bureaucratic nor professional. They believe that such an organization has the following characteristics:

1. Professionals negotiate with significant others in their organization to create their own roles and do not fit neatly into the established roles in the organization.
2. Professionals tend to cluster within an organization; this leads to spontaneous internal differentiation rather than differentiation legislated from the top of the organization.
3. The various professionals in an organization have different interests, goals, and so forth; this leads to internal competition and conflict.
4. Through political means the different professionals seek to affect the policies and goals of the organization.
5. Power is constantly shifting rather than located in a particular office.

In a sense then, there is no irreconcilability between professionalization and bureaucratization, since professionals in organization can—in at least some cases—create an entirely different kind of organization that conforms to neither of these models.

Building on the work of Bucher and Stelling and others, Benson[27] offers

---

[25] Bengt Abrahamsson, *Military Professionalization and Professional Power* (Beverly Hills, CA: Sage Publications, 1972). See also, Jacques van Doorn, "The Officer Corps: A Fusion of Profession and Organization," *European Journal of Sociology*, 6 (1965), 262–265.

[26] Rue Bucher and Joan Stelling, "Characteristics of Professional Organizations," *Journal of Health and Social Behavior*, 10 (1969), 3–15. A number of studies point in essentially the same direction, including Joan Stelling and Rue Bucher, "Autonomy and Monitoring in Hospital Wards," *Sociological Quarterly*, 13 (1972), 431–46; Celia Davis, "Professionals in Organizations: Some Preliminary Observations on Hospital Consultants," *The Sociological Review*, 20 (1972), 553–567; Stephen Green, "Professional/Bureaucratic Conflict: The Case of the Medical Profession in the National Health Service," *The Sociological Review*, 23 (1975), 121–141.

[27] J. Kenneth Benson, "The Analysis of Bureaucratic-Professional Conflict: Functional Versus Dialectical Approaches," *Sociological Quarterly*, 14 (1973), 376–394.

what he calls a "dialectical approach" to the study of professionals in organizations. Here, he seeks to integrate the earlier view of inevitable conflict with the newer view of the relationship between professional and organization as a negotiated reality. He begins with the assumption that every organization contains fundamental contradictions. In this context, the relationship between the participants is subject to political negotiations. In seeking to understand this process of negotiation, we must understand the commodities each party uses as negotiating items, including money, prestige, authority, and autonomy. We must understand the base of power of each of the parties involved in the negotiation, their strategies, and the factors that serve to determine the outcome of the negotiation. If we do uncover conflict among professionals and the organization, it may well be tied to other conflicts endemic to the organization, including conflict among diverse interest groups, between the central administrative elite and various subunits, among specific occupations or segments within occupations, or between the organization and the broader public.

Conflict between professionals and organizations may be brought to the fore by a variety of events. Increasing specialization may be seen by some groups as in their best interests, while others may be threatened by it. Similar conflict within the organization may be produced by changes in the role of the organization, technological change, centralization, or rigidification of organizational rules.

Benson's basic point is that the bureaucratic-professional conflict that does exist is part of the ongoing dialectic of organizational life. Organizations are being reconstructed from day to day by their participants. Those participants are constantly negotiating with each other; as a result there will be times when bureaucratic-professional conflict will arise, although there is no necessary contradiction between professionals and organizations. Such a position moves us away from the simple idea that professionals and organizations are structurally incompatible and toward the examination of conditions that may give rise to that conflict. It also places bureaucratic-professional relations within the broader context of ongoing life within organizations.[28]

We will now turn to a few examples of conflicts that *do* exist between bureaucracies and professionals. Our goal will be to isolate some of the conditions that give rise to this conflict.

Company doctors.   Walters has examined the conflicts facing Canadian doctors who are employees of companies.[29] She identified four areas of conflict for the company physician. First, there is the issue of absenteeism. The management of companies expects "company doctors to prevent unnecessary absence from work and to return the worker, at least to light duties, as soon as possible."[30] The workers, on the other hand, are not anxious to return to work, even to lighter duties. In general, company doctors seem to adopt the

[28]Robert Perrucci, et al., "Whistle-Blowing: Professionals' Resistance to Organizational Authority," *Social Problems,* 28 (1980), 149–164.

[29]Vivienne Walters, "Company Doctors' Perceptions of and Responses to Conflicting Pressures from Labor and Management."

[30]Ibid., 2.

management position by, for example, trying to catch malingering workers and by coming to view a return to work as therapeutic for the worker.

The second area of conflict is over preemployment physicals designed to determine whether potential employees are healthy enough to be hired. Basically, the doctors are pressed by the company to "err on the side of safety by certifying doubtful cases as unfit to work" and to "identify with their companies and try to protect them from 'bad risks.' "[31] This conflicts with basic medical practice. Futhermore, it was still possible for management to choose not to accept a doctor's recommendation. People who showed signs of becoming dedicated workers might be hired even though the physician expressed health reservations about them. In times of a shortage of labor, management might also be more inclined to ignore a doctor's advice not to hire someone.

A third area of conflict is workers' compensation for work-related illnesses and injuries. It is in the interest of workers to have as many health problems as possible classified as eligible for workers' compensation, but the antithetical interests of management are:

> . . . to keep assessments as low as possible, to resist an extension of the range of illnesses subject to compensation, and to oppose any case where the occupational basis of worker's illness or disability is open to doubt. In consequence, this has been an area of bitter and lengthy disputes between workers and management.[32]

Needless to say, it is a bitter dispute in which company doctors find themselves in the middle.

Finally, there is the issue of health hazards in the workplace. The conflict here is over the workers' and union's demand that *all* health hazards be removed from the workplace and the management's view that workplaces cannot be totally free of health risks. Thus the management objective is to set an "acceptable" level of risk and to provide employees with needed health equipment. But from the worker-union point of view there is no such thing as an acceptable level of risk. Once again, physicians find themselves caught in the middle of this dispute.

In general, Walters found that the autonomy of physicians was limited by their employing organization. In the conflicts discussed above, it was management that had the greatest power, and physicians were therefore biased in the direction of their employers' priorities. As a result, company doctors often serve to buttress management control over workers.

Military psychiatrists. Psychiatrists are supposed to be concerned with the mental health of their patients but patients are secondary for military psychiatrists—they are engaged primarily in providing services to the military.[33] Thus they are merely advisors on such matters as discharges, special

---

[31]Ibid., 4.

[32]Ibid., 6.

[33]Arlene K. Daniels, "The Captive Professional: Bureaucratic Limitations in the Practice of Military Psychiatry," *Journal of Health and Social Behavior,* 10 (1969), 255-265. See also, Arlene K. Daniels, "Military Psychiatry: The Emergence of a Subspecialty," in Eliot Freidson and Judith Lorber, eds., *Medical Men and Their Work* (Chicago: Aldine/Atherton, 1972), pp. 145–162.

duty for soldiers, and military legal matters. Moreover, they are not even free to make diagnoses on the basis of their professional judgment. They are constrained by a variety of military rules (for example, rules guiding separation from the military) that have an important impact on the kind of diagnosis they make. They are often asked to justify the decisions of a commanding officer or a military court, and the need for such justifications affects the kinds of diagnoses they make. In effect, these constraints transform them from counselors to control agents within the military. In addition to these constant constraints upon them, there are a variety of shifting or variable contingencies that affect their action. One is the "climate of opinion" at any given time. If, for example, there is a manpower crisis in the military, there will be a great deal of pressure on military psychiatrists to be very conservative in classifying soldiers as unfit. Because of logistics, psychiatrists are generally prevented from making recommendations that would involve transfers of patients to distant places. Finally, the character of a commanding officer at any given time has a great effect on the practice of military psychiatry. Some commanding officers place greater restraints on the activity of psychiatrists than do others, depending on how they interpret military regulations. In short, the psychiatrist who works in the military is a "captive professional."

Military chaplains.   Military chaplains are in a position similar to that of military psychiatrists. They are, in a sense, members of two professions: the professional clergy and the military. As professional clergy, chaplains are supposed to preach and act in accord with the notion of universal brotherhood. Yet as members of the military they are asked to contribute to an organization whose goal is to develop itself into the most effective destructive force possible. Like military psychiatrists, chaplains generally must be more responsive to the immediate pressures of the military than the more distant professional expectations. Although chaplains are often unwilling to admit the existence of this stress, or to the fact that they are generally directed by military requirements, their actions indicate that their primary orientation while in the military is to the needs and demands of that organization.[34]

Industrial scientists.   In the case of military psychiatrists and military chaplains, we discussed general and pervasive bureaucratic-professional conflict. In the case of industrial scientists, we will examine some of the more specific forms taken by this conflict. Kornhauser points out four areas of conflict between industrial scientists and their employing organizations.[35] First, there is the issue of recruitment. "In most government establishments (especially military) and in commercial enterprises . . . personnel matters tend to be controlled by an administration that represents the organization rather than the profession."[36] This stands in opposition to the professional notion that only a peer can evaluate competence of another professional. Many or-

[34]Gordon Zahn, *The Military Chaplaincy: A Study of Role Tension in the Royal Air Force* (Toronto: University of Toronto Press, 1969).

[35]William Kornhauser, *Scientists in Industry: Conflict and Accommodation* (Los Angeles: University of California Press, 1962).

[36]Ibid., p. 45.

ganizations, furthermore, seek to hire lesser scientists who might ultimately become administrators. Professionals, on the other hand, would prefer to hire the best qualified scientists without regard to their managerial potential. Second, there is the problem of how the professional scientist's work is to be organized. Organizations tend to prefer "task forces" made up of professionals from various disciplines to work on a specific problem; scientists are likely to prefer groups of individuals from the same discipline. Third, there is the question of who should lead a professional subgroup within an organization. Professional scientists would like their manager to be the most scientifically qualified individual, while organizations tend to seek administrators who exhibit managerial rather than scientific qualities. Finally, there is the conflict between the professional notion of free and total communication and the organization's desire for secrecy. If scientists in an organization make a discovery, they would like it published so that all those in the profession may see and use their contribution. The organization, however, would prefer that these discoveries be kept secret so that the benefits belong exclusively to the organization.

An organization uses monetary rewards and is generally incapable of rewarding professionals with the symbols they desire. Thus professional scientists can rarely find bureaucratic life totally rewarding. They must operate on two levels, simultaneously trying to gain economic rewards from the organization and seeking symbolic recognition from their professional colleagues. The organization, however, acts in a number of ways to prevent the achievement of professional recognition. One example is the openness-versus-secrecy conflict discussed above. Another problem is that an organization pays professionals to solve problems of immediate importance to it, not esoteric questions that will bring no recognizable payoff. Thus scientists must reconcile what they feel needs to be researched with the more insistent demands of the organization. In such a situation, the organization will frequently discourage or forbid independent research; and if they choose to stay in the organization, professional scientists must then work on such research on their own time. This strain is what Kornhauser has called the conflict between pure and applied research. The American Association for the Advancement of Science has noted that "what is essential to the proper growth of science is often in conflict with the conditions of its service to military and political and, it may be added, industrial affairs."[37]

Electronic data processing personnel. Danziger[38] studied a group he considered a profession (or at least an emergent profession): electronic data-processing personnel (EDP) within American local governments. EDP personnel (for example, computer programmers and system analysts) were found to have constructed a "skill bureaucracy" with three distinguishing characteristics: "(1) it is an organizational subunit which provides services to particular clients; (2) it has a relative monopoly within certain areas of both services provision and technical expertise; and (3) its members have an external,

---

[37]Ibid., p. 18.
[38]James N. Danziger, "The 'Skill Bureaucracy' and Intraorganizational Control," *Sociology of Work and Occupations*, 6 (1979), 204–226.

professionalized reference group."[39] Danziger found that EDP personnel constructed a skill bureaucracy that had considerable autonomy within the organization and were even seeking to expand its domain. Despite the lack of
significant external control, the EDP unit was found to adequately serve the
organization. However, because the EDP unit is primarily interested in
achieving its own objectives, it does not provide the larger organization with
as many benefits as it might. Danziger foresees a time in the near future when
conflict between EDP units and the larger organization will escalate. The organization will seek to get more gains from its investment in EDP and it will
seek to more rationally manage such a department. Such efforts are likely to
be resisted by EDP personnel who have become accustomed to the autonomy
offered by their "skill bureaucracy."

In sum, we conclude that while professionalization and bureaucratization are not necessarily incompatible, the fact remains that in at least some
situations bureaucratic-professional conflict does exist. Given this reality, we
turn now to a discussion of the methods employed in coping with this conflict.
Our first concern is with the actions an employing organization may take to
cope with the conflict.

Coping With Bureaucratic-Professional Conflict: The Employing Organization

It is clear that in at least some cases the conflict between professionals
and organizations can never be completely eliminated. In fact it may well be
that this conflict, like many others, has a variety of functions for both professionals and organizations. There are, however, a number of steps an organization can take to reduce the dysfunctional aspects of the conflict.

Barber makes some suggestions on ways an organization can accommodate its professionals.[40] For example, it can place them into separate substructures where they can perform their specialized activities relatively free of
organizational constraints. Or it can set up a separate authority structure for
them with the head of the professional group being a qualified professional.
Barber also suggests a separate reward structure that would enable them to
achieve professional recognition while continuing to serve the organization.
Included in this separate reward structure would be the opportunity to attend
professional meetings, salary increases based strictly on professional accomplishments, and time off with pay to further professional education. Yet although these changes would help alleviate the conflict, they would not eliminate the inherent problems. Even if professionals had separate substructures,
they still would not possess the authority or organizational knowledge to have
control over their clients. Such a separation, furthermore, would enhance the
segregation of professionals within the organization and would do little to increase their authority. The suborganization, even with a professional head,
would ultimately be responsible to higher-level bureaucrats. Professional

[39]Ibid., 206.

[40]Bernard Barber, "Some Problems in the Sociology of the Professions," in Kenneth Lynn,
Professions in America (Boston: Beacon Press, 1967), pp. 15–34.

heads[41] would find themselves in an extremely difficult position: inevitably they would have to decide whether they were primarily professionals or bureaucrats, and whatever choice they made would alienate some segment of the organization and reduce their effectiveness.

The dual ladder.   The dual ladder is one of the preferred methods that employing organizations use to resolve professional-bureaucratic conflict. In all organizations, there is a hierarchy of statuses leading to positions of increasing authority. Professionals, because of the nature of their occupations, are ordinarily barred from this ladder, a condition that has led some organizations to set up a second ladder. This ladder also has a hierarchy of positions, but these do not carry with them increasing authority. Instead, they carry greater salaries, status, autonomy, or responsibility. Organizations realize that if professionals were to move up the traditional ladder, they would be moving out of the area of their expertise; the second ladder allows them to be rewarded and experience some mobility *within* their professional area.

Although there has been widespread adoption of the dual ladder, Goldner and Ritti contend that—at least as far as engineers are concerned[42]—this idea is based on the false assumption that professionals are interested in professional rewards rather than power. Goldner and Ritti found that engineers do want power and that they identify with their employing organization rather than the profession. Further, the professional ladder at best can only resolve the conflict (if one exists) between individual professionals and their employing organizations; it cannot resolve the basic conflict between the profession as an institution and the employing organization.

If the professional ladder does not function the way it is supposed to, what then is its function? Goldner and Ritti note that it performs the function of "cooling out" professionals in organizations; it keeps them in the organization and productive even though they cannot aspire to the normal definition of success in organizations—power. But "cooling out" generally occurs after the fact, as when an individual has been fleeced by a confidence man. In organizations, the construction of a dual ladder allows professionals to be "cooled out" even before they have actually failed in their quest for power (as most will). The organization has redefined success for the professional from increasing authority to moving up the professional ladder.

The professional ladder might even be viewed as a face-saving device for professionals. Goldner and Ritti contend that organizations may even find it functional to define nonprofessions as professions, and in so doing continue to get high performance from employees, even though they have failed in their quest for power. For example, if older salespersons have failed to achieve power, the organization can keep them productive by defining them as professionals. By the same token, individuals in certain occupations would

[41]David Luecke, "The Professional as Organizational Leader," *Administrative Science Quarterly*, 18 (1973), 86–94.

[42]Fred Goldner and R.R. Ritti, "Professionalization as Career Immobility," *American Journal of Sociology*, 73 (1967), 489–502.

find it functional to define themselves as professionals since this "explains" why they have not succeeded in terms of their search for power.

Segregation of professionals.   Hammond and Mitchell's study of the campus ministry suggests a radical solution to the professional-bureaucratic conflict.[43] The Protestant Church handles radical ministers by sending them to college campuses where their ideology is accepted and where it does not affect the church-going public. Generalizing from this example we can see how organizations can reduce the conflict between themselves and professionals by housing them in a physically separate structure. The only contact between the organization and its professionals is then through the leaders of the professional suborganization. Although this will ease the conflict for most of the professionals, it will not eliminate the basic conflict between the two groups.

Although it can never solve the problem, the organization must seek to maximize the creativity of its professionals while minimizing its control over them, for if it imposes too much control, it will stifle the creativity it seeks. Nevertheless, organizations have goals and must be sure that their professionals are contributing to the achievement of those goals: they cannot allow professionals to operate totally independently. The organization must set broad limits for professionals and then allow them to operate autonomously within these limits. Most organizations find it difficult to grant professionals such autonomy, but it is clear that they must if they are to progress as much as they would like.

Coping With Bureaucratic-Professional Conflict: Professionals

Just as the organization can take steps to reduce this conflict, professions and individual professionals can also act to resolve the dilemma. Vollmer and Mills suggest that one means for professionals is to "sell out" to the organization by becoming primarily bureaucrats.[44] This would certainly eliminate the conflict, but few professionals are willing to take this step and few organizations would like to see it happen.

Resolutions open to the professions.   Professional schools can offer courses on the structure and operation of complex organizations in an effort to prepare new professionals for life in such structures. They will then know what to expect and, perhaps, how to handle some of the dilemmas that will confront them. Professional schools often continue to socialize their students as if they were going to become free professionals. But most new professionals will work in organizations, and they need to be prepared for the possibility of conflict.

The profession can restructure itself so that there are symbolic rewards for those who work in organizations. For example, it could offer greater recognition for applied research by, for example, accepting more of such papers

---

[43]Phillip G. Hammond and Robert E. Mitchell, "Segmentation of Radicalism: The Case of the Protestant Campus Minister," *American Journal of Sociology,* 71 (1965), 133–143.

[44]Vollmer and Mills, *Professionalization,* p. 276.

for presentation at national meetings and for publication in professional journals. Those professionals who achieve high status in their employing organization might also receive some recognition from their professional association. These kinds of changes are occurring within some professions, particularly in science and engineering. For example, the professional administrator's position is beginning to be viewed as a "valued activity" and is achieving high status in professional associations. Further,

> in the scientific society, journals and conferences in applied science have been organized; permanent sections of the society have been established in applied areas; employment clearing houses have been created to facilitate contacts of industrial and governmental employers with scientists; and large grants have been solicited from industry to finance society activities.[45]

Resolutions open to individual professionals. There are also mechanisms to reduce professional-bureaucratic conflict available to individual professionals. For one thing, before taking a position professionals can select the setting (for example, highly bureaucratic, autonomous) that is most comfortable for them. In a study of aerospace scientists and engineers, Miller found that conflict was minimized because professionals tended to find their way into the setting best suited to them.[46] Thus self-selection, as well as careful organizational selection, helps prevent the development of bureaucratic-professional conflict.

It has generally been assumed that professionals in organizations must either identify with the organization or the profession. Gouldner (following Merton) calls those who identify with the profession cosmopolitans and those who identify with the employing organization locals.[47] Yet there is no reason to assume that these are the only possibilities.[48] Reissman, for example, identifies four types of orientation: the functional bureaucrat who identifies with the profession and not organization; the job bureaucrat who identifies with employing organization and not profession; the specialist bureaucrat who identifies with both; and the service bureaucrat who identifies with neither.[49] The most important type for our purpose is the specialist bureaucrat, or the type Glaser has called the "local-cosmopolitan."[50] Much of the conflict is

---

[45]Kornhauser, *Scientists in Industry*, p. 198.

[46]George Miller, "Aerospace Scientists and Engineers: Some Organizational Considerations," in Phyllis Stewart and Muriel Cantor, eds., *Varieties of Work Experience: The Social Control of Occupational Groups and Roles*, pp. 114–127.

[47]Alvin Gouldner, "Cosmopolitans and Locals: Toward an Analysis of Latent Social Roles-I," *Administrative Science Quarterly*, 2 (1957), 281–306.

[48]Paul J. Baker and Mary Zey-Ferrell, "Local and Cosmopolitan Orientations of Faculty: Implications for Teaching," *Teaching Sociology*, 12 (1984), 82–106.

[49]Leonard Reissman, "A Study of Role Conceptions in Bureaucracy," *Social Forces*, 27 (1949), 305–310; Loether calls those who identify with neither profession nor organization "indifferents;" see, Herman J. Loether, "Organizational Context and the Professorial Role," in Phyllis L. Stewart and Muriel G. Cantor, *Varieties of Work* (Beverly Hills, CA: Sage, 1982), pp. 137–152.

[50]Barney Glaser, "The Local-Cosmopolitan Scientist," *American Journal of Sociology*, 69 (1962), 249–259. For a somewhat different usage of this concept see, Albert I. Goldberg, "The Relevance of Cosmopolitan/Local Orientations to Professional Values and Behavior," *Sociology of Work and Occupations*, 3 (1976), 331–356.

resolved by those who can identify with *both* occupation and organization.

A much more radical alternative open to professionals is to abandon professional associations for the much more militant labor unions. Semiprofessionals (for example, teachers) have long been attracted to the benefits of unionization. In the more established professions, it is among college professors that unions have made the greatest inroads.[51] However, with the recession in college teaching in the 1970s and 1980s, there has been a decline in interest in unionization and collective bargaining.[52]

Benign Conflict?

It may well be that the conflict between professionals and organizations is not undesirable and hence should not be eliminated. Kornhauser notes that "the tension between the autonomy and integration of professional groups, production groups, and other participants tends to summon a more effective structure than is attained where they are isolated from one another or where one absorbs the other."[53] With little research on this point, we need more comparative studies of organizations in which accommodation has and has not been attempted. Nonetheless this notion is in line with sociological work that emphasizes the functions of social conflict. From this work, one might hypothesize that the conflict makes for unity in the professional subgroup. One might also hypothesize that the conflict leads to greater feedback between pure and applied research. In any event, it must not be concluded that the conflict between professionals and their employing nonprofessional organizations is necessarily dysfunctional.

FREE PROFESSIONALS

The major free professionals have been physicians and lawyers in private practice. Although the trend is away from free professionals and toward organizational involvement,[54] there remains a significant proportion in some professions who are still largely free of organizational control. Free of organizational constraints, they are also free of most of the problems faced by professionals in organizations. They retain to a degree both their autonomy and their commitment to their occupation. They are, however, faced with a series of rather distinctive problems. For free professionals, these problems primarily revolve around their relationships with clients.

---

[51]Gus Tyler, "The Faculty Joins the Proletariat," *Change* (Winter, 1971–1972), 40–55.

[52]Loether, "Organizational Context and the Professorial Role."

[53]Kornhauser, *Scientists in Industry*, p. 198.

[54]The same trend, but even more pronounced, is occurring in England; see, D.G. Gill and G.W. Horobin, "Doctors, Patients and the State: Relationships and Decision-Making," *The Sociological Review*, 20 (1972), 505–520.

Conflict With Clients

Although conflict with clients is characteristic of free professionals and threats to autonomy are characteristic among professionals in nonprofessional organizations, the distinction is not as clear as we have tried to make it. First, free professionals are also confronted with threats to their autonomy. While they retain their freedom, free professionals are unable to avail themselves of the resources an organization can provide. This lack of resources constitutes a threat to their autonomy.[55] They may, for example, lack the equipment they need, or they may have to handle so much detail work that they are left with less time to work on professional matters. Second, just as free professionals may experience threats to their autonomy, professionals in organizations are likely to experience conflict with clients.[56] Third, many professionals fall into both categories. Such professionals would experience conflict with clients primarily in private practice and threats to autonomy while working in an organization. Fourth, while professionals employed in nonprofessional organizations also have clients,[57] it is not clear exactly who they are—individuals in need of professional services or the employing organization. In spite of these ambiguities, we continue to adhere to the general view that professionals in nonprofessional organizations are characteristically confronted with normative conflict (threats to their autonomy), while the distinguishing conflict for free professionals is with their clients.

Physicians and patients.   In Freidson's view, the struggle between patients and physicians seems to have occurred throughout history,[58] a conflict inherent in the very structure of their relationship. Here is the way Freidson describes it:

> The basic doctor-patient relationship may be seen as a conflict of perspectives and a struggle for control over services. From their perspective, patients believe they need a particular service; from theirs, the physicians seek to employ their own criteria of need and propriety.[59]

Freidson found that physicians talked incessantly about the problems they had with patients."[60]

The privacy of the relationship between physician and patient makes it generally free of external constraints. This lack of formalized rules of interac-

[55]Eliot Freidson, *The Profession of Medicine* (New York: Dodd, Mead, 1970).

[56]Eliot Freidson, *Doctoring Together: A Study of Professional Social Control* (New York: Elsevier, 1975); Eliot Freidson, *Patients' Views of Medical Practice* (Chicago: University of Chicago Press, 1980; originally published in 1961).

[57]Arlene Kaplan Daniels, "Advisory and Coercive Functions in Psychiatry," *Sociology of Work and Occupations*, 2 (1975), 55–78.

[58]Eliot Freidson, "Dilemmas in the Doctor/Patient Relationship," in Caroline Cox and Adrianne Mead, eds., *A Sociology of Medical Practice* (London: Collier-Macmillan, 1975), pp. 285–292.

[59]Freidson, *Doctoring Together*, p. 45.

[60]Ibid., p. 48.

tion makes conflict much more likely. We must also realize that physicians and patients bring very different worlds of experience to their interaction and that they have different reference groups. In the interaction, patients desire highly personalized treatment, but physicians, for the sake of efficiency as well as their own peace of mind, usually deal with patients impersonally.[61] That is, they treat patients as types of disease, rather than as individuals. Whatever form the interaction takes, patients will have doubts about physicians' diagnoses, decisions, and advice. Finally, it should be pointed out that the ever-present possibility of crisis makes the doctor-patient relationship fraught with conflict. The patients' health can decline precipitously, or the treatments prescribed by physicians can have some unfortunate effects. These crises threaten to plunge even the most harmonious doctor-patient relationship into conflict.

Although patients certainly contribute to conflict with physicians, Bloor and Horobin place much of the blame for the conflict on physicians, arguing that they place patients in a "double bind."[62] On the one hand, doctors make it clear that they dislike trivial visits from patients. By sanctioning those who take up their time with unimportant matters, physicians are encouraging patients to assess their own illness in order to be sure a visit is really necessary. This leads to increasing knowledge about health matters, making patients more capable of self-diagnosis. Thus, when they do visit doctors, they are more likely to question their judgments. It is here that the double bind occurs, since physicians do not want patients to question their judgments. Yet in pressing patients to diagnose their own ailments before visiting the office, doctors are creating the kind of questioning clients they so dislike.

Although there is a tendency to blame physicians for the strain in the doctor-patient relationship, it is clear that there are other factors involved in the conflict. A recent study by David Hughes of the relationship between physicians and cardiology patients in England has clarified one source of this strain—the inability of patients to adequately explain their problems to physicians.[63] Physicians enter interactions with patients with preconceived ideas about information that is relevant, in this case whether or not there is a cardiological problem. Patients, however, are not sure what is relevant information. The need for physicians to get important information, and the inability of patients to know what is important and what is unimportant, creates strain in the relationship. Physicians are seen by Hughes as structuring the interaction not so much to control patients as to elicit the relevant information. The source of this structuring is in Hughes' view more the incapacities of patients than the need for power of physicians.

Although strain is ubiquitous in the doctor-patient relationship, the nature of the strain is dependent on the nature of the participants.[64] Hanley and

[61]Freidson, *Patients' Views of Medical Practice*, p. 175.

[62]M. J. Bloor and G.W. Horobin, "Conflict and Conflict Resolution in Doctor/Patient Interaction," in Cox and Mead, *A Sociology of Medical Practice*, pp. 271–284.

[63]David Hughes, "Control in the Medical Consultation: Organizing Talk in a Situation Where Co-Participants Have Differential Competence," *Sociology*, (1982), 361–376.

[64]Freidson, *Doctoring Together*, p. 49.

Grunberg outline three types of patients (the hostile, the passive-dependent, and the manipulative-seductive) and three types of doctors (the omnipotent, the anxious, and the detached), and they discuss the nature of the strain in each of the nine possible relationships.[65] In only two of the nine possible relationships is there no real strain. The perfect relationship for doctors exists when they are detached and are dealing with passive-dependent patients: there is no strain of personalities and detached doctors are given virtual carte blanche by such patients. The perfect relationship for patients exists when they are manipulative and are dealing with anxious doctors: in this situation patients can completely dominate the relationship. *In all of the other relationships there is considerable strain.* When hostile patients meet "omnipotent" doctors, physicians are thwarted by patients and there is a rapid termination of the relationship. In the relationship between passive-dependent patients and anxious doctors both try to please, but insecurities and guilt in both lead to strain and eventual termination.

Lawyers and clients. In contrast to lawyers who work in large organizations and have corporations as clients, lawyers who work on their own and have individuals as clients are generally marginal members of the legal profession.[66] Much of their professional life is spent in seeking out clients who are deemed undesirable and unprofitable by the large law firms. Some must even engage in the unethical behavior of "ambulance chasing" in order to make a living.[67] Ambulance chasers are those lawyers who actively pursue customers involved in accidents and offer them their services, whereas those in the large law firms can generally sit back and wait for the clients to come to them.

Carlin's study of lawyers in private practice catalogs a long list of devices employed to build up a clientele.[68] Young solo lawyers may at first rely on friends and relatives, but they soon find that they cannot build practices on this basis alone. Thus they join organizations, cater to members of their ethno-religious group, become involved in politics, and rely on "brokers" (for example, another lawyer, a police officer, a minister) to find clients. Life for them is generally a constant struggle to get and keep an adequate clientele, and they must engage in a number of activities that they may consider nonprofessional and/or distasteful because they do not have the prestige and administrative apparatus of a law firm. This is in line with the findings previously cited by Engel, which point out that solo practice is a threat to professional status, in this case, of the lawyer.

In a study of the relationship between lawyers and clients over injury claims, Rosenthal found a basic conflict of interest.[69] From the lawyers' point

---

[65]F.W. Hanley and F. Grunberg, "Reflections on the Doctor-Patient Relationship," *Canadian Medical Association Journal,* 86 (1962), 1022–1024.

[66]John P. Heinz and Edward O. Laumann, *Chicago Lawyers: The Social Structure of the Bar* (New York: Russell Sage Foundation; and Chicago: American Bar Foundation, 1982).

[67]Kenneth Reichstein, "Ambulance Chasing: A Study of Deviation and Control Within the Legal Profession," *Social Problems,* 13 (1965), 3–17.

[68]Jerome Carlin, *Lawyers on Their Own* (New Brunswick, NJ: Rutgers University Press, 1962).

[69]Douglas Rosenthal, *Lawyer and Client: Who's in Charge?* (New York: Russell Sage, 1974).

of view, their income was maximized by a quick settlement of a suit. On the other hand, it was in the clients' interest to extend the case over a period of years. Such conflicts of interest are common in lawyer-client relationships.

Hosticka has added to our knowledge of the "power struggle" between lawyer and clients in his study of a legal-services-for-the-poor program funded by the federal government.[70] Although there is a power struggle here, as in all professional-client relationships,[71] the vast majority of the power in this specific situation rests with the lawyers. The clients are poor, often on welfare and living in substandard housing, faced with chronic problems, and defensively responding to the initiatives of others (for example, landlords suing to get back rent). The lawyers, of course, are perceived as high-status, highly educated professionals.

The lawyers move immediately to establish their control over the interaction and to maintain that control throughout the encounter. It is at this point, however, that

> there is often a "power struggle" as the client tries unsuccessfully to control the description of the case. The struggle consists of the client beginning a description, the lawyer interrupting to ask a question, the client answering the question, then changing the subject, the lawyer interrupting with another question, and so on, until the client lapses into brief answers to questions posed by the lawyer. A large number of the remaining questions contain their own answer, indicating that the lawyer is seeking confirmation of developed views on the subject.[72]

While most clients acquiesced to the efforts of lawyers to control interaction, some resisted by persisting in putting forth their version of the story. Lawyers tended to regard such persistent clients as hostile and in a few cases walked out on such situations where they were unable to control the interaction. Interestingly, lawyers also tended to work harder for persistent clients. Because of limited time, the lawyers seemed to give a disproportionate amount of their time to cases in which demands were made on them. Conversely, little attention was devoted to cases in which few demands were made of the lawyers.

Coping With Conflicts With Clients

In this section, we will examine some of the ways in which the free professionals in medicine and law cope with their conflict with clients. Interestingly, we find that in a surprisingly large number of cases the professionals seek to accommodate themselves to the demands of their clients.

Doctors, for example, often follow a carefully defined set of rules designed to avoid antagonizing the patients. After all, in the end physicians are dependent for their livelihood on a steady flow of patients. Thus, they are

---

[70]Carl J. Hosticka, "We Don't Care About What Happened, We Only Care About What Is Going to Happen: Lawyer-Client Negotiations of Reality," *Social Problems*, 26 (1979), 599–610.

[71]Fisher shows how the power lies with physicians in their relationships with patients; see, Sue Fisher, "Doctor-Patient Communication: A Social and Micro-Political Performance," *Sociology of Health and Illness*, 6 (1984), 1–29.

[72]Ibid., 604.

careful to appear interested in everything the patient has to say, no matter how trivial. Further, they are not supposed to argue with patients' personal prejudices. They at least should always appear to be immersed in the discussion. Finally, they are to "beware of bare statements, or bare truth, or bare logic."[73]

In some cases physicians must go even further in accommodating themselves to the needs and desires of patients. General practitioners, in particular, must be responsive to the lay culture. It is by pleasing this culture that they get and keep patients. "Whether their motives be to heal the patient or to survive, professionally, they will feel pressure to accept or manipulate lay expectations, whether by administering harmless placebos or by giving no unpopular drugs."[74] Many patients visit physicians for the first time on a "tryout" basis. The patients assess the doctors' performance and may even compare their assessment with those of others who have used the same doctors. Only if their assessment is favorable will the patients return to the doctors. This obviously puts a great deal of pressure on physicians to attempt to please their patients.

Professionals can, of course, take far more aggressive and independent stands. Rosenthal found a variety of such actions in his study of legal injury claims. Lawyers could simply refuse cases that promised to be too difficult or that held out a small monetary return. They could "farm out" cases that didn't look very promising to specialists for a fee. They could themselves specialize, handling only those cases that they preferred and found most lucrative. Too, it is possible for lawyers to take a variety of very questionable actions in order to cope with the basic conflict of interest between themselves and their clients. It is possible, for example, to bribe some insurance adjusters to settle a case quickly and profitably; or cut corners to reduce the time required on the case; or attempt to persuade clients, often falsely, that a quick settlement is in their best interests. Finally, they could present their case fairly to the clients and seek an approach that is in the interests of both of them. Thus there are a variety of rather independent actions open to professionals in seeking to cope with client conflict, although some of them are highly unethical or illegal.

Although a variety of independent actions are open to professionals in coping with client-centered conflict, in many cases they are forced to accommodate their interests to the wishes of the client. And though they have often surrendered to clients, they usually deny it, arguing that such a surrender hurts professional performance. With this ideology, professionals have hoped to bolster their power vis-a-vis the clients. However, research has indicated that the compromise between professionals and clients not only exists, but is likely to lead to improved performance by professionals.

Rosenthal studied the relationship between 59 Manhattan residents who made personal injury claims and their lawyers.[75] He sought to determine which of two models of professional-client relations was superior. One model was the "traditional approach," which accords ultimate power to the profes-

[73]L.J. Henderson, "Physician and Patient as a Social System," *The New England Journal of Medicine,* 212 (1935), 821–823.

[74]Eliot Freidson, "Client Control and Medical Practice," *American Journal of Sociology,* 65 (1960), 378.

[75]Rosenthal, *Lawyer and Client: Who's in Charge?*

TABLE 8.1   Actions Taken by Clients in Personal Injury Cases

ACTION	PROPORTION OF THE SAMPLE TAKING THE ACTION
1. Seeks quality medical examination of the injuries.	76%
2. Makes wishes and concerns about the case clear to the lawyer.	39%
3. Follows up with the lawyer to be sure his case is getting his attention.	31%
4. Seeks a second legal opinion.	27%
5. Collects information to help the lawyer.	22%

SOURCE: Adapted from *Lawyer and Client: Who's in Charge?* by Douglas Rosenthal, © 1974 by RussellSage Foundation.

sional; the other was the "participatory model," "which assumes that client welfare and the public interest are best served where clients participate actively in dealing with their problems and share control and decision responsibility with the professional."[76]

He found five types of client activities that might have an impact on an injury claim decision. Those five actions, with the proportion of the respondents taking each of them, are presented in Table 8.1. Only two clients took all five actions, while eight took none of them.

An index of client activity was developed and it was related to case outcome. In developing the index of case outcome, the opinions of a series of experts on what settlement the client should get was compared to what the client actually got. Contrary to the expectations of many, participating clients did not do more poorly—in fact, those who actively participated got better recoveries than those who did not. Not all forms of client activity were useful. Making follow-up demands of the lawyers and making wishes clear were most highly related to successful case outcome, while seeking a second legal opinion and marshaling evidence were weakly related.

The relationship between client participation and successful outcome was not perfect. Some clients who participated did poorly, while some who did not participate did well. Yet 75 percent of those who were active on their cases got good results, while only 41 percent of those who were inactive got similar results. Rosenthal argues that the legal process is so complex that lawyers can use all the help they can get. He concludes that "neither lawyer nor client should be in charge, but that professional service should be a matter of shared responsibility."[77] On the basis of his research, Rosenthal goes on to build what he calls a "participatory model" of professional-client relations. It has the following elements:

1. Clients are active participants in the professional-client relationship (informed of choices open to them as well as the attendant risks; involved in making decisions and sharing responsibility for those decisions).

[76]Ibid., p. 2.
[77]Ibid.

2. Clients should surrender the notion of the professional as invincible.
3. Clients understand the choices open to them and make a positive contribution in the making of those choices.
4. Clients recognize that conflicts of interest between professionals and clients are inevitable and can be resolved by collaborative efforts.
5. Standards of professional and client performance can be defined and maintained by collaborative efforts of professionals and laypersons.
6. The public can be given more information about problems requiring professional help and encouraged to shop around among available professionals.

Although Rosenthal believes in the participatory model, he recognizes that there are costs involved in such an approach: it will take more of the clients' time and energy, it may cost more, and it may increase the ability of clients to pressure the lawyers into more immoral, illegal, or unfortunate actions.

Although some of these problems are far-fetched, the fact remains that this new approach will entail costs. Yet given the changing nature of client-professional relations, is there any choice? We think not. The participatory model will solve many problems involved in professional-client relations and, if we can generalize from Rosenthal's findings, it will also give us higher-quality decisions. It should also be noted that Rosenthal's findings are not idiosyncratic. At least some support is to be found in Hosticka's research (discussed above) in which he concluded that lawyers devoted more time and energy to those cases in which the clients persistently followed their interests.

In concluding this section on the conflict between free professionals and their clients, we must underscore Freidson's point that no matter what efforts are undertaken, there will always be a residue of conflict that cannot be eliminated:

> The patient, properly educated or not, will find occasion to resist the doctor. The doctor cannot accommodate himself to the patient beyond a certain point without ceasing to be a professional expert, but his expert status does not by itself stimulate patient cooperation in the areas where conflict is most likely to occur.[78]

THE PROFESSIONAL SCIENTIST

Earlier we discussed the scientist as one of the professionals likely to be found in organizations. But in this post-industrial society where scientific knowledge, in particular, is becoming ever more important, we need to devote considerably more attention to the professional scientist.[79] Our focus here is the conflict engendered among scientists by their institutionalized efforts to compete for fame, even preeminence, within their chosen fields. While competition is a reality of life in science, it contradicts the profession's formal norms such as

[78]Freidson, *Patients' Views of Medical Practice*, p. 186.

[79]For a historical discussion of the emergence of this profession see, Joseph Ben-David, *The Scientist's Role in Society: A Comparative Study* (Chicago: University of Chicago Press, 1984).

communality and disinterestedness. In fact, much of what really goes on in science is in opposition to the formal norms of the scientific community. In the course of discussing scientific competition we will also analyze the general gap between formal norms and actual behavior.

In this section we are offering a sociological view of scientific innovation and creativity. We are arguing that it is the social pressure to compete for recognition that is an important, even crucial, factor in the development of scientific breakthroughs. Such a perspective stands in contrast to widely held views about scientific achievements. One generally held idea is that scientific developments are the product of the intellectual genius working in virtual isolation. This image has been buttressed by the mass media, which see the lonely scientist as a romantic and dramatic figure. Scientists have also contributed to this image by their own behavior and their descriptions of their work. Take, for example, Isaac Newton's rather humble description of his achievements:

> I do not know what I may appear to the world; but to myself I seem to have been only like a boy playing on the seashore, and diverting myself in now and then finding a smoother pebble or a pretty shell than ordinary, whilst the great ocean of truth lay all undiscovered before me.[80]

Closely related to this image of the isolated scientist is the idea that scientific breakthroughs are the products of individuals with an extraordinary intellectual capacity which we often label as genius. Albert Einstein has come to be the very symbol of the scientific genius. This idea fits well with the view of the isolated scientist, since the genius is assumed to be best suited to working alone, unplagued by the inadequacies of less brilliant colleagues and laypeople.

There is still a third conception of the scientist and scientific development which we need to differentiate from the one taken here. This view differs from the individualistic bias of the two outlined above; it errs in the direction by being too socially deterministic. Here scientific developments are seen as the almost inevitable products of prior social and scientific developments, of the "ripeness of the time." The scientist has simply added the small, often anticlimactic, final touch. An extreme version of this point of view argues that the individual scientist really makes no difference. In our opinion, this perspective accords too little significance to the individual, while the first two are overly individualistic.

A more complete conception of scientific achievement must embrace the three points of view outlined above as well as adding another crucial ingredient: the social setting of the scientist. In this view "science in fact develops within a community of interacting scientists."[81] But this is not to reject the other conceptions. Scientific breakthroughs can be made by scientists who work alone, although they must be dependent on the work of peers and predecessors, even if they do not have actual physical contact with them. The genius is certainly necessary and, all other things being equal, scientific geniuses

---

[80]In Jonathan R. Cole and Stephen Cole, *Social Stratification in Science* (Chicago: University of Chicago Press, 1973), p. 1.

[81]Ibid.

are more likely to make breakthroughs than are their less intellectually capable colleagues. Scientists are also dependent on the work that has come before them, although their additional contributions, even if they are small, may be crucial.

Although we accept the importance of all these factors, sociologists place primary emphasis on the social processes involved in scientific creativity. As we will see, the thrust of sociological thought and research on this issue leads to the conclusion that it is the process of competition for scientific recognition that is crucial in the creation of scientific developments.

Normative Structure of Science

We need to begin with a discussion of the basic normative structure of science. As with much else in the sociology of science, the seminal work on the normative structure of science was done by Robert Merton, and Norman Storer has performed a useful service for us by organizing (and expanding on) Merton's original formulations.[82] Table 8.2 provides us with an overview of the basic normative structure of science, the guidelines that scientists are supposed to follow in their craft. Let us briefly examine each of the six basic norms of science enumerated in Table 8.2.

The norm of objectivity.   The scientist is expected to evaluate past and on-going scientific developments from an objective, rather than a subjective, point of view. This means that scientific work is, in Merton's terms, to be evaluated on the basis of "preestablished impersonal criteria."[83] Implied here is the idea that a scientific idea will receive the recognition it deserves whether it is produced by a Noble-prize-winning physicist at Harvard University or an unknown technician at a remote junior college.

The norm of organized skepticism.   It is the responsibility of scientists to be skeptical, especially to be critical of the work of their colleagues, in particular the work that forms the basis of their own studies. If they fail to do this, and incorporate others' false or erroneous ideas, then they are held responsible for this failing by the larger scientific community (assuming, of course, that their failure is discovered). The discovery of this kind of error is made more likely by another aspect of this norm, which makes it necessary for scientists to publicly expose errors in the work of others. Further, scientists are supposed to take a similarly skeptical attitude toward their own work; they must critically analyze it from all sides in order to expose its weaknesses.

The norm of emotional neutrality.   Scientists are expected to adopt an emotionally neutral stance toward their own work as well as the work of their peers. Overly committed scientists may fail to see the problems involved in those ideas or in the utility of a new or different set of ideas because of their commitment to a given point of view. Scientists who are overly committed to one theory would be more tempted to bias their methods or their findings.

[82]Norman W. Storer, *The Social System of Science* (New York: Holt, Rinehart and Winston, 1966).

[83]Robert K. Merton, *The Sociology of Science* (Chicago: University of Chicago Press, 1973).

TABLE 8.2   The Basic Normative Structure of Science

	POINT OF REFERENCE		
Focus of the Norm	The Body of Scientific Knowledge 1.	Interaction among Scientists 2.	The Scientist's Psychological State 3.
Orientation	Objective	Organized Skepticism	Emotional Neutrality
	4.	5.	6.
Action	Generalization	Communality	Disinterestedness

SOURCE: From *The Social System of Science* by Norman W. Storer. Copyright © 1966 by Holt, Rinehart and Winston, Inc. Reprinted by permission of Norman W. Storer.

The norm of generalization.   The norms of objectivity, organized skepticism, and emotional neutrality relate to the way scientists orient themselves to a variety of objects. The last three norms, on the other hand, are concerned with the action of scientists. The norm of generalization underscores the fact that scientists are supposed to aim toward the development of general, and generalizable, knowledge. They are expected to take isolated bits of data and combine them into more general hypotheses, propositions, and laws. Ultimately, of course, these are supposed to be combined into still more general theories, such as Darwin's theory of evolution, Mendel's theory of genetics, and Einstein's theory of relativity.

The norm of communality.   The norm of communality (or "communism," as Merton originally called it) means that scientists must recognize that their work is dependent upon the contributions of predecessors as well as peers. This is epitomized in Isaac Newton's well-known statement: "If I have seen farther, it is by standing on the shoulders of giants."[84] A corollary of this norm is that scientists are supposed to have humility. As Merton has emphasized, scientific knowledge constitutes "a common heritage in which the equity of the individual is severely limited."[85] Scientists are expected to share their work with colleagues doing work in the same area. They should publish their work as soon as they feel it is ready for public exposure, so that other scientists can react to it, expand on it, even refute it.

The norm of disinterestedness.   Finally, scientists are expected to be interested in the good of the larger scientific community, not in receiving financial reward or in increasing their own fame.

The Scientist's Real World

These six norms constitute a very romantic image of scientists. There is, of course, a gap between this model and actual behavior, and this section is

[84]Ibid., p. 303.
[85]Ibid., p. 273.

devoted to the conflicts brought about by this disparity. We begin by discussing the antecedent issue of what causes this gap to exist.

As Storer has pointed out, the normative system of science is purely structural and tells us little about what actually happens in science and what causes those things to occur.[86] It was Merton himself who saw the weaknesses in his static formulation and developed a conception of how the system actually moves, how it operates. The motive force is seen by Merton to be the ambition to achieve professional recognition. In part, this ambition is derived from a psychological desire to succeed. But in addition, and more important sociologically, professional recognition is an institutionalized aspect of the structure of science that serves to reinforce the basic psychological drives.

In his work on the battles over priorities in scientific discovery, Merton emphasizes the real world in science and the centrality of competition in that life. It is of considerable interest to scientists to be the first to discover something, to establish their priority in a scientific discovery. The rewards in science, primarily recognition from the larger scientific community, go to the individual or individuals who are the first to make and publicly announce a discovery. Someone who makes the same discovery later is relegated to the dustbin of scientific history. It is through original discoveries, through what Kuhn calls scientific revolutions, that the great scientific advances are made.[87]

It is important to reiterate that the drive for recognition is not simply a result of the psychologic drive for success. It is also derived from, and is an integral part of, the normative system of science.

> To say that these frequent conflicts over priority are rooted in the egotism of human nature, then explains next to nothing; to say that they are rooted in the contentious personalities of those recruited by science may explain part, but not enough; to say, however, that these conflicts are largely a consequence of the institutional norms of science itself comes closer, I think, to the truth. . . . It is these norms that exert pressure upon scientists to assert their claims.[88]

The norms of science constrain the behavior of scientists in a variety of ways. As students, scientists internalize these norms; thus they have a great impact on what they do in later life. In addition, other scientists enforce the norms and in overt and covert ways lead scientists to conform to the desire to achieve recognition from peers for original contributions.

What are scientists after in their drive for recognition? To answer this question we must look at the reward system in science. Financial gains are supposed to be of little importance to scientists, as well as to professionals in general. But today it is more and more possible for scientists to strive for, and be rewarded with, money. In spite of this, few have the option of becoming rich.

Money aside, at the top of the reward list in science is *eponymy,* or the affixing of a scientist's name to an aspect of his or her field. "Eponymy is . . . the most enduring and perhaps the most prestigious kind of recognition

[86]Norman W. Storer, "Introduction" to Merton, *The Sociology of Science,* pp. xi–xxxi.

[87]Thomas Kuhn, *The Structure of Scientific Revolutions,* rev. ed. (Chicago: University of Chicago Press, 1970).

[88]Merton, *The Sociology of Science,* p. 293.

institutionalized in science."[89] A scientist may be recognized for part, or all, of something he or she has discovered (the *Copernican* system, *Halley's* Comet). Even more impressive would be to have one's name affixed to an entire age (the *Newtonian* epoch, the *Einsteinian* era). Or a new science, or a branch of science, can be named for a scientist (*Freudian* psychiatry). There are other ways in which a scientist can be rewarded with eponymy. Minor subspecialties within a science can be named after an individual, or specific laws, theories, or instruments.

There are, of course, many other rewards of significance to scientists that serve to motivate them toward making important breakthroughs.

1. Prizes and medals—Perhaps the most sought-after prize is the Nobel Prize.[90]
2. Nomination to exclusive and prestigious professional societies.
3. Citations in analyses of the history of one's field.
4. Citations in textbooks and in others' research.
5. Fellowships—Among the most prized are Guggenheim and Ford Foundation fellowships.
6. Editorships of important journals in the field—This enables one to serve as a "gatekeeper," deciding what work should and should not be published.
7. Appointment to well-known chairs in universities.
8. Honorary degrees.
9. Appointment as consultant to various governmental, industrial, or international bodies. (This reward also brings additional income.)
10. Recognition by scientific peers and the public.

Merton maintains that in many ways the drive for recognition stands in opposition to the normative system, even though it is itself derived from that system. He acknowledges that science has a more human side, even some dysfunctional aspects, but he believes that most of these dysfunctions are kept largely in check by the existence of counterbalancing norms. For example, the communality of science leads scientists to have a sense of humility that counteracts the egotism spawned by the rush for priorities. Fraud and plagiarism, which are made distinct possibilities by the desire for recognition,[91] are largely prevented by the existence of the norm of communality.

The contradiction between at least some scientific norms and the pressure toward priority gives scientists a sense of ambivalence toward their desire to compete for recognition:

> To insist on one's originality and claiming priority is not exactly humble and to dismiss one's priority by ignoring it is not exactly to affirm the value of originality; as a result of this conflict, scientists come to despise themselves for wanting that which the institutional values of science had led them to want.[92]

[89]Ibid., p. 300.

[90]Harriet Zuckerman, "Nobel Laureates in Science: Patterns of Production, Collaboration, and Authorship," *American Sociological Review*, 72 (1967), 391–403; Harriet Zuckerman, *Scientific Elite* (New York: The Free Press, 1977).

[91]L.S. Hearnshaw, *Cyril Burt: Psychologist* (London: Hodder and Stoughton, 1979).

[92]Merton, *The Sociology of Science*, p. 305.

In other words, scientists are literally compelled by the norms of science to be ambitious *and* to be ashamed of those ambitions.

This is not the only type of ambivalence[93] in science. Other forms of ambivalence include the following:

1. Scientists are expected to make their knowledge available to peers as rapidly as possible, but they are also admonished not to publish shoddy or incomplete work by rushing into print.

2. Scientists are warned against being caught up blindly in the latest scientific fads, but they must simultaneously avoid becoming ossified. They must be flexible, open to new ideas, but must avoid blindly following the scientific bandwagon.

3. Scientists are expected to believe that their scientific contributions should, and will be, esteemed. Yet at the same time they are warned not to work in order to enhance their personal standing and esteem.

4. Scientists are not supposed to advance claims for new knowledge until they are, in their minds, beyond reasonable dispute. But once they advance those ideas, they are expected to shift gears and defend them no matter how great the opposition.

5. Scientists are supposed to make every effort to know the work of their predecessors and contemporaries. At the same time they are taught that too much erudition can be a substitute for creativity or can stultify creativity.

6. Scientists are expected to pay scrupulous attention to detail, but they must not become so bogged down in minutiae that they fail to see the broader significance of their work.

7. Scientific knowledge is supposed to be universal. Yet science is often wrapped up in the political aspirations of the scientist's nation. Thus, scientists often see their work used as political tools by their nations, sometimes to the detriment of the overall scientific community.

8. It is the responsibility of scientists to train the next generation of scientists, but they must not allow teaching to sap all of their energies, leaving them little time for original, creative research.

9. The scientific craft is learned best when neophytes apprentice themselves to masters, yet they ultimately must gain autonomy, become scientists on their own.

As we can see, the focus in the sociology of science has gradually moved from the normative structure to the real world of scientists. Spurred on by James Watson's[94] expose of the way he and his colleague Francis Crick made one of the most important discoveries of our time, the DNA double helix—and won a Nobel Prize in the process—sociologists could no longer ignore the "real" behavior of scientists.

Watson made it clear that he and Crick were highly ambitious men who were not going to allow a few norms to stand in their way in their race to establish priority in the discovery of the structure of DNA. Watson's description led many to realize that the desire for recognition, the need to compete, and a great deal of ambition were far more valid descriptions of the behavior of sci-

---

[93]Robert K. Merton, "The Ambivalence of Scientists," in Norman Kaplan, ed., *Science and Society* (Chicago: Rand-McNally, 1965), pp. 112–132.

[94]James D. Watson, *The Double Helix* (New York: New American Library, 1968).

entists than the abstract normative system. Science emerges, in Watson's work, as a world no better and no worse than those of business, politics, and the like.

Merton responds that this is not news. He argues that the "dog-eat-dog" world of science has been with us since the beginning of the scientific endeavor; competition for priority within science has been institutionalized from the beginning.[95] The only difference in our time, he says, is that there are now many more scientists, so a given discovery is likely at any time to be made by a number of people. It is the realization that competition exists that has increased in recent years, not the competition itself.

A phenomenon that highlights the reality of life in science, rather than its normative structure, is the "Matthew Effect,"[96] the tendency to give recognition to already famous scientists (for example, Nobel Prize winners) while those who have made as important or even more important discoveries get significantly less acknowledgment. This, of course, stands in contradiction to the basic norms of science, in particular the objectivity of scientific activity. Yet the Matthew Effect exists in spite of these norms. For example, in collaborative work, it is often the most prestigious of the coauthors who gets credit for the discovery. It also occurs in the case of simultaneous multiple discoveries when the more famous of the scientists is the one who receives recognition for an accomplishment. The Matthew Effect obviously has negative consequences for lesser-known scientists. Furthermore, it leads to the rather uncritical acceptance of work by noted people.

The cult of the personality in science performs some positive functions as well. Scientific idols can set the course for an entire field and lead it into some uncharted areas into which it might not otherwise venture. They also keep the field exciting by continually igniting intellectual ferment. They are particularly important in influencing the direction taken by young scientists. Publishing with scientific leaders obviously gains attention for the work of young scientists.[97] Because they already have high status, famous scientists can afford to tackle high-risk problems that have a limited hope of success. Thus, in his later life, Albert Einstein devoted himself to the kinds of issues others avoided.[98] Moreover, famous scientists, their status secure, are less likely to deluge the field with a series of lower-quality research papers. They know what not to publish. Thus scientific heroes have both positive and negative consequences for science.

There is research that warns us to be careful in applying the Matthew Effect. A study by Cole and Cole found that the quality of a piece of work is more important in gaining recognition for it than are the variables associated with the Matthew Effect (such as whether the author possesses awards, works in a prestigious department, or is a widely known figure in the field.)[99] Later,

[95]Merton, *The Sociology of Science*, pp. 334–335.

[96]Ibid., p. 381.

[97]Stephen Cole, "Professional Standing and the Reception of Scientific Discoveries," *American Journal of Sociology*, 76 (1970), 286-306.

[98]Ronald Clark, *Einstein: The Life and Times* (New York: Avon Books, 1971).

[99]Stephen Cole and Jonathan Cole, "Scientific Output and Recognition: A Study in the Operation of the Reward System in Science," *American Sociological Review*, 72 (1967), 377–390.

the Coles found that the initial reception of a paper appears to be determined more by its quality than by the position of the author in the stratification system of science.[100] However, the speed of diffusion of a paper is affected by the position of the author in the scientific hierarchy. High-quality papers by either high- or low-ranking scientists are about equally likely to be diffused early, but lesser-quality papers by top-ranking scientists are more likely to be disseminated early than those of low-ranking scientists. These studies suggest that Merton may have exaggerated the significance of the Matthew Effect.

A view seems to be emerging in which science is no longer seen in terms of a single set of norms, but rather in terms of norms and counternorms. As early as 1963, Merton and Barber made this observation: "Behavior oriented wholly to the dominant norms would defeat the functional objectives of the role. Instead role behavior is alternately oriented to dominant norms and to subsidiary counter-norms in the role."[101] In contrast to the impersonal character of the dominant norms, the counternorms of science are distinctly personal. Personal elements are increasingly less likely to be seen as dysfunctional, as destructive of good science, but rather as an integral part of the scientific enterprise.

The importance of counternorms in science has been empirically demonstrated in Mitroff's[102] study of the scientists involved in the analysis of rocks brought back from the moon. Of prime importance is his finding that in contrast to the norm of emotional neutrality, there was strong emotional involvement in the work: "*Every one of the scientists interviewed on the first round of interviews indicated that they thought the notion of the objective, emotionally disinterested scientist naive.*"[103] They were committed to their work in at least three different senses: (1) they believed that scientists had to be committed to their theories in order to test them adequately; (2) "Scientists were affectively involved with their ideas, were reluctant to part with them and did everything in their power to confirm them;"[104] (3) commitment was found to pervade the whole process of science from the discovery of scientific ideas to the testing of those ideas. Said one of the scientists about the most committed of his peers:

> The commitment of these guys to their ideas while absolutely infuriating at times can be a very good thing too. . . . It's true that these guys are a perpetual thorn in the side of the profession. . . . [But] we need them around. They perpetually shake things up with their wild ideas, athough they drive you mad with the stick-to-itiveness that they have for their ideas.[105]

[100]Ibid.

[101]Robert Merton and Elinor Barber, "Sociological Ambivalence," in E.A. Tiryakian, ed., *Sociological Theory: Values and Sociocultural Change* (Glencoe, IL: The Free Press, 1963), pp. 91–110.

[102]Ian Mitroff, "Norms and Counter-Norms in a Select Group of the Apollo Moon Scientists: A Case Study of the Ambivalence of Scientists," *American Sociological Review*, 39 (1974), 579–595.

[103]Ibid., 587.

[104]Ibid., 586.

[105]Ibid., 589.

In fact, such commitment to both norms and counternorms is, almost by definition, a state of ambivalence. Scientists cannot choose between one or the other but are constantly confronted with a tug-of-war between the two sets of norms.

Just as the norm of emotional neutrality has a counternorm of personal commitment, the norm of communality is opposed by the counternorm of solitariness–the belief that discoveries are one's property and that secrecy may have to be practiced to retain control over that property. Mitroff found that about a fifth of his sample acknowledged that stealing was a minor, or sometimes even a major, problem. By stealing, however, the scientists did not mean conscious theft (which was regarded as an insignificant problem), but rather the unconscious and unintended use of another scientist's ideas.

Mitroff argues that solitariness and secrecy are not merely protective devices, but true counternorms within science. As such, they perform a number of vital functions: for example, without secrecy science would be chaotic since it would be almost constantly disrupted by priority disputes. In addition, secrecy plays the useful function for scientists of acknowledging that they are indeed doing something worthwhile, something worth protecting. Even stealing, as dangerous as it is, performs a similar function by affirming the value of what one is doing. Said one scientist:

> It is only when I began to do something significant and important that people began to *steal* [italics added] from me . . . *You know you're doing something significant when people want to steal it.*[106]

So, we can see that the actual practice of science is far more human, personal, and informal than was indicated in the early work in the sociology of science, which focused on the normative structure of science. The gap that exists between the ideal and the real behavior of professional scientists causes conflict. One type of conflict—the drive for recognition and the resulting competition—exists as a reality alongside the formal norms of science: objectivity, disinterestedness, emotional neutrality, communality, and so on. That conflict is the force behind the creativity and progress of professional scientists.

CONCLUSIONS

In this chapter we have examined the distinctive worklife conflicts of three types of professionals. We have seen that professionals employed in organizations, particularly nonprofessional organizations, tend to be confronted with conflict between their professional norms and the norms of the employing organization. Although this conflict exists, we have also seen that there is no simple and direct inverse relationship between professionalization and bureaucratization. Although this conflict may be functional for both organization and professional, we discussed a number of ways in which the various parties involved can cope with the conflict. Among the devices open to the employing

[106]Ibid., 593.

organization are the dual ladder and the physical segregation of professionals. Professions can help ease the conflict by rewarding contributions to employing organizations and training new members to adapt to those organizations. Individual professionals can cope by choosing a setting best suited to their needs or by adapting in various ways to the conflict, such as by attempting to fuse the roles of professional and bureaucrat. More radical is the propensity of at least some professionals to join labor unions.

The second part of the chapter was devoted to a discussion of "free" professionals, their distinctive conflicts and resolutions. The free professional is most often confronted with conflict with clients. We examined a variety of ways in which the professional can cope with this conflict. The most surprising conclusion to be drawn from this section is that, contrary to what many professionals say, the quality of professional service seems to be better when there is a more questioning clientele and hence a greater chance of professional-client conflict.

Finally, we dealt with professional scientists and the conflict between the norms of scientific behavior and the reality of life within science. In our view, this conflict is an important source of innovation and creativity in science.

NINE
CONFLICT IN THE MARGINAL PROFESSIONS

In this chapter we turn to a discussion of a number of occupations that, despite great effort,[1] have failed to win full professional recognition. Marginal to the established professions, their basic conflicts stem from their inability to become fully established *professions*. We will examine several such occupations, including pharmacists, chiropractors, funeral directors, business executives (especially personnel managers), and paraprofessionals.[2] But the main focus in this chapter will be the female semiprofessions: nurses, schoolteachers, social workers, and librarians. These occupations constitute the most important, and sociologically most interesting, marginal professions. Our focus throughout will be on the efforts of the marginal professions to win professional recognition, the barriers to such recognition, and the efforts made by people in these occupations to cope with the conflicts engendered by their failure.

The relative standing of professionals, semiprofessionals, and marginal professionals is well illustrated by a study by Lorber and Satow of a ghetto,

---

[1]Cohen and Wagner write of social work's "obsession with professionalism." See, Marcia B. Cohen and David Wagner, "Social Work Professionalism: Reality and Illusion," in Charles Derber, ed., *Professionals as Workers: Mental Labor in Advanced Capitalism* (Boston, MA: G.K. Hall and Co., 1982), p. 155.

[2]Unlike other occupations discussed in this section, paraprofessionals are not close to the professional end of the continuum. However, they are discussed here because they were largely created by the professions and occupy a position marginal to them—they often perform the "dirty work" the professionals prefer to avoid.

hospital-based community mental health center.[3] Employed in this center were (professional) psychiatrists, (semiprofessional) social workers, and paraprofessionals (marginal professional). The center was stratified in a variety of ways. The psychiatrists earned more money than the others. Social workers and paraprofessionals were required to punch a time clock and work on a fixed schedule; psychiatrists were not. However, the most important dimension of stratification was the types of patients assigned to each occupation. The psychiatrists were assigned the most desirable cases, "people who were verbal, intelligent, highly motivated, and most likely to come regularly for at least one year."[4] The least desirable patients, "the least cooperative and verbal and those with numerous problems of everyday living . . . 'problem patients'—were assigned to paraprofessionals."[5] Social workers, reflecting their status below psychiatrists but above paraprofessionals, got the middle-ranking patients. The irony of this stratification system was that the least trained group (paraprofessionals) "had to work with the most complicated and difficult cases, including some with severe psychopathology."[6] Furthermore, it was the paraprofessionals who had the heaviest case load.

One result of this system was the dissatisfaction felt by both social workers and paraprofessionals with their work. Yet it was these people who saw the bulk of the patients, and as a result the treatment suffered: "patients were treated predominantly by dissatisfied, time-clock-oriented social workers, or by minimally trained and barely supervised paraprofessionals."[7] This leads Lorber and Satow to conclude:

> Victims of occupational stratification in their own lives, these ghetto residents who sought help with their problems of daily living or with severe emotional difficulties were victims of the occupational stratification of their helpers as well.[8]

The existence of, and differences among, professionals, semiprofessionals, and marginal professionals reflects the rigid stratification system at the upper end of the occupational continuum.

THE FEMALE SEMIPROFESSIONS

In this section we discuss four of the most interesting and conceptually important occupations in the workworld—schoolteacher, social worker, nurse, and librarian. These occupations are collectively labeled the *female semiprofessions*. While most of the section is devoted to a discussion of why these occupations are marginally professional (are, in other words, semiprofessions) we should

---

[3]Judith Lorber and Roberta Satow, "Creating a Company of Unequals: Sources of Stratification in a Ghetto Community Mental Health Center," *Sociology of Work and Occupations*, 4 (1977), 281–302.

[4]Ibid., 288–289.

[5]Ibid., 289.

[6]Ibid., 292.

[7]Ibid., 295

[8]Ibid., 296

TABLE 9.1   Female Semiprofessions: 1972 and 1982 (% female)

YEAR	LIBRARIANS*	NURSES (REGISTERED)	SOCIAL WORKERS**	ELEMENTARY SCHOOLTEACHERS
1972	82%	98%	55%	85%
1982	81	96	66	82

*also includes archivists, curators
**also includes recreation workers
SOURCE: U.S. Bureau of the Census, *Statistical Abstract of the United States*, 104th ed. (Washington, D.C., 1983), p. 419; percentages are rounded.

first discuss the reasons *female* precedes *semiprofession*. First of all, as is clear in Table 9.1, such occupations have for years been dominated by women.[9] Despite a small decline recently in the predominance of females in most semiprofessions, numerical preeminence continues.

From Table 9.2 it is clear that females have made some inroads into male-dominated professions, although these occupations remain highly sex-segregated. While we see a pattern of substantial gains for females in male professions, there is clearly a great distance to go in all of them. Greater changes in the future are foreshadowed by the growing numbers of women in professional schools. In addition to being numerically dominated by women, the female semiprofessions have been sex-labeled as female domains.[10] We discussed the concept of sex-labeling at length in Chapter 5, which dealt with the general status of women in the workworld. Of all the sex-labeled occupations in American society, the semiprofessions are among the most rigidly demarcated. The nurturant, supportive, tender, helping, caring character[11] of the semiprofessions seems to fit neatly with the stereotypes of female behavior and the roles they are expected to perform in American society.[12] Thus, it is the numerical predominance and the seeming fit between occupational and sex roles that have earned for these occupations the label of the female semiprofessions.[13]

Professional Marginality

Put in simplest terms, males have won the most prestigious, powerful, and highest-paying established professions for themselves and have relegated females with professional aspirations to the less prestigious, less powerful, and lesser-paying semiprofessions. In other words, the existence of male-domi-

[9]John G. Richardson and Brenda Wooden Hatcher, "The Feminization of Public School Teaching: 1870–1920," *Work and Occupations*, 10 (1983), 81–99.

[10]Jeff Hearn, "Notes on Patriarchy, Professionalization and the Semi-Professions," *Sociology*, 16 (1982), 184–202; Valerie Kincade Oppenheimer, *The Female Labor Force in the United States* (Berkeley, CA: University of California Press, 1970).

[11]Bonnie Bullough and Vern Bullough, "Nursing as a Profession," in Phyllis L. Stewart and Muriel Cantor, eds., *Varieties of Work* (Beverly Hills, CA: Sage Publications, 1982), pp. 213–224.

[12]Athena Theodore, *The Professional Woman* (Cambridge, MA: Schenkman Publishing Co., 1971), p.1.

[13]Not everyone calls these occupations semiprofessions. For example, see Bullough and Bullough, "Nursing as a Profession."

**TABLE 9.2 Females in Male-Dominated Professions: 1972 and 1982
(% female)**

YEAR	PHYSICIANS	LAWYERS AND JUDGES	ENGINEERS	DENTISTS
1972	9%	4%	1%	2%
1982	15	15	6	3

SOURCE: U.S. Bureau of the Census, *Statistical Abstract of the United States,*
104th ed. (Washington, D.C., 1983), p. 419; percentages are rounded.

nated professions and female-dominated semiprofessions is illustrative of a
patriarchal society.[14] Theodore catches the essence of this process of sex-
labeling in both the professions and the semiprofessions:

> Those professions in which males are concentrated are more highly professiona-
> lized than those in which females are concentrated and are therefore more pres-
> tigious. Thus male and female professions are stratified on the occupational con-
> tinuum according to how the sexes are ranked in the society. . . . Both males and
> females are considered to be social deviates if they trespass into the territory that
> is typed for the opposite sex."[15]

The most obvious question is: Why have the semiprofessions been
denied full professional status? Following our discussion of power and the
professions in Chapter 4, it is clear that the answer lies in the lack of power of
the semiprofessions to overcome the power of those forces opposing their efforts to professionalize.

The irony here is that the female semiprofessions have control over
areas of indeterminacy and uncertainty,[16] the bases of professional development. Thus, they have the raw material with which to win professional status.
A large proportion of the tasks within the female semiprofessions are *indeterminate.* Though it is certainly true that some semiprofessional tasks can be,
and have been, routinized, the same is also true of established professions—
and that has not prevented them from gaining, and retaining, professional
status. The nurses' relationship with patients, the educational process that
takes place between schoolteachers and pupils, and the helping relationship
that exists between social workers and clients are not very amenable to
routinization. In addition, semiprofessionals have also controlled areas of
uncertainty—the health of the patient, the education of the young, and the welfare of the poor. In sum, the semiprofessions possess the bases for
professionalization—control over areas of uncertainty and indeterminacy.

The failure of the semiprofessions to become established professions
cannot be traced to a lack of ideological efforts to win that prestigious label. In
fact, the semiprofessions have developed a rather elaborate ideological system
to rationalize their right to professional recognition. This ideological position
has been widely broadcast and disseminated in the media. In fact, few occupa-

[14]Hearn, "Notes on Patriarchy."

[15]Theodore, *The Professional Woman,* p. 4.

[16]Librarians would seem to be an exception here.

tions have spent as much time developing and broadcasting their ideological positions on professionalization as have the semiprofessions. Thus, it is not from a lack of trying, or a lack of ideological justifications, that the semiprofessions have failed to win the professional label.

Why, then, have they failed? The semiprofessions have the characteristics needed to professionalize, and they have attempted to win that status. Why are they still semiprofessions? Let us examine some of the barriers to the professionalization of the semiprofessions.[17] The semiprofessions have failed to professionalize not so much because of their own lack of power, but because of greater power that has operated against them from a variety of quarters. The first and most important factor is obviously the opposition from powerful male elites. Male elites have simply found it in their best interest to keep the status of the female semiprofessions comparatively low. Freidson has pointed out that the professions occupy their position because they are allowed to by societal elites.[18] If they wish, societal elites can allow that status to lapse, or they can even actively remove it. In aiding the established professions, the elites have often operated against the interest of other occupations, including the semiprofessions. They use their influence to drive competing occupations out of the same area of work, to discourage others by conferring advantages on the chosen occupation, and to require still others to be subordinated to the professions.[19] Thus, a large portion of the nurses' problems can be traced to the advantages conferred upon physicians and disadvantages imposed on nurses by societal elites.

Further complicating the plight of the semiprofessions is the fact that once the professions are established, they become aligned with societal elites in containing the demands and aspirations of the semiprofessions. Katz has demonstrated how the established profession of medicine acts to keep the semiprofession of nursing in a subordinate position.[20] Within the hospitals the physicians have come to occupy the most important positions, far above the nurses and any other occupation within the hospital system. This results, according to Katz, in a "caste-like system" that "puts an unscalable wall between the physicians and the semiprofessionals in the hospital."[21] Nurses must "know their place"; for example, they must not give information directly to the patient but instead transmit it to physicians, whose job it is to pass that information on, if they so desire. They must not sit at the doctors' table during lunch. Physicians hold nurses in low esteem and frequently treat them as if they were "nonpersons." And another part of this male "conspiracy," male hospital administrators, support physicians in this subordinating process. Male patients—and female patients who accept the male ideology—are also unwilling to accept nurses as full professionals with the autonomy and authority that goes with such a title. Thus, male professionals, acting in concert with

---

[17]Alfred Kadushin, "Prestige of Social Work: Facts and Factors," *Social Work*, 3 (1958), 37–43.

[18]Eliot Freidson, *The Profession of Medicine* (New York: Dodd, Mead, 1970).

[19]Ibid., p. 72.

[20]Fred E. Katz, "Nurses," in Amitai Etzioni, ed., *The Semiprofessions and their Organization* (New York: Free Press, 1969), pp. 54–81.

[21]Ibid., p. 69.

male elites, have conspired (sometimes consciously, most often unconsciously) to keep the female semiprofessions in subordinate positions.

The form of opposition to the semiprofessional varies from one occupation to another. In public schools, for example, male administrators (in particular, principals) treat teachers like employees and are unwilling to allow them freedom and authority. Becker found that teachers are in a much weaker position vis-a-vis principals than are established professionals in their relationship with their peers.[22] Physicians in a clinic, for example, are likely to comply with routine decisions made by the physician in charge.[23] However, when the physician in charge makes judgments about patients, these judgments are taken by the doctors as suggestions with the final decision left to the particular doctor. No such differentiation between routine and core duties is made in the case of schoolteachers: they must accept the principal's authority totally. This is exemplified by the comments of one teacher interviewed by Becker: "After all, he's the principal, he is the boss, what he says should go, you know what I mean. . . . he's the authority, and you have to follow his orders, that's all there is to it."[24] Another teacher said, "I think that teachers feel that they are being treated as underlings, and they are not sufficiently consulted . . . in many instances, teachers have not been consulted in areas of their own specialty."[25] For social workers and librarians it is the largely male administrators, and to a lesser extent male clients, who are unwilling to accord these occupations professional status. In general, we can say that the most important reason for the failure of the semiprofessions to gain professional status has been the power of the male opposition.

Male opposition is, of course, intimately related to the fact that these occupations have been, and continue to be, "female" in both number and orientation. In general, high-status, high-power positions have been denied to females in all areas of life, not just the workworld. It should come as no surprise that female occupations are denied professional status given the power and prestige that such a label carries with it. Scotch's description of the general attitude toward social work could easily be extended to all of the semiprofessions:

> Social work has always been characterized as a woman's profession. Partly this reflects the preponderance of women as practitioners. But it also represents a derogation of social work activity as being soft-minded and impractical and therefore "feminine" in quality.[26]

[22]Howard S. Becker, "The Teacher in the Authority System of the Public School," *Journal of Educational Sociology,* 27 (1953), 128–41.

[23]Mary Goss, "Influence and Authority Among Physicians in an Outpatient Clinic," *American Sociological Review,* 26 (1961), 39–50.

[24]Becker, "The Teacher in the Authority System of the Public School," 133.

[25]Ronald Corwin, *Militant Professionalism: A Study of Organizational Conflict in High Schools* (New York: Appleton-Century-Crofts, 1970), p. 109.

[26]Bernard Scotch, "Sex Status in Social Work: Grist for Women's Liberation," *Social Work,* 16 (1971), 5–11.

Because the image of femininity has been a liability, the semiprofessions have tended to welcome the entry of males into these occupations. It is hoped that this would help change the occupations' images and aid the quest for professional recognition. This is true in social work, where males number over one-third of the total workforce. As Scotch has observed, men "were welcomed not as a source of competition but as a means of overcoming the female image and of raising the profession's status."[27]

However, the entry of males has done little to alter the status of the occupation. In fact, males in social work are likely to move on much more quickly to administrative positions within the occupation, leaving the semiprofessional activities to women. This dynamic—true among all the female semiprofessions—is perhaps most notable among schoolteachers, where males move up the ladder to principal and beyond. This process has led Hearn to generalize: "The semi-professions can be seen as one relatively easy route by which men can reach managerial positions."[28]

Semiprofessionals are almost always employees of large organizations, and there are a variety of factors associated with this that impede their effort to win professional recognition.[29] Although it has long ceased being the norm, physicians and lawyers, the paradigmatic professionals, were often private entrepreneuers who were not beholden to administrative superiors. The semiprofessions, however, are all creatures of organizations and as a result face barriers to professional recognition. For example, they are often forced to compromise their own interests, and often the interests of their profession, to the demands of the organization. Moreover, the semiprofessions often are "one of the lower levels of authority and power within the organization."[30] It is this status within the organization that differentiates semiprofessionals from established professionals who, even though they are now increasingly employees of organizations, stand at or near the top of those organizations.

That employed semiprofessionals are often forced by the organization to act at variance with their professional orientation is borne out in a description by Wasserman of the plight of the social worker:

> The social worker in such a bureaucracy is caught up in this brutal intersection of contradictory values. If he [sic] actually tries to help his clients and "bucks" the organization, he often suffers from emotional and physical fatigue and becomes cynical and defeatist about the nature of social work. If he adapts to the bureaucracy, he will at best experience massive frustrations; at worst he becomes a "mindless functionary."[31]

[27]Ibid., 6.

[28]Hearn, "Notes on Patriarchy," 195.

[29]There are exceptions, such as social workers in private practice: see, Michael Cohen, "The Emergence of Private Practice in Social Work," *Social Problems,* 14 (1966), 84–93; Laura Epstein, "Is Autonomous Practice Possible?" *Social Work,* 18 (1973), 5–12.

[30]Henry Wasserman, "The Professional Social Worker in a Bureaucracy," *Social Work,* 16 (1971), 89.

[31]Ibid., 95

Another factor militating against the drive of semiprofessionals toward professional status is the nature of their clientele. Although the semiprofessions cannot be said to perform "dirty work," many serve what are considered to be low-status clients. The social worker is viewed as dealing, in general, with the poor, unacceptable minorities, and so forth. Teachers, and librarians to a lesser extent, deal with children, and children are generally considered low-status clients within the workworld. While the sick represent a wider range of status positions, the nurse is seen as handling the manual chores associated with sick patients (cleaning bedpans, dispensing pills, and the like).

For these and undoubtedly many other reasons the female semiprofessions have failed, despite great effort, to gain recognition as established professions. This failure has, in turn, had adverse consequences for the practice of the semiprofessions. For example, their salaries have been, and continue to be, appallingly low. The median salary for social workers in 1982 ranged between $13,656 and $19,392; the average annual salary for public school teachers in 1982–83 was between $14,285 in Mississippi and $26,045 in the District of Columbia;[32] average maximum salaries for public librarians in 1982 ranged between $22,776 and $23,424; and the annual salaries for general duty nurses was between a low of $10,600 in Vermont and a high of $25,100 in Wyoming.[33] For comparison purposes, recall that the average net income for physicians in 1982 was about $90,000.[34]

Not only are the semiprofessions comparatively poorly paid, but they are also relatively powerless within their employing organization and with their clients. They are regarded as dispensable and very easily replaced. Denied professional recognition, they subjected to control from all sides. "They will also be less able to insist on complete freedom from control, whether by the public, public groups of layman, or their administrative superiors."[35] It seems incontrovertible that semiprofessionals are subjected to a variety of external controls that are not experienced by established professionals.

The attitudes of semiprofessionals reflect the lack of complete professionalization. Scott discovered this in his study of social workers where he found four types of professional orientation:

1. Professionals—those with graduate training and responsiveness to professional groups.

[32]We have omitted the average pay of teachers in Alaska ($33,953) because of the unusual economic characteristics of that state. Alaska will also be excluded in the salaries for nurses.

[33]John W. Wright, *The American Almanac of Jobs and Salaries* (New York: Avon Books, 1984), pp. 186, 194, 199, 640–641.

[34]Ibid., p. 355.

[35]Nina Toren, "Semi-Professionalism and Social Work: A Theoretical Perspective," in Etzioni, ed., *Semiprofessions*, p. 154. See also, Nina Toren, *Social Work: The Case of a Semiprofession* (Beverly Hills, CA: Sage Publications, 1972)

2. Reference group only—those without graduate training, but responsive to the professional groups.
3. Training only—those with graduate training but responsive to the employing organization.
4. Bureaucrats—those who both lack professional training and are responsive to the employing organization.[36]

Scott found that 56 of the 79 individuals he studied could be classified into the nonprofessional categories of (3) training only and (4) bureaucrats. This means that a vast majority of respondents did not have autonomy and were not likely to be concerned about it. When he asked his respondents about routine supervision by superiors in the organization, half felt this to be "a good arrangement," and the other half found it to have both "advantages and disadvantages." None felt that this was "not a good arrangement." Thus social workers, in the main, are subjected to external control and accept it. One could contrast this to the established professions, in which all efforts aimed at outside control by nonprofessionals are likely to be bitterly fought.

They may want to be like the professions, but the reality of the worklife of semiprofessionals forces them to behave differently, and many have come to accept this fact. For those who accept it, the conflict is lessened, but for those who continue to try to emulate professionals the conflict continues.

Coping With Professional Marginality

We have explored a number of reasons why the semiprofessions have failed to gain professional recognition. Let us turn now to the question of how semiprofessionals can adapt to their situation and thereby cope with their distinctive conflict.

One method, of course, is to continue to strive for professional recognition. This seems to be relatively unwise, given the seemingly insurmountable barriers. A somewhat less difficult course would be to define a new goal that acknowledges the fact that the model created by the established professions of medicine and law is unrealistic in the modern world, A new label might be "bureaucratic professionalization." Such a goal recognizes that the old ideal of professional autonomy is unrealistic in a bureaucratic setting; instead, the focus is on an ideology that seeks to compromise autonomy and bureaucratic control. By redefining goals to eliminate the pursuit of the impossible model of the free professions, the semiprofessions can eliminate much of the frustration and conflict involved with trying to be like doctors and lawyers.

A much more extreme solution is a rejection of the whole idea of professionalization and the adopting of a much more activist, real-world orientation. This is a course of action espoused by Richan and Mendelsohn: "The search for professionalism, the very concept of professionalism, in social work is bankrupt. It has failed to deliver in the past and offers no promise for delivery in the future."[37] They reject not only the idea of professionalization

---

[36]Richard Scott, "Professional Employees in a Bureaucratic Structure: Social Work," in Etzioni, ed., *Semiprofessions*, pp. 82–140.

[37]Willard C. Richan and Allan R. Mendelsohn, *Social Work: The Unloved Profession* (New York: New Viewpoints, 1973), p. 62

for social work, but the whole notion that stands behind the professions: "Social work needs to understand how other professions have come to distort their high ethical callings and become ingrown and self-aggrandizing, in order to avoid following in their footsteps."[38] Richan and Mendelsohn contend that social work has tended to withdraw from the real world into professionalization: "It is professionalism that is eroding activism. It is intellectual pretentions and failure to deliver on its promises that are spelling the doom of social work."[39]

Unionization involves a rejection of professionalization, at least in part. The semiprofessions have also been moving in the direction of greater unionization as a tool to solve many of their worklife problems.[40] The most impressive gains have been made among schoolteachers, particularly in the large urban areas.

While some see unionization as leading to the demise of professionalization, it is at least possible that the two can coexist. Dorros sees teachers as both professionals and laborers:

> Teachers are coming to realize that by taking appropriate collective action in line with their status as labor they can actually protect or enhance their status as professionals. But if they forget their role as professionals in their rush to achieve the benefits of organized labor, they may destroy all vestiges of professionalism in teaching.[41]

Unionization is viewed as being more realistic for teachers than efforts to emulate the free professions:

> For many years many teachers hitched their hopes to the objective of becoming "professional like doctors and lawyers," This was an unrealistic goal primarily because most doctors and lawyers are private entrepreneurs while most teachers are public employees. Teaching has, and will continue to have, many of the characteristics of labor. Among these are employer-employee relationship, compensation in wages rather than fees, and a work role in a large organization.[42]

The success of the unionization of schoolteachers has had an effect on all the other semiprofessions. For example:

> . . . now that the colleagues in the teaching profession have entered the collective bargaining arena and thus have set the precedent, there is evidence that social workers no longer consider unionizing as unprofessional. Rather, they recognize

[38]Ibid., p. 134

[39]Ibid., p. 93

[40]On the issue of unionization of semiprofessionals see, Corwin, *Militant Professionalism;* Joseph A. Alutto and James A. Belasco, "Determinants of Attitudinal Militancy among Nurses and Teachers," *Industrial and Labor Relations Review,* 27 (1974), 216–227; Milton Tambor, "Unions and Voluntary Agencies," *Social Work,* 18 (1973), 41–47; Joseph S. Hopkins, "Unions in Libraries," *Library Journal,* 94 (1969), 3403–3407.

[41]Sidney Dorros, "Teachers as Labor; Teachers as Professionals," *The High School Journal,* 54 (1971), 414.

[42]Ibid., 413; see also, R.D. Coates, *Teachers' Unions and Interest Group Politics* (London: Cambridge University Press, 1972).

that collective bargaining may produce many gains, such as reduced case loads, greater job security, improved procedures for dealing with grievances, and increased salaries and benefits.[43]

Thus, the American Federation of State, County, and Municipal Employees (AFSCME) claims to represent over 200,000 professionals (and semiprofessionals), of which the majority are likely to be social workers.[44] Unionization clearly will play an even greater role within the semiprofessions in the coming years. Indeed, there are signs that unions are making inroads in the established professions such as college teaching and even in medicine and law. Yet unionization will not come easily to the semiprofessions. At the moment, the union movement as a whole is very weak. Many of the traditional factors that have stood in opposition to the unionization of a variety of white-collar clerical occupations must be overcome.[45] Women have generally proven to be resistant to unionizing drives, and the semiprofessions are heavily overrepresented by females. And white-collar workers have derived much of their status from their ability to differentiate themselves from blue-collar workers. Joining unions would threaten this status. For these and other reasons, barriers to the unionization of the semiprofessions will continue.

Notwithstanding the foregoing, the semiprofessionals' characteristic form of coping with their marginality remains their formal obedience to authorities in the organization; meanwhile the semiprofessionals quietly do what they think should be done in given situations. Lacking formal power, semiprofessionals have compensated by developing informal power. This is not a very good resolution of the situation, but it is time-honored and will probably continue. Rushing's study of psychiatric nurses illustrates this well.[46] He found that while nurses accept the authority of physicians, they also accept the norm that they help the patient. Some nurses in his study had completely surrendered authority over the patient to doctors because of their superior status, knowledge and competence. However, most tried to intervene in doctors' decisions, but interestingly never by confronting physicians directly with their knowledge about the patient. Rather than challenge the authority of doctors, some presented physicians with information about the patient that seemed to contradict the physicians' evaluation, but even these nurses were careful not to contradict doctors: "I will tell him things about the patient that are contrary to the order given. I just let him know about these things in hopes that he will change the order."[47] Still other nurses asked physicians questions in the hope that in answering the physicians would see their error. These attempts at influence represent the subordination of nurses to doctors, and the deference nurses feel they owe them. Nurses are supposed to be experts on the patient, yet they are unwilling to openly question the judgments of physicians even in their area of expertise. How can an occupation with

[43]Tambor, "Unions and Voluntary Agencies," 41.

[44]Personal communication, AFSCME.

[45]See Chapter 11 for a more complete discussion of this issue.

[46]William Rushing, "Social Influence and the Social-Psychological Function of Deference: A Study of Psychiatric Nursing," *Social Forces*, 41 (1962), 142–148.

[47]Ibid.

these characteristics be considered a profession? In contrast, physicians who are confronted by nurses with judgments they doubt would be quick to express their dissatisfaction.

Males In The Female Semiprofessions

The numerical predominance of women and the nature of the tasks has traditionally made the semiprofessions a comfortable haven for most women. An interesting issue here is the degree to which males can adjust to a predominantly female occupation. When they are employed in semiprofessions they face a variety of peculiar problems. They must be able to work in an occupation that is (1) defined as feminine and (2) dominated by females. Segal's study of male nurses focuses on both aspects of this problem.[48] He studied a private psychiatric hospital in Boston that had 103 nurses, 22 of whom were males. The male nurses were likely to be placed in wards that had male or senile patients. The male nurses were also likely to be in higher administrative positions within the hospital. This did not alleviate the status tensions of male nurses since they continued to feel that they did not receive the prestige and respect they deserved. Unlike female nurses, they "compared themselves to the doctors and aspired to decrease the social distance between the doctors and themselves."[49] However, they were rebuffed in their efforts to identify with doctors. On the other hand, they tried to disassociate themselves from the male aides below them in the hospital hierarchy, whom they considered to be blue-collar workers, while viewing themselves as "professional men". They wanted a clear line drawn between themselves and the aides, but this was impossible because they frequently performed work very similar to the aides' work. There was also considerable strain in the relationship between male and female nurses. The males were likely to see themselves as at least as capable as female nurses, while female nurses were rather derogatory in their comments about male nurses.[50] The female nurses were more likely to see a role for male nurses in the aspects of nursing the females found difficult or distasteful. In effect, the females wanted to relegate the males to hospital chores that were traditionally performed by the aides. The male nurses resisted this definition because they would soon have found themselves being supervised by female nurses. This continuing threat of female supervision causes a great deal of status anxiety among male nurses, for males in our society are not supposed to be supervised by females. Another aspect of the male nurses' problem is that society does not define the occupation as an acceptable mobility step for males. That this view is also accepted by the male nurses is evidenced by Segal's finding that "40 percent of the men and only 10 percent of the women located themselves in a stratum below the middle class."[51]

In the case of male nurses there is a reversal of the usual position of minority groups in occupational life. Most frequently females find themselves in

---

[48]Bernard Segal, "Male Nurses: A Case Study in Status Contradiction and Prestige Loss," *Social Forces,*" 41 (1962), 31–38.

[49]Ibid., 34.

[50]Ibid., 35.

[51]Ibid., 37.

male occupations, and hence confronted with a host of problems. The female doctor who succeeds in her position in spite of the difficulties is likely to be praised by society. However, the male nurse who succeeds is more likely to be looked down upon. America is dominated by male values, and the female who succeeds in the male world has accomplished something in terms of our values, while the male who succeeds in the female world is not conforming to major values and is therefore unlikely to receive favorable recognition for his accomplishments.[52] This is true not only of male nurses but also of successful male hairdressers, clothing designers, and so forth. In effect, male nurses "are involved in a status contradiction between characteristics ascribed to men in our society and characteristics that are supposed to inhere among members of the nursing profession."[53] In many ways the male in the female occupation is in a far more uncomfortable situation than the female in a male occupation. However, there is evidence that males can adapt to this strain by developing an identity with nursing that is consistent with their sex identity as males.[54] For example, male nurses tended to choose specialties that served to minimize sex discrepancies. They chose specialties such as administration, anesthesia, and operating room nursing that, among other things, had higher status; higher potential for autonomy, authority, and responsibility; and required a high degree of technical ability.

OTHER MARGINAL PROFESSIONS

We turn now to a disparate group of occupations that share with the semiprofessions a lack of professional status and a desire to be accorded professional recognition. This group also shares the conflict that results from the failure to achieve its desired goal. In all of the occupations to be discussed here efforts have been made to achieve professional recognition, but they have failed. This failure, as was true of the semiprofessions, is traceable both to the lack of power of the marginal professions and the greater power of the forces that oppose the professionalization of these occupations. Pharmacists and chiropractors have been opposed by physicians; funeral directors and business executives by the public; and paraprofessionals by both established professionals and semiprofessionals as well as by the public.

Pharmacists.   Pharmacists work in a variety of settings including independent retail stores, large-scale chain drug stores, hospitals, and various types of research settings. Given their professional training, pharmacists claim to be professionals. However, pharmacy is still considered a marginal profession by most people. Denzin and Mettlin argue that pharmacy has taken on a number of characteristics of professions, "but . . . failed to escape the margi-

---

[52]Susan Hesselbart, "Women Doctors Win and Male Nurses Lose," *Sociology of Work and Occupations,* 4 (1977), 49–62.

[53]Segal, "Male Nurses," 37.

[54]Donald Auster, "Occupational Values of Male and Female Nursing Students," *Sociology of Work and Occupations,* 5 (1978), 209–233.

nality associated with professions which still contain within themselves elements of an occupation."[55]

There are several factors that cause this occupation to retain its status as a marginal profession. For one thing, pharmacists engaged in their own enterprises continue to advertise, a singularly nonprofessional act. (Interestingly, however, we now see more and more lawyers and doctors advertising.) Also, the level of commitment and altruism among pharmacists seems lower than among established professionals. Perhaps most damning is the fact that pharmacists have not been able to achieve "control over the social object around which their activities are organized—e.g., the drug."[56] It is the physician, rather than the pharmacist, who controls the dispensation of drugs. Thus the pharmacist, like many other marginal professions, is plagued by control from an established profession. Finally, because of its numerous specialities, pharmacy has not been able to build a strong organization to control its members.

It has been generally assumed that the marginally professional status of the pharmacist stems from the difficulty of bridging the business and professional roles. Hence it is assumed that pharmacists who are employed in hospitals or research centers are more professional than those who own their own businesses, or who work in drug stores for a salary. McCormack catches the essence of the conflict between the business and professional roles:

> The role of the pharmacist is unstable to the degree that it is beset by the cross-pressures of the business and professional world . . . the collective or service objectives of a profession are at odds with pecuniary goals of a business. . . . The pharmacist faces decisions which involve a choice of one or the other. How these decisions are made will depend to some degree on his value-system—whether he sees himself as a professional performing a social service or acting in the capacity of a seller.[57]

In her study of pharmacy students, McCormack found them engaged in an effort to resolve this conflict through compromise. Most of the students she studied wished to own retail drug stores in medium-sized cities and carry out their business in residential, rather than business, districts. "There was a decided disinclination to run a small business in a large city or commercial district where conditions would be strongly competitive and the conflict between professional and commercial demands greatest."[58] In effect, these student pharmacists attempt to resolve the conflict between professional and business norms by blunting the conflicting normative systems and thereby reducing the discrepancy.

A study by Carol Kronus has cast some doubt on these findings.[59] Basi-

[55]Norman K.Denzin and Curtis J. Mettlin, "Incomplete Professionalization: A Case of Pharmacy," *Social Forces*, 46 (1968), 376.

[56]Ibid., 377.

[57]Thelma H. McCormack,"The Druggist Dilemma: Problems of a Marginal Occupation," *American Journal of Sociology*, 61 (1956), 308.

[58]Ibid., 311.

[59]Carol Kronus, "Occupational Values, Role Orientations and Work Settings: The Case of Pharmacy," *Sociological Quarterly*, 16 (1975), 173–183.

cally, Kronus found altruism and interest in income to be similarly important to pharmacists with both business and professional orientations. As a result, she rejects the idea that the service orientation stands in contrast to economic or prestige values. She finds pharmacists about equally motivated by economic and service values. Kronus offers two reasons for her rejection of the idea that there is necessary conflict between business and professional roles in pharmacy. First, she argues that the ideology of service is no longer the exclusive domain of the professionally oriented individual. Many businesses now profess an orientation of public service and altruism in order to sell products and justify price increases. In effect, the service ideology has become commercialized and this has served to reduce, or eliminate, the ability to use it to discriminate between those with a business orientation and those with a professional orientation.

Second, she argues that most pharmacists are no longer independent entrepreneurs but instead are salaried employees. This new status has served to blunt the pressure and drive for high profits, since employees are less interested in profits than owners. This changed status of the retail pharmacist from proprietor to employee helps to account for why there is, according to Kronus, little difference between them and professionals in terms of their orientation toward money.

Despite the results of the Kronus study, we believe it is clear that pharmacy *is* a marginal profession. In fact, Kronus' own study demonstrates this fact. She found that of the fifty-three pharmacists she categorized only eleven (21 percent) could be called "professional pharmacists." The rest were "dualists," oriented toward both professional and business roles (36 percent), "business pharmacists" (23 percent), and "indifferents" (21 percent)—oriented to neither business nor profession.

Quinney's study of prescription violation among retail pharmacists shows a similar professional-business distribution as the study by Kronus.[60] However, unlike the Kronus study, the Quinney research seems to indicate that the difference between professional pharmacists and business pharmacists is a meaningful one. Quinney studied twenty retail pharmacists who were, according to state records, prescription violators and sixty additional pharmacists who were selected at random. He found that the retail pharmacist was torn between professional and business norms, and it was this conflict, and the way it was resolved, that accounted for prescription violation. Business pharmacists were most likely to violate prescription rules, while none of the professional pharmacists violated prescription rules. Professionalism seems to be a potent force in preventing normative and legal violations by pharmacists.

Pharmacy possesses some characteristics of a profession, but others inhibit its effort to win professional recognition. Most people seem unwilling to accord a business person the professional label. More important, perhaps, is the fact that, to the public, the pharmacist appears to be in an occupation that is under the control of the omnipotent physician. It also seems clear that the

[60]Earl R. Quinney, "Occupational Structure and Criminal Behavior: Prescription Violation by Retail Pharmacists," *Social Problems*, 11 (1963), 179–185.

pharmacist has been adversely affected by the trend toward pharmacies becoming little more than "pill dispensaries" rather than the old-fashioned pharmacy where drugs were actually mixed by the pharmacists. Also adversely affecting the pharmacist's desire to be considered a professional is the trend toward pharmacies becoming mini-department stores in which virtually everything including hardware, food, toys and electrical appliances are sold. The pharmacist is increasingly simply another employee of a large, chain store–type system.

Chiropractors. Physicians have long opposed chiropractors,[61] accusing them of quackery and charlatanism; and the public has accepted much of this propaganda. When people compare physicians to chiropractors, they generally believe that the chiropractor has less knowledge, less technical competence, a narrower scope of practice. Furthermore, the chiropractor earns, on the average, far less income than the physician—the 18,000 chiropractors in the United States earn on the average between $25,000 and $35,000 per year,[62] roughly one-third of the income of physicians; and the chiropractor has far lower prestige. Physicians clearly have a vested interest in opposing chiropractors and denying their claims for equivalent status. After all, chiropractors, were they to gain widespread acceptance, would become more active competitors for patients. Thus physicians generally refuse to recognize chiropractors as doctors and have, in the past, even officially condemned them.

Chiropractors have sought to overcome the opposition of physicians, as well as of the public as a whole, through a variety of means.[63] They united to counter negative publicity. They actively participated in civil, civic, and fraternal activities in order to gain the acceptance of the community. They successfully attempted to change licensing laws in their favor by engaging in campaigns to educate the public about the benefits to be derived from their services. Chiropractors also developed a number of rationalizations to deal with the conflict caused by their marginal professional status, and, as with all rationalizations, there is some truth in their claims.

> Chiropractors have a new type of healing art which the medical monopoly wants to keep from the public in order to prevent financial loss to themselves; until chiropractors obtain sufficient public support to get the laws changed, they are justified in technically violating them; they are bringing relief and health to the suffering sick, many of whom medicine has failed to help.[64]

This statement by a chiropractor is certainly accurate in its claim about the opposition of the medical profession because of its fear of financial loss, but it seems also to be a justification for illegal activities. In fact, Wardwell found a tendency on the part of chiropractors to use deviant means such as secret

[61]Walter Wardwell, "A Marginal Professional Role: The Chiropractor," *Social Forces,* 31 (1952), 339–348.

[62]Wright, *The American Almanac of Jobs and Salaries,* p. 658.

[63]Walter Wardwell, "The Reduction of Strain in a Marginal Social Role," *American Journal of Sociology,* 61 (1955), 16–25.

[64]Ibid., 21.

remedies and fee splitting. Such behaviors served only to exacerbate the problem for chiropractors, since they provided further rationales for those who wanted to keep them in their marginal professional status. And impeded by opposition from the medical profession, chiropractors have lacked anything like the amount of power needed to win professional recognition.

In a more recent study, Rosenthal has questioned the idea that chiropractors are a marginal profession.[65] In his view, chiropractors were defined as marginal because they lacked the characteristics that physicians considered important. Thus, he feels that the definition of chiropractic as marginal was, at least in part, a political act; a result of the power of the medical profession. But that is precisely the point! Chiropractors were, and are, defined as marginal because it was in the self-interest of medicine to foster such a definition.

However, Rosenthal more successfully makes the point that various changes in chiropractic since the 1950s have served to make it less marginal, at least in the sense of its basic characteristics. Chiropractors have generally stopped making exaggerated claims for their treatments. They are now licensed in all fifty states, and in many states chiropractors control the licensing. The Council of Chiropractic Education is recognized by the U.S. Office of Education as an accrediting body for chiropractic schools. Among federal employees, chiropractic services are covered by Medicare and Workmen's Compensation, and some private insurance companies will reimburse claims for such services. There is now evidence that at least some forms of chiropractic adjustments are clinically effective.

As a result of all these changes, Rosenthal concludes that things are improving for chiropractors:

> Despite opposition from medicine, chiropractic survives and grows. New schools are opening, more patients seek chiropractic treatments, and there appears to be growing public acceptance. And there are reports of more frequent—though still clandestine—collegial relationships between chiropractors and physicians.[66]

However, Rosenthal admits that chiropratic is still confronted with much opposition from the medical profession. As a result, Rosenthal concludes, "In some ways, then, chiropractic remains on the fringes."[67]

Funeral directors.   The funeral director represents an interesting marginal profession. Funeral directors have engaged in rather elaborate efforts to become recognized as professionals, but these efforts have largely failed, Why? The problem is similar in part to the pharmacist: the funeral director "is pulled by two opposing forces, the one a vision of itself as a profession, and the other a view of itself as a business that has to meet an array of monthly expenses."[68] Here is the way one funeral director put it:

[65]Saul F. Rosenthal, "Marginal or Mainstream: Two Studies of Contemporary Chiropractic," *Sociological Focus*, 14 (1981), 271–285.

[66]Ibid., 274.

[67]Ibid., 283.

[68]Christopher Beattie "Professionalism and Marginality: The Case of the Ontario Funeral Director," in Audrey Wipper, ed., *The Sociology of Work: Papers in Honour of Oswald Hall* (Ottawa: Carleton University Presses, 1984), p. 146.

The funeral director supplies his own facilities, often at great cost. This presents an opening to say that he is in it for gain. It seems that he has to make a fast buck in order to keep up his establishment. This is the main problem for the funeral director.[69]

Further increasing the strain is the ongoing movement of funeral directors away from their own businesses and into becoming employees of mass mortuaries.

In addition to the professional and business roles, Pine argues that the funeral director is also expected to be administrator and manager.[70] "Because of these multiple tasks, the rights and duties of a funeral director are not well-defined. And occupational conflicts may arise because different segments of society expect him to perform or refrain from performing different tasks."[71]

Perhaps the greatest barrier to professionalization among funeral directors is the fact that they perform "dirty work." That is, they deal with one of the things that is most feared in our society, the dead body. In this, they suffer in comparison to the physician. The physician deals with the living body and seeks to keep it alive—obviously a very desirable task as far as society is concerned.

Society is unlikely to grant high status and high power to an occupation that deals with such a socially feared area. People generally transfer their hostility[72] and fears about death to the funeral director. As a result, funeral directors not only are denied professional status but are often viewed as being different from normal people: "[The funeral director] may be thought abnormal for having such an occupation; he may be perceived as unclean; finally, he may be a source of humor—witness such radio and TV characters as Digger O'Dell, Herman Munster, and Morticia Adams."[73] This, needless to say, is a source of frustration and conflict in the field.

Business executives.   A very different sort of occupation, business executives have also failed to win professional recognition.[74] Personnel management, for example, has achieved some of the formal characteristics of a profession.[75] It became a full-time occupation in the early 1900s. Soon afterwards, professional training schools were set up at a number of places; core academic programs were developed, academic degrees awarded, and university bureaus devoted to personnel research were established. A few years later the

---

[69]Ibid., p. 159

[70]Vanderlyn R. Pine, *Caretaker of the Dead: The American Funeral Director* (New York: Irvington Publishers, 1975).

[71]Ibid., p. 37.

[72]David R. Unruh, "Doing Funeral Directing: Managing Sources of Risk in Funeralization," *Urban Life,* 8 (1979), 256.

[73]Pine, *Caretaker of the Dead,* p. 38.

[74]Bernard Barber, "Is American Business Becoming Professionalized? Analysis of an Ideology," in E. A. Tiryakian, ed., *Sociocultural Theory, Values and Sociocultural Change: Essays in Honor of Pitirim A. Sorokin* (New York: Harper Torchbooks, 1967), pp. 121–145.

[75]George Ritzer and Harrison M. Trice, *An Occupation in Conflict: A Study of the Personnel Manager* (Ithaca, NY: New York State School of Industrial and Labor Relations, Cornell University, 1969).

first national personnel association was formed. Personnel administration developed a formal code of ethics, one of the defining characteristics of a profession. However, the field has not been able to win the support of the law—in other words, one does not need to be licensed to become a personnel administrator.

There are several reasons why personnel administrators have not achieved professional standing. For one thing, they are regarded as employees of an organization and under the command of their superiors. Though personnel administrators are apt to be viewed by superiors as experts in "people problems," most superordinates feel themselves equally capable in that area. The general public as well remains unconvinced that the personnel manager has distinctive expertise. This point, in fact, can be extended to virtually all managerial personnel: managerial work has little that distinguishes it sharply from the normal day-to-day activities of most people in our society.

In sum, the concept of professionalization, developed from the free professions of medicine and law, has little to do with the managerial employees of an organization. Indeed, it can even be argued that it has little to do with the contemporary professional who is an employee of an organization rather than operating free of organizational control.

While the concept of professional*ization* may not apply to managers in general, and personnel managers in particular, the concept of professional*ism* does. As was pointed out in Chapter 4, professionalization refers to occupations while professionalism relates to individuals. Personnel administrators as individuals *can* develop a higher degree of professionalism.[76] In a study of British personnel administrators, Watson concluded that while professionalization was problematic, professionalism was a viable option: " *'Being professional' or having 'a professional approach' is the emphasis which is often preferable to 'being a member of a profession.'* "[77]

Paraprofessionals.   Finally, we come to a wide range of occupations that we have generally classified under the heading of "paraprofessional." People who fill these positions generally serve as assistants to professionals (such as physicians and lawyers) or semiprofessionals (such as teachers and nurses). They perform a wide range of tasks, most frequently those requiring less skill, experience, and training. They are attractive to professionals because they perform many ancillary tasks at low cost. For example, paralegals might "help draft legal documents such as wills, mortgages, divorce papers, trusts . . . organize, index and summarize documents and files, prepare different types of tax forms, draft organizational documents for corporations, and assist in all aspects of pretrial work for criminal and civil cases."[78] The formal training of paralegals can vary greatly, from a brief, three-month course at a business college to a degree from a four-year college. In 1980, the starting salary for paralegals averaged just over $15,000 per year.[79]

[76]Ibid.

[77]Tony Watson, *The Personnel Managers: A Study in the Sociology of Work and Employment* (London: Routledge and Kegan Paul, 1977), p. 133.

[78]Wright, *The American Almanac of Jobs and Salaries*, p. 377.

[79]Ibid., pp. 377–378.

Thus, paraprofessionals are the most marginal of the marginal professions. They are creatures of the established professions and semiprofessions and exist to serve their needs. They have no hope of ever achieving professional recognition.

The plight of paraprofessionals is well illustrated by the history of one subtype—indigenous nonprofessionals.[80] A product in the 1960s and 1970s of the so-called New Careers Movement, the indigenous nonprofessional was created mainly by professionals to serve as a "bridge between the middle-class-oriented professional and the client from the lower socio-economic groups."[81] Indigenous nonprofessionals are recruited from the group being served and act as aides to, and as links for, the professional.[82] They were—and to some degree still are—found in a variety of areas (education, public health, community mental health.)

The New Careers Movement involved a number of essential elements. It assumed that the tasks performed by professionals could be broken down into smaller, simpler tasks that could be handled by less experienced people. Those hired were to be trained on the job, but the job was not supposed to be a dead end. Attached to that position, at least theoretically, was a career ladder leading ultimately to the possibility of becoming a professional. The people in this category were supposed to free professionals so that they could perform more general functions such as supervision, planning, and training. Because indigenous nonprofessionals came from the same groups that were served, it was hoped they could perform some traditional professional functions more effectively, and they were expected to develop new functions, since they were peers and could act in a more subjective manner toward clients. Although the New Careers Movement was committed to the development of new functions and roles for indigenous nonprofessionals, it was simultaneously committed to the idea of not adversely affecting the position and status of the professional.

As the program was designed, it appeared that indigenous nonprofessionals should have been a boon to both needy clients and harried professionals. The clients were being helped, at least in part, by peers who presumably understood their needs. Furthermore, new careerists were in a position to act as "advocates" for their new constituency, making the helping agency more responsive to their needs. Such a program would also seem welcome to professionals—they would be aided by subordinates who constituted no threat to their powerful position. Despite these promises, the New Careers Movement ran into some profound difficulties that created conflicts for indigenous nonprofessionals.

The basic problem lay in the way the New Careers Movement was

[80]This section is based on George Ritzer, "Indigenous Non-professionals in Community Mental Health: Boon or Boondoggle?" in Paul M. Roman and Harrison M. Trice, *Psychiatric Sociology* (New York: Jason Aronson, 1973), pp. 215–234.

[81]F. Reiff and F. Reissman, "Indigenous Non-professional: A Strategy of Change in Community Action and Community Mental Health Programs," *Community Mental Health Journal Monograph,* 1 (1970), 3–31.

[82]Being necessarily recruited from the group being served is what distinguished indigenous nonprofessionals from other paraprofessionals.

conceptualized. It was originally launched to patch up a failing system, not really to change that system. Basically, the movement sought to coopt into the existing service delivery system some of the actual, or potential, enemies of that system. The primary goal was to defuse an explosive situation, and any real gains in service were seen as incidental. Not all of those involved in the New Careers Movement were conscious of this objective, but it is certain that at least some of them were. Haug and Sussman agree with this position: "The 'new careers' movement, although probably not developed as cooptation, may be discussed from this perspective."[83]

Not only was the New Careers Movement ill conceived, but it was subverted from the beginning. The jobs given to indigenous nonprofessionals were often meaningless, such as tying children's shoelaces or taking attendance. Not only did new careerists lack meaningful jobs, they also did not achieve the promised careers. The new careerists were told that they could become professionals by demonstrating superior performance on the job and by undertaking job-associated training. In fact, it can be argued that that idea was a cruel joke. It implied radical changes in the way professionals were trained, and the established professions were clearly not about to allow such revolutionary transformations. From its inception, one of the major problems that plagued the New Careers Movement was an inadequate training program. Although a lack of funds also contributed to this failure, professionals helped destroy these programs. The training that occurred was oriented toward turning the indigenous nonprofessional into the middle-class model of respectability. This was in line with the general orientation of cooptation that surrounded the New Careers Movement: the selection of new careerists tended toward those who already conformed to the middle-class ideal. This eased the training process as well as the process of cooptation. Similarly, the indigenous nonprofessionals were used to cope with the demands of their peers within the community in order to defuse their opposition to the established system.

The indigenous nonprofessionals are the most marginal of professionals discussed in this section. In reality, they are low-status workers who have been granted nothing but a lofty title by the professions. Control by established professions is a problem for all marginal professions; but this area of conflict is most striking in the case of the indigenous nonprofessionals. In truth professionals made it clear from the beginning that the new careerist was to remain in subordinate positions.

> Without supervisory professionals, to train, direct, and assist mental health "support" personnel, there may be a dispersion and waste of talents and services that could be to the detriment of those seeking help.[84]

---

[83]Marie Haug and Marvin B. Sussman, "Professional Autonomy and the Revolt of the Client," *Social Problems*, 17 (1969), 158.

[84]L. J. Crowne, "Approaches to the Mental Health Manpower Problem: A Review of the Literature," *Mental Hygiene*, 53 (1969), 176–177.

CONCLUSIONS

In this chapter we have examined the plight of those in a variety of marginal professions—pharmacists, chiropractors, funeral directors, business executives, paraprofessionals and, most important, the female semiprofessions. We have detailed the barriers to professional recognition in these occupations. In all cases we found that they simply lacked the power to overcome barriers to professional recognition—in particular, opposition from established professions and other groups. Thus, for example, while nurses certainly possess a modicum of power, they are no match for the powerful physicians who oppose any significant increase in their status. Many marginal professionals (pharmacists, business executives, and to a lesser extent funeral directors) are thwarted by their need to fuse business and professional roles. "Dirty work" also constitutes a barrier for funeral directors. Paraprofessionals and the female semiprofessions are plagued by their subordinate status vis-a-vis established professionals, primarily physicians. The female semiprofessions must also overcome problems posed by the fact that most members, obviously, are women laboring in a male-dominated workworld.

TEN
CONFLICT AMONG MANAGERS, OFFICIALS, AND PROPRIETORS

In the first part of this chapter, we deal with the role conflict confronting managers and officials. *Role conflict* may be defined "as the simultaneous occurrence of two or more role expectations such that compliance with one would make the other more difficult."[1] By *managers* we mean the broad category of business executives.[2] While managers operate in profit-making organizations, *officials* perform essentially the same functions in such nonprofit-making organizations as hospitals, labor unions, and the government. The second section of this chapter deals with *proprietors* who are the owners of businesses, most often rather small businesses. In addition to their entrepreneurial role, they perform a number of managerial and even manual functions.[3] While they, too, are faced with role conflict, their most defining source of conflict is their marginality, primarily their marginal economic position.

MANAGERS AND OFFICIALS: ROLE CONFLICT

It is our basic thesis that role conflict constitutes the most basic occupational conflict for managers and officials. This holds for the company president, the personnel manager, the general manager, the foreman, the president of the

---

[1]Daniel Katz and Robert L. Kahn, *The Social Psychology of Organizations*, 2nd ed. (New York: John Wiley and Sons, 1978), p. 204.

[2]Peter F. Drucker, *The Changing World of the Executive* (New York: Truman Talley Books, 1982).

[3]Richard Hall, *Occupations and the Social Structure*, 2nd ed. (Englewood Cliffs, NJ: Prentice-Hall, 1975), p. 137.

United States, the president of a labor union, the administrator of a hospital, and the manager of a baseball team. Although managers and officials are confronted with a number of other occupational conflicts (for example, alienation, conflict with clients, professional marginality), it is role conflict that is most characteristic of people in this category. There are a number of reasons why this form of conflict is experienced. For one thing, managers and officials are inevitably found in organizations, with a variety of significant others above, below, and beside them in the organization.[4] This structural reality is a necessary, but not a sufficient, condition for the existence of role conflict. To this, we must add the fact that managers and officials wield, in varying degrees, power within the organization:

> The most important and unyielding necessity of organizational life is not better communications, human relations, or employee participation, but power. . . . Without power there can be no authority, without authority, there can be no discipline; without discipline, there can be difficulty in maintaining order, system, and productivity.[5]

Power is wielded by managers and officials and it is crucial to the functioning of organizations. But power is also often the center of conflict in organizational life as various managers and officials vie for it or seek to defend themselves from those who wield it.[6] Another factor that makes role conflict a defining reality for managers and officials is the multitudinous roles they fill. Because they occupy many roles and are confronted with a wide array of frequently conflicting role expectations, managers and officials are particularly prone to role conflict. Before we turn to an examination of the role conflicts confronting, and resolutions employed by, the manager and official, we will first examine these various roles.

Mintzberg finds on the basis of his own research, as well as his analysis of various other studies of the manager and official, that they perform ten basic roles.[7] These ten roles are divided among three broad types of role constellations—interpersonal, informational, and decisional. Let us briefly examine each of the ten in an effort to understand the roles of managers and officials and to see the potential for role conflict that exists among them.

Interpersonal roles.   These roles stem from the managers'[8] authority posi-

---

[4]Unlike professionals, semi- and unskilled, and deviant occupations, we find no "free" workers in this occupational group. Managers and officials, by definition, are employed in organizations.

[5]Robert N. McMurry, "Power and the Ambitious Executive," *Harvard Business Review,* 51 (November/December, 1973), 140.

[6]Alonzo McDonald, "Conflict at the Summit: A Deadly Game," *Harvard Business Review,* 50 (March/April, 1972), 59–68.

[7]Henry Mintzberg, "The Manager's Job: Folklore and Fact," *Harvard Business Review,* 53 (July/August, 1975), 49–61.

[8]We shall, for convenience sake, often simply use the term "manager" to describe both managers and officials.

tion within the organization and their interpersonal relations with others in the organization. They include:

1. Figurehead role. Includes primarily ceremonial interpersonal duties such as greeting a visiting dignitary, taking an important customer to lunch, or attending a community function. Although sometimes time-consuming, this role requires little more from the manager or official than time, patience, and charm.
2. Leadership role. Involves the hiring, training, motivating, and encouraging of the managers' personal staff.
3. Liaison role. Entails contacts with peers in the organization who are not within the manager's particular unit.

Informational roles.   As a result of their wide number of contacts, managers or officials are privy to a great deal of information, far more than their more specialized subordinates. Dealing with this information entails three subordinate roles:

4. Monitor role. Managers must be continually in contact with various people in the organization in order to obtain necessary information. They obtain much of this informally in contacts with subordinates, peers throughout the organization, and friends. This is primarily "soft" information that arrives in the form of gossip and hearsay. Despite its source, this information is important to managers in order to be able to function adequately.
5. Disseminator role. Managers must not only receive this information, they must also pass it on to subordinates who otherwise might not be privy to it.
6. Spokesperson role. Here managers must communicate at least some of their information, often "laundered" for public consumption, to various significant others outside the organization.

Decisional roles.   These roles entail the utilization of the information received to make decisions that affect the organization. They include:

7. Entrepreneurial role. Here managers make a set of decisions relative to the overall status of their organization and its position in the larger society. They are here initiating a set of changes that they hope will improve the general status of the organization.
8. Disturbance-handler role. In addition to initiating change, managers must also react to external events and make decisions relative to them. Thus, they must decide what to do in the event of a strike, the bankruptcy of a major customer, or a supplier failing to fulfill a contract.
9. Resource allocation role. Managers or officials must decide who gets what within the organization. Such decisions would involve such factors as money, power, and people.
10. Negotiator role. Here managers or officials must negotiate decisions with a variety of significant others. For example:

The president of the football team is called in to work out a contract with the holdout superstar; the corporation president leads his company's contingent to negotiate a new strike issue; the foreman argues a grievance problem to its conclusion with the shop steward.[9]

Although all these roles exist, at least theoretically, for all managerial and official personnel, there is considerable variation in the degree to which they focus on each. Thus, we can expect a sales manager to spend more time on the interpersonal role, the production manager on decision roles, and the personnel manager on informational roles. Whatever the specific mix, it is quite clear that the multiplicity of roles confronting the manager and official makes role conflict an ever-present reality of occupational life. Before we can get to a discussion of these conflicts, we first need some basic definitions derived from role theory.

Role theory.   The definitions used here are the ones employed in what many consider to be the major study of an occupation using role theory— Gross, Mason, and McEachern's study of the role of the school superintendent.[10] They define a *position* as "the location of an actor or class of actors in a system of social relationships."[11] A *role* is a set of expectations applied to the incumbent of a particular position. According to Gross, Mason and McEachern, "An *expectation* is an evaluative standard applied to an incumbent of a position"[12] and, "A *role behavior* is an actual performance of an incumbent of a position which can be referred to an expectation for an incumbent of that position."[13]

A *position* relevant to this chapter is plant manager. In this position an individual is expected to fill many *roles,* including ultimate decision maker in the plant, agent for community relations, and communication link with top management. These roles constitute the *expectations* of a number of people in the plant for the individual who holds the position of plant manager. When the plant manager makes decisions, is involved in community relations, or acts as a communication link, the manager is exhibiting *role behavior.* It should be clear that the same concepts can be applied not only to managers and officials, but to any and all occupations.

Role conflict.   In their book, *Organizational Stress: Studies in Role Conflict and Ambiguity,* Kahn et al. have pointed out five types of role conflict: role overload, inter-sender, person-role, inter-role, and intra-sender.[14] In this section each of these types of role conflict is discussed in terms of our hypothetical plant manager.

Role overload occurs when the focal role is confronted with a large number of expectations and finds it difficult if not impossible to satisfy all of them

[9]Mintzberg, "The Manager's Job," 59.

[10]Neal Gross, Ward Mason, and Alexander McEachern, *Explorations in Role Analysis: Studies of the School Superintendency Role* (New York: Wiley, 1958).

[11]Ibid., p. 48.

[12]Ibid., p. 58 (Italics added).

[13]Ibid., p. 64 (Italics added).

[14]Robert L. Kahn et al., *Organizational Stress: Studies in Role Conflict and Ambiguity* (New York: Wiley, 1964), pp. 18–21.

in a given period. For the plant manager it is simply a case of too many role expectations. Figure 10.1 offers a schematic representation of role overload.

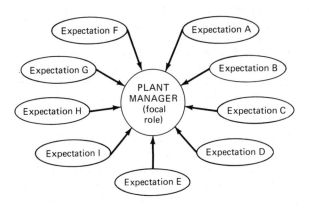

FIGURE 10.1

Inter-sender role conflict is a situation in which the focal role is confronted with conflicting expectations from two or more significant others. The situation is such that the fulfillment of one expectation makes it difficult or impossible to satisfy the other. In our example of the plant manager, such a situation would occur when the manager of the accounting department wants the plant manager to cut personnel costs, while the personnel manager wants the plant manager to approve the hiring of more minority group members, who might require additional training. This is an overly simplistic illustration, however; very frequently there are a large number of significant others, each having conflicting expectations of the focal role. Figure 10.2 gives a schematic representation of this conflict.

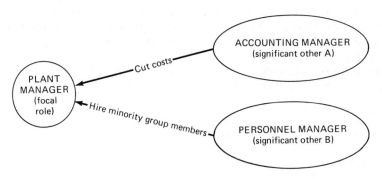

FIGURE 10.2

Person-role conflict occurs when the expectations associated with a particular role violate the focal role's moral values, needs, or aspirations. In the case of the plant manager, this may occur when the manager is expected to give preferential treatment to minority group members in terms of hiring when this conflicts with his or her principles of egalitarianism. The plant manager may feel that all applicants should be given an equal chance to a job. Person-role conflict is illustrated in Figure 10.3.

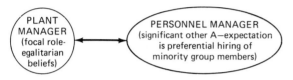

FIGURE 10.3

A fourth type of role conflict outlined by Kahn et al. is *inter-role conflict.* This occurs when the expectations attached to one role conflict with the expectations of the same individual in another role. Let us take the plant manager's roles as decision maker and in community relations. In the former, the plant manager may be expected to give preferential treatment in the hiring of minority group members, but in the role in community relations, the plant manager may be expected to reassure the community that the plant is not giving preferential treatment to minorities. Schematically this conflict is seen in Figure 10.4.

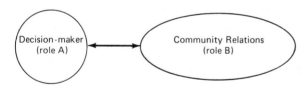

FIGURE 10.4

Intra-sender role conflict occurs when one significant other has conflicting expectations of the focal role. The expectations are such that to satisfy one expectation would make it virtually impossible to satisfy the other. As an example, one might examine a hypothetical relationship between the plant manager and a superior, the company president. The president might expect the plant manager to cut personnel costs, but also expect him or her, because of government pressure, to hire more minority group members. The hiring of minorities may be costly, because minority employees may require extra training as well as an allowance on the part of management for errors made in adjusting to work settings from which they have previously been excluded. Schematically, this example of intra-sender role conflict appears in Figure 10.5.

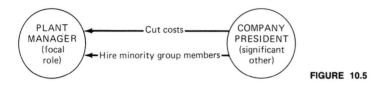

FIGURE 10.5

For illustrative purposes, a situation in which there are only two conflicting expectations has been outlined. In the real world one would be more likely to find situations in which a significant other had many expectations of the focal role, and many of these might conflict with one another.

Another concept by Kahn et al. deserves mention, although it is not directly related to role conflict. *Role ambiguity* occurs when the focal role receives an inadequate amount of role-related information. A focal role will find it difficult to satisfy the expectations of significant others when these expectations are ambiguous. Thus, plant managers are faced with role ambiguity when they are unsure what others expect of them.

Because they are in relatively high positions in an organization, managers and officials are particularly subject to conflicting expectations from significant others within the organization. Professionals are far less likely to suffer from role conflict, because by definition fellow professionals are their major significant others. Similarly, those in manual occupations such as assembly-line work are also not as likely to face role conflict. One of the basic tenets of organizational structure is that those in semi- and unskilled occupations have only one superior and are not subject to the conflicting demands of several supervisors. Although semi- and unskilled employees face little role conflict, this is not to say that they suffer none. For example, when the boss demands a certain level of productivity and peers set a norm of lower productivity, workers are faced with inter-sender role conflict. However, semiskilled or unskilled employees in an organization suffer far more from alienation than they do from role conflict. Lower level white-collar clerical and sales workers may also experience role conflict and/or ambiguity even though, as we will argue later, the people in these occupations are more likely to suffer from status panic and conflict with customers, respectively.

Evidence that role conflict exists in occupations other than managers and officials is found in Morris, Steers, and Koch's study of role conflict and ambiguity among professional, secretarial/clerical, and blue-collar employees in a major university,[15] as well as a study by Parkington and Schneider of em-

[15]James H. Morris, Richard M. Steers, and James L. Koch, "Influence of Organization Structure on Role Conflict and Ambiguity for Three Occupational Groupings," *Academy of Management Journal*, 22 (1979), 58–71.

ployees of a large commercial bank.[16] Thus, role conflict is faced by virtually everyone in organizational life, but it is our position that it is particularly acute for managers and officials. We will now discuss the five types of role conflict in more detail.

Role Overload

Business executives. Because of the nature of their position at the top of achievement-oriented organizations, business executives are subject to virtually every type of role conflict, and are particularly prone to role overload. William H. Whyte, Jr. notes that the executives he studied worked an average of 45 to 48 hours per week in the office.[17] But the executive's work does not stop there. Whyte's executives worked 4 nights a week entertaining or catching up on office work, or in conferences. During the day the executive's lunch hour is rarely passed idly—it is usually spent in conference. Add to this trips to outlying corporate locations and early morning and weekend work, and it is not unusual for the business executive to put in 70 to 80 hours per week on the job. More recent work has tended to confirm Whyte's conclusions. For example, in her study of corporate managers, Margolis found managers who worked 60 to 70 hours per week to be common:

> Most left for work around seven thirty in the morning and did not return home for eleven or twelve hours. Usually they brought back with them two or three more hours of work. This homework typically involved catching up on correspondence or on business periodicals and trade journals, but occasionally it included report writing or communications with fellow workers. One man reported regularly receiving business related telephone calls until eleven o'clock at night.[18]

A study of upper level managers—general managers who hold multifunctional responsibilities—also revealed role overload.[19] Many of those studied worked 60 (or more) hours per week "and some confided that the job could absorb 120 hours if they did not set some limits on themselves."[20] Said one general manager:

> It never ceases to amaze me how many people want to see me each day, and how many different problems they come up with. We could schedule meetings all day and all night if we didn't try to control it.[21]

Kotter recognizes that all managerial positions have similar demands, "but general management jobs seem to be unique with respect to the overall diversity of demands."[22]

[16]John J. Parkington and Benjamin Schneider, "Some Correlates of Experienced Job Stress: A Boundary Role Study," *Academy of Management Journal*, 22 (1979), 270–281.

[17]William H. Whyte, Jr., *The Organization Man* (Garden City, NY: Anchor Books, 1957).

[18]Diane Rothbard Margolis, *The Managers: Corporate Life in America* (New York: William Morrow and Co., Inc., 1979), p. 58.

[19]John P. Kotter, *The General Managers* (New York: Free Press, 1982).

[20]Ibid., p. 19.

[21]Ibid.

[22]Ibid., p. 22.

To view life at the very top of an organization, let us look at the way the president of a broadcasting company describes his day and the role overload in which he is involved—and which he seems to enjoy immensely:

> My work day starts between 4:30 and 5:00 in the morning . . . I dictate in my library until about 7:30. Then I have breakfast. The driver gets there about 8 o'clock and often times I continue dictating in the car on the way to the office . . . I talk into a dictaphone. I will probably have as many as 150 letters dictated by 7:30 in the morning. I have five full-time secretaries, who do nothing but work for (me). I have seven swing girls, who work for me part-time. This does not include my secretaries in New York, Los Angeles, Washington, and San Francisco. They get dicta-belts from me every day. . . . I get home around 6:30, 7:00 at night. After dinner with the family I spend a minimum of two and a half hours each night going over the mail and dictating. I should have a secretary at home just to handle the mail that comes there. . . . Although I don't go to the office on Saturday or Sunday, I do have mail brought out to my home for the weekend. I dictate on Saturday and Sunday. When I do this on holidays, like Christmas, New Year's, and Thanksgiving, I have to sneak a little bit, so the family doesn't know what I'm doing.[23]

This description is extraordinary and few executives, even those at the top, approximate the routine outlined in it. Yet many business executives do work extremely long hours and are faced with an enormous number of role expectations. For those who do not approximate this description, the model described above is one that they are supposed to emulate.

Those at the top of the organization are not the only employees who experience role overload. For example, Chisholm, Kasl, and Eskenazi studied quantitative role overload (too much work to do), qualitative role overload (too much difficult and challenging work to do), and inter-sender role conflict among 324 workers employed at Three Mile Island during a nuclear accident in March, 1979.[24] The authors also included 298 workers employed at a nearby nuclear plant as a control group. The employees at Three Mile Island experienced more quantitative and qualitative role overload as well as more inter-sender role conflict than their counterparts in the control group. However, when looking at the differences in experiences between supervisory and nonsupervisory personnel at both plants, only quantitative role overload proved to be statistically different. Supervisors at both plants were more likely than nonsupervisors to experience quantitative role overload and this type of role conflict was more prevalent among supervisors than either of the other two types of role conflict studied. Perceived workplace hazards, the need to be in two places, and lack of information were all found to be predictive of the supervisors' experience.

As the preceding discussion indicates, personnel not at the top of the organization may, on occasion, also experience role overload, In fact, in a study of environmental stress among 339 upper, middle, and lower level business/industrial managers, Ivancevich, Matteson, and Preston found that it

[23]Studs Terkel, *Working* (New York: Pantheon, 1974), pp. 390–391.

[24]Rupert F. Chisholm, Stanislav V. Kasl, and Brenda Eskenazi, "The Nature and Predictors of Job Related Tension in a Crisis Situation: Reactions of Nuclear Workers to the Three Mile Island Accident," *Academy of Management Journal*, 26 (1983), 385–405.

was the middle level manager who was most likely to experience such stress.[25] Several sources of environmental stress were studied including both quantitative and qualitative role overload and inter-sender role conflict—and middle level managers were more likely than managers at the other levels to experience these three stressors. Consequently, middle level managers were also more likely to report being dissatisfied with both intrinsic (challenge and responsibility) and extrinsic (pay and working conditions) characteristics of their jobs.

While structural/environmental characteristics of one's job are important sources of stress, Ivancevich et al. found that these stressors are mediated by the manager's personality. In other words, environmental stressors including quantitative and qualitative role overload will affect managers differently depending on the type of personality they bring to the job. In their study, Ivancevich et al. looked at the conditioning effects of two types of personalities on environmental stress, including one type of role overload: quantitative. Individuals in the study were divided into Type A and Type B personalities. The Type A person was competitive, achievement oriented, aggressive, and pressured by time and responsibility demands. The Type B person was reserved, less competitive, less aggressive, and so forth. The authors found that managers with Type A personalities were more adversely affected by environmental stressors in a variety of ways. For example, quantitative role overload was negatively related to both intrinsic and extrinsic job satisfaction and positively related to both systolic and diastolic blood pressure more for Type A than Type B personalities.

The extent to which managers may experience role overload has also been found to be related to the amount of discretion they can exercise on the job. In a cross-cultural and longitudinal study of U.S. and Swedish male workers—including managers—Karasek found that excessive job demands in themselves do not lead to experiences of mental strain (exhaustion after work, depression, nervousness, anxiety, etc.).[26] In both the U.S. and Swedish cases, workers with jobs characterized by excessive job demands *and* low decision latitude were more likely to experience mental strain than any other category of workers. Hence, it is not simply overburdened managers (or workers) who are likely to be adversely affected by role overload but overburdened managers who do not have the authority, discretion, power, and/or control congruent with the demands placed upon them.

Elected public officials.   Elected public officials also face role overload, as well as all the other forms of role conflict. Mitchell notes that at all levels, politicians complain of the number of demands made upon them.[27] Rather than detail the demands which can possibly be made upon the elected politician, let us note the comments of a former United States Senator on the role overload which confronted him:

[25]John M. Ivancevich, Michael T. Matteson, and Cynthia Preston, "Occupational Stress, Type A Behavior, and Physical Well Being," *Academy of Management Journal,* 25 (1982), 373–391.

[26]Robert A. Karasek, Jr., "Job Demands, Job Decision Latitude, and Mental Strain: Implications for Job Redesign," *Administrative Science Quarterly,* 24 (1979), 285–309.

[27]William C. Mitchell, "Occupational Role Strains: The American Elected Public Official," *Administrative Science Quarterly,* 3 (1958), 211–28.

... the volume of business that is done in my office ... is so great as almost to break me and my whole staff down. In mail alone we receive from 200 to 300 letters every 24 hours. And this in addition to telegrams and long-distance calls and personal visits. ... I can say to you truthfully that even if I had four times the amount of time I have I could not possibly perform adequately and fully the duties imposed upon me. ... In the departments of government there are always delays or injustices or matters overlooked in which a Senator can be of very great assistance to his constituents. The flood of duties in my office has reached such proportions, and is so steadily increasing, that I am almost totally unable to enter into the study of any legislative matters. That means that frequently I have to inform myself concerning matters of importance by listening to arguments on the floor of the Senate. And yet even my presence on the floor is only intermittent, so great is the burden of my office duties. ...[28]

One of the defining characteristics, then, of managers and officials is role overload. Business executives and politicians have been discussed in these terms. Virtually all managers and officials are particularly subject to role overload.

Inter-Sender Role Conflict

Business executives.   Business executives are supposed to make decisions and because of this role they are subjected to a great deal of conflicting pressure. Top-level decisions affect many subgroups within the organization and each subgroup strives to affect the executives' decisions. Kahn et al. have composed the following list of groups of significant others that may make conflicting demands on any manager in an organization:

1. Management or company in general
2. Person's direct supervisor(s)
3. Co-workers within organization
4. Person's subordinates
5. Union or its representatives
6. Extraorganizational associates (such as clients, customers, suppliers)
7. Others (such as family, friends).[29]

When the expectations of one of these groups conflict with the expectations of another, inter-sender role conflict exists. Although everyone in an organization is faced with such role conflict, some types are more typical of the business executive. For example, one of the current vogues in business is the delegation of some of the executive's authority to subordinates. Delegation performs two functions: it gives subordinates who may someday occupy the executive's position experience in making decisions, and it frees some of the executive's time for other types of work. Many subordinates have come to expect executives to delegate some of their authority to them. Conflicting with this expectation is the accepted organizational reality that the executives' superiors will hold them responsible for decisions made by them or their subor-

[28]Ibid., 222–223.

[29]Kahn et al., *Organizational Stress*, p. 56.

dinates. Thus executives are expected by their superiors to be responsible for decisions coming from their office and are faced with a dilemma: should they delegate decision making and risk their status in the organization if the decision made by their subordinate is a poor one? Or should they deny their subordinates authority and therefore fail to fulfill their subordinates' expectations?

Although inter-sender conflict occurs at all levels of organizational life, it is particularly acute at the top because that is where the major decisions are made. This is not to say that other, lower-level managers are not confronted by inter-sender role conflict. Middle managers are often caught in a crossfire between their superiors and their subordinates. Subordinates tend to feel that middle managers have little influence with top management and are indecisive because they are, at least to some degree, not in a powerful enough position to make more decisions. Thus, middle managers feel pressure from subordinates to exert more influence and to make more decisions. On the other hand, top managers see middle-level managers as unrealistic in their expectations and often as meddlers in their prized right to make decisions. Top management is not anxious to delegate decisions, at least important decisions, to "unrealistic" middle managers.[30]

Lower level, first-line supervisors are also subject to inter-sender role conflict. W. Earl Sasser, Jr. and Frank S. Leonard describe first-level supervisors as caught in a crossfire of demands, constantly trying to balance the shifting and, more often than not, conflicting demands, values, and priorities placed upon them by both management and the workforce.[31] Sasser and Leonard describe the first-level supervisor's position:

> The first-level supervisor is a "person caught between"—primarily between middle management and the work force. Both groups have very different values and priorities. Middle managers tend to be interested in cost, efficiency, and performance; workers tend to be more interested in wage rates, security, and comfort. Managers usually believe that hard work leads to advancement; workers often see little point in exerting themselves. To management, the labor contract and work rules seem restrictive; to labor, they seem protective from unreasonable management demands. Managers are concerned about the status of their positions; workers want recognition for work well done. Managers usually identify strongly with the company; workers often have little company loyalty.[32]

Officials. David A. Whetten has studied the inter-sender role conflict faced by the directors of sixty-seven manpower agencies in New York State.[33] In general, the agencies served to link the needs of the underprivileged members of the community (poor, unemployed, and the like) with the public and

---

[30]Emmanuel Kay, "Middle Management," in James O'Toole, ed., *Work and the Quality of Life: Resource Papers for Work in America* (Cambridge, MA: The M.I.T. Press, 1974), pp. 106–29. For a discussion of inter-sender conflicts facing the general manager see, Hugo E. R. Uyterhoeven, "General Managers in the Middle," *Harvard Business Review*, 50 (March/April, 1972), 75–85.

[31]W. Earl Sasser, Jr. and Frank S. Leonard, "Let First-level Supervisors Do Their Job," *Harvard Business Review*, 58 (March/April, 1980), 113–121.

[32]Ibid., 116.

[33]David A. Whetten, "Coping with Incompatible Expectations: An Integrated View of Role Conflict," *Administrative Science Quarterly*, 23 (1978), 254–271.

private organizations in the community that could provide the needed services, employment opportunities, and training. Whetten found that the directors of these agencies faced conflicting expectations from (1) the staff of the organizations; (2) local community leaders; and (3) the state and regional administrators, all of whom, in one way or another, controlled resources (political and/or economic) necessary for the effective operation of the agency. Community leaders based their judgment of the agency's effectiveness on various characteristics that served to enhance the agency's visibility in the community (such as the total number of community organizations with which the agency was involved). The staff of the agency rated effectiveness on the quality of services provided. Finally, the state and regional administrators based their evaluations on the quantity of placements made by the agency. Of these conflicting expectations, the gap between the staff and the regional administrators was found to create the most problems for the directors. Not only were the directors of these agencies likely to experience conflicting expectations related to organizational effectiveness, but the conflict-riddled position that these officials found themselves in led to feelings of insecurity, perceived powerlessness, and uncertainty.

School superintendents.   Gross, Mason, and McEachern's study of school superintendents focused on four situations in which the school superintendent faced inter-sender role conflict.[34] The first situation involved a hiring situation; 71 percent of the respondents felt that this situation exposed them to role conflict. They felt that a local politician, school board member, or personal friend might ask them to recommend a friend or relative. On the other hand, community groups such as the PTA or the teachers might feel they should not give special consideration to any interest group, but should base their decision solely on merit. A second area of conflict involved the allocation of the school superintendents' time. Fifty-three percent of the respondents felt that they were confronted with role conflict over how they spent their time. Professional associations expected them to attend meetings and participate on committees. Local groups such as the Chamber of Commerce and the Rotary Club expected the superintendents to be active in their programs. Further, the school board and staff members expected them to devote the bulk of their time to the needs of the board and staff.

The third conflict situation for superintendents concerned salary recommendations. The PTA and local teachers' associations undoubtedly expected superintendents to fight for the maximum possible salary increases. Other groups, however, wanted them to hold the line on salary increases. These groups included property owners, those who lived on fixed incomes, and local taxpayers' associations. Also, political figures were likely to resist salary increases because the resulting higher taxes would reduce their chances of reelection. Eighty-eight percent of the school superintendents perceived role conflict over this situation.

The fourth and final conflict situation involved the school budget, which

---

[34]Gross et al., *Explorations in Role Analysis*, pp. 258–280; see also, Donald J. McCarty and Charles E. Ramsey, *The School Managers: Power and Conflict in American Public Education* (Westport, CT: Greenwood Publishing Corp., 1971).

91 percent of the responding superintendents viewed as a situation involving role conflict. Such groups as taxpayers' associations, local politicians, and the city council were likely to expect superintendents to give priority to the community's financial resources when making budgetary decisions. On the other hand, groups such as the teachers and the PTA were perceived as expecting superintendents to give priority to educational needs.

However, even in those situations which appear to be laden with discord, there are those who do not perceive any conflict. Further, it is true that in every occupation there are always long periods of quiescence interrupted by periods of crisis and distress. Although we have chosen to emphasize the conflict aspect of occupational life here and in the rest of the book, it is not denied that much of occupational life is relatively routine. However, in our view, in looking at conflict in occupational life one can learn much about the nature of the workworld.

Person-Role Conflict

Navy disbursing officers. A third type of role conflict is person-role conflict, illustrated by Turner's study of Navy disbursing officers.[35] The disbursing officer's chief function is to serve as a paymaster at his location; he is also in charge of other types of expenditures. There are certain rules of action which disbursing officers have internalized as norms of behavior. Conflict for them generally occurs when their superiors expect behavior which contradicts their normative orientation. This is *person-role conflict* because the stress centers on the contradiction between what the disbursing officers feel they should do and the expectations of superiors. The major source of conflict for disbursing officers is commanding or executive officers. Turner points out that they "have little knowledge of and patience with disbursing regulations, and . . . are generally not accustomed to being asked by a subordinate to discuss the advisability of an order they have issued."[36] The conflict facing disbursing officers is complicated by the fact that their immediate supervisors are likely to support the demands of the commanding or executive officer; if disbursing officers do not accede to these demands, they are threatened with notations on their permanent fitness report. Thus powerful forces within the Navy expect them to go against the regulations and their own view of how the job should be handled.

School superintendents. In the Gross et al. study of school superintendents, there are elements of person-role conflict on the issue of teachers' salaries. The superintendents studied by Gross et al. favored higher salaries for teachers:

> . . . most of them are acutely aware of and concerned about the relative lag in teacher salary increases as compared to those of other occupational groups. . . .

[35]Ralph H. Turner, "The Navy Diburshing Officer as a Bureaucrat," *American Sociological Review,*" 22 (1974), 342–348.

[36]Ibid., 343–344.

Most superintendents are former teachers and know from firsthand experience the difficulties of maintaining a "middle class" standard of living on a "lower class" wage level.[37]

Despite their own predisposition to increase teacher salaries, there are powerful forces within the community which oppose such increases. Thus, on this issue the school superintendent is exposed to person-role conflict as well as inter-sender role conflict.

Business executives.   White-collar crime constitutes a major source of person-role conflict for some business executives. They are frequently placed in a position in which an action that may be profitable for the company conflicts with their own morality. As Sutherland shows in his classic work on white-collar crime, these behaviors may include:

> . . . misrepresentation in financial statements of corporations, manipulation in the stock exchange, commercial bribery of public officials directly or indirectly in order to secure favorable contracts and legislation, misrepresentation in advertising and salesmanship, embezzlement and misapplication of funds, short weights and measures and misgrading of commodities, tax frauds, misapplication of funds in receiverships and bankruptcies.[38]

It is not out of the question that an organization would expect its executives to perform actions that would improve the company's financial position even though the actions might be unethical or illegal. With these demands posed, executives must face a conflict between their own morality and the demands of business life.

Inter-Role Conflict

Heads of professional organizations.   In inter-role conflict, the expectations attached to one role conflict with those of another role. Etzioni points out that the institutional head of a professional organization is subject to this type of conflict[39] Professional organizations are organizations whose major goal is to institutionalize knowledge and sustain its creation. Under this heading, Etzioni includes research centers, schools, universities, and hospitals. When individuals are the heads of such organizations they have two basic roles: expert and administrator. They must fill the role of expert so that the major goals of the organization will be kept in the forefront and so they can be responsive to the needs of the professionals in their organization. On the other hand, they must also be administrators because "organizations have to obtain funds to finance their activities, recruit personnel to staff the various functions, and allocate the funds and personnel which have been recruited."[40]

---

[37]Gross et al., *Explorations in Role Analysis,* p. 168

[38]Edwin H. Sutherland, "White Collar Criminality," in Gilbert Geis, ed., *White Collar Criminal* (New York: Atherton Press, 1968), p. 42.

[39]Amitai Etzioni, *Modern Organizations* (Englewood Cliffs, NJ: Prentice-Hall, 1964), p. 82.
[40]Ibid.

If they underemphasize their administrative role, institutional heads "may endanger the integration of the professional organization by overemphasizing the major goal activity, neglecting secondary functions, and lacking skill in human relations."[41] If institutional heads overemphasize their administrative roles, they will alienate the professionals and tend to lose sight of the major goals of the organization.

Publishing managers. The managers of companies engaged in publishing books, particularly high quality books, are confronted with two frequently conflicting roles. In one role they are expected to identify with the literary world and emphasize the goal of publishing material that is of great cultural value. This role is primarily oriented toward satisfying the expectations of prestigious authors. In the other major role, publishing managers are expected to make a reasonable profit for the company. The problem is that the role of profit-earner is often in direct conflict with the role of publisher of culturally valuable books.[42]

Prison supervisors. The supervisors of prisons are particularly subject to inter-role conflict. They are at the top of the hierarchy and have two major roles to fulfill; one is that of chief custodian, with the expectation they they focus on "maintaining discipline and control over inmates."[43] Their other major role requires them to focus on treatment and rehabilitation of prisoners. Historically, the custodial role came first, with the treatment role coming to the fore more recently. Built into these two roles is an inherent conflict. As Grusky, in his study of prison officials, comments:

> If he stressed discipline by establishing new restrictive rules and hence curtailing the inmate's freedom, he would be seen as decreasing the probability of achieving the . . . treatment goal, since such a policy would serve to increase inmate resentment toward the officials. On the other hand, if he was overly permissive in his policies, discipline and control would break down and he would not be able to sustain the custodial goal.[44]

The supervisors' problems were exacerbated by divisions among their subordinates in their emphasis on the two goals. Some were oriented toward the custodial functions and others were more concerned with treatment. In spite of this conflict, supervisors were faced with the problem of maintaining a cohesive staff.

Elected public officials. Elected public officials are confronted with inter-role conflict. Two of the conflicting roles the politician is expected to fill are

---

[41] Ibid.

[42] Michael Lane, "Publishing Managers, Publishing House Organization and Role Conflict," *Sociology*, 4 (1970), 367–383.

[43] Oscar Grusky, "Role Conflict in Organizations: A Study of Prison Camp Officials," *Administrative Science Quarterly*, 3 (1959), 456.

[44] Ibid.

administrator and partisan.[45] Mitchell contends that the conflicts between these two roles "are contrary at every relevant choice point."[46] For example, as administrators, politicians are expected to be affectively neutral, but as partisans they are supposed to be affectively involved with their constituents. The plight of politicians is complicated by the fact that they have two other roles attached to their positions: executive and judicial. Mitchell contends that the offices with the greatest number of roles are likely to have the greatest inter-role conflict. Executive political positions such as mayor, governor, and president have more roles and, therefore, more inter-role conflict than legislative or judicial positions. Another important variable is the heterogeneity of the constituency. If the constituency is highly heterogeneous, the politician is likely to have more roles to fill and therefore a greater likelihood of inter-role conflict.[47]

Inter-Position Conflict

Before discussing the final type of role conflict developed by Kahn et al., it is necessary to point out a conceptual omission in their typology of role conflict. Kahn and his colleagues define inter-role conflict as a situation in which the "role pressures associated with membership in one organization are in conflict with pressures stemming from membership in other groups."[48] However, what they are describing is a conflict between positions, not a conflict between roles. There is, therefore, another type of conflict to add to the five developed by Kahn and his colleagues—*inter-position conflict*. A typical inter-position conflict for those in high-status occupations is between their occupational and family positions. In fulfilling the demands of their occupation, many individuals find that they cannot adequately handle their family responsibilities. In their study of union business agents, for example, Rosen and Rosen found that the demands of the job resulted in "considerable psychological, as well as physical, isolation from family and friends."[49]

Gross, Mason, and McEachern also discuss this inter-position conflict for the school superintendent:

> Over 90 percent of the superintendents in discussing the impact of their jobs on their families reported that their wives were concerned about the infinitesimal amount of time they were able to spend with their families. Many superintendents also said that their children expect them to be at home "like other fathers."[50]

[45] Mitchell, "Occupational Role Strains," 214.

[46] Ibid., 215.

[47] As with most other types of role conflict, managers and officials are not the only ones who experience inter-role conflict. For example, Olson studied inter-role conflict among twenty-seven mothers with preschool children. See, Joan Toms Olson, "Role Conflict Between Housework and Child Care," *Sociology of Work and Occupations*, 6 (1979), 430–456.

[48] Kahn et al., *Organizational Stress*, p. 20

[49] Hjalmar Rosen and R. A. Hudson Rosen, "Personality Variables and Role in a Union Business Agent Group," *Journal of Applied Psychology*, 41 (1975), 132.

[50] Gross et al., *Explorations in Role Analysis*, p. 263.

Intra-Sender Conflict

The final form of role conflict is intra-sender, or conflicting expectations from one significant other. Let us use the example of personnel executives to illustrate this type of conflict. Within any unionized organization there are personnel officers (often called labor relations managers) who are in charge of relations with the union. Although they are managers, they are subordinate to personnel managers, who have broad responsibility for all the personnel functions. Personnel managers frequently have contradictory expectations of labor relations managers. They expect labor relations people to maintain harmonious relations with the union. They also expect them *not* to "sell out" to the union; they expect labor relations staff to be tough on the handling of grievances and in contract negotiations. These dual expectations are laden with conflict for labor relations managers. If they are too soft with the union, the union will win too many grievances and get too good a contract. On the other hand, if they are too hard on the union, it will upset union-management harmony and possibly lead to lengthy and costly strikes or slowdowns. Thus labor relations managers must attempt to balance these conflicting expectations.

Another example of intra-sender role conflict experienced by personnel managers emerges from conflicting signals currently being sent out by the judicial system with reference to wrongful discharge.[51] The right to discharge an employee has long been, and continues to be, the prerogative of management. Historically and currently the judicial system still upholds the manager's right to fire employees for economic reasons, that is, personnel cutbacks or incompetence. However, as Ewing points out, we are currently witnessing an increase in the number of discharges for noneconomic reasons: for example, for refusing to participate in illegal price fixing; for refusing an employer's order not to serve on jury duty; for refusing to take a polygraph test; and for challenging a company's violation of a legal statute. The decisions that are emerging from the judicial system at this time are conflicting and confusing. As Ewing notes:

> One day the law seems to tell managers, "Go ahead and fire a trouble maker if you want to." The next day it seems to say, "Watch it, you'll get yourself and your company in trouble."[52]

Elsewhere, Ewing refers to this period as "a pretzel palace of contradictory decisions, inconsistent opinions, and hazy precedents."[53] Until firm precedents are established and consistent decisions emerge from the judicial system, personnel managers will continue to experience intra-sender conflict from the judicial system.

[51]David W. Ewing, "Your Right to Fire," *Harvard Business Review*, 61 (March/April, 1983), 32–42.

[52]Ibid., 32

[53]Ibid., 41.

Role Ambiguity

Finally, although it is not actually role conflict, some mention must be made of role ambiguity. Mitchell discusses role ambiguity in his analysis of the elected politician: "Instead of being pulled in opposite directions by well known forces, the elected official is often in the position of a lost hunter seeking direction."[54] This ambiguity applies to both the politicians' administrative and partisan roles. In their administrative role the ambiguity stems from inadequate knowledge of means they may utilize in the attainment of goals. The ambiguity surrounding the partisan role concerns a difficulty in discovering what are the goals of the community. These types of ambiguity would also seem to occur in all managerial and official positions. Of course, other sources of role ambiguity exist for the manager as well.

Nicholson and Goh have shown how role ambiguity is related to various structural variables depending on the organizational setting within which a manager is employed.[55] For twenty-one supervisors employed in the production department of a manufacturing organization, role ambiguity was found to be negatively related to formalization (the importance of rules and procedures) and participation in decision making (the amount of influence the manager has on decisions made in the organization). On the other hand, for twenty-one supervisors employed in the data processing research and development department of a large utility company, role ambiguity was found to be positively related to span of subordination (the extent of exposure to multiple authority figures). Hence, role ambiguity is not only related to various structural factors, but it is also found to vary according to work environment.

Much of the role ambiguity confronting the business executive stems from inadequate communication from below. Many studies have shown that for a variety of reasons subordinates restrict information flow up through the organization's hierarchy. In his classic study of government agencies, Blau found that subordinates were unwilling to ask superiors questions, for in asking questions subordinates were confessing their ignorance to the people who evaluated them.[56] To circumvent this, subordinates with problems would consult with more knowledgeable peers in other departments. The questioning subordinates thus became indebted to their more knowledgeable peers, but deemed this indebtedness preferable to letting superiors know about their ignorance. This example is not unusual and presents a problem for managers and officials in virtually every organization.

Attempts have been made to ease this problem by emphasizing two-way communications in organizations. However, this overlooks the fact that the interests of subordinates are frequently not compatible with the interests of superiors. Because of this incompatibility, subordinates will almost always attempt to restrict communication to superiors, and therefore superiors must

[54]Mitchell, "Occupational Role Strains," 218.

[55]Peter J. Nicholson, Jr. and Swee C. Goh, "The Relationship of Organizational Structure and Interpersonal Attitudes to Role Conflict and Ambiguity in Different Work Environments," *Academy of Management Journal,* 26 (1983), 148–155.

[56]Peter M. Blau, *The Dynamics of Bureaucracy,* 2nd ed. (Chicago: University of Chicago Press, 1963).

always make some decisions in the face of ambiguity. This is complicated by the fact that other groups in the organization also find it to their benefit to restrict information flow. In Simon's view, this is one of the reasons managers can never optimize, but must almost always be restricted to satisfactory types of decisions.[57]

However, when two-way communication is established, there is evidence that, for subordinate managers at least, role conflict and role ambiguity is less severe. This is the finding by Quick who studied forty-six junior officers, managers, and staff personnel as well as fifteen executive officers of a nationally based insurance company who were all involved in a goal-setting training program.[58] Quick found that there were statistically significant declines in both role conflict (inter-sender) and role ambiguity experienced by the junior officers and staff five months following the goal-setting training program. Eight months after the training session both role conflict and ambiguity, while slightly more intense than after 5 months, were still significantly less than prior to the goal setting session. Hence, Quick concludes that periodic goal-setting sessions among managers at various levels in the organization help to reduce role conflict and ambiguity by clarifying the subordinate manager's role in the organization and by facilitating the communication of compatible and consistent role expectations.

Let us turn now from a discussion of the types of role conflict to the methods employed to resolve these conflicts.

Role Conflict Resolution

The theory of role conflict resolution developed by Gross, Mason, and McEachern offers a major conceptual base for the study of occupations. The Gross group hypothesized that there were four basic devices for resolving role conflict:

1. Conformity to expectation A.
2. Conformity to expectation B.
3. Performance of some compromise behavior which represents an attempt to conform in part to both expectations.
4. Attempt to avoid conforming to either of the expectations.[59]

Based on these hypotheses, the authors went on to develop a theory of role conflict resolution. Their goal was to be able to predict which of the means an individual would adopt. With information on three factors, they believed that they would be able to predict modes of role conflict resolution. The first factor is *legitimacy*, or the right others have to expect the focal role to behave in conformity with their expectations. Using only the legitimacy dimension, the following predictions are made: (1) where expectations A and B are

---

[57]Herbert Simon, *Administrative Behavior*, 2nd ed. (New York: Free Press, 1957).

[58]James C. Quick, "Dyadic Goal Setting and Role Stress: A Field Study," *Academy of Management Journal*, 22 (1979), 241–252.

[59]Gross et al., *Explorations in Role Analysis*, p. 284.

both perceived as legitimate, they predict some sort of compromise behavior; (2) when expectation A is perceived as legitimate and expectation B is perceived as illegitimate, they predict conformity to A; (3) when expectation A is perceived as illegitimate and expectation B as legitimate, they predict conformity to expectation B; (4) where both expectations A and B are perceived as illegitimate, they predict some sort of avoidance behavior.

However, there is more than one factor involved, and this complicates the power to make predictions. The second factor is the ability of the significant others to *sanction* the focal role for nonconformity to their expectations. Considering sanctioning ability alone, the authors predict: (1) compromise behavior where both A and B have strong negative sanctions; (2) conformity to A when A has strong negative sanctions and B does not; (3) conformity to B when A has weak negative sanctions and B has strong negative sanctions; (4) no prediction where both significant others have weak negative sanctions.[60]

When the Gross group tried to look at both factors together, they found that they were unable to make predictions in a number of situations, specifically when "the legitimacy and sanctions elements predisposed him (the focal role) to undertake different behaviors."[61] What was needed was some knowledge of what predisposes an individual to give primacy to one factor over the other. They posited three distinct *individual orientations* to role conflict situations. The first is a *moral orientation,* where the individual tends to emphasize legitimacy and minimize sanctioning ability. The second is the *expedient orientation,* in which the actor gives primacy to sanctioning ability over legitimacy. The third is the *moral-expedient,* where the individual sees a net balance between sanctioning ability and legitimacy. To ascertain which of the three types each respondent fit into, the authors constructed a series of questions which they felt differentiated among them.

On the basis of the ratings of the significant others on legitimacy and sanctioning ability, and knowledge of the individual's orientation, Gross et al. were able to predict 91 percent of the role conflict resolutions correctly.[62]

A study of personnel managers conducted by Ritzer and Trice was designed to expand on the theory of role conflict resolution developed by Gross, Mason, and McEachern.[63] The major finding of this study was that independent action is a fifth alternative available in the resolution of role conflict. *Independent action* was operationally defined as listening to both significant others in an inter-sender role conflict, but then making one's own decision. Surpris-

---

[60]Ibid., p. 287.

[61]Ibid., p. 289.

[62]The impressive results led to a series of follow-up studies including Delbert Miller and Fremont Shull, "The Prediction of Administrative Role Conflict Resolution," *Administrative Science Quarterly,* 7 (1962), 143–160; H. Ehrlich, J. Rinehart, and J. Howell, "The Study of Role Conflict: Explorations in Methodology," *Sociometry,* 25 (1962), 85–97; Alvin Magid, "Dimensions of Administrative Role and Conflict Resolution Among Local Officials in Northern Nigeria," *Administrative Science Quarterly,* 12 (1967), 321–338.

[63]George Ritzer and Harrison M. Trice, *An Occupation in Conflict: A Study of the Personnel Manager* (Ithaca, NY: New York State School of Industrial and Labor Relations, Cornell University,1969), pp. 46–57. For a replication of some aspects of this study in another society see Sergio Ferrari, "The Italian Personnel Manager," *Management International Review,* 15 (1975), 67–74.

ingly, independent action proved to be not only a viable alternative, but the most frequently chosen of the five modes of resolving role conflict. As a matter of fact, in eleven of the twelve situations employed in the study, independent action was chosen significantly more often than the next most frequently chosen alternative.[64]

This brief review of the literature on the theory of role conflict resolution leaves us with two important tools for analyzing the resolution of role conflict by managers and officials. First, the theory has given us five types of actions one may employ in resolving role conflict. Second, the literature has indicated a number of variables which can help us explain why an individual in an occupation chooses a particular resolution. Many of the variables discussed in the preceding pages really relate to the power of significant others. Using some general measure of the power of significant others we can hypothesize the following about role conflict resolution:

1. If significant other A has more power than significant other B, the focal role will resolve the conflict by conforming to expectation A.
2. If significant other B has more power than significant other A, the focal role will resolve the conflict by conforming to expectation B.
3. If both significant others have a great deal of power, the focal role will seek to compromise or withdraw.
4. If both significant others have little power, the focal role will take independent action.

These hypotheses have received some empirical support in the Ritzer and Trice study of personnel managers. The theory of role conflict resolution gives us the types of actions an individual may take in resolving role conflict and provides an explanation of why a particular action is taken. One of the problems, for our purposes, with this explanation is that it focuses on the social-psychological level. It helps explain why an individual chooses a particular resolution, but fails to explain why a mode of resolution is chosen by the occupation as a whole. For example, later in this chapter there is a discussion of the way in which the Navy disbursing officer resolves the conflict between regulations and orders from the top. Most, if not all, such officers resolve the conflict between regulations and orders from the top in the direction of orders from above. This is due, in part, to the power of superiors, but it has also become a norm within the occupation. Thus at the occupational level the resolution of role conflict is determined by a combination of the power of the significant others and norms within the occupation. In sum, the preceding discussion enables us to understand better the means employed in managerial and official occupations for resolving role conflict.

School superintendents   The school superintendents studied by Gross et al. employed each of these resolutions, although differentially across the four cases employed in the study. The hiring situation was seen as a conflict be-

---

[64]For a discussion of far more specific behaviors used to cope with role conflict see, Douglas T. Hall, "A Model of Coping with Role Conflict: The Role Behavior of College-Educated Women," *Administrative Science Quarterly,* 17 (1972), 471–486.

tween basing hiring decisions on merit or giving preferential treatment to some individuals. Eighty-five percent of the superintendents resolved this conflict in the direction of a decision based on merit rather than on the basis of personal preference, while 10 percent resolved it in the other direction, allowing the preferences of some significant others to determine their decision. The remaining 5 percent chose to attempt to compromise between merit and the preferential expectations of significant others. The time-allocation situation was seen as an example of inter-role conflict. In terms of how they spent their time, the superintendents were torn between their work role and their family role. Sixty-six percent of those superintendents who perceived a conflict on this issue resolved it in favor of their work role. One who did so explained his decision in this way:

> The school board and the PTA would get sore if I didn't, and I'd worry too. I don't think I'd be able to do a good job as superintendent of schools if I didn't.[65]

Only 8 percent of the superintendents resolved this conflict by giving greater priority to the demands of their family; the remaining 26 percent compromised. According to Gross et al.: "One superintendent used the device of showing up just frequently enough at important meetings in the community to avoid the charge of not being interested in school and community affairs."[66]

The question of teacher salary increases was the third situation discussed by Gross, Mason, and McEachern. Of those who perceived role conflict in this situation, 64 percent conformed to the expectation of giving the highest possible salary increase, while 9 percent conformed to the expectation that they give the lowest possible salary increase. This situation was seen, therefore, as involving inter-sender role conflict. Of the remaining superintendents, 21 percent sought to compromise by satisfying both demands to some degree, while 6 percent withdrew from the situations. One of those who withdrew placed the problem in the hands of the school committee, stating that

> ... it's a hot potato so I let the school committee handle it. The teachers feel I should represent them; I'd hang myself by getting involved. But I go along with the school committee recommendation 100 percent, whatever they decide.[67]

Of the compromisers, some acted as intermediaries while others acted as salespeople. As has been pointed out before, Gross et al., ignore the possibility of independent action. However, thirteen of those who were classified as compromisers were in reality independent actors. Three of these compromisers were described as follows: "When exposed to the salary dilemma (they) rejected both sets of expectations and substituted a new criterion in making their recommendations. . . . One of the superintendents recommended that the salary increases be contingent on a cost of living index."[68] The other ten

[65]Gross et al, *Explorations of Role Analysis*, p. 266.
[66]Ibid., p. 267.
[67]Ibid., p. 271.
[68]Ibid.

superintendents, whom we would classify as independent actors, "resolve(d) the salary dilemma by trying to modify the expectations of those with whom they had initially agreed."[69] The actions of these thirteen superintendents are qualitatively different from the actions of those who compromised. They were being innovative in their approach, rather than merely seeking a middle-ground position.

The fourth situation that confronted the superintendents involved the budget. This, too, was a case of inter-sender role conflict, with 69 percent of the superintendents conforming to the expectations of those who emphasized educational needs and 3 percent going along with those who stressed the financial resources of the community. In addition, 27 percent sought to compromise, while only 1 percent withdrew in the face of this conflict.

Personnel managers. The Ritzer and Trice study of personnel managers was designed as a test of the theory of role conflict resolution developed by Gross and his associates.[70] Two cases were designed to expose the respondents to inter-sender role conflict. The first case involved a storm that forced a number of employees to miss work and lose pay. Respondents were then given six situations in which they were asked to make a decision in the face of incompatible expectations from significant others in their organization. The six situations based on the first case were:

1. The man immediately above you in the personnel department is in favor of paying employees for the time lost, but the top company official at your location is opposed.

2. The manager of the accounting department is in favor of paying employees for the time lost, but the man immediately above you in the personnel department is opposed.

3. The top company official at your location is in favor of paying employees for the time lost, but the manager of the accounting department is opposed.

4. The manager of the accounting department is in favor of paying employees for the time lost, but your immediate subordinate whose knowledge would be relevant to the situation is opposed.

5. Your immediate subordinate is in favor of paying employees for the time lost, but the top company official at your location is opposed.

6. Your immediate subordinate is in favor of paying employees for the time lost, but the person immediately above you in the personnel department is opposed.

After each of these situations, the respondents were given the following choices of action:

1. Recommend pay for the time lost (operationalization of conform to expectation A of Gross et al.).

2. Do not recommend pay for the time lost (conform to expectation B).

3. Talk to the two parties and attempt to resolve their differences (compromise).

[69]Ibid., p. 272.
[70]Ritzer and Trice, *An Occupation in Conflict*, pp. 46–57.

4. Listen to both, but make your own recommendation (independent action).
5. Hold your recommendation in abeyance (withdraw).

A second case was also employed in which personnel managers had to decide what to do about some changes recommended by an outside consultant, including changes in the personnel function. The same six situations were employed, although this time the significant others made recommendations concerning action on the consultant's suggestions. The only changes in the choices of action open to personnel managers after each situation were that the conform to expectation A alternative read "Recommend the changes," and the conform to expectation B alternative read "Do not recommend the changes." Table 10.1 summarizes the findings for the two cases.

There are some rather striking findings here in terms of the theory of role conflict resolution and the way individuals in managerial and official occupations resolve the role conflict inherent in their occupations. The major finding, as pointed out previously, is that independent action is a viable means of resolving role conflict. As a matter of fact, for the personnel managers in the Ritzer and Trice study it was by far the dominant choice. If individuals in such a traditionally passive occupation choose independent action in resolving role conflict, then individuals in higher-status official and managerial positions are even more likely to be independent decision makers.

The findings on independent action in role conflict situations are also interesting because they reveal an entirely different means of resolving conflict in occupational life: adherence to a *mythical occupational image*. Publicly, personnel managers deny that they ever make decisions. Personnel managers are described as:

> . . . glorified clerks . . . they have no backbone and always find some way to accommodate the wishes of the strongest forces acting on them . . . the personnel officer is traditionally nonactivist, not a positive force . . . he isn't sufficiently assertive.[71]

This theme of passivity is repeated over and over in the literature describing personnel managers and mentioned by practicing managers when asked about their role in the organization. Nevertheless, such observers as William Whyte have noted that in reality personnel managers play a dynamic and assertive role within organizations. Whyte reports: "Engineers in particular, but also personnel men and some other specialists, are expected to be innovators, to get operating people to adopt new products, machines, processes, and systems of doing work or organizing relations among men."[72]

In a study of personnel managers in Great Britain, one of the respondents indicated his lack of passivity, his interest in power: "In this job I've an advisory role rather than an executive one yet I like power. It's not overt power, it's influence, I like influencing the totality!"[73]

---

[71]O. Glenn Stahl, "Tomorrow's Generation of Personnel Managers," paper presented at the Public Personnel Association, International Conference, Victoria, B.C. October, 1967.

[72]William F. Whyte, *Men at Work* (Homewood, IL: Dorsey Press and Richard D. Irwin, 1961), p. 561.

[73]Tony J. Watson, *The Personnel Managers: A Study in the Sociology of Work and Employment* (London: Routledge and Kegan Paul, 1977), p. 98.

TABLE 10.1   Comparison of Resolutions of Two Role Conflict Cases for Personnel Managers

BEHAVIORAL ALTERNATIVES	PERCENT IN CASE ONE	PERCENT IN CASE TWO
Conform to Expectation A	15	11
Conform to Expectation B	10	9
Compromise	24	17
Independent Action	50	62
Withdraw	1	1
	100	100

The question is, why do most personnel administrators contend that they are merely passive advisors when they do make decisions? The answer is that they are preventing role conflict by adhering to a mythical occupational image. If they were to state they were decision makers, relations with line (production) managers would be severely strained. Part of the ideology of line managers is that they make all the critical decisions in the organization, whereas in fact staff officers such as the personnel managers are making an increasing number of decisions for them. This reality is handled by both parties through adherence to mythical occupational images: line managers believe they make all the decisions and staff managers believe they are merely advisors. To forestall conflict with line managers, personnel administrators are content to accept a passive public image and are prepared to fight anything that threatens to reveal the real power that they wield within the organization.

Controllers.   The controller, like the personnel manager, is a staff officer, and as a staff officer is also supposed to be an advisor rather than a decision maker. However, because they control monetary matters, controllers are generally more powerful figures than personnel managers. Nevertheless, their authority is supposed to be very limited. A study by Henning and Moseley indicates that this view of the controller, like the view of the personnel manager, is largely mythical.[74] They interviewed controllers, their superiors, and peer executives in twenty-five medium-sized firms. It was found that controllers had much authority in making government reports and internal auditing and comparatively little in budgeting and making accounting reports. Thus like personnel managers, controllers do have a great deal of authority, at least in some areas. More important, there is a difference between controllers' perceptions of their own authority and the perceptions of superiors and peers. According to Henning and Moseley: "These data suggest that controllers generally perceive themselves as having more authority than either their superiors or peers perceive them to have."[75] Thus, we can see that when dealing with others within their organization, staff officers downplay their authority in order to avoid conflicts.

[74]Dale A. Henning and Roger L. Moseley, "Authority Role of a Functional Manager: The Controller," *Administrative Science Quarterly,* 15 (1970), 482–489.
[75]Ibid., 487.

Prison camp officials.   The prison camp supervisor is confronted with a conflict between custodial and treatment orientations. Grusky contends that the prison camp supervisor's typical resolution is to take a position of administrative neutrality. As one supervisor commented: "Another thing I found out is that you can be custodially-minded as well as treatment-minded. You don't have to be one or the other."[76] This neutrality tended to enhance the supervisors' position within the camp. Both the treatment-oriented and custodial-oriented factions were forced to work through them if they wanted to extend their influence throughout the organization. Prison camp officials are, therefore, typically compromisers in the face of the role conflict inherent in their position.

Prison welfare officers.   Prison welfare officers are in a position very similar to that of prison camp officials. They too, are confronted with a conflict between simply serving as custodians or attempting to treat and rehabilitate the prisoners. As welfare workers, they are in a less powerful position than the prison official and are more likely to conform to the expectations of those significant others with the greatest power. Those who are oriented to custodial goals seem to have the greatest power. Thus, Priestly found that prison welfare officers "appear to be becoming more involved with running the institution than meeting the needs of prisoners either collectively or individually."[77] Welfare officers rationalize their abandonment of their traditional treatment orientation by contending that the only way they can help prisoners is by working within the custodial system. Of course, it is questionable whether they can really help prisoners in that context.

Priestly also found other types of resolutions employed by prison welfare officers. Some withdrew from the situation either by psychologically identifying with researchers and academics outside the system or by actually quitting their jobs. Some were even found taking more independent action in seeking to change the prison system from within. The dominant resolution for prison welfare officers, however, was conformity to the custodial role.

Elected public officials.   Mitchell has noted that politicians tend to withdraw in the face of inter-role conflict.[78] When in this situation the politician typically takes a "no comment" position, at least until the situation becomes clearer in terms of expectations and alternative actions.

Navy disbursing officers.   In the person-role conflict faced by Navy disbursing officers, they are generally not able to take a compromise position. When confronted with a clash between regulations and the orders from above, the disbursing officers tend to resolve the conflict by obeying the order. They do so because of the sanctions superiors may impose on them if they fail to follow orders. Further, in following orders from the top, they know they cannot be held responsible for violating a rule. The Navy has recognized the

[76]Grusky, "Role Conflict in Organizations," 458.
[77]Philip Priestly, "The Prison Welfare Officer—A Case of Role Strain," *British Journal of Sociology,* 23 (1972), 232.
[78]Mitchell, "Occupational Role Strains."

inherent dilemma of disbursing officers and provided them with two possibilities for withdrawing from the conflict. They can point out the discrepancy between orders and rules to their superiors and, if no understanding is reached, they can bring the problem to the attention of a board for a decision. Or, they can bring the conflict to the attention of the commanding officer "who may order the disbursing officer to make the expenditure 'under protest,' the commanding officer thereby assuming full financial liability."[79] However, these two withdrawal possibilities are infrequently utilized. Rather, the disbursing officer finds a variety of ways to get around the formal rules and fulfills orders in a variety of informal ways.

There are many other studies of occupations which describe specific modes of resolving role conflict. The basic point is that wherever there is a role conflict in occupational life, individuals seek in a variety of ways to resolve the problem of incompatible expectations. All of these idiosyncratic resolutions can be categorized as either conformity to expectation A, conformity to expectation B, compromise, independent action. or withdrawal.

Drinking and drugs.   Alcohol and drugs are generally used throughout society as a means of coping with a wide range of stresses and strains.[80] Roman found that drinking among middle- and upper-level managers and officials provides a way of coping with the stress and role conflict associated with their positions. According to Roman: "Escape through drinking may be extremely functional when one is putting in a heavy energy investment in daily work activities. The expectation of rewarding escape at 5 o'clock allows one to endure stress."[81] Drinking and drugs certainly have dysfunctions, especially when they are abused, but we cannot ignore the fact that they are used in coping with a variety of stresses, most notably in this context the conflicts associated with middle- and upper-level management positions.

PROPRIETORS: ECONOMIC MARGINALITY

In 1980 there were approximately 8.2 million people officially classified as self-employed.[82] This represents an increase of over 1 million workers since 1972 and reverses a 25 year decline in the number of workers classified as self-employed.

The self-employed tend to be white males who are somewhat older than

[79]Turner, "Navy Disbursing Officer," 345.

[80]H.M. Trice and Paul Roman, *Spirits and Demons at Work: Alcohol and Drugs on the Job* (Ithaca, NY: Cornell University Press, 1972). For a specific discussion of the functions of drinking and drugs in another occupation, the military, see, Clifton D. Bryant, "Olive-Drab Drunks and GI Junkies: Alcohol and Narcotic Addiction in the U. S. Military," in Clifton Bryant, ed., *Deviant Behavior: Occupational and Organizational Bases* (Chicago: Rand-McNally, 1974), pp. 129–145.

[81]Paul Roman, "Settings for Successful Deviance: Drinking and Deviant Drinking Among Middle- and Upper-Level Employees," in Bryant, *Deviant Behavior*, p. 119.

[82]The information in this section is based on T. Scott Fain, "Self-employed Americans: Their Number Has Increased," *Monthly Labor Review*, 103 (November, 1980), 3–8. The 8.2 million figure does not include 2.1 million workers who are incorporated self-employed and who are officially classified as wage and salary workers. The figure also does not include 1.5 million workers who are self-employed in their second job and approximately 760,000 unpaid family workers. See Fain pp. 7–8 for a discussion of the incorporated self-employed.

the average wage and salary worker. During the 1970s, the proportion of blacks who were classified as self-employed remained constant. In 1972, 5.5 percent of proprietors were black and as of 1980 this figure had not changed. Women make up 25 percent of the self-employed. Women are underrepresented in this category but gains have been made.

In terms of the total number of self-employed, the percentage of farm workers fell from 23.4 in 1972 to 17.2 by 1980. Those classified as self-employed service workers remained constant at about 9.2 percent. During this same period we witnessed a substantial increase in the percentage of blue-collar workers classified as self-employed. By 1980, slightly more than 25 percent of the self-employed were blue-collar workers compared to 20.7 percent in 1972. The biggest gains occurred among the crafts, with carpenters and other construction workers leading the way. The white-collar self-employed category also continued to grow from 46.8 percent in 1972 to 48.3 percent by 1980. Among this group, sales workers experienced one of the largest gains.

One of the great American dreams, and myths, is the idea that one can escape low-status jobs in organizations by going into business for oneself. The desire to be one's own boss has been uncovered in many studies of workers, especially those in blue-collar occupations.[83] Every year many people quit their jobs and with their life savings in hand open their own businesses—a grocery store, a filling station, a newspaper stand. Most of these efforts are, of course, doomed and in a short period of time ex-proprietors return to their old jobs (if they are still available), having lost time, savings, and perhaps even pension rights. Furthermore, they are likely to be deeply in debt. Despite this reality, many people follow the same route each year in a desperate effort to avoid low-status work in organizations.

The futility of most such efforts is clear in a study by Mayer and Goldstein of ninety small businesses.[84] Of these businesses, almost 50 percent (forty-four businesses) had closed after only 2 years. Although most of those who open businesses are likely to do badly, those whose background is solely in manual work are likely to do worse than those with some white-collar experience. Of those with only manual work experience, 60 percent did not last even 2 years as proprietors. Worse, 90 percent of those businesses that managed to survive the first 2 years were ranked as either "marginal survivors" or "only limited successes." Only two of the forty-nine businesses begun by ex-manual workers were clearly successful, and then only after some very difficult times.

Why does such a high proportion of businesses fail? First, they are generally undercapitalized. New proprietors often have little money and hence have little to fall back on in the first few months in business—generally considered to be the most difficult. Second, those who enter business have generally had little or no experience in being a proprietor. They have no idea what to expect or how to cope with the problems that do arise. Third, many enter business on the spur of the moment, with little advance planning. They have

[83]See, for example, Ely Chinoy, *Automobile Workers and the American Dream* (Boston: Beacon Press, 1955).

[84]Kurt B. Mayer and Sidney Goldstein, "Manual Workers as Small Businessmen," in Arthur Shostak and William Gomberg, eds., *Blue Collar World: Studies of the American Worker* (Englewood Cliffs, NJ: Prentice-Hall, 1964), pp. 545–558.

been nursing a dream of their own business and when one becomes available they buy, almost unthinkingly. Mayer and Goldstein conclude that "it would appear that the dream of business ownership is tarnished. It continues to lure substantial numbers of workers into an adventure in which most of them fail."[85]

Although the idea of becoming a successful small proprietor seems largely mythical, there are at least two exceptions to this generalization. First, obviously there have been a few hard-driving individuals who have built huge businesses with little or no initial experience and capital. The mass media periodically features such individuals as Ray Kroc who built a single hamburger stand into a multibillion-dollar business—McDonald's.[86] Boyd and Gumpert found support for the idea that owning one's own business can be lucrative.[87] In their study of 450 chief executives of established small companies, Boyd and Gumpert found that approximately 75 percent of the respondents earned over $40,000 annually, about 60 percent earned over $50,000 annually, and 20 percent earned over $100,000 per year. But the few who are successful constitute a destructive role model for the vast majority of those who seek to open their own business. They distort the fact that the earnings of the majority of the self-employed are less than the average earnings of wage and salary workers[88] and that a vast majority who attempt to open their own business will ultimately fail.

The second exception is the growing trend toward franchises such as McDonald's, Wendy's, Holiday Inn, and the like.[89] In 1970 there were approximately 396,000 franchise establishments. By 1983 the number had increased to about 465,000 units.[90] Sales had grown much more dramatically from $120 billion in 1970 to $436 billion in 1983.[91] A good portion of this growth was accounted for by franchise restaurants. In 1970, there were about 33,000 franchise restaurants with sales of about $4.6 billion. In 1983, there were over 70,000 franchise restaurants doing over $38 billion in sales.[92]

In contrast to the other available openings, proprietorship of one of these franchise outlets seems like a good opportunity. However, one cannot buy one of these major outlets for a few thousand dollars. As of 1982, the cost of a Burger King franchise was $500,000 while a McDonald's outlet was between $250,000 and $325,000.[93] And the cost of such franchises is rising rapidly. Furthermore, the licenses generally expire after a certain length of time, after which licensees must match their initial investment. In return for this investment and a yearly fee, franchise holders receive a number of benefits:

[85]Ibid., p. 557.

[86]Ray Kroc, *Grinding it Out* (New York: Berkley Medallion Books, 1977).

[87]David P. Boyd and David E. Gumpert, "Coping with Entrepreneurial Stress," *Harvard Business Review*, 61 (March/April, 1983), 44–64.

[88]T. Scott Fain, "Self-employed Americans: Their Number Has Increased."

[89]Stan Luxenberg, *Roadside Empires: How the Chains Franchised America* (New York: Viking, 1985).

[90]*Statistical Abstract of the United States: 1984*, p. 806.

[91]Ibid.

[92]Ibid.

[93]Peter G. Norback and Craig T. Norback, *The Dow Jones-Irwin Guide to Franchises*, rev. ed. (Homewood, IL: Dow Jones-Irwin, 1982).

1. A well-known name
2. A building and a piece of real estate
3. Formulae for making the products
4. A ready-made clientele
5. The benefit of the nationwide advertising undertaken by the franchiser
6. A line of products that is known to sell well
7. Efficient equipment provided by the franchiser
8. A set of guidelines for running the operation
9. Help from the franchiser, if needed. (In McDonald's case this also includes a degree program at their $2-million-dollar "Hamburger University." A "Bachelor of Hamburgerology" awaits the graduate!)

By the same token, the franchise arrangement offers a number of advantages to franchisers:

1. They are able to expand rapidly on other people's capital. As of 1982, McDonald's had 4859 franchises in the United States and eighty-nine internationally.
2. The risk of loss is shifted from the franchiser to franchisee.
3. There is reduced corporate vulnerability. Taxes, government regulation, and code enforcements are generally less stringent on small businesses than large corporations. It is easier to frustrate efforts at unionization. (In any case, most of the workers are teenagers who stay for only a few months.) The franchisee has the legal and financial liability as well as the responsibility for coping with customer complaints.
4. The franchise holders, with a great deal of their money on the line, will police themselves very carefully. [94]

For all these reasons we are likely to witness a continuing expansion of these types of franchise operations.

It could be argued that such franchise arrangements obviate the basic reason why people enter their own businesses. With a great deal of control from the central office, regular inspection, detailed rules, almost self-operating machines, and the like, there is comparatively little independence left. Are the franchisees little more than employees of the franchisers? That question is left for the reader to ponder. In trying to answer this question the reader might consider this description of the control central management at McDonald's wields over its franchisees:

> In the field, licensees and managers are incessantly hounded by roving inspectors (called "field supervisors") to make sure that the restaurant floor is mopped at proper intervals and the parking lot is tidied up hourly. If a manager tries to sell his customers hamburgers that have been off the grill more than ten minutes or coffee more than 30 minutes old, Big Brother . . . will find out. Headquarters executives calculate exactly how much food each restaurant can be expected to

[94]Richard Peterson, *The Industrial Order and Social Policy* (Englewood Cliffs, NJ: Prentice-Hall, 1973).

throw away each day, and are ready to chastise a chronically deviant manager who has no good explanation.[95]

But the hard-driving individual success and the franchise are exceptions to our general theme that success as an independent proprietor is extremely difficult to achieve. Let us return to this basic theme by focusing on the well-known phenomenon of the husband and wife who devote a large portion of their lives to a marginally successful, and difficult to operate, small business. Reflecting the difficulty of this task, Terkel calls the owners of the small grocery and gift store in question "Ma and Pa Courage." To make it, they must sell a wide array of goods, including food, crayons, bandages, costume jewelry, buttons, and so forth—it is a modern version of the old country store. The owners describe some of their major problems:[96]

Crime.

We have thirteen hundred dollars worth of bad checks. We allow a little bit of credit to old stand-bys for about a week.

We had magazines and books, but we took'em out two years ago because the theft was so bad.

We had thirteen hundred dollars of books stolen in the last three months of the last year we handled books. A lot with cases of food. . . . I caught a guy one evening puttin' two dozen eggs in his Eisenhower jacket.

We've had several hold-ups

Hard work, long hours.

There usually isn't that much sleep. We used to average two, three hours. That went on for ten years that way. Now we get an average of four hours. . . . In the morning I mop the floors, haul fifteen to twenty cases of soda from the basement, throw it in the cooler. For the first three hours you have your variety of salesmen, your breadmen and your milkmen . . . then your evening trade starts. We switch hours between meals. I wouldn't say we're tired at the end of the day, we just drop. (Laughs)

Economic marginality.

When we first opened the store, our insurance was $398 a year. Now it's jumped to $1,398. They say you're too high a risk. Your lights have went up, your gas, all your utilities. Your mark-up on your profit has decreased. . . . With costs up, your overhead is 10 percent, now you're workin' on 2 percent profit. Instead of coming out of the hole, you're going into the hole. It's impossible to survive unless you're doing something else on the side.

[95]"The Burger That Conquered the Country," *Time,* (September 17, 1973), pp. 84–85.
[96]Terkel, *Working,* pp. 414–421.

The problems associated with owning one's own business can also be discussed at a more general level. In the study by Boyd and Gumpert, they found that loneliness, total immersion in the business, conflicts with partners and subordinates, and a compelling need to achieve were major sources of stress for successful businesspeople. With reference to loneliness, the small entrepreneur does not have the social network that many executives have as a result of working in a large organization. In addition, long hours inhibit, if not on occasion prevent, outside contacts with family and friends. And long hours are common. Boyd and Gumpert found that 60 percent of the entrepreneurs in their study worked 50 hours or more per week, while 25 percent worked 60 or more hours per week. Furthermore, 66 percent worked weeknights and 55 percent worked on Saturdays.

For the majority of small businesspeople who are not successful it is our position that the biggest problem faced by these individuals centers around relations with customers and economic marginality. To compete, at least to some extent, with large chain stores, small proprietors must concentrate on personalizing their relationships with their customers. Since they cannot compete with the chains on the basis of price, they must excel in catering to the customer's personal and business needs. One way is to be concerned with the personal welfare of one's customers, or at least to feign such concern. Ma and Pa Courage emphasize the "personal touch." "How's the kids?" "Work goin' okay?" "Sorry to hear you lost your job."[97] In competing with the large chain stores, Ma and Pa emphasize other things as well:

> Chain stores don't bother me. People gotta have a place where they can run for a loaf of bread, a dozen eggs, or somethin' for a snack, a pint of ice cream or a bottle of soda. Instead of goin' in the chain store and standing in line. The cold indifference. They still get the personal touch here, the chatter back and forth, the gossip and the laughter.[98]

Though these personal touches are of some help in competing with the chain stores, one still gets the feeling that such small proprietorships are fighting a losing, rear-guard action against the irreversible trend toward larger size, greater efficiency, and more impersonality.

CONCLUSIONS

This chapter is divided into two sections. In the first, we dealt with role conflict and role conflict resolution among managers and officials. We analyzed in some detail each of the major forms of role conflict in this occupational category—role overload, inter-sender role conflict, person-role conflict, inter-role conflict, and intra-sender role conflict—as well as role ambiguity. Following a discussion of several examples of each of these phenomena, we turned to the modes of role conflict resolution—conformity to expectation A,

[97]Ibid., p. 415.
[98]Ibid.

conformity to expectation B, compromise, withdrawal, and independent action.

The second section dealt with proprietors, primarily small entrepreneurs. Many proprietors have been driven out of business by their inability to compete with the large chain stores. The defining conflict for proprietors is their economic marginality. Those few who manage to survive are generally undercapitalized and can only survive through hard work, long hours, etc. We also examined a new type of proprietor—the franchise owner. Ownership of franchises (such as McDonald's, Burger King, Kentucky Fried Chicken, and Pizza Hut) is an increasing outlet for those who aspire to proprietorship. However, these are very different from traditional small enterprises. The owner is controlled, to a large degree, by the franchiser. Also, one needs a large amount of initial capital to qualify for such a franchise, which rules out proprietorship for a large portion of the population.

ELEVEN

CONFLICT IN A RANGE OF WHITE- AND BLUE-COLLAR OCCUPATIONS

In this chapter we examine the distinctive conflicts and modes of conflict resolution of four rather distinct occupational types—white-collar clerical workers, salespeople, the skilled crafts, and "free" semiskilled and unskilled workers. These types of jobs are unified by the fact that their position in the occupational continuum stands between the managers, officials, and proprietors discussed in the last chapter and those in semiskilled and unskilled occupations in organizations analyzed in the next chapter. White-collar clerical workers and salespeople rank at the bottom of the white-collar category, while the skilled crafts stand at the top of the blue-collar occupations. Free semiskilled and unskilled occupations are discussed in this chapter rather than the next to differentiate these positions from semi- and unskilled positions in organizations, which tend to experience different types of work conflict. This chapter, then, is a transition between the high-status occupations discussed previously and the lower-status occupations analyzed in Chapter 12.

WHITE-COLLAR CLERICAL WORKERS

Social Changes

Although not all white-collar clerical workers are female, we will focus on females in this section since they constitute the vast majority of all office workers in the United States. Overall, 80.7 percent of clerical and kindred workers in 1982 were female.[1] More specifically, in 1982 women constituted over 95 percent of all receptionists, secretaries, and typists, and approximately 92 percent of all bank tellers, bookkeepers, and telephone operators.[2] In general, they are performing traditional female roles, but in the workworld rather than the family. According to Benet: "Their work is supplementary and custodial rather than productive: it is low in status and in pay."[3] One of the reasons for the low status is that women are often required to do tasks that are not related to clerical work, but are related to traditional female sex roles—they are often expected to be the "office wife:"

> Clerical workers are often expected and sometimes required to make morning coffee and run personal errands for the boss. One woman clerk was told by her boss to go and try on a nursing bra for his wife, who didn't have the time to purchase one. And many clerks resent the assumption that they should provide a "shoulder" for the boss to cry on.[4]

Benet has labelled the "female office" the "secretarial ghetto."[5] Let us examine the historical background of this "ghetto" as well as its contemporary character in terms of its distinctive conflicts and the efforts to cope with these conflicts.

The early clerical occupations were dominated by males. In 1870, only 3.5 percent of the 76,639 office workers in the United States were female.[6] In fact, office work was considered a good place for a man to begin his career. He worked closely with the boss, gained valuable experience, and could stand in for him on various occasions. Thus, when it was dominated by males, the clerical occupation was of fairly high status and offered considerable upward mobility. The working environment of early offices was very different from the contemporary office.

Lockwood analyzes the British countinghouse of the nineteenth century, comparing it to the modern office of the twentieth century to highlight the enormous changes that have affected the clerical worker.[7] The early countinghouse was small, with an intimate relationship between the workers resulting in part from the comparative lack of a division of labor:

> The most simple division of tasks in the older office was that between the employer or partners, who made the important business decisions, the bookkeeper-cashier, who dealt with financial records, and the ordinary clerk, who was re-

[1]U.S. Bureau of the Census, *Statistical Abstract of the United States: 1984,* 104th edition (Washington, D.C., 1983), p. 419.

[2]Ibid.

[3]Mary Kathleen Benet, *The Secretarial Ghetto* (New York: McGraw-Hill, 1972), p.1

[4]Mary Frank Fox and Sharlene Hesse-Biber, *Women at Work* (Chicago: Mayfield Publishing Co., 1984), p. 109.

[5]Benet, *The Secretarial Ghetto.*

[6]Fox and Hesse-Biber, *Women at Work,* p. 101.

[7]David Lockwood, *The Blackcoated Worker: A Study in Class Consciousness* (London: George Allen and Unwin, 1958). For a contemporary study of white-collar work in Great Britain see, K. Prandy, A. Stewart and R.M. Blackburn, *White-Collar Work* (London: MacMillan, 1982).

sponsible for correspondence, filing, elementary bookkeeping entries and routine office matters.[8]

Clerks, bookkeepers, and owners had very personal relationships with each other.

Since the work was not highly specialized, the recruiting process was not oriented toward obtaining highly, and specifically, trained personnel. Rather, the goal was to obtain a person with a good general education in such fields as Latin, Greek, geography, science, arithmetic, French, even a little poetry. In other words, people with a "superficial secondary education" were sought. Since the major job requirements were quick and accurate arithmetic and legible handwriting, little specialized education was required. Training was largely on the job, individual and informal.

Despite their few skills and low pay, the clerks (called "blackcoated workers") set themselves apart from the working class, from blue-collar workers. They aspired to managerial careers and despite their lack of means were fond of copying the gentlemanly manners of their superiors. In addition, other factors differentiated them from the working class, including their middle-class background, greater education, cleaner and more mental work, mode of dress (black coats), proximity and ties to the employer, responsibility for confidential matters and often for subordinates, and secure and progressive salaries. Lockwood concludes: "If economically they were sometimes on the margin, socially they were definitely part of the middle class."[9] Thus this worker, like his American counterpart, gained considerable status by being able to set himself apart from blue-collar workers.

Status Panic

A variety of social changes over the last hundred or so years has conspired to radically change the old-time office. As a result, the relatively high status clerical workers once possessed has dramatically declined; the distinguishing conflict of the white-collar clerical worker is now "status panic."[10] Let us examine a number of changes that have led to this status anxiety among clerical workers.

The first factor is the sheer increase in numbers of people in this occupation. Once a fairly select group, the clerical category has been inundated with a flood of workers prompted by the growth of bureaucracies and the burgeoning need for clerical workers to process the lifeblood of any bureaucracy—information! In 1900, clerical and kindred workers composed only 3 percent of the workforce, but by 1982 the proportion had multiplied more than six times to 18.5 percent.[11] Both computer- and noncomputer-based clerical occupations have been expanding rapidly, but the biggest growth between 1972 and 1982 was in the number of computer operators

[8]Lockwood, *The Blackcoated Worker*, p. 20.

[9]Ibid., p. 35.

[10]C. Wright Mills, *White Collar* (New York: Oxford Universiy Press, 1951).

[11]Philip M. Hauser, "Labor Force," in Robert E. L. Faris, ed., *Handbook of Modern Sociology* (Chicago: Rand McNally, 1964), p. 183; *Statistical Abstract of the United States. 1984*, p. 417.

which almost tripled in the decade.[12] This flood of workers has helped to reduce the status of the white-collar worker. Related to the increasing number of clerical workers is the increasing size of the office and office staffs. Once a small and select group within the organization, white-collar workers now make up a large segment of many organizations. This, too, has had a negative effect on their status within the organization.

A second factor in the declining status of the clerical workers is technological change. The early blackcoated worker performed his work with a pen, paper, and his mind. As improved technology entered the office, the skills needed to perform clerical tasks declined. The typewriter and the adding machine tended to transfer the skill from the worker to the machine. The invention of the dictaphone led to the development of the typing pool in the 1920s. The typist now got no closer to the boss than his voice on a dictaphone belt. More recently, the coming of the computer to the office has radically altered the nature of white-collar work. The word processor serves to "deskill" white-collar clerical work. An expert typist who makes few, if any errors, is no longer required. All errors are easily corrected on the display screen *before* the final draft is printed. There are even electronic spellcheckers that can pick out spelling errors before they find their way into a final draft. Such deskilling of clerical work by building various skills into the technology helps to further erode the status of the occupation.

A third, and perhaps central factor in the decline in the status of the clerical workers, was the influx of females. In 1890, only 15 percent of all clerical jobs in the United States were held by females. As we have seen, by 1982 that number had grown to over 80 percent of all clerical workers.[13] Table 11.1 details the proportion of females in selected clerical occupations and the change in that percentage between 1962 and 1982. It is clear that women constitute the vast majority of most types of white-collar clerical workers and that this predominance is, in general, increasing.

However, it is important to point out that the status of the clerical worker was under attack earlier in history as well. The work was considered "unmasculine" even before the entry of large numbers of females, and their introduction was but the final blow to the attacks on the "fake gentility" of the clerical worker.[14] The first women who entered the occupation were given lower-status positions than those held by males. These positions required less skill, knowledge, responsibility, prestige, and pay. As time passed, technological advances created new, relatively unskilled positions and a large proportion of these went to women. Two major technological developments—the telephone and the typewriter—largely became preserves of female employees, and that remains true to this day.[15]

The increasing number of clerical workers in bureaucracies, technological change, and the growing feminization of the occupation have all come together in recent years to produce the new "factorylike" office. Here is the way C. Wright Mills describes it:

[12]*Statistical Abstract of the United States: 1984*, p. 419.

[13]Ibid.

[14]Benet, *The Secretarial Ghetto*; see also Lockwood, *The Blackcoated Worker*.

[15]Benet, *The Secretarial Ghetto*.

TABLE 11.1   Percentage of Women in Selected White-Collar Clerical Occupations: 1962–1982

OCCUPATION	1962	1982
Bank Tellers	71.5%	92.0%
Bookkeepers	85.4	91.8
Cashiers	82.5	86.8
Secretaries	98.5	99.2
Typists	94.8	96.6
Office Machine Operators	72.9	74.6

SOURCES: Stuart Garfinkle, "Occupations of Women and Black Workers, 1962–1974," *Monthly Labor Review*, 98 (1975), 28; *Statistical Abstract of the United States: 1984*, p. 419.

The modern office with its tens of thousands of square feet and its factory-like flow of work is not an informal, friendly place. The drag and beat of work, the "production unit" tempo, require that time consumed by anything but business at hand be explained and apologized for. Dictation was once a private meeting of executive and secretary. Now the executive phones a pool of dictaphone transcribers whom he never sees and who know him merely as a voice. Many old types of personnel have become machine operators, many new types began as machine operators.[16]

According to Mills, a machine-like atmosphere is pervasive.

The new office is rationalized: machines are used, employees become machine attendants; the work, as in the factory, is collective, not individualized; it is standardized for interchangeable, quickly replaceable clerks; it is specialized to the point of automization.[17]

A number of other factors are involved in reducing the status differential between white- and blue-collar workers.

White-collar salaries have been leveled, while there has been a corresponding increase in blue-collar salaries.[18]

White-collar workers now find themselves more likely to be unemployed.[19]

White-collar workers no longer have a significant say in the decision making of top executives.

Blue-collar workers have obtained increasing power, especially through their involvement in labor unions.

[16]C. Wright Mills, *White Collar*, pp. 204–25. For a similar point of view see the Department of Health, Education, and Welfare's *Work in America* (Cambridge, MA: The M.I.T. Press, 1973), pp. 38–40.

[17]Mills, *White Collar*, p. 209.

[18]Harry Braverman, *Labor and Monopoly Capital: The Degradation of Work in the Twentieth Century* (New York: Monthly Review Press, 1974), pp. 296–297.

[19]Fox and Hesse-Biber, *Women at Work*, p. 106.

Some highly skilled blue-collar occupations require more skill and training than many white-collar occupations.

Blue-collar work has become much cleaner, especially in automated factories. In such factories it may now be impossible to see any differences between white- and blue-collar work.[20]

Norval Glenn has found empirical support for the contention that the status differences between white- and blue-collar occupations have been diminishing.[21] While Glenn found that being a white-collar worker had some slight effect on occupational prestige in a 1947 study, by 1963 that effect had largely disappeared. As a result of changes such as these, Braverman sees white-collar clerical workers, along with manual workers, as part of the proletariat.[22]

Glenn and Feldberg have studied the proletarianization of clerical work.[23] Clerical workers were usually included in the middle class because of "clean physical surroundings, and emphasis on mental as opposed to manual activities, reliance on workers' judgment in executing tasks, and direct personal contact among workers and between workers and managers."[24] Proletarianization in this context is defined by the loss by clerical work of these distinctive characteristics, "*as work is organized around manual rather than mental activities, as tasks become externally structured and controlled and as relationships become depersonalized.*"[25] In their view, office workers have become proletarianized, although not at uniform rates for all types of clerical workers and in all types of organizations.

First, organizational and technological changes in the office have served to proletarianize clerical work. The growing size of organizations and various technological changes, especially the revolutionary impact of the computer, have served to trivialize old skills (such as stenography, bookkeeping) and reduced the opportunity to learn new skills. The new skills required of clerical workers tend to be more mechanical, lower level and narrower than the skills required of their predecessors. The routine jobs require little mental activity and are, as a result, very demanding, in the sense that the worker "experiences great pressure to work quickly, accurately, and to maintain the pace set by the machine."[26] Furthermore, there is now less opportunity for people in such routine occupations to experience upward mobility. In these ways, clerical workers have come to increasingly resemble semiskilled and unskilled workers.

Second, the methods of controlling clerical workers have grown more rational and more impersonal. In the old office, clerical workers were

[20]Mills, *White Collar*, p. 249.

[21]Norval D. Glenn, "The Contribution of White Collars to Occupational Prestige," *The Sociological Quarterly*, 16 (1975), 184–189.

[22]Braverman, *Labor and Monopoly Capital*, p. 355.

[23]Evelyn Nakano Glenn and Roslyn L. Feldberg, "Degraded and Deskilled: The Proletarianization of Clerical Work," *Social Problems*, 25 (1977), 52–64.

[24]Ibid., 53.

[25]Ibid.

[26]Ibid., 57.

controlled through face-to-face contact with superiors. This is not possible in the huge, modern office with the result that formal, administrative controls are implemented. Thus, for example, work is reduced to numerical production and the supervisor can see at a glance at a computer screen whether a clerical worker has processed a sufficient number of words. This is not simply a different form of control over clerical workers, it constitutes an increase in external control. Thus, in quality and quantity of external control, clerical workers have come to resemble manual workers.

Finally, personal relationships within the office have been altered, again in the direction of greater similarity between office and factory work. The face-to-face relationships between supervisor and subordinate in the old office have been replaced by impersonal relationships within the modern office. At the same time, the ability to maintain personal relationships with other clerical workers has also been undermined by a variety of factors. There is less need for cooperation among workers since those in the work group often do the same job rather than a set of interrelated jobs. Clerical units are often physically separated from one another. Workers must stay at their work stations making it impossible for them to interact with other clerical workers. Finally, clerical workers performing standardized operations feel vulnerable to replacement with the result that they are reluctant to talk openly with other people in the organization. They are afraid that such openness could further jeopardize their already precarious position in the organization.

Thus, in terms of the organization of clerical work, the methods by which it is controlled, and the social relationships on the job, it seems clear that clerical work has undergone a considerable amount of proletarianization in recent years. It is this proletarianization that is a major factor in the declining status of the clerical worker and the increase in their status panic.

Nevertheless, research by Grandjean and Taylor has questioned the perspective on status panic offered here.[27] Grandjean and Taylor state: "Ritzer suggests that the job dissatisfaction of clerical workers can be traced to 'status panic.'"[28] In contrast to this, they argue that the dissatisfaction of office workers can be traced to "perceived impediments to advancement and accomplishment" within the opportunity structure of the organization.[29] They proceed to test these alternative perspectives in a study of female secretaries, stenographers, and typists in a federal agency. They conclude that their data show far more support for the opportunity structure than the status panic argument:

> The results show that the adequacy of training programs, the utilization of office workers' skills, and (indirectly) sex discrimination, at least as these are perceived by the workers themselves, are by far more influential in determining job satisfaction than are variables related to status, status insecurity and deference.[30]

---

[27]Burke D. Grandjean and Patricia A. Taylor, "Job Satisfaction Among Female Clerical Workers: 'Status Panic' or the Opportunity Structure of Office Work?" *Sociology of Work and Occupations*, 7 (1980), 33–53.

[28]Ibid., 36.

[29]Ibid., 40.

[30]Ibid., 49.

Although a useful effort to test a theoretical idea empirically, the research by Grandjean and Taylor is far from a definitive test of the status panic theory. One problem is that there are a number of questionable operationalizations of theoretical ideas. However, the most critical weakness lies in the differentiation between the opportunity structure and status panic theories. In fact, it should be argued that the lack of a perceived opportunity structure is *one* cause of status panic among clerical workers. The loss of opportunities for advancement and accomplishment is one of the changes that has taken place in clerical work as a result of the broader changes discussed above (such as larger organizations, technological change, deskilling, proletarianization, and so forth). It would be better to think of perceptions of declining opportunity structures as a cause of increasing status panic, rather than conceiving of these perceptions and status panic as alternative causes of job dissatisfaction.

Responses To Status Panic

Let us turn now from a discussion of status panic to some of the resolutions employed by clerical workers to cope with this problem.

Informal group structures. Frequently, white-collar workers respond to status threats by developing informal group structures that perform a variety of functions. Studies by Homans and Gross cast considerable light on some of these groups and their functions. In the main, both studies indicate that to to compensate for external status threats, white-collar workers turn their attention inward and get satisfaction from informal relations with peers.

Gross studied an office of 100 white-collar workers in a manufacturing firm of 1,600 employees.[31] Within this office, he found eleven cliques made up of thirty-seven office workers. Within a clique no member was a competitor of another member—that is, no two clique members did the same work and had the same supervisor. The functions of the office cliques revolved around their ability to yield to their members informal work gratification. Thus they served as media of communication, enabling members to find out what was happening in the rest of the organization. Second, they allowed highly specialized clerks to understand the significance of their role in the organization. Finally, the clique's congeniality and noncompetitiveness gave its members a great deal of satisfaction. All in all, the Gross study reveals a turning inward of white-collar workers in an effort to escape the external threats and gain a measure of informal satisfaction.

Status games. Homans' study of clerical workers reveals other functions of informal office groups in the face of external threats.[32] Homans found two groups of workers, the cash posters and the ledger posters. We need not go into detail about the nature of these two occupations other than to point out that they are different but related clerical operations. Both the cash posters

---

[31]Edward Gross, "Cliques in Office Organizations," in Neil J. Smelser, ed., *Readings on Economic Sociology* (Englewood Cliffs, NJ: Prentice-Hall, 1965), pp. 96–100.

[32]George Homans, "Status Among Clerical Workers," *Human Organization*, 12 (1953), 5–10.

and the ledger posters were classified at the same pay grade, although it was generally agreed that the ledger posters had more status. Because of the differences in their work and their status, the two work groups formed separate informal groups. Homans concentrated on the ledger posters and found them to be generally satisfied with their work. Specifically, they liked such things as the friendliness on the job, the superiors, the pay, security, responsibility, variety, opportunity for outside contacts, and the chance to solve problems. Despite their satisfacton they, like most white-collar workers, were faced with a status problem. Although they were supposed to have more status than cash posters, they received no more pay. They frequently complained when they were taken off their jobs to do lower-status cash posting. The separation of the informal groups was very functional, especially for the ledger posters. By excluding lower-status cash posters, they were able to maintain an elite informal group. Thus they were able informally to gain the greater status they were unable to gain in a formal manner on the job.

In his analysis of the modern office, Lockwood found a great concern for status and status symbols among white-collar workers.[33] Not only are they of great concern to the workers, but any effort to alter the structure of the extant status system is likely to be met by great resistance. Moreover, since these workers are highly oriented toward getting ahead, while chances of truly meaningful advances are becoming increasingly remote, slight changes in status or the acquisition of small symbols of status advancement are of great importance to the clerk. Blocked, in most cases, from any real advance, the clerical worker focuses on and gains satisfaction from the most symbolic of changes. Thus, a new desk, or even a new blotter, is likely to be cherished as a sign of advancement by the recipient and envied by peers who have not been similarly blessed. Another reason for the importance of such symbols is that many clerical jobs seem to be alike. Thus, anything that sets one's job apart from the others is likely to be highly prized. Competition for symbolic advancement has come to replace the largely disappearing chances for real advancement.

In his study of seven Parisian insurance companies, Crozier found a similar interest in status games.[34] In these games the workers sought to differentiate themselves from those above and below them. The French clerical world, like the American and the British, is highly stratified and the workers seem to like it that way. Efforts to eliminate the stratification system were opposed and even where they were successful, the workers simply set up even finer gradations among themselves. Much of the French clerical workers' involvement in their employing organization can be traced to their involvement in the stratification system and their enjoyment of status games. Crozier expected to find the French clerical workers to be a dehumanized lot, but instead, because at least in part of the status games, they seemed to be able to "flesh out" a meaningful worklife.

[33]Lockwood, *The Blackcoated Worker.*

[34]Michael Crozier, *The World of the Office Worker* (Chicago: University of Chicago: Press, 1971).

Formality. While informal relationships offer one way of alleviating status threats for white-collar workers, formality offers another. By becoming experts on the formal rules, white-collar workers are able to define for themselves specific areas of proficiency which differentiate them from blue-collar workers and make them safer from the encroachment of modern technological advancements. This also serves to reduce the threat from another source, the client. With their expertise, clerical workers gain status vis-á-vis the client and by rigidly following the rules they remain safe from criticism by superiors. This is the "bureaucratic personality" described by Merton, with its "unchallenged insistence upon punctilious adherence to formalized procedures."[35] Most studies of the bureaucratic personality, "red tape," the civil service mentality, and so forth, have emphasized the factors within the structure of a bureaucracy as the main causes. This is not debated here; instead, the goal is to point out that devices such as the bureaucratic personality are in part created by insecure bureaucrats in order to give themselves a greater measure of security and status.

Unionization. In the face of their external threats one might think that white-collar workers would turn to unions for self-defense, especially for protection against the general trends toward proletarianization. Many blue-collar unions have been able to improve pay and working conditions; why could not white-collar unions do the same? Despite logical reasons for the formation of white-collar unions, there has not been much unionization at this occupatonal level,[36] mainly because the concept of a union in itself constitutes a status threat to white-collar workers. To put it another way, joining unions is something the proletariat does. In joining unions, white collar workers believe they would be confirming and reinforcing their proletarianization, not fighting against it.

> The overwhelming majority of salesmen, typists, file clerks, and professionals will not join because they consider it beneath their dignity, because they feel differently from blue-collar workers about their jobs and their status, because they are afraid it will hurt their advancement, and because the face of the labor movement seems to them crude and exploitative.[37]

Although unionization might represent confirmation of proletarianization, it would also give white-collar workers more power to fight against unwanted changes in their work. Nevertheless, white-collar workers generally continue to ignore unionization because of what Bruner calls their "will-o'-the-wisp dig-

---

[35]Robert Merton, *Social Theory and Social Structure* (New York: Free Press, 1957), pp. 195–206.

[36]For studies of the more successful white-collar unionism in Great Britain, see Nigel Nicholson, Gill Ursell, and Paul Blyton, *The Dynamics of White Collar Unionism: A Study of Local Union Participation* (London: Academic Press, 1981); K. Prandy, A. Stewart and R.M. Blackburn, *White-Collar Unionism* (London: MacMillan, 1983).

[37]Dick Bruner, "Why White Collar Workers Can't Be Organized," in Sigmund Nosow and William H. Form, eds., *Man, Work and Society* (New York: Basic Books, 1962), p. 188.

nity."[38] Thus, as we saw in Chapter 3, as of 1978 less than 9 percent of all white-collar workers belonged to unions. Astonishingly, this percentage represents a decline from 1956 when 12.9 percent of white-collar workers were unionized.[39] On the other hand, white-collar membership in labor unions as a percentage of total membership has risen from 13.4 percent in 1956 to 18.7 percent in 1978.[40] This growth, however, is attributable to the overall growth in white-collar workers rather than to inroads in organizing such workers.

In large measure, labor unions' failure to attract white-collar workers is due to management efforts to prevent the unionization of its white-collar workforce. Management often gives as much as, or even more than, what the employees would get if they joined a union. For example, on the issue of pay one executive said: "My unionized blue-collar workers never get a thing that is not passed on and more to my office employees—and without the latter having to pay union dues."[41] On fringe benefits, another executive said: "Our aim is to gradually widen the fringe benefit gap in favor of white collar employees."[42] In addition, in their effort to keep unions out, employers give their white-collar workers special privileges, greater job security, promises of advancement, and plenty of opportunity to voice their grievances.

What is the future of white-collar unionization? It seems likely that some inroads will be made, but how great they will be remains to be seen. Despite more interest in white-collar members and more sophisticated organizing techniques, the union movement continues to have its problems, even in blue-collar sectors. The mood of the country in the 1980s is conservative and largely uninterested in unionizaton. The fact is that many white-collar workers have never been approached by a union. Jurisdictional disputes among various unions continue to impede unionization efforts. Finally, there are a number of unions that cannot adapt to the changing conditions and address themselves to this group of workers in a more modern way. On the other side, most managers continue to oppose unions and act to keep them out. It would seem, on balance, that it would take major social changes, or a major upheaval like the Great Depression, to impel large numbers of white-collar workers to join unions.

It is interesting to note that one of the few areas of gain in recent years in white-collar unionization is among grocery clerks, an occupation that is, at best, a marginal white-collar occupation. Estey calls these workers members of the "dirty white collar group."[43] Success among these workers is not easily transferable to the secretary, the stenographer, or the computer specialist. The same can be said of the increasing success in unionizing blue-collar gov-

[38]Ibid., p. 190.

[39]Albert A. Blum, "The Office Employee," in Blum et al., eds., *White Collar Workers* (New York: Random House, 1971), p. 7.

[40]*Statistical Abstract of the United States: 1984,* p. 439.

[41]Blum, "The Office Employee," p. 26.

[42]Ibid.

[43]Martin Estey, "The Retail Clerks," in Blum et al., *White Collar Workers,* pp. 46–82.

ernment workers such as post office employees, police officers, firefighters, sanitation workers, and low-status hospital workers.[44]

SALESPEOPLE

Unlike their brethren in white-collar clerical work, salespeople are not increasing rapidly. Between 1970 and 1982 the percentage of the labor force in this occupational category increased from 6.2 percent to only 6.6 percent.[45] About half of all salespeople are found in retail trade, but the percentage found in this latter area has actually declined, in part as a result of the development of self-service retail outlets. In contrast, sales positions in insurance and real estate are growing more rapidly, with the increasing insurance-consciousness of the population and the burgeoning construction of residences and offices. Thus there is a shift underway in the distribution of people in sales occupations. Females continue to dominate in retail sales, and there has been a dramatic increase in their representation in the more lucrative area of real estate sales, up from 36.7 percent of real estate salespeople in 1972 to just over 50 percent in 1982.[46] Although females have also made great strides in insurance sales (from 11.6 percent in 1972 to 26.2 percent in 1982[47]), they clearly continue to lag well behind males in this more lucrative sales area. Overall, females account for 45.4 percent of all sales workers, dramatically less than the 80.7 percent of all clerical workers.

One of the defining characteristics of sales occupations is their great insecurity. No matter how long they have been on the job, salespeople must continue to sell or they will rapidly be in danger of losing their jobs. Such positions hinge on sales and when the sales cease, so does income, and ultimately employment. One car salesman reflects this insecurity:

> Say I've been working at this place twenty years, okay? Most people's jobs, after twenty years you got seniority. You're somebody. After twenty years at this job, I go in tomorrow as if I started today. If I don't sell X amount of cars a month, I've gotta look for another job.[48]

Conflict with Customers

Although salespeople are always in highly insecure positions and are confronted with a variety of other types of stress, the basic problem is conflict with customers.[49] The workday is spent in interaction with customers, and suc-

---

[44]David Lewin and Shirley B. Goldenberg, "Public Sector Unionism in the U.S. and Canada," *Industrial Relations,* 19 (1980), 239–256.

[45]*Statistical Abstract of the United States: 1984,* p. 417.

[46]Ibid., p. 419.

[47]Ibid.

[48]Studs Terkel, *Working* (New York: Pantheon, 1974), p. 227.

[49]Although most observers of the salesperson would agree with this position, a somewhat opposing argument can be found in Alan Richardson and Meryl Stanton, "Role Strain among Salesgirls in a Department Store," *Human Relations,* 26 (1973), 517–536.

cess on the job is directly related to success in handling them. They must seek to control customers, but much of the power in the relationship lies with the customers.[50] There are two basic types of salespeople: those who seek out customers and those who are sought out by them. The door-to-door salesperson of encyclopedias, vacuum cleaners, cosmetics, and insurance falls into the first type. They must often ring a number of doorbells before a responsive customer is found. Part of the sales pitch is spent in selling the customers on the idea that the salesperson should be allowed into the house. Fast talking, subterfuges, or offers of free gifts are frequently employed. Once in the door the most important part remains, selling the product.

The second type of salesperson has only to sell the item. Car salespeople, salespeople in department stores, and so forth, don't have to gain entrance since the customers come to them. They must still sell their product, because their income is frequently determined in large part by commissions on sales. Many salespeople are paid a small salary, but this is generally not enough to live on. Thus the livelihood of salespeople depends on their ability to sell to customers, who have the balance of power. Customers can refuse to allow salespeople even to talk to them, or can walk out without buying anything after the salesperson has invested a good deal of time. It is not unusual for a customer to take up a good part of a used-car salesperson's day and then decide not to buy a car. This time spent by the salesperson is totally wasted since no income has been derived.

Coping with Conflict with Customers

There are an almost infinite number of ways in which salespeople may seek to wrest control of a situation from the customers, ranging from the "hard sell" to the "soft sell." Basically, salespeople attempt to manipulate their performance to suit the particular situation. With some types of customers they are likely to take a vigorous approach, while with others a relaxed manner works better.

Store salespeople. Mills discusses the almost infinite variety of approaches used by female salespersons in large stores.[51] He notes that this variety is a function of the nature of the salesperson, the customer, and the store. The "wolf" is one of the most aggressive, prowling the store and pouncing on customers, rather than waiting for them to come to her. One salesperson stated: "Every well-dressed customer, cranky or not, looks like a five-dollar bill to me."[52] An even more aggressive wolf is an "elbower," who is determined to get every customer: "While attending to one, she answers the question of a second, urges a third to be patient, and beckons to a fourth from the distance. Sometimes she will literally elbow her sales colleagues out of the way."[53]

[50]Shirley S. Angrist, "Selling Real Estate: Redefinition and Persuasion," in Audrey Wipper, ed., *The Sociology of Work: Papers in Honour of Oswald Hall* (Ottawa: Carleton University Press, 1984), p. 144.

[51]Mills, *White Collar*, pp. 161–188.

[52]Ibid., p. 175.

[53]Ibid.

Dalton offers us an excellent example of the procedures employed by the elbower as well as the enmity such behavior is likely to engender among coworkers:

> Mrs. Brown's most galling behavior to the group was her practice of getting sales claims on as many prospective buyers as possible. She thus deprived the other saleswomen of a chance at the buyers. For instance, as she was serving one person, she would see another coming through the door—which she nearly always faced even when busiest. Quickly she would lay a number of items before the first person with the promise to be back in a moment, then hurry to capture the second customer. If the situation were right, she might get her claim on three or four buyers while two or more of the saleswomen were reduced to maintaining the showcases, and setting things in order so as not to appear idle.[54]

The "charmer" is the salesperson who relies on her looks and smile to make sales. The "ingenue" is new to the job and relies on her self-effacing manner and the help of more experienced saleswomen to make sales. The "collegiate" is a part-time college student who relies on "her impulsive amateurishness" to make a living. The "drifter" is more concerned with gossiping with her colleagues than with making sales. The "social pretender" alienates her colleagues with her "airs," but she is attractive to wealthy customers in particular. The saleswoman who lasts to be an "old-timer" is either the "disgruntled rebel or a completely accommodated saleswoman. In either case, she is the backbone of the salesforce, the cornerstone around which it is built."[55]

Automobile salespeople.   As in virtually all sales occupations, automobile (especially used car) salespeople's major sources of conflict are customers and the agencies in which they work.[56] In the end, the power to close a deal lies with the agency. Thus, salespeople may make a deal with customers, but they must get it approved by the agency. If the agency disapproves a deal that does not meet its specifications, this leads to a mortifying situation. Says one salesperson:

> The only person harder to convince than the customer is the house . . . to get the house to sign off the car . . . they always want more money. "Make him go a little higher" is all they ever think about.[57]

The agency can also keep salespeople ignorant of things like the price of a particular car, or the commission on a certain sale. But even though the agency is a source of conflict to salespeople, it is sometimes an aid to them in making a sale. In many cases, they can use the agency as "the scapegoat, the forces of evil, the bad guys, especially when contrasted with the customer's

---

[54]Melville Dalton, "The Ratebuster: The Case of the Saleswoman," in Phyllis Stewart and Muriel Cantor, eds., *Varieties of Work Experience* (New York: Schenkman, 1974), p. 210.

[55]Ibid., p. 177.

[56]Joy Browne, *The Used Car Game: A Sociology of the Bargain* (Lexington, MA: Lexington Books, 1973).

[57]Ibid., p. 68.

friend, the salesman."[58] We will see the utility of this approach as we turn to salespeople's major source of stress—customers.

The sources of automobile salespeople's conflict with customers are manifold. First, of course, they need the income from the sale far more than the customers need the car, at least from a particular agency. Second, and related, customers have virtually all the power in the situation. No matter what automobile salespeople do, the customers ultimately decide whether or not to buy a car. Third, there is a widespread stereotype in American society that auto salespeople are dishonest. Said one, "Every guy who comes in here is sure he's getting cheated, is getting charged . . . too much for the car he buys. And every guy is sure that he's getting . . . too little for the car he's selling you."[59] To make a sale, this feeling must be overcome. Finally, the customers' ignorance about cars does not make them compliant and submissive, but often rather aggressive and unpleasant. These, and other factors, account for the conflict between automobile salespeople and customers.

For their part, automobile salespeople develop a set of stereotypes about used-car buyers, and most of them are uncomplimentary. Such unflattering views provide salespeople with justifications for their actions. Browne found five such stereotypes and five corresponding rationalizatons. First, the customer is viewed as misinformed, even ignorant, and therefore likely to make unfair demands. This is seen by the salesperson as justification for rejecting customer demands. Second, the customer is viewed as innocent, childlike, and therefore highly malleable. This entitles salespeople, from their point of view, to manipulate the customer. Third, the customer is seen as evil, disloyal, even prone to larcenous behavior. Salespeople take this as an excuse to give the customer a hard time. Fourth, the customer is seen as being out to get salespeople and this entitles salespeople to reciprocate and "get" the customer before the customer "gets" them. Finally, and more positively, the customer is seen as a source of income that is to be protected by the salesperson. All these stereotypes reflect, in one way or another, the conflict inherent in the automobile salesperson-customer relationship.

According to Miller's study of the used-car salesperson, the sales process can be broken into four stages in which we can examine the coping mechanisms employed by the salesperson.[60]

The contact may be either random or solicited by the salesperson. Customers who are unsolicited are not ideal. Many are not really in the market for a car while others are, but salespeople are reluctant to deal with them because the customer controls the negotiation and the sale. Much more important are recruited customers who are clearly in the market and whom the salesperson is able to control. Thus, one of the defining characteristics of a good salesperson is the ability to recruit customers.

In discussing the way the used-car salesperson deals with customers once they have been recruited, we are dealing with a sociological approach known as *dramaturgy.* Derived primarily from the work of Erving Goffman, this ap-

---

[58]Ibid., p. 73.

[59]Ibid., p. 45.

[60]Stephen Miller, "The Social Base of Sales Behavior," *Social Problems,* 12 (1964), 15–24.

proach views social life as similar to a theatrical stage.[61] Life is seen as a social drama in which we all put on performances to convey a desired image of ourselves. In the workworld we find that workers of every type put on dramaturgical performances to gain control over the work setting and to cope with work-related conflicts. Let us turn to a discussion of the way the used-car salesperson copes with conflict with clients through dramaturgical manipulation; later in this chapter and in Chapter 13 we will see this technique employed in various semiskilled and unskilled, and deviant, occupations.

The dramaturgical approach of the used-car salesperson can be seen in the next three stages: the pitch, the close, and cooling.

The pitch is the verbal approach used by used-car salespeople with customers. The salespeople vary what they say on the basis of what they think the customer wants to hear and what they think will help make the sale. In discussing a trade-in, taking a test drive, and seeking the customer's old car, salespeople are able to discover things about the customer which help in selling the car. Salespeople seek to find out what the customer is thinking at all times. They accomplish this by "taking the role" of the customer as well as by keeping the customer talking. At all times "the salesperson desires to keep control, in fact, achieve mastery of his relationship with the customer."[62]

The close is marked by salespeople figuratively changing sides telling the customer, in effect, "that he has gotten the best of the deal."[63] In addition, salespeople now say they will act in behalf of the customer in trying to get sales managers to "OK" such a magnificent deal. Salespeople feign a battle with sales managers and return telling the customer how much trouble they had closing the deal. Throughout the entire drama it is emphasized that the buyer is the shrewdest negotiator imaginable.

Cooling is the last stage. After the purchase, salespeople try to disengage from the customer. They now have nothing to gain from him and seek to pass him on to others in the organization so they can move on to other sales.

> The buyer is ushered to the service department where he is literally promoted from the role of buyer to that of owner and presented with the purchased automobile. The salesman foists the customer on the agency and the service manager now enters into a relationship with owner . . . The "cooling" of the buyer becomes a continuing feature of the service manager's role.[64]

The salesperson-customer conflict is an ongoing, ever-present reality. It seems to vacillate between high drama and low comedy. In either case, we should not be surprised to find that it is the dramaturgical ability of the salesperson that determines how it will turn out.

Having discussed two occupational groupings that stand at the bottom of the white-collar world, we turn now to the skilled craftspeople at the top of the blue-collar world.

[61]Erving Goffman, *The Presentation of Self in Everyday Life* (Garden City, NY: Anchor Books, 1959); *Stigma* (Englewood Cliffs, NJ: Prentice-Hall, 1963).

[62]Miller, "The Social Base of Sales Behavior," 10.

[63]Ibid., 20.

[64]Ibid., 21.

SKILLED CRAFTS

The skilled crafts encompass a wide array of strategically important occupations in society including construction workers,[65] carpenters, electricians, machinists, tool and die makers, and plumbers. As a result of technological advances and other factors, the percentage of craft workers in the total labor force declined from 13.5 percent in 1975 to 12.8 percent in 1982.[66] Because of the significance of their tasks, the skilled crafts have developed some of the most powerful unions in the United States. And it is these unions that have made skilled craftspeople among the highest paid hourly workers in America. In fact, they often earn more money per week than clerical workers and sales workers. In 1982, the median weekly earnings for a full-time craft worker was $375, while it was only $248 for clerical workers and $317 for sales workers. While they earned a good deal more than clerical and sales workers, craft workers earned not much less than managers ($430) and professionals ($410).[67]

Although they may earn a higher dollar amount per year, skilled craftspeople suffer in comparison to white-collar clerical (and sales) workers on a variety of dimensions, such as the need to punch a time clock and their lower job security.[68]

Although at one time virtually all workers were skilled craftspeople, the history of the modern skilled craftsperson can be traced to fourteenth-century Europe.[69] It is at this time that we find the first craftsperson who "owned not only the tools but also the raw materials and, in some cases, the workshop."[70] These early craftspeople were organized into guilds which served to further their interests as well as assuming a responsibility to the community for quality goods at a fair price. They worked on an individual basis mainly because there were as yet no large industries, and since there were no industries the major work organization was the occupation and its guild. It is from involvement in the guilds and lack of involvement in industry that the craftspeople developed their sense of autonomy. However, the old guild system broke down in the wake of modernization:

> The regulated economy of the guild town disintegrated with the growth of a centralized state organization, unification of large economic areas and radical changes in the technique of production and distribution which came in the seventeenth and eighteenth centuries. Commercializaton and later mechanization

[65]Marc Silver, "The Structure of Craft Work: The Construction Industry," in Phyllis Stewart and Muriel Cantor, eds., *Varieties of Work* (Beverly Hills: Sage, 1982), pp. 235–252; Jack Haas, "Learning Real Feelings: A Study of High Steel Ironworkers' Reactions to Fear and Danger," *Sociology of Work and Occupations*, 4 (1977), 147–170.

[66]*Statistical Abstract of the United States: 1984*, p. 417.

[67]Ibid., p. 434.

[68]Gavin Mackensie, *The Aristocracy of Labor: The Position of Skilled Craftsmen in the American Class Structure* (London: Cambridge University Press, 1973).

[69]Arthur Salz, "Occupations in Their Historical Perspective," in Nosow and Form, *Man, Work and Society*, pp. 58–63.

[70]Ibid., p. 62.

of industry resulted in a regrouping of occupations and eventually in the creation of a new occupational order.[71]

That new occupational order forced the vast majority of skilled craftspeople into large industries in which their old notions of autonomy were opposed: the principles of formal organizations stood in direct contrast to the principle of autonomy. Some skilled craftspeople have avoided employment in formal organizations and continue to work on their own, but their problem is more one of survival than of autonomy—they have many of the problems of a small proprietor.

Threats to Autonomy

Skilled craftspeople are in many ways similar to professionals. Like professionals they feel a sense of autonomy: after all, only they know how to perform their particular tasks. Despite this ideology, their autonomy is continually threatened. One reason is that significant others do not accept the view that they have the general systematic knowledge of professionals. Because they have less status and little theoretical knowledge, laypeople are much more likely to question skilled workers than professionals. But the most important threat to their autonomy stems from the fact that, with the growth of huge industries, they are increasingly employees of organizations, subject to control from above, frequently from superiors with little knowledge of their specialty. As we have seen in the case of professionals, it is difficult to sustain autonomy within an organization. In the case of skilled workers it is even harder to maintain because of their lower status and lack of a powerful professional association.

While we contend that skilled craftspeople are "like" professionals, Stinchcombe goes further in his discussion of "professional" construction workers,[72] in which he argues that construction workers go through a process of technical socialization and as a result are recognized as being competent in their area by the public. He sees the construction union as analogous to a professional association and as an agency that ensures that those who are trained by it are hired preferentially.

Stinchcombe further points out that for a number of reasons that relate to the structure of the construction industry, it cannot be, and is not, run bureaucratically. For one, the amount and kind of work done are highly variable—there are periods when there is much work and periods when much of the workforce is laid off. The kind of work required also varies from one site to another. In addition, the work is widely dispersed geographically. For all these reasons it would be inefficient to organize construction work bureaucratically, and thus, according to Stinchcombe, it is organized professionally. Decisions are made autonomously by the work crews rather than dictated from the top. The construction industry has an attenuated organizational

[71]Ibid., pp. 62–63.

[72]Arthur Stinchcombe, "Bureaucratic and Craft Administration of Production: A Comparative Study," *Administrative Science Quarterly*, 4 (1959), 168–187.

structure with relatively few bureaucrats employed. Communication is not from the top down, but built into the contracts. Further, the contracts specify only goals of the work and prices; how the job is to be performed is left to the construction worker. Stinchcombe contends that these specifications do not have to be there because of the "professionalized culture" of the construction workers.

While Stinchcombe is correct in his analysis of the construction industry, he is using the term "professional" far too liberally. Skilled craftspeople have many characteristics in common with professionals, but these crafts lack a number of aspects of the professional model. Most importantly, it is clear that a blue-collar occupation cannot (in our society at least) gain enough power to win professional recognition. Nevertheless, skilled craftspeople face many of the same problems as professionals employed in organizations.

The threat of management.   Management, generally in the form of immediate supervisors, poses the greatest threat to the skilled craftsperson's autonomy.[73] Most craftspeople take a great deal of pride in their work and feel that since only they have the skills, only they should judge their work. Yet management frequently has different goals, and this is the source of the conflict. Management feels that only it has the "big picture," and that therefore it must supervise the activities of all its workers, including skilled craftspeople. Knowing it must meet a deadline, management may request its skilled craftspeople to work harder or to take shortcuts. Squeezed by cost pressures, management may force skilled workers to cut a variety of corners. As a result of these kinds of pressures, Riemer concludes that "we are beginning to see an increase in shoddy workmanship in the construction of our public and private buildings."[74]

The threat of customers.   In the case of at least some skilled craftspeople, customers constitute another threat to autonomy.[75] As Glaser points out, customers have far more power in their relationships with skilled workers than clients do in their dealings with professionals.[76] In his study of the relationship between building subcontractors and their customers, Glaser found that a major source of the power of customers is their ability to get numerous bids from different subcontractors. Knowing that they must compete with others, subcontractors are likely to be highly responsive to customers, at least until they obtain a contract. Once they have that, subcontractors have considerable power and are able to do such things as leaving one job unfinished to handle another more pressing or more lucrative job. Yet customers retain their own

[73]Jeffrey W. Riemer, "Worker Autonomy in the Skilled Building Trades," in Phyllis Stewart and Muriel Cantor, eds., *Varieties of Work*, p. 231. See also, Jeffrey Riemer, *Hard Hats: The Work World of Construction Workers* (Beverly Hills, CA: Sage Publications, 1979).

[74]Riemer, *Hard Hats*, p. 163.

[75]Riemer also mentions nonunion workers and the general public as threats to the unionized skilled craftsperson. Jeffrey Riemer, "Worker Autonomy in the Skilled Building Trades," p. 232.

[76]Barney G. Glaser, *The Patsy and the Subcontractor: A Study of the Expert-Layman Relationship* (Mill Valley, CA: The Sociology Press, 1972).

bases of power until the end of the relationship. A major source of this power lies in the fact that customers do not pay until the job is completed. In general, customers can constitute a threat to the autonomy of skilled craftspeople.

Coping with Threats to Autonomy: Formal Means

The major function of skilled trade unions is to prevent managerial encroachment on autonomy. Because they are among the strongest unions,[77] the skilled trades unions have been unusually successful in warding off this threat. To examine how this operates, let us look at the history of the International Typographical Union (ITU), which until recently[78] was extremely successful in protecting the autonomy of typographers on the job. According to Perlman and Taft, the ITU had "the most complete control over job conditions of any union in the world."[79] All workers in the composing room, even foremen, had to belong to the ITU before they could be considered for a job. The inclusion of foremen meant that they were far more responsive to the union than they were to management. If a foreman violated union regulations, he was subject to a fine. In this way, a major managerial tool was brought under the union's control, and this fact alone severely restricted management's power to dictate terms to the skilled workers. The ITU, however, went far beyond this in its efforts to maintain the autonomy of its members.

In the printing industry it was the workers, not management, who ran their workplace, the composing room. Management had only the broad right to determine the way the work was supposed to be done. The job, however, belonged to the printer, not to the foreman or the shop. A good example of the printer's control over his job was the way in which replacements were selected if the worker decided to take a day off. In almost every other job it is the company that determines the substitute; in the printing industry the regular printer decided who would temporarily replace him. An even clearer example of the printer's power was the fact that no nonunion employee was allowed on the shop floor. This meant that the union could prevent the owner of the company from setting foot in the composing room. Lipset et al. point out that this rule was rarely enforced:

> Yet its existence is a reminder of a power relationship, and it may be invoked when the workers in a given shop have a grievance. In one New York newspaper some time ago the men stopped working when a well-known anti-labor columnist who had written articles attacking the ITU walked into the composing room to deliver his copy.[80]

The ITU controlled hiring in the printing industry. Union rules, which

---

[77]Jeffrey W. Riemer, "Worker Autonomy in the Skilled Building Trades," p. 230.

[78]Michael Wallace and Arne Kalleberg, "Industrial Transformation and the Decline of Craft: The Decomposition of Skill in the Printing Industry, 1931–1978," *American Sociological Review,* 47 (1982), 307–324.

[79]Seymour Martin Lipset, Martin Trow, and James Coleman, *Union Democracy* (Garden City, NY: Anchor Books, 1962), p. 24.

[80]Ibid., p. 26.

were accepted by management, stated that workers must be hired (or fired) in accord with the union's seniority list. The union had a list of substitute workers and when a permanent opening occurred it had to be given to the substitute with the most seniority "regardless of the employer's or foreman's opinion of the relative capabilities of available men."[81] When there was to be a reduction in force the company had to lay off the employee with the least seniority.

The ITU had a series of laws which determined "conditions of employment, maximum length of work-week or work day, . . . closed shop, use of reproduced material, control over all composing-room work, and other work conditions."[82] These laws were defined by the union as nonnegotiable; that is, management had to accept them if they wished to be in the printing business. If management objected to any portion of union law, or wished to lay off a worker with seniority, it had to make its appeal within the union structure. It could appeal to the local union, the national union, or to the convention, but the final decision rested with the union. There were many disputes between publishers and the union on this issue, but in general the union was able to maintain its control. According to Lipset et al.: "In large measure printers have demanded and won the right to be treated as independent craftsmen who control their own work and maintain and enforce their own standards of workmanship."[83]

Although the ITU was more successful than other craft unions in protecting its members' autonomy, it is not completely different from other craft unions. Almost all craft unions have been able to employ a variety of techniques to protect member autonomy. Most are able to control job entry through the apprenticeship system. (Apprenticeship usually involves the lengthy training of the neophyte by an established journeyman.) This program performs a variety of functions for the skilled trades. Management may only hire as skilled craftsmen those who have successfully completed the program. The training of new skilled workers is determined by the union and its members, not the management: this keeps the number of skilled tradesmen low, giving them high job security and wages. Finally, the union sets the wages for apprentices and prevents them from competing with journeymen when they near the end of their training program. Many skilled trade unions also utilize a union shop and this in fact gives them control of the selection of new employees. Under this system employers may hire whom they wish, but the employee is required to join the union within a specified period of time. Skilled trade unions frequently have hiring halls in which unemployed members are referred to employers who have reported vacancies. Legal changes made it necessary that these hiring halls accept nonunion workers, but these nonmembers were referred only on a token basis.

There are a number of other devices employed by skilled trade unions, in particular, to increase the autonomy of their members. Some have rules that determine the number of workers that must be used on a given job. Such

[81]Ibid., p. 24.
[82]Ibid., p. 25.
[83]Ibid., p. 31.

efforts to set work crews, which management generally feels forces them to use unneeded manpower, are common among railroad workers and musicians. A variant of this is union efforts to set up "make-work" requirements. For example, painters may be forbidden to use rollers, although it is more efficient to do so. Other skilled unions attempt to set the work pace as well as wages, hours, and working conditions. Seniority rules are utilized in virtually all types of unions, skilled and nonskilled, to give the union control of hiring and firing.

Although skilled crafts unions have been, and continue to be, important in protecting the autonomy of skilled workers, it is important to point out that in general their strength is declining. Both Riemer in his study of the building trades and, much more strikingly, Wallace and Kalleberg in their study of printers show a decline in the power of the skilled crafts unions. Based on their analysis, Wallace and Kalleberg contend that it "is likely that the erosion of craft skills in the composing room, indeed the total elimination of many printing jobs, will continue into the foreseeable future."[84] What trends like these mean is that skilled crafts unions are less and less able to protect not only the autonomy of craft workers, but their very existence in the workworld.

Coping with Threats to Autonomy: Informal Means

In addition to the formal methods employed by the unions, skilled craftspeople employ a variety of informal means to protect their sense of autonomy. Note that the emphasis here is on the sense of autonomy rather than the autonomy itself. The union structure is a much more important contributor to actual autonomy than is the informal organization. Nevertheless, the informal organization does also, to some degree, contribute to actual autonomy. However, the preeminent function of the informal organization in the skilled trades is the preservation of a feeling, or sense, of autonomy.

The printers, once again, are the best example of the development of such an informal organization. Lipset et al. point out that printers traditionally considered themselves an elite blue-collar occupation because of their great skill and their high degree of literacy. They were one of the first cohesive, informal work groups, and this informal structure, after first serving to preserve the autonomy of its members, was soon transformed into a formal union. Later, an elaborate informal structure coexisted with the formal union hierarchy. It fulfilled a variety of social functions, some of which were related to the preservation of autonomy. For example, there were a series of informal norms, violations of which were punished by the group. As mentioned earlier, since foremen were members of the union, this was an important method of preventing encroachment on autonomy by first-line supervisors. If the foremen tried to interfere with the printers' traditional activities, they were likely to be sanctioned severely by the informal group. This was a weapon that was peculiar to the printing industry, since in few other industries were members of management also members of the union.

The fact that there was a high degree of informal, off-the-job interaction

---

[84]Wallace and Kalleberg, "Industrial Transformation and the Decline of Craft," 322.

among printers also helped preserve their sense of autonomy. Social interaction did little to preserve actual autonomy, but it did give printers a sense of their different and elite status among blue-collar workers. As Lipset et al. point out, the informal relations among printers were almost unbelievably elaborate:

> Social clubs, organized leisure activities such as bowling leagues, and union newspapers are of course not unique to the printers, although we know of no other occupation which has as many and diverse forms of organized extravocational activities as the ITU. . . . many printers reported that their best friends are other printers, that they regularly visit the homes of other printers, that they often meet in bars, go fishing together, or see each other in various places before and after work. . . . there is also more socializing among printers on the job than we find in most occupations.[85]

Control over uncertainty.   Crozier's study of a French bureaucracy reveals another aspect of the informal autonomy of skilled craftspeople[86] in a discussion of the relationship between the unskilled production workers and the skilled maintenance employees. The maintenance workers, because of the nature of their work, are free and independent from control by production workers. On the other hand, the production workers are highly dependent on the maintenance employees. The autonomy of the maintenance workers and the dependency of the production workers center around machine stoppages. When a machine breaks down only the maintenance workers have the skill to fix it and they cannot, because of their skill, be directly supervised by anyone in the organization. Hence in this central event in the life of an industrial organization, maintenance people are almost totally autonomous, while production workers cannot fix the problem themselves and therefore must rely on the maintenance people. Also, the breakdown of the machines is a highly important event for production workers:

> Production workers are displeased by the consequences of a machine stoppage. It disrupts their work; it is likely to make it necessary for them to work harder to compensate for lost time; and if it lasts long enough, they will be displaced, losing friendship ties and even status.[87]

Because they have power over both production workers and supervisors in this situation, maintenance workers emerged as the most powerful figures on the shop floor. Their power stemmed from their ability to control uncertainty, specifically the centrally important event of machine breakdown. Although they have power, it is not legitimate power. Thus they are insecure in their power position due to threats to that power from other actors on the shop floor. Nevertheless, their skilled status has given them a great deal of autonomy within the French bureaucracy studied by Crozier. This finding may also be generalizable to other industrial settings in the sense that many skilled

---

[85]Lipset et al., *Union Democracy*, p. 78.

[86]Michel Crozier, *The Bureaucratic Phenomenon* (Chicago: University of Chicago Press, 1967).

[87]Ibid., p. 109.

craftspeople have the rather unique ability to control uncertainty and hence gain informal power in the organization.

Although the discussion in this section has focused on only two skilled crafts, there is evidence that many skilled trades utilize these devices to protect autonomy. A look at the formal and informal organization of carpenters, plumbers, electricians, and others shows many of the same protective mechanisms. They all have strong unions, apprenticeship programs, and strong informal organizations. One of the major goals of each of these devices is the protection of the skilled craftsman's autonomy.

FREE SEMISKILLED AND UNSKILLED OCCUPATIONS

We have already discussed free professionals such as physicians and lawyers in private practice. Similar to free professionals, those in free semiskilled and unskilled occupations may either work outside bureaucracies (for example, the independent taxi driver), or if they are employees of organizations, much of their worklife takes place outside the bureaucratic structure per se (for example, a bus driver).

Conflict with Customer/Clients

Individuals in free unskilled or semiskilled occupations face many of the same problems that confront free professionals. Customer/clients represent the major source of stress for free professionals as well as those in "free" unskilled or semiskilled occupations.[88] The problems of the latter are much greater, however, since they are of lower status and therefore do not possess the authority that professionals have in dealing with clients. Those in unskilled or semiskilled occupations must be able to handle their customer/clients without this authority.

Taxi drivers. The problem of dealing with customers is perhaps greatest for taxi drivers. As Davis points out, the relationships between drivers and their customers are "fleeting."[89] It is this characteristic which differentiates the taxi driver-customer relationship from most other service relationships, where there usually are a series of constraints that keep interaction within certain boundaries. However, most of these constraints are lacking in the driver-passenger relationship. In general, "the cab-driver's day consists of a long series of brief contacts with unrelated persons of whom he has no foreknowledge, just as they have none of him, and whom he is not likely to encounter again."[90] Cab drivers are never confronted with the same role-set—it varies from day to day. Control of interaction is in the hands of the customers and

[88]Richard A. Peterson, John T. Schmidman and Kirk W. Elifson, "Entrepreneurship or Autonomy?: Truckers and Cabbies," in Phyllis L. Stewart and Muriel G. Cantor, eds., *Varieties of Work*, pp. 181–198.

[89]Fred Davis, "The Cabdriver and His Fare: Facets of a Fleeting Relationship," *American Journal of Sociology*, 65 (1959), 158–165.

[90]Ibid., 159.

thus the drivers are subject to such things as "stick-ups, belligerent drunks, women in labor, psychopaths, counterfeiters, and fare-jumpers."[91] As Henslin puts it, "the cabbie regularly confronts passengers who threaten his self, his routine, and sometimes his property or even his life."[92]

The taxi drivers' inability to control their customers is also tied to their lack of esoteric skill. Most people who ride in cabs also can drive and also know their way around the city. Therefore, cabbies are subject to much second-guessing about their driving ability as well as the routes they select. States Henslin: "Some passengers berate him for not going fast enough or for missing a green light, while others withhold the tip as a sanction against something they did not like about the driver."[93]

The power of the passengers is reflected in a variety of other problems they pose for the drivers:

> The cabbie must also put up with persons who are "playing." (In "cabby-ese" this refers to those who call in and have a cab dispatched to a location where no one desires a cab.) Other callers are present when he arrives but refuse to enter the cab. Still others, "bucket loads," skip out without paying their fare. Other passengers demand services he is unwilling to provide, such as locating a prostitute or entering an area of the city which the driver considers to be unsafe after dark.[94]

Of course, the ultimate threat posed by the passengers is to the safety of the drivers. The fact is that drivers are constantly in danger of being mugged, robbed, even murdered. The drivers are ever aware of the threat posed by strangers who are sitting behind them in a perfect position to do harm. The drivers are defenseless since they are usually prohibited by law from carrying weapons, although some drivers violate this law for their own protection.

Taxi drivers are, in Goffman's terms, frequently treated as if they were "nonpersons." That is, customers behave as if the drivers were not even present. Because they are at times treated like nonpersons, they are unable to control interactions:

> Passengers sometimes do not adjust their behavior to his presence—any more than they would for a steering wheel of an auto. When intimate arguments are fought out in the cab between lovers, for example, it is as though the cab driver was merely a non-human extension of the steering wheel, a kind of machine which guides the cab. Such interaction in all its varied aspects–the tones and loudness of voice, the words used, the subjects spoken about–takes place as though the individuals were in private, with no third person present. The effect on the cabbie of some types of non-person treatment is challenging of the self since others are not acknowledging his self but acting as though he did not exist.[95]

[91] Ibid.

[92] James Henslin, "The Underlife of Cabdriving: A Study in Exploitation and Punishment," in Phyllis Stewart and Muriel Cantor, eds., *Varieties of Work Experience*, p. 69.

[93] Ibid., p. 70.

[94] Ibid.

[95] Ibid., p. 69.

On other occasions, because of the fleeting nature of the relationship, drivers become confidants on extremely personal matters. They are people "to whom intimacies can be revealed and opinions forthrightly expressed with little fear of rebuttal, retaliation, or disparagement."[96]

Tips represent an important source of income for the drivers, as well as symbols of success.[97] Given their inability to control their customers, they are also unable to control this important source of economic and symbolic reward.

It should be pointed out that while taxi drivers are subject to the control, even abuse, of clients, they are largely free of organizational control. Peterson, Schmidman, and Elifson found that self-employed taxi drivers (and truck drivers) were motivated to buy their own cabs by a desire to be autonomous; in fact, they acted "more out of a desire for autonomy than out of a desire for entrepreneurship."[98] As a result, taxi drivers do not have to cope with the high degree of alienation that confronts fellow unskilled or semi-skilled workers (see Chapter 12) who spend their workdays within an organization. In support of this position, Peterson found that the taxi drivers' "level of subjective alienation was as low as many of the free professionals and markedly lower than that of blue-collar workers generally."[99] This freedom from organizational control has the positive consequence of reducing alienation and the negative effect of increasing conflict with clients.

Bus drivers.   Although their stress is not as great as that of taxi drivers, bus drivers must also cope with conflict with passengers. There is less contact, less privacy, less danger, and no tip in the bus driver-passenger relationship. The absence of these factors serves to reduce, but not eliminate, the conflict. An interesting example of this conflict is offered by Toren in her study of Israeli bus drivers.[100] She found conflict was exacerbated when the passengers were relative newcomers to Israel and unfamiliar with urban life in general and the norms of bus travel in particular. Such passengers cause great trouble for the driver because they continually violate the norms. One driver described his plight this way:

> They don't know how to behave! They don't know what it means to stand in line; they haggle about the fare as if they were in the market; sometimes they even jump through the windows. . . . These passengers want me to give information and advice, to be a social worker and a father, and sometimes also a driver![101]

[96]Davis, "The Cabdriver and His Fare," 160.

[97]Peterson, Schmidman and Elifson, "Entrepreneurship or Autonomy?: Truckers and Cabbies," p. 193.

[98]Ibid., p. 195.

[99]Richard A. Peterson, *The Industrial Order and Social Policy* (Englewood Cliffs, NJ: Prentice-Hall, 1973), p. 88.

[100]Nina Toren, "The Bus Driver: A Study in Role Analysis," *Human Relations*, 26 (1973), 107-112.

[101]Ibid., 103.

Although this is an extreme situation, urban American bus drivers face similar problems with immigrants, foreign visitors, rural tourists, and others. This, of course, says nothing of the far more common type of conflict with the belligerent native urban passengers the drivers are likely to encounter many times during the day.

Waitresses and waiters.   Waiters,[102] waitresses,[103] and more specifically cocktail waitresses,[104] stand somewhere between taxi drivers and bus drivers in terms of conflict with customers. They are more troubled than bus drivers, but face less conflict than taxi drivers. Customers are certainly very important to waiters and waitresses, determining to a large extent how well their work night (or day) goes. Customers create all sorts of problems, including drunkenness, belligerence, complaints to the boss about service, and in the case of waitresses, sexual advances. Much conflict surrounds the desire of waiters and waitresses to be respected and the customers' propensity to act superior to them. Finally, as is also true of the taxi driver, the tip is significant to waiters and waitresses both as symbols of success and as a source of income. The customer controls the size of the tip and, indeed, whether or not a tip is left. This is a continuing source of stress to waiters and waitresses:

> Tips? I feel like Carmen. It's like holding out a tambourine and they throw the coin. (Laughs) There might be occasions when the customers might make it demeaning—the man about town, the conventioneer. When the time comes to pay the check, he would do little things, "How much should I give you?" He might make an issue about it. I did say to one, "Don't play God with me. Do what you want." Then it really didn't matter whether I got a tip or not. I would spit it out, my resentment—that he dares make me feel I'm operating only for a tip. He'd ask for his check. Maybe he's going to sign it. He'd take a very long time and he'd make me stand there, "Let's see now, what do you think I ought to give you?" He would not let go of that moment. And you know it. You know he meant to demean you. He's holding the change in his hand, or if he'd sign, he'd flourish the pen and wait. These are the times I really get angry. I'm not reticent. Something would come out. Then I really didn't care. "Goddamn, keep your money!"[105]

Emergency medical technicians.   In his book *Running Hot,* Donald Metz discusses emergency medical technicians, the people who staff ambulances

[102]Gerald Mars and Michael Nicod, *The World of Waiters* (London: George Allen and Unwin, 1984).

[103]Suellen Butler and William B. Snizek, "Waitress-Diner Relationships," *Sociology of Work and Occupations,* 3 (1976), 209–221; Suellen Butler and James K. Skipper, Jr., "Waitressing, Vulnerability, and Job Autonomy: The Case of the Risky Tip," *Sociology of Work and Occupations,* 7 (1980), 487–502; Suellen Butler and James K. Skipper, "Working for Tips: An Examination of Trust and Reciprocity in a Secondary Relationship of the Restaurant Industry," *The Sociological Quarterly,* 22 (1981), 15–27; Suellen Butler and James K. Skipper, Jr., "Working the Circuit: An Explanation of Employee Turnover in the Restaurant Industry," *Sociological Spectrum,* 3 (1983), 19–33.

[104]H. L. Hearn and Patricia Stoll, "Continuance Commitment in Low-Status Occupations: The Cocktail Waitress," *Sociological Quarterly,* 16 (1975), 105–114.

[105]Terkel, *Working,* p. 295.

and deal with medical emergencies.[106] Metz describes this as a low-status occupation in which workers are *"free from close supervision."*[107] The major source of stress for emergency medical technicians is the patient. Many of the patients are very ill, or in danger of dying, when they enter the ambulance. At the beginning of their careers, technicians have a deep emotional involvement with patients, but after a relatively brief period of time the mortally ill patients begin to blur into one another and the technicians develop a more detached attitude toward the patients as well as routine methods of dealing with them. Nevertheless, the nature of the work makes the sick patient a continuing source of stress to the emergency medical technicians.

At times, emergency medical technicians find themselves in adversary relationships with patients. On the one hand, there are times when the technicians arrive on the scene only to find that the patient really does not require conveyance to a hospital. However, it is often the case that family, bystanders, and perhaps even the patient want the patient to be taken to a hospital. Adding to the conflict here is the fact that the technicians are always afraid of making a mistake and not transporting a patient who really should have been taken to the hospital. On the other hand, there are patients who are reluctant to go to the hospital even though the technician thinks such action is necessary.

Dead and dying patients represent a particular source of stress to emergency medical technicians. For one thing, technicians do not like the fact that society defines dealing with dead bodies as "dirty work." For another, there are likely to be a variety of unpleasantries involved since the body may have undergone some decomposition. Most importantly, it is not easy to define someone as dead since the line between death and dying is ambiguous. Here there is great pressure on the technician, especially when a patient has just died. It is possible for the technician to misdefine someone as dead.

Then there are a variety of types of patients who are dangerous to the emergency medical technician. Among these are patients with communicable diseases, belligerent drunks, the emotionally unstable, or patients with weapons.

Janitors. Apartment building janitors face problems in dealing with their tenants.[108] The technical aspects of the job are relatively easy to master and present no real problem—the major source of anxiety is the attainment of the social skills needed to control the building's tenants. Janitors seek to gain respect and recognition from the tenants and a good deal of their time is spent in "training" the tenants to give them respect. Gaining respect from tenants depends to a large extent on their social class. Upper-class tenants seem to be easier to get along with because they do not perceive janitors as status threats. On the other hand, tenants who are in occupations as marginal as

---

[106]Donald L. Metz, *Running Hot: Structure and Stress in Ambulance Work* (Cambridge, MA: Abt Books, 1981).

[107]Ibid., p. 66.

[108]Raymond L. Gold, "In the Basement—the Apartment-Building Janitor," in Peter L. Berger, ed., *The Human Shape of Work* (New York: Macmillan, 1964), pp. 1–49.

janitorial work are often regarded as troublemakers. Another factor affecting the ability of janitors to handle their tenants is the nature of the owner of the building or the real estate agent. If these individuals grant the janitors autonomy, they will be better able to train recalcitrant tenants. If they are not granted this authority, their task is much more difficult.

Police officers.   The major source of stress for police officers is the public and the threat the public poses to police and their authority.[109]

> The policeman cannot permit his authority to be challenged successfully . . . no matter what the social status of the individual and no matter what the situational context in which the encounter takes place, the policeman's authority is the crux of police-citizen encounters.[110]

In trying to maintain order, police officers are thrust into circumstances where there is unpredictable danger. They know what might happen when they are chasing a robber, but such tasks are not a major portion of their job. More time is spent in dealing with such things as interpersonal disputes[111] (such as family squabbles), weapons calls, and fights in public places;[112] situations that, in the police view, are "unpredictable, high-risk, and have a high potential for injury or something more serious."[113] They are generally not welcomed under such conditions and must use their own discretion in a situation that is "one of conflict and in an environment that is apprehensive and perhaps hostile."[114] In such situations they are dealing with areas in which the law is ambiguous (such problems as disorderly conduct, disturbing the peace) and therefore does not provide them with firm guidelines. They frequently must depend on the cooperation of injured parties, but injured parties are often unwilling to cooperate,[115] regarding it as a personal matter or feeling unwill-

---

[109]Although most observers see the problems of the police officer primarily in their relations with the public, there are other points of view. For example, Galliher sees the basic problem as role conflict. Police officers stand between a dominant social class that wishes them to regulate the behavior of the lower classes and those members of the lower class that resent such regulation and use the police as a scapegoat for their antagonism toward the upper classes. Even more generally, Galliher sees the police officer as a victim of the class conflict endemic to capitalist society. See, James F. Galliher, "Explanations of Police Behavior: A Critical Review and Analysis," *Sociological Quarterly,* 12 (1971), 306–318; Egon Bittner, "The Police on Skid Row," *American Sociological Review,* 32 (1967), 699–716.

[110]James R. Hudson, "Police-Citizen Encounters that Lead to Citizen Complaints," *Social Problems,* 18 (1970), 193.

[111]Douglas A. Smith and Jody R. Klein, "Police Control of Interpersonal Disputes," *Social Problems,* 31 (1984), 468–481; see also, Donald Black, *The Manners and Customs of the Police* (New York: Academic Press, 1980), especially Chapter 5.

[112]Philip A. Russo, Jr., Alan S. Engel, and Steven H. Hatting, "Police and Occupational Stress: An Empirical Investigation," in Richard R. Bennett, ed., *Police at Work: Policy Issues and Analysis* (Beverly Hills, CA: Sage, 1983), pp. 89–106.

[113]Ibid., p. 94.

[114]James Q. Wilson, *Varieties of Police Behavior* (Cambridge: Harvard University Press, 1968), p. 21.

[115]Bell reports in one study of domestic violence that in 76 percent of the incidents, no criminal complaints were initiated; see, Daniel J. Bell, "The Police Response to Domestic Violence: A Replication Study," *Police Studies: An International Review of Police Development,* 7 (1984), 141.

ing to get involved with the law over such an issue. Thus police officers are expected to do something, but the victims are unwilling to help. In such crises they are supposed to handle the situation in a routine manner, but such impersonal behavior often exasperates the participants.

Police officers are thus frequently in the position of being unable to satisfy the public's needs. This is extremely frustrating to the public because it occurs in a situation that is both important and emotionally charged. When police officers are dealing with the lower class they tend to judge beforehand that their complaints are not legitimate, and this further increases public hostility. In sum, the police deal with the public in an environment they feel is charged with suspicion, emotion, hostility, and uncooperativeness.

Police officers see themselves as continually called upon to make "quick decisions about what their (people's) behavior has been in the past or is likely to be in the future."[116] They must rapidly evaluate such factors as social class, race, appearance, status, and influence. They must be ever alert to danger signals. This constant possibility of danger[117] may make them tense and likely to overreact when there is some danger.

It is interesting to note that the policewoman is placed in an extraordinarily conflict-laden position. She must deal with the same conflicts as the patrolman as well as an additional set derived from being a female in a "male" occupation. Martin describes the dilemma of the patrolwoman:

> . . . in addition to the recurrent uncertainties faced by all officers in dealing with often reluctant citizens, police women face contradictory expectations and inappropriate behavior by citizens. As an officer the policewoman is required to take control and act with authority. As a woman she is expected to act in a different fashion—as a subordinate seeking displays of chivalry and deferential behavior.[118]

Coping With Customer Conflicts: Typologies

In the preceding section we dealt with a number of examples of conflict with customers and/or clients faced by those in free unskilled and semiskilled occupations. We now examine a variety of efforts to cope with this conflict. The first type of coping mechanism entails developing typologies of client/ customers. Mennerick contends that typologies perform at least five functions: they facilitate work, increase control, increase gain, reduce danger, and restrict interaction with those who are considered to be morally unacceptable.[119] In the following discussion we will focus on the use of typologies to increase control over the customer/client.

[116]Wilson, *Varieties of Police Behavior*, p. 38.

[117]Robert E. Little, "Cop-Killing: A Descriptive Analysis of the Problem," *Police Studies: An International Review of Police Development*, 7 (1984), 68–76.

[118]Susan Ehrlich Martin, *Breaking and Entering: Police Women on Patrol* (Berkeley: University of California Press, 1980), pp. 158–159.

[119]Lewis Mennerick, "Client Typologies: A Method of Coping with Conflict in the Service Worker-Client Relationship," *Sociology of Work and Occupations*, 1 (1974), 396–418. Mennerick shows that typologies are used by a wide array of service occupations, not just those considered to be semi- and unskilled; see, Lewis Mennerick, "Client Typologies and Occupational Role Autonomy: Correctional System Personnel," in Phyllis Stewart and Muriel Cantor, eds., *Varieties of Work*, pp. 257–267.

Taxi drivers.   In the discussion of taxi drivers, the symbolic and economic importance of the tip has already been pointed out. Despite its importance, drivers have no control over whether they will get a tip or how large it will be. To reduce this uncertainty, they develop typologies of passengers[120] on the basis of the size and likelihood of a tip. The *sport* is generally a local celebrity who will treat the driver well and is likely to give a large tip. The *blowhard* is a phony sport who talks big, but does not tip as well as the sport. The *businessperson* is the staple of the taxi business since he or she is the most frequent user of a cab. Although businesspersons are not big tippers, they are generally fair ones. The *lady shopper* also frequently uses the taxi, but she is a notoriously low tipper. The *live one* is generally an out-of-towner who is, at least potentially, the source of the largest tip.

By placing the passenger in one of these types drivers do nothing to increase the size of their tip, but they at least have an idea of what to expect from each passenger.

Waiters.   Waiters also were found to use typologies in dealing with customers, although not all these types relate to tipping behavior.[121] Someone who is known to be a good tipper may be referred to as "good for a drop," while customers who do not tip at all are said to have "stiffed" the waiter. Other kinds of customers are also typified:

> Awkward customers are variously described as "bastard," "bitch," and so on. "Prostitute" is a term applied to women whose appearance suggests that they have been hired from an escort agency. "Peasants" are people whose conduct and appearance give the impression that they are not accustomed to dining out. A "snob" is someone who knows (or *thinks* he knows) how to behave and tries to draw attention to the fact whenever he can.[122]

Typologies such as these enable waiters to better deal with their customers.

Emergency medical technicians.   Metz found that emergency medical technicians also use typologies in dealing with patients. "Good runs" are those in which the technicians are able to use their professional skills with patients and/or those in which something interesting happens. "Shit runs" are those in which the technicians are wasting their time. Various types of patients are involved in shit runs. *Walkers* are those patients who are able to walk to the ambulance thereby demonstrating that they do not need emergency help. While walkers are at least able to pay for the ambulance service, *twenty-sevens* (the company code for bums and drunks) are not. They, too, lack serious symptoms and are seen by the technicians as a waste of time. *Regulars* are patients who call ambulances over and over even though they have no medical problem at all. Finally, there are the *fakers* who "get themselves in an ambulance call and then put on a show to justify it."[123] By being able to put patients into

[120]Davis, "The Cabdriver and His Fare," 158–165.

[121]Mars and Nicod, *The World of Waiters.*

[122]Ibid., p. 54.

[123]Metz, *Running Hot,* p. 122.

the last four categories, emergency medical technicians are able to reserve their emotional energies for the truly needy patients.

Janitors.   Apartment building janitors simply divide tenants into two types, "good" and "bad." Bad tenants unnecessarily disturb janitors at home and in their work routine; ask for immediate service or service the janitors are not supposed to supply; ask them to do several things when they had called to request only one thing; are uncooperative in following building rules; do not appreciate what janitors do; will not recognize that janitors are the owners' representatives; and are lazy, argumentative, and conniving. In short, they are inconsiderate of janitors. The "good" tenants, on the other hand, have none of these negative characteristics.

Coping With Customer Conflict: Workers' Actions

In addition to using typologies, those in free unskilled and semiskilled occupations cope with their client conflict through direct action.

Janitors.   Janitors are not satisfied with passively categorizing their tenants as either good or bad. They actively try to change bad tenants into good ones, keep the good tenants in line, and employ a number of ways of "training" them. The ability to train tenants comes with janitorial experience. If tenants make unreasonable demands, janitors may respond by stalling. If tenants are disrespectful in making a demand, janitors may refuse to do anything until they are asked in a "proper" manner. They try to prevent tenants' carelessness by threatening to force them to pay for the needed repairs. They may seek to train tenants to tip them for services rendered. As with taxi drivers, the tip signifies respect for the janitors' position and their abilities.

Janitors dislike being bothered in their off-hours and they seek through a variety of responses to prevent such interference, which they regard as unnecessary and unwarranted. They may try to bring bad tenants into line by refusing to receive packages for them. No matter what devices they use, janitors will find that some tenants are untrainable. When this occurs they try to rationalize their failure by contending that there is something "wrong" with the tenant. They may also deal with the untrainables by making small concessions that keep them from complaining, or the janitors may act as if such tenants did not exist. If all these fail, janitors may resign themselves to the fact they have some untrainable tenants and accommodate themselves to them.

Bus drivers.   The Israeli bus drivers described by Toren seek to control interaction with the newcomers to the city by training them in the norms of riding a bus:

> The driver may have to convince these passengers that it is not customary to cook and eat on the bus. Less dramatic is the need to explain the basic rules of the game—that fares are fixed and have to be paid, that buses operate according to a time schedule, and that the driver has to comply with traffic regulations.[124]

[124]Toren, "The Bus Driver," 110.

324   CONFLICT IN A RANGE OF OCCUPATIONS

Because of the fleeting character of their relationship, bus drivers have far less need to train, and far less interest in training their customers than do janitors. Nevertheless, some training must be undertaken, especially in extreme cases.

Taxi drivers. Taxi drivers have developed a number of dramaturgical techniques which help to increase the size or likelihood of a tip, such as fumbling with change or making change in such denominations that the passenger is forced to tip. Such devices as telling hard-luck stories, opening doors, fancy driving, or calling the passenger "sir" or "madam" may also enhance the tip. Making up fictitious charges for services rendered is the most direct, and dishonest, means employed to increase income.[125] Davis concludes, however, that these devices and the typing of passengers do not in the end give the driver a great deal of control over the tipping behavior of the passengers.

Henslin also analyzes the relationship between cab driver and fare, but he focuses on the "trust" between the two.[126] His analysis is an effort to directly apply the dramaturgical approach to the study of the driver-passenger relationship. Thus, trust is defined by Henslin in this way: "Where an actor has offered a definition of himself and the audience is willing to interact with the actor on the basis of that definition, we are saying trust exists."[127] Henslin asks what determines whether drivers will accept passengers; he answers that potential passengers are accepted if they want a destination or service which the driver is able and willing to provide, if they will reimburse the driver adequately for the service, and if the risks involved are not too high. If potential passengers do not meet these criteria, they will not be accepted. Because passengers may be potential threats to drivers, the drivers expend much effort evaluating potential passengers. They are acutely aware of words or actions which seem to indicate that potential passengers are up to no good. In Goffman's terms, the drivers pay close attention to the passengers' "front" behavior. They analyze the setting in which the passengers present themselves (such as, at a taxi stand, poor neighborhoods), their appearance, and their manner. If these three aspects of the passengers' front behavior (setting, manner, appearance) are not coherent, they become wary of them as possible passengers. Thus by paying close attention to certain symbols, drivers can be sure they only admit to their cab those passengers they can trust.

A number of factors help drivers define trustworthy passengers. Drivers are much more likely to trust passengers who have phoned the company for a cab. The nature of the neighborhood is another important factor—the better the neighborhood where passengers are picked up or to which they are going, the more likely the driver is to trust them. Passengers picked up during the day are more likely to be trusted than those picked up at night. This accounts

[125]Vaz also documents the existence of underreporting of earnings by taxi drivers to their bosses. Edmund W. Vaz, "Institutionalized Stealing Among Big-City Taxi-Drivers," in Audrey Wipper, ed., *The Sociology of Work: Papers in Honour of Oswald Hall*, pp. 75–91.

[126]James Henslin, "Trust and the Cabdriver," in Marcello Truzzi, ed., *Sociology and Everyday Life* (Englewood Cliffs, NJ: Prentice-Hall, 1968), pp. 138–158.

[127]Ibid., p. 140.

for why many taxi drivers prefer to work during the day despite the fact that they generally can earn more at night. During the day drivers have a better chance to look over passengers and assess their trustworthiness. Females are perceived as being more trustworthy than males, obviously because of the lesser physical threat they pose. Thus drivers will pick up females in situations in which they would never pick up males. Drivers also consider the variable of age important: the very old and the very young are considered less threatening and are therefore more likely to be trusted. Finally, there are a number of more subtle factors (such as sobriety, the way the passenger sits, etc.) which the driver examines in an effort to determine whether a passenger is worthy of trust.

More generally, the taxi driver seems to develop a distinctive personality, a particular way of dealing with passengers in order to cope with the stress:

> Cabbies frequently develop a veneer of hardness, an outward crust which helps deflect painful threats to the self. This veneer manifests itself in the commonly perceived belligerency of cab drivers—the shaking fist and the cursing mouth, or the "Don't-tell-me-how-to-get-there" attitude. These are part of the cabbies' attempt to maintain control over threatening passengers and a situation over which he actually has little control.[128]

Waiters.   Mars and Nicod have recently provided a wealth of information on the ways in which waiters dramaturgically deal with customers.

> . . . waiters must always aim to meet the expectations of their customers. They do this by offering an idealised view of their situation, which involves concealing or underplaying activities, facts and motives which are incompatible with the impression they are attempting to put over. They are actors putting on a performance.[129]

Mars and Nicod found that the nature of the performance varied by the type of restaurant.

Focusing on middle-ranking restaurants, they revealed a number of different efforts undertaken by waiters to create the "right" impression for customers by concealing a variety of things. For example, waiters would want to conceal the fact that little effort is involved in the preparation of the food. For another, there is an effort to hide the fact from customers that waiters are confronted with a chronic shortage of cutlery. Some waiters resort to hoarding silverware or stealing needed pieces from their peers. Waiters also seek to conceal the fact that they have to perform such "dirty work" as clearing away dirty dishes and throwing away half-eaten food. Then, waiters try to conceal the discrepancy between the appearance and the reality of their jobs. For example, although they purport to serve fresh-brewed coffee, waiters may in fact use instant coffee. Although strict hygienic standards may appear to be

[128]Henslin, "The Underlife of Cabdriving: A Study in Exploitation and Punishment." p. 70.

[129]Mars and Nicod, *The World of Waiters,* pp. 35–36.

applied, in fact that are many examples of unhygienic practices such as "reusing unwashed dishes, using spittle to clean cutlery," and the like.[130]

In dealing with customers, it is in the interest of the waiter to "get a jump on the customer" and gain control over the interaction. As one waiter put it:

> In this game, you've always got to be one step ahead. If you let the customer get the upper hand, before you know where you are he'll be treading all over you— and then it'll be too late to do anything about it.[131]

It is important for the waiter to take the initiative and gain control over the situation because the customers have most of the power in the relationship. There are clearly a wide range of strategies open to waiters in their effort to gain control over customers. Waiters can try to ingratiate themselves, be particularly helpful and attentive, impress the customers with their knowledge of the menu, and serve extra large portions or bring extra items. On the other hand, it may sometimes be effective for waiters to remain distant from customers by such devices as lowering their voices in the presence of customers to communicate their subordinate status or addressing them as "sir" or "madam." Waiters can go further and be subtly disrespectful or even disdainful of customers. Finally, if all else fails, waiters may feel themselves forced to publicly humiliate customers even though such actions are likely to cost them all hope of a tip. The essential point here is that there is a struggle going on between waiters and customers and in that struggle waiters have a variety of dramaturgical tools at their disposal.

Police officers.   In addition to typologies, police officers employ a wide variety of devices to control the public. In cases of law enforcement, the police perceive themselves to be in danger and act to eliminate that danger as expeditiously as possible. They seek to arrest lawbreakers as quickly as they can, thereby reducing the risk to themselves. They may even engage in a variety of police abuses (such as distorting the facts to expedite arrest and conviction) to successfully complete their mission. In all this they are equipped with rather clear guidelines of how they are supposed to act in dealing with someone who breaks the law.[132] Unfortunately, the same is not true of the more common situations such as family violence and street fights. With guidelines unclear, police officers must depend on a wide range of dramaturgical techniques to handle the situation while minimizing the danger to themselves.

CONCLUSIONS

In this chapter we examined the conflicts and modes of conflict resolution of four occupational groups. The white-collar clerical occupation, once a relatively high-status "male" occupation, has suffered a marked diminution in sta-

---

[130]Ibid., p. 42.

[131]Ibid., p. 65.

[132]Paul Chevigny, *Police Power: Police Abuses in New York City* (New York: Vintage Books, 1969), pp. 276–277.

tus as a result of social changes such as increasing numbers, technological change, and the influx of females. The distinctive conflict that has developed from this is "status panic" among white-collar clerical workers. They have attempted to deal with this in a variety of ways, most notably through the development of artificial status hierarchies and competition for informal status positions. Salespeople must cope with conflicts caused by customers who are far less dependent on a sale than they are. Customers have the power in this situation and salespeople attempt to wrest it from them, primarily through the use of various dramaturgical devices. Skilled craftspeople are forced to deal with a variety of threats to their autonomy. It is the union that constitutes the first line of defense against such encroachments. Finally, we discussed free semi-skilled and unskilled workers and their distinctive conflicts with clients/customers. We also examined their methods of dealing with this conflict, especially the use of typologies and dramaturgical methods.

TWELVE
CONFLICT IN SEMISKILLED AND UNSKILLED OCCUPATIONS IN ORGANIZATIONS

Having concluded the last chapter with a discussion of free semiskilled and unskilled occupations, we turn in this chapter to an analysis of semi- and unskilled occupations found in organizations. Included in this latter category are laborers, machine operators, and, most importantly, assembly-line workers.

ALIENATION

In our view, alienation is the basic source of stress for semiskilled and unskilled workers in organizations. The concept of alienation is derived from the work of Karl Marx. Yet sociologists have almost always used the concept for their own purposes and largely ignored what Marx intended in his use of the term.[1] The use of the concept by American sociologists has had several defining characteristics. First, it has never been used in the radical political manner that Marx intended. Melvin Seeman pointed out that in his construction of at least one aspect of alienation he "clearly departs from the Marxian tradition by removing the critical . . . element in the idea of alienation."[2] Thus, in the hands of American sociologists alienation was deradicalized. Second,

[1]Joachim Israel, *Alienation: From Marx to Modern Sociology* (Boston: Allyn and Bacon, 1971.)
[2]Melvin Seeman, "On the Meaning of Alienation," *American Sociological Review*, 24 (1959), 512.

American sociologists endeavored to make alienation amenable to empirical research by making it clearer and more rigorous so that it could be operationalized, measured, and statistically analyzed. This led them to a conception of alienation that is different from Marx's conceptualization. As a result, there are, as we will see, few empirical tests of alienation directly from a Marxian theoretical perspective. Finally, and most important from a theoretical point of view, American sociologists have almost always transformed Marx's primarily structural theory of alienation into a social-psychological theory. It is not that a social-psychological approach is not valuable, but this has tended to drastically alter the Marxian approach. Let us examine Marx's structural theory and then turn to the American social-psychological orientation and the research on work in unskilled and semiskilled occupations that it has spawned.

Marx's Theory of Alienation from Work

In the *Economic and Philosophic Manuscripts of 1844*, Marx begins his analysis of alienated labor in the following way:

> We proceed from an economic fact of the present. The worker becomes all the poorer the more wealth he produces, the more his production increases in power and size. The worker becomes an even cheaper commodity the more commodities he creates. With the *increasing value* of the world of things proceeds in direct proportion the *devaluation* of the world of men.[3]

Marx begins his analysis of alienated labor with this contradiction. He sees the increased productive power of labor, yet he also sees the corresponding debasement of the worker. Through increased productivity, the worker can produce more than ever yet the rewards go to the capitalist, while for the worker there is only increasing privation. Marx takes the position that this contradiction exists because the capitalists, not the laborers, own and control the workers' activity and the products of this activity.[4]

In capitalism, alienation from work is the result of the lack of ownership and therefore control over those aspects of life that make the human being a *species being*. Marx's concept of species being is crucial not only to understanding alienation, but also to his criticisms of capitalist society and his image of the communist alternative. Species being can be loosely translated into the

---

[3]Karl Marx, *The Economic and Philosophic Manuscripts of 1844*, Dirk J. Struik, ed. (New York: International Publishers, 1844/1964), p. 107.

[4]There is much support in the current literature to substantiate the notion that Marx's analysis of alienation from work rests on the dual concepts of ownership and control. Peter B. Archibald, "Using Marx's Theory of Alienation Empiricially," *Theory and Society*, 6 (1978), 119–132; Ernest Mandel and George Novak, *The Marxist Theory of Alienation* (New York: Pathfinder Press, 1970); Bertell Ollman, *Alienation*, Second Edition (Cambridge: Cambridge University Press, 1976); Wayne Plasek, "Marxist and American Sociological Conceptions of Alienation: Implications for Social Problems Theory," *Social Problems*, 21 (1974), 316–328; Ron J. Stanfield, "Marx's Social Economics: The Theory of Alienation," *Review of Social Economy*, 37 (1979), 298–312; Adam Schaff, *Alienation as a Social Phenomenon* (New York: Pergamon Press, 1980); Michael H. Best and William E. Connolly, *The Political Economy* (Lexington, MA: D.C. Heath and Company, 1982).

idea of human potential. People have yet to fully achieve species being, but it is possible that they will in the future. Prior to capitalism, the difficulties involved in simply surviving made it impossible for people to approach their human potential. Throughout history various societies (for example, feudalism) have prevented the expression of species being. Capitalism, too, impedes species being, but it also provides the tools (such as advanced technologies) that could eventually allow people to reach their human potential.

What is species being? To Marx, species being is a state of natural interconnectedness. People are intimately tied to their activities (their work), their products, other people, as well as their self-expression. Capitalism (as well as all other known societies) serves to destroy this natural interconnectedness. Hence, from Marx's point of view, capitalism needs to be overcome. In its place, he would prefer a communist society. What is communism? From Marx's perspective, *communism* is a society in which there is natural interconnectedness, in which species being fully exists for the first time. Clearly, none of the societies that now call themselves communist approximate this model. In fact, they impede species being as much as, or more than, capitalist societies. Were Marx alive today he would be a critic of *both* contemporary capitalist *and* communist societies.

It is the structure of ownership and control inherent in the social organization of capitalist production that destroys species being.[5] As originally conceptualized by Marx, it is this destruction of natural interconnectedness, of species being, that is *alienation*. More specifically, alienation from work is caused by structural factors that reach their peak in the social organization of capitalist production.[6] Consequently, alienation for Marx is not reducible to social-psychological phenomena. However, while Marx's main focus was on structural causes of alienation, he was certainly cognizant of the social-psychological consequences of alienation.[7] Although Seeman and others refer to these social-psychological consequences as alienaton, in Marx's work they are "simply" the consequences of structural alienation. Under capitalism, the worker may feel powerless, isolated, estranged, but from a Marxian perspec-

[5]In addition to cited works by Archibald, Plasek, and Schaff see the following: George Ritzer, *Toward an Integrated Sociological Paradigm: The Search for an Exemplar and an Image of the Subject Matter* (Boston: Allyn and Bacon, 1981); Richard Schacht, *Alienation* (New York: Doubleday, 1970).

[6]We do not mean to imply that alienation from work cannot or does not exist in modern socialist/communist societies. It can and does, but a thorough examination of this topic falls outside of the space limitations of this book. For an introduction to the theoretical dimensions of the problem see, Ben Agger, ed., *Western Marxism: An Introduction* (Santa Monica, CA: Goodyear Publishing Company, Inc., 1979).

[7]Several observers argue that, for Marx, alienation is *both* objective and subjective. Schacht describes the objective manifestations of alienation as taking on a structural-relative character while subjective alienation takes on a perspective-relative character. In a similar vein, Schaff refers to objective alienation as alienation and subjective alienation as self-alienation. Archibald also argues that according to Marx alienation from work is both a structural and a psychological phenomenon. Writes Archibald: "Thus in Marx's own usage alienation does sometimes appear to be structural, as with the definition of alienation 'as appropriation' " (p. 124). However, Archibald is quick to point out that Marx also often referred to the psychological reactions of individuals to structural conditions as indications of alienation.

tive it is wrong to define alienation in terms of these feelings; rather, alienation is an objective/structural social condition.

Implicit in our interpretation of Marx's theory of alienation from work is the notion that objective/structural alienation can be thought of as an independent causal variable with corresponding dependent, subjective, social-psychological manifestations. There are several authors[8] who conceptualize Marx's theory of alienation in this way, but the clearest exposition of this position is found in Schaff.

> We must look for sources of subjective alienation in appropriate phenomena of objective alienation; to overcome a given subjective alienation it is necessary to eliminate its source in the domain of objective alienation.[9]

Alienation can be seen as an independent, structural variable with various corresponding social-psychological manifestations appearing in the minds, the consciousness, of individual actors.[10]

What, for Marx, is the structural source of alienation? It can be nothing other than the structure of capitalist society, a structure that blocks the natural interconnectedness of species being: it stands between people and their products, their productive activity, other people, and even themselves. One key element of that structure is the social class system in which workers must sell their labor time to capitalists who own the means of production. Because of the capitalists and their system, workers do not have control over their products, their activities, their social relationships, and even themselves.

Empirical Research on Marx's Theory of Alienation

Although it has not often been done, Marx's largely structural theory of alienation from work can be studied empirically.[11] Maurice Zeitlin studied the

---

[8]See, Ritzer, *Toward an Integrated Sociological Paradigm*; Schacht. *Alienation*; Archibald, "Using Marx's Theory of Alienation Empirically."

[9]Schaff, *Alienation as a Social Phenomenon*, p. 214.

[10]There is a "casual" connection between objective and subjective alienation. However, it should be added that we are not, nor is Schaff, arguing for a simple, undirectional, non-dialectical approach. Hence, the independent-dependent relationship between objective and subjective alienation is only one moment in a complex totality of mutual interaction. People are not totally determined and inevitably constrained by the external structural of objective alienation. While the structure of capitalism may shape and influence people's attitudes and behavior, people, according to Marx, are endowed with consciousness, creativity, and intentionality and can act back upon the structural source of their oppression. As Marx and Engels note, "circumstances make men just as much as men make circumstances;" Karl Marx and Frederick Engels, *The German Ideology*, Part One, C. J. Arthur, ed. (New York: International Publishers, 1970), p. 59.

[11]We disagree with those who argue that alienation is basically a philosophic/normative concept and hence not amenable to empirical verification. See the following: Ollman, *Alienation;* John Goldthorpe et al., *The Affluent Worker in the Class Structure* (Cambridge: Cambridge University Press, 1969); Igor S. Kon, "The Concept of Alienation in Modern Society," *Social Research*, 34 (1967), 507–528. To be sure, alienation for Marx was a normative concept. The moral revulsion and disdain that Marx had for the alienation of work under capitalism is widely recognized and clearly etched in the passion of his work. Yet Marx was not simply a philosopher of morality and ethics. We would argue that Marx recognized the advantages of the empirical approach and incorporated certain elements into his general methodology. See the following: Archibald, "Using Marx's Theory of Alienation Empirically;" Lloyd Easton, "Alienation and Empiricism in Marx's

relationship between alienation (partly structural) and revolution among industrial workers in Cuba shortly after the Castro revolution.[12]

Rhodes tested the relationship between objective and subjective alienation among a group of students.[13]

In a study of middle and lower echelon workers in administrative bureaucracies in Belgium, Bacharach and Aiken also conceptualized alienation as an objective phenomena.[14]

Finally, Walczak studied a national cross-section of all adult workers employed in the United States,[15] utilizing objective/structural alienation as his independent variable.

Although we do have some research that focuses on Marx's structural theory of alienation, we really know very little about this type of alienation among semi-skilled and unskilled workers in the United States. This is an important failing in the field that points to the need for much more research on the structural aspects of alienation among such workers.

Social-Psychological Studies of Alienation

While the empirical studies of structural alienation in semiskilled and unskilled occupations are few, this is not the case with social-psychological studies of alienation.[16]

Although there are many pieces of social-psychological research to choose from, we focus here on Robert Blauner's definition of alienation, which breaks it down into four social-psychological components.[17] The first

Thought," *Social Research*, 37 (1970), 402–427; Z.A. Jordan, *The Evolution of Dialectical Materialism* (New York: St. Martin's Press, 1967); Al Szymanski, "Marxism and Science," *Insurgent Sociologist*, 3 (1973), 25–38; Richard Schacht, "Alienation, the 'Is-Ought' Gap and Two Sorts of Discord," in Felix Geyer and David Schweitzer, eds., *Theories of Alienation: Critical Perspectives in Philosophy and Social Science* (The Netherlands: Martinus Nijhoff, 1976). In fact, we would agree with Archibald who claims that it is wrong to even ask whether alienation is a normative or a descriptive concept, for it is both.

[12]Maurice Zeitlin, "Alienation and Revolution," *Social Forces*, 45 (1966), 224–236.

[13]Lewis A. Rhodes, "Objective and Subjective Alienation of Labor: The Student Case," Paper presented at the International Sociological Association meetings in Sweden, 1978.

[14]Samuel B. Bacharach and Michael Aiken, "The Impact of Alienation, Meaninglessness, and Meritocracy on Supervisor and Subordinate Satisfaction," *Social Forces*, 57 (1979), 853–870.

[15]David Walczak, "An Empirical Test of Karl Marx's Theory of Alienation from Work," Unpublished Ph.D. Dissertation, University of Maryland, 1982.

[16]There have been several empirical studies which are concerned with various dimensions of the workworld but which center on alienation from society and not alienation from work. As a result, we will not consider these studies. The interested reader should consult the following examples: Charles M. Bonjean and Michael D. Grimes, "Bureaucracy and Alienation: A Dimensional Approach," *Social Forces*, 49 (1970), 622–630; Melvin Kohn, "Occupational Structure and Alienation," *American Journal of Sociology*, 82 (1976), 111–180; Donald V. Nightingale and Jean-Marie Toulouse, "Alienation in the Workplace: A Comparative Study in French and English-Canadian Organizations," *Canadian Journal of Behavorial Science*, 10 (1978).

[17]Robert Blauner, *Alienation and Freedom* (Chicago: University of Chicago Press, 1964). This approach has been used in many studies. More recent are William A. Rushing's *Class, Culture, and Alienation* (Lexington MA: Lexington Books, 1972), and Melvin L. Kohn and Carmi Schooler, *Work and Personality: An Inquiry Into the Impact of Social Stratification* (Norwood, NJ: Ablex, 1983).

element is *powerlessness,* or the feeling of domination by other people, or objects, and the feeling of being unable to reduce or eliminate that control. *Meaninglessness* is the second aspect of alienation and involves people's inability to see their role in relation to other roles and their purpose in the organization. Third, alienated people suffer from *isolation;* they lack a feeling of belonging to the work situation and identification with the workplace. Finally, alienation involves *self-estrangement*—feeling unable to express one's unique abilities, potentialities, or personalities in one's work. According to Blauner: "Further consequences of self-estranged work may be boredom and monotony, the absence of personal growth, and a threat to self-approved occupational identity."[18]

Assembly-line workers. The occupation that epitomizes social-psychological alienation is assembly-line work, in which the major source of alienation is the omnipresent assembly line. Assembly-line workers perform their assigned tasks (such as tightening a bolt, fastening a fender) at set intervals and no variation is allowed. For 8 hours every workday they perform the same task at set intervals. Respite comes when the line breaks down, an event many workers hope for and sometimes contribute to by sabotaging the machinery. Walker and Guest have said that the assembly-line worker is "the classic symbol of the subjection of man to the machine in our industrial age."[19] In Blauner's estimation, it is the automobile assembly-line industry in which "technological, organizational and economic factors" combine to produce the most alienating work environment.[20] More recently, a scathing critique of work on a French automobile assembly line concluded that such work is "destructive to health, reasonable existence, and human dignity."[21]

A spot-welder on one automobile assembly line describes his job this way:

> I stand in one spot, about two- or three-feet area, all night. The only time a person stops is when the line stops. We do about thirty-two jobs per car, per unit, forty-eight units an hour, eight hours a day. Thirty-two times forty-eight times eight. Figure it out, that's how many times I push that button.[22]

Says another welder: "What's there to say? A car comes, I weld it. One hundred and one times an hour."[23] Another assembly-line worker describes the effect such work had on him:

> Sometimes I felt just like a robot. You push a button and you go this way. You become a mechanical nut. You get a couple of beers and go to sleep at night.

[18]Blauner, *Alienation and Freedom,* p. 26.

[19]Charles R. Walker and Robert Guest, *Man on the Assembly Line* (Cambridge, MA: Harvard University Press, 1952), p. 9.

[20]Blauner, *Alienation and Freedom,* p. 182.

[21]John Calder, Introduction to Robert Linhart, *The Assembly Line.* Translated by Margaret Crosland (Amherst, MA: University of Massachusetts Press, 1981), p. 10.

[22]Studs Terkel, *Working* (New York: Pantheon Books, 1974), p. 159.

[23]Barbara Garson., *All the Livelong Day* (Hammondsworth, England: Penguin, 1977), p. 88.

Maybe one, two o'clock in the morning, my wife is saying, "Come on, come on, leave it." I'm still workin' that line. Three o'clock in the morning, five o'clock. Tired. I have worked that job all night. Saturday. Sunday, still working. It's just ground into you. My wife taps me on the shoulder.

Tappin' me didn't mean nothin'. (Laughs)[24]

Assembly-line operations in settings other than the automobile industry are just as alienating. United States Department of Agriculture chicken inspectors are required to inspect up to seventy birds per minute which adds up to over 35,000 daily. Line hypnosis is an assembly-line affliction where the inspectors "lose awareness and concentration" and the "birds become just a blurred yellow vision."[25]

These, of course, are but a few descriptions—several volumes could be filled with such images of assembly-line work. What is it about the assembly line that makes it such a nightmare for many people?[26]

For one thing, assembly-line workers are almost totally powerless. They are unable to control the pace of the line. The machine pace is set by the organization and is designed to get the maximum productivity from each employee. Once the speed of the line is set, there is little the workers can do to affect it, and consequently they are unable to control their own work pace. This is perhaps the most demoralizing aspect of their job, and differentiates their work from virtually all other occupations. There is some degree of powerlessness in virtually all occupations, but most workers are able to have some control over the pace of work or the variety of work. Even the lowliest clerks can generally vary their own work pace and make their work more interesting by changing the tasks they perform.

Assembly-line workers are also characterized by an inability to control their immediate supervisors. For one thing, it is difficult for them to interact with their foremen. The combination of noise, job pressure, and need for continual attention to the line make it almost impossible to communicate with anyone. Even if assembly-line workers could communicate with their supervisors, they would have little chance of affecting their behavior. In fact, they have few resources which they can use to gain something from their superiors, for they have few skills and are easily replaceable. Their almost total unimportance to the organization further increases the assembly-line workers' sense of powerlessness. They lack even the power to withdraw occasionally, because their absence from the line would be noticed immediately. It is also hard for them to quit, because they have few skills and would find it extremely difficult to find other positions.

For a variety of reasons, assembly-line workers find their jobs meaningless. They are unable to see what their very specialized task has to do with the work of others on the line or of those who work at other levels in the organization. They also are unable to see what tightening their bolts have to do with

[24]Terkel, *Working*, p. 175.

[25]Kathy Sawyer, "On the Chicken Line: Trying to Catch the Bad Ones, Quickly," *The Washington Post* (September 2, 1979), p. A1.

[26]For a dissenting view on this see, William H. Form, *Blue-Collar Stratification: Autoworkers in Four Countries* (Princeton, NJ: Princeton University Press, 1976), especially pp. 113–137.

the finished product (and in many cases they do not even know what the finished product is). Finally, the intrinsic nature of the job contributes to a feeling of meaninglessness. It is so specialized, uninteresting, and unimportant that it is difficult for anyone to derive any satisfaction from their work.

The assembly-line workers' problems are compounded by their isolation. The noise and demands of the line prevent interaction on the job, making it difficult for an informal work group to develop. The workers are also isolated from all levels of management in order to allow managers to maintain what they consider to be proper distance from workers. Assembly-line work is frequently found in large plants, and plant size also serves to inhibit the development of personal relationships. Huge cafeterias, parking lots, and rest rooms are scarcely designed to encourage social interaction.

Finally, those on the assembly line are particularly prone to self-estrangement. The work is boring and monotonous, requiring continual attention but little real involvement in the task or the organization. Hence, the workers spend a good part of their time daydreaming. No real skills or abilities are needed and they are unable to express themselves in their work.

The focus here on semiskilled and unskilled occupations is not to say that workers in other types of occupations are not alienated. Studies have demonstrated that even high-status professionals,[27] semiprofessionals,[28] and white-collar bank employees[29] can also be alienated. Nevertheless, the bulk of the evidence indicates that unskilled and semiskilled workers are more likely to be alienated and more likely to exhibit a high degree of alienation.

Alienation and Technology

Blauner's previously cited study examines alienation in four types of industries and points out the effect of technology on alienation. The automobile worker's alienation is attributed to the technology of the assembly line.[30] As we have seen, the machine controls the pace of work; the speed is set by external forces and is invariable; the line requires constant attention; interaction is made impossible because of the nature of assembly-line work; the contributions of individuals are small and they don't know how they contribute to the final product; and few skills or abilities are needed to perform the work. Blauner compares the automobile industry to three other industries (printing, textiles, and chemicals) in an effort to determine the relationship between technology and alienation.

[27]George Miller, "Professionals in Bureaucracy: Alienation Among Industrial Scientists," *American Sociological Review,* 32 (1967), 755–768.

[28]Leonard Pearlin, "Alienation From Work: A Study of Nursing Personnel," *American Sociological Review,* 27 (1962), 314–326.

[29]Louis A. Zurcher Jr., et al., "Value Orientation, Role Conflict, and Alienation from Work: A Cross Cultural Study," *American Sociological Review,* 30 (1965), 539–548.

[30]In a cross-cultural study comparing different technologies in four societies, Form has reaffirmed the primacy of technology in determining worker's actions. See William H. Form, "Technology and Social Behavior of Workers in Four Countries: A Sociotechnical Perspective," *American Sociological Review,* 37 (1972), 727–738.

Printers.   Printing, a skilled occupation discussed in Chapter 11, is the least alienating of the four occupations Blauner studied. Perhaps the major reason is that printing had been virtually untouched by technological change at the time of Blauner's study. (Since that time computer technology has radically transformed printing, but we will restrict ourselves to Blauner's discussion of the technology of printing as it existed several decades ago.) Much of the work was still done by hand or by traditional machine methods. Other factors also contributed to the relative lack of alienation among printers. Printing plants were comparatively small; management, generally, was by traditional rather than bureaucratic means; there was high job security; and, as we saw in the last chapter, labor unions in printing were quite powerful. Above all, however, is the fact that the machine had not taken over the printing industry and the printers retained their traditional skills and control over the means of production. The printers' job was complex and required the mastery of a series of diverse skills. An apprenticeship period of from 4 to 6 years was necessary before one could be considered a journeyman printer. The complexity and diversity of the work militated, at least until recently, against its standardization and mechanization. The skill required enabled printers to set their own pace and determine their own techniques, tools, and the sequence in which they would perform their tasks. Each occupation in printing was different and this gave the printer great latitude in terms of decision making, initiative, and judgment. Further, printers were relatively free to try out new ideas, move about the plant, and work without supervisory control. Because of these factors, printing was by far the most meaningful occupation in the Blauner study. It allowed those in the occupation the opportunity for self-actualization. As a result, printers were highly pleased with the intrinsic aspects of their work. Blauner neatly summarized the position of the printer at the time:

> In some ways, the printer is almost an anachronism in the age of large-scale industrial organizations. His relation to his work is reminiscent of our picture of the independent craftsman of preindustrial times. Craft technology, favorable economic conditions, and powerful work organizations and traditions result in the highest level of freedom and control in the work process among all industrial workers today.[31]

Textile workers.   Blauner found textile workers more alienated than printers, but less alienated than automobile assembly-line workers. This is because at the time the textile industry, technologically, was a throwback to the early days of industrialization. The basic job in this industry was tending a number of machines which did most of the production. The jobs themselves required little skill because most of the necessary skill had been built into the machines. Because textiles was a machine industry, the workers were faced with unvarying work pressure, an inability to control that pressure, and an inability to choose techniques or to move around freely. Further, the technology which forced each worker to handle several machines also had the need, built in, for close supervision. In a craft technology, close supervision is not

---

[31]Blauner, *Alienation and Freedom*, p. 56.

needed and is even resented, because of the strong sense of craftsmanship among skilled workers. In the assembly-line technology, close supervision is not needed because the machines control the work pace and the quality. In the textile industry, however, neither the machines nor the norms of craftsmanship insured quality or quantity production. Further, the textile industry was composed mainly of small, marginal firms that had to get maximum productivity to stay in business. Despite these alienating aspects of textile work, it was not as alienating as the automobile assembly line. Blauner accounts for this in several ways, citing the traditional, more personalized nature of the organization; the social cohesion of the workers resulting from their life in small Southern towns; the small size of the plants, which allowed for considerable interaction; and the fact that most textile workers (almost half of whom were females) had few career ambitions. Above all, however, is the fact that the machine-tending technology allowed the workers more freedom than their counterparts on the assembly line.

Workers in continuous-process industries.   Most theories have accepted the notion that as technology advances work will become increasingly alienating, but Blauner found that in the technologically advanced continuous-process industry there is, in fact, a decline in alienation. In continuous-process industries such as chemicals

> . . . the flow of materials; the combination of different chemicals; and the temperature pressure, and speed of the process are regulated by automatic control devices. The automatic controls make possible a continuous flow in which raw materials are introduced at the beginning of the process and a large volume of the product continually emerges at the end stage.[32]

Few employees are needed in such industries, and these employees are generally thinly spread throughout the numerous buildings that make up a particular plant. Because the number of employees is already minimal and because the amount of production is determined by the machine, not the individual, there is a high degree of job security in continuous-process industries. The employee does little physical work; instead, "the work of the chemical operator is to monitor these automatic processes: his tasks include observing dials and gauges; taking readings of temperatures, pressures, and rates of flow; and writing down these ratings."[33] Employees have a great deal of responsibility for the maintenance of smooth operations and for the care of expensive machinery. In performing these tasks, they work in small groups of from three to seven people. There is little standardization of work and most of the time is spent in waiting for, or trying to prevent, a breakdown and trying to repair it when it occurs. Because of the nature of their jobs chemical workers have considerable freedom in terms of time and movement. There is no continuous pressure; rather, the work routine is highly erratic. The work environment is relaxed and employees can set their own pace except in the case of an emergency. They are also free to determine the quality of their work and

[32]Ibid., p. 125
[33]Ibid., p. 133.

the methods they will employ. There is much free time and few employees and this provides the basis for the development of highly cohesive work groups. There is ample chance for advancement in the organization for those who are deserving. All these factors, which stem primarily from the nature of the continuous-process technology, enable chemical workers to be less alienated than assembly-line or textile workers.

Other studies.   Shepard has replicated and expanded upon Blauner's research.[34] In the replication phase, Shepard compared craft, assembly-line, and automated, continuous-process workers in the automobile and oil industries on five (rather than four) dimensions of alienation. In general, Shepard found the same curvilinear relationship between alienation and technology uncovered by Blauner. That is, alienation increases as we move from craft to assembly-line technology, but decreases as we move from the assembly-line to automated, continuous-process technology.

Shepard extended Blauner's research by attempting to discover whether the relationship between alienation and technology also held for white-collar clerical workers. Without going into details, we can simply say that the same basic relationship existed (that is, computer workers were less alienated than office machine operators and nonmechanical clerks) although not nearly as strongly as is the case for blue-collar workers. Similar support for the Blauner thesis in white-collar work has been reported by Kirsch and Lengermann.[35]

Other Alienation from Work Studies

While the social-psychological conceptualization of alienation has been widely utilized, not everyone concerned with alienation from work has followed the Seeman/Blauner tradition.

Aiken and Hage do not utilize the Seeman/Blauner approach, but they do conceptualize alienation as an individually perceived, subjective reaction.[36] In fact, Aiken and Hage's alienation scale is really a job satisfaction scale. Many sociologists have been prone to equate alienation and job satisfaction, but for our purposes it is best to keep these concepts distinct.[37] It should not be assumed that just because people are dissatisfied with their work that they are alienated. As we have seen, alienation has very specific structural and social-psychological characteristics.

[34]Jon Shepard, *Alienation and Automation: A Study of Office and Factory Workers* (Cambridge, MA: M.I.T. Press, 1971). For further confirmation of Blauner's thesis on blue-collar workers see, Stephen Cotgrove, "Alienation and Automation," *British Journal of Sociology*, 23 (1972), 437–451; Michael Fullan, "Industrial Technology and Worker Integration in the Organization," *American Sociological Review*, 33 (1970), 1028–1039.

[35]Barbara A. Kirsch and Joseph J. Lengermann, "An Empirical Test of Robert Blauner's Ideas on Alienation in Work as Applied to Different Type Jobs in a White-Collar Setting," *Sociology and Social Research*, 56 (1972), 180–194.

[36]Michael Aiken and Gerald Hage, "Organizational Alienation: A Comparative Analysis," *American Sociological Review*, 31 (1966), 497–507.

[37]See, for example, George M. Torrance, "The Underside of the Hospital: Recruitment and the Meaning of Work Among Non-Professional Hospital Workers," in Audrey Wipper ed., *The Sociology of Work: Papers in Honour of Oswald Hall* (Ottawa, Canada: Carleton Unversity Press, 1984), pp. 211–231.

In any case, Aiken and Hage argue that they are interested in studying alienation from work and alienation from expressive relations, two categories that they see as comparable with Marx's notion of alienation from the process of production and alienation from fellow workers. They operationally define alienation from work, that is, the process of production, in the following manner:

> How *satisfied* are you with the progress you are making towards the goals which you set for yourself in your present position? On the whole, how *satisfied* are you with your present job when you consider the expectations you had when you took the job?[38] [Emphasis added]

These are but two questions in the Aiken and Hage alienation from work scale; the other five components in this scale also measure one's satisfaction with various components of the job. To measure alienation from expressive relations Aiken and Hage operationally define this concept in terms of employee satisfaction with one's supervisor and with one's fellow workers.

Aiken and Hage proceed to relate alienation to two components of formal organizations—centralization and formalization. The findings indicate that alienation, as conceptualized by them, is positively related to both dimensions of formal organization.

Aiken and Hage use a social-psychological measure of alienation, albeit one that is different from the Seeman/Blauner tradition. Another approach is to view alienation in behavioral, rather than social-psychological terms. Thus, for example, absenteeism[39] and turnover[40] rates have been used as behavioral indicators of psychological alienation.

COPING WITH SOCIAL-PSYCHOLOGICAL ALIENATION

Workers' Actions

There is a rich literature in occupational sociology on the efforts of individuals in unskilled and semiskilled occupations in organizations to flesh out their worklives. Let us now turn to a discussion of worker actions directed at coping with alienation in these occupations.

Sailors.   In a study of the sailor aboard ship, Zurcher describes the "underlife" that develops there to make life more palatable.[41] Some of the informal practices are recognized by the authorities on board, while others per-

---

[38]Aiken and Hage, "Organizational Alienation," 501.

[39]Frank Hull, "Organizational Level Correlates of Alienation as Indicated by Absenteeism and Turnover Rates." Paper presented at the Annual Meeting of the Southern Sociological Society, 1979.

[40]Frank Hull, Nathalie S. Friedman and Theresa F. Rogers, "The Effect of Technology on Alienation from Work: Testing Blauner's Inverted U-Curve Hypothesis for 110 Industrial Organizations and 245 Retrained Printers," *Work and Occupations,* 9 (1982), 31–57.

[41]Louis A. Zurcher, Jr., "The Sailor Aboard Ship: A Study of Role Behavior in a Total Institution," *Social Forces,* 43 (1965), 389–400.

sist although they often conflict with the smooth running of the ship. Examples of the first type are bypassing chains of command to cut red tape, use of the grapevine for information, and the use of "unofficial, pirated, or home-made parts to maintain machinery in full operation."[42] All these functions do help in the operation of the ship and grant a measure of individuality to the sailor. But there are also what Goffman calls "secondary adjustments," which seem to be dysfunctional for the ship while they are functional for the sailor in retaining some individuality within a total institution. Examples of such secondary adjustments are deals to get a better bunk, snacks, haircuts, first priority on leaves, private use of the ship's property, and deviations from the prescribed mode of dress.

Letter carriers.   The letter carrier is another example of an occupation in which people seek to make their worklives more meaningful through a variety of informal practices.[43] Despite the formal rules and supervision, the actual work behavior of letter carriers is quite different from their formal job description. Because they are on their own most of the time, they have little difficulty reorganizing their work routine to suit them better. For example, the work route is designed to take 8 hours to complete, but carriers are normally able to complete it in much less time. When the route is being timed, they are careful to follow the rules of the post office exactly, but once the routine has been set they utilize a variety of shortcuts which may violate formal rules, but which enable them to complete their route sooner. Such "illegal" shortcuts as criss-crossing streets, using personal automobiles, walking on lawns, and failing to deliver all the mail enables letter carriers to have an hour or more of free time each day.

A threat to these informal practices is the substitute carrier, who may not know the informal norms of mail delivery and therefore may do the work more efficiently than the regular carrier without breaking the rules of the post office. To protect themselves from this, carriers have instituted a norm, which is known to the substitutes, that substitutes must take longer than regulars to do the job. If substitutes violate this norm, the regular carriers have a number of sanctions at their disposal. They may not tell the substitutes how to work the route, or they might "forget" to tell them of some vicious dogs to be wary of, or they might actively interfere with substitutes' work by placing the sacks of mail they need in the wrong pick-up boxes.

Assembly-line workers.   As mentioned earlier, the occupation that best embodies all the characteristics of alienation is the automobile assembly-line worker. Two recent studies by Runcie[44] and Houbolt[45] analyze the various

[42]Ibid., 394.

[43]Dean Harper and Frederick Emmert, "Work Behavior in a Service Industry," *Social Forces*, 42 (1963), 216–225.

[44]John F. Runcie, "By Days I Make the Cars," *Harvard Business Review*, 58 (May/June, 1980), 106–115.

[45]Jan Houbolt, "An Empirical Critique of Blauner's Concept of Powerlessness on the Automobile Assembly Line." Paper presented at the Annual Meeting of the Eastern Sociological Society, 1982.

means developed by the assembly-line worker for coping with alienation from work.

Runcie spent 5 months as an employee in an automobile assembly plant in a medium-sized city in the Midwest. In general, Runcie found that workers cope with the monotony and boredom of the assembly line in one of two ways: workers either take off (physical withdrawal) or stay in the plant and find ways to make their jobs more meaningful.

In terms of withdrawal, Runcie cites the high absentee rate in the plant. As one utility worker suggested, "People take time off because they're bored. They get tired of the same old routine."[46] Runcie notes that during particular times of the year, for example deer-hunting season, so many workers were absent that other workers were asked to work two shifts. However, even during the rest of the year, absenteeism was still a problem. Runcie says, "On many mornings the line could not start due to the shortage of workers. Often we would stand around waiting for the company to find people to fill the holes in the line."[47]

Absenteeism is not the only method used by automobile assembly-line workers to cope with alienation. While on the job, workers have devised several ways of coping. Although not a major coping technique, Runcie found that sabotage does exist. Automobile assembly-line workers do, on occasion, let cars go by without doing their work. According to Runcie: "Sometimes they take their frustrations out on the car or the tools themselves—breaking tools, banging tools against the bench, or causing air wrenches to emit high-pitched shrieks."[48] As we will see shortly, psychological mechanisms and games are also utilized by workers to cope with alienation. Further, as one worker told Houbolt:

> I've taken my portable television and watched a football game or baseball. I've had it down there several times. I can watch it by getting ahead on the job.[49]

Both Runcie and Houbolt found that drugs are also used by workers as a means of coping with alienation. In relation to drug-taking and supervisor indulgence, one worker told Houbolt:

> As long as you do that job without stopping the line, that's the main thing. Basically they don't give you too much trouble. Guys drink, smoke pot right on the line, as long as you do your job it's all right. You're not supposed to, but you keep it hid . . . but the foreman also knows it's going on.[50]

As a means of coping with boredom one worker said, "If I smoke (marijuana), I can stare at a spot on the floor all day long and not get bored."[51] While drugs

[46]Runcie, "By Days I Make the Cars," 109.

[47]Ibid.

[48]Ibid.

[49]Houbolt, "An Empirical Critique of Blauner's Concept of Powerlessness on the Automobile Assembly Line," 3.

[50]Ibid.

[51]Runcie, "By Days I Make the Cars," 109.

are taken on the job, often with tacit supervisory knowledge, as a means of coping with alienation, drug-taking can lead to serious risks involving production and the health and safety of the worker. While many workers may be able to "run their jobs as good as when they're straight,"[52] many cannot. One worker told Runcie:

> On second shift I've seen them take a guy and hide him 'cause he was so messed up. I don't like to get stoned when I'm working 'cause I don't know if I've done the whole car or not.[53]

It has been suggested that alcohol is a drug also used by employees as a means of coping with alienation from work. However, recent empirical evidence casts doubt on a simple and direct relationship between alienation and drinking behavior. Fennell, Rodin, and Kantor found only a modest relationship between job stress and frequency of drinking.[54] More relevant to the discussion here on alienation is a recent study by Seeman and Anderson.[55] They studied the relationship between three types of alienation and frequency as well as quantity of alcohol consumed. Alienation from work was defined in terms of self-estrangement, or the lack of intrinsic satisfaction in one's work, as well as a generalized sense of societal powerlessness—or the lack of control or sense of mastery over one's life outside of the workplace. The third type of alienation was social isolation, or the respondent's lack of attachment to relatives, friends, and neighbors.

Seeman and Anderson found that societal powerlessness, not alienation from work (self-estrangement), was consistently related to both frequency of alcohol consumption and the average amount of alcohol consumed on each occasion. In terms of at least one dimension (network support) of the isolation type of alienation, Seeman and Anderson found, contrary to expectations, that workers who were integrated into a network of friends tended to drink *more* per occasion than those who were isolated.

Seeman and Anderson also analyzed the interrelationship of the various types of alienation. They found that drinking behavior is most troublesome for those who experience high societal alienation (powerlessness), are tied into a network of support, and intrinsically involved in their work.

In addition to alienation from work, Seeman and Anderson studied the effects of four other work-related variables. Neither job satisfaction, attitudes toward status attainment, career mobility, nor substantive complexity at work were found to be related to frequency or quantity of alcohol consumption. Thus, although the relationship is neither simple nor clear-cut, alienation (societal powerlessness) seems to be the best predictor of occupationally related drinking problems.

---

[52]Ibid.

[53]Ibid.

[54]Mary L. Fennell, Miriam B. Rodin and Glenda K. Kantor, "Problems in the Work Setting, Drinking, and Reasons for Drinking," *Social Forces*, 60 (1981), 114–132.

[55]Melvin Seeman and Carolyn S. Anderson, "Alienation and Alcohol: The Role of Work, Mastery, and Community in Drinking Behavior," *American Sociological Review*, 48 (1983), 60–77.

Working fast and getting ahead on the job is another method used by workers to cope with alienation. Workers can get ahead on the assembly line by working as fast as possible, thereby getting ahead of themselves and gaining time for a breather. This allows them to exercise a measure of control over their work. Other methods for exercising "control" over the line include trading jobs, alternating jobs, and doubling or tripling up on jobs. One worker in the Houbolt study describes the doubling-up process as follows:

> One guy will just do thirty jobs, a half hour's worth, and the other guy will do whatever he wants for that hour and then catch up the next half hour. He can leave the line and wander around. Now that's against the rules, but the foreman just looks the other way.[56]

Besides allowing the worker a modicum of control over the production process, doubling up gives the worker a break from the monotony and boredom of the assembly line. Further, these shortcuts allow free time for other activities which may include reading a newspaper, napping, letter writing, or playing checkers.

Restriction of output.   The richest descriptions of informal practices designed to alleviate alienation come from studies of the effort to restrict production. The famous studies at the Hawthorne plant of the Western Electric Company in Chicago, first brought these informal practices to light.[57] In one portion (the "bank wiring room") of the studies there was a complicated incentive system that was based on both group and individual productivity. The individual incentive system was designed to get high productivity from workers by tying their earnings to their productivity. By also tying earnings to group productivity, it was felt the group as a whole would prevent slacking off by any of its members. However, both these techniques failed to maximize productivity. An informal group norm developed that defined what was a "proper day's work." The individuals chosen for this portion of the study had been from the same department, but they had not been friendly previously. As soon as they were involved in the research, friendships were established and two cliques developed. Despite the cliques, all the workers shared the norm of how much should be produced. Those who turned out too much work were called "rate busters" and those who turned out too little were labeled "chiselers." No one was supposed to "squeal" on anyone else, nor were they supposed to act "officiously."[58] The group had a variety of sanctions at its disposal. If individuals deviated from the norm, they would be "binged" by fellow workers. (Binging was a sharp punch on the arm.) The group also used less direct means of sanctioning, such as name calling: "If a person turned out

[56]Houbolt, "An Empirical Critique of Blauner's Concept of Powerlessness on the Automobile Assembly Line."

[57]Fritz Roethlisberger and William J. Dickson, *Management and the Worker* (New York: Wiley, 1964).

[58]Rodman reports a similar treatment of squealers by Canadian infantry recruits. See, Hyman Rodman, "Informal Behaviour of Infantry Recruits," in Audrey Wipper, *The Sociology of Work: Essays in Honour of Oswald Hall*, pp. 99–100.

too much work, he was called names, such as 'Speed King' or 'The Slave.' "[59]

In his analysis of this portion of the Hawthorne studies, Homans feels that the workers' restriction of output is a reflection of the "conflict between the technical organization of the plant and its social organization."[60] In the face of technical norms and orders from the top, "the industrial worker develops his own ways of doing his job, his own traditions of skill, his own satisfactions in living up to his standards."[61] Industrial workers also develop subgroups to protect themselves from technical norms and especially from technological changes that might disrupt their work routine or the routine of the informal group. The sentiments of the informal organization and its protective practices serve to make the worklife of the industrial worker more meaningful. More generally, we can say that these practices are designed to help the worker cope with alienation caused by technological changes in the workplace.

Beating the system.   The informal group in industry also attempts to deal with alienation by developing methods of "beating the system." Roy's study of a machine shop shows that much cheating was done in order to make the production quota and that a great deal of loafing, swindling, and conniving also existed.[62] Roy was a participant observer and noted that

> . . . we machine operators did "figure the angles," we developed an impressive repertoire of angles to play and devoted ourselves to crossing the expectations of formal organization with perseverance, artistry, and organizing ability of our own.[63]

For example, the workers would take longer to do a job when it was being timed in order to set piecework rates. They would run the machines at slower speeds or utilize extra movements such as "little reachings, liftings, adjustings, dustings, and other special attentions of conscientious machine operation and good housekeeping that could be dropped instantly with the departure of the time-study man."[64] When the time-study person made a job difficult, the workers revised it to make it easier. The set process was streamlined even though it might be harder on tools or reduce the quality of production. A variety of devices were needed to keep these practices from supervisors and inspectors. Finally, there were collusive arrangements with other groups in the plant to beat the system.

Runcie illustrates this point in terms of a truck-driving job he had while

---

[59]George C. Homans, "The Western Electric Researches," in Amitai Etzioni, ed., *Readings on Modern Organizations* (Englewood Cliffs, NJ: Prentice-Hall, 1969), p. 110. Rodman reports that Canadian infantrymen who do not keep up with their work are called "leadswingers." Rodman, "Informal Behaviour of Infantry Recruits," p. 98.

[60]Homans, "The Western Electric Researches," p. 111.

[61]Ibid., p. 113.

[62]Donald Roy, "Efficiency and 'the Fix': Informal Intergroup Relations in a Piecework Machine Shop," *American Journal of Sociology,* 60 (1954), 255–266.

[63]Ibid., 257.

[64]Ibid.

employed in the automobile assembly plant. In this job, Runcie, as well as two others, were expected to move cars from one section of the repair floor to another. Runcie notes:

> Although three of us were assigned to the task, most of the time two were sufficient; we were only needed if a car had to be moved. We worked out a schedule so that two of us were available at any one time, with the third hiding out of sight, reading a newspaper, napping, or eating lunch.[65]

In collusion with the other two workers, loafing was informally established to the point that Runcie claims during an 8-hour shift on this job: "I actually worked a total of about two and one-half hours."[66]

These activities may be viewed as protective devices. Although protection cannot be minimized, the preeminent function of these activities is to deal with alienation by enhancing the meaningfulness of work for semiskilled and unskilled workers. The informal group, its norms, its cohesiveness, and its efforts to beat the system all serve to make work more meaningful, less alienating.

The informal practices discussed in this section are functional both for the worker and management. Even though some of the informal mechanisms may be contrary to the immediate goals of management, they do tend to reduce alienation, turnover, absenteeism, sabotage, and the like. Without such informal practices management might find itself confronted with a disgruntled group of workers who strike out at management in a variety of ways. Given this, it may be that management should encourage the development of such groups rather than act to prevent their development. If it did encourage informal group development, it might well find that these groups work even more often with the organization than against it.

Games workers play. In another study, Roy examined informal group processes which are not aimed against management but do nevertheless serve to make the worklife less alienating, more meaningful.[67] Roy himself admits that in this study he was interested in how machine operators prevent themselves from "going nuts." He was a participant observer in a group of machine operators who were engaged in work that was repetitious and very simple and that required long hours and a 6-day week. Roy is concerned with devices these operators used to find some meaning in this essentially meaningless occupation. First they found that they could make a little game out of their work: they varied their activity by changing the colors of the material or die shapes used or engaging in some maintenance work on the machinery. These little games, however, were of secondary importance to the informal group activities that took place on the job. Roy observed a variety of minor group processes that served to pass the day more pleasantly and interestingly. During the morning "peach time" was announced, at which point one worker took

---

[65]Runcie, "By Days I Make the Cars," 108.

[66]Ibid.

[67]Donald Roy, " 'Banana Time': Job Satisfaction and Informal Interaction," *Human Organization*, 18 (1959–1960), 158–169.

out two peaches and divided them among the four workers. Then there was "banana time." The same man who brought the peaches also brought one banana, which was for his own consumption. However, regularly each morning one of the workers would steal the banana and consume it gleefully while yelling "banana time!" The person who brought the banana would regularly protest and just as regularly another worker would admonish him for protesting so vociferously. As the day progressed there was "window time," "lunch time," "pick-up time," "fish time," and "Coke time." Through these rather pathetic little devices workers on an essentially meaningless job endeavored to make their worklife less alienating.

Roy has also pointed to still another game designed to cope with alienation among machine operators—sex play![68] He found that sexual relations between coworkers and various types of games with sexual overtones helped workers deal with undesirable aspects of their jobs. Here is just one example of such a game to give the reader a flavor of this form of activity and its significance on the job:

> I recall a factory job in my early work experience in which the massive boredom of performing simple repetitive operations as a member of a cooky-machine crew was alleviated by the lewd antics of a moronic operative. . . . This mentally but not sexually defective fellow would rescue the rest of us from our pit of painful boredom at intervals by flashing an erection and whirling back and forth with it, to and from the oven, quite gracefully in fact, and by responding to the cheers, laughter, and obscene suggestions of his workmates by imbecilic grinning.[69]

Runcie also found games to be a technique workers used to cope with the boredom and monotony of the automobile assembly line. Runcie and his fellow workers played "football" with a foam rubber ball wrapped in electrical tape and "basketball" where workers threw various production materials, such as screws, nuts, and bolts, etc., into a styrofoam cup. Another game played was called "hooting." Runcie describes the game as follows:

> A worker hoots at the top of his lungs, others pick up the cry and the hooting goes up and down the line until it dies out sometime later.[70]

While these games are not directed at management, Houbolt describes a game that was directed at what was perceived as undeserved abuse by a foreman.

> So what we ended up doing was that every time we had the slightest problem, OK . . . we would go "Yoohoo," and have the foreman checking out the problem. Just like the rules say. We had him running around all day, all of us, we all joined in. We call ourselves the Odd Squad. At the end of that day, the next day, we gave him a hard time up to lunch. After lunch we didn't see him anymore.[71]

[68]Donald Roy, "Sex in the Factory: Informal Heterosexual Relations Between Supervisors and Work Groups," in Clifton D. Bryant, ed., *Deviant Behavior* (Chicago: Rand-McNally, 1974), pp. 44–66.

[69]Ibid., p. 45.

[70]Runcie, "By Days I Make the Cars," 109.

[71]Houbolt, "An Empirical Critique of Blauner's Concept of Powerlessness on the Automobile Assembly Line," 5.

As Houbolt points out, this game tortured the foreman without violating the formal rules of the organization. Such incidents are quite amusing until one realizes that these are adults striving desperately to cope with a meaningless and alienating worklife.

Most analysts who have examined the games workers play, and more generally the range of informal group practices, see them as efforts to reduce alienation (and a variety of other discontents on the job). They have usually been seen as social mechanisms developed by workers in opposition to management. A very different perspective on this is taken in a recent study by Burawoy in which he concludes that these games "are usually neither independent nor in opposition to management."[72] Furthermore: "Management, at least at the lower levels, actually participates not only in the organization of the game, but in the enforcement of its rules."[73] Rather than challenging management, the organization, and ultimately the capitalist system, these games actually serve to support them. For one thing, playing the game serves to create consent among the workers about the rules on which the game is based and, more generally, to the system of social relations (owner-manager-worker) which define the rules of the game. Second, since the managers and workers are both involved in the game, the system of antagonistic social relations to which the game was supposed to respond is obscured.

Burawoy argues that such methods of generating active cooperation and consent are far more effective ways of getting workers to cooperate in the pursuit of profit than coercion (such as, firing those who do not cooperate). In the end, Burawoy believes that games and other informal practices are all methods of gaining acceptance of the system by workers and eliciting their contributions to ever-higher levels of profitability.

Psychological Coping Mechanisms

Assembly-line workers. Many alienated automobile assembly-line workers seek, psychologically, to flesh out their worklives. For example, mental games and daydreaming are quite common. In his job, Runcie claims he tried to pass the time by counting the number of cars he had already completed as well as the number of cars still to come. Not all mental games are this conscious, however. Runcie notes:

> One time I realized that I was doing my job to the rhythm of an aria from an opera I had heard the last weekend. Another time I found myself a thousand miles away, driving an imaginary automobile down a highway I had not been on for years. How many chassis went by during my mental lapses—and whether I even did my job—I don't know and never found out.[74]

Some workers sing songs or recite multiplication tables, while others daydream. One worker told Runcie:

---

[72]Michael Burawoy, *Manufacturing Consent: Changes in the Labor Process Under Monopoly Capitalism* (Chicago: University of Chicago Press, 1979), p. 80.

[73]Ibid.

[74]Runcie, "By Days I Make the Cars," 109.

There's not much you can do, I guess. You just do the work. Daydream, that's the best. Gettin' out of this place. Gettin' off the line for about six hours. Just put your mind in a different place, say you're not here. I daydream about when I was a kid. Then you sit and laugh, and people look at you like you're crazy or something.[75]

Although the work routine itself offers little hope, many rationalize their plight by focusing on extrinsic job factors such as the high pay and job security: the job is a means to an end and not an end in itself, since the activity of work is fundamentally unrewarding.[76] Real advancement is virtually impossible for most assembly-line workers, so advancement becomes "the search for security, the pursuit of small goals in the factory, and the constant accumulation of personal possessions."[77] Another major psychological "out" for this worker is the projection of "[his] unfulfilled ambitions upon [his] children."[78] He cannot improve his own worklife, so he concentrates on his children, seeking to prevent them from working in a factory and encouraging them to go to college: "I never had a chance, but I want my kids to go to college and do something better than factory work."[79] However, these psychological resolutions and the resulting actions are only marginally successful. Many children, despite their fathers' aspirations, do finally go into blue-collar work. More important, for our purposes, the deemphasizing of the job and focusing on other factors only serves to increase the assembly-line worker's alienation. Work becomes little more than "a necessary evil to be endured because of the weekly pay check."[80]

Telephone operators.   Individuals in unskilled and semiskilled occupations sometimes attempt to cope with their alienation by overemphasizing the status or importance of their job. For example, the work of telephone operators is similar in many ways to assembly-line work, yet most operators consider themselves white-collar employees.[81] Ignoring the intrinsic similarities to blue-collar jobs, they emphasize the cleanliness of the work, their better manners, and superior dress. One operator contends: "It's not like manual labor, it's more like office work."[82] Another states: "It's the same as any business office. In fact, I think they [telephone operators] should be called communication secretaries because they do a great deal of work for business firms."[83] Others in the telephone company have a more realistic appraisal: "I tell you I simply can't see that they [operators] are classified as white collar people . . . it's just

---

[75]Ibid.

[76]Ely Chinoy, *Automobile Workers and the American Dream* (Boston: Beacon Press, 1955).

[77]Ibid., p. 124.

[78]Ibid., p. 126.

[79]Ibid., p. 127.

[80]Ibid., p. 130.

[81]Joel Seidman et al., "Telephone Workers," in Sigmund Nosow and William H. Form, *Man, Work and Society* (New York: Basic Books, 1962), pp. 493–504.

[82]Ibid., p. 498.

[83]Ibid.

like an assembly-line. . . . But if you say that they all resent it—they don't want to admit it because it degrades them."[84]

Psychiatric attendants. Another psychological mechanism employed in manual occupations to deal with alienation is generally called a *mythical occupational image.* Low-status workers may "seize upon some aspect of their work which is highly valued, either throughout society or in the work subculture, and build a self-image around it."[85] Simpson and Simpson's study of the psychiatric attendant is perhaps the best example of the utilization of this device. Most of the psychiatric attendants gave extrinsic reasons (salary, not qualified for anything else, and so forth) for taking their jobs, but gave intrinsic reasons (interest in patients, for example) for staying on the job. When the activities the attendants say are most important are compared to the activities they say are most time-consuming, some interesting differences appear. For example, 52 percent of the psychiatric attendants report housekeeping and miscellaneous activities as most time-consuming, yet only 7.8 percent report this activity as most important. Conversely, 28.4 percent of the respondents reported interaction with patients as their most important activity, yet only 4.9 percent reported this activity as most time-consuming. Thus, attendants stress their activities that relate to the care of the patient while they spend the majority of their worktime on housekeeping and miscellaneous chores. By focusing on the highly valued aspect of patient care, the psychiatric attendants are able to maintain a highly favorable self-image. Although all attendants are not satisfied with their work, this exaggerated self-image serves to make the job more tolerable.

Night watchmen. Trice's study of the night watchman also presents evidence that those in manual occupations emphasize a minor, but highly valued, aspect of their work.[86] The night watchman is required to move around his location in order to be sure that there is no trouble. This, however, tends to be dull, routine, and alienating since there is rarely anything wrong. To enhance their occupational self-image, the watchmen chose to focus on several aspects of their job which were regarded by society as being very important. For example, almost all felt that fire prevention was their most important task, despite the fact that for years there had been no fire at the location Trice studied. They also emphasized that they were management surrogates, "representing the company to anyone who came or went in the building."[87] This image was held despite the fact that rarely, if ever, did anyone come into the building during the hours that they were on duty. In sum, an occupational self-image which emphasizes highly valued aspects of the job

[84]Ibid., pp. 498–499.

[85]Richard L. Simpson and Ida Harper Simpson, "The Psychiatric Attendant: Development of an Occupational Self-Image in a Low-Status Occupation," *American Sociological Review*, 24 (1959), 389.

[86]Harrison M. Trice, "Night Watchman: A Study of an Isolated Occupation," *ILR Research*, 10 (1964), 3–8.

[87]Ibid., 7.

makes work in manual occupations less alienating to the individuals in these occupations.

It is interesting to ponder whether this emphasis on a highly valued aspect of the job is really accepted by individuals in the occupation, or whether it is merely for public consumption. If it is truly believed, this involves an enormous task of self-deception. The workers must hold this belief although most of the things they do and are expected to do contradict it. Further, if they do believe in their mythical occupational image, they will be confronted with much status inconsistency, for they will think they have high status while virtually everyone else in the organization has a more realistic view of their position. This is exemplified by the individual in the telephone company who said that he could not see how operators could classify themselves as white-collar workers when their work more closely resembles that of the assembly line. If the individuals in manual occupations hold their image merely for public relations purposes, they are faced with other problems. They cannot enhance their own job satisfaction if they do not really believe in the occupational image they are trying to project. Further, they are unlikely to convince anyone else if they do not believe it themselves. One must question whether occupational myths can ever be truly successful. How can people convince themselves that their self-image is true when they are constantly faced with evidence to the contrary? How can they convince others when they clearly see that the image does not reflect reality? The lack of success of such mythical occupational images points up the frustration of those in semiskilled and unskilled occupations. Despite the difficulties inherent in them, mythical occupational images are an important part of the life of individuals in manual occupations in organizations. As Dubin notes, these occupational myths (or fictions, as he calls them) "are necessary in order that action within the formal organization may proceed."[88] Everyone knows they are untrue, but "the truth, however, is disturbing, so by a kind of silent agreement among members of the organization, this truth is clothed in fiction."[89]

Unions as Coping Mechanisms

Only about 17.3 million Americans belong to labor unions, but the union movement's greatest strength is among unskilled and semiskilled workers.[90] Manual workers can utilize labor unions to compensate for and reduce the alienating aspects of their worklives. As individuals, blue-collar workers were, historically, powerless vis-a-vis management. As a matter of fact, one of the most important reasons for the development of unions was the almost total control of management over workers. Once a union is formed, management is no longer able to fire, promote, demote, or punish workers at will, and if it acts without just cause, workers can bring grievances against it which the union will generally actively support. The mere existence of the possibility of the expensive grievance process has reduced management's dictatorial power.

[88]Robert Dubin, "Organization Fictions," in Robert Dubin, ed., *Human Relations in Administration*, 3rd ed. (Englewood Cliffs, NJ: Prentice-Hall, 1968), p. 494.

[89]Ibid., p. 496.

[90]Paul O. Flaim, "New Data on Union Members and Their Earnings," *Employment and Earnings*, 32 (1985), 13.

As a group, through the collective bargaining process, union members have a good deal of power over management, which can no longer arbitrarily set wages, hours, and working conditions. Instead, these conditions must be agreed upon by both parties during labor negotiations. If management does not present a reasonable offer, the union can call a strike which, in most organizations, would severely cripple or totally halt production. It is not only the strike, but also the mere threat of one, which gives the union a good deal of leverage in its dealings with management.

Besides lessening feelings of powerlessness, the union may help to reduce the other three social-psychological dimensions of alienation: meaninglessness, isolation, and self-estrangement. If semi- and unskilled workers seek some meaning in their worklives, they may turn to the union. By being active in the union, they can see their role in relation to other roles within the union structure. Further, they can get a clear idea of the purpose of the union and what is their part in the attainment of its objectives. This is especially true in small local unions. The union can also help alleviate the manual workers' feelings of isolation. If they do not feel as if they belong in the work setting, they can get a feeling of belonging within the union, where they find themselves in an organization with their peers and where all strive for a mutual goal.

Finally, workers may be able to alleviate some of their feelings of self-estrangement by becoming involved in the union. It has been pointed out before that they are frequently unable to express their abilities, their potential, or their personality on the job. The union offers an alternative: frequently, capable workers who have been barred from managerial positions have been able to utilize their administrative skills and fulfill their desire for leadership within the union. At the local level there are low-level administrative positions available and above them are such positions as union secretary, treasurer, vice president, and president. For those who demonstrate exceptional administrative ability there is the possibility, at least, of high-level positions within the national union or even within the AFL-CIO. The union constitutes one of the few remaining sources of upward mobility for talented blue-collar workers.

Union dysfunctions. In all fairness we should point out that in many cases unions fail to fulfill the function of reducing worker alienation, and that occasionally they have instead increased it. Some unions have developed their own hierarchies, which have not been responsive to the needs and demands of the membership. Illustrative of this is the fact that in his book on unions, Hall took as his major theme the "amazing separation that exists between union leaders and union rank and file."[91] In such unions it is not unusual to find leaders who have remained in power for 30 or even 40 years. They have retained their power by systematically excluding members from a say in how the union should be run and by making deals with management which serve their own ends without serving the members' needs. Sociologists who have studied unions have often explained this phenomenon in terms of Robert Michels' "Iron Law of Oligarchy." That is, once in power leaders become more con-

[91]Sylvia Kopald, cited in Burton Hall, "Introduction," in Burton Hall, ed., *Autocracy and Insurgency in Organized Labor* (New Brunswick, New Jersey: Transaction Books, 1972), p. 2.

cerned with maintaining their position than in pursuing the goals they had promised to attain. This problem is especially acute in unions because of the huge gap between the pay of union leaders and the pay that they received as workers, or would receive again if they should fail to be reelected. Once in power, union leaders have a number of devices under their control to solidify their position. They have patronage to dole out, union funds to support their reelection campaigns, and control of the union press with which they can extol their virtues and downgrade those of their opponents.

However, Lipset et al.'s study of typographers has indicated that the "Iron Law of Oligarchy" is neither iron, nor a law.[92] They found that in the typographical workers union there was a substantial turnover of leadership— but they quickly pointed out that there were a number of historical peculiarities and differences in the nature of printers which accounted for this unusual situation. These peculiar conditions exist in few other unions, and therefore many unions *are* characterized by an oligarchical structure.

In those unions which are oligarchical and not responsive to the needs of the members, alienation is increased rather than decreased. Hence many workers who turn to the union to reduce alienation find to their dismay that alienation has increased.

In general it may be concluded that when unions are run with the focus on the needs of the members they may serve to reduce the alienation of manual workers. However, alienation may be increased when they are designed to serve the interests of the leaders. Most unions probably fall between these extremes and hence serve to reduce the alienation of manual workers to some degree.

Employing Organizations and Coping with Alienation

Alienation is costly to employers of unskilled or semiskilled workers. The question management has always had to deal with is: Is the cost of the solution greater than the cost of the problem? In human terms, reducing alienation is certainly a worthwhile investment, but unfortunately management often tends to think more in terms of profit margins than in terms of human work satisfaction. Even looking at the problem of alienation from the perspective of profits indicates that alienation is economically costly. Walker and Guest, among others, found that turnover and absenteeism are highly related to the repetitiveness of work on the assembly line.[93] Sabotage of the assembly line, and glee when the machine breaks down accidentally, are not uncommon in mass-production factories. Many of the workers are careless and this results in low quality, even where the quality is ostensibly set by the machine. An alienated worklife is also likely to lead to hostility toward management, which might take the form of involvement in the union or even wildcat strikes. Given these and other costs, some organizations have sought to reduce the alienation of their unskilled employees.

[92]Seymour M. Lipset, Martin Trow, and James Coleman, *Union Democracy* (Garden City, NY: Anchor Books, 1962).

[93]Walker and Guest, *Man on the Assembly Line.*

Managerial manipulation.   Unfortunately, many of these efforts have been more manipulative than sincere. The most blatant example of managerial manipulation was developed by the human relations school of management theory. This approach was a reaction to the scientific management theory of F.W. Taylor (see Chapter 14 for more on Taylor's ideas), who felt that the needs of the laborer and the needs of the organization could be united if pay was tied to productivity. Since workers were supposedly motivated by economic desires, they would produce more under such an arrangement and the company would be more profitable. But in the original human relations study at the Hawthorne plant of the Western Electric Company in Chicago it became quite clear that people were not driven solely, or even primarily, by economic motives. The finding, for example, that the group acted to restrict productivity indicated that social factors were also very important in understanding human behavior in the workplace. This led to the conclusion that if the group was content and understood what management was trying to do, it would be more likely to produce up to its maximum capabilities.[94]

An offshoot of this conclusion was the development of a variety of techniques to make the group happier and therefore more productive. Communication was deemed of the utmost importance. The emphasis, however, was on communicating what management wanted rather than on communicating the needs of the workers. It was also felt that if workers were allowed to participate in decision making, they would be more productive. However, this participation often took the form of asking what the workers wanted and then ignoring their desires in the ultimate decision, which remained in the hands of top management. At its extreme the human relations approach came to be known as "cow sociology": as long as the workers were content (as well-fed cows) they would be productive. To make them content, management piped in music, painted walls brightly, and provided comfortable rest rooms. But these devices were extrinsic to the job, and it was the nature of the job that was the basic source of the worker's alienation.

One of the basic assumptions of the human relations school (and scientific management) was that there was no irreconcilability between the goals of management and the goals of workers. However, management's goal of the highest possible profit *is* often contrary to the needs of the workers.

In opposition to the "harmony" view of the human relations school there has developed the structural school in the sociology of organizations. The structuralists recognize "the inevitable strains—which can be reduced but not eliminated—between organizational needs and personal needs; between formal and informal relations; between management and workers, or, more generically, between ranks and divisions."[95] There is inevitable conflict between the worker and the organization which can never be eliminated, but it

[94]Recent statistical evidence calls into question this conclusion. See, Richard Herbert Franke and James D. Kaul, "The Hawthorne Experiments: First Statistical Interpretation," *American Sociological Review,* 43 (1978), 623–643. Franke and Kaul suggest that it was not human relations that led to an increase in productivity, but rather managerial discipline (firing two workers), the economic adversity of the depression (scarcity of jobs and the threat of unemployment), and longer rest periods (reduction of worker fatigue).

[95]Amitai Etzioni, *Modern Organizations* (Englewood Cliffs, NJ: Prentice-Hall, 1964).

can be reduced to manageable proportions. Because of the nature of blue-collar work, alienation can never be eliminated without a restructuring of the entire organization. Such a reorganization would also be necessary to eliminate the conflict between management and the worker.

One such reorganization worthy of mention at this point is employee ownership of firms. Employees do not buy firms in order to reduce alienation (they generally buy them to save their jobs), but that could be one of the byproducts of their action. Although it is clear that the purchase of organizations by their employees preserves jobs,[96] it is less clear whether employee ownership leads to a decrease in feelings of alienation.[97] One of the reasons for the failure of employee ownership to reduce alienation may be that employees in such firms come to view managers as *de facto* owners; they do not see themselves as the owners.[98]

COPING WITH STRUCTURAL ALIENATION

The preceding examples of coping with alienation have dealt with actions taken independently by the workers, unions, or management. Primarily, these actions have focused on attempting to alleviate the psychological manifestations of alienation. Most of these coping mechanisms are limited, for they address the issue of alienation *only* at the individual level. As a result, they can be seen as only temporarily relieving workers' *feelings* of boredom, monotony, meaninglessness, powerlessness, and so forth. These coping mechanisms help the worker gain some meaning from otherwise routine, meaningless work, but they do not change or alter the structural dimensions of alienation as suggested by the Marxian theory of alienation. These actions do not alter the decision-making processes relating to the structural dimension of control over one's work. However, some companies have come to more meaningfully cope with alienation by altering the structural dimension of worker decision making and control. As the president of one firm that has made such an effort notes:

> More and more companies are finding that to continue to operate they have to have better contact with all their people. You have to stop the alienation. And you don't stop that except by getting at the root causes of alienation.[99]

From our point of view, industrial democracy can be seen as such an attempt.

[96]Corey Rosen, "Job-Creating Performance of Employee-Owned Firms," *Monthly Labor Review,* 106 (1983), 15–19.

[97]David J. Toscano, "Toward a Typology of Employee Ownership," *Human Relations,* 36 (1983), 582.

[98]Tove Helland Hammer and Robert N. Stern, "Employee Ownership: Implications for the Organizational Distribution of Power," *Academy of Management Journal,* 23 (1980), 78–100.

[99]David W. Ewing and Pamela Banks, "Participative Management at Work: An Interview with John F. Donnelly," *Harvard Business Review,* 55 (January/February, 1977), 117–118.

Democratization[100]

The principles of authoritarian control from the top, highly circum-scribed worker autonomy, and minute specialization have served to make American industry a bastion of autocracy within a supposedly democratic society. The external control of the worker by increasingly sophisticated machinery has created a lack of control by workers over their workplace. These principles and developments seem to be combined in their most extreme form in the assembly line, which has become, as a result, the symbol of all that is wrong with work in America, in particular blue-collar work.[101] These symbols and the efforts to cope with the abuses caused by them received a great deal of attention in the 1970s. A variety of forces coincided to spark this surge in interest during this period. We will examine these changes and then turn our attention to more recent developments in the 1980s that have served to overturn many of the changes put in place during the 1970s.

Prior to the 1970s, management played its part in the pursuit of greater and greater profits by doing such things as speeding up the assembly line, reducing the content of many jobs until there was little left but the most minute tasks, and increasing the size of its bureaucracies (for example, through the development of conglomerates) so that the worker was further and further removed from the top of the organization. These developments stood in opposition to a variety of trends in the larger society. The workforce, in particular the younger members, were better educated and were entering the workworld with higher expectations about their work and their role in it. But the jobs they were entering were not changing and were still attuned to the older type of workers who seemed more satisfied with, or were at least less likely to manifest their resentment to, traditional work. Along with their greater education, the new workers also seemed to be adopting a new value system that deemphasized money and focused on the ability to learn, to develop one's potential, and to gain more control over one's work. For example, a plant manager at the General Motors car assembly plant at Tarrytown, New York suggested:

> It was during this time that the young people in the plant were demanding some kind of change. They didn't want to work in this kind of environment. The union didn't have much control over them, and they certainly were not interested in taking orders from a dictatorial management.[102]

The failure of management to respond to these new workers led to a rebellion against traditional work.

---

[100]This discussion is drawn, in part, from George Ritzer, "Work-linked Equity in Sweden: Implications for America," in Irving Louis Horowitz, ed., *Equity, Income and Policy: A Comparative Developmental Context* (New York and London: Praeger, 1977), pp. 49–69.

[101]For white-collar workers, it is the bureaucracy, organized on the same principles, that has become a similar symbol of oppression and lack of freedom on the job.

[102]Robert H. Guest, "Quality of Work Life—Learning from Tarrytown," *Harvard Business Review*, 57 (July/August, 1979), 78.

In effect, the workers were rebelling against the very principles that had made industry and bureaucracy so efficient, at least until the 1970s. A Swedish observer catches the essence of this when he argues that the worker was reacting against

> ... the principles [of] job simplification, repetition and close control. The worker is viewed as one more interchangeable part, programmed to perform a small task that is precisely specified on the basis of time and motion studies. He is assumed to be a precise element in the production process, motivated primarily by his economic needs and characterized primarily by a predictable degree of strength, agility and perseverance; innovation and dealing with variations in the flow of production are considered beyond his scope and are left to specialists. In order to energize and coordinate some dozens of hundreds of atomized human "parts" in a plant, a rigorous and highly detailed control system is called into play, exemplified in its most extreme form by the balanced, intricately interwoven network of conveyors that constitutes an automobile assembly line.[103]

As a result of the social changes discussed above, this once highly rational system was proving to be less and less efficient. Workers were finding their jobs increasingly dull, tiring, and destructive of their self-esteem. Resentment against the technology and employers grew, bringing with it such costly problems as poor quality, high absenteeism, and high turnover. To cope with these problems, management fell back on its old principles and developed even simpler jobs, even tighter controls, and even faster lines. The workers' reaction was predictable—they found their work even more monotonous, exhausting, and demeaning. The problems of turnover, absenteeism, and quality grew correspondingly. Although this destructive process occurred in many settings, both blue- and white-collar, it was most pronounced on the assembly line. The effects of these problems on the assembly line were great, because it proved to be most vulnerable to serious disruption by these developments. In sum, the most rational technological and bureaucratic developments had failed to keep pace with changes in society, with the result that they were no longer rational. What worked in Detroit in the early 1900s ceased to operate efficiently in Tarrytown, New York (and many other places throughout the world) in the early 1970s.

Since the term "industrial democracy" has been used to denote a variety of things, we need to clarify the term. Industrial democracy embraces three developments that need to be carefully separated.[104] The first is *interest-group democracy*, a situation in which the relationship between union and management brings at least a measure of democracy to the workplace. Through the union the workers have a say, at least theoretically, in how their work is done, and the binding agreement between labor and management prevents arbitrary management action. The second type, *representative democracy*, results

---

[103]Lars Bjork, "An Experiment in Work Satisfaction," *Scientific American*, 232 (1975), 17.

[104]Eric Trist, "Work Improvement and Industrial Democracy," Paper presented to the Conference of the Commission of European Communities on "Work Organization, Technical Development and Motivation of the Individual," Brussels, Belgium, 1974.

from the institutionalization of a variety of formal committees in which representatives from different levels within the organization meet to discuss issues of mutual interest and sometimes even make decisions. The major example of this is the Yugoslavian workers' councils, although a large number of companies in the Western world have joint committees on a variety of matters of mutual concern to managers and workers. Finally, *work-linked* democracy involves the ability of workers to influence, and sometimes even decide upon, how *their own work* is to be performed. As we will see, all three types of industrial democracy gained strength in the United States in the 1970s, and each played a role in other countries (for example, Norway, West Germany, and Great Britain) as well. Before turning to developments in the United States, we would like to direct our attention to the development of industrial democracy in Sweden which, in the middle 1970s, became the world's laboratory for studying efforts to cope with the aforementioned problems.

Work-Linked Democracy in Sweden

Although no one knows exactly how many programs in industrial democracy were undertaken in Sweden in the 1970s, the undeniable fact is that there were many such efforts. The generally peaceful relations between union and management created a high degree of interest-group democracy. There were also numerous examples of representative democracy, with a wide variety of joint work-management committees existing throughout the industrial world. As of April 1973, Swedish companies with 100 or more employees were required to allow two employee representatives to sit on the board of directors. Thus, democratization took place across a broad front in Sweden. Parenthetically, it should be noted that not everyone was happy with these efforts. Many considered them to be unsuccessful. Nevertheless, there existed an almost universal commitment throughout Sweden to the principles of industrial democracy.

While commitment to industrial democracy was widespread in Sweden, the major experiments were in the area of work-linked democracy. Work-linked democracy efforts ranged from small-scale attempts at job rotation and job enlargement to the program in the Volvo plant at Kalmar in which about $30 million was invested in a plant that had been designed and built on the principles of work-linked democracy. From the Volvo plant case, we can derive a number of insights into the nature of work-linked democracy and see the extent to which Swedish workers gained some real, structural control over various decision-making processes that affect their worklife.

Volvo.   No company has been more active in the area of work-linked democracy than Volvo. The company's general manager enunciated the following company policy:

> Here at Volvo, in fact all over Sweden, we are trying to create small groups of workers who develop into skilled and proud craftsmen, small groups under one large umbrella—craftsmen who set their own work pace, their own coffee

breaks. It costs more, but there is evidence that it decreases the rate of absenteeism.[105]

This general policy was implemented in different ways by the various semi-autonomous units within Volvo.[106] At the Torslanda plant, a large-scale job rotation program was undertaken: "One group will assemble fuel pipes on Monday; fit side windows on Tuesday; fit car interiors on Wednesday; assemble rear parts on Thursday; and fit fuel pipes again on Friday."[107] Such a program is not unusual, but Volvo went further. At the Volvo Lundwerken plant work-linked democracy was implemented:

> Groups of up to nine workers are given a work assignment and they decide for themselves who does what. The teams elect their own foremen—on a rotating basis—and they do their own training, with the cost of the training borne by the company. Production problems are discussed with management at monthly meetings.[108]

At Volvo Skövde:

> . . . the assembly line has been replaced by small "work groups." Built-in "buffer zones" give workers and/or the work groups a chance to determine their own work pace as well as rest periods. The work groups are fully responsible for quality control, processing of raw materials, and tool inventories. Each work group takes care of transport of motors from one workshop to another.[109]

While these efforts to build workplace democracy and replace the traditional methods of doing work are important, they can be seen as mere preludes to Volvo's most important contribution to workplace democracy—its plant at Kalmar. While we focus on Kalmar, the reader should bear in mind that Volvo has not stopped with this effort. For example, in 1980 it built a new Tuve truck assembly plant near Gothenborg which incorporated many of the ideas developed earlier.[110]

The Kalmar plant was created on the basis of the following mandate from the corporate general manager:

> Produce a factory which, *without sacrificing efficiency and economic result* [italics ours], provides the possibility for the employee to work in groups, to communicate freely, to carry out job rotation, to vary the rate of work, feel identification

---

[105]Derek Norcross, "Sweden's Newest Export—Industrial Democracy," *Parade* (December 13, 1974), p. 15.

[106]Pehr Gyllenhammer, *People at Work* (Reading, Mass.: Addison-Wesley, 1977); Pehr Gyllenhammer, "How Volvo Adapts Work to People," *Harvard Business Review,* 55 (July/August, 1977), 102–113.

[107]Joseph Mire, "Improving Working Life—The Role of European Unions," *Monthly Labor Review,* 97 (1974), 6.

[108]Ibid.

[109]Ibid.

[110]Paul Bernstein, "Efficiency is Up and Absenteeism Down at New Volvo Plant," *World of Work Report,* 8 (1983), 94–95.

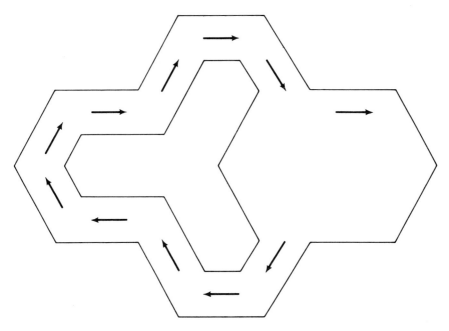

Arrows depict path of cars under construction

FIGURE 12.1

with the products, to be aware of quality, and also be in a position to influence their working environment.[111]

Before discussing this plant, some preliminary warnings need to be given. First of all, Volvo, unlike many of its admirers, did *not* consider the Kalmar plant to be the ultimate answer to industrial ills. Second, the factory was built with the clear directive from the general manager that efficiency *not* be reduced. Third, this development, like many others in Sweden, was the result of a management initiative aimed at coping with pressing problems such as turnover, absenteeism, difficulty in recruiting young workers, and so forth.

Figure 12.1 gives an overview of the Kalmar plant, while Figure 12.2 gives a more detailed picture of one section of it.

The star, or hexagonal, shape of the factory has a number of implications for the work that takes place within it. With the center of the plant devoted to material storage, the actual assembly of the cars takes place along the outer walls. Thus the assembly work is done in close proximity to the numerous windows that let sunlight in and give the workers a pleasant view of the surroundings. More important, the angular construction of the walls allows each group to have its own relatively well-defined area. Each angle represents

[111]Agis Salpukas, "Swedish Auto Plant Drops Assembly Line," *The New York Times* (November 12, 1974), p. 31.

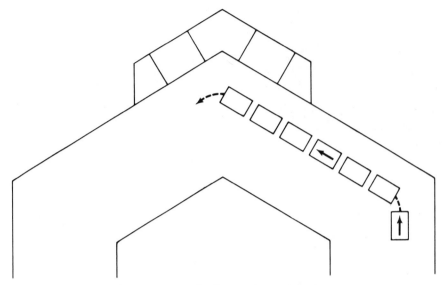

Arrows depict path of cars under construction

FIGURE 12.2

the end of one group and the beginning of another. Each of these groups performs a different part of the general process—electrical system, instruments, safety equipment, and so forth. Each team includes about twenty workers. The differentiation of function, along with the physical structure of the building, gives each group the feeling that it is set apart from those groups that precede and succeed it in the production process. This sense of independent identity is enhanced by the fact that each group has its own entrance, changing room, rest rooms, coffee break area, even its own sauna. All this is aimed at creating an environment in which autonomous or semi-autonomous work groups develop. In other words, the goal is the creation of something akin to a set of old-style skilled workshops under the roof of one large factory. With this method, the anonymous feeling of working in a huge impersonal setting is greatly reduced.

The atmosphere in the plant is remarkable. It is light, colorful, and airy. Great pains have been taken to reduce the noise level. It has none of the noisy dinginess that is characteristic of most American automobile assembly plants. As one observer has noted, the plant generally looks like a large, modern supermarket.

All of this, of course, does not produce cars. The structure of the plant as well as the philosophy ruled out the possibility of an assembly line. To move the cars in the process of being assembled through the various stations, the Volvo engineers developed an electrically driven carrier system. Each car is on a separate carrier that can be controlled by either a central computer or manually by the employees as they work on the car. The workers in each group therefore have the ability to move the car through their work area in any way they decide. They can collectively work on it as it stands still or moves slowly through their area, or they can set the carrier to move through their area at a set pace, in much the same way as on the traditional assembly line. The one major constraint on workers is that they must produce a set number of cars per hour. The workers in each group have the possibility, if they want, of working quickly and filling up the two-car buffer zone that exists between them and the next group. If they can fill the buffer zone, they will have time for a 10-minute coffee break. Incidentally, the electric carriers have the ability to tilt the car at about a 90-degree angle so that the formerly odious task of working under the car is made far easier and can be done like all the rest of the work.

The workers themselves have the ability to determine how the work within their group is to be done. (There is ordinarily only one foreman for every two groups.) They can decide to do a single task, or rotate among a number of tasks, or assemble a car collectively; they can use either the "straight-assembly" or the "dock" method. In the straight-assembly method, each individual works at a set station doing a particular task or set of tasks. This is much like the traditional assembly line in that the workers do their tasks as the carriers roll by. In the dock method, the workers work on the car as a team. They can follow the car through the entire process in their area, and when they are finished they return to the starting point and begin again on a new car. This method reduces the repetition of tasks to once every 40 minutes. In either case, the team is free to choose the method it prefers as long as productivity remains at the prescribed level.

Although foreigners were apt to see the "Kalmar concept" as the answer to industrial problems, the Volvo people did not share this exalted conception. In fact, as a result of Volvo's decentralization, different parts of the company did very different things in an effort to cope with their particular problems. As one Volvo official involved in corporate planning put it:

> Today we find not one Volvo model for socio-technical-administrative changes (as is often presumed) but a number of different models, or rather change processes. There is a wide range of approaches with different strategies involved. We thus find different developments—and results—in each plant where factors such as environment and cultural traditions play a crucial role.[112]

Furthermore, the developments at Kalmar are but one element in the future planning at Volvo:

> Within Volvo we look upon Kalmar as *the first step* [italics ours] to a new generation of production technology rather than the ultimate solution to assembly-work problems. At the moment we are are using this as a base to make further development work to be implemented in old as well as in new plants.[113]

Almost as a warning to overeager Americans the Volvo people warned: "We

[112]Berth Jonsson, "Strategy Towards Flexible Production Design." Paper presented at the Conference of Equilibrium Technology, Salzburg, Austria, 1975, 3.

[113]Ibid., 9.

will fail when we try to uncritically copy solutions."[114] Although most workers seemed relatively satisfied with these developments, others quickly became dissatisified with the developments and this dissatisfaction stood as still another warning to foreigners anxious to build "Kalmars" of their own. One Kalmar worker said: "This is certainly different from other jobs I've had. But there is a certain amount of monotony. It can't be avoided."[115] Although hard information is difficult to obtain, one source reports that the Kalmar plant had a comparatively low (10 percent) absenteeism rate in 1979.[116]

Industrial Democracy in the United States

Various forms of industrial democracy have been attempted in the United States since the early part of the eighteenth century.[117] In 1980 Zwerdling provided a guide to firms that had recently attempted some form of industrial democracy.[118] While not all these experiments were successful, Zwerdling discusses work-linked and representative democracy at such firms as General Foods, Rushton Mining, and McCaysville Industries. Workers have been represented on the boards of directors of such firms as Eastern Airlines, Pan American World Airways, and Chrysler.[119] Walton suggested that a significant minority of the *Fortune* "500" companies attempted some significant democratization projects.[120] General Motors, Proctor & Gamble, Exxon, TRW, Mars, Inc., DuPont, Alcoa, Texas Instruments, Weyerhaeuser, and Rockwell have all engaged in some form of industrial democracy. Among these organizations, General Motors was certainly among the leaders in industrial democracy experiments in the United States. In the late 1970s it was estimated that General Motors was engaged in over fifty "quality-of-work life" projects. This prompted one observer of the American scene to suggest that the efforts by General Motors were not only likely to have been the "most extensive of any company in the United States" but may have been more extensive than the efforts of Volvo in Sweden.[121]

Earlier, we noted that coping mechanisms were primarily actions taken by the worker, the unions, or management. With reference to industrial democracy, the current evidence suggests that not only is there a large measure of cooperation among these groups, but that successful implementation can only be achieved with a high degree of cooperation. Initiative for various pro-

[114]Ibid., 4.

[115]Salpukas, "Swedish Auto Plant Drops Assembly Line," p. 31.

[116]Bernstein, "Efficiency is Up and Absenteeism Down at New Volvo Plant," 95.

[117]Henry P. Guzda, "Industrial Democracy: Made in the U.S.A.," *Monthly Labor Review,* 107 (1984), 26–33.

[118]Daniel Zwerdling, *Workplace Democracy: A Guide to Workplace Ownership, Participation, and Self-Management Experiments in the United States and Europe* (New York: Harper Colophon Books, 1980).

[119]Carey W. English, "Companies Learn to Live with Unions in Board Rooms," *U.S. News and World Report* (January 30, 1984), p. 63.

[120]Richard E. Walton, "Work Innovations in the United States," *Harvard Business Review,* 57 (July/August, 1979), 91.

[121]Ibid.

jects usually comes from management. However, once initiated these projects are successful only with the cooperative efforts of the workers and the unions (where, of course, the workers are represented by a union).[122] A vice president of General Motors notes that a "key concept of our quality-of-worklife process is union participation."[123] General Motors is not an isolated case; union and management cooperation was also essential in the development of a quality-of-worklife program established between American Telephone and Telegraph and the Communication Workers of America.[124]

Although there are other examples of industrial democracy in the United States, perhaps nowhere else were these more developed than in the various quality-of-worklife projects undertaken at many General Motors assembly plants throughout the country.

General Motors.   The various projects at General Motors can be seen incorporating all three types of industrial democracy. In 1973 General Motors and the United Auto Workers negotiated a national agreement committing both managerial and union interest groups to mutually explore ways of improving the quality-of-worklife. This was the first time a major U.S. management-labor contract formally and explicitly addressed the quality-of-worklife issue.[125] With the National Committee to Improve the Quality of Work Life, the traditional adversary relationship between interest groups was transformed into one where cooperative efforts were aimed at improving the quality-of-worklife. The goal was to bring a measure of dignity and decision-making power to the worker at the factory floor.

Perhaps nowhere were the quality-of-worklife projects better exemplified than in the long-term, wide-reaching experiment at the General Motors assembly plant in Tarrytown. The initiative for establishing the program was originally taken by management.[126] In 1971, when the company decided to move the hard and soft trim departments to a new location in the plant, management started in the traditional manner, that is, from the top down. However, two production supervisors, sensing managerial desire for new approaches, made an important suggestion:

> Why not ask the workers themselves to get involved in the move? They are experts in their own right. They know as much about trim operations as anyone else.[127]

The workers were shown the various plans for the change and were given cer-

---

[122]Edward E. Lawler III and John A. Drexler, Jr., "Dynamics of Establishing Cooperative Quality-of-Worklife Projects," *Monthly Labor Review,* 101 (1978), pp. 23–28.

[123]Stephen H. Fuller, "How Quality-of-Worklife Projects Work for General Motors," *Monthly Labor Review,* 103 (1980), 37; see also, Irving Bluestone, "How Quality-of-Worklife Projects Work for the United Auto Workers," *Monthly Labor Review,* 103 (1980), 39–41.

[124]Michael Maccoby, "Helping Labor and Management Set Up a Quality-of-Worklife Program," *Montly Labor Review,* 107 (1984), 28–32.

[125]Robert Guest, "Quality of Work Life—Learning from Tarrytown."

[126]Ibid.

[127]Ibid., 79.

tain decision-making powers over the set-up of various jobs. The plans were initiated and the change instituted. The following year employees were involved in the complete rearrangement of the chassis department.

Early in 1977, a quality-of-worklife effort was launched on a plant-wide scale. Between early 1977 and December, 1978 a number of training sessions were conducted. The trainees learned:

> . . . first, about the concept of QWL [quality-of-worklife]; second, about the plant and the functions of management and the union; third, about problem-solving skills important in effective involvement.[128]

Over 3300 workers, union representatives, supervisors, and managers participated in the sessions.

With the introduction of the all-new 1980 X model General Motors cars, employees were given a chance to exercise their newly acquired skills. Together, managers and workers evaluated many of the anticipated assembly processes. The workers, in conversations with supervisors and technical people, were involved directly in establishing the best ways of setting up various jobs involved in the assembly process.

Through a series of regularly scheduled meetings, workers were kept informed of information needed to make intelligent, responsible problem-solving decisions:

> . . . following the plant manager's regular staff meetings, the personnel director passes on critical information to the shop committee. The safety director meets weekly with each zone committeeman. Top union officials have monthly "rap sessions" with top management staff to discuss future developments, facilitate alterations, schedule changes, model changes, and other matters requiring advanced planning. The chairman of Local 664 and his zone committeemen check in with the personnel director each morning at 7:00 a.m. and go over current or anticipated problems.[129]

At Tarrytown, information was disseminated, communication channels were opened, and workers were encouraged to participate and involve themselves in various decision-making processes.

However, despite these changes at Tarrytown, the "intrinsic nature of repetitive conveyor-paced jobs has not substantially changed."[130] Thus, unlike at Volvo-Kalmar, the basic source of worker alienation at General Motors has *not* been altered by democratization. However, structural changes (teams, committees, contracts) have been implemented and decision-making powers altered so that the workers have more say and control over the work process than in the past.

Efforts in industrial democracy like those at General Motors can be seen as attempts to not only help make the worker feel more powerful but also to

[128]Ibid., 83.
[129]Ibid., 84–85.
[130]Ibid., 87.

alter the structural arrangement by which work is performed and decisions are made. As such, these projects can be conceived of as attempts to alter the objective/structural forces that cause alienation as suggested by the Marxian theoretical formulation. In essence, these projects are aimed at changing the ways Americans work so that they are more involved in decisions that affect not only their immediate work processes but other areas in the organization as well. While these changes may be seen as more localized and more pragmatic than the various attempts at industrial democracy in Europe, they can at least be seen as initial attempts to structurally alter the way blue-collar work is performed in the United States.

The question still remains as to the effect of these structural changes on reducing psychological and behavioral indicators of alienation. Does an increase in the participation in decision making and/or an increase in the control over one's immediate work process decrease feelings and behavioral manifestations of alienation?

Research on Industrial Democracy

Research carried out primarily in the 1940s and 1950s by a variety of social psychologists all pointed to the significance of, and benefits to be derived from, worker participation.[131] Blumberg concluded, after carefully reviewing this body of work, that "there is hardly a study in the entire literature which fails to demonstrate that satisfaction in work is enhanced or that other beneficial consequences accrue from a general increase in workers' decision-making power. Such consistency of findings, I submit, is rare in social research."[132]

A body of literature with similar implications is to be found in Europe, generally aligned with the Tavistock Institute of England. Among many others, studies were undertaken in British coal mining,[133] an Indian textile factory,[134] and Norwegian metal working, pulp and paper, fertilizer and chemicals.[135] The dominant figure in the Tavistock tradition, Eric Trist, offers the following as the major conclusions to be derived from the long history of his group's research into industrial democracy:

1. High productivity and a high quality of working life are not necessarily antithetical.

2. The evidence indicates that industries must move away from coercive management.

[131]See, for example, L. Coch and J. R. P. French, Jr., "Overcoming Resistance to Change," *Human Relations,* 1 (1948), 512–532.

[132]Paul Blumberg, *Industrial Democracy: The Sociology of Participation* (New York: Shocken, 1968), p. 323.

[133]Eric Trist and K. W. Bamforth, "Some Social and Psychological Consequences of the Long-Wall Method of Coal-Getting," *Human Relations,* 4 (1951), 3–38.

[134]A. K. Rice, *Productivity and Social Organization: The Ahmedabad Experiment* (London: Tavistock, 1958).

[135]F. E. Emery and E. Thorsrud (in collaboration with E. L. Trist), *The Form and Content of Industrial Democracy* (London: Tavistock, 1969).

3. Technology is not deterministic. That is, different types of work groups and working arrangements are possible within the same technological setting.
4. Increased democracy through the development of semi-autonomous and autonomous work groups leads to improved job satisfaction, self-development, and occupational learning. At the same time, management gains high productivity and quality.
5. Management must reassess its ideology that views the worker as unreliable, unmotivated, and narrowly responding to money.

In a review of virtually every major piece of research done on industrial democracy up to the time of his essay, Singer contends that the bulk of the evidence points to the fact that increased participation by employees in decision making leads to increased acceptance of managerial ideas, greater cooperation between management and subordinates, greater acceptance of change, higher productivity, better morale, heightened motivation to achieve organizational objectives, and reduced turnover, lower absenteeism, fewer grievances, and a reduction in stress and tension.[136]

More recent findings seem to echo the positive reviews of Blumberg, Trist, and Singer. With reference to the various General Motors projects, Bluestone suggests these projects have resulted in:

> ... a more constructive collective bargaining relationship; a more satisfied workforce; improved project quality; a reduction in grievance handling, absenteeism, labor turnover, and disciplinary layoffs and discharges.[137]

Bluestone continues that from the workers' point of view this all adds up to more self-fulfilling work and the enhancement of human dignity. Walton[138] reports that similar findings emerge from the quality-of-worklife project undertaken at another General Motors plant. Mutual trust between union and management, pride in one's work, commitment to the job and organization as well as equality, flexibility, and informality at work have all resulted from the changes brought about by the quality-of-worklife project. Compared with similar plants, Walton reports that production has not decreased.

While these are glowing, positive reports, not all findings are so favorable. In their study of quality-of-worklife projects, Lawler and Drexler[139] report that in two of the organizations the projects created tension and worsened the relationship between the local and the international unions participating in the projects. Further, "expected gains in performance have not yet been realized in some cases, and this, combined with slow progress, has led to some disagreement about the worth of the projects."[140]

In a review of the quality-of-worklife project at Harman International

---

[136]Jack Singer, "Participative Decision-Making about Work," *Sociology of Work and Occupations,* 1 (1974), 347–371.

[137]Irving Bluestone, "How Quality-of-Worklife Projects Work for the United Auto Workers," 41.

[138]Richard E. Walton, "Work Innovations in the United States."

[139]Edward E. Lawler and John A. Drexler, "Dynamics of Establishing Cooperative Quality-of-Worklife Projects."

[140]Ibid., 28.

Industries in Bolivar, Tennessee, Macy suggests that while there have been gains, there have also been losses.[141] On the positive side, grievances and absences due to lack of work decreased. Further, jobs became more secure, product quality and productivity rose, there was a decline in minor accidents and overall accidents decreased at a rate faster than the industry average. On the negative side, workers reported more incidence of both physical and psychological stress, perhaps reflecting the added responsibilities and decisions resulting from increased participation. Further, workers reported less satisfaction with pay levels and pay equity which again probably stems from the additional responsibilities which accompany quality-of-worklife projects.

The aforementioned results reflect a large number of indicators and are, in general, mostly favorable. However, what are the results of the changes on feelings of control and alienation? Specifically, do the changes in the way work is structured lead to increased feelings of participation and a corresponding decrease in feelings of psychological alienation?

In terms of increased participation, most employees are skeptical at first. Initially, old timers at Tarrytown reported they were

> ... wondering about management's motives. We could remember the times management came up with programs only to find there was an ulterior motive and that in the long run the men could get screwed.[142]

Management and union leaders also seem dubious at first.

While skepticism and doubt seem typical at the beginning of such changes, once sincerity and trust develop, most employees feel that participation, decision making, and control do increase. While still cautious, the chairman of the local union involved in the quality-of-worklife project at Tarrytown remarks

> I no longer believe that what's going on is a "love-in" at Tarrytown. It's not a fancy gimmick to make people happy. And even though we have barely scratched the surface, I'm absolutely convinced we are on to something. We have a real and very different future. The guys in the plant are beginning to participate and I mean really participate.[143]

At the Bolivar plant, Macy reports an increase in work-group participation, more employee influence over task-related decisions and more work improvement ideas provided by employees.[144] From the above, it appears that an improved climate of participation in decision making has followed from the structural changes in the way work is organized.

National empirical studies relating industrial democracy specifically to changes in worker's feelings of alienation are rare. However, we can get an insight into this relationship from two recent studies.

---

[141]Barry A. Macy, "The Quality-of-Worklife Project at Bolivar: An Assessment," *Monthly Labor Review*, 103 (1980), 41–43.

[142]Robert H. Guest, "Quality of Work Life—Learning from Tarrytown," 79.

[143]Ibid., 85.

[144]Macy, "The Quality-of-Worklife Project at Bolivar."

Nightingale studied the effects of improved quality-of-worklife and employee participation on job satisfaction, general life satisfaction, organizational commitment, and societal alienation.[145] Approximately 1000 employees were studied in twenty industrial organizations in Canada. Of these organizations, ten were organized along traditional hierarchical lines while the remaining ten were formally participative. Formally participative organizations are those which give "rank-and-file employees the right to participate in decision-making."[146] These decision-making rights are contractually binding on all parties and sanctioned by legal arrangements beyond the organization or by the organizational charter or other collective agreements between union and management. In Nightingale's study, formally participative organizations include producer cooperatives, firms with worker representation on the board of directors, and companies with worker's councils wherein employees have the right to determine wages, hours, work assignments, pace of work, and so forth, and participate in other matters of organizational policy. Nightingale found that employees in formally participative organizations were more satisfied with their jobs and life in general, they were more committed to the organization and experienced less societal alienation. Task enrichment—that is, greater autonomy, utilization of skills, variety, novelty, and mental effort—as well as the extent to which workers were free of conflicting demands, were found to be the two most important predictors of the four outcome variables.

In another study, Whitehorn investigated the extent to which self-managed factories in Yugoslavia were associated with lower levels of both societal and work alienation than the more traditionally organized bureaucratic firms in Canada.[147] Contrary to expectations, Whitehorn found higher levels of societal alienation among Yugoslavian workers than their Canadian counterparts. However, alienation from work was found to be lower among Yugoslavian workers. Whitehorn suggests that the high level of societal alienation and low levels of alienation from work among Yugoslavian workers indicates that the self-managed factory does reduce worker alienation, but it does so amidst conditions of perceived alienation from society.

In the United States, empirical findings relate more specifically to the behavioral manifestations of alienation, that is, absenteeism and turnover, than to psychological alienation. However, in his evaluation of the quality-of-worklife project at Harman International Industries, Macy found that changes in the organization of work did lead to reduced levels of alienation from work.[148]

In terms of behavioral outcomes, Bluestone reported that a reduction in absenteeism and turnover was associated with several of the General Motors quality-of-worklife projects.[149] Macy found that at the Bolivar plant discharges

[145]Donald V. Nightingale, "Work, Formal Participation and Employee Outcomes," *Sociology of Work and Occupations,* 8 (1981), 277–296.

[146]Ibid., 278.

[147]Alan Whitehorn, "Alienation and Industrial Society: A Study of Workers' Self-Management," *Canadian Review of Sociology and Anthropology,* 16 (1979), 206–217.

[148]Macy, "The Quality-of-Worklife Project at Bolivar."

[149]Bluestone, "How Quality-of-Worklife Projects Work for the United Auto Workers."

and retirements (involuntary turnover) decreased by 95 percent while voluntary turnover rates decreased by 72 percent.[150] In reference to the quality-of-worklife project at Tarrytown, Guest suggests that absenteeism went down from 7¼ percent to between 2 and 3 percent.[151]

While we do not have definitive data, it would appear that industrial democracy helps to reduce psychological and behavioral manifestations of alienation.

The Future of Industrial Democracy in the United States

Given this overview of efforts to democratize work, we come to the issue of the present and the future prospects of industrial democracy in the United States. The fact is that with the end of the decade of the 1970s came a significant decline in interest in, and attention to, industrial democracy. What factors served to limit (at least for the immediate future) the development of industrial democracy in this country?

For one thing, we must recognize that while some workers want democratization, not all are in favor of such a development. In one study, while a majority of American workers surveyed preferred to work in employee-managed companies, 45 percent did not wish to work in such firms.[152] The basic reason lies in the American workers' acceptance of the traditional managerial prerogative of decision making. In addition, many workers in the United States aspire to one day join the ranks of management or own their own businesses. Hence worker self-management was rejected by some workers who see it as a potential threat to their aspirations. Such employee attitudes serve as a formidable barrier to the growth of industrial democracy in the United States.

Some workers may prefer simplistic repetitive work to the greater complexity and responsibility that comes with democratization. When given the chance to change their work, at least some people will not want to change. We should not force people to change their working pattern in a direction *we* think is best for them. We must beware of *ethnomorphizing* or imposing our values (that is, the values of executives or academicians) on workers who may well not share our orientation.[153] We can easily fall into the elitist trap of arguing that workers do not know that democracy is good for them and that what we need to do is to *educate* them into accepting our way of thinking.

While workers may create various barriers to industrial democracy, managers pose another set of barriers. Managers often resist the usurpation of their traditional prerogatives to make basic decisions. As Best and Connolly point out, surrendering control to workers poses a threat not only to managerial prerogatives, but ultimately to the system of the private ownership of the

[150]Macy, "The Quality-of-Worklife Project at Bolivar."

[151]Guest, "Quality-of-Worklife—Learning from Tarrytown."

[152]Ain Haas, "Workers' Views on Self-Management: A Comparative Study of the United States and Sweden," in Maurice Zeitlin, ed., *Classes, Class Conflict, and the State: Empirical Studies in Class Analysis* (Cambridge, MA: Winthrop Publishers, 1980), pp. 276–295.

[153]Singer, "Participative Decision-Making about Work."

means of production.[154] However, it should be borne in mind that in the majority of experiments in industrial democracy management *has* retained ultimate control:

> Workers are allowed to participate in corporate decision making only if they do not infringe on the prerogatives of company leaders. When quality of work life programs fail to meet management's goals, the programs are scuttled and any gains in workers' satisfaction are lost.[155]

While managers may fear that worker participation in the decision-making process may erode their traditional power base, recent empirical evidence suggests that power equalization within an organization may actually lead to greater managerial perception of authority and control.[156] Hence, managers' concerns over the erosion of power as a result of democratization may be unfounded.

Another barrier to democratization is the continuation of the traditional adversarial relationship between labor and management. To be successful, industrial democratization must involve at least some measure of labor-management cooperation.

Democratization has also been impeded by the fact that at least some efforts are not motivated by a sincere managerial concern for real worker participation; in other words, they are another form of managerial manipulation of the worker:

> To the extent that participative management schemes withhold meaningful influence, authority, and allotment of the ensuing profits, labor cannot be faulted for viewing such experiments as shams, as sophisticated attempts at behavior modification.[157]

American unionists may well react negatively to the similarities between industrial democracy and the old human relations movement. In fact, the two *do* have much in common. One Dutch observer of industrial democracy has made this point:

> The current situation is one in which allowing the workers a certain measure of participation is considered to have a useful function in that it can help achieve the goals of the enterprise, which latter, however, are not open to discussion at all.[158]

American unionists may also be swayed by the argument made by many Euro-

---

[154]Michael Best and William Connolly, *The Politicized Economy.*

[155]Sar A. Levitan and Clifford M. Johnson, "Labor and Management: The Illusion of Cooperation," *Harvard Business Review,* 61 (September/October, 1983), 9.

[156]Klaus Bartolke, et al., "Worker Participation and the Distribution of Control as Perceived by Members of Ten German Companies," *Administrative Science Quarterly,* 27 (1982), 380–397.

[157]Levitan and Johnson, "Labor and Management: The Illusion of Cooperation," 10.

[158]J. J. Ramondt, "Personnel Management and Shop Floor Consultation," in *Participation and Self-Management;* Vol. IV (Zagreb, Yugoslavia: Institute for Social Research, 1973), 241.

pean unionists, in particular those from Great Britain, who argue that work-linked democracy is simply another tool to buttress the capitalist system. Swedish managers have been unequivocal on this issue: "We cannot, or will not, introduce reforms which are inimical to capitalism."[159] Observes Ramondt: "A striking feature of these forms of consultation is that they tend to reinforce power rather than to bring about a redistribution of power."[160]

Another barrier to industrial democracy in the United States is the lack of legislative support for the process. This stands in contrast to the Swedish case where industrial democracy is embedded in the law.[161] As mentioned earlier, 1972 legislation in Sweden gave unions the right to representation on the boards of directors of most firms employing more than 100 persons. A 1973 law gave union officials the right to stop unsafe and dangerous work. In 1974, restrictions were placed on traditional managerial rights to hire and fire workers. In 1976, Sweden passed the Act on Employee Participation in Decision Making which prevented management from refusing to discuss any labor relations issues on the grounds that it has the exclusive right to make such decisions. Currently, Swedish lawmakers are discussing a bill that would set up funds derived from payroll taxes and taxes on corporate profits. Worker representatives would oversee these funds and be responsible for investment decisions. Through these funds, workers could purchase control of capitalist enterprises. This process could lead to the end of the distinction between labor and management. To further democratization in the United States, similar legislative changes would be needed.[162] However, the strength of the free enterprise ideology in the United States is likely to continue to bar such legislative changes.

Although all of the above are important causes of the decline in interest in industrial democracy in the United States in the 1980s, two other factors are of overwhelming importance. The first is the decline in a number of important American industries which has led workers to be more concerned with simply keeping their jobs than with democratizing them. The second is the growth of automation and robotization which has meant that instead of democratizing work, management is seeking to eliminate as many jobs and human workers as possible. As a result of these two developments, the hopes of the 1970s for democratizing work have been replaced in the 1980s by a rear-guard action by workers to hold on to their jobs. Most workers do not now have the luxury of worrying about such "niceties" as democratic work environments.

In the end, management in the 1980s seems to be in the process of making the decision that automation and robotization are preferable to democra-

---

[159]Lars Erik Karllson, "Industrial Democracy in Sweden," in Gerry Hunnius, David Garson and John Case, eds., *Workers' Control: A Reader on Labor and Social Change* (New York: Vintage, 1973), p. 179.

[160]Ramondt, "Personnel Management," 241.

[161]Andrew Martin, "From Joint Consultation to Joint Decision-Making: The Redistribution of Workplace Power in Sweden," in John A. Fry, ed., *Industrial Democracy and Labour Market Policy in Sweden* (Elmsford, NY: Pergamon Press, 1979), pp. 5–14.

[162]Steven Deutsch, "Work Environment Reform and Industrial Democracy," *Sociology of Work and Occupations*, 8 (1981), 180–194.

tization. Both processes are aimed at solving the same set of problems—alienation, absenteeism, turnover, sabotage, and the like. Democratization attempts to solve these problems by reducing the level of worker alienation. Automation and robotization deal with the problems by largely eliminating the workers. Robots will never feel alienated, be absent, quit, or sabotage the production process. In this sense, management of the 1980s sees technological change as a more effective response to alienation than the efforts at democratization that gained popularity in the 1970s.

CONCLUSIONS

In this chapter we have focused on the problem of alienation among semiskilled and unskilled workers in organizations. We discussed a variety of approaches to alienation, including the structural orientation of Karl Marx and the social-psychological approach of most American sociologists. We turned to a description of the problem of alienation primarily among automobile assembly-line workers. Because of the nature of their work, they suffer from extraordinarily high levels of powerlessness, meaninglessness, isolation, and self-estrangement. The high degree of alienation of such workers was compared to the lower levels of alienation of those who work with other technologies—craft (printing), machine-tending (textiles), and continuous process (chemicals).

We discussed actions undertaken by workers themselves to deal with alienation. Among these actions are efforts to beat the system, games workers play on the job, and restriction of output. Although these efforts may help workers get through the work day, they do not deal with the sources of the problem and may, in fact, help buttress the system that creates alienation. For another, we analyzed some of the psychological mechanisms employed by workers to cope with alienation. Among these are mental games, daydreaming, rationalizations of various sorts, and the development of mythical occupational images. We briefly discussed some of the ways unions can help cope with alienation, although we showed how they may well exacerbate the problem rather than help workers deal with it. We also discussed efforts undertaken by management, although many of these turned out to be insincere efforts to manipulate workers rather than serious attempts to deal with the sources of alienation.

The most serious efforts to deal with the structural sources of alienation involve the democratization of work. Our primary focus was on two automobile companies—Volvo in Sweden and General Motors in the United States. Although these efforts were of great importance in the 1970s, they seem to have lost momentum in the 1980s. The decline of "smokestack industries" in the United States has led more workers to be concerned with keeping their jobs than with worrying about democratization. Management seems to be in the process of moving from trying to deal with worklife problems through democratization to dealing with them by replacing many semiskilled and unskilled workers with robots and automated technologies.

THIRTEEN
CONFLICT IN DEVIANT
OCCUPATIONS*

The basic element of deviance, as it is typically defined in sociology, is norm-violating behavior. Thus, deviance is any type of human action that violates the accepted and prevailing rules of conduct of a group or of the larger society. Deviant activity can occur at many levels within a society, ranging from isolated and sporadic rule violations by individuals to the more organized and continuous rule violations of groups, such as illegal gambling operations.[1] For the purposes of this chapter, it is important to note that many deviant activities are organized as occupations. This chapter, then, deals with only one aspect of deviance as it occurs within society; that is, those sets of deviant activities that meet the definition of an occupation offered in the first chapter of this book.

Some occupations are obviously deviant because their activities are typically defined as *illegal* in American society. Examples are bank robbery and prostitution. There are, however, many other occupations that involve *legal* rule-violating behavior. Stripping, for example, is legal in most areas of the United States, but strippers are often treated as deviant because the occupationally required activities in which they engage are violations of other,

---

*This chapter was written primarily by Gale Miller.

[1]A very nice overview of the social organization of deviance and deviants in modern society is found in Joel Best and David F. Luckenbill, *Organizing Deviance* (Englewood Cliffs, NJ: Prentice-Hall, Inc. 1982).

less formalized norms that relate to the nature of the female role and the nature of human sexuality within society. Thus, a deviant occupation need not necessarily involve illegal activities.

In other cases, the central activities of an occupation are not violations of prevailing norms, but related aspects of the occupation are perceived as norm-violating. Buerkle and Barker note, for example, that the occupation of jazz musician is sometimes perceived and treated as deviant because of popular conceptions about the lifestyle and culture associated with the occupation.[2]

An occupation will be treated as deviant if it meets one or more of the following criteria:

1. It is illegal.
2. One or more of the central activities of the occupation is a violation of nonlegalized norms and values.
3. The culture, lifestyle, or setting associated with the occupation is popularly presumed to involve rule-violating behavior.

Unlike some occupations discussed in previous chapters, few deviant occupations can be easily divided into "free" and "organizationally based" types. This difficulty is partly related to the low level of bureaucratization that characterizes these occupations, because most of them are found within small-scale organizations (such as night clubs, brothels, or small retail stores where stolen items are bought and sold) or they are organized as informal and sometimes temporary alliances of two or more people committed to similar goals.[3] An example of the latter arrangement is the shifting networks and arrangements of upper-level drug dealing and smuggling operations.[4] Indeed, even those deviant occupations that are often publicly depicted as highly bureaucratized (such as the so-called Mafia) do not appear to be so rigidly organized when studied close up.[5] At the same time that deviant occupations are seldom bureaucratized, most cannot be classified as free because the small-scale organizations are important sources of constraint and opportunity in the lives of workers. Rather than dividing deviant occupations into types, then, this chapter is organized around the common problems that are shared by persons involved in a variety of deviant occupations.

---

[2]Jack V. Buerkle and Danny Barker, *Bourbon Street Black* (New York: Oxford University Press, 1973). For a more complete discussion of the distinction between deviant and marginal occupations see, Patrick C. Easto and Marcello Truzzi, "The Carnival as a Marginally Legal Work Activity," in Clifton D. Bryant, ed., *Deviant Behavior* (Chicago: Rand-McNally, 1974). pp. 336–353.

[3]For general discussions of the bureaucratization of deviant occupations see, Donald R. Cressey, *Criminal Organization* (New York: Harper and Row, 1972); James A. Inciardi, *Careers in Crime* (Chicago: Rand-McNally, 1975); Mary McIntosh, *The Organization of Crime* (London: The Macmillan Press, Ltd., 1975); Gregory R. Staats, "Changing Conceptualizations of Professional Criminals," *Criminology*, 15 (1977), 49–65.

[4]Patricia A. Adler and Peter Adler, "Relationships Between Dealers," *Sociology and Social Research*, 67 (1983), 260–278.

[5]Francis A. J. Ianni with Elizabeth Reuss-Ianni, *A Family Business* (New York: New American Library, 1972); Gale Miller, *Odd Jobs* (Englewood Cliffs, NJ: Prentice-Hall, Inc., 1978).

In the previous chapters we have generally separated the discussion of types of conflict from the discussion of modes of resolution. In this chapter we will deal with the two simultaneously. The worker in a deviant occupation is confronted with conflict with clients, customers and victims and seeks to cope, primarily, through dramaturgical manipulation. We have examined dramaturgy in a variety of places throughout this book as the *reliance of workers on their ability as performers to manipulate a situation in their favor.*[6] In this chapter we will examine this more intensively than in any earlier discussion.

COPING WITH CONFLICT WITH CLIENTS, CUSTOMERS, AND VICTIMS

As with conventional occupations involving direct interaction with customers, one source of occupational insecurity for members of deviant occupations is the social setting in which the customer is found. The problem of controlling the customer and the setting is more important for members of deviant occupations, however, because many deviant occupations are illegal and if customers take advantage of the deviant occupational member, there is no legal recourse available. If a "john" "skips out" on the prostitute without paying, for example, she cannot summon the police to her aid, because such an action would be an admission of criminal activity and she would be punished. Thus it is vital that members of deviant occupations involving direct contact with customers develop manipulative or dramaturgical skills that allow them to control the interactional setting and the customer.

Although dramaturgical skills are important features of many deviant occupations, the nature and type of skills required are varied. A major reason for this variation is the diversity of work settings and relationships that make up these occupations. Strippers, female impersonators, and other entertainers, for example, work on a stage that is somewhat separated from their audiences. Most of the manipulative skills of these workers, then, are related to the problem of controlling boisterous and rowdy audience members. Prostitutes, on the other hand, must deal directly with customers and they, therefore, develop a different set of skills that will allow them to control the problematic aspects of these encounters, such as physical threats and the problem of a customer who demands too much time and attention. Members of other deviant occupations, such as bank robbers, must deal with the problem of unwilling victims who, based on their intense fear or desire to be heroic, may act in unpredictable and dangerous ways. Thus, although members of deviant occupations may be publicly depicted as unconventional or immoral, they too develop dramaturgical skills that are useful in dealing with the problems found in the relationships of their everyday work lives.

It should also be noted that not all deviant occupations are characterized by high rates of success at dramaturgical manipulation. Lemert's study of the systematic check forger indicates that many check forgers spend more of their

---

[6]Erving Goffman, *The Presentation of Self in Everyday Life* (Garden City, NY: Anchor Books, 1959).

lives in prison than outside.[7] This pattern is, to a great extent, related to the high degree of dramaturgical failure. Lemert discovered that instead of writing bad checks intermittently, the forgers were more inclined to go on "sprees" of bad-check writing. Such an approach obviously enhanced the possibility of detection both by "marks" and the police, and their blunders frequently led to arrest. Thus, deviant occupations vary in the type of dramaturgical skill that is required and the success of occupational members in utilizing the necessary dramaturgical skills.

Stage entertainers. Many deviant occupations are organized as stage performances which include comedic, musical, and dance performances as well as explicit sexual displays. Although the performances are often highly routine, the performers must deal with audiences that frequently include people who are interested in disrupting the show by heckling, and, in some cases, physically assaulting the performers. Where possible, the entertainers attempt to segregate themselves from the audience so that little or no interaction can occur, but this strategy is seldom fully successful and so they develop other ways of dealing with audiences. The most common strategy is to attempt to publicly embarrass the offending audience members. The specific techniques used vary depending on the audience and performance.

In the case of stripping, the primary technique is the direct insult. The insults or "put-downs" are seldom spontaneous; rather, most are standardized within the occupation and learned through the informal socialization that takes place among strippers.[8] The strategy for dealing with troublemakers varies with the sex of the troublemaker. For males, the typical strategy is to make an insulting reference to his sexual capacities. Female troublemakers are handled differently. The strippers assume that hostile females are reacting against the bodily exposure of the performance, and, consequently, they react by flaunting their bodies and nudity. In some cases, dramaturgical manipulation is not effective in controlling the audience and the stripper must react in a direct way.

Part of the reason the stripper does not develop an extensive array of dramaturgical skills is because she is not alone on stage. There are usually comedians who introduce the strippers and entertain the audience between acts. Although few of them like to admit it, one function of the burlesque comic is to intervene between the audience and the strippers in an effort to control the situation.[9]

The primary mechanism through which the comic controls the audience involves the creation of a "gamelike" atmosphere. That is, he "tries to manipulate his behavior to show the audience that the striptease is a game after all and people should laugh as they watch the show."[10] This atmosphere is cre-

[7]Edwin Lemert, "The Behavior of the Systematic Check Forger," *Social Problems,* 6 (1958), 141–148.

[8]Jacqueline Boles and A. P. Garbin, "Stripping for a Living: An Occupational Study of the Night Club Stripper," in Clifton Bryant, ed., *Deviant Behavior,* pp. 312–335.

[9]Marilyn Salutin, "The Impression Management Techniques of the Burlesque Comedian," *Sociological Inquiry,* 43 (1973), 159–168.

[10]Ibid., 163.

ated through the use of two dramaturgical techniques. First, the comic regularly praises the audience and the "super-masculine" qualities of its membership. ("The girls will be really turned on when they see you out there, yessiree. . . ."[11]) A second technique is to play the role of eunuch—that is, showing no sexual interest in the strippers, thereby reducing the problems of hostility and resentment from the audience.

If, however, the audience is not controlled through such techniques, the comic has a serious problem. Whether the problem stems from a silent and sullen audience or from a boisterous heckler, the comic responds in the same manner—that is, through degradation of the offender. In other words, the comic utilizes the same "putdown" techniques as do the strippers. In the case of an unresponsive audience, the comic degrades them by transferring his failure to them. Thus, he may respond with "You guys are a ship leaving a sinking rat."[12] In the case of a disruptive heckler, the comic typically attacks him through the use of put-downs that cast doubt on his sexual competence. The comic attempts to control the situation in such a way that problems will not develop, but if they do arise, he responds in much the same manner as the stripper.

David M. Petersen and Paula Dressel have recently studied the male strip show.[13] There are some similarities between the male and female stripper in terms of their relationship to the audience. For example, neither the female nor the male stripper need to develop a wide variety of dramaturgical skills because neither is on stage alone. The female stripper is accompanied by a male burlesque comic while the male stripper is accompanied by a female announcer. The comic and announcer both try to control the crowd. However, this is where the similarities end. The audience attending a female strip show is both male and female and the manipulative techniques used to control the audience can vary according to the sex of the trouble maker. The audience at a male strip show is typically exclusively female. Traditionally, females have been socialized to repress their sexuality and to be sexually passive in their interpersonal relationships. Males are taught to be sexually aggressive and assertive. In an attempt to overcome the sexual inhibition of many women in the audience, the announcer at the male strip show tries to encourage, not discourage, sexual assertiveness.

The female announcer uses a variety of dramaturgical techniques to encourage the women in the audience to become assertive and boisterous. Prior to the show, the announcer might state "It's equal rights night. Ladies, we're gonna let the guys work for us for a change."[14] Another technique used by the announcer is to toast various women in the audience who are celebrating a significant event in their life, such as marriage, divorce, or birthday. The announcer might try to generate excitement in the audience in the following way:

[11]Ibid., 162.

[12]Ibid., 163.

[13]David M. Petersen and Paula L. Dressel, "Equal Time for Women: Social Notes on the Male Strip Show," *Urban Life,* 11 (1982), 185–208.

[14]Ibid., 190.

> "Put your hands together for (woman's name). She's celebrating her divorce tonight. (Crowd applause.) It (marriage) sucks, doesn't it? (Woman in spotlight turns thumbs down.) How many of you ladies have been married once? (Hands raised.) Twice? (Fewer hands raised.) You learned the first time, didn't you?"[15]

Women frequently respond with calls of "bring out the men." The announcer then teases and excites the audience by encouraging them to interact with the male strippers. Women are encouraged to tip the male dancer in exchange for a kiss and/or a hug. The announcer might suggest that personal contact after the show may be a realistic possibility.

While the announcer plays an important part in creating an atmosphere that encourages sexual assertiveness among the women in the audience, the performer plays an equally important part in maintaining the fabricated atmosphere. Costumes and make-up are used so as to reinforce the sexual nature of the performance. Eye contact is used, not to distance oneself from the audience, but to break down the social distance. The following is a typical example:

> The best thing I can do is stare them (audience members) down, and I try to get into a sexual thing. I try to get turned on and to find someone who looks good to me and get her turned on. I look at her and let her know I want to do illicit things to her. . . . I'm trying to be bad. I'm trying to get up there and tell the women I'm going to give it to them every way they can get it.[16]

Most of the dramaturgical skills used by the female announcer and the male stripper are aimed at encouraging the women to transcend their traditional gender roles and become more assertive. Resultantly, male dancers are frequently subjected to the audience's excessive verbal and physical abuse. With reference to the former, a male dancer states:

> Some women are really sarcastic and heckle you. Some of them can be real nasty and say things that are rude and shouldn't be said.[17]

Petersen and Dressel report that male dancers have had their G-string pulled off. The dancers have been burnt with lit cigarettes, stabbed with needles, and bitten.

Male stripping has only recently begun gaining popularity in the United States. However, if the excessive audience behavior encouraged by the announcer and sustained by the performer becomes much more violent, we will probably soon witness the transformation of the announcer from one who attempts to encourage the audience, to one who attempts to control and discourage it using techniques similar to those currently utilized by the burlesque comic. Similar to the female stripper, in the future the male stripper may also have to develop dramaturgical skills that will protect him not only from verbal assaults, but from physical threats as well.

[15]Ibid., 191.
[16]Ibid., 195.
[17]Ibid., 201.

The dramaturgical manipulation of the female impersonator is somewhat more involved and the specific strategy is highly dependent on the setting of the performance and the audience. There are two types of nightclubs that hire female impersonators: tourist clubs and gay clubs.[18] Tourist clubs cater to "straight" audiences who often come to the shows to satisfy their curiosity and interest in seeing the bizarre. A major problem with such audiences is putting them at ease because many are threatened by the presence of a man in woman's clothes. The typical strategy is to begin the performance in a humorous fashion. For example, the performer might make fun of himself in order to get the audience to relax and enjoy the show. In some cases, the tension is more intense and it is necessary for the performer to deal more directly with the audience.

One source of tension is the straight audience's inability to see the performer as a man in woman's clothing; instead, they react to him as a unique type of human being who is both male and female. In this case, it is necessary for the performer to make his sexual status clear to the audience. He may break the illusion of the performance by occasionally removing his wig or in some other way indicate that he is a man. In other cases, the female impersonator must deal with belligerent members of the audience and he responds to these situations in a similar way as the stripper, through the use of standardized "put downs." Newton gives an example of this type of response to a customer who insisted upon being called "sir." The performer replied, "Sir . . . ? I'm more 'sir' than you'll ever be, and twice the broad you'll ever pick up."[19]

The gay audience demands that the performer present himself in a "glamorous" way and that his performance be of high quality. It also expects the performer to be able to deftly banter with the members of the audience because part of being a quality performer involves being able to effectively exchange insults. Finally, the gay audience expects the performer to express the values of the gay subculture. There are a number of ways of expressing these values but one of the most effective is to "put down" the "straight" members of the audience. The important point is that the dramaturgical style of the performer must be adapted to the needs and expectations of the audience.

Prostitutes. Although prostitution is often described as an exclusively female occupation, men and boys are also involved and each type is characterized by somewhat different problems and relationships.[20] There are, however, some commonalities that cut across the divisions of prostitution and it is these commonalities that are of concern in this section.

A major source of insecurity in the prostitute's life stems from his or her

---

[18]Esther Newton, *Mother Camp* (Englewood Cliffs, NJ: Prentice-Hall, Inc., 1972).

[19]Ibid., p. 66.

[20]See, David J. Pittman, "The Male House of Prostitution," *Transaction,* 8 (1971), 21–27; Robin Lloyd, *For Love or Money* (New York: Ballentine Books, 1976); Jennifer James, "Prostitutes and Prostitution," in Edward Sagarin and Fred Montanino, eds., *Deviants* (Morristown, NJ: General Learning Press, 1977), 369–428; Barbara Sherman Heyl, "Prostitution," in Freda Adler and Rita James Simon, eds., *The Criminology of Deviant Women* (Boston: Houghton Mifflin Company, 1979), pp. 196–212.

relationship with the customer who is frequently called the "square" or the "john." The fact that the prime years of the occupation are very short makes it inherently insecure. If he or she is to make big money, the prostitute must do it during the few years in which he or she is physically most attractive; after this he or she will either have to find other work or be relegated to the lowest form of prostitution, streetwalking. Even during the prime years the prostitute's relationship with customers is fraught with insecurities. For one thing, it is difficult to build up a clientele, let alone a steady, high-paying group of customers. This is a particularly serious problem for those prostitutes who do not work in organizations (such as massage parlors, hotels, and brothels) where some or all of their customers are procured by someone else.

Whether the prostitute works in an organization or not, however, he or she must deal with a work situation in which the power lies with the customer. Some may "stiff him or her" (refuse to pay for services), while some take too much time, causing the prostitute to lose considerable income. There is also the constant threat of physical assault. Consequently, it is important that the prostitute manipulate the interactional setting and the customer in order to protect himself or herself.

For many high status prostitutes who do not solicit customers on the street, in bars, hotels, or other public places an important dramaturgical skill is the ability to use the telephone to attract customers. In part, this involves the cultivation of an appealing telephone "voice," but may also include a telephone "pitch" through which the prostitute attempts to attract the customer.

A sob story over the phone is a typical device: "Either it's the rent or she needs a car, or doctor's bills, or any number of things."[21] Other, lower-status prostitutes, must go out and actively recruit clients in such places as bars. Many of these prostitutes will use a ploy similar to those used over the phone. Winick and Kinsie cite a procedure used by a prostitute who works hotel lobbies.[22] Her technique involved approaching a man by claiming that they had met somewhere else, such as a resort area. Very often this leads to an extended conversation and the "john" may ask her for a date and she accepts. After the first date or two the prostitute confronts the "john" with her problem, usually it is a financial crisis of some kind, and if he will agree to give her the money, she will consent to have sexual relations with him. This is, perhaps, the most elaborate approach used by prostitutes at this level. A more typical pattern is for the prostitute to simply ask any man who seems interested if he would like a "date" or would like to "have some fun."

For the high-status prostitutes, setting is extremely important, as is appearance. As Greenwald states in regard to call girls, "In the circle in which they move the girls have to make a good appearance. They must, for example, be able to walk in and out of the finest hotels without attracting undue attention because of dressing too poorly or too garishly. . . . Call girls' apartments are generally in expensive neighborhoods."[23] Since the lower-status

---

[21]James H. Bryan, "Apprenticeships in Prostitution," *Social Problems,* 12 (1965), 287–297.

[22]Charles Winick and Paul M. Kinsie, *The Lively Commerce: Prostitution in the United States* (New York: Signet, 1971).

[23]Harold Greenwald, "The Social and Professional Life of the Call Girl," in Simon Dinitz et al., eds., *Deviance* (New York: Oxford University Press, 1969), p. 401.

streetwalker caters to a different clientele, he or she sports a different appearance—one that will attract clients. Cleanliness of both body and working environment are emphasized, especially for higher-status prostitutes.

One of the most serious problems for the streetwalker is the threat of assault by the customer. He or she has no legal protection from such assaults. The typical pattern in handling this problem is to attempt to control as many aspects of the social setting as possible. Gray states that female prostitutes attempt to work in pairs or larger groups in order to minimize their vulnerability.[24] They also refuse to ride in the cars of customers or to go to customers' residences. Both of these places are highly isolated and vulnerable. Instead, most women streetwalkers insist upon the use of public transportation and "trick hotels" where they are less isolated. "But even experienced girls at times may misjudge a trick or take chances, especially if there appears to be a considerable sum of money involved. These are the times that the girls are most vulnerable and may find themselves in dangerous situations."[25] Thus, the streetwalker must constantly be aware of the dangers that are present in the social setting and attempt to control them as much as possible. There are, however, severe limits on the extent to which she can anticipate and control all of the dangers that she faces.

One of the most interesting dramaturgical skills developed by prostitutes involves the ability to take the customer's money without engaging in sexual relations. In some cases, prostitutes "rip off" their customers by working with a confederate. While the prostitute entertains the customer, the confederate steals his money. In other cases, the prostitute may use more direct means such as flirting with a potential customer and in the process pick his pocket.

The dramaturgical skills associated with prostitution are more varied than those associated with stage entertainment because prostitution involves a wider variety of work settings and relationships. Prostitutes also differ from stage entertainers because they confront their customers face-to-face and often alone, whereas the stage entertainer works in public and at a distance from his or her customers. At the same time that the dramaturgical problems of the prostitute may be seen as more difficult than those of the stage entertainer, he or she still deals with a voluntary customer. This is not the case for others, such as bank robbers, who must develop appropriate social skills for controlling their victims.

Bank robbers.   Although bank robbers do "case" banks (observe the bank and the persons in it) before a robbery, they do not always emphasize aspects of banks that are commonly presumed to be important. Letkemann indicates that bank robbers seldom worry about the architectural design of banks—instead they assume that most banks are relatively standardized.[26] A second element of the bank that is ignored by the bank robber is the alarm system. Rather than attempting to find and shut off the alarm system of the

---

[24]Diana Gray, "Turning-Out: A Study of Teenage Prostitution," *Urban Life and Culture,* 1 (1973), 401–425.

[25]Ibid., 421.

[26]Letkemann, *Crime as Work* (Englewood Cliffs, NJ: Prentice-Hall, 1973).

bank, the bank robbers assume that the alarm has gone off as soon as they enter the bank. The objective is to complete the robbery before the police arrive, usually in only a few minutes. The importance of casing is not, then, a way of gaining information about the design of the bank or its alarm system; rather, casing provides the robber with information about the typical flow of activities and persons in the bank. In a sense, casing is an "assessment of risk" involved in the holdup and this assessment involves two dimensions. First, the bank robber must be able to assess the probability of a group of policemen being present, one policeman or a guard does not present a problem. He notes the traffic that goes in and out of the bank at different times of the day. According to Letkemann: "The danger lies in the customer noting that something is wrong before he or she has entered. Such a customer cannot be prevented from leaving at that point and becomes the first 'alarm.' "[27] A second dimension of risk assessment involves the probability that personnel will resist the bank robbery. It is assumed that persons who own property that is being stolen and people who feel an important responsibility for protecting the property under their care are most likely to resist. One of the reasons that professional bank robbers do not rob small grocery stores, for example, is because the owner is likely to be present and to resist. In the case of banks, the assessment of resistance primarily involves the bank manager and his characteristics. It is assumed that older, more experienced bank managers are least likely to resist the bank robber. Younger, less experienced bank managers, on the other hand, are more likely to be oriented toward bravery and playing the role of "hero."

Once the bank robber has entered the bank he must manipulate all of the persons inside the bank in a very short time. This involves two important elements: first, surprise and vulnerability are vital. That is, the bank robber attempts to disrupt the social setting to the extent that the persons in the bank are temporarily shaken, but not so shaken that they will panic. This is accomplished through the presence of guns, which tend to frighten the persons in the bank, and, more importantly, through the behavior of the bank robber. Upon entering the bank it is important that this person assert control over the situation; this is usually accomplished through a series of loud and self-confident orders ("This is a hold-up;" "Hit the ground"). It is not so important what he says, however, as the way he says it; that is, the commands must be sufficiently loud so that everyone can hear and they must carry a sense of determination and mastery of the situation. In some cases, the bank robber may use profanity because such words are often associated with physically threatening behavior and victims are likely to react to them by conforming to the bank robber's demands.

A second problem faced by the bank robber is the tension that arises during the robbery. Not only does the robber have to deal with his own anxiety, but he must also control the victims who may panic or otherwise respond to the situation by defying the robber. To a great extent, managing the tensions of the situation involves the continued use of direct commands that reflect the bank robber's self-confidence and determination. Another way ten-

---

[27]Ibid., p. 95.

sion is managed is through the physical manipulation of the bank personnel and customers. By making the victims lie face-down on the floor, the bank robber has more control over the situation and can better anticipate and deal with resistance by the victims. These procedures are not always successful, however, and the bank robber must be prepared to spontaneously respond to unplanned contingencies. One of Letkemann's respondents tells of a bank robbery in which a woman was so surprised by the robbery that she lost all awareness of the situation and the demands being made upon her. Instead of remaining with the other victims, she slowly began to walk toward the door of the bank. Thus, tension was increased for both the bank robbers and the other victims and it was necessary for the bank robbers to reassert control. This was done by slapping the woman, thereby ending her temporary state of shock, and forcing her to join the other victims.

Recently, Luckenbill has developed an analytic model of robber-victim relations.[28] Central to the model is the establishment of victim compliance with the robber's demands. He states that the successful robberies involve four stages: (1) establishing co-presence with the victim; (2) establishing a common robbery frame; (3) the transfer of goods; and (4) leaving the robbery scene. Although there are a variety of ways of accomplishing the stages of successful robbery, Luckenbill states that all must be accomplished or victims will not comply with the demands of the robber. Depending on the circumstances, uncompliant victims make it impossible for the robber to complete the robbery or increase the likelihood that the robber will have to resort to greater violence to achieve his or her ends.

Other deviant occupations. It is clear from the preceding studies that success at bank robbery, prostitution, and stage entertainment requires that workers develop dramaturgical skills to minimize the risks associated with these occupations. In each of the cited cases, however, the workers acknowledge the deviant label that is associated with their work roles and settings. Another important way in which members of deviant occupations deal with problems posed by clients, customers, and victims is to create an image of themselves and their activities as legitimate. One example of such a person is the fence who often hides his or her illegal operations behind a legitimate front, such as a retail store.[29] In this way, the fence protects him- or herself from arrest and creates a setting in which the customer is kept ignorant of the source of the goods being sold.

The medicine huckster and the spiritual reader also try to create an image of themselves and their actions as legitimate. Joseph Simoni and Richard Ball show how the medicine huckster in Mexico creates an image of legitimacy through an elaborate six-stage sales pitch which includes the expert use of refined communication skills and detailed displays.[30] Such dramaturgical skills

---

[28]David F. Luckenbill, "Generating Compliance," *Urban Life,* 10 (1981), 25–46.

[29]Carl B. Klockars, *The Professional Fence* (New York: Free Press, 1974); Marilyn Walsh, *The Fence* (Westport, CT: Greenwood Press, 1974).

[30]Joseph J. Simoni and Richard A. Ball, "The Mexican Medicine Huckster," *Sociology of Work and Occupations,* 4 (1977), 343–365.

and props help to reduce the customers' fears, anxieties, and apprehensions and convince them that the huckster is a credible and competent source of a medicinally useful product. With reference to the spiritual reader, John Heeren and Marylee Mason show how legitimacy is created by the skillful use of various linguistic and paralinguistic devices.[31] For example, visionary utterances are presented by the reader as fact. The certainty of the vision is communicated in a rapid and unhesitating tone of voice. The specific words chosen by the reader are also important. "I see for you," is more convincing than "I say to you." Other linguistic devices aimed at getting the client to confirm the visionary statements or to fill in missing details all help the spiritual reader create an image of competence and legitimacy.

COPING WITH OTHER CONFLICTS

Dealing with clients, customers, and victims is not the only problem faced by members of deviant occupations. They must also deal with the problems created by police and, very often, other persons who control the settings of their work.

Coping with the Police.

Although persons in virtually all deviant occupations must deal in some way with the insecurity stemming from relations with others, only those in illegal occupations must contend with the insecurity born of the ever-present possibility of police detection. However, all persons involved in illegal occupations do not spend a great deal of time worrying about police detection and arrest. For example, many low-level drug dealers spend little time worrying about police detection and arrest because they assume that the police are little interested in their activities and that the police are too inept to catch them.[32] They also believe that most drug arrests are "accidental;" such as, "after stopping a motorist for a traffic offense, a patrolman will spot drugs under the dashboard . . ."[33] When a local drug dealer is arrested, however, often the other dealers become "paranoid" and take greater precautions in protecting themselves from arrest.

Persons involved in illegal occupations who do worry about the police use both dramaturgical and more direct methods to avoid detection and arrest.

The most direct means employed is the payoff; and nearly all those employed in illegal deviant occupations pay off or attempt to pay off the police, the courts, and highly placed politicians. Payoffs are used at different levels for different purposes. The small-time operator may merely pay off the local

[31]John Heeren and Marylee Mason, "Talk About Visions," *Deviant Behavior*, 2 (1981), 167–186.

[32]Patricia A. Adler and Peter Adler, "The Irony of Secrecy in the Drug World," *Urban Life*, 8 (1980), 447–465.

[33]Ibid., 452.

cops on the beat, while bigger operators also give money to top police officials, who then unofficially declare them off limits to the local policeman.[34] If the individual in an illegal occupation is caught by the police, then efforts are frequently made to buy off the courts so that he will not be convicted. At a still higher level, politicians are paid off to prevent the passage of unfavorable legislation or to influence them into persuading lower-level judges and policemen to leave certain individuals alone. Scott indicates the importance of the fix in his discussion of the bookie establishment, commonly called a "horse room." "Obviously, then, horse rooms cannot operate unless a political 'fix' has been arranged. Whenever the police crack down or an antigambling reform administration takes office, the horse books are often the first and most obvious targets, since their operation and location is common knowledge in a community."[35] A more dramatic example is found in John Gardiner's discussion of payoffs ranging from the small-scale bribes offered street cops to the mayor's weekly salary.[36] These operations are important because they show that only a portion of payoffs are direct. In addition to direct bribes, city officials were led to others in and out of the community who were also interested in exchanging money for political favors. In this way an extensive network of corruption was created and sustained for a number of years, and during that time racketeering operations were protected from interference by local police.

Although the fix is ubiquitous, it is rarely totally effective, particularly at the level of the small-time operator where periodic police crackdowns or reform movements by idealistic new administrators are common. Just as important for the small-time operator are those police officers who refuse to be bought. In his study, Whyte notes the omnipresence of the police payoff, but also mentions a number of policemen who were labeled by the racketeers as "untouchables."[37] A racketeer discussed one of these: " 'When O'Leary was around here, we didn't make no money for six months. What a hell of a six months that was. No profits at all. We had to pay out all the profits to take care of the pinches.' "[38] In addition to the honest cop, another threatening figure to the individual in an illegal deviant occupation is the rookie cop. "The racketeers fear the rookies. It is hard to do business with them. Their actions are unpredictable."[39] Thus, despite the success of the payoff, the individual in an illegal deviant occupation must employ other means of reducing the insecurity caused by the police.

A second direct means for handling the insecurity related to the police and the courts is to make arrangements for protection before an arrest. Milner and Milner, as well as Gray, indicate that one of the functions of the

[34]William J. Chambliss, *On the Take* (Bloomington, IN: Indiana University Press, 1978).

[35]Marvin Scott, *The Racing Game* (Chicago: Aldine, 1968), p. 143.

[36]John A. Gardiner with David J. Olson, "Wincanton: The Politics of Corruption," in the President's Commission on Law Enforcement and Administration of Justice, *Task Force Report: Organized Crime*, Appendix B (Washington, D.C.: Government Printing Office, 1967); John A. Gardiner, *The Politics of Corruption* (New York: Russell Sage Foundation, 1970).

[37]William Foote Whyte, *Streetcorner Society* (Chicago: University of Chicago Press, 1967).

[38]Ibid., p. 132.

[39]Ibid.

pimp is to protect the prostitute if she is arrested.[40] That is, it is part of his obligation to the prostitute to provide for her bail and to help in her court-room defense, if she chooses to plead innocent to the charges. Thus, the pimp is an important figure in helping to minimize the insecurity created by the police. A similar service is often provided by the manager of a massage parlor or brothel when the prostitutes who work there are arrested.[41]

The burglar uses a similar technique, but his preplanning involves arrangements with bondsmen and attorneys. As Shover indicates, this arrangement may necessitate further involvement in criminal activity:

> When the good burglar is arrested—as he frequently is—he can count upon receiving the services of both a bondsman and an attorney, even if he has virtu-ally no ready cash. In lieu of a cash down payment the thief will be able to gain his release from confinement, and also preliminary legal representation, on the basis of his reputation and a promise to deliver the needed cash at a later date. He will then search for one or more suitable burglaries (or some type of crime) which holds out the promise of a quick and substantial reward—so that he can pay his attorney and bondsman.[42]

Another direct means of controlling the police and other law enforce-ment officials is to develop occupational and friendship relations with them. Tatro, for example, notes that the fortuneteller is often immune from arrest and prosecution when a local politician is one of his clients.[43] Fortunetellers also protect themselves by becoming members of the local community. By "giving elaborate parties, joining lodges, sending their children to respected private schools, securing church positions for themselves and their families, and by engaging in expensive recreational pursuits" they legitimate their ac-tivities to others and, ultimately, may protect themselves from legal action.[44] Finally, the fortuneteller may become more directly involved with political officials by making deals with them. "A local politician may cultivate the friendship of the fortuneteller and request that the reader secure votes for him in exchange for his obtaining political favors for the reader."[45]

Members of deviant occupations do not always utilize direct means of control of the police, they also utilize dramaturgical means. In part, this is ne-cessitated by the limited effectiveness of the direct means, such as when the police cannot be bribed or the offender has no friends in important political positions. In other cases, members of deviant occupations may use dramaturgical manipulation because it creates fewer problems for them. That is, it is simpler to manipulate settings and persons than to attempt to bribe an

[40]Christian Milner and Richard Milner, *Black Players: The Secret Life of Black Pimps* (New York: Bantam Books, 1973) and Diana Gray, "Turning Out."

[41]Peter Whittaker, *The American Way of Sex* (New York: Berkley Publishing Corp., 1974).

[42]Neal Shover, "The Social Organization of Burglary," *Social Problems*, 20 (1973), 511.

[43]Charlotte R. Tatro, "Cross My Palm With Silver: Fortunetelling as an Occupatonal Way of Life," in Bryant, ed., *Deviant Behavior*, pp. 286–299.

[44]Ibid., p. 293.

[45]Ibid., p. 292.

official. Consequently, indirect means may be used first, and direct means later when and if dramaturgical manipulation fails.

There are a number of ways in which persons and situations can be manipulated to protect members of deviant occupations. The most direct form involves the manipulation of the victim in such a way that no complaint is made to the police.

In the confidence rackets, "cooling out" is frequently employed to prevent the mark from going to the police. One example of this is the wire racket,[46] an example of a long-term con game. A sucker is selected who the mob is sure has the money needed and is likely to be willing to use illegal means to make more. With its victim selected, the mob begins the buildup. One approach is to have a member of the gang (the "steerer") engage the sucker in conversation and then point out a passerby (who is another member of the gang) as a professional gambler who can give tips on future horse races and who happens to be indebted to the steerer. Another approach is to have the steerer and the sucker find a wallet that belongs to the professional gambler. When returning the wallet the sucker is informed that the gambler is in a position to give tips on horse races. Whatever means are used, the initial contact has been made. In the next step, known as the "convincer," the sucker is allowed to win a number of bets and even allowed to collect several hundred dollars. He is then introduced into a gambling club in which he is told it will be safer to place his bets, still with tips from the professional gambler. Ultimately, he wins a big bet, which he has placed with an IOU. The manager of the club tells him that he cannot collect until he has shown he has the cash he bet. The sucker goes to the bank, secure that he has made a big "killing." When he returns, he is convinced that he should deposit all his money in the club. Then the con man is ready for the big step, relieving the sucker of all of the money he has just deposited. The usual technique is to give him a tip worded in such a way that he will lose, but due to his "misunderstanding" of the instructions. For example, he is told "to place everything on a certain horse." The gambler knows that the horse has already come in second, but words his instructions so that the sucker will bet all his money on the horse to win. After the sucker loses all his money he is told that it was his fault—he had been instructed to bet on the horse to "place" (come in second). Finally, the gambler tries to "cool the sucker out" (in this case, by telling him it was his own fault) so that he will not go to the police. Sometimes the sucker is cooled out so well that he never knows he has been taken and returns again and again to lose his money.

Another technique for avoiding detection and apprehension is to use a "stand-in" to do the actual dirty work. The "pigeon passer" frequently uses this technique.[47] He attempts to cash counterfeit or discarded parimutuel tickets. One variation is to pick up discarded losing tickets and attempt to get them cashed. This is most successful with inexperienced or easily cowed cashiers. The pigeon passer picks up losing tickets from early races and waits for

[46]Edwin Sutherland, *The Professional Thief* (Chicago: University of Chicago Press, 1937). See also, Erving Goffman, "On Cooling the Mark Out," *Psychiatry*, 15 (1952), 451–463.

[47]Scott, *The Racing Game.*

that number to show up in a later race. The inexperienced cashier, faced with a long line of winners impatient to collect, is anxious to please them and thus only glances at the ticket presented to him to be sure it has the winning number. He may not notice that although it has the right number, it is from the wrong race. A variation on this approach is to present the cashier with a "pigeon" included among a number of legitimate winning tickets. Still another variation is to pass counterfeit tickets. This is the most risky of the approaches, although all are fraught with danger. There is always the possibility of detection by the cashier. In the first two approaches the pigeon passer can claim ignorance and probably get away with it, unless he has been caught doing the same thing a number of times before. The pigeon passer who passes counterfeit tickets is in greater danger because being caught involves not only the anger of the cashier but the notification of the track police. Many cashiers have ultraviolet lights that help them determine whether a ticket is counterfeit.

Another dramaturgical means for handling problems with the police is the obvious one of eliminating the evidence of the crime. A fence acts as a "middleman" between the thief and the buyer of the stolen goods. His primary task is, then, the distribution of stolen items. The fence may be involved in the distribution of stolen goods on a full-time basis, but more frequently he engages in these activities as a secondary aspect of a legitimate job.[48]

The fence protects the thief by taking the stolen items from him and thereby eliminating the problem of evidence. This is often done through the use of a "drop." Once the items are stolen, the thief takes them to a previously specified place where they are left. Later, the fence picks up the stolen merchandise and sells them. The fence either pays the thief before the crime or waits until a later date when it is safer to pay him.

The fence also utilizes dramaturgical means to protect himself. Klockars finds that one common technique used by warehouse owners is to mix the stolen items in with legitimate goods, thus minimizing the risks of police detection. The fence may also destroy any identifying marks, such as brand names or serial numbers, from the merchandise. In this way, incriminating evidence of his activities is eliminated.

In some types of criminal activity it is not sufficient to eliminate the evidence; the thief must be able to successfully confront the police in order to get away. Letkemann describes an example of how this is done by some bank robbers. After robbing the bank and using a stolen car, the bank robbers return to a predetermined place, abandon the stolen car, and bury the money. The robbers then take their own car which "contains everything associated with an innocent fishing trip—beer, fishing rods, and some fish bought earlier at the market" to a nearby police roadblock.[49] They tell the police that they are on a fishing trip and usually they are allowed to pass through the roadblock. They later return to collect the money. If the police arrest them, they have eliminated the evidence of the crime and have a legitimate excuse for being in the area. Consequently, the chances of criminal conviction are minimized.

[48]Shover, "The Social Organizations of Burglary." See also, Carl B. Klockars, *The Professional Fence.*

[49]Letkemann, *Crime as Work,* p. 106.

Coping with Other Nonclients.

To this point, we have only considered the various means that are utilized to control threats from the police and other agencies of law enforcement. Many deviant occupations are not illegal, however, and the occupational members do not have to handle problems involving the police. This does not mean, however, that they have no problems with persons other than clients. Both legal and illegal deviant occupations involve relations with persons who act to control the occupation and its members. One example of this type of controlling agent is the nightclub manager.

In some cases a nightclub owner is also the manager, although the more typical pattern is for the club to be managed by a person who is in the employ of the club owner. In either case, performers are dependent on the management in most aspects of their worklives. "It is the manager who decides on salary, hiring and firing, and content of performance; he even monitors the off-stage behavior . . . ."[50] Given the dependence of the performers on management, it should not be surprising that they have few means, either direct or dramaturgical, for dealing with this threat to their occupational security. If the manager also operates as the emcee, the performers may attempt to control him by ridiculing him in front of the audience and "by little conspiracies among themselves."[51] This type of dramaturgical manipulation is not very effective, however, and the performer runs the added risk of being fired.

The key to the powerlessness of some performers (strippers, comics, female impersonators, for example) in relation to the nightclub manager is their lack of occupational cohesion. Newton finds that female impersonators do not have a shared system of values and norms that make is possible for the performers to collectively control the conditions of their work. Rather, they compete with each other to gain favors from the management at the expense of the other performers and this type of activity is encouraged by the management in an effort to solidify their control. Newton summarizes the lack of occupational solidarity in this way: "Cut-throat motives of gain and competition were allowed free play and even encouraged in a very loosely structured situation whose only certainties were uncertainties."[52]

Although stripping is characterized by a shared system of values and norms that constrain the relations among the strippers, there is no collective orientation toward management that aids them in controlling their work setting. As Boles and Garbin note, "Job security is extremely tenuous. A house girl does not have a contract with the club where she is employed, and she can be fired 'on the spot.' In fact, one club owner fired all of his house girls one night as they reported for work because 'he was in a peeve.' "[53] The absence of a collective orientation toward the management is further exacerbated by the fact that a majority of the strippers are "house girls"—that is, they are full-time employees of one nightclub and do not travel the nightclub circuit. Consequently, many identify with the nightclub and not the occupation. This

[50]Newton, *Mother Camp,* p. 122.

[51]Ibid., p. 124.

[52]Ibid., p. 114.

[53]Boles and Garbin, "Stripping for a Living," p. 326.

commitment is best reflected in the "maternalistic" attitudes that many house girls have toward nightclub managers. Given the absence of a collective orientation toward management, the financial power of the nightclub manager, and the limited identification of many of the strippers, it should not be surprising that strippers have little power in their work setting and few means of manipulating the setting to their advantage. Indeed, emotional involvement with nonoccupational members appears to be a significant factor in limiting the occupational control of members of other deviant occupations as well. One occupation in which emotional involvement is crucial in determining social control is that of prostitution and the relationship between the prostitute and the pimp.

Because pimp-prostitute relationships are based on many combinations of concern for respect, business, and love, the techniques used by prostitutes to control pimps are varied. The most autonomous prostitutes are those who have a strict business relationship where they and their pimps are partners. The least autonomous are those women who have an intense emotional commitment to their pimps and can, therefore, be manipulated by pimps who withhold their affection unless the women are submissive. Between these extremes are a number of relationships allowing for varying degrees of manipulation by the prostitutes. The ultimate resource available to the prostitute is the termination of the relationship and the ultimate resource of the pimp is the use of violence. Indeed, resort to these extremes is not uncommon. Milner and Milner, as well as Gray, note, for example, that beatings not only occur, but they are accepted as a necessary fact of life by pimps and prostitutes alike.[54] On the other hand, the pimp who relies exclusively on physical force to control his prostitutes is likely to command little honor from others and his control is limited by his inability to supervise his prostitutes all of the time. The most effective pimps develop less violent ways of controlling their prostitutes on an everyday basis.

Madams try to control prostitutes in their employ and this effort is most evident in the house rules that are presented to the new prostitute as nonnegotiable. The limits of these rules are most evident when they are broken because the madams often refuse to fire rule violators. In the male house of prostitution described by Pittman, for example, two members of the house broke the rules by becoming emotionally involved and decided to set up their own residence. Although the "madam" was angry and predicted that the relationship would not last, he also requested that they continue to work at the house.[55] But prostitutes may attempt to control madams in other ways which do not violate the house rules. In her study of a female house of prostitution, Heyl notes that one of the most popular strategies used by these women was to engage in a type of work "slow-down".[56] This was done by doing only the minimal amount needed to be attractive to customers and to encourage them to spend their money. Thus, the women abided by the rules and could not be

[54]Milner and Milner, *Black Players*; Gray, "Turning-Out."

[55]Pittman, "The Male House of Prostitution."

[56]Barbara Sherman Heyl, *The Madam as Entrepreneur* (New Brunswick, NJ: Transaction Books, 1979).

fired, but they did only the minimal amount necessary to keep their jobs. Another popular strategy was to claim illness in order to get the night off. Indeed, this strategy was used so often that the madam in this house referred to it as "the whorehouse syndrome" and, like similar ploys by other workers, it could be effective in gaining worker control.[57]

These women were able to get by with work restriction because the madam needed them to keep her business operating. Although she could always find replacements for those who left, the interim period could be a difficult time and then when a replacement was found, the madam was faced with the prospect of training her. Thus, as long as the prostitutes were not too extreme in their work restriction, the madam tended to allow them autonomy. Those women who took their protests to the extreme were either fired or their pimps were informed and asked to remedy the problem. There is, then, a limit to the autonomy that a madam will allow prostitutes and, like the other relationships described in this section, much of the prostitute's and madam's time is directed toward the negotiation of those boundaries.

IDEOLOGY AND DEVIANT OCCUPATIONS

Many occupations are characterized by cultures that emphasize values and orientations that make them distinctive from other occupations. One element of occupational cultures is the value systems that are contained within them. The value systems may be vague and general or they may be concrete and limited to only certain aspects of the occupation. The value systems may also be highly integrated or they may be made up of values that are disconnected and, perhaps, inconsistent. Thus, there are a variety of characteristics that may be present within the culture of any single occupation. It is not our purpose here to discuss the full range of value systems that are found in either conventional or deviant occupations. Rather, we intend to concentrate on only one aspect—the ideological aspect. Our definition of occupational ideology is similar to Salamon's approach, in which he claims:

> The value systems may be seen, at least in part, as ideological, in that they contain a view of the occupation, its role in the society, the nature of the contribution it makes to the general good, the relationship between the occupation and other related lines of work, and the conditions necessary to ensure an adequate flow of "suitable" recruits to the occupation. . . . Value systems may also be seen as ideological in that they supply ordered, coherent perspectives to the sorts of situations and difficulties that members of . . . occupations are likely to experience. They thus supply a framework for marshalling and interpreting social situations.[58]

The basic feature of occupational ideologies is that they contain relatively integrated perspectives that define the nature of the relationship be-

[57] Ibid.

[58] Graeme Salamon, *Community and Occupation: An Exploration of Work/Leisure Relationships* (London: Cambridge University Press, 1974).

tween the occupation and its members with the larger society. It should be noted that all deviant occupations do not have "coherent perspectives" that are passed on through the socialization process, but many do, and the occupational ideology is important in helping members handle the problems that they encounter in their worklives. For example, Hayano notes that professional gamblers tend to look at all aspects of their lives in terms of chance and luck.[59] As they say, "life's a gamble."[60] Such an ideology is useful for the gamblers because they live in a world of great financial uncertainty and it helps them to place their wins and losses in a general perspective.

A second important point is that the ideology must be accepted by the occupational members. Bryan's studies of call girl socialization, for example, indicate that although the instructor attempts to socialize the novice into a value system that emphasizes loyalty to other call girls and contempt for customers, few of the novices accept the value system and many violate its most basic tenets early in their careers.[61] If an ideology is to be an effective device in helping occupational members deal with recurrent problems and stresses, it is crucial that the ideology be accepted by the occupational members.

A related point is that different segments of a deviant occupation may hold to different ideologies; indeed, contradictory ideologies may be found in the same deviant occupation. In drug dealing, for example, some dealers justify their work as "turning people on" to new experiences and a new consciousness and, in this way, contributing to social change. Other dealers define their work as a business which involves selling goods for which there is a public demand. Thus they describe their primary motives as providing quality goods and making profits. As one drug dealer states, "All of society is based on a capitalist rip-off, and that's just the way things go."[62]

Finally, it should be noted that occupational ideologies do not need to conform to established fact in order to be effective in helping occupational members deal with their problems or to justify the occupation. The key factor is that the ideology be accepted by the members of the occupation and not whether it accurately describes the objective situation. We move now to a consideration of a few occupational ideologies that are found in deviant occupations and a consideration of the ways these ideologies operate to justify the occupational activities of the members.

Hustling and pimping.   Hustling, in its simplest form, is the practice of manipulating others to one's own advantage. The concept of hustling does not necessarily entail illegal or even unethical activity; indeed, hustling and the related manipulative techniques are an important part of many conventional occupations, such as the diverse occupations that involve direct sales to customers. Given the emphasis on hustling in American society, it should not be surprising that many deviant occupations are also based on the ability to manipulate others for gain. Not all deviant occupations that are based on

[59]David M. Hayano, *Poker Faces,* (Berkeley, CA: University of California Press, 1982).

[60]Ibid., p. 134.

[61]James Bryan, "Apprenticeships in Prostitution," and "Occupational Ideologies and Individual Attitudes of Call Girls," *Social Problems,* 13 (1966), 441–450.

[62]John Langer, "Drug Entrepreneurs and Dealing Culture," *Social Problems,* 24 (1977), 383.

hustling are characterized by well-developed ideologies, however. Both Sutherland and Polsky note that con men and poolroom hustlers seldom feel the need to justify their occupational activities to others.[63] Such justification is rarely necessary because the members of these occupations seldom interact with "outsiders" except as a part of their work; thus, the con man and the poolroom hustler encounter few occasions in which justification is necessary. There is, however, one "hustling occupation" that is characterized by an integrated ideology, the occupation of pimping.

The pimp is a paradox in our society.[64] Looked at in one way, he is an American hero, or at least an anti-hero—the self-reliant man who lives by his skills and ingenuity. Similarly, the pimp is not subordinate to any other person in either his economic or social life; instead, he uses others to his advantage. Viewed in another way, however, the pimp violates many of the most important moral rules in American society. First, he consciously violates the assumption that men should be the "protectors and providers" for their women. Second, the pimp violates shared values about the purposes of wealth. Rather than saving his money in an effort to attain financial and social stability and security, the pimp and his subculture stress conspicuous consumption. Thus, the pimp is a man who simultaneously incorporates and violates many of the basic values in our society.

For the pimp, however, there is no paradox. The ideology of the occupation is sufficiently integrated that the apparent contradictions of pimping are really overlapping dimensions of a distinctive subculture and lifestyle. At its most general level, it involves a world view that emphasizes social life as a game of unequal exchange. This aspect of the ideology is best summarized in a common pimping cliché: " 'There are the givers, the takers, and the givers-and-takers. After that comes the undertakers.' "[65] The pimp is both a giver and a taker. Although his lifestyle is based on the use of women to his advantage, he is used by other persons as well. For example, "the man who sells them Cadillacs, cocaine, television sets, jewelry, and clothes" is using the pimps in the same way as the pimps use their women.[66] The giver-and-taker relationship is not limited to the pimp, however; it also applies to the relationships that exist between the pimp and the prostitute and between the prostitute and her trick. That is, the prostitute is used by the pimp, but she uses the trick to her advantage. The trick, on the other hand, is used by the prostitute but he takes advantage of the pimp's desire for material goods. As mentioned above, an effective ideology need not be an accurate assessment of the objective situation, and this is clearly the case with the ideology of pimping. The prostitute, for example, is not used in the simple and clear-cut way that is claimed in the pimp's ideology. Indeed, the requirement that the prostitute have a pimp before she is totally acceptable to the other prostitutes indicates that she is not totally exploited by him. Even though the prostitute-pimp relationship is more complicated than is assumed by the ideology, the ideology is

[63]Sutherland, *The Professional Thief;* Ned Polsky, *Hustlers, Beats, and Others* (Garden City, NY: Anchor Books, 1969).

[64]Milner and Milner, *Black Players.*

[65]Ibid., p. 211.

[66]Ibid., pp. 212–213.

still effective in defining the desired relationships among the prostitutes, pimps, and tricks and it also serves to justify many of the activities of the pimps.

At a less general level, there are two other aspects of the ideology that need further discussion. The first involves the need for the prostitute-pimp relationship. The ideology of pimping emphasizes the ubiquitousness of exchange in all social relationships, and this emphasis includes the relationship between husband and wife. The most basic division of the world in the pimping ideology involves the traits that differentiate men from women. Women are seen as "biological beings" who are concerned with attaining material security for themselves. Indeed, this biological factor is presumed to be sufficiently important that women are willing to exchange their bodies for personal security. Men, on the other hand, are assumed to be "intellectual beings" who are oriented toward leadership and control. Sexually, men are presumed to have very strong sexual desires and impulses which impel them toward involvement with a diversity of women. Thus the "natural" relationship between men and women is one of control and leadership by the man over the woman. This relationship is further necessitated by the "incomplete" nature of women. That is, according to this ideology it is assumed that women are not whole unless they have a man to control them and a man to care for. As the Milners state:

> In her pristine state, woman is only half of a completed unit. Without a man she is nothing. Her being is a vessel to nurture the thoughts and the seed which her man implants in her. Without his seed she cannot bear children, and without his Pygmalion-like efforts to shape her mind, she cannot be productive or happy. She is the natural student of man, who provides her with "direction."[67]

The problems of the modern world can be attributed, according to this ideology, to the disruption of the natural relationship between men and women. And this disruption is best reflected in modern marriage. According to the pimp's ideology, the modern marriage reflects the domination of women over men and this unnatural relationship creates the need for prostitutes. Specifically, the institution of marriage is the result of a basic need of women for security and their willingness to exchange sexual favors for it. Under "natural" conditions, men would be unwilling to marry, because their independence and need for diverse sexual experiences would prohibit it, but modern women have tied sexuality to marriage. Thus men find it necessary to marry in order to fulfill themselves sexually, and as a result even the institution of marriage is based on an exchange relationship. Unfortunately, according to this ideology, few wives fulfill their obligations under the informal contract of marriage. Rather, shortly after marriage the wife begins to refuse her implicit duty as a sexual partner and because of this development and the fact that most husbands are insufficiently manly to insist upon their "rights," it becomes necessary for the husband to seek other sexual outlets—that is, prostitutes.

[67]Ibid., p. 164.

A second, and related, aspect of the ideology of pimping involves the relationship between the pimp and his prostitutes. Specifically, this relationship reflects the "natural" order of male-female relations. The man is dominant in this relationship and the woman is submissive, even to the point of selling her body to provide him with a livelihood. But the dominance of the pimp goes beyond the occupational elements of the relationship. Indeed, all aspects of the relationship are "ideally" controlled by the pimp. Given the more general ideology of pimping, it is assumed that such a relationship is the best and that it should make both parties happy. The fact that many prostitutes rebel against the domination of the pimp is not taken as an indication of unhappiness, but it is assumed that women often try to test their strength against the man. Although a woman who can successfully dominate her man is doomed to unhappiness, the ideology states that women make the effort anyway and that their efforts for control must be stopped at all costs. Thus, physical punishment is justified under these circumstances if no other means of control are available to the pimp.

Obviously, the ideology just described is chauvinistic and self-serving for the pimps. It is important to keep in mind, however, that such an ideology helps to solve the paradox that is implicit in pimping as a way of life. That is, the pimp is presumed to be a self-reliant and independent man who embodies only the best qualities of manhood. At the same time, he is not violating any of the "natural" rules involving male-female relations. It is assumed that the contemporary American value that men should provide for women is false. Indeed, many claim that such a value is just another reflection of the extent to which women have come to control the lives of their men. Thus, the pimp is a "real" man and his relationship with the prostitutes is natural and proper. There is an ideology of pimping because of the importance of maintaining the relationship with the prostitute. That is, because the pimp does not provide a clear-cut good or service in exchange for the money received from the prostitute, it would seem that the relationship must be based on something less concrete. One such basis could be an ideology that stresses the "naturalness" of the prostitute-pimp relationship. The findings of Gray in her study of teenage streetwalkers implicitly supports this position.[68] Gray claims that most of the prostitutes in her sample tend to accept the physical punishment of the pimp as something they need. At least implicitly, these assertions suggest that these women accept the right of the man to control them and to be supported by them.

One of the outcomes of the ideology of pimping is that it helps to explain away much of the presumed immorality of the pimp's activities and lifestyle. Put differently, one of the functions of the ideologies of many deviant occupations is that they "neutralize the stigma" that is associated with the occupation and its members.[69] Thus the pimp is transformed through t he ideology from a hustler who exploits women in the pursuit of material accumulation into a real man who represents the "natural" relationship between men and women.

[68]Gray, "Turning-Out: A Study of Teenage Prostiution."

[69]Gresham M. Sykes and David Matza, "Techniques of Neutralization: A Theory of Delinquency," *American Sociological Review*, 22 (1957), 664–670.

Pimps are not the only persons who must deal with the stigma attached to their occupation, nor are they the only persons who utilize an occupational ideology to legitimate their activities. For example, Ken Levi has recently studied the neutralization techniques used by the novice hit man.[70]

Stripping.   The central moral issue that confronts the stripper involves the problem of public nudity and its related social and sexual implications. Thus the moral issue goes beyond public nudity; rather, the act of stripping in public challenges many of the cultural values and practices that give meaning to sexuality and sexual relations in the United States, as well as other societies. As Salutin states:

> Strippers are viewed as "bad," then, because they strip away all decorum with their clothes. They taunt the public with their own mores by teasing them and turning them on. The privacy of the sex act disappears as does its personal quality, that is, the physical touching of one another and the sharing of affection. In burlesque theaters and in the strip bars, open to the public for the price of admission, the sex act is made a packaged commercial deal.[71]

Thus strippers constitute an occupation that is based on the violation of shared norms and values within society.

Equally important, the occupation, and the stripper herself, are often seen as a threat to many persons within the society. It should not be surprising, then, that the occupation of stripping is characterized by an ideology that justifies the stripper's activities and neutralizes the stigma attached to her performance.

One ideological solution to the moral issue surrounding stripping is to emphasize the entertainment dimension of the occupation. Several studies report that many strippers identify with persons in the more legitimate occupations asssociated with show business and entertainment.[72] These studies also indicate, however, that such an identification and justification of the occupation is primarily limited to feature performers and others who are not exclusively employed by a single nightclub. Those women who work for one nightclub exclusively (usually house girls) tend to justify their occupational activities on different grounds.

House girls are, in part, distinct from features because of their primary identification with and commitment to the personnel and regular customers who populate the nightclubs in which they work. Because of their attachment to the nightclub, house girls are more likely to adopt an ideology that emphasizes the educational and community service aspects of their activities. As Boles and Garbin note:

[70]Ken Levi, "Becoming a Hit Man: Neutralizaton in a Very Deviant Career," *Urban Life* 10 (1981), 47–63.

[71]Marilyn Salutin, "Stripper Morality," *Transaction,* 8 (1971), 13.

[72]Boles and Garbin, "Stripping for a Living;" James Skipper and Charles McCaghy, "Strippers: The Anatomy and Career Contingencies of a Deviant Occupation," *Social Problems,* 17 (1970), 391–405.

The strippers, especially the house girls, feel they are performing a therapeutic service for men, in particular, and a protective service for society, in general. Most of them say their performances permit the men watching to fantasize about having intercourse with them providing a therapeutic function by relieving sexual tension. Many of the girls believe there would be more sex crimes if it were not for strip shows. There is a tendency for both house girls and features to believe they provide educational instruction and information for women in attendance at the club.[73]

As with most ideologies, there is a certain amount of evidence to support the position taken by the house girls. Boles and Garbin indicate that the claim that women in the audience are often interested in learning about sexual techniques and seductiveness is particularly supported by the fact that several strippers in their sample had previously been approached by women desiring such information. Similarly, their claim that they provide an educational service for young men who are largely ignorant of the female anatomy and sexual techniques is given some support by the large number of college-age males who attend stripping shows.[74] Finally, the fact that some male members of the audience use the stripper's performance as an occasion for masturbation also lends superficial support for the therapeutic claim of the ideology.

Given the stigmatized nature of the occupation and the characteristics and activities of the audiences, it should not be surprising that the occupation is characterized by an ideology claiming "that society needs strippers in the same way it needs teachers and doctors."[75]

The male stripper is also viewed in a negative way by society. Paula Dressel and David Petersen found that male strippers thought many people perceived their show to be "cheap" and "crude."[76] As a result, male strippers have developed four primary justifications for stripping. Similar to the ideology developed by female strippers, the male strippers' justifications center around the entertainment value of their work and the community services they provide. One male stripper notes:

It's a nightclub act, not just a strip joint. We don't always take our clothes off. . . . It's entertainment.[77]

In terms of community services, the male strippers see themselves providing women with an outlet similar to what men enjoy. Equal rights for women is an important component of the male strippers' ideology. As one male stripper put it:

They want to experience something they haven't seen before. They want to see something they've been denied and to have their rights to like men.[78]

[73]Boles and Garbin, "Stripping for a Living," 324.

[74]Salutin, "Stripper Morality."

[75]Ibid., 18.

[76]Paula L. Dressel and David M. Petersen, "Becoming a Male Stripper: Recruitment, Socialization, and Ideological Development," *Work and Occupations,* 9 (1982), 387–406.

[77]Ibid., 402.

[78]Ibid., 401.

Related to this is the idea that the male strip show provides a sexual outlet and sexual diversion for the women in the audience. Finally, women can attend these shows and act with little inhibition in a safe and secure environment. A dancer suggests:

> They can act themselves without any restrictions. They can do what they feel, oblivious to everything.[79]

Cockfighting.   One of the most comprehensive and ingenious ideologies associated with a deviant occupation is found among cockfighters, that is, persons who breed, train, and bet on a special type of chicken that has been bred for fighting.[80] These birds are equipped with special spurs (or "gaffs") which are used to cut and stab the opponent during the fight. According to McCaghy and Neal: "The gaff's blade is perfectly round; it tapers and curves from the socket on the leg to an extremely sharp point, and its length may range from 1¼ to 3 inches."[81] Because of the use of such equipment and the fact that the birds are sometimes allowed to fight to their deaths, cockfighting is often condemned as a brutal sport that should be outlawed, and those who participate in the sport are described as inhumane thugs. Not surprisingly, the ideology associated with cockfighting is largely directed toward these charges.

An important part of that ideology is an attack on those who condemn the sport as inhumane. One part of this counterattack is the claim that those who piously condemn cockfighting are hypocrites who are involved with equally inhumane acts on a regular basis, such as attending boxing matches where the object of the contest is to hurt a human opponent. Equally important, however, are the respectable qualities that the cockfighters find in the history of their sport and work. They note that some of the most respected and influential people in the history of the country have been involved in this line of work and those persons who attend cockfights today are described as clean-cut, respectable, and wholesome people. Indeed, cockfighting is sometimes described as an important source for preserving traditional values, because the whole family can participate in breeding, training, and fighting the cocks. Thus, the elderly, children, and wayward husbands are kept at home and in the family through their common interest in cockfighting. Finally, the cockfighters note that their birds are bred to be fighters and attempts to keep them from the ring will make them miserable; indeed, some argue that the cocks find self-actualization in their battles. Presumably, the birds share with human beings a desire to achieve their natural potential.

Thus, just as members of conventional occupations develop explanations that justify the meaninglessness, inhumanity, and inequalities associated with their work, so members of deviant occupations develop their own ideologies. The ideologies found in the latter occupations have an added im-

---

[79]Ibid., 402.

[80]Charles H. McCaghy and Arthur G. Neal, "The Fraternity of Cockfighters: Ethical Embellishments of an Illegal Sport," *Journal of Popular Culture*, 8 (1974), 557–569.

[81]Ibid., 558.

portance, however, because these workers must deal with public condemnation and legal harassment. Their ideologies are used, then, as sources for maintaining the dignity of the workers and countering the attacks of others.

A Note on Occupational Deviancy

In this chapter we examined deviant occupations in considerable detail, but deviance also occurs in otherwise "straight" occupations. Various forms of deviant behavior can be found throughout the "straight" (nondeviant) workworld. Any work behavior is considered deviant when it violates "legal codes, formalized expectations, customary standards, and informal social norms."[82]

We find numerous examples of deviant behavior among physicians, including fee splitting, kickbacks, use of quack remedies, and charging for work never done.[83] Lonn Lanza-Kaduce discusses the case of unnecessary surgery as an example of deviance among doctors.[84] Lawyers, in particular those involved in politics, have had a number of their abuses highlighted by the Watergate scandal.[85] Among managers we find such abuses as false advertising, bribery, criminal fraud, illegal political contributions, tax evasion, and price fixing.[86] Proprietors of business often engage in easy credit schemes that plunge buyers deeply into debt.[87] Another abuse is the bait and switch, in which the proprietor advertises a low-price item, but when the customer comes into the store, the sale item is downgraded; or in another form of this technique, the customer is strongly encouraged to buy a higher-priced item. Salesmen have been found to "fiddle," that is, overcharge, short change, or short-deliver their customers.[88] Semiskilled workers often take shortcuts on the production process that may seriously impair the quality of the finished product.[89] Recently, property theft and production deviance, that is, slow or

[82]Clifton D. Bryant, ed., *Deviant Behavior*, p. 17.

[83]For a general overview of professional deviance see, H. Kirk Dansereau, "Unethical Behavior," in Bryant, ed., *Deviant Behavior*, pp. 75–89.

[84]Lonn Lanza-Kaduce, "Deviance Among Professionals," *Deviant Behavior*, 3–4 (1980), 333–359.

[85]Jerome Carlin, *Lawyer's Ethics* (New York: Russell Sage Foundation, 1966). For a discussion of the way politicians attempt to deal with their deviance see, James Boyd, "The Ritual of Wiggle," *The Washington Monthly*, 2 (1970), pp. 28–43.

[86]For a review of the literature on white-collar crime see, Donald J. Shoemaker and Donald R. South, "White-Collar Crime," in Clifton Bryant, ed., *Deviant Behavior*, pp. 189–200. For examples of crime at the upper echelons of the corporate hierarchy see the following: Walter Kiechel III, "The Crime at the Top in Freuhauf Corp," *Fortune* (January 29, 1979), pp. 32–35; Peter W. Bernstein, "The Rise, Fall, and Rise of Irving Kahn," *Fortune* (July 28, 1980), pp. 58–62; Peter W. Bernstein, "Prison Can be Bad for Your Career," *Fortune* (July 28, 1980), pp. 62–67; Irwin Ross, "How Lawless Are Big Companies," *Fortune* (December 1, 1980), p. 56–64.

[87]David Caplovitz, "The Merchant and the Low-Income Consumer," *Jewish Social Studies*, 27 (1965), 48.

[88]Jason Ditton, "Learning to 'Fiddle' Customers," *Sociology of Work and Occupations*, 4 (1977), 427–449.

[89]Joseph Bensman and Israel Gerver, "Crime and Punishment in the Factory," *American Sociological Review*, 28 (1963), 588–598.

sloppy work, absenteeism, and tardiness have been found among all occupational levels in specific manufacturing, retail, and service (hospital) sectors of the economy.[90] Finally, police deviance such as bribes and shakedowns have received much publicity in the media.[91]

Recently, Gerald Mars has analyzed much of the literature on occupational deviancy with a classificatory scheme emphasizing the strength of occupational cultures and the extent to which members of occupations share common interests.[92] He describes four types of occupational deviancy: hawks, donkeys, wolves, and vultures. "Hawks" are persons in occupations that have weak cultures and little common interests and, consequently, they are most likely to have an individualistic approach to occupational deviancy, emphasizing their own self interests. Hawks include salespeople, managers, independent professionals, cab drivers, and many waiters.

"Donkeys" are persons who work in occupations with strong cultures but few shared worker interests. These workers often have boring jobs that are highly supervised and much of their deviance may be understood as a way of striking back at management. As Mars states in regard to a grocery store cashier who regularly stole five times her daily wage: "Her motive was simply that she hated being treated like a programmed robot and fiddling made her job much more interesting; it gave her new targets and a sense of challenge as well as hitting her boss where it hurt."[93]

Mars classifies persons who work in occupations involving strong cultures and many shared worker interests as "wolves." These occupations are most characteristic of traditional working-class jobs, such as mining teams, garbage collection crews, and longshore gangs. Such groups are tightly organized and individuals are controlled by their commitment to the groups and the fact that most of their work occurs in the presence of their coworkers. Thus occupational deviance in these jobs is usually a group effort involving the same sort of teamwork that is required to do other aspects of the jobs. An example of deviance committed by wolves is the routine pilferage of ships' cargoes committed by longshoremen.[94]

Finally, Mars discusses "vultures." Vultures are persons working in occupations that have weak cultures, but where workers share many common interests: "Workers in these occupations are, therefore, members of a group of co-workers for some purposes only and they act individualistically and competitively for others."[95] Typically, vultures' jobs involve traveling and, during this time, their behavior cannot be observed by supervisors. People

[90]Richard Hollinger and John Clark, "Employee Deviance," *Work and Occupations*, 9 (1982), 97–114; Richard C. Hollinger and John P. Clark, "Deterrence in the Workplace," *Social Forces*, 62 (1983), 398–418.

[91]Ellwyn Stoddard, "The Informal 'Code' of Police Deviancy," *Journal of Criminal Law, Criminology and Police Science*, 59 (1968), 201–213; Maurice Punch, "Developing Scandal," *Urban Life*, 11 (1982), 208–230.

[92]Gerald Mars, *Cheats at Work* (London: Unwin, 1982).

[93]Ibid., p. 31.

[94]William W. Pilcher, *The Portland Longshoremen* (New York: Holt, Rinehart and Winston, 1972).

[95]Gerald Mars, *Cheats at Work*, p. 32.

who drive delivery trucks are an example and the practice of not delivering all the goods ordered by their customers is typical of the way in which vultures work. They can get by with "shorting" their customers because they have regular customers who trust them and, therefore, do not watch them unload their trucks or count the number of delivered items. If they are caught, the drivers say that they made a mistake. Most of the time they do not get caught and the leftover items are sold to others at a reduced rate.

Deviance occurs throughout the workworld and is not restricted to those in deviant occupations. Indeed, it may be that deviance in "straight" occupations is a more serious problem than the activities of people involved in deviant occupations.

CONCLUSIONS

In this chapter we have examined a wide array of deviant occupations. We discussed the conflicts caused by customers and clients and the efforts to resolve these conflicts by entertainers, prostitutes, and bank robbers. Client conflict is not the only problem for those in deviant occupations. The police are a source of stress for those in deviant occupations and individuals in these occupations employ a variety of direct (bribes) and indirect (dramaturgical) devices to cope with this conflict. There are also other outside agents who are a source of conflict for deviant workers. We saw how the nightclub manager exercises considerable unwanted control over the stripper, the comic, and the female impersonator and that pimps and madams are often a source of similar problems for the prostitute. We also discussed the use of ideologies by those in deviant occupations to justify or rationalize their activities both to themselves and to those around them. Finally, we briefly considered an issue that has received relatively little attention from occupational sociologists–deviance within conventional jobs. This chapter suggests that deviance is pervasive in modern society and it involves the degraded and honored alike.

FOURTEEN
CONTEMPORARY WORK-
RELATED PROBLEMS

In a sense, a very large portion of this book has been concerned with problems associated with work in America. Many of the chapters (8-13) have been focally concerned with the kinds of conflicts various kinds of workers experience on the job. In Chapter 5 we examined in detail the problems experienced by women in the workworld. Throughout the book we have encountered a wide range of specific problems such as occupational deviancy, difficulties associated with technological change, union corruption, career immobility, and so forth. We close this book with a discussion of three additional problems—racism in the workworld, occupational safety and health problems, and the overarching problems caused by the rationalization of society in general and work in particular.

RACISM IN THE WORKWORLD

It is no longer radical or revolutionary to contend that America is a racist society. We know that the educational institution operates in such a way that black children do not get as good an education as white children. We are also familiar with the fact that the political institution is often structured in such a way that blacks do not have an adequate voice in political decisions, even those that directly affect their lives. It is also clear that blacks are discriminated against in the institution of medicine, since they die younger, receive poorer-quality care, and are likely to suffer from curable diseases that have all but disappeared in the white community.[1]

In this section we deal with the racism that pervades still another institution—the occupational domain. Before proceeding, however, it is necessary that we first define the concept of racism:

> Racism is any set of beliefs that organic, genetically transmitted differences (whether real or imagined) between human groups are intrinsically associated with the presence or the absence of certain socially relevant abilities or characteristics, hence that such differences are a legitimate basis of invidious distinctions between groups socially defined as races.[2]

Although the focus in this section will be on racism affecting blacks, it is clear from this definition that all other racial groups are confronted with basically the same problem.

It is important to underscore the point that from a sociological perspective races are *socially* defined. Thus, races need not be different organically and genetically, they merely need to be so defined. Racism occurs in this country because whites define blacks as a race and attribute to them the possession or nonpossession of important abilities and characteristics. On the basis of these perceptions, the white majority makes judgments about blacks that adversely affect blacks in the workworld, as well as in every other social institution. Whites stereotypically perceive blacks as " 'lazy,' 'apathetic,' 'dumb,' 'shiftless,' 'good-timers.' "[3] Given this stereotype, whites have taken a number of actions that have discriminated against black workers. It is to these acts and their adverse effects that we now turn.

Exclusion of Blacks from the Workworld

One dimension of occupational racism is the exclusion of blacks from the workworld. This exclusion may be either total or partial. When people are totally excluded (at least for a time) they are either *not in the labor force* or they are *unemployed*. A person may also be *underemployed*. Let us look at each of these forms of occupational exclusion.

Not in the labor force. In 1983, approximately 7.3 million blacks were considered not to be in the labor force. Of these, 5.7 million were classified as not wanting a job while 1.6 million were classified as wanting a job but not currently looking. Table 14.1 lists the various reasons why blacks either did not want a job or wanted a job but were not looking in 1983. Of particular interest is the nearly half-million blacks who wanted a job but were not looking because they thought they could not get one.[4] A further breakdown of

---

[1]Louis Knowles and Kenneth Prewitt, eds., *Institutional Racism in America* (Englewood Cliffs, NJ: Prentice-Hall, 1969).

[2]Pierre van den Berghe, *Race and Racism: A Comparative Perspective* (New York: John Wiley & Sons, 1967), p. 11.

[3]Stokeley Carmichael and Charles Hamilton, *Black Power* (New York: Vintage Books, 1967), p. 36.

[4]Paul A. Flaim, "Discouraged Workers: How Strong are Their Links to the Job Market?" *Monthly Labor Review*, 107 (1984), 8–11.

TABLE 14.1   Blacks Not in Labor Force by Reason: 1983 (in thousands)

Total not in labor force	7,278
Do not want a job now	5,707
Current activity:	
Going to school	1,050
Ill, disabled	694
Keeping house	2,238
Retired	1,049
Other activity	676
Want a job now	1,571
Reason for not looking:	
School attendance	393
Ill health, disability	187
Home responsibilities	332
Think cannot get a job	470
Other reasons*	189

*Includes small number of men not looking for work because of "home responsibilities."

SOURCE: *Employment and Earnings* 31, 1 (Washington, D.C.: U.S. Department of Labor, 1984), p. 197.

these individuals shows that 54.4 percent had looked for work in the past but had given up because they could not find work.[5] As a middle-aged unemployed machine operator states:

> People say we do not want to work, but that's not true. I want to work, but I can't find a job. . . . employers have made me discouraged.[6]

The second major reason these individuals do not think they can get a job is because they think no jobs are available. Some 28.6 percent of these individuals feel this way. An unemployed black teenager's response is typical:

> I really don't think the business people have enough jobs, if you really want to know how I feel about it. I have looked and I don't know where else to look. I go to (the) unemployment (office), no response. Answer ads in the paper, no response. So I really don't think there are any jobs, or at least I'm not supposed to have one.[7]

There are several other reasons why blacks who want to work do not think they can get a job. Approximately 9.2 percent claim they lack sufficient education or training. Another 4.5 percent feel they cannot get a job because employers consider them to be too young or too old, while 3.4 percent cite

---

[5]*Employment and Earnings,* 31 (Washington, D.C.: U.S. Department of Labor, 1984), p. 198.
[6]Lloyd Gite, "No Prospects for Work," *Black Enterprise* (August, 1983), 17.
[7]Jill Nelson, "The People Behind the Statistics," *Black Enterprise* (May, 1982), 63.

other personal handicaps as the main reason they are unable to get a job.[8] However, it is clear that discouragement and doubt stemming from years of defeat in the workworld top the list. Many blacks have been turned down often in efforts to secure employment. After a series of such disappointments it is little wonder that a significant number of blacks have given up hope of finding work and are, as a result, not included in the labor force.

Unemployed. Many blacks continue to try and find work but are unsuccessful and are therefore considered unemployed. From the end of World War II until 1980, the number of unemployed blacks in the United States had been roughly twice that of whites. As shown in Table 14.2 (page 406), in recent years the unemployment ratio between blacks and whites has been increasing.

In contrast, the unemployment rate for other minority groups has been lower than that of blacks. For example, in 1983, the unemployment rate for four major minority groups was as follows:[9]

Mexican	14.7%
Puerto Rican	15.9
Cuban	11.9
Hispanic (Other)	13.7

As a result, the unemployment ratio between whites and these minority groups is lower than between blacks and whites.

Table 14.2 demonstrates the greater likelihood of black unemployment. Another dimension of this problem is that blacks are likely to be unemployed for a longer period of time than whites. In 1983, the mean number of weeks spent out of work by unemployed blacks was 22.3 weeks.[10] In contrast, unemployed whites spent an average of 19.4 weeks out of work. Further, of those blacks who were unemployed during 1983, nearly 27.5 percent were unemployed for 27 weeks or more whereas 23 percent of unemployed whites were out of work for this period of time. The duration of unemployment increases the hardship and frustration experienced by blacks. As one youth notes:

> I've been to record shops, hamburger places, department stores—you name it. I've had applications in some of these places almost a year now. They tell me to just fill it out and hand it in. Nothing changes. You just build more frustration as you go on.[11]

What are the factors that account for the high rates of black unemployment (as well as total exclusion from the labor market)? One is the nature of the capitalistic system. It seems true that no capitalistic system can

---

[8]*Employment and Earnings,* 1984, p. 203.

[9]Ibid., p. 202.

[10]Ibid., p. 171.

[11]Gordon Witkin, "Where Joblessness Reigns Supreme," *U.S. News and World Report* (January 18, 1982), p. 54.

TABLE 14.2   Comparison of Black and White Unemployment: 1981–1984

YEAR	BLACK	WHITE	RATIO: BLACK TO WHITE
1981	15.6%	6.7%	2.3 to 1
1982	18.9	8.6	2.2 to 1
1983	19.5	8.4	2.3 to 1
1984(Feb)	16.2	6.7	2.4 to 1

SOURCE: 1981 adapted from *Monthly Labor Review*, 2 (106), 1983, 60. 1982, 1983, and 1984 adapted from *Monthly Labor Review*, 4 (107), 1984, 61.

run without at least some unemployment. But this explanation does not tell us why blacks are more likely to be unemployed than whites.

Two important reasons are the lower levels of education among blacks and employer discrimination against them. Blacks have not gotten as much (or as high quality) education as white Americans. In 1968 blacks represented 6.0 percent of the total enrolled in college.[12] By 1976, this figure had increased to about 10.5 percent. Since then, enrollment of blacks in college has remained essentially unchanged. Further, in 1970 the median school years completed for all persons 25 years or over was 12.1. For blacks the average was 9.8.[13] As of the early 1980s, this gap had been significantly reduced, but blacks are still slightly behind whites in terms of the median number of school years completed. In 1982 the figure for all persons was 12.8 while for blacks it was 12.7.[14]

Before one can enter college, one needs a high school degree. While the gap between black and white high school drop out rates continues to narrow, blacks are still more likely to drop out of high school than whites.[15]

At the other end of the continuum, little improvement has been made among blacks receiving advanced degrees. In fact, the number of doctorates conferred on blacks and other minorities has actually declined since 1975. Blacks and other minorities received 12.1 percent of all doctorates conferred in 1975.[16] By 1981, this had dropped so that of the doctorates conferred, 10.6 percent went to blacks and other minorities. It is obvious that this statistic is exaggerated because blacks and other minorities are combined. William F. Brazziel estimates that the percentage of blacks receiving doctoral degrees has averaged less than 4 percent over the last few years.[17] In a society in which academic credentials are more and more important for obtaining even lower-level jobs, many blacks are excluded because of the lack of academic credentials. Even those who have them (a high school or college diploma, or an ad-

[12]U.S. Bureau of the Census, *Statistical Abstract of the United States: 1984*, 104th ed. (Washington, D.C., 1983), p. 163.

[13]Ibid., p. 144.

[14]Ibid.

[15]W. Vance Grant and Thomas D. Snyder, *Digest of Education Statistics: 1983–84* (Washington, D.C.: National Center for Education Statistics, 1983), p. 71.

[16]Ibid., p. 600.

[17]William F. Brazziel, "Baccalaureate College of Origin of Black Doctorate Recipients," *The Journal of Negro Education*, 52 (1983), 102–109.

vanced degree) are often less well-trained than white peers who are, as a result, more likely to be hired.

The other side of this equation is employer discrimination. In the past, many employers had formal, blatant barriers to black employment. In recent years, however, because of government legislation, these formal barriers have been dismantled. But informal discrimination remains in many employing organizations.

In a survey of employed black, middle-income workers, nearly 60 percent of the respondents said they experienced racial discrimination while at work.[18] Racial discrimination was more prevalent among men (64.6 percent) than women (54.2 percent). As one climbs the income hierarchy, reports of racial discrimination increase. Nearly 75 percent of those earning $35,000 or more a year reported experiencing racial discrimination on the job.

Blacks also experience racial discrimination in hiring practices. This takes numerous forms. For one thing, information about job openings is passed by word-of-mouth only among friends of white employees. Another is employing an all-white hiring staff, subtly discouraging those blacks who do manage to apply. As one observer notes:

> It is common . . . for blacks and whites who become friends in the CETA (Comprehensive Employment and Training Act) programs to go job hunting together. One, the black, will go in and get nothing. . . . "We don't have anything," they tell him. "Check with us later." The other, the white one, goes in. He gets better treatment. "Sit down," they say. "Here's an application." He might even get an interview.[19]

Another subtle form of discrimination that has arisen in recent years in response to government pressure is *tokenism*. So that they seem to be complying with government pressure, employers hire a token black or two, usually in highly visible positions within the organization. In this way, the organization appears to be doing something about discrimination without taking any really meaningful action. In the survey cited earlier, over 31 percent of the black employees questioned agreed that their company treats them as tokens.

There are several other reasons why black unemployment rates are so much higher than those of whites. For one thing, the character of the labor force is changing. The great boom in the economy during and immediately after World War II was a great impetus to black employment, but by 1950 a series of changes were underway that adversely affected the employability of the black worker. It was about this time that the flow of whites from rural to urban America exceeded the exodus of blacks in the same direction. These ex-farmers came to compete with blacks for a variety of less-skilled jobs and because they were white, they often won out.[20]

[18]Joel Dreyfuss, "Speaking Out About Work," *Black Enterprise* (August, 1982), 51–56.

[19]Charles Stafford, "Black Teen-agers: No Jobs, No Cures," *St. Petersburg Times* (August 29, 1982), p. 21A.

[20]Charles C. Killingsworth, "Negroes in a Changing Labor Market," in Arthur M. Ross and Herbert Hill, eds., *Employment, Race and Poverty* (New York: Harcourt, Brace and World, 1967), pp. 49–75.

Another factor has been the comparative decline of blue-collar jobs, in particular low-status jobs, that have been relatively easy for blacks to enter.[21] Between 1948 and 1977, over 1.2 million jobs in the manufacturing and wholesale sector were lost in the four major industrial centers of New York, Chicago, Philadelphia, and Detroit.[22] Fully two-thirds of these losses have occurred since 1967. Furthermore, many blacks were unable to qualify for the white-collar jobs that came into existence. While traditional blue-collar jobs were declining, jobs in knowledge and information intensive industries such as advertising, data processing, consulting, and research and development grew by approximately 220,000 between 1948 and 1977 in the aforementioned cities. Most of the jobs created were high-skilled white-collar positions, many of which blacks were not trained for. Hence, not only has there been a decline in the types of jobs within which blacks have been disproportionately overrepresented, but the new jobs that were created were typically out of reach for those affected.

A third change operating to increase black unemployment was the decentralization of American industry, with many plants moving from the Northern urban centers where blacks were likely to live, to Southern and Western rural locales where blacks were likely to be less well-represented in the labor force. More recently, many of these industries have lost jobs to foreign competition, further compounding the problem of black unemployment.

Underemployment.   In addition to being more likely to be unemployed, or not in the labor market at all, more blacks are likely to be *underemployed.* Among the underemployed are those, like migrant workers, who are only likely to work intermittently during the year. Thus migrant workers might, for example, begin work in the spring in Florida and work their way north as the summer progresses, ending up, perhaps, in upper New York State or New England. But with the arrival of fall, migrant workers are likely to be unemployed until the growing season begins again.[23] Another type of underemployed black is one who works, either voluntarily or involuntarily, less than 35 hours per week. What is of greatest interest to us is the involuntary part-time workers.[24] These are people who want to work on a full-time basis, but can only find part-time work. There are roughly 40 percent more blacks than whites in this category. In 1983, 8.9 percent of blacks in the labor force were involuntarily on shortened workweeks, while for whites it was only 6.3 percent.[25] Still another form of underemployment is found in low-paying occupations that require little from the workers. It is clear that an untold number of blacks are in this category.

[21]Most analyses of unemployment focus on blue-collar workers, but white-collar workers, even professionals, experience unemployment; see, Paula Goldman Leventman, *Professionals Out of Work* (New York: Free Press, 1981).

[22]John D. Kasarda, "Caught in the Web of Change," *Society,* 21 (1983), 41–47.

[23]William H. Friedland and Dorothy Nelkin, *Migrant: Agricultural Workers in America's Northeast* (New York: Holt, Rinehart & Winston, 1971).

[24]Sylvia Lazos Terry, "Involuntary Part-Time Work: New Information from CPS," *Monthly Labor Review,* 104 (1981), 70–74.

[25]*Employment and Earnings,* 31 (1984), p. 164.

The National Urban League computes what it calls a "Hidden Unemployment Index" which includes those who are underemployed in part-time jobs because they were unable to find full-time jobs, as well as those who have become discouraged and given up looking for work. In 1983, the Urban League computes that about one-third of the black population falls into this category, more than double the number of whites in this group.[26] These statistics indicate that the efforts to deal with the high rates of unemployment and underemployment in the black community have not been notably successful.

Employing the unemployed. The difficulties involved in bringing the un- (and under-) employed into the workworld can be divided into two broad categories.[27] The first involves a set of difficulties posed by the employing organization, its employees, and its union, if there is one. The employing organization must rethink its basic personnel policies. Screening, training, and discipline policies must be revised, as must rules relating to entry, upgrading, and layoffs. For example, screening, traditionally oriented toward eliminating from consideration those people who lack the necessary qualifications, must be radically changed so that people can be hired even though they lack certain qualifications. Naturally, such a shift proves difficult for many administrators. Managers at all levels find it difficult to adapt to a set of ground rules that are antithetical to the ones they are accustomed to operating under. To this must be added the racism of many managers, which serves to increase their opposition to the "unemployables." But management is not the only source of opposition. A union, if there is one, is also apt to be opposed to the way this discrimination in favor of minority groups affects the status quo.

The problem of the unemployables' behavior patterns brings us to the other set of difficulties—the difficult time many of these people have in adapting to their new environment. The fact is that many of them have developed a lifestyle designed to cope with a life without work. If they have never had a real opportunity to develop a method of coping with work, and suddenly find themselves with a job, many of them simply try to transfer their traditional techniques for dealing with the absence of work to the workworld. Needless to say, many of these techniques do not work well in the new situation—techniques such as outward aggression and hostility, ignoring the rules, anxiety about adequacy, dependence on drugs and alcohol, and the like. The point is that it is difficult for unemployables to adapt to work, and it is difficult for the organization to adapt to them. A program to bring "unemployables" into the workworld can be effective, but it requires great patience and effort on the part of everyone.

Blacks in the Workworld

Let us now turn to a brief discussion of those blacks who have jobs. Tables 14.3 and 14.4 detail the changing composition of the black workforce since 1972. Data are included that compare the position of black and white

[26]James D. Williams, ed., *The State of Black America: 1984* (New York: National Urban League, 1984), p. 2.

[27]Harland Padfield and Roy Williams, *Stay Where You Were: A Study of Unemployables in Industry* (Philadelphia: J.B. Lippincott, 1973), p. 32.

TABLE 14.3 Comparison of Occupational Distribution of Black and White, Males and Females Using Old Census Bureau Classification: 1972–1980

OCCUPATION	BLACK MEN		WHITE MEN		BLACK WOMEN		WHITE WOMEN	
	1972	1980	1972	1980	1972	1980	1972	1980
Professional and technical	6.4%	8.2%	14.3%	16.1%	10.6%	13.8%	14.9%	17.0%
Managers and administrators	4.0	5.6	14.0	15.3	2.1	3.4	4.8	7.4
Clerical	7.6	8.4	6.8	6.2	22.7	29.3	36.2	36.0
Sales	1.7	2.5	6.6	6.4	2.5	2.8	7.8	7.3
Private household	0.3	0.1	—	—	16.4	7.4	3.0	1.9
Other service	15.8	16.4	7.3	7.9	27.6	25.4	16.2	16.0
Crafts	14.8	17.6	21.2	21.5	0.9	1.4	1.3	1.9
Operatives	17.4	15.5	12.1	10.7	14.8	13.8	12.5	9.4
Transport equipment operatives	10.3	9.9	5.7	5.4	0.4	0.7	0.4	0.7
Laborers	17.4	13.0	6.8	6.5	0.9	1.4	0.9	1.2
Farmers and farm managers	1.0	0.4	3.4	2.6	—	—	0.4	0.4
Farm laborers	3.5	2.4	1.7	1.5	1.1	0.5	1.5	1.3
Total	100.2	100.0	99.9	100.1	100.0	99.9	99.9	100.5

SOURCE: Adapted from Diane Nilsen Westcott, "Blacks in the 1970's: Did They Scale the Job Ladder?" *Monthly Labor Review*, 105, 6 (1982), 29–38. Totals reflect rounding errors.

TABLE 14.4 Comparison of Occupational Distribution of Black and White, Males and Females Using New Census Bureau Classification: 1983

OCCUPATION	BLACK MEN	WHITE MEN	BLACK WOMEN	WHITE WOMEN
Executive, administrative, managerial	5.8%	13.5%	4.9%	8.3%
Professional specialty	6.4	12.1	11.2	14.3
Technicians and related support	2.0	2.8	3.4	3.3
Sales	4.7	11.5	7.3	13.5
Administrative support, including clerical	8.2	5.6	25.6	30.5
Private household	0.2	0.1	5.7	1.7
Protective service	4.1	2.4	0.7	0.5
Other service	14.3	6.3	24.2	15.3
Precision production, craft, and repair	15.7	20.5	2.1	2.2
Machine operators, assemblers, and inspectors	11.6	7.6	11.5	6.8
Transportation and material moving occupations	10.7	6.5	0.9	0.7
Handlers, equipment cleaners, helpers, and laborers	11.3	5.6	1.9	1.5
Farming, forestry, and fishing	5.2	5.5	0.6	1.4
Total	100.2	100.0	100.0	100.0

SOURCE: *Employment and Earnings,* 31, 1 (Washington, D.C.: U.S. Department of Labor, 1984), p. 177. Totals reflect rounding error.

males and females. Table 14.3 uses the old census bureau occupational classification while Table 14.4 uses the new system (see Appendix).

The picture that emerges from the broad categories listed in Tables 14.3 and 14.4 is one of general improvement in the occupational position of blacks. For example, both black males and females made gains in the professional category between 1972 and 1980. In fact, during this period the number of black males in the professional category grew at a faster pace than that of white males.[28]

The improvement noted in this general category obscures the picture that emerges from an analysis of the specific professions within which blacks are employed. Although the percentage of male and female black professionals has increased, blacks tend to be overrepresented in the lower-prestige, lower-paying, less-powerful semi-professions. In 1983, while 9.3 percent of all those employed in the United States were black, 18.2 percent of all social workers and 15.7 percent of all recreation workers were black.[29] In contrast, only 2.7 percent of all lawyers and judges as well as engineers were black. Within the health profession, blacks were underrepresented among the high-status, high-paying occupations of physician (3.2 percent) and dentist (2.4 percent), while they were overrepresented among dietitians (21 percent).

[28]Diane Nilsen Westcott, "Blacks in the 1970's: Did They Scale the Job Ladder?" *Monthly Labor Review,* 105 (1982), 29–38.

[29]Unless otherwise noted, all the statistics in this section are taken from *Employment and Earnings,* 1984, pp. 178–179.

Among nurses, only 6.7 percent of all registered nurses are black while nearly 18 percent of all licensed practical nurses are black.

The teaching profession provides another example. In 1972, 2.9 percent of the teachers in higher education were black.[30] This figure increased to 4.4 percent in 1975. Since then no improvement has been made. Hence, in 1983, blacks represented only 4.4 percent of all college and university teachers. The rarity of black college and university teachers has led one observer to suggest: "Black college professors are approaching the status of an endangered species."[31] On the other hand, nearly 12 percent of prekindergarten and kindergarten teachers and over 11 percent of elementary schoolteachers were black in 1983.

A recent article by William H. Exum highlights several additional problems confronting black college and university teachers.[32] For example, blacks are not evenly distributed across academic disciplines. Blacks are overrepresented in the social sciences and education while they are underrepresented in the natural sciences. Furthermore, blacks are underrepresented in the nation's more prestigious colleges and universities, that is, those that are private or that grant doctorates. Blacks are also underrepresented in 2-year colleges. On the other hand, blacks are overrepresented in black colleges and universities. Blacks in academia are overrepresented in the lower ranks and in nontenurable positions, even when controlling for the year in which the Ph.D. was received and when one began teaching. Finally, black faculty earn less than their white counterparts.

Black men and women have also made gains in the managerial category, but were still much less likely to be employed in this field than their white counterparts. In 1983, white men were more than twice as likely to be employed as managers than black men. Compared to white women, the situation for black women is similar.

In a study of white and black nonfarm employed males, Kluegel found that blacks were less likely than whites to hold authority positions such as manager or foreman.[33] For those blacks in authority positions, the authority that they actually wielded was found to be approximately half of that exercised by whites in similar positions. Young black managers ranging in age from 20–44 were more likely than older black men (45–65) to be in positions of authority and they exercised more authority while on the job. However, compared to young white managers, young blacks were still greatly underrepresented in positions of authority and exercised much less authority on the job. Hence, while young black males are in a better position than older black males, relative to whites, blacks still have a way to go to gain equality in the authority structure.

---

[30]Rodney J. Reed, "Affirmative Action in Higher Education: Is It Necessary?" *Journal of Negro Education*, 52 (1983), 332–349.

[31]Andrew Billingsley, "Building Strong Faculties in Black Colleges," *Journal of Negro Education*, 51 (1982), 4–15.

[32]William H. Exum, "Climbing the Crystal Stair: Values, Affirmative Action, and Minority Faculty," *Social Problems*, 30 (1983), 383–399.

[33]James R. Kluegel, "The Causes and Cost of Racial Exclusion from Job Authority," *American Sociological Review*, 43 (1978), 285–301.

A recent study by Fernandez of male and female, white and minority managers gives further insight into the current plight of the black manager.[34] Twenty-one percent of all managers interviewed believe that minority managers are placed in dead-end jobs. Over 51 percent of the black managers felt this way, while only 11 to 26 percent of Asians, Hispanics, and Native Americans felt this was the case. One black manager commented that "even though I have a technical degree I am in personnel and I see no getting out."[35]

Racist stereotypes are also regularly experienced. Nineteen percent of all managers interviewed agreed that minorities face racial stereotypes on the job. Fully 52 percent of black men and 44 percent of black women felt this way. Again, the other minority managers interviewed were much less likely than blacks to experience racial stereotypes on the job.

Blacks, more than the other minority managers, also felt that they were excluded from informal work groups, that they must outperform their colleagues, and that they are bypassed by their subordinates. Over 36 percent of all managers agreed that minorities are excluded from informal work groups. Over 70 percent of the black men and 59 percent of the black women felt this was the case. A black female manager noted: "My peers never invite me to informal discussions, meetings, and luncheons, and many times they discuss issues related to my job."[36] Black managers also felt that they must outperform their counterparts. Over four-fifths of the black men and women felt this way. A white, middle-level manager stated: "Most minority executives are superminorities—mediocrity is the privilege of the white male."[37] A black manager concurs:

> I cannot afford to be average or meet the minimum requirements for a position. It's almost mandatory that I am from the right school with a little higher degree and be blessed with the favoritism of my boss.[38]

Finally, 20 percent of all managers agreed that white subordinates are uncomfortable with minority managers and bypass them in favor of the minority manager's superior. Forty-three percent of all black managers agreed that bypassing was done, while the range for other minorities who felt this way was 8 to 23 percent.

The problems facing the new black manager are underscored in the description by one such manager, Edward Jones, of his initial experiences in an all-white organization: "I found myself enveloped in almost unbearable emotional stress and internal conflict."[39] The firm that had recruited Jones was a fairly progressive organization that employed a relatively high proportion of black employees. Yet when he entered the formal training program, he found himself the only black trainee in a department of over 8000 employees. His

---

[34]John P. Fernandez, *Racism and Sexism in Corporate Life* (Lexington, MA: D.C. Heath and Company, 1981).

[35]Ibid., p. 64.

[36]Ibid., pp. 53–54.

[37]Ibid., p. 62.

[38]Ibid., pp. 56–57.

[39]Edward W. Jones, Jr., "What It's Like to Be a Black Manager," *Harvard Business Review,* (July/August, 1973), 108.

initial apprehension about being a token black was increased during the training period when he was called upon to be the resident expert on all matters relating to blacks or the civil rights movement. Once he had completed the training program, Jones moved from one position to another. In general, he found himself the victim of covert rather than overt racism. The problem was that the company, despite its commitment to increasing the number of black managers, was not able to cope with problems of covert discrimination. Said Jones: "Do they expect a person to be stupid enough to come right out and say, get out, blackie; we don't want your type here?"[40] The fact is that very few white managers would make such a statement, but many would say and do a number of things that covertly reflected their underlying racism.

But racism was only part of the problem for the black managers. The difference between the culture from which most blacks come and the middle- and upper-class white culture that pervades the managerial levels of most organizations is also a factor. Jones described his difficulty in coping with these cultural differences:

> I was extremely tense and ill at easy. Levels of sensitivity, polish, and tact which were foreign to me were now necessities of life. The world of white business presented me with an elaborate sociopolitical organization that required unfamiliar codes of behavior.[41]

This black manager was able to cope with the racism and the other forms of stress and managed to succeed within his employing organization. It is important to note, however, that success was difficult. The level of stress he encountered can help us understand why so many other black managers have been unsuccessful in their efforts to adapt to the realities of white organizational life.

Between 1972 and 1980 we witnessed an increasing proportion of black men entering craft occupations and a corresponding decrease in the proportion of black men categorized as semiskilled and unskilled workers. However, there are still far more blacks than whites in these latter occupations and by 1983 fully one of every three employed blacks were in the semiskilled and unskilled category.

For black women, the biggest movement has been away from private household service work. Since 1972, there has been a 66 percent decrease in the number of black women in this occupation. By 1983, only 5.7 percent of all black females in the labor force were classified as private household service workers. The movement out of service work was paralleled by black women entering clerical work. In 1983, 30 percent of the black women who worked were classified as administrative support workers, including clerical employees.

[40]Ibid., 111.
[41]Ibid., 113.

TABLE 14.5 Comparison of Median Weekly Earnings for Full-Time, Wage and Salary Workers by Selected Categories of Race and Sex: 1979–1983

YEAR	BLACK WOMEN TO WHITE WOMEN	BLACK WOMEN TO WHITE MEN	BLACK MEN TO WHITE MEN
1979	93.0%	57.0%	76.1%
1980	91.7	57.4	75.1
1981	92.9	58.9	76.1
1982	91.4	58.3	73.5
1983	92.2	59.5	75.3

SOURCE: Data for 1979, 1980, and 1981 from U.S. Bureau of the Census, *Statistical Abstract of the United States: 1982–83*, 103rd ed. (Washington, D.C., 1982), p. 404. Data for 1982 and 1983 from *Employment and Earnings*, 31, 4 (Washington, D.C.: U.S. Department of Labor, 1984), p. 78.

Income Differences

Given that blacks are overrepresented in the semiprofessions, semi-skilled and unskilled occupations, and clerical work, it is of little surprise that blacks continue to earn less money than whites. In 1970, median weekly earnings for full-time wage and salary black male and female workers was approximately 73 percent of whites. By 1975, blacks were earning about 82 percent of white earnings. Since 1975, blacks have continued to earn about four-fifths of what whites earn.

When disaggregated according to sex, the picture is less sanguine. In 1970, the earnings of black women averaged about 50 percent of white males. By 1975 black women were earning approximately 58 percent of white male earnings. As can be seen from Table 14.5, steady, although very modest gains have been made since 1979. By 1983, black women were earning only 60 percent of what white males earned. Relative to white women, black women also continue to earn less. Since 1979, black women have been earning between 91 and 93 percent of white female earnings.

Over the last 5 years, earnings for black men have averaged roughly 75 percent of white men. This is an improvement since 1970 when black men earned about 70 percent of whites, but black men continue to earn much less than white males. It is clear that blacks continue to face a wide array of significant problems within the workworld.

SAFETY AND HEALTH HAZARDS

For many workers—far more than one might believe—work is hazardous. The hazards associated with the work world take a number of forms. For one thing, various types of work can be *unsafe* and have the possibility of causing the worker physical harm. A machine operator can lose a limb because of a careless move. Lumberjacks can break various bones falling from a tree. Steelworkers have been scalded while others have been crushed to death. Construction workers can fall from scaffolds to their death, and truck drivers can die in fiery crashes. Firefighters have died as a result of defective protective equipment used while putting out fires. Another form of hazard exists for many people who have threatening forms of interaction on the job. The most obvious examples are the soldier and the police officer, but there are many other examples. The shopkeeper or the gas station attendant must deal with thieves, while the social worker must deal with the danger of forays into some of the rougher urban areas.[42]

Then there are workers who are confronted with a variety of *unhealthy* conditions that can bring on debilitating, and in some cases fatal, illnesses. Some of these diseases are even more likely to kill or cripple people than on-the-job accidents. The best known example is black lung disease among coal miners. There are about 100,000 cases of this disease in the country today and approximately 4,000 people die from it each year. There are many other examples. People who work with uranium run a risk of contracting cancer due to their exposure to radioactivity. Over 80,000 workers were exposed to radiation in 1980. This constitutes both an increase in the number of people exposed as well as the amount of radiation each worker was exposed to; the exposure rate has nearly quadrupled since 1969.[43] Another major occupational health hazard is asbestos. A large number of the one-half million people who have worked with asbestos can expect to contract cancer and other diseases.[44] In a study conducted at a Bethlehem Steel shipyard, it was found that over 86 percent of the shipyard workers who worked with asbestos showed signs of lung damage. The director of the research project suggested that this is "a major, major public health problem."[45] Lambrinos and Johnson enumerate a few of the 16,500 *known* toxic substances present in the workplace:

> Everyone knows about asbestos. But there is also benzene, to which leukemia and brain cancer have been linked. An estimated 3 million workers have been exposed to benzene. A half-million workers have been exposed to cotton dust, 1.5 million to airborne arsenic, and 3.5 million to vinyl chloride, all proven causes of illnesses.[46]

No one is sure precisely how many workers die each year from work-related accidents and illnesses. Deaths due to illnesses and disease are obviously more difficult to measure than deaths due to accidents:

> Incidence rates of occupational disease . . . understate the total impact of the work environment on workers' health. This is so because statistics virtually ex-

[42]John E. Mayer and Aaron Rosenblatt, "Encounters with Danger: Social Workers in the Ghetto," *Sociology of Work and Occupations*, 2 (1975), 227–245.

[43]Joanne Omang, "A-Worker Exposure Soars, Group Says," *Washington Post* (September 5, 1981), p. A6.

[44]Jeanne M. Stellman and Susan M. Daum, *Work is Dangerous to Your Health* (New York: Vintage Books, 1973), p. XIV.

[45]"Lung Damage Found in 86% of Ship Workers," *Washington Post* (July 9, 1979), p. C2.

[46]James Lambrinos and William G. Johnson, "Robots to Reduce the High Cost of Illness and Injury," *Harvard Business Review*, 62 (May/June, 1984), 24.

clude chronic types of illnesses, as well as illnesses having a long latent period whose relationship to the job often surfaces only after retirement or death.[47]

The fact is that we really have no firm idea how many people die each year from diseases contracted on the job. For example, how many fatal cancers are traceable to exposure on the job, perhaps decades before the disease manifested itself, to carcinogens?

We have a better idea of how many people are killed each year on the job, but even here there is a considerable disparity in available data. Between 1955 and 1973 about 14,000 workers were killed on the job every year.[48] If we take a conservative estimate, about 11,000 workers were killed on the job in 1982.[49] This is a rate of eleven workers for every 100,000 and it marks a significant decrease from 1955 when the rate was twenty-four workers killed for every 100,000 at work.

Hilaski reports that there were 5.7 million occupational injuries and illnesses in 1978, a decline of 15 percent in the injury and illness rate over 1972.[50]

Lambrinos and Johnson estimate that about a fourth of all disabled people in the United States are disabled as a result of injuries incurred on the job.[51] Norman Root found that five general types of injuries accounted for over 75 percent of all occupational injuries: sprains and strains; cuts and lacerations; contusions, crushing, and bruises; fractures and burns.[52]

Frenkel, Priest, and Ashford analyzed workers' perceptions of occupational hazards on the job.[53] Contrary to Hilaski's finding of a decline in the rate of total injuries and illnesses actually reported, Frenkel et al. report an increase in occupational hazards *perceived* by workers on the job. For example, in 1969, 38 percent of the workers reported citing one or more safety and health hazards in the workplace. By 1977 this figure had doubled to 78 percent. The authors attribute this discrepancy to greater worker sensitivity to the many potential hazards encountered on the job.

There are several reasons why these statistics on occupational injuries and illnesses may underestimate the actual incidence of such occupational hazards. As Hilaski points out, since many occupational illnesses are indistinguishable from illness in general (for example, cancer), it is hard to assign cause specifically to one's occupation.[54] Harmful exposure to cancer-causing

[47]Harvey J. Hilaski and Chao Ling Wang, "How Valid are Estimates of Occupational Illness?" *Monthly Labor Review*, 105 (1982), 27.

[48]*Statistical Abstract of the United States: 1984,* p. 442.

[49]Ibid; for an even more conservative estimate see, Janet Macon, "BLS' 1982 Survey of Work-Related Deaths," *Monthly Labor Review*, 107 (1984), 43–45.

[50]Harvey Hilaski, "Understanding Statistics on Occupational Illnesses," *Monthly Labor Review*, 104 (1981), 25–29.

[51]Lambrinos and Johnson, "Robots to Reduce the High Cost of Illness and Injury."

[52]Norman Root, "Injuries at Work are Fewer Among Older Employees," *Monthly Labor Review*, 104 (1981), 30–34.

[53]Richard L. Frenkel, W. Curtiss Priest, and Nicholas A. Ashford, "Occupational Safety and Health: A Report on Worker Perceptions," *Monthly Labor Review*, 103 (1980), 11–14.

[54]Harvey Hilaski, "Understanding Statistics on Occupational Illnesses."

agents can occur on and off the job making the origin difficult to specify. In addition, there is often a time lag between exposure, onset of the illness and diagnosis. Government employees who were exposed to atomic radiation in the 1950s are only now beginning to experience the effects and fight for compensation. Hilaski points out that lack of medical expertise in occupational hazards and variability in individual worker susceptibility are also reasons why the true incidence of occupational injury and illness may be higher than actually reported.[55] Employee tenure is another reason. Frenkel et al. found that less than 30 percent of workers with less than 3 months tenure reported a serious work hazard whereas approximately 70 percent of the workers with 5 to 10 years tenure were likely to report such a hazard.[56] This is so even though less experienced workers (both male and female) are more likely to experience an injury or illness on the job.[57]

In 1978, Root and Sebastian analyzed private sector, job-related accidents and illnesses by occupational level.[58] In general, blue-collar workers were most likely to experience a job-related injury. Blue-collar workers (craftsmen; operatives, including transport equipment operatives; and nonfarm laborers) accounted for 77 percent of all injuries yet made up only 40 percent of all employment.[59] Professional and technical workers, managers, sales, and clerical workers make up the white-collar category and comprise 48 percent of the labor force. However, this group accounted for only 12 percent of all occupational injuries. Service workers make up 12 percent of the work force and accounted for 11 percent of all such injuries.

The Federal Government and Safety and Health

The federal government has tended to be lax in terms of its control over hazardous work conditions. It was not until 1970 that comprehensive legislation on this matter was passed. The Occupational Safety and Health Act of 1970 recognized, for the first time, "the right of the government to inspect, cite, and penalize employers for infringements of the right of workers to labor under safe and healthy conditions."[60] The federal agency created in 1971 to deal with these problems was the Occupational Safety and Health Administration (OSHA). It is widely believed that OSHA was founded to mollify labor and that there was no real intention of dramatically altering health and safety

---

[55]Ibid.

[56]Richard Frenkel, et al., "Occupational Safety and Health: A Report on Worker Perceptions."

[57]Norman Root, "Injuries at Work are Fewer Among Older Employees."

[58]Norman Root and Deborah Sebastian, "BLS Develops Measure of Job Risk by Occupation," *Monthly Labor Review*, 104 (1981), 26–30.

[59]David R. McCaffrey, "Work-related Amputations by Type and Prevalence," *Monthly Labor Review*, 104 (1981), 35–41.

[60]Patrick G. Donnelly. "The Origins of the Occupational Safety and Health Act of 1970," *Social Problems*, 30 (1982), 13.

conditions in the workplace.[61] However, the degree of its activity has been shaped by the philosophy of the president in power. During the Carter administration (1976–1980), OSHA tended to be very active. A number of improvements in occupational safety and health were made and workers grew more aware of, and knowledgeable about, hazards on the job. Under the Reagan administration "the agency has throttled down or off on many of its regulatory controls, shrinking the scope of work-place inspections and putting a hold on . . . health and safety standards the agency is supposed to produce."[62] In the first 2 years of the Reagan administration, the number of serious citations given to industry was halved and penalties levied dropped from $25 million to $5 million. OSHA's power was curtailed even though there is at least some evidence that it has been effective in reducing injury rates, at least in larger firms.[63] Although some gains have been made over the years, the fact remains that major health and safety hazards remain and less rather than more is being done about them. A former official of the AFL-CIO sums up the problem: "You can have a carnage in the work place and no one cares. If we did, we'd have a program that works."[64]

Barriers to Coping with Safety and Health Problems

Our focus in this section will be on some of the major barriers to effective action on health and safety matters by management and government officials. There are at least four basic barriers to meaningful action.[65]

First, on the one side is management's desire to keep costs down and still keep profits up, as well as its desire to control what goes on in the workplace. Opposed to this is the workers' desire to maximize their own control as well as to improve working conditions, including health and safety conditions.[66] That action that has been undertaken, despite this conflict, has been aimed at eliminating immediate safety hazards rather than the long-run, and perhaps most dangerous, health hazards.

This is related to the second source of conflict—the lack of clear and unequivocal evidence of the role of occupational variables in health hazards. As we have seen, it is very difficult to unravel the relationship between work-related factors and other variables in the etiology of such chronic, long-term illnesses as cancer, hypertension, heart disease, and so forth.

[61]Kitty Calavita, "The Demise of the Occupational Safety and Health Administration: A Case Study of Symbolic Interaction," *Social Problems*, 30 (1983), 437–448.

[62]Kathy Sawyer and Pete Earley, "OSHA Befriends Industry, but Draws New Fire," *Washington Post* (July 5, 1983), pp. A1, A2.

[63]William N. Cooke and Frederick H. Gautschi, III, "OSHA, Plant Safety Programs, and Injury Reduction," *Industrial Relations*, 20 (1981), 245–257.

[64]Sawyer and Earley, "OSHA Befriends Industry, but Draws New Fire," p. A12.

[65]Nicholas A. Ashford, "Work, Health and Safety: An Arena of Conflicts," *Monthly Labor Review*, 98 (1975), 3–11.

[66]Carl Gersuny, *Work Hazards and Industrial Conflict* (Hanover, NH: University Press of New England, 1981).

The third conflict revolves around the appropriate role for public policy. The issues are whether something should be prohibited until it is proven to be safe, or allowed to continue until it is proven hazardous.

Finally, the various forces working on these problems in our society are virtually unrelated and, at times, are at odds with each other. Ashford gives the following example of this in the area of pesticides:

> General environmentalists succeeded in eliminating DDT for use as pesticide because it posed serious ecological dangers to wildlife and to the consumer. These efforts resulted in the increased use by farmers of parathion, which deteriorates in the environment much faster than DDT. However, parathion may be very much more harmful than DDT for the workers who handle it. Because mechanisms did not exist to coordinate the resolution of problems in the work environment with those of the general environment, control of pesticides in the work environment came very much later.[67]

There are other problems of coordination in the efforts to deal with health and safety hazards. For example, those working to prevent these problems are not working in unison with those oriented toward treating them once they have occurred.

We can close this section with a hopeful note. That is, robots are increasingly being employed in unsafe and unhealthy work settings.[68] There is a long way to go here, however. Robots now handle only a small proportion of dangerous jobs. Furthermore, management does not usually install robots for health and safety reasons, but rather to save money in terms of the cost of production. Lambrinos and Johnson argue that corporations should take a broader view and take into consideration future costs such as health expenditures and litigation expenses. If they do, they state, "it *could be* the basis for a surge in the use of robots for hazardous jobs in the plant."[69]

Occupational Stress and Burnout

Another important work-related hazard is *stress*. Whereas the types of occupational hazards discussed previously have primarily physical effects— that is, physical illnesses, cuts, bruises, amputations—stress is basically a negative mental/psychological reaction to one or more of a multiplicity of job-related factors. A psychological reaction to job conditions receiving much attention today is *job burnout*. Job burnout can be seen as an advanced, more intense form of occupational stress. More specifically, burnout is a negative "internal, psychological experience involving feelings, attitudes, motives, and expectations . . . (that) concerns problems (of) distress, discomfort, dysfunction, and/or negative consequences."[70]

Job stress and burnout cut across the occupational spectrum. Professionals like physicians, brain surgeons, lawyers and college professors are all sub-

---

[67]Ashford, "Work, Health, and Safety," 4.

[68]Lambrinos and Johnson, "Robots to Reduce the High Cost of Illness and Injury."

[69]Ibid., 28.

[70]Christina Maslach, "Understanding Burnout: Definitional Issues in Analyzing a Complex Phenomena," in Whiton Stewart Paine, ed., *Job Stress and Burnout: Research, Theory and Intervention Perspectives* (Beverly Hills, CA: Sage, 1982), p. 32.

ject to stress and burnout.[71] Managers, from chief executives through the middle layers, are subject to this occupational hazard.[72] Ivancevich, Matteson, and Preston found that it was not upper-level managers who were most likely to experience stress but rather middle-level managers.[73] Ivancevich et al. also studied stress among operating room and surgical nurses. Medical surgical nurses experience more stress than operating room nurses due mainly to work overload and time pressures. Many other workers experience stress and burnout on the job (for example, teachers[74] and police officers[75]).

The symptoms and causes of occupational stress and burnout are many including fatigue, headaches, increased alcohol and drug consumption, depression, increased interpersonal conflict, distrust, and so forth.[76] Loss of enthusiasm, loss of self-confidence, and indecision quickly follow. As a burned out corporation vice president states:

> I just can't seem to get going . . . I can't get interested in what I'm supposed to do. I know I should get rolling. I know there's a tremendous amount of work to be done. That's why they brought me in and put me in this job, but I just can't seem to get going.[77]

As with the symptoms, the job-related causes of stress and burnout are many. Carroll and White argue that personal, work group, and organizational variables are important sources of stress.[78] These authors suggest that variables external to the organization (family, community, legislative) and the broader cultural and world-wide context must also be considered.

The number of hours worked during the day can certainly lead to stress and eventually burnout. The unremitting pressure of 12- to 16-hour days can easily led to exhaustion, irritability, a sense of being overwhelmed. For the middle manager, lack of opportunity for advancement can lead to pressure, tension, frustration, and hostility to others involved in the promotion hierarchy. Recalling the stress of his earlier managerial days, one chief executive said:

> It is universal that middle management—and especially young middle management—should always feel discontented. They always look ahead and see

[71]Carol Krucoff, "Confronting On-the-Job Burnout," *Washington Post* (August 5, 1980), p. B5.

[72]Herbert Benson and Robert L. Allen, "How Much Stress is Too Much?" *Harvard Business Review*, 58 (September/October, 1980), 87.

[73]John M. Ivancevich, Michael T. Matteson and Cynthia Preston, "Occupational Stress, Type A Behavior, and Physical Well Being," *Academy of Management Journal*, 25 (1982), 373–391.

[74]Robert I. Sutton, "Job Stress Among Primary and Secondary Schoolteachers: Its Relationship to Ill-being," *Work and Occupations*, 11 (1984), 7–28.

[75]Jeannie Gaines and John M. Jermier, "Emotional Exhaustion in a High Stress Organization," *Academy of Management Journal*, 26 (1983), 567–586.

[76]Jerome F.X. Carroll and William L. White, "Theory Building: Integrating Individual and Environmental Factors Within an Ecological Framework," in Paine, ed., *Job Stress and Burnout*, p. 44.

[77]Harry Levinson, "When Executives Burn Out," *Harvard Business Review*, 59 (May/June, 1981), 73.

[78]Carroll and White, "Theory Building."

no opportunities for promotion coming, and they complain that they are not consulted and don't know what is going on.[79]

Also with reference to chief executives and managers, Levinson discusses several other job factors that are related to stress. Managers in large complex organizations must cope with numerous people including the "least capable among the employees, with the depressed, the suspicious, the rivalrous, the self-centered, and the generally unhappy."[80] The manager is responsible for balancing these various personalities with the goals and priorities of the organization. According to Levinson: "That frustration, carried to extremes beyond stress, can—and does—cause managers to burn out."[81] Hence, within the organization interpersonal relationships can be a source of burnout and stress. Furthermore, there is the pressure experienced when there is the need to cut back staff, trim jobs, demote and discharge employees. Add to this a controversial public issue, a hostile press, and an angry community and it might not be long before the chief executive finds him/herself on involuntary, permanent vacation in the stress ward of the nearest local hospital.

While occupational stress and burnout are serious problems, we should not lose sight of the fact that the unhealthy and unsafe working conditions discussed earlier in this section are far more pressing. There seems to be a great deal of attention to stress and burnout because they are problems that afflict high-status professional and managerial personnel. There is a danger that the far more serious health and safety hazards that afflict blue-collar workers will be relegated to secondary importance.

THE RATIONALIZATION OF WORK

Thus far in this chapter we have discussed two fairly specific occupational problems—racism and safety and health hazards. We could go on enumerating a wide range of additional problems of similar magnitude associated with the contemporary workworld. However, rather than take that course we have opted to close this chapter, and the book, with a discussion of a much more general problem, one that touches virtually every occupation and every worker—the rationalization of work.

This discussion is based on the work of the great German sociologist, Max Weber. Weber devoted himself to the question of why the Western world had rationalized to so much greater an extent than the rest of the world. Following Weber, we may define rationalization[82] as a historic process by which large-scale structures (for example, bureaucracies, technologies, markets) emerge and come to be characterized by an emphasis on *calculability, efficiency,*

---

[79]Herbert Benson and Robert L. Allen, "How Much Stress is Too Much?" 91.

[80]Harry Levinson, "When Executives Burn Out," 77.

[81]Ibid.

[82]This is clearly a very different definition of rationalization than ones we use more commonly (for example, in psychology the idea that people utilize "rationalizations" to explain things to themselves and others).

predictability, non-human technology, and *control.* Ultimately and paradoxically, these rational structures come to have a series of *irrational consequences.* Although Weber was interested in the benefits to be derived from rationalization, what most concerns us is his orientation toward the problems created by rational social structures.

Taking Weber at his word, it is difficult to argue that he had a general theory of the increasing rationalization of (Western) society. He was critical of theorists (like Marx and Hegel) who he believed offered general theories of society moving toward some inevitable future objective. He tended to shy away from studies of, and generalizations about, society as a whole. He preferred, instead, to do comparative studies of more specific structures and institutions such as bureaucracy, law, stratification, the city, religion, the polity, and the economy. Thus, there is no single general theory of rationalization presented clearly and systematically in Weber's work.[83] But it is possible to make some general statements about the process of rationalization from Weber's scattered, specific works. However, we always must be wary of going too far with this for, as Weber says in the *Protestant Ethic and the Spirit of Capitalism,* rationalization "covers a whole world of different things" and "the history of rationalism shows a development which by no means follows parallel lines in the various departments of life."[84]

In many places and in many ways, Weber not only describes rationalization in general terms, but also worries about its overall effect on the future of society.[85] However, it is in Weber's work on bureaucracy, which he clearly regarded as the best example of rationalization, that we get the clearest statements on the inevitability of rationalization, its advantages as well as Weber's fears about what it means for people and the larger society. We will examine some of Weber's thoughts on bureaucracies because his views on them exemplify his general perspective on a rational society.

On the one hand, Weber saw many advantages in the bureaucracy:

> From a purely technical point of view, a bureaucracy is capable of attaining the highest degree of efficiency, and it is in this sense formally the most rational known means of exercising authority over human beings.[86]

On the other hand, while Weber lauded bureaucracies for their efficiency and effectiveness, he also fretted a great deal about the progressive increase in bureaucratization/rationalization:

> No machinery in the world functions so precisely as this apparatus of men and, moreover, so cheaply . . . Rational calculation . . . reduces every worker to a cog

---

[83]Rogers Brubaker, *The Limits of Rationality: An Essay on the Social and Moral Thought of Max Weber* (London: George Allen and Unwin, 1984), p. 9; Stephen Kalberg, "Max Weber's Types of Rationality: Cornerstones for the Analysis of Rationalization Processes in History," *American Journal of Sociology,* 85 (1980), p. 1147.

[84]Max Weber, *The Protestant Ethic and the Spirit of Capitalism* (New York: Charles Scribner's Sons, 1958), p. 78.

[85]Max Weber, *Economy and Society* (Totowa, NJ: Bedminster Press, 1968).

[86]Ibid., p. 223.

in this bureaucratic machine and, seeing himself in this light, he will merely ask how to transform himself into a somewhat bigger cog ... The passion for bureaucratization drives us to despair.[87]

Appalled as he was by bureaucratization/rationalization, Weber saw no way out; we are imprisoned in an "iron cage" of rationalization. He described bureaucracies as "escape proof" and "practically unshatterable." There really is no viable alternative to bureaucracies: "The needs of mass administration make it today completely indispensable. The choice is only between bureaucracy and dilettantism in the field of administration."[88] Weber concludes that "the future belongs to bureaucratization."[89]

Not only did Weber see no hope within contemporary capitalist society, but he felt that revolutions, specifically socialist revolutions, would not help, but would make things much worse:

> When those subject to bureaucratic control seek to escape the influence of existing bureaucratic apparatus, this is normally possible only by creating an organization of their own which is equally subject to the process of bureaucratization.[90]

Socialism would bring with it "a tremendous increase in the importance of professional bureaucrats,"[91] bureaucracies, and rationalization in general. At least in capitalism we find a variety of partially autonomous and countervailing rational systems.

In general, then, Weber has a gloomy view of bureaucratization, rationalization, as well as the future of the world:

> Not summer's bloom lies ahead of us, but rather a polar night of icy darkness and hardness, no matter which group may triumph externally now.[92]

In the next several pages we will discuss each of the six basic characteristics of rationalization with special reference to the workworld and the settings within which work takes place. This discussion is premised on the idea that Weber's ideas are not only still relevant to modern society, but even more applicable than they were in Weber's day. This is reflected in the fact that the bureaucracy, on which Weber lavished so much attention and concern, is even more ubiquitous and more worrisome than it was at the turn of the century. Furthermore, while the bureaucracy continues to be important, it has been supplanted by even better examples of rationalization. Ritzer, for example, argues that the modern fast-food restaurant can be seen as a contemporary

---

[87]Ibid., p. iii.

[88]Ibid., p. 223.

[89]Ibid., p. 1401.

[90]Ibid., p. 224.

[91]Ibid.

[92]Max Weber, in Hans Gerth and C. Wright Mills, *From Max Weber* (New York: Oxford University Press, 1958), p. 12.

paradigm case of rationalization.[93] Thus, not only are the examples of Weber's day still with us, but very contemporary developments can be better understood within the context of his theory of rationalization. We will use the fast-food restaurant (an important work setting for millions of teenagers) to illustrate each of the dimensions of rationalization. We will also bring in a number of other examples from the workplace at appropriate points in the discussion.

Calculability. By *calculability* we mean an emphasis on quantitative rather than qualitative measures—an emphasis on things that we can count. Quality is notoriously difficult to evaluate. How do we assess the quality of a hamburger? of the work of a physician? of executive ability? of putting hubcaps on cars on an assembly line? Instead of even trying to assess quality, in an increasing number of cases a rational society seeks to develop a series of quantifiable measures that it takes as surrogates for quality. The urge to quantify everything possible gave great impetus to the development of the computer, and that desire, in turn, has been spurred by the widespread use and increasing sophistication of the computer.

To illustrate the emphasis on calculability, let us begin with the fast food restaurant. McDonald's expends far more effort telling us how many billions of hamburgers it has sold than it does in telling us about the quality of those burgers. Relatedly, it touts the size of its product (the "Big Mac") more than the quality of the product (it is *not* the "Good Mac"). The bottom line at fast food restaurants consists of a series of quantifiable ends—number of customers processed, the speed of service, the amount of profits. Conversely, there is little concern for the quality of the "dining" experience, of the service provided, or of the overall activities involved in producing a profit.

Turning to the workworld, the most general point is that occupations are increasingly controlled and evaluated quantitatively. There is a tendency to shy away from the evaluation of the quality of work and a tendency to substitute quantitative for qualitative measures.

Let us discuss in this context the occupation of college professor and its twin responsibilities of teaching and research. The quality of both teaching and research is difficult to measure with the result that there has been a tendency to emphasize quantitative variables associated with both.

To make evaluation of teaching easier, qualitative judgments by students are replaced by quantified scores, generally based on the results of student surveys. Of course, such scores involve a series of qualitative judgments made by students about teaching, but the problems involved in these qualitative assessments are generally ignored. There are many problems involved in relying on such scores, but the most important is that high scores may not reflect high quality classes or teachers. For example, easy graders who teach "gut" courses in which students learn little may receive high scores. Conversely, tough graders who teach rigorous courses in which students learn a

[93]George Ritzer, "The McDonaldization of Society," *Journal of American Culture,* 6 (1983), 100–107.

great deal may receive low scores. Here, as elsewhere, quantity is not a good measure of quality, but because of the difficulties involved in assessing quality we are willing to accept quantitative measures.

Not only are quantitative measures used to evaluate teaching performance, but they are also used to evaluate the research and writing of a college professor. The quality of a research article or a monograph is difficult to evaluate, so the emphasis has come to be placed on quantitative measures of academic productivity. One crude measure is the sheer number of articles and books published. Another measure that is gaining increasing support is the number of times an academician's works are cited by colleagues. The theory is that the higher the quality of the work, the more likely it is to be useful to, and cited by, other academicians. These measures are flawed in that they seek to reduce the elusive quality of a work or works to a single number. Furthermore, they generally assume that more work is better work. A person who publishes a lot of mediocre work would tend to get a high score in these rating systems. This even includes a high citation score since the mediocrity of the work may lead many to criticize it. This points out a more general problem in the citation count method and that is that it tells us nothing about why a work is cited by others. A work that is lauded by a number of people gets the same citation score as a work that is roundly criticized by a similar number of people.

Thus, in both their teaching and their research, there is a tendency to evaluate college professors quantitatively rather than qualitatively.

Efficiency.   The process of rationalization leads to social structures in which a great deal of emphasis is placed on *efficiency,* on finding the best, or optimum, means to any given end or objective. Whatever a group of people defines as an end, and everything they so define, is to be pursued by attempting to find the best means to achieve the end. Thus, in turn-of-the-century Germany, Weber saw the bureaucracy as the most efficient means of handling the wide array of administrative tasks.

One of the most interesting and important aspects of efficiency is that it often comes to be not only a means, but an end in itself. This "displacement of goals" is a major problem in a rationalizing society. We have, for example, the bureaucrats who slavishly follow the rules even though their inflexibility negatively affects the organization's ability to achieve its goals. Then there are the bureaucrats who are so concerned with efficiency that they lose sight of the ultimate goals the means are designed to achieve.

For many modern families, the fast food restaurant is a highly efficient method of obtaining much of the food that they need to survive. It is certainly far more efficient (or so it seems) than going to the market to buy food, taking it home, cooking it, eating it, and then cleaning up after the meal is over. Many of the steps involved are eliminated or abbreviated by taking one's meals at a fast food restaurant. Recognizing this, the restaurants themselves are organized so that diners can be fed as efficiently as possible. They offer a limited, simple menu so that food can be cooked and served in an assembly-line fashion. There is little or no wait involved as long as the customer does not have an unusual request (a "rare" hamburger). A recent development in fast food restaurants, the addition of the drive-through window, constitutes an effort to increase still further the efficiency of the dining experience. The family now can simply drive through, pick up its order, and eat it while driving to the next, undoubtedly efficiently organized, activity. Gone are such inefficient steps as parking the car, getting out, walking to the restaurant, waiting in line, carrying one's order, cleaning up after oneself, walking back to the car, getting in and driving away.

The example we will use from the workworld is the scientific management developed by Frederick W. Taylor in the late 1800s and early 1900s. Taylor's ideas were of overwhelming significance in shaping blue-collar work in the United States and in recent years they have come to be applied as well to white-collar occupations.

Taylor was obsessed with the idea of efficiency and many of those who later came to practice Taylor's principles were called "efficiency experts." Taylor started from the premise that there was a need for "greater national efficiency" and that his principles could help us achieve that goal, first with manual workers and later throughout the social world.[94] Taylor argued that previous efforts to create greater efficiency had focused on finding more efficient workers who were either born with the needed skills or who had gained them earlier in training programs conducted outside the organization. Instead, Taylor sought to develop a system of training within the organization so that people were made competent to do their work. In so doing, Taylor argued, we would "be on the road to national efficiency."[95]

Because Taylor believed that the nation was suffering a great loss because of "inefficiency in almost all . . . daily acts,"[96] he took as his goal the remedying of this situation—through the development of systematic training and management techniques. Furthermore, he felt that there was a science to this training and management which involved clearly defined laws, rules, and principles. He was a true believer in these principles arguing that "whenever these principles are correctly applied, results must follow which are truly astounding."[97] He believed that "every single act of every workman can be reduced to a science."[98]

The principles of scientific management and the efficiency they would produce stood in stark contrast to the management principles that preceded it and produced so much inefficiency. In various ways, Taylor regarded these earlier principles as irrational. For example, he often talked of them as being dominated by a "rule of thumb." Obviously, in the place of a rule of thumb Taylor wanted more calculable procedures. He also saw earlier managers as relying on such nonrational factors as "good will," "ingenuity," and the initiative of workers.[99] In any case, management was only able to obtain these con-

---

[94]Frederick W. Taylor, "The Principles of Scientific Management," in Taylor, *Scientific Management* (Westport, CT: Greenwood Press, 1972), pp. 5–8.

[95]Ibid., p. 6.

[96]Ibid., p. 7.

[97]Ibid.

[98]Ibid., p. 64.

[99]"Taylor's Testimony Before the Special House Committee," in Taylor, *Scientific Management*, p. 39.

tributions from workers "spasmodically" and "irregularly."[100] To be obtained more routinely, these abilities had to be built into the organization system rather than being the private possession of the workers.

Taylor's ideas on efficiency are best viewed in his thoughts on time and motion studies. The goal of such studies, indeed the goal of scientific management in general, is to get each worker to operate at maximum efficiency. Taylor outlined a series of basic steps involved in time and motion studies.[101] First, find a number of different workers, preferably at different locales, who are particularly skillful at the task at hand. Second, a careful study must be made of the elementary motions used by these workers as well as their implements. Third, each of the elementary steps is to be studied with a stop-watch and the quickest way of doing each of these steps is selected. Fourth, the work is to be made even more efficient by eliminating "all false moves, slow movements, and useless movements."[102] Fifth, after all the unnecessary movements have been eliminated, all of the quickest and most efficient movements and the best tools are to be put together in one whole series. Once this "one best way," this one most efficient way, has been defined, the organization is on its way:

> This one new method, involving that series of motions which can be made quickest and best, is then substituted in place of the ten or fifteen inferior series which were formerly in use. This best method becomes standard, and remains standard, to be taught first to the teachers . . . and then by them to every workman in the establishment until it is superseded by a quicker and better series of movements.[103]

In this way, all workers, and ultimately the organization as a whole, would be made more efficient. Although Taylor was interested in efficiency at all levels, he focused most of his attention on increasing the efficiency of blue-collar workers.

Much of the efficiency that we find in blue-collar work (and other occupations) today is traceable to the legacy of Taylorism—time and motion studies and scientific management.

Predictability.   A third dimension of rationality is *predictability*, or the effort to insure that there are no surprises from one time or place to another time or place. People, services, places, and things are expected to be the same, or at least similar, from time to time and place to place. To insure such predictability, rational social structures must emphasize such things as discipline, order, systematization, formalization, routines, consistency, and methodical operation.

Fast food restaurants offer a high degree of predictability. The "logo," physical symbols (such as Ronald McDonald, Roy Rogers, Big Boy), physical structures, and menus are the same or similar from one setting to another.

[100]Ibid.
[101]Taylor, "The Principles of Scientific Management," pp. 117–118.
[102]Ibid., p. 117.
[103]Ibid., p. 118.

The food is indistinguishable from one setting to another as a result of carefully controlled and uniform raw materials, technologies, cooking procedures, serving procedures, and restrictions on how long food can be retained before it must be disposed of. The people doing the serving are also virtually indistinguishable from one setting to another. Generally teenagers, they are required to wear the same uniform and to talk and act in a predictable manner. Guidelines for employee action and demeanor are developed by the company, taught to franchise owners and managers, who in turn enforce these guidelines on employees. Furthermore, the structure of the fast food restaurant makes the behavior of customers quite predictable. Customers are unlikely to demand steak with bearnaise sauce at a fast food restaurant, or to linger over their meal for hours, or to demand their hamburgers served on fine china.

For another work-related example of predictability, let us look at the bureaucracy and the bureaucrat. One of the great assets of the bureaucracy as compared to other administrative structures is its great predictability and the great predictability of those who work in bureaucracies. In other types of organizations, decisions can be made on the whim of the administrator. The operation of the organization may be haphazard and a procedure followed in one case may be entirely different from procedures followed in other cases. Indeed, there may be *no* procedures at all. The result is that the client is totally unable to predict the response of the administrator or whether he/she is going to be able to get the desired goods or services from the organization.

The bureaucracy, of course, is set up to prevent this; to ensure great predictability. The objective is to limit or even eliminate whimsical individual decision making. This is done by the development of a wide range of formalized procedures and rules by which the organization must operate. The individual bureaucrat is required to operate in accord with these procedures. In fact, the nature of the individual is supposed to be irrelevant to the operation of the organization. One individual can be replaced by another with *no change* in the way the organization operates. It is the position, and the rules and procedures that surround the position, that matter, not the particular individual who happens to be occupying a position at a given moment. Since decision making is built into the organization and its rules and procedures, there is great predictability in the operation of the organization. The client of the organization can predict what is going to happen to him/her on the basis of knowledge of the rules and procedures of the organization, of what has happened to others involved with the organization under similar circumstances, and what his/her experiences were in past encounters with the organization. Bureaucracies and bureaucrats operate in a predictable fashion from one time or place to another time or place.

Nonhuman for human technology. In spite of the herculean efforts of rationalizing social structures, there are important limits to the ability to rationalize what human beings think and do. Seemingly no matter what these structures do, people still retain at least the ultimate capacity to think and act in a variety of unanticipated, incalculable, inefficient, and unpredictable ways. Thus, in a rational society there is great interest in developing and using *nonhuman technologies* (rules, organizational structures, machines, etc.) to limit individuality and ultimately to replace humans altogether. After all, technologies lack the ability to think and act independently—nonrationally. With the replacement of humans by machines (robots), rationalization is raised to new heights.

Fast food restaurants do not yet have robots to serve us food, but they do have teenagers whose ability to act autonomously is almost completely eliminated by the constraints imposed by a wide range of techniques, procedures, routines, and machines. There are numerous examples of this including rules that prescribe all the things a counterperson should (and should not) do in dealing with customers. Then there are the machines that determine the actions of workers, or even take the actions for them, such as the drink dispensers that shut themselves off when the cup is full; buzzers, lights and bells which indicate when food (such as french fries) is done; and cash registers which have the prices of each item programmed into them. These technologies are designed to constrain human action and build as much decision making as possible into the system. The idea is to minimize, if not eliminate, the thought and creativity of the worker. More and more, it is the technologies, and not the people who run them, that "make decisions."

Because of such technologies, people often feel as if they are dealing with human robots when they relate to the personnel of a fast food restaurant. When "human" robots are found, mechanical robots cannot be far behind. Once people are reduced to a few robot-like actions, it is a relatively easy step to replace them with mechanical robots.

The automobile assembly line, and the current replacement of assembly-line workers with robots, is a good example of the replacement of human with nonhuman technology. It is Henry Ford who is credited with the invention of the assembly line in 1913. Ford derived his idea from the overhead trolley used by Chicago meatpackers to butcher cattle. As the steer moved along the trolley, specialized butchers performed specific tasks and by the end of the trolley line the cattle had been completely butchered.

Given the model of the assembly line, and Ford's desire to cut costs and deal with his inability to find enough skilled workers, he developed a series of principles for the construction of the automobile assembly line.

1. If it can possibly be avoided, a worker is not to take any unnecessary steps or stoop over to do the task. In other words, movements are reduced to an absolute minimum.
2. Tools and men are to be placed in order of the sequence of operation in question.
3. Parts are to travel the least possible distance in the process of assembly.
4. Work slides are to be used to carry a part from one step in the operation to the next.
5. Workers are not to carry parts along, but they are to be conveyed by mechanical means. At first gravity was used, but later electrical conveyors were employed.
6. The necessity of thought on the part of the worker is reduced to the absolute minimum.

7. Complex series of operations are eliminated and the worker does "as nearly as possible only one thing with only one movement."[104]

In the automobile assembly line, skill was taken from the individual worker and built into the mechanical system. Ford was well aware of this process:

> I have heard it said, in fact I believe it is quite a current thought, that we have taken skill out of work. We have not. We have put in skill. We have put a higher skill into planning, management, and tool building, and the results of that skill are enjoyed by the man who is not skilled . . .
> We have to recognize the unevenness in human mental equipments. If every job in our place required skill the place would never have existed. Sufficiently skilled men to the number needed could not have been trained in a hundred years. A million men working by hand could not even approximate our present daily output. No one could manage a million men.[105]

As we saw in chapter 12, although the assembly line is a rational technology, many people who work on it have not adjusted well to it. Individual workers have reacted negatively to it and these reactions are manifested in such things as tardiness, absenteeism, turnover, restriction of output, sabotage, and strong feelings of alienation. These reactions are part of the reason that management has sought to further rationalize assembly-line work. This has led them to robots and the ongoing process whereby human workers are being replaced by mechanical robots. This is a relatively easy process since the human workers had already been reduced to human robots on the job doing simple, repetitive tasks. It is with robots that we reach the ultimate stage of the substitution of nonhuman for human technology. Up to now, technologies have simply controlled workers making them more efficient and predictable. Now they are actually replacing human workers and in the process raising rationality to new levels.

Control.   Rational systems are oriented toward, and structured to expedite, *control* in a variety of senses. At the most general level, we can say that rational structures are set up to allow for greater control over the uncertainties of life—birth, death, food production and distribution, housing, religious salvation, and many others. More specifically, rational systems are oriented toward gaining greater control over the major source of uncertainty in social life—other people. Among other things, this means control over subordinates by superiors and control of clients and customers by workers.

Fast-food restaurants certainly have great control over the process of food production and distribution. In fact, it could be argued that their control is too great since they are successfully delivering a massive number of calories to people who don't need them and whose health is even adversely affected by

---

[104]Henry Ford, in collaboration with Samuel Crowther, *My Life and Work* (Garden City, NY: Doubleday, Page and Co., 1922), p. 80.

[105]Ibid., p. 78.

them. Clearly, the fast food restaurant has great control over its employees dictating the vast majority of their actons while they are on the job. Similarly, the actions of customers are also highly controlled. One of the interesting aspects of the control that fast food restaurants exert over customers is the amount of work they get them to do for no pay. Included here would be serving as a "waiter"—picking up and delivering one's own food—and as a "busperson"—cleaning up after oneself.

In the last three sections we have examined aspects of the workworld (scientific management, bureaucracies, assembly lines) that are all designed to exercise massive control over those who work within them. Just to take one example, let us return to Taylor and scientific management. Taylor recounted one of the now-famous stories of how he got one man, Schmidt, to follow the principles he had developed for the one best way of carrying pig iron. Schmidt was told that if he wanted an increase in pay, when his supervisor told him

> . . . to pick up a pig and walk, you pick it up and you walk, and when he tells you to sit down and rest, you sit down. You do that right straight through the day. And what's more, no back talk. Now a high-priced man does just what he's told to do, and no back talk. Do you understand that? When this man tells you to walk, you walk; when he tells you to sit down, you sit down, and you don't talk back at him. Now you come to work here tomorrow morning and I'll know before night whether you are really a high-priced man or not.[106]

Taylor feels he is able to exert this kind of extreme control over workers because he has a very low opinion of them:

> Now one of the very first requirements for a man who is fit to handle pig iron as a regular occupation is that he shall be so stupid and so phlegmatic that he more nearly resembles in his mental make-up the ox than any other type. The man who is mentally alert and intelligent is for this very reason entirely unsuited to what would, for him, be the grinding monotony of work of this character.[107]

Irrationality of ratonality.   While those who foster rationalization certainly intend it to involve increasing calculability, efficiency, predictability, substitution of nonhuman for human technology, and control, the same cannot be said for the irrationalities that seem to be an inevitable byproduct of the process. We can think of the *irrationality of rationality* in several ways. At the most general level, it can simply be seen as an overarching label for all the negative effects of rationalization. More specifically, it can be seen as the opposite of rationality, at least in some of its senses. For example, there are the *in*efficiencies and *un*predictabilities that are often produced by seemingly rational systems.

Thus, although bureaucracies are constructed to bring about greater efficiency in organizational work, the fact is that there are notorious inefficiencies such as the "red tape" associated with the operation of most bu-

---

[106]Taylor, "The Principles of Scientific Management," p. 46.
[107]Ibid., p. 59.

reaucracies. Or take the nuclear arms race in which the focus on negotiating treaties on the basis of the quantity of arms, rather than the qualitative fact that both the United States and the Soviet Union have many times the number of missiles they need to destroy each other, has made the possibility of nuclear war more likely; it has made all of our lives more unpredictable.

Of greatest importance, however, is the variety of negative effects that rational systems have on the individuals who live in, work with, and are served by them. We might say that *rational systems are not reasonable systems*. Reason here can be conceived of as the ability of human beings to think and act; to be self-reflective and creative; to control what they do and their lives in general. Reason implies a truly human rationality as opposed to the inhumanity of the technocratic rationality associated with the rational social structures we have been discussing throughout this section.

In these terms, rational structures are irrational because they are *dehumanizing*. It is dehumanizing both to work and to eat in a fast food restaurant. Workers are not expected to think, be self-reflective or creative in their work. What they do on the job is determined by the system in which they work. Similarly, the customer has few options to choose from: the idea is to reduce eating to the barest, animal (that is, nonhuman) essentials.

Other dimensions of the irrationality of rational systems are *demystification* and *disenchantment* leaving our lives without mystery, excitement, or ultimate purpose. Thus, in the fast food restaurant, there are few mysteries for either workers or diners. Food is limited in variety and sophistication. Preparation is very simple as far as workers are concerned, and customers know exactly what they are getting. Food is seen as something to be gobbled down as quickly as possible so that one can get on to the next activity. Fine dining, or even eating slowly and enjoying simple foods, are no longer ends in themselves. Eating is a means to other ends (for example, survival, or something to get out of the way of other activities) and is not valued in itself.

Other aspects of the irrationality of rational systems relate to their totalitarian implications. For one thing, rationalization, as we've seen in the cases of Ford's assembly line and Taylor's scientific management, is someting which is imposed by those at the top on those at the bottom of the organization. Top executives seek to be free of rationalization while they impose it on the rest of the organization, especially those at the bottom. This puts great constraints on lower participants and leaves people at the top free to control them. Thus those at the bottom lose control over the rational system in which they exist. This, in turn, makes for the possibility of an authoritarian system in which those at the bottom are rigidly controlled by top executives. Furthermore, there is the possibility, envisioned by Weber and others, that such a rational system would take on a life of its own so that everyone, including those at the top of the organization would come to be controlled by it.

In some senses, perhaps the ultimate irrationality of rationality is that it demands that people leave behind their most distinctive human characteristics—their ability to think and act creatively. The object is to take these distinctive human abilities and build them into the rational system. The result is that the individual is asked to behave as mindlessly as possible in the work setting. The irrationality here is that this constitutes an enormous waste of human abilities. Untold individual contributions are lost because the individual is expected to behave in this way.

In addition to these irrational aspects of rational systems, we can also detail some more direct negative effects on people. For example, the fast food restaurant's seemingly rational way of feeding large numbers of people quickly and cheaply has had many unforeseen and irrational consequences— such as weight gain because of the highly caloric nature of the food, increased cholesterol levels, heightened blood pressure as a result of the high salt content of the food; it has played a key role in the destruction of the family meal and perhaps ultimately of the nuclear family itself.

Turning to the workworld, we can see these irrationalities manifested quite clearly in a variety of settings, but none more so than the automobile assembly line. The assembly line is certainly a rational system, but it is also clearly an unreasonable system as far as the workers on the line are concerned. They are not expected to think or act creatively; in fact they are supposed to act as mindlessly as possible, to be human automatons. It is certainly a dehumanizing experience to work on automobile assembly lines; to work as an automaton is not a human way of working. Work is demystified and disenchanted. The work is so simple that no skills are needed and the workers do not feel that they are working for any higher objective than the paycheck at the end of the week. Top management personnel in automobile factories have resisted rationalization while they have been most successful in imposing it on workers on the line. The assembly-line system certainly exerts almost total control over the workers and the more general bureaucratic system exerts similar control over everyone else in the organization—even those at the top. It could be argued that everyone in the organization is controlled by a rational system.

What has been depicted to this point is an inexorable process of the rationalization of society in general, and work in particular. But what of the future? While it is possible to continue to predict further increases in rationalization in some work settings, there are also some trends worth noting that might lead to derationalization in at least some settings in the workworld.

For example, it is likely that the jobs that have been most subject to rationalization, lower-level blue-collar occupations, are precisely the ones that are now being eliminated by recent advances in rationalization. The workforce of the future is likely to be increasingly dominated by white-collar and service workers whose work has in the past proven more resistant to rationalization. Furthermore, as more and more simple tasks are taken over by computerized operations of one sort or another, more workers are going to be freed from the need to perform these tasks. It would seem that this would free more people to do mental work while the machines do the manual tasks, and such mental work has proven more resistant to rationalization. However, we must be wary of underestimating the process of rationalization. Mental tasks that seem resistant too rationalization may well be rationalized in the future. Thus, while there are some trends toward some derationalization we must be cautious about making such a prediction for the future. The progress of rationalization has been too long-running and all-encompassing to this point to allow us to dismiss it as a force to be reckoned with in the future.

APPENDIX
OCCUPATIONAL STRUCTURE: REVISIONS IN U.S. CLASSIFICATION SCHEME

Many of the occupational changes described in Chapter 2 are based on the 1970 census occupational classification system. Since that time the U.S. Department of Labor has adopted a new occupational classification scheme that was used for the first time in the collection of the 1980 census. The old and new classification systems are presented in Table A.1 (page 436).

To put it mildly, these are major changes. More forcefully, "the new occupational categories are so radically different that their implementation represents a break in historical data series."[1] The reader will note the absence in the 1980 classification system of some common terms used to identify major occupational groups. Most importantly, occupations are no longer classified by the census according to familiar terms like white-collar, blue-collar, professional and technical, craft, or operative. In addition, many occupations classified in one major group in 1970 have been reclassified. An obvious example is "cashiers," which was classified as clerical work in 1970 and in 1980 is categorized under the heading of sales occupations. Another example is "therapy assistance," which was classified as professional and technical work in 1970 but is now classified as service work. There are many other reclassifications.

[1]Gloria Peterson Green, Khoan tan Dinh, John A. Priebe and Ronald R. Tucker, "Revisions in the Current Population Survey Beginning in Jauary 1983," *Employment and Earnings*, 30 (Washington, D.C.: U.S. Department of Labor, 1983), 8.

TABLE A.1   Occupational Groupings Based on the 1970 and 1980 Census Classification Systems

1970	1980

White-collar workers
  Professional and technical workers
  Managers and administrators, except farm
  Sales workers
  Clerical workers
	Managerial and professional specialty
	  Executive, administrative, and managerial
	  Professional specialty

Blue-collar workers
  Craft and kindred workers
  Operatives, except transport
  Transport equipment operatives
  Nonfarm laborers
	Technical, sales, and administrative support
	  Technicians and related support
	  Sales occupations
	  Administrative support, including clerical

Service workers
  Private household workers
  Other service workers
	Service occupations
	  Private household
	  Protective service
	  Service, except private household and protective

Farm workers
  Farmers and farm managers
  Farm laborers and supervisors
	Precision production, craft, and repair

	Operators, fabricators, and laborers
	  Machine operators, assemblers, and inspectors
	  Transportation and material moving occupations
	  Handlers, equipment cleaners, helpers, and laborers

	Farming, forestry, and fishing

SOURCE: Gloria Peterson Green, Khoan tan Dinh, John A. Priebe and Ronald R. Tucker, "Revisions in the Current Population Survey Beginning in January 1983," *Employment and Earnings,* 30, 2 (Washington, D.C.: U.S. Department of Labor, 1983), p. 10.

In Table A.2 we present the percent distribution as of January, 1985 of employed civilians by occupation using the new census occupation classification system. We will not engage in comparisons with the old occupational classification scheme because "any comparisons with historical data are not possible without major adjustments" and further because "only about 35 percent of the occupational categories are directly or nearly comparable between

TABLE A.2 Employed Civilians by New Occupational Categories (percent distribution)

OCCUPATION	JANUARY 1985
Total, 16 years and over (thousands)	97,262
Percent	100.0
Managerial and professional specialty	24.3
Executive, administrative, and managerial	11.5
Professional specialty	12.7
Technical, sales, and administrative support	31.3
Technicians and related support	3.2
Sales occupations	11.9
Administrative support, including clerical	16.2
Service occupations	13.7
Private household	1.0
Protective service	1.6
Service, except private household and protective	11.1
Precision production, craft, and repair	12.2
Operators, fabricators, and laborers	15.7
Machine operators, assemblers, and inspectors	7.5
Transportation and material moving occupations	4.2
Handlers, equipment cleaners, helpers, and laborers	4.0
Farming, forestry, and fishing	2.8

SOURCE: *Employment and Earnings*, 32, 2 (Washington, D.C.: U.S. Department of Labor, 1985), p. 35.

the two systems."[2] We present the data so the reader will become familiar with how the distribution of occupations has changed. Since this is the system the U.S. Department of Labor will use to classify occupations, it will therefore be important for future comparisons and trends. Although we present this new schema, this book continues to be informed by the more traditional occupational schema.

[2]Ibid., 8, 10.

NAME INDEX

Downs, A., 42
Dressel, P..L., 145, 377, 397
Drexler, J. A., 363, 366
Dreyfuss, J., 407
Drucker, P. F., 173, 177, 258
Dubin, R., 175, 350
Duff, R. W., 144
Duman, D., 67
Duncan, D., 158
Duncan, G. J., 150
Duncan, O. D., 187
Durkheim, E., 17, 18, 40

Earley, P., 419
Easton, L., 331
Eddy, E. M., 185, 186
Edwards, R., 14
Eekelaar, J., 80
Ehrlich, H., 278
Ehrlich, J. L., 186
Einstein, M. E., 38
Eisen, A., 204
Ekstrom, C., 65
Elifson, K. W., 315, 317
Ellis, J., 140
Emery, F. E., 365
Emmert, F., 340
Engel, A. S., 320
Engel, G., 207
Engels, F., 331
English, C. E., 362
Epstein, C., 110
Epstein, L., 242
Epstein, N., 39
Eskenazi, B., 266
Esland, G., 2
Esposito, A. I., 113, 114, 115
Estey, M., 302
Etzioni, A., 63, 306, 240, 272, 344, 353
Evan, W. M., 31
Ewing, D. W., 275, 354
Exum, W. H., 412

Faflick, P., 36
Faia, M. A., 54
Fain, T. S., 285, 287
Faris, R. E. L., 294
Faulkner, R., 124, 126, 170
Faunce, W. A., 18, 29, 33
Feldberg, R. L., 297
Fennell, M. L., 342
Ferber, M., 107, 114
Fernandez, J. P., 413
Ferrari, S., 278
Fielding, A., 66, 80, 89
Fisher, S., 222
Flaim, P. O., 46, 350, 403

Flude, R. A., 178
Foner, A., 196, 197, 198, 199, 200, 201
Ford, H., 19, 430, 431
Ford, J., 127
Form, W., 160, 162, 301, 334, 335, 348
Fox, M. F., 96, 99, 110, 293, 296
Fox, R., 134
Franke, F. H., 353
Freeman, J., 96
Freeman, R. B., 45, 47, 48, 49, 53
Freidson, E., 3, 64, 71, 72, 73, 74, 76, 80, 87, 211, 219, 220, 223, 225, 240
French, J. R., Jr., 365
Frenkel, R. L., 417, 418
Friedland, W. H., 34, 408
Friedman, N. S., 339
Friedmann, E. A., 195, 198
Friedrich, O., 35, 36, 38
Fry, J. A., 371
Fuller, S. H., 363

Gaines, J., 421
Galliher, J. F., 320
Garbarino, J. W., 50
Garbin, A. P., 193, 376, 389, 396, 397
Gardiner, J. A., 385
Garfinkle, S. H., 306
Garson, B., 333
Garson, D., 371
Gautschi, F. H., III, 419
Geer, B., 130
Geis, G., 272
Geison, G. L., 63, 84
Gelfand, T., 67
Gerstl, J. E., 31, 78
Gersuny, C., 419
Gerth, H., 424
Gerver, I., 399
Geyer, F., 332
Gies, J., 6, 7
Gilbert, N., 79
Gill, D. G., 218
Ginzberg, E., 112, 127
Gite, L., 404
Glaser, B. G., 124, 151, 217, 310
Glenn, E. N., 297
Glenn, N. D., 297
Goffman, E., 139, 307, 375, 387
Goh, S. C., 276
Gold, R. L., 319
Goldberg, A. I., 217
Goldenberg, S. B., 303
Goldman, D. R., 175
Goldner, F. H., 180, 215
Goldstein, M. S., 74
Goldstein, P. J., 191
Goldstein, S., 286
Goldthorpe, J., 331

SUBJECT INDEX